Computer-Aided Software Engineering

Issues and Trends for the 1990s and Beyond

Thomas J. Bergin
The American University

IDEA GROUP PUBLISHING
Harrisburg, U.S.A. • London, U.K.

Senior Editor: Mehdi Khosrowpour
Series Editor: Thomas J. Bergin
Managing Editor: Jan Travers
Printed at: BookCrafters

Published in the United States of America by
    Idea Group Publishing
    Olde Liberty Square
    4811 Jonestown Road, Suite 230
    Harrisburg, PA 17109
    Tel: (717) 541-9150
    Fax: (717) 541-9159

and in the United Kingdom by
    Idea Group Publishing
    3 Henrietta Street
    Covent Garden
    London WC2E 8LU
    Tel: 071-240 0856
    Fax: 071-379 0609

Copyright © 1993 by Idea Group Publishing. All rights reserved. No part of this book may be reproduced in any form or by any means, electronic or mechanical, including photocopying, without written permission from the publisher.

Library of Congress Card Catalog No. 91-76951

British Cataloguing in Publication Data
A Cataloguing in Publication record for this book is available from the British Library

ISBN 1-878289-15-2

Other IDEA GROUP Publishing Books

- Architecture and Planning of Enterprise-Wide Information Management Systems/Targowski
- Computer-Aided Software Engineering: Issues and Trends for the 1990s and Beyond/Bergin
- Emerging Information Technologies for Competitive Advantage and Economic Development
- Expert Systems and Related Topics: Selected Bibliography and Guide to Information Sources/Palmer
- Global Issues of Information Technology Management/ Palvia/Palvia/Zigli
- Global Information Technology Education: Issues and Trends/ Khosrowpour & Loch
- Information Technology and Organizations: Challenges of New Technologies/Khosrowpour
- Information Technology Resources Utilization & Management: Issues and Trends/Khosrowpour/Yaverbaum
- Management Impacts of Information Technology Szewczak/Snodgrass/Khosrowpour
- Managing Expert Systems Turban/Liebowitz
- Managing Information Technology in a Global Society
- Managing Microcomputer Technology as an Organizational Resource Khosrowpour/Amoroso
- Managing Information Resources in the 1990s
- Microcomputer Applications for Managers: A Hands-on Approach/Breslawski, et al.
- Partners Not Competitors: The Age of Teamwork and Technology/ Oliva
- Strategic Information Technology Management: Perspectives on Organizational Growth and Competitive Advantage/Mahmood
- Strategic Management: An Integrative Context-Specific Process/ Mockler

IDEA GROUP PUBLISHING

SERIES In
Software Engineering
Management

Senior Editor:
Mehdi Khosrowpour
Pennsylvania State University

Series Editor:
Thomas J. Bergin
The American University

First release of this series
Computer-Aided Software Engineering: Issues and Trends for the 1990s and Beyond

For more information, or to submit a proposal for a book in this series, contact:

Mehdi Khosrowpour, Senior Editor
Idea Group Publishing
Olde Liberty Square
4811 Jonestown Road, Suite 230
Harrisburg, PA 17109
Tel: (717) 541-9150 Fax: (717) 541-9159

Table of Contents

Section I: Integrated CASE 1

CHAPTER 1
Integrated CASE Environments 3

    Gene Forte, *CASE Outlook*

CHAPTER 2
Integrating CASE Using Existing Tools 59

    Hasan H. Sayani, *Advanced Systems Techonlogy Corp.*
    Cyril P. Svoboda, *Advanced Systems Technology Corp.*

CHAPTER 3
An Integrated CASE Model for Forward and 94
Reverse Software Engineering

    Shirley A. Becker, *The American University*
    B.J. Gleason, *The American University*
    Anita J. LaSalle, *The American University*

Section II: Managing the Transition to CASE 129

CHAPTER 4
Factors Influencing the Adoption of CASE 130

    Mary Sumner, *So. Illinois University-Edwardsville*

CHAPTER 5
Development Effectiveness: The Quest for 156
Improvement

    Robert Schooley, *University of Tulsa*
    John Parkinson, *Ernst & Young*
    Roy Youngman, *Ernst & Young*
    J. Philip Vidrine, *Ernst & Young*

CHAPTER 6
Current Limitations in CASE Methodology 176
and Recommendations for Improvement

> Oscar Gutierrez, *University of Massachusetts*

CHAPTER 7
The Adoption and Implementation of 211
CASE Technology

> Cyrus H. Azani, *University of District of Columbia*
> Reza Khorranshahgol, *The American University*

CHAPTER 8
Assessing User Experience with CASE Tools: 227
An Exploratory Analysis

> Gordon C. Everest, *University of Minnesota*
> Macedonio Alanis, *State of Nuevo Leon, Mexico*

**Section III: Methodology Issues in Existing 247
CASE Tools and Methods**

CHAPTER 9
Flexible CASE Tools for Information 248
Systems Planning

> Robert A. Stegwee, *University of Groningen*
> Ria M.C. van Waes, *Coopers & Lybrand*

CHAPTER 10
Integrating Project Planning Tools into 293
a CASE Architecture

> Vijay K. Kanabar, *University of Winnipeg*

CHAPTER 11
Object-Oriented Analysis with CASE 318

> Christopher G. Jones, *Utah Valley Community College*

CHAPTER 12
CASE and Expert Systems Integration Issues 360

    Ludwig Slusky, *California State University, LA*
    Parviz Partow-Navid, *California State University, LA*

CHAPTER 13
Using CASE in Expert System Design 379

    David C. Chou, *West Texas State University*

CHAPTER 14
CASE in Business and Administrative 400
Information Systems

    J. Christopher Westland, *University of So. California*

CHAPTER 15
Simulation for CASE: Use of a Prototype and 427
Experimentation to Assess the Effectiveness
of a CASE Method

    James R. Warren, *The American University*

CHAPTER 16
The Impact of Computer-Aided Software 473
Engineering on Software Development:
An Experiment

    Mary J. Granger, *George Washington University*
    Roger Alan Pick, *Louisiana Tech University*

Section IV: Case Studies of CASE Usage 507

CHAPTER 17
COBOL-TO-Ada Transition: A System 508
Re-Engineering Case Study

    Reginald Hobbs, *Army Research Laboratory*

CHAPTER 18
Measuring the Effects of CASE 542

    Raoul J. Freeman, *California State University*

CHAPTER 19
A Case Study with MicroSTEP 552

    Ismail Bayraktar, *Agent Systems Inc.*
    Murat M. Tanik, *Southern Methodist University*

CHAPTER 20
A Methodology for MicroSTEP Based on 569
the Rapid Prototyping Paradigm

    David Key, *U.S. Military Academy-West Point*
    Murat M. Tanik, *Southern Methodist University*

CHAPTER 21
Integrating Computer-Aided Software 594
Engineering Technology into the Information
Systems Curriculum: a Case Study

    David Jankowski, *California State University, San Marcos*
    Douglas L. Dean, *University of Arizona*

Section V: CASE and the Future 615

CHAPTER 22
Critical Factors Influencing the Future 616
of Computer-aided Software Engineering

    Robert L. Crosslin, *The American University*
    Thomas J. Bergin, *The American University*
    Jack W. Stott, *University of Maryland, Balt. Co.*

Authors' Biographies 637
Index 646

PREFACE

The purpose of this project is to start the process of evaluating CASE, by publishing ideas, research results, and opinion, about the use of CASE in organizations, especially the continued evolution of computer-aided software engineering as a methodology, a strategy, and as a set of software development support tools. The text is divided into five sections.

In the first section, *Integrated CASE*, the authors provide insights into the evolution of CASE tools, as well as identifying some of the problems on the road to an integrated CASE environment, i.e., an environment in which all tools communicate directly and efficiently with a central repository which stores information on all activities performed in all phases of the supported life cycle.

In the first chapter, "Integrated CASE Environments," Gene Forte surveys CASE integration issues and provides an analysis of the present state of the industry, including a reference model for a layered CASE architecture. Gene also discusses the state of CASE standards, and the role and features of an integrated CASE repository. In "Integrating CASE Using Existing CASE Tools," Hasaan Sayani and Cy Svoboda examine the requirements, and suggest a general method, for integrating CASE tools with a central repository which contains a metamodel for all linked tools. The authors describe work done to approximate an integrated CASE environment using existing CASE tools, including a semantic-based repository, and bridge-tools to diagramming, spreadsheet, and language entities.

In "An Integrated CASE Model for Forward and Reverse Software Engineering," Shirley Becker, B.J. Gleason and Anita La Salle describe a "layered' model which incorporates traditional approaches to software (re)engineering as well as approaches based on developments in expert systems. Each layer of this model defines a set of specific services available through CASE tools. The authors believe that such a layered model shows great promise for achieving the goal of an integrated CASE environment. In the final chapter of this section, Chris Westland discusses how business information systems can be restructured to integrate the products of the development phases into an improved "seamless" methodology. Westland believes that such changes can be achieved with minor extensions to the underlying methodologies and slight extensions in present CASE tool capabilities.

The second section, *Managing the Transition to CASE*, focuses on the problems inherent in managing change. Organizations wishing to take advantage of the power (or potential power) of CASE, must have, or create, environments which support doing things differently. The chapters in this section explore the management and methodological issues necessary to successful CASE implementation. In "Factors Influencing the Adoption of CASE," Mary Sumner describes the organizational and support factors that are associated with the successful transition to computer-aided software engineering. Using a case study approach, Sumner also identifies some of the barriers to successful CASE. In "Development Effectiveness: The Quest for Continuous Improvement," Robert Schooley et al, explain that introducing technology into an organization's culture requires a comprehensive structured approach. Based on their experience, the authors argue that a change as important as CASE adoption must be introduced gradually, i.e., the change must be managed from an evolutionary and not a revolutionary perspective.

In "Current Limitations in CASE Methodology and Recommendations for Improvement," Oscar Gutierrez identifies and discusses the problems caused by the mismatch between current CASE tool capabilities and the emerging business-oriented paradigm. Gutierrez concludes that active user involvement is necessary for effective CASE implementation. In "The Adoption and Implementation of CASE Technology," Cyrus Azani and Reza Khorramshahgol identify a systematic and comprehensive methodology for effective adoption and implementation of CASE technology. These authors argue that the organization's structure and culture must be incorporated into any plan to implement CASE, and that continuous evaluation of these factors must parallel the usual monitoring of technical capabilities (in the marketplace). In the final chapter of this section, Gordon Everest and Macedonio Alanis report on their research into user experiences. In "Survey of CASE User Experiences," they report on the organizational characteristics and experience of nineteen large organizations using CASE. The authors identify a set of critical success factors for successful CASE adoption.

The third section of the book, *Methodology Issues in Existing CASE Tools and Methods*, examines the relationship between

CASE tools and system development methodologies. In "Flexible CASE Tools for Information Systems Planning," Robert Stegwee and Ria van Waes examine the planning phase of the life cycle. Having concluded that current CASE tools do not adequately support the planning phase, the authors propose a meta-model for the meta-data in the CASE encyclopedia/repository, based on their research. In "Integrating Project Planning Tools into the CASE Architecture," Vijay Kanabar states his belief that one of the key advantages of CASE is potential improvements in project planning and estimation that could result from improved use of project data (stored in the repository). This chapter describes the experience of using CASE tools to estimate the effort for projects developed using fourth generation tools. The third chapter in this section, "Object Oriented Analysis with CASE," by Chris Jones addresses emerging developments in CASE tools that support object-oriented analysis. After an overview of the object approach, Jones examines available tools and provides an in depth review of OOATool, one of the first commercial object-oriented analysis CASE tools.

In "CASE and Expert Systems Integration Issues," Ludwig Slusky and Parviz Partow-Navid state that current CASE toolsets are often inadequate for complex software development projects. The authors believe that expert systems can provide a consistent interface and support for navigating between methodological tasks. Slusky and Partow-Navid investigate the issues related to the integration of expert systems and CASE toolsets. In "Using CASE in Expert Systems Design," David Chou proposes the inclusion of knowledge engineering toolkits into CASE tools. Chou believes that expert systems development would be facilitated if existing CASE tools and repositories were expanded to include information/knowledge identified during the expert systems analysis and design processes.

In "Simulation for CASE: Use of a Prototype and Experimentation to Assess the Effectiveness of a CASE Method," James Warren describes a prototype simulation environment which produces performance simulations of IS designs automatically from annotated data flow diagrams. The prototype provides model-based expert advice in the use of the stochastic simulation model as well as help in interpreting its output. Based on experimental results, Warren concludes that embedding simulation capabilities in CASE workbenches should result in better designed information systems. The final chapter of this section,

"The Import of Computer-Aided Software Engineering Development: an Experiment," by Mary Granger and Alan Pick, reports on the results of an experiment to assess the impact of CASE on software quality. Since much of the literature identifies CASE as the answer to classical software development problems and failures, the authors tested this thesis through an experimental study. The process used, and the results gained, provide insight into proper usage of current CASE tools, as well as the characteristics that might improve the quality of future tools.

The fourth section, *Case Studies of CASE Usage*, provides an in-depth look into the use of specific CASE products in specific environments. In "COBOL-TO-ADA Transition: A System Re-Engineering Case Study," Reginald Hobbs describes an effort to develop a re-engineering strategy for converting Army Management Information System applications from COBOL to Ada. The purpose of the project was to develop a method as well as to test various software systems. In "Measuring the Effects of CASE," Raoul Freeman reports on an empirical study to measure the effect of CASE in systems development. Although it is too early to assess the results of his research, Freeman explains his use of function point analysis to measure differences in software developed with and without CASE tools.

"A Case Study with MicroSTEP," by Ismail Bayraktar and Murat Tanik, describes the use of the MicroSTEP CASE tool, which supports the development of requirement specifications through the use of flow diagrams. The authors describe the characteristics of MicroSTEP, and the process of creating an insurance tracking application. In "A Methodology for MicroSTEP Based on the Rapid Prototyping Paradigm," David Key and Murat Tanik describe a methodology for rapid prototyping using MicroSTEP. The resulting MicroSTEP Rapid Prototyping Methodology (MRPM), which provides users with a structured development method supporting a wide range of software applications, is described in detail.

The final chapter in this section, "Integrating Computer-Aided Software Engineering Technology Into the Information Systems Curriculum: A Case Study," by David Jankowski and Douglas Dean, describes the authors' efforts to integrate CASE technology into a university information systems curriculum. The critical success factors for CASE integration are described along with some of the difficulties encountered.

The purpose of the final section, CASE and the Future, is to provide some guidance for assessing the future of CASE methodologies and tools. Although all of the chapters in this book provide some insights into the future of CASE from various foci, this final chapter, "Critical Factors Influencing the Future of CASE," attempts to provide a common perspective. Robert Crosslin, Jack Stott and I surveyed the authors of this book as to the factors which they believed would most influence CASE development in the future. These factors were then shared with colleagues in Europe. The result of these surveys identify a wide range of technical, economic and implementation factors of importance to CASE tool users and developers.

Thomas J. Bergin
The American University

Acknowledgments:
Many people deserve our appreciation for their contributions to making this book a reality. Mehdi Khosrowpour was the person who saw the need for it and supported it. The authors did a remarkable job in creating high quality chapters. Robert Crosslin and Anita La Salle pitched in to help review drafts when I was overwhelmed. Most importantly I owe a great debt to our managing editor, Jan Travers, whose patience was beyond the call of duty.

T.J.B.

Section I

Integrated CASE

CHAPTER ONE

Integrated CASE Environments

Gene Forte
CASE OUTLOOK

As the CASE industry matures we are moving beyond the notion of software automation as a set of independent tools. Further improvements in software quality and productivity require not only higher levels of automation for specific tasks, but also a more integrated software environment. The move toward integrated CASE environments is driven by the need to share and manage the complex information created and used by many developers and many tools in large software development projects. Of course, creating an integrated CASE environment is in itself a major software undertaking, complicated by lack of standards on which to base inter-tool interoperability and generalized CASE environment services. However, the need for integration is so critical that, in spite of obstacles, many major government and private undertakings are underway, and we are beginning to see significant progress in this area. This chapter is a survey of CASE integration issues and a report on the current state-of-the-industry, including:

- The reasons CASE integration is critical to the success of CASE
- The forces affecting the acceptance and technical progress of CASE integration
- The dimensions of integration in a CASE environment

- *The facilities needed to support team engineering*
- *A comparison of open and closed approaches to integration*
- *A reference model for a layered CASE integrated architecture*
- *The role and features of a CASE repository*
- *Examples of some commercially available integration frameworks*
- *The status of industry standards for CASE integration*
- *Future trends in CASE tools environments.*

DEFINING CASE INTEGRATION

We all have an intuitive notion of software integration, and as developers we have specific opinions about what we would like to see in the next generation of CASE tools. But, if we had the task of long-range planning for integrating a wide variety of CASE tools (some of which do not yet even exist), exactly what would our expectations be for a robust, fully-integrated CASE environment? Perhaps a simple definition is a good place to start:

An integrated CASE environment addresses all aspects of software development and maintenance as a single complex system.

The software development system includes the traditional technical development activities of analysis, design, construction and testing. But it also includes related activities such as:

- Requirements definition, including interactions with the users and other constituents of the system
- Delivery and maintenance of the system
- Long-range systems and information resource planning
- Support functions such as quality assurance and documentation
- Planning, management and improvement of the development process

There are many industry forces driving the growing demand for tighter integration among software development tools (see Figure 1). Among them is the mere fact that there are many more tools available, and passing data among them is becoming a larger problem. Increasing project scale and software complexity are making it more difficult to manage large software development efforts using ad hoc, manual approaches. Iterative methodologies exacerbate the "ripple effect" and make automatic proliferation and checking of design changes a practical necessity. From a management perspective, expectations of higher quality, better project control and

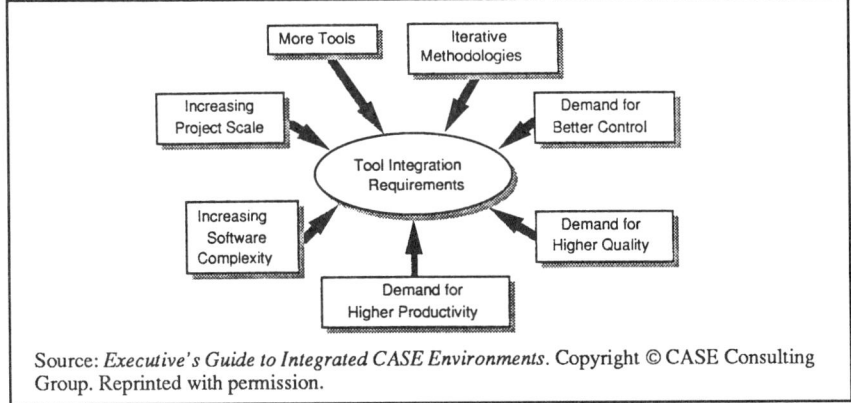

Figure 1: Forces for Integration

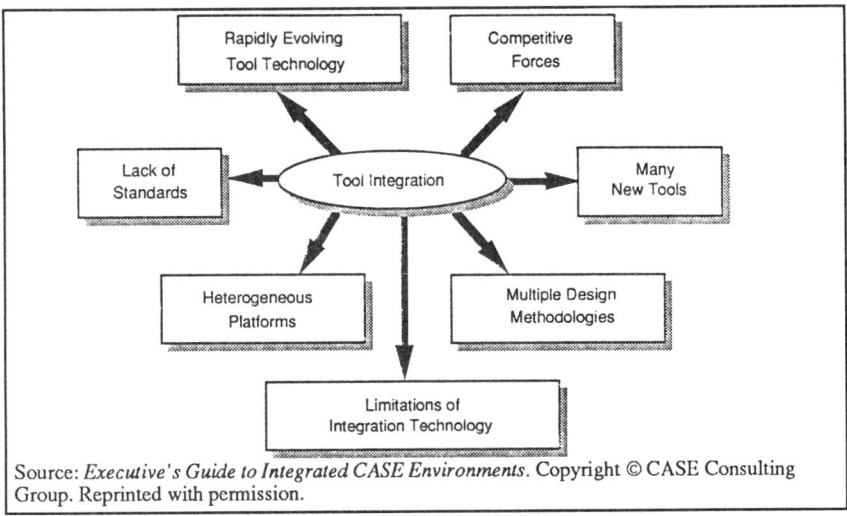

Figure 2: Barriers to Integration

predictability, and higher productivity are creating a growing demand for better integration.

At the same time, there are powerful barriers to integration, as shown in Figure 2. Creating an environment in which a variety of tools, methodologies and processes can coexist requires the definition of a common tool interface, common services and a common semantic definition for the underlying design representations. This is not only a difficult technological challenge but also sensitive to competitive pressures and the "Not Invented Here" syndrome. To complicate matters further, the technology itself is evolving so rapidly, and so many new products are being introduced, that it is difficult to anticipate the needs of the next generation of tools. Hence, standards for CASE integration have been slow to mature. This, combined with the need to operate in heterogeneous environments (networks with workstations from many manufacturers), has slowed the delivery of fully-integrated CASE environments.

Who and What Needs To Be Integrated?

Our concept of CASE integration must circumscribe more than just the interconnection of "point tools." Dealing with all development activities as a single system requires that we explicitly address the interactions among all the people, tasks, deliverables and intermediate work products involved in systems development (see Figure 3). Nor can we realistically hope to simplify the integration task by insisting on a single method, process or set of tools for all development scenarios. In fact, one of our primary expectations is that the integrated CASE environment will provide a measure of stability as we switch among various tools and methodologies in response to changing needs. Therefore, a viable general-purpose integration approach must be able to integrate:

- A variety of design notations, techniques and methods
- Many types of hardware platforms, operating systems and development system topologies
- A wide range of intermediate deliverables and end products
- Unique and widely varying development processes and procedures

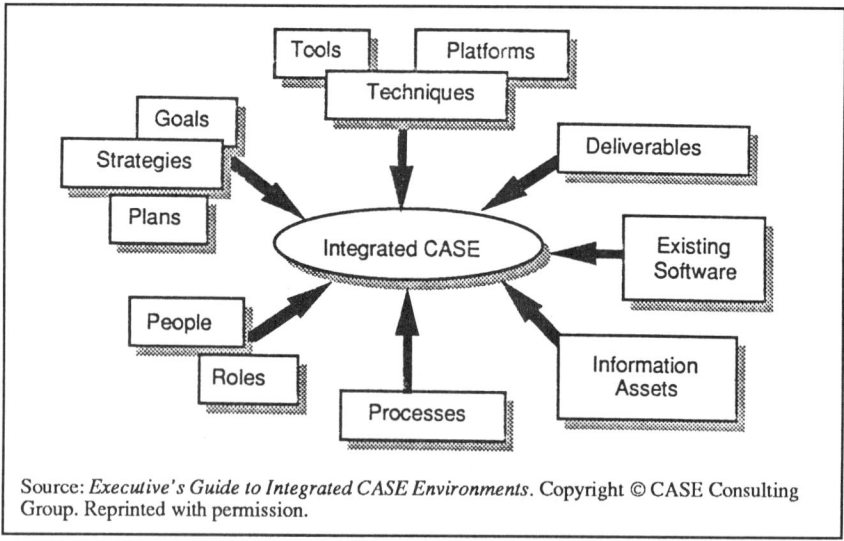

Source: *Executive's Guide to Integrated CASE Environments.* Copyright © CASE Consulting Group. Reprinted with permission.

Figure 3: Integration Requirements

- Large teams of developers with different skill levels, specialties and roles.

In addition, a CASE environment should help us ensure that our information architecture, our existing software components and models, and our newly generated application requirements remain consistent with our business goals and objectives.

CASE Constituents

Who are the users of an integrated CASE environment? They include everyone associated with software development including business planners, systems architects, software analysts, software designers and programmers, project and program managers, documentation specialists, QA specialists, database administrators, and software tools specialists. In addition, the CASE environment itself must be configured and maintained by a specialist, the CASE environment administrator.

One way to look at integrated CASE is to view it as an application environment, much like a database management system. Then we can regard the software development process as a series of application tasks, and the associated CASE tools as a set of applications to automate these tasks. CASE "applications" would then include tools for:
- Enterprise modeling
- Information resource management
- Strategic systems planning
- Requirements capture and analysis
- Conceptual design
- Analytical modeling
- Rapid prototyping
- Architectural design
- Detail/algorithm design
- Program construction
- Testing and debugging
- Quality assurance
- Documentation
- User training
- Problem report tracking
- System maintenance (defect removal and feature enhancement)
- Project estimating, planning and tracking

Capers Jones, President of Software Productivity Research (Burlington, MA), has estimated that there are over 100 potential discrete CASE tools that could be brought to bear on the software development process (Jones, 1987). These are appearing in the marketplace at a prodigious rate; there are hundreds of CASE vendors offering tools for almost every facet of software engineering. Our problem is changing from a lack of tools, to the need for a tool box big enough to organize and manage them effectively. So the role of the CASE integration environment (the toolbox) is becoming more crucial.

The User View

What would a fully-integrated CASE environment look like to a software developer? First, she would be able to simultaneously execute virtually any combination of tools in separate windows. Each tool would access a common design database describing the system of interest, acting as a task-specific "engine" to translate between the underlying representation and a particular view. Because of the common database, changes made using one tool view would be immediately reflected in all other views. The user could, at any time, request information about all the impacts of a proposed change. This might require cooperative analysis by several tools and the consolidation of their findings.

The environment would manage relationships between design objects at any level of granularity (systems, components, diagrams, processes, entities, modules, data elements, etc.). These "links" could be defined automatically by the CASE tools, or explicitly by the user. At any time, the current state of the system could be depicted in up-to-date design documents automatically produced by document processing tools integrated with the project database. Tools could cooperate in complex user-defined tasks, such as the impact analysis described above. Once defined by the user, these composite tasks could be placed on menus and would behave as "standard" commands, or they could be associated with specific events (like edit sessions) and be invoked automatically.

The CASE integration framework would also permit the CASE administrator or QA specialist to define company-specific workflow requirements and process rules. It would then monitor projects to ensure the procedures were being followed, and would capture predefined metrics used by QA specialists to determine how to improve the process further.

The CASE integration framework would operate transparently across heterogeneous platforms, so each developer would see a virtually identical development environment, despite differences in location, platform manufacturer, compute power and operating system.

THE SOFTWARE FACTORY PARADIGM

Having described what we mean by Integrated CASE in general, let's step back for a moment and explore the issue of CASE integration from a results-oriented perspective.

Our goal is to achieve higher quality, reliability and productivity, in software development—i.e., to build better systems faster and at a lower cost. Experience of the early adopters of CASE technology indicate that we must do more than introduce a set of discrete software tools. We must change our basic approach to systems development. In software, as in many other fields, it is the way we apply both methods and tools (the process) that leads to the improvements we desire.

We need to build software according to an orderly, well-defined process using the best tools at each step. We also need to employ "best practices" and ensure that they are employed consistently on every project. We should avoid building each new application from scratch because many functions are common from application to application. In a sense, we need to regard software development more as a manufacturing process than an art form or a craft. A model that has been proposed by Michael Jackson and others for an efficient software process is the "Software Factory." Although this may at first conjure up the notion of assembly line programmers, the analogy is really closer to the "flexible manufacturing cell" concept: work-in-process is transformed by skilled professionals using a variety of versatile, programmable machines to create customized products from standard components and processes.

How does the Software Factory paradigm apply to integrated CASE? A good factory produces high quality goods efficiently, which is also what we are after in software development (Hewitt and Durham, 1989). In order to do so, the factory must be well tooled, precise and efficient, the workpieces must be moved efficiently and safely between machines, and the production process must be well planned and managed. In the Software Factory, the efficient machines are discrete CASE tools. The CASE integration framework supports the "safe" (i.e., complete and uncorrupted) movement of the correct work products (design documents, code modules, etc.) between machines (tools). The production process is defined by management (with the technical assistance of the Quality Assurance function), but is supported and enforced by the CASE environment. In summary, the CASE framework provides the opportunity to turn the software development process from a series of discrete, loosely connected steps, into a well-integrated process flow. Let's take a closer look at how CASE integration improves the software development process.

Sharing Data Among Multiple Tools

As the number of tools available in the CASE environment grows, the need for tighter integration becomes more critical. To eliminate the need to re-enter information, each discrete tool must pass its data to every other tool that can make use of it, usually through a translation filter of some type (top half of Figure 4). When requirements change or design iteration occurs on a project where there are many software development tools, this becomes very cumbersome. A single requirement or design change could necessitate many data transfers to update all the tools. Not only is this time consuming (and boring), there is a high probability that components will get out of synchronization through human error, i.e., some component of the design will not be regenerated when impacted by

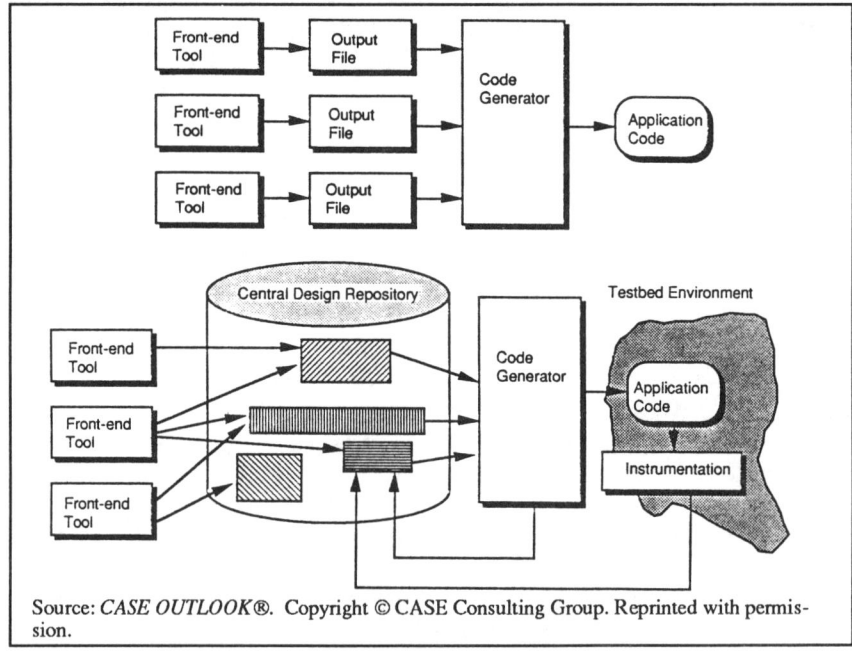

Source: *CASE OUTLOOK®*. Copyright © CASE Consulting Group. Reprinted with permission.

Figure 4. Data Sharing Among CASE Tools

a change elsewhere in the system.

A preferable arrangement is to have all tools access a single design repository (database) in which the design specifications are stored in a language- and representation-neutral form (bottom half of Figure 4). This also facilitates two-way information exchanges, so design documents can be "back-annotated" with more detailed information supplied in later stages of development.

Reducing Apparent Complexity

The apparent complexity of the software development process increases when the number of tools increases, especially if the tools are inconsistent and require the memorization of large numbers of commands and interaction styles. An integrated CASE environment places a common user interface over the tools to give them a more consistent look and feel. It also allows some low level actions to be automated or combined into higher level tasks, reducing the required learning curve in the short term and operator errors in the long term.

New Development Life Cycles

While we have traditionally attempted to manage complexity by trying to develop software in a strictly top-down manner (top half of

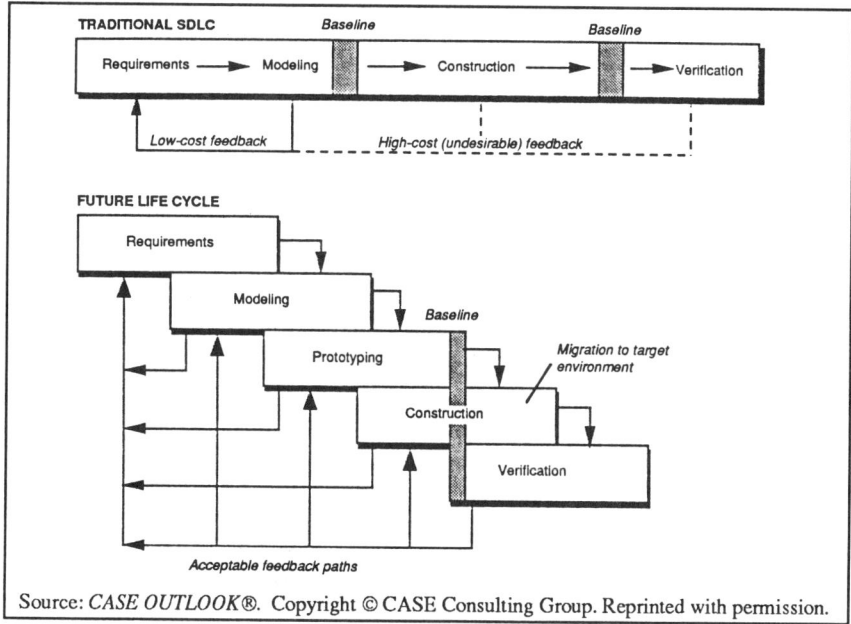

Figure 5. New Development Life Cycles

Figure 5), experience indicates that real projects tend not to follow this ideal pattern. Starting with a complete requirements specification and continuing linearly and irreversibly through successive stages of refinement is only feasible for very well-understood systems. Unfortunately, most software development projects exhibit an iterative pattern, with continuous ripple effects occurring at all levels of the design specifications and code. This is partly a result of the way people prefer to work, partly due to inherent uncertainty in the requirements (even in the minds of the ultimate users), and partly due to limitations on what we can know at each stage of development (before later decisions are confronted). In some cases this iteration is planned for and managed, in other cases it results in chaos.

Rather than forcing us to live with an unworkable process, new approaches to CASE are trying to deal with the complexity of information flow through better notations and data management techniques. CASE tools that reduce the cost of code construction (through simulation and automatic generation) open up the possibility of more iterative development methodologies (bottom half of Figure 5). The iterative (or Rapid Prototyping) technique has several benefits:

- It uncovers the real system requirements by giving developers and users a live prototype to observe and test under simulated conditions of use.
- It manages complexity by encouraging the development of core functions before all the "bells and whistles" are added.
- It reveals design and implementation considerations that can later impact the requirements or the system architecture.
- It provides early feedback on the quality of the overall design.
- Subsequent stages of development tend to be overlapped, reducing the overall time to completion.

However, the rapidity of change, the overlapping phases and the feedback effects of Rapid Prototyping are extremely difficult to manage effectively without a high degree of integration among all the tools being employed.

Diagramming versus Modeling

The first generation of CASE tools provided facilities to create and edit diagrams, and to perform checks for consistency and completeness within each diagram. To build greater quality into our software, we need to better assess the correctness and quality of our overall designs early in the development process. To do so, second-

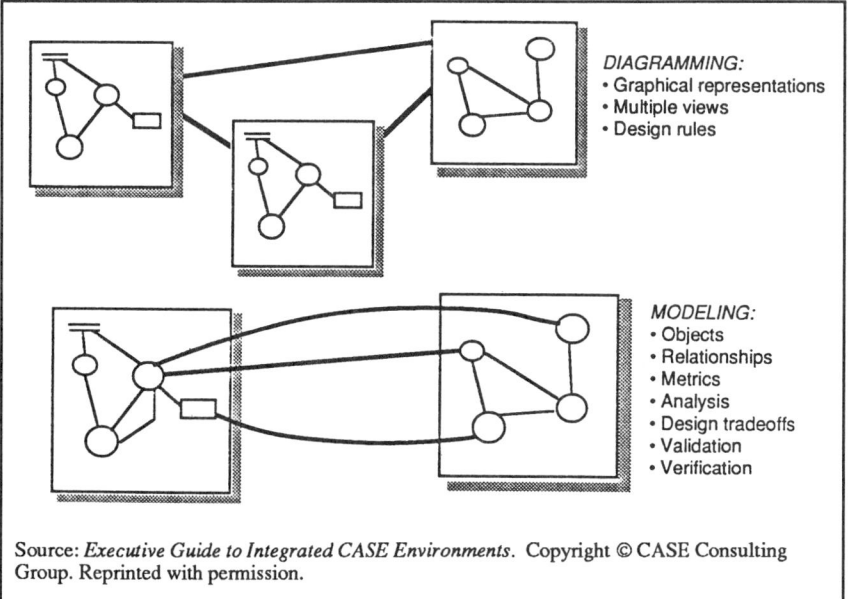

Source: *Executive Guide to Integrated CASE Environments.* Copyright © CASE Consulting Group. Reprinted with permission.

Figure 6: Diagramming vs. Modeling

generation CASE tools provide the capability to do true modeling, i.e., support multiple representations in which the various views of a system are not independent, but related according to the rules of the chosen methodology (see Figure 6). Such multi-dimensional models come closer to a complete specification of the system, and may even be executable to give greater feedback about the correctness of the design (simulation).

True modeling with complete design verification in a context of changing requirements requires the ability to manage relationships at a low level of granularity, e.g., between a dataflow on a DFD and an entity on an ER diagram. In all but the smallest projects, this requires a high degree of automation and integration among tools. The addition of metrics associated with design models opens up the possibility of making quantitative design tradeoffs, the way electronics and mechanical engineers do for their designs.

Improving Information and Process Integrity

By automating many of the information management chores associated with software development, an integrated CASE environment also improves the integrity of the design specification, the work products, and the software development process itself. These chores include:

- Managing multiple versions of each development work product
- Explicitly managing relationships between all versions of all design objects, deliverables and user requirements
- Keeping track of configurations that make up baselines and making sure they are complete (all work products completed)
- Imposing check-in and check-out procedures for quality assurance
- Making sure that design verification steps are carried out consistently
- Notifying team members of significant events such as milestone completions, version updates, and requirement changes.

Managing Information Assets

To make the goal of reusability (i.e., building software from pre-existing components) a reality, we must have a strategy for reuse, an effective means to share information assets (the items being reused), and an efficient way to preserve them from one project to the next. The integrated CASE environment includes a common database called the "repository" which acts as the central facility to manage information assets such as source code modules, executable libraries, business models, system models, user interface models, composite task definitions, process rules, and so on. In effect, the repository is the global database that manages the information we acquire and create—not just about specific applications—but about systems development in general within our particular application domain. Thus, it contains both general process and methodology definitions, and very specific reusable elements (at all levels of abstraction) that apply to our business, including unique elements that create competitive advantage.

The integrated CASE environment provides a framework in which we can manage software development, changing it from an ad hoc, non-repeatable process to a flexible manufacturing facility which we can fine-tune and improve over time. We're expecting a lot from the integrated CASE environment—how can we provide such a robust environment within a context of intense competition, immature standards and rapid technological change?

DIMENSIONS OF INTEGRATION

The broad range of facilities required for full CASE integration can be grouped into three major areas:

Integrated CASE Environments

- Presentation integration—providing access to all the tools through a graphical user interface with a common look-and-feel
- Data integration—sharing data among tools, keeping track of relationships and dependencies among data elements, and managing the context of each developer
- Control integration—enabling tools to send and receive messages, to respond to user- or tool-initiated events in the environment, to coordinate their activities, and to perform user-defined composite tasks comprising sequences involving multiple tools

When assessing degrees of integration, these three areas may be viewed as relatively independent dimensions (see Figure 7). The degree of integration exhibited in a particular environment can then be plotted in the resulting three-dimensional space (Wasserman, 1990). Individual tools can also be plotted, based on the characteristics of their accessible interfaces. Such a representation provides information about the relative difficulty of integrating various tools.

When tools are separated by some distance as shown in Figure 7, they must be made compatible either by reducing the capability of one or adding to the capability of the other in each of the three dimensions. One way to add to a tool's capability is to "encapsulate" it with code that adds the missing facilities (see Figure 8). The resulting extended interface then becomes compatible (at a common point in integration space) with the other tool.

From this perspective, a CASE framework is an integration platform for a wide variety of CASE tools that today exist at various

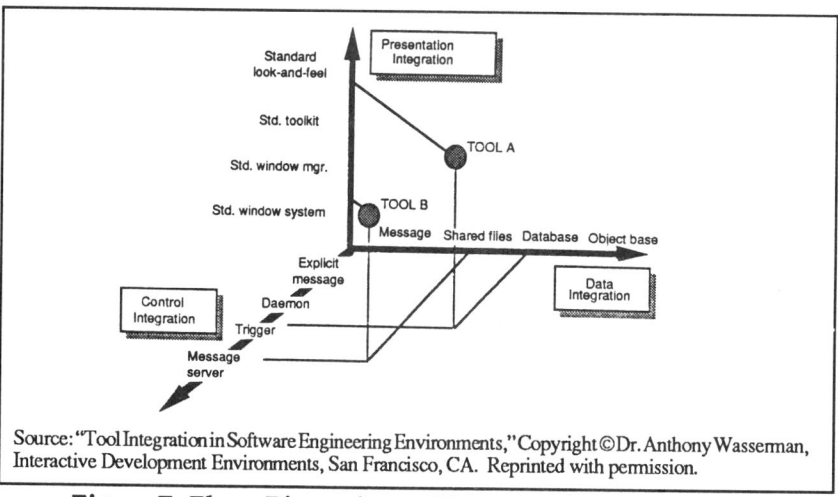

Source: "Tool Integration in Software Engineering Environments," Copyright © Dr. Anthony Wasserman, Interactive Development Environments, San Francisco, CA. Reprinted with permission.

Figure 7: Three Dimensions of CASE Tool Integration

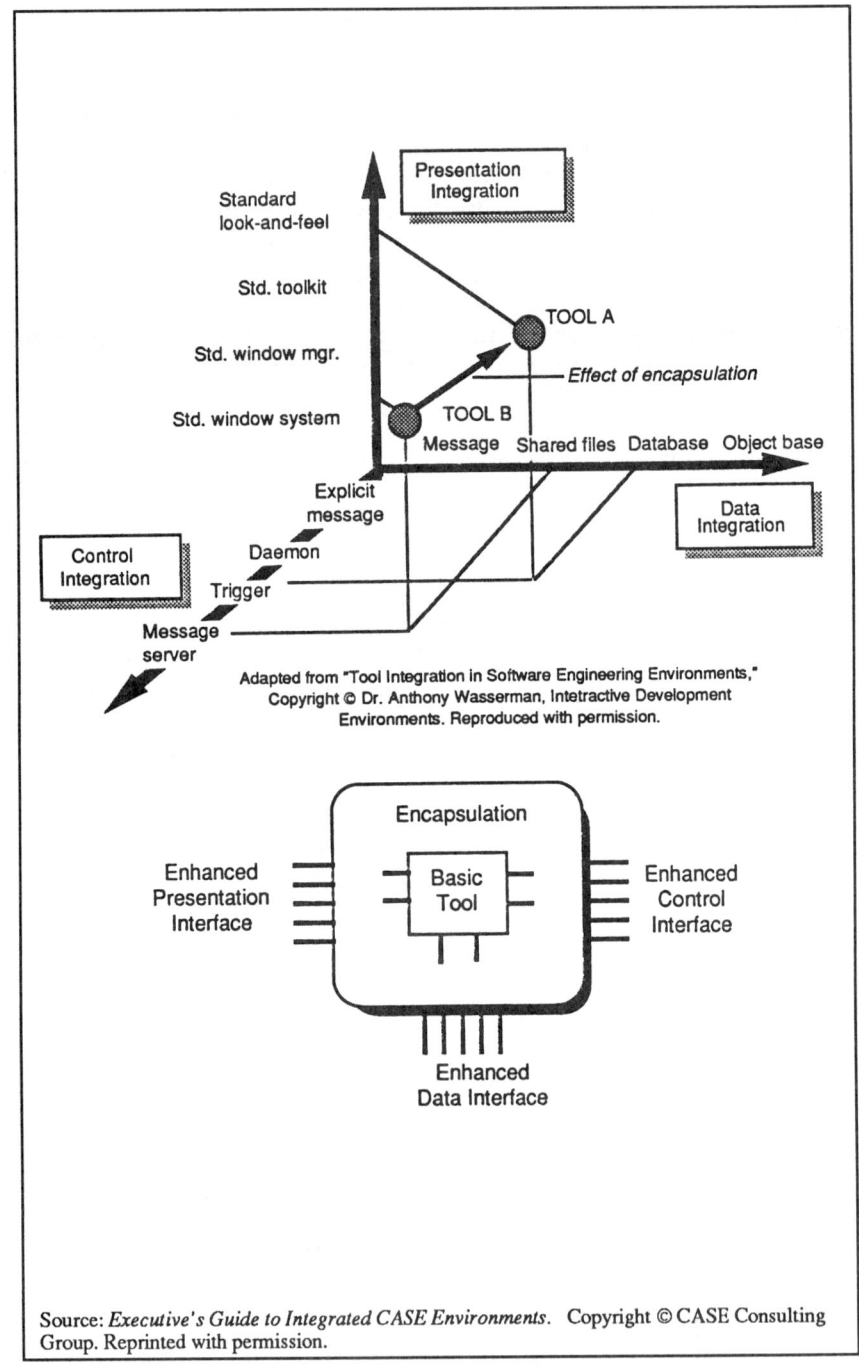

Figure 8: Tool Encapsulation

points in integration space. Such a framework provides facilities addressing each dimension of integration. Unfortunately, the variation among tools means that it is impossible to define a framework that can immediately integrate existing products. However, a defined interface provides a target for tool vendors to build their tools toward in the future. In the meantime, the encapsulation technique can make existing tools compatible with a CASE framework, if it is sufficiently flexible.

INTEGRATED PROJECT SUPPORT ENVIRONMENTS

While providing an integration mechanism between discrete CASE tools is a major requirement for effective software development, providing communication and coordination among multiple software developers is also a major challenge for large projects. It is this area of software engineering where the European community has traditionally placed most of its CASE efforts, so it is not suprising to see the first commercially available Integrated Project Support Environments, or IPSEs, emerge from European consortia and vendors (more on specific products later).

IPSEs deal with many of the administrative aspects of software development and tend to be "horizontal" in nature (i.e., extending across the entire development life cycle) and support multiple roles (e.g., analysts, designers, programmers, project managers, documenters, etc). More recently, second generation IPSEs and second generation tool integration frameworks have tended to merge toward the same functional goal of providing complete support for interactions among both tools and tool users. Consequently, we will ignore the historical genesis of these two terms and base further discussion on the idealized mature CASE environment, which we will continue to refer to as an IPSE for convenience.

General IPSE Capabilities

An IPSE must support tool integration across the life cycle and across all the roles associated with software development and management. Besides the common data management facilities, the IPSE should provide a common tool interface that is general enough to support existing and future tools. It should, wherever possible, support "standard ways of doing things," e.g., supporting the native windowing system of the user's computing platform.

An IPSE must be flexible enough to support an organization's traditional processes and to evolve with the company as it improves its process through continuous quality improvement techniques. To ensure enough flexibility to support evolution, an IPSE must be highly extensible, i.e., it should be possible to define new object types and relationships and to redefine message and link management facilities to meet new requirements. Extensibility should include the ability to customize the IPSE to support a variety of development methodologies and life cycles, as well as the organization's unique processes, procedures and standards.

An IPSE should provide a high degree of availability to the users. This means it must have effective data sharing, archiving and recovery mechanisms to ensure that all users have access to tools and data whenever they need them. The IPSE should also manage information in a manner that makes results reproducible. For example, configuration management facilities should ensure that any module or system version can be recreated on demand. This requires accurate version control and historical system build information. The same requirements apply to other design documents such as diagrams, test data sets, test procedures, manual revisions, etc.

An IPSE should support a software reuse strategy by providing a place to manage long-term information assets such as data definitions, business rules, and reusable models and code modules. It should also provide a mechanism to categorize and retrieve reusable components.

The IPSE must provide facilities for CASE environment administration, including control of access and security mechanisms, archiving and recovery facilities, and direct manipulation (without intervening CASE tools) of design database contents. Administrative facilities should also allow CASE administrators to define and modify the repository "meta model" (discussed later) and to maintain process descriptions and procedures.

A robust integrated CASE environment supports multi-developer, multi-workstation team environments consisting of a variety of computing platforms. Let's look at specific features of an IPSE in more detail.

Common User Interface

A common user interface facility presents a similar look and feel for all tools in the CASE environment. It allows any tool to be accessed without having to leave the CASE environment or a currently executing tool. It should support the full complement of window-oriented, direct manipulation attributes made popular on the Macintosh and now incorporated into de facto standards such as Motif, Open Look, DECwindows and IBM's CUA. It should be easy to register new tools in the environment without making changes to the tool's source code. The IPSE should provide a common graphical user interface for tools that don't already have one, yet allow tools with unique GUIs to maintain their distinctive look-and-feel.

Tool Interface

The IPSE provides discrete tools with common access facilities to project data and to other tools. This eliminates redundant services, such as security enforcement, that would otherwise be duplicated in each tool. Access services must support multiple simultaneous users operating multiple tools on a host or across a network with appropriate priority and locking mechanisms. Tools that plug into the CASE framework are of two general types: vertical tools and horizontal tools. Vertical tools address one specific aspect, task or phase of the software development life cycle, such as analysis, design, construction, etc. Horizontal tools are used throughout the development process, for example, project management and documentation tools. Both types of tools can employ a similar tool interface, although horizontal tools tend to generate a large number of short transactions with the central design database while vertical tools tend to generate very long transactions by checking out part of a design and checking it back in several days later. Because of this, vertical and horizontal tools may use different access procedures, and vertical tools may have an intermediate local database to enhance interactive performance.

Tool Communications and Control

An IPSE provides control facilities to allow inter-tool communication and interaction through messages and event and data triggers (i.e., user-defined actions taken in response to specified events or data states). It also allows the user to define and execute composite tasks comprising multiple tools used in sequence or concurrently. Control facilities also help manage the software development process itself by initiating actions, defined by triggers and process rules, that enforce the company's development standards.

Repository

An IPSE should include a common data management facility, or repository, that permits tools to share both the design-related information and the project-related information generated and used during systems development. By keeping the information in a representation-independent form, redundancy is eliminated, and cross-tool data integrity is maintained.

The repository also acts as a long-term database management facility for all project-related information, managing information assets that have value beyond the completion of the development project, e.g., system documentation to be used during maintenance, reusable models and modules that can be employed in future projects, metrics collected on the project, etc. Individual CASE tools may have their own internal data that is managed privately, but information that is to be stored with the rest of the environment or preserved for extended periods is managed in the repository.

In the most general case, the repository must operate across a heterogeneous network of workstations and hosts from multiple hardware vendors and executing multiple operating systems. An integrity enforcement mechanism should be built into the repository to increase the accuracy of the project database. It should manage all data entries (either directly by users or via CASE tools) against a consistent set of data validation rules, design rules (object relationships), security rules and process control procedures.

The repository also stores meta data, i.e., information about the design data, such as dependencies between entities (objects) and between design documents, when documents were created and by whom, the security level associated with a document, revision levels, what components make up a baseline, how to build and configure a system, etc. The repository meta data facility is also the storage mechanism for the rules that define specific notations and methods. The "meta model" tells individual CASE tools how to interpret and make use of each other's data. It also describes process rules that define the procedures and deliverables at each stage of the development life cycle.

Object Management

An IPSE must provide the traditional data management facilities, such as source file version control, but it must be able to operate on a much wider variety of object types in order to manage the complete spectrum of software development deliverables. These deliverables include specification documents for all stages of the life cycle (including graphical design representations), source code modules, executables, test plans and suites, documentation files, project management files, process and program metrics, and so on. Many of these objects are in non-textual formats. All data management facilities should apply consistently across all standard and user-defined objects.

Key object management features are:

- The ability to define objects of arbitrary size and granularity (i.e., not restricted to file-level)
- The ability to manage versioned links between any set of objects
- The ability to associate objects into collections that can be manipulated and versioned as a single object

Compared to conventional DBMS facilities, object management facilities can provide better support for cross-checking, greater data integrity, more advanced configuration management and traceability features, better tool performance, and greater flexibility in accommodating new tools and methods. In effect, an object management system (OMS) is a special-purpose database tuned to the specific requirements of software design automation. A similar evolution has taken place in other design automation fields, such as mechanical and electrical CAD.

Configuration Management

Traditionally, configuration management has referred to the ability to keep track of the latest version of each source and library component required to build a system (see Figure 9). Version management is the process of maintaining the latest version of a source module, along with all its predecessors. For reasons of space efficiency, versioning systems save only the differences between versions and rebuild antecedents from the latest version and the

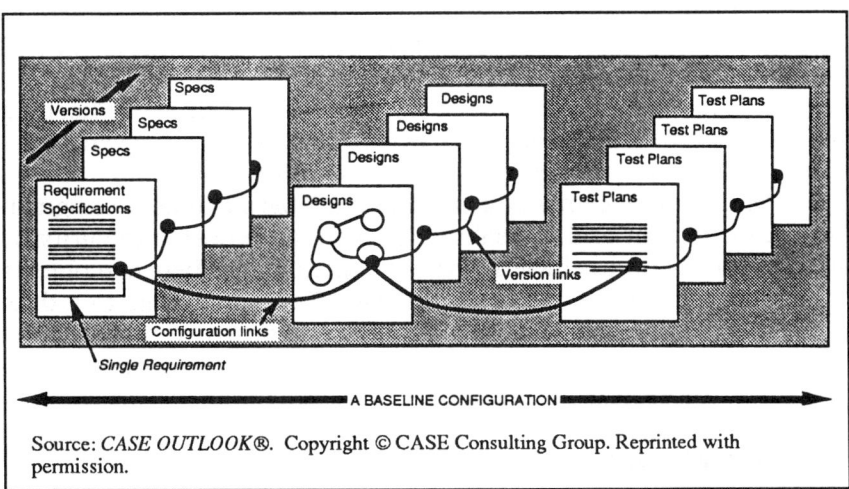

Source: *CASE OUTLOOK®*. Copyright © CASE Consulting Group. Reprinted with permission.

Figure 9: Configuration Management and Traceability

difference information. More sophisticated systems permit the version sequence to be split, so that multiple descendents can be derived from a single precedent. At some later point in the version chain the two variant paths can be merged.

Build facilities that manage the compile and link process are usually considered part of configuration management. They automatically select the correct component and tool versions for a specified system version, and also keep track of dependencies between modules so that only modified components and their dependents are recompiled.

Newer CASE environments expand the notion of configuration management to include all data items associated with a project including requirements documents, design representations, test plans, test data, test results, project plans, problem reports, engineering change proposals, etc. These objects are versioned and have explicit dependencies and relationships maintained in the CASE repository. For practical reasons, it is critical that these facilities be able to operate over a network of dissimilar workstations.

Traceability

Object link management facilities provide the ability to do full traceability from system requirements through analysis and design documents, code modules, executables, test suites and documentation files. A developer should be able to generate summary reports such as traceability matrices, or to navigate through a network of requirements and related work products in either the forward (requirements to code) or reverse (code to requirements) direction. Traceability enhances system quality by helping to ensure that all requirements have been met and that no unspecified features have been introduced. It also aids in system maintenance by keeping design documentation aligned with system versions, even when multiple versions are being supported simultaneously.

The link management facilities that enable advanced configuration management and traceability also enhance design integrity by allowing the IPSE to efficiently track dependencies between objects at arbitrarily small levels of granularity. Thus, a change to a data element or a process transformation in one design representation could trigger analysis of related representations, so that inconsistencies could be detected immediately and automatically.

Context Management

In team software development projects, individuals rarely need

Integrated CASE Environments 23

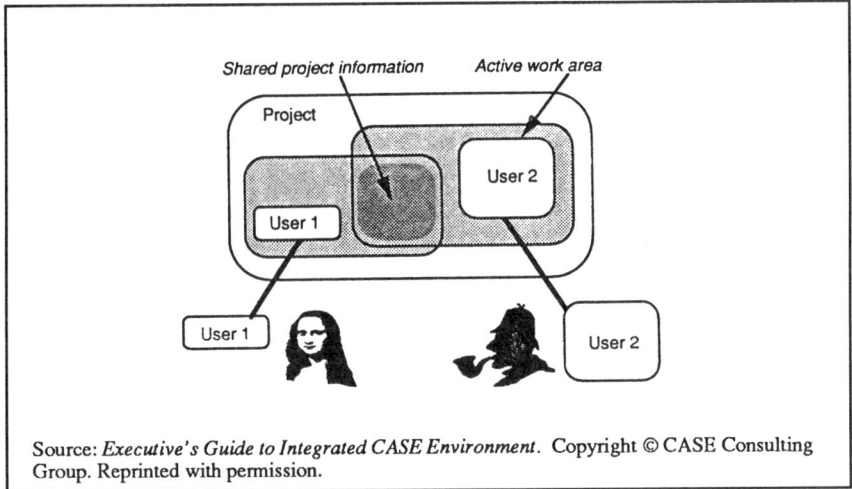

Source: *Executive's Guide to Integrated CASE Environment.* Copyright © CASE Consulting Group. Reprinted with permission.

Figure 10: Context Management

to access the entire system design at any one time. In fact, the "divide and conquer" strategy seeks to make each developer's area of responsibility disjoint from all the others, except at well-defined interfaces. To reduce the complexity and amount of information that the developer must deal with, the IPSE should be able to make selective views, or subsets, of the project database visible to each developer. In addition, a developer should be able to work with and modify her subset without fear of impact to any other part of the project until she is ready to merge that subset back into the larger system. The ability to selectively view portions of the overall system design and to transfer subsets into a separate workspace is commonly called "context management" (depicted in Figure 10). In many cases, subset workspaces (or contexts) overlap to some degree, so the IPSE must provide a way to merge them back into a single baseline, detecting any inconsistencies in the process.

Context management can also include security mechanisms that attach permissions to tools and components of the design that are specific to the developer. This places limits on the areas of a project that a developer can view, and the tools she is able to use. By controlling the scope presented to the developer, context management reduces apparent complexity and the possibility of inadvertent errors.

Work Flow Control

A key success factor for improving software development quality

24 Forte

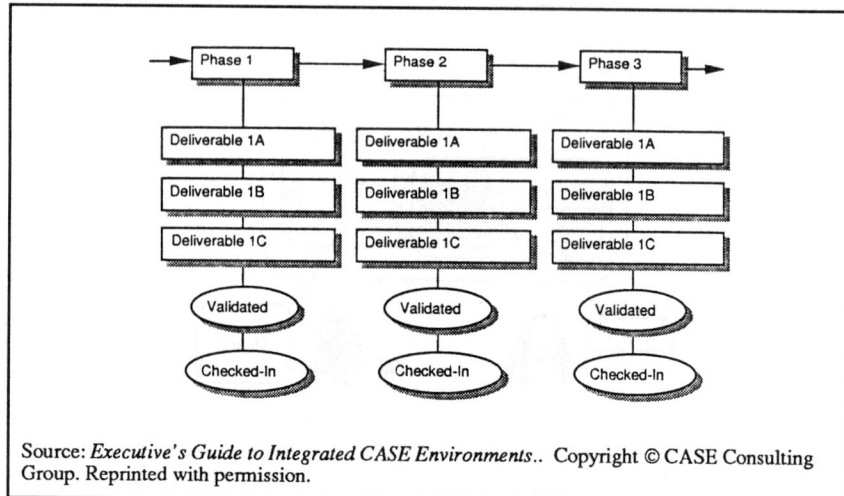

Source: *Executive's Guide to Integrated CASE Environments..* Copyright © CASE Consulting Group. Reprinted with permission.

Figure 11: Work Flow Control

and productivity is process maturity. The Software Engineering Institute has proposed a model of software development organizations comprising five levels of process maturity ranging from Initial (completely ad hoc process) to Optimized (continuous process improvement). To move from the Initial, or uncontrolled, state to the Optimized state, an organization must clearly define its software development process, put a Quality Assurance organization in place to monitor and enforce it, develop metrics to measure it, and place a high emphasis on long-term process improvement, rather than promoting only short-term, project-oriented results.

Though not a substitute for management attention to process issues, an IPSE can support movement toward process maturity in several ways. It can provide a mechanism for defining, documenting and monitoring the development process. Many of the process features can be automated or enforced by the environment, e.g., an orderly design document check-in/check-out process, or regular design analysis and reporting. The IPSE can enforce rules that specify what deliverables are required at each stage of development, and can ensure that all related documents are kept up-to-date (see Figure 11). The team communications facilities of an IPSE can be used to involve QA personal at critical points in the project, and ensure that they receive the correct deliverables.

Network Transparency

Figure 12 depicts today's state-of-the-art, large-scale software

Integrated CASE Environments 25

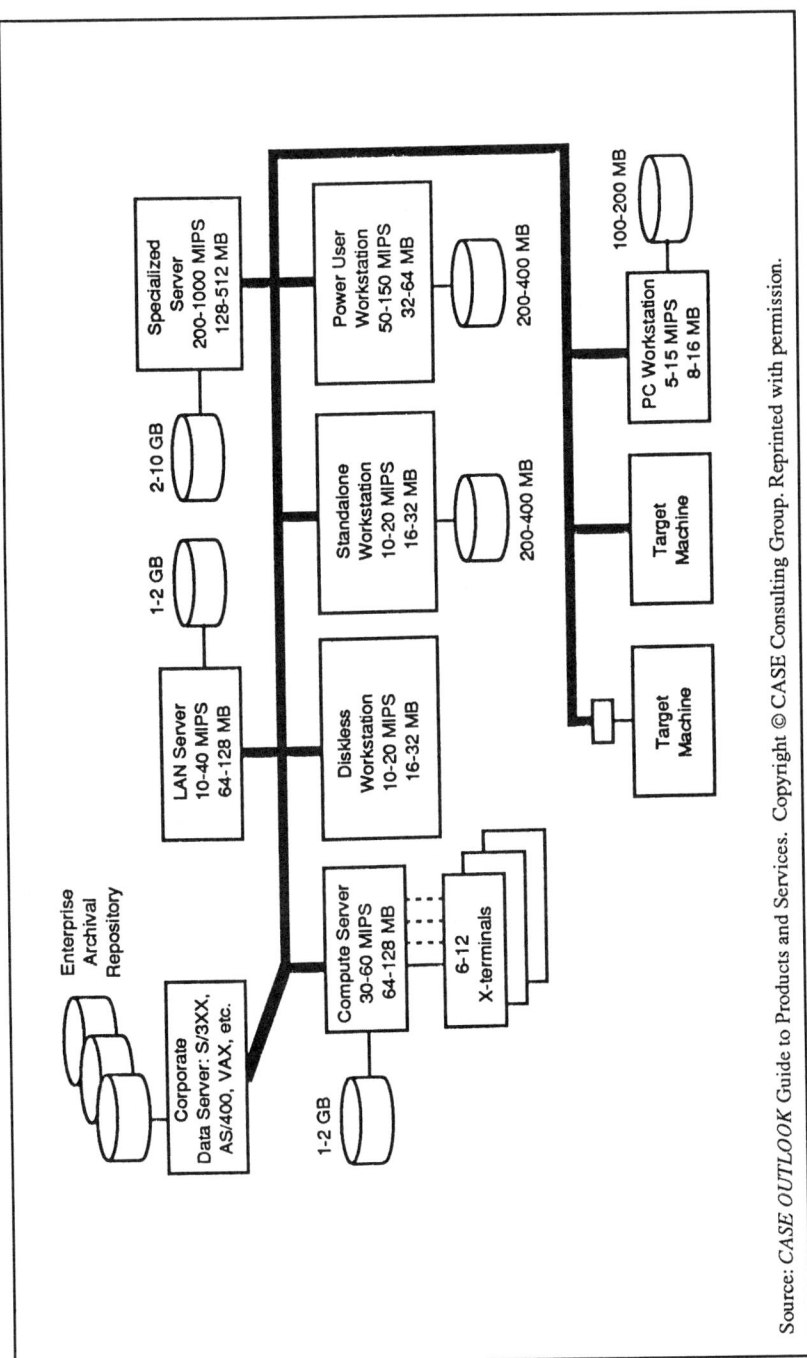

Source: *CASE OUTLOOK* Guide to Products and Services. Copyright © CASE Consulting Group. Reprinted with permission.

Figure 12: CASE Network Topologies

development computing plant. The CASE environment must be integrated with networking facilities so that access to data located anywhere in a heterogeneous network is transparent to the CASE user. This allows users to execute tools on remote workstations, to physically distribute design information while keeping it under configuration control, and to access specialized computing platforms when needed for special tasks such as system builds, simulation or computation-intensive design rule checking and analysis. Remote tool execution also supports debugging on target hardware from a developer's familiar CASE platform, rather than forcing her to learn a new environment.

Operating System Portability

Finally, an IPSE should be independent of the underlying operating system and computing platform so that platforms can be mixed in response to resource demands, and so that technology changes in these areas have a minimal impact on the development organization. An IPSE should make it possible to employ either a generic (platform-independent) user interface, or the native interface associated with each platform, depending on the user's preference.

OPEN VS. CLOSED ARCHITECTURES

There are several strategies for implementing an integrated CASE environment. The most direct approach is to design all the tools and their underlying database (or repository) as a single monolithic system. This approach has merit from the standpoint of quality control and time to market, provided the vendor has sufficient resources. However, the size and complexity of the task is so great that, to date, no vendor has delivered a fully integrated CASE environment as described here, although there are a few that come close (see below).

If we limit our scope to a portion of the full CASE environment and to limited application domains, there are several vendors that have been able to deliver highly integrated products. For example, in the commercial segment Texas Instruments' Information Engineering Facility, KnowledgeWare's Information Engineering Workbench, Andersen Consulting's Foundation, CGI's PacBase and PacLan, Softlab's Maestro II, American Management Systems' LPS, and Intersolv's APS Series address the software development life cycle from planning through code generation and integration. However, these products have proprietary architectures and tend to be targeted to a fairly narrow application domain. Typically, they support only a single methodology, or are methodology independent (as opposed to providing flexible methodology support).

Each of these companies is addressing the issue of how to modularize their products so they can evolve with the technology and the marketplace, with Softlab perhaps the furthest along in this respect with their flexible Object Management System and metamodel facilities. Some companies, exemplified by Futuretech Systems, VSF Ltd. and Ipsys, have based their CASE workbench on an internal, methodology-free specification language with a meta-model description facility, giving the workbench a great amount of flexibility in supporting new methods, or the unique variations of their individual customers.

Even considering the success of some of the monolithic workbench products, to meet the needs of the larger software development context (project management, configuration management, testing, quality control, etc.) as well as the desire for domain-specific specialty tools, we believe an open tool integration facility is still required. Once a robust integration framework is in place, it opens the way for incorporation of more and more specialized tools for targeted tasks and application domains. Consequently, over the long term we expect a migration toward open frameworks permitting tools from multiple vendors to be integrated into a consistent CASE environment.

A Model for Open Integration

An open approach to integration is desirable because it provides the greatest choice of tools for users while minimizing the risk of obsolescence due to changes in technology. On the other hand, it is also the most difficult to achieve since it requires well-defined standards for CASE integration.

The CASE open integration model is a reference model that we can use as a basis for developing standards, just as the OSI reference model for systems interconnection serves as a basis for networking and telecommunications protocol standards (see Figure 13). The CASE reference model is layered to provide flexibility to accommodate changes in the underlying platform, database and operating system technology, tools and methodologies, and to permit operation in a heterogeneous environment. It provides a stable environment within which tools may be modified or replaced, as CASE technology and the needs of the user evolve (Nolan, 1988).

The top layers of the model tend to be application domain specific, i.e., tailored to a particular type of software or industry. For

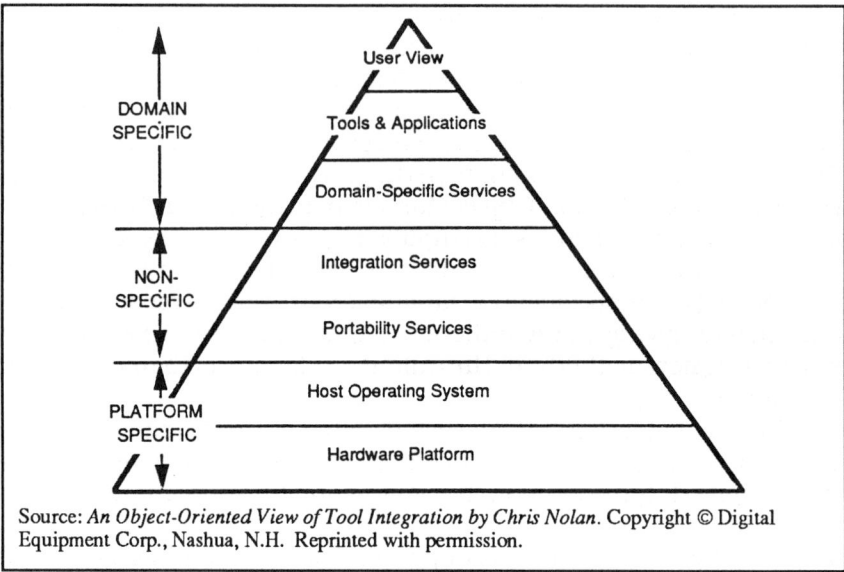

Figure 13: CASE Open Integration Reference Model

example, aerospace software designers require different tools and services and prefer to work with different methodologies and notations than software developers in the financial services industry. Currently there is a trend toward industry-standard graphical user interfaces, such as Motif, Open Look, and the underlying X-Windows system. However, CASE tool environments will eventually emerge that add value by customizing or extending the user interface and the tool set for particular vertical niches.

At the bottom of the architecture is the hardware platform itself with its unique operating system and services. Above it is a portability layer that isolates the higher levels of the CASE framework from platform specifics, typically by implementing a "generic" operating system on top the vendor-specific operating system. In the middle are domain- and platform-independent services that comprise data and control integration facilities.

With this reference model in mind, what might a typical CASE integration framework architecture look like? Like the reference model, it would be highly layered to maintain flexibility and independence from technology and methodology changes (see Figure 14a). The layers would map to the three major areas of integration: presentation, data and control integration (Figure 14b). The specific facilities found in each layer of an open integration platform are discussed below.

Integrated CASE Environments 29

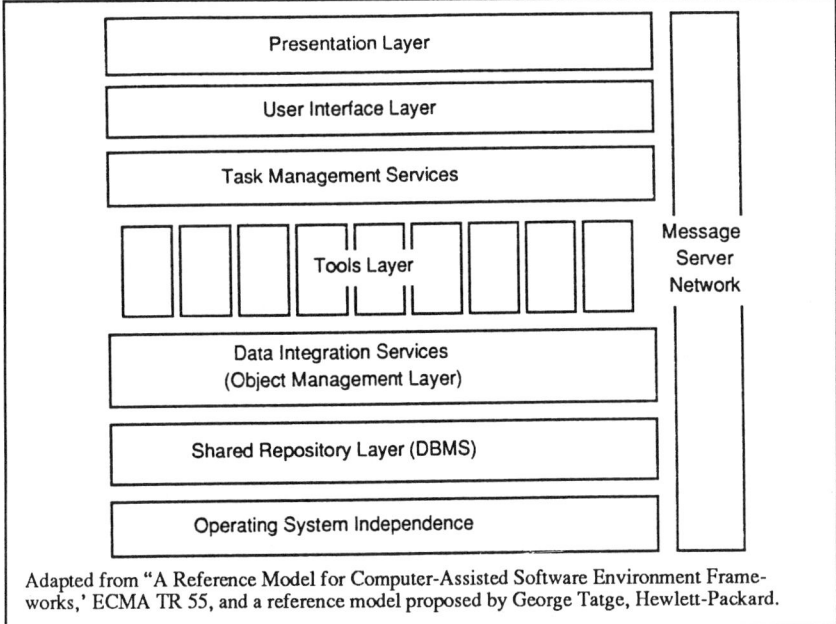

Figure 14a. Typical CASE Open Integration Framework Architecture

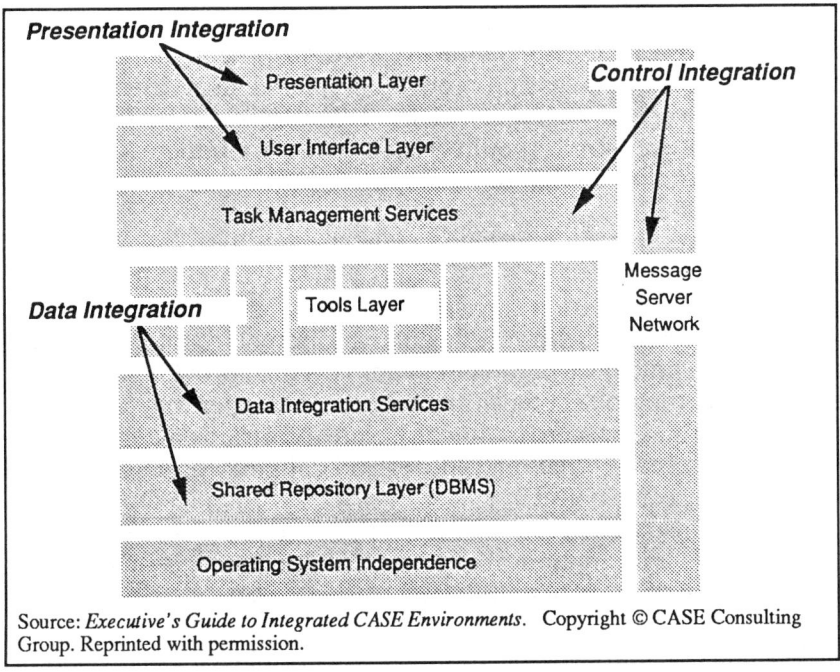

Figure 14b. Mapping the Architecture to the Dimensions of Integration

Presentation Layer

The presentation layer defines a common "look-and-feel" seen by the user across all tools in the CASE environment. A similar way to access all tools, similar window controls, menus, help messages, error messages, and interaction styles reduce the learning curve of the developer. Consistency also reduces confusion and errors when using many tools. Important presentation styles include OSF's Motif, Sun's Open Look, Microsoft's Windows, Apple's Mac OS, and IBM's Presentation Manager.

User Interface Layer

The user interface layer supplies the underlying mechanisms for a graphical user interface, such as a window manager, scroll bars, buttons, select boxes, pop-up menus, dialog boxes, and so on. In the UNIX environment, the most important GUI is X-Windows, while CUA is the de facto standard under IBM's SAA. Besides a library of graphics primitives called "widgets," X-Windows also provides a client-server protocol that enables local display of a remotely executing X-Windows process. In practical terms, this means that CASE tools with an X-Windows user interface layer can execute in a distributed fashion over a network. For example, a debugger could execute on a remote target platform (X-Window client) while the user controls the debug session from a graphical user interface (X-Window server) executing on a local workstation. In fact, each window on a workstation could actually control a remote X-Window process executing on different computing platforms.

Data Integration Services Layer

The data integration services layer (also called the object management layer) provides a very flexible way for tools to interface to the repository. The object paradigm is employed to provide maximum extensibility (new object types and relationship types may be defined using inheritance properties), and to isolate tools from having undesirable effects on each other (procedures and data may be encapsulated within tool-specific objects).

This is also the layer where meta data is defined and managed. Meta data is information about the CASE environment that, for example, can include definitions of:

- The objects that can be modeled and managed in the CASE environment

- Design rules for each method employed
- Definitions of the procedures and deliverables that make up the firm's unique software engineering process

To support the definition and maintenance of meta data, this layer provides a set of services that allow a CASE administrator to inspect, modify and place access controls on the meta data.

The data integration services layer also provides "trigger" or event notification facilities that alert the other tools and services in the rest of the environment when data changes or events occur. The data integration services layer also participates in context management by introducing the notion of repository "views" and workspaces associated with individual developers. Also, some of the data distribution and access security facilities are implemented at this layer.

Of course, depending on the specific implementation, there is some overlap of functionality across layers. The partitioning will be different for different framework implementations. For example, security enforcement might be located partially in the data integration services layer and partly in the repository layer. The partitioning decisions are based on what features the framework implementor feels can be made independent of the next lower layer.

Data Repository Layer

The shared repository provides common data and relationship (link) management for all the tools in the CASE environment. The repository must be able to manage a very wide variety of object types, not just text and code. Any type of textual, graphical, or binary information associated with software development will eventually be managed by the CASE repository. In the future, this may also include object types like voice mail and video. In addition to the objects themselves, the repository stores information about relationships among objects. This ranges from the business relationships depicted in an enterprise data model, to the relationships among development team members defined by the organization's software development process standards. The traditional configuration management dependencies are expanded in scope to include relationships among all the development intermediate and deliverable products such as dataflow diagrams, E-R diagrams, structure charts, test data, test plans, test results, requirements documents, user documentation, project plans, etc. Full versioning and naming conventions apply to all these work products and may be supported and enforced by the repository itself.

The repository supports arbitrary groupings of objects into

aggregations that the developer may find useful. For example, an aggregation of all the requirements, design documents, source modules, make files and test suites might be designated as an official "baseline configuration." Once identified as a composite object, it can be managed as a single entity with its own versions, security level, dates of creation and modification, and so on.

The repository also takes care of the more traditional database management services such as transaction management, roll back in the event of system failure, multi-user access arbitration, archiving and access security.

Message Server Network

The message server provides a software communications path among all the tools in the environment. Messages are "multicast" via a discriminating message delivery mechanism. This means that tools can specify what type of messages they need to receive (via tool registration) and the message server will only deliver a particular message type to the appropriate subset of tools. This greatly enhances efficiency, which becomes important in an environment with a large number of tools and many developers.

The message server also distributes knowledge of special events such as event and data triggers throughout the environment. The message server operates across physical networks transparently and incorporates security provisions to control the type of information being passed, and where it can go.

Task Management Services

The task management services layer allows the developer to define and execute composite tasks that require the cooperation and synchronization of several tools. This layer provides a user interface for task definition and presentation, and services for tool synchronization and execution management.

This layer also supports the definition of a standard software development process. The associated tasks and triggers can be used to monitor and enforce the process, in many cases performing some of the required procedures automatically.

Operating System Portability Layer

Finally, a platform portability layer isolates the CASE framework from the specifics of a particular operating system and computer architecture by interpreting between generic service calls made at higher levels, and the platform-specific calls to the native

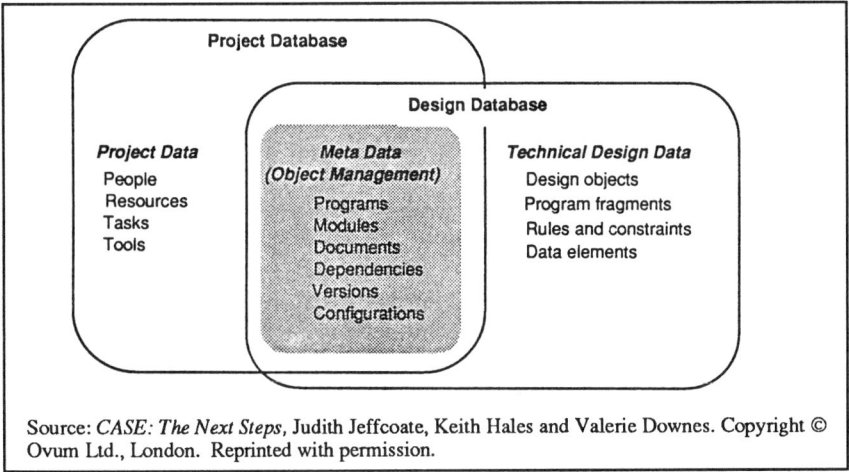

Figure 15: Repository Contents

operating system. As operating systems themselves become more standardized through industry specifications such as POSIX and X/OPEN, this layer could shrink and ultimately disappear.

REPOSITORY: THE CORE OF CASE INTEGRATION

The repository is the central data integration facility for a CASE environment. As such, it contains a broad range of information, or object types, including the traditional information involved with system design and project management. In addition, it introduces another level of information, called "meta data," that previously was managed manually (see Figure 15).

Meta data includes definitions of the types of objects that can be stored in the repository. It also includes information about the relationships and dependencies among the objects, version and configuration information (which versions of which objects make a baseline), audit information (when created, owner, why modified, etc.), access privileges and composite task definitions. The repository also provides a facility to store a variety of rules related to the software development activity. These include rules defining specific methods, design notations and techniques, process (work flow) procedures and required deliverables, QA requirements and security rules.

Repository Services

In addition to storing a wide variety of object types, the repository provides a set of services to support the administration and use of the repository data. Of course, multi-user access is supported through appropriate locking mechanisms. Other services allow the repository contents to be decomposed into subsets which may be hierarchically related. Subsets may also be re-merged or consolidated into larger aggregates. The repository has facilities for importing from, or exporting to, other databases or tools.

Most of the time, repository information is accessed through the CASE tools. However, the repository administrator may want to access information directly to produce special reports or to reconfigure information. For example, when a new project starts up, rather than starting with an empty project repository, the administrator may load it with selected information from the corporate repository based on previous projects. The ability to browse in several modes is valuable. Some reports might lend themselves well to a relational view using SQL queries. Alternately, the administrator may need to navigate based on object types or relationships between objects in order to find desired information. For example, maintaining the meta model that describes valid design rules and modeling notations is most conveniently done via entity-relationship or object-oriented views of the repository contents. The repository also has services supporting security enforcement, relationship management, and transaction control which it uses to maintain its own contents. These services may also be used by individual CASE tools.

Work flow control (i.e., managing the software development process itself) can be implemented within the task management layer through inter-tool communications and event triggers, as described above. Alternately, it can be managed through repository rules associated with data triggers. More advanced solutions will use a combination of both techniques.

Repository Model Levels

A CASE repository not only deals with a broad range of information types, but also contains information at several conceptual levels (see Figure 16). The lowest level is the operational level, i.e., the data used by the daily operation of the application. In current CASE systems, this data is not managed strictly within the repository, but rather in a separate database management system associated with the application. The operational level is mentioned here for completeness, and because trends indicate that CASE repositories may in the future become far more dynamic and interact directly with operational systems. This would allow applications to bind data definitions, network configurations and other information at run time

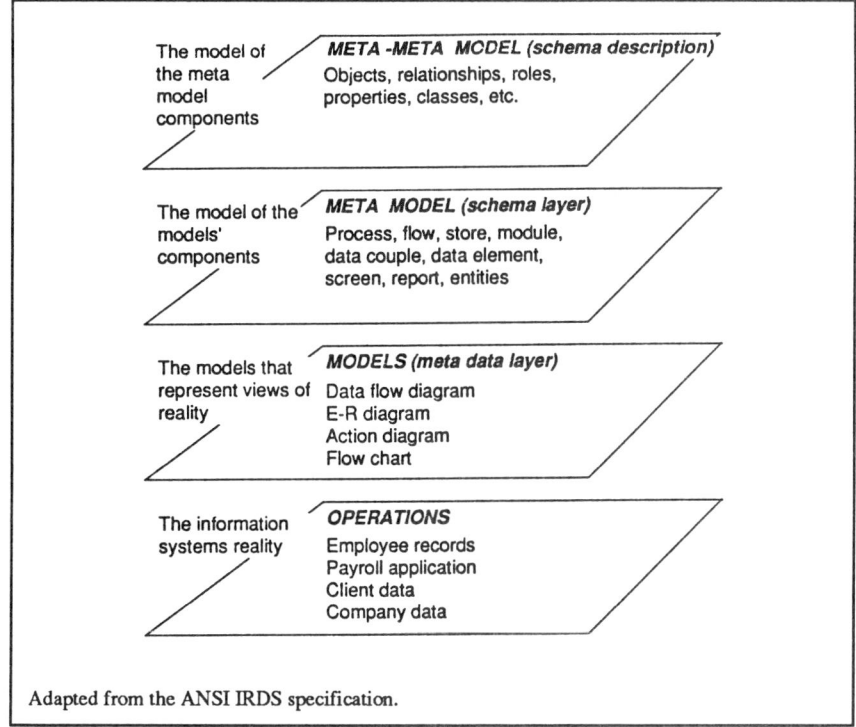

Figure 16: Repository Conceptual Levels

rather than at system generation time. In this sense, the repository would become part of the actual executing application itself.

The next higher level is the "model layer," (also called the meta data level) which contains the specific models of applications. This layer would define the data flow diagrams, E-R diagrams, action diagrams, structure charts, state transition diagrams, flow charts, etc., that describe the system of interest.

Above the model layer is the "meta model" layer (also called the schema layer) which describes the types of modeling notations and rules available to the developer in specifying an application. It contains descriptions of object types such as "process, data flow, control flow, store, module, data couple, screen, report format," etc. In addition, it contains rules about how these types can be meaningfully arranged and related to describe systems. Usually, the object and relationship types are described in terms of entity-relationship or object-oriented notations. Integrity rules and actions can be associated with specific object types, object aggregations and events.

The meta model layer provides the CASE environment with a great amount of flexibility to accommodate the evolution of software development methods and tools, and to adapt to the unique aspects of different organizations. The alternative to a meta model layer is to embed the methodology, design notations, design rules, etc. directly into the code of the CASE framework and the individual tools. This not only makes it more difficult for the CASE environment to evolve, but it results in fragmentation of the integrity checking rules and generally yields a lower level of confidence in the completeness and correctness of designs. Most emerging CASE workbenches and environments include a repository with a meta model layer built on top of a commercial database management system, either relational or object-oriented.

Some repositories allow access to the meta model by a specialist (the repository manager), while others hide the meta model and do not allow modifications to it, meaning that, as far as the customer is concerned, the model (and therefore the method) is fixed. IBM's Repository Manager (part of AD/Cycle) and DEC's CDD/Repository permit access to the CASE meta model. The ANSI Information Resource Directory Services (IRDS) repository standard also defines a meta model layer.

The next layer is called the "meta-meta model" layer. This highly conceptual layer describes what components and capabilities are available for creating meta models. While it may seem that this progression could go on forever, it appears that the meta-meta layer provides a sufficient degree of abstraction to deal effectively with CASE environments. The meta-meta layer provides another degree of freedom for extending the meta model and also simplifies the definition of design rules and integrity checking. For example, a set of meta model object types may be grouped as "flow from" objects and another grouped as "flow to" objects. It then becomes a simple matter to introduce a design rule that says only "flow from" and "flow to" objects may connect with a "process" object type, rather than specifying all possible combinations of permissible connections between pairs of object types.

Implementing a Repository

CASE vendors have a variety of options for implementing the functions required in a CASE repository. One approach is to build the repository from the ground up, including all the DBMS facilities, and a few vendors (e.g. Softlab) have done this. Most vendors build CASE-specific capabilities on top of commercial relational, network or object-oriented database management systems. Often, the CASE-specific implementation is partitioned into a meta model layer, as described above, and other facilities such as tool integration, link management, and administration. The meta layer presents an E-R interface to the repository administrator for defining and maintaining the organization's approved methods and notations.

A few vendors have implemented special-purpose E-R databases from the ground up to support CASE in an effort to achieve better performance and integrity than possible using general-purpose DBMSs. However, the cost of developing and evolving the underlying DBMS as well as the CASE tools technology is prohibitive to most vendors. In addition, improvements in relational technology to some degree have closed the gap between these approaches. One technology that appears to have considerable promise for CASE repositories is object-oriented databases (OODBMS). OODBMSs inherently provide many of the capabilities needed for CASE and other design automation and engineering disciplines. As the underlying database technology, an OODBMS requires far less special-purpose code to be added on top to meet the CASE repository requirements, yet it offers the promise of industrial strength and commercial support, leaving CASE vendors free to concentrate on specific tools for design tasks.

Why Object Oriented?

The object-oriented paradigm offers a great degree of flexibility in the form of abstract data types and encapsulation, inheritance and polymorphism. These characteristics support greater extensibility, allowing the repository to accommodate new design notations, new methods, new processes and new tools. OODBMSs tend to be easier to evolve and maintain because design rules and methods can be closely associated with object types. Because OODBMSs have characteristics of a network database, it is possible to efficiently store and retrieve representations of multi-part relationships, which is inefficient with standard relational databases.

OODBMSs provide many of the unique services needed by a repository, and the mechanism of polymorphism allows these generic services to operate on a wide range of object types, including those defined by the user. This makes it easier to introduce new tools and methods requiring new object types without affecting the existing environment. OODBMSs, like object-oriented languages, are based on a message-passing paradigm which is very useful for implementing the required communication among the large number of CASE tools in a robust environment.

Although OODBMSs seem suited as a foundation for CASE repositories, the products themselves are relatively new. As with relational database technology, OODBMS vendors will experience a learning curve in which the responsiveness, robustness and integrity of the technology improve dramatically. This process has already begun, but most CASE vendors are approaching OODBMS technology carefully, and hedging their bets by pursuing relational repositories as their mainline technology for the present.

CURRENT APPROACHES TO INTEGRATION

Full CASE integration is a difficult challenge full of technical and marketing risks. For this reason, CASE integration is being introduced to the marketplace in stages (see Figure 17). There are still many CASE tools that are essentially standalone products, leaving it up to the user to incorporate their output into the next stage of development. Many tools have export facilities that can load internal data into a flat file that can be parsed by a translator and restructured into a form needed by another tool. This, of course, requires that the user build the translator, unless she can find one that already exists from the vendor or another user. Tool user groups are often good sources for such tool "bridges."

Point-to-point bridges are not good long-term solutions, however, because they become extremely cumbersome when many tools are used, and when iterative development cycles are employed. They also create a significant opportunity for data corruption, for example, when the translation process gets out of sync (i.e., part of a design gets updated and passed on to subsequent tools and another part does not).

Other partial integration solutions provide a common user interface so that tools can be easily invoked and present the same look-and-feel, thus reducing user learning curve. Control integration strategies provide tool-to-tool communication and synchronization, but each tool administers its own internal database, so there is little or no data sharing.

Data integration strategies provide common DBMS facilities for all tools in the environment, and ultimately will include semantic definition of the design information so that all tools can interpret each other's data as appropriate. In fact, the most promising solution is to record all design information in a completely normalized (non-redundant), representation-independent format that is interpreted by each tool.

The goal of CASE integration frameworks is to combine all these aspects of integration into a single layered architecture. Although no commercially available open CASE framework meets all the requirements discussed above, there are some useful products now on the

Integrated CASE Environments 39

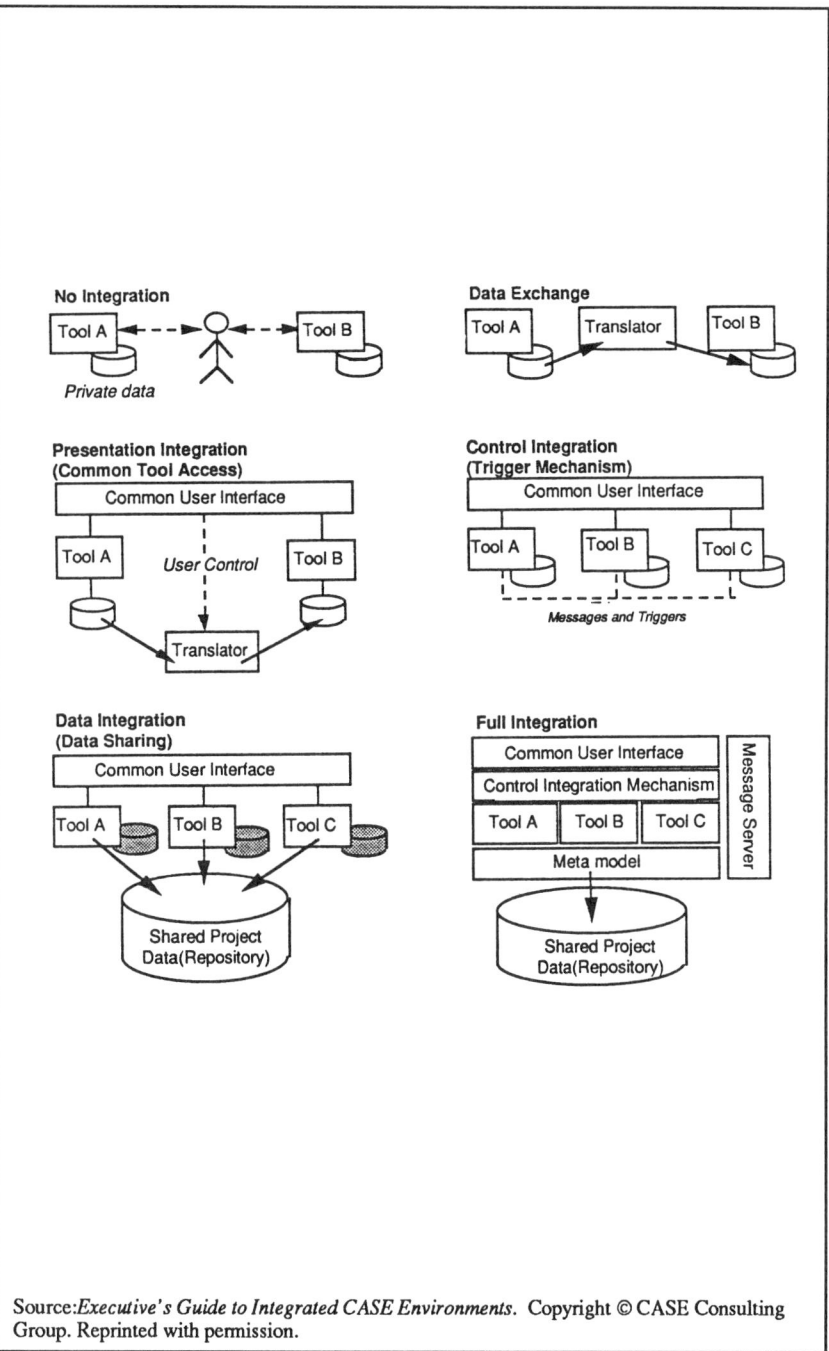

Source:*Executive's Guide to Integrated CASE Environments*. Copyright © CASE Consulting Group. Reprinted with permission.

Figure 17: Steps toward Full Integration

market that provide significant added value to a toolkit of discrete CASE tools.

Texas Instrument's Information Engineering Facility

IEF is an example of a proprietary integrated CASE toolset for developing large-scale information systems. It provides a set of tools that implement the Information Engineering methodology as developed by James Martin Associates under contract to TI. IEF project teams build information systems by creating a set of diagrams that model business information and activities. Then IEF automatically generates all the code implied by the model including database schema definitions, screen maps, JCL, transaction controls and Cobol or C code. IEF addresses the entire systems life cycle, from initial planning through code generation and maintenance.

IEF is integrated through a proprietary, mainframe-based central repository (encyclopedia in IEF terms) which maintains all design components. IEF's encyclopedia consists of a repository engine, meta model and object-oriented tool interface built on top of the standard DB2 relational DBMS from IBM. Multiple developers can share contents of the repository and upload or download portions of a project model for development on individual workstations. A "subsetting" facility allows developers to select portions of a large model based on scoping criteria such as entity types, subject areas, functions, processes, business areas, etc. Locking mechanisms establish model ownership on an object level. Owners may modify objects, and other developers may view but not modify locked objects. Merge facilities identify and help resolve inconsistencies when model subsets are re-merged. The repository provides model version control on individual components and component collections. Administrator, security and report facilities are also provided.

IEF is partitioned into workstation tools and host-based tools. The workstation includes toolsets for planning, analysis, design, construction (code generation), and implementation (installing, testing and debugging) with a local (single-user) encyclopedia and linkage (upload/download) to host encyclopedias. Design models are typically developed on multiple workstations and consist of three types of graphical representations: data models (entity-relationship, dataflows, physical data models), interaction models (processes, screens, etc.), and activity models (menu dialogs, activity decomposition, transaction synchronization, etc.). All model components are continuously checked for consistency and completeness so that valid models are guaranteed to generate executable code. Applications can be generated and executed on the workstation; alternately, the design can be uploaded to a host and generated and tested in the mainframe environment. IEF provides facilities for enterprise modeling , business systems planning, and business re-engineering as well as for systems analysis and design. Business models include organizational charts, planning matrices, functional dependency diagrams, and business area diagrams.

The host supports the central, multi-user IEF encyclopedia with import/export facilities to foreign repositories, IBM's CSP/ESF and generic public interfaces. A model management toolset is provided for partitioning, merging and versioning large project design databases. There is also a reverse engineering toolset for capturing existing Cobol data structures, IMS/DB DBD macros and SQL DDL. Host construction and implementation toolsets are provided for each supported target platform/operating system. IEF supports cross development from the PC to the IBM, DEC and Tandem mainframe environments using Cobol as the target language; IEF also supports development for Unix targets and will offer C and Ada code generation in the future.

TI has indicated that it will maintain links to IBM's Repository Manager and DEC's CDD/Repository; a Public Interface is available with an import/export utility, giving users and third party tool vendors access to repository data. However, IEF is not an "open CASE environment" in the sense that it is not easy for customers to obtain interoperability between their own choice of tools and IEF. To a large degree, this reflects TI's strategic priority to provide a working end-to-end solution first (albeit a closed one). We expect to see gradual "opening up" of the IEF environment with facilities such as a modifiable metamodel, more encyclopedia administrator access facilities, third-party tool invocation facilities, and so on. IEF would also benefit from the addition of more extensive configuration management, project management, process management and regression testing tools.

Hewlett Packard's HP SoftBench

HP's SoftBench primarily addresses the presentation and control dimensions of CASE integration. It has three major components: an integrated programmer's workbench for C and C++, tool integration facilities and services for distributed computing.

The program construction toolkit includes a syntax-directed source editor, an automatic program builder (similar to the UNIX make facility), compilers, a static analyzer, an interactive debugger and a development manager for file access and context management. All these tools operate in the SoftBench environment with a Motif

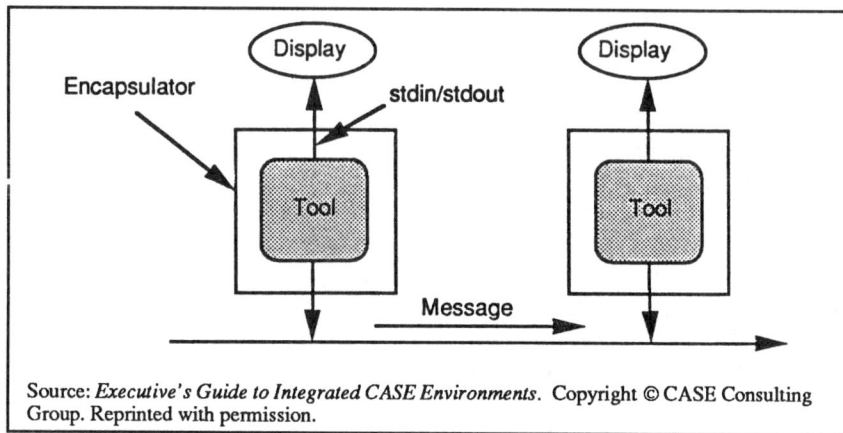

Source: *Executive's Guide to Integrated CASE Environments*. Copyright © CASE Consulting Group. Reprinted with permission.

Figure 18: Hewlett Packard's HP SoftBench

user interface, and are well integrated. For example, during compilation, errors are displayed on the screen and the source editor is automatically invoked and positioned to the offending source code line. The debugger is also linked to the editor so the developer can specify breakpoints and variables and track program execution in symbolic terms, and also view the currently executing code with the program editor.

The tool integration platform provides a message server allowing tools to communicate with each other and to coordinate their actions through event triggers (see Figure 18). Each tool registers with the environment, indicating what types of messages it needs to receive. The message server then routes messages originating from any tool only to the appropriate receivers wherever they are located on a network. In this way, many tools can be accommodated without suffering performance degradation. Distributed computing services also include support for remote procedure calls (RPC) and X-Window client-server protocols, and the NFS and RFA distributed file systems.

A special tool, called HP Encapsulator, assists developers wanting to integrate existing non-HP tools into the SoftBench environment. HP Encapsulator can adapt any tool with a programmatic interface to operate within the SoftBench environment by wrapping it in an interface layer. To the tool integrator, HP Encapsulator appears as a high-level language in which she describes the tool interface and indicates the type and format of messages sent and responded to by the tool. The tool integrator can also define tool events that send triggers to other tools. For example, UNIX tools using "stdin/stdout" I/O, commonly used with pipes, can be encapsulated to give them a Motif user interface and to allow them to communicate via the SoftBench message bus. The tool source code does not have to be modified, provided there is programmatic access to all the desired tool functionality. Typically, encapsulation requires from 2 days for simple tools, to a few weeks for complex tools, depending on the experience of the tool integrator.

Because of the ease of incorporating existing tools into the CASE environment, HP SoftBench has enjoyed rapid acceptance in the marketplace. It has been ported (by HP) to Sun's SPARCstation and has been licensed by IBM for its RS/6000 workstations. Sun and DEC have also announced integration products (ToolTalk and ACAS respectively) similar in concept to HP SoftBench. The integration portion of all these products is essentially a multicast message server based on the work of Tim Rice at Brown University.

Sun's Network Software Environment (NSE) and Tooltalk

NSE provides facilities to manage the relationships among objects in the CASE environment (see Figure 19). It supports typed objects, a limited inheritance scheme, distributed access to objects (via NSF) and a notification facility similar to HP SoftBench's event triggers.

NSE's link facility maintains a database of dependencies among objects in the environment. These are established by direct user manipulation or in response to tool requests. The link facility is

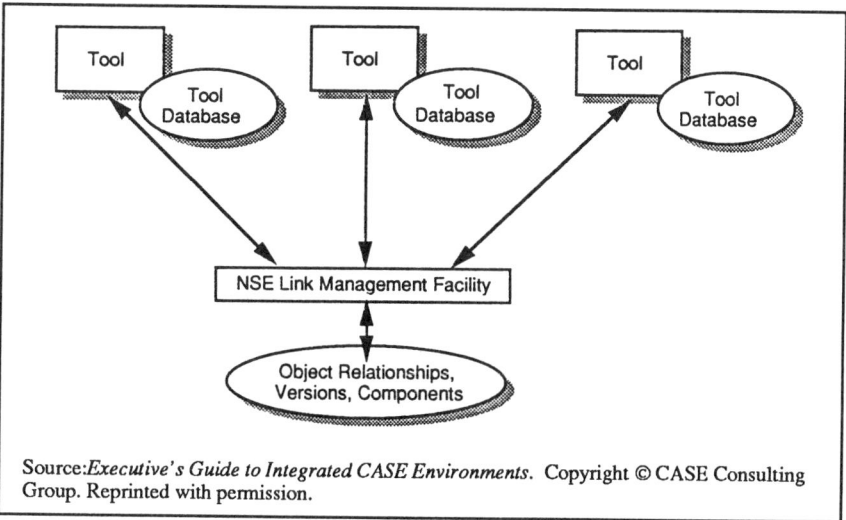

Source:*Executive's Guide to Integrated CASE Environments.* Copyright © CASE Consulting Group. Reprinted with permission.

Figure 19: Sun's NSE

44 Forte

integrated with a version and configuration management system that supports object aggregations called components. Components can be used to define baseline configurations which can also be placed under version control. Parallel development is supported with multiple antecedents and a "reconcile" function to re-merge parallel paths. Under NSE, each CASE tool maintains its own database of development work products (objects), but may establish links to any other tool's objects through the link facility.

More recently, Sun has started to replace NSE with a facility called ToolTalk that is similar to HP SoftBench. It provides a multicast message server based on a model of communicating objects. It is reportedly closer in capability and concept to the specification for a true Object Request Broker, as defined by the Object Management Group. In fact, the CASE integration problem is increasingly being viewed as a special case of the generalized need to integrate applications across heterogeneous networks. Thus, HP SoftBench, ToolTalk and DEC's ACAS (described below) are all precursors to more general-purpose facilities expected to become part of the network operating system (actually, ACAS may already fulfill that role as part of NAS).

Sun has also announced SPARCworks which includes the Sun programming tools (editor, debugger, etc.) integrated with ToolTalk, making it roughly functionally equivalent to HP SoftBench.

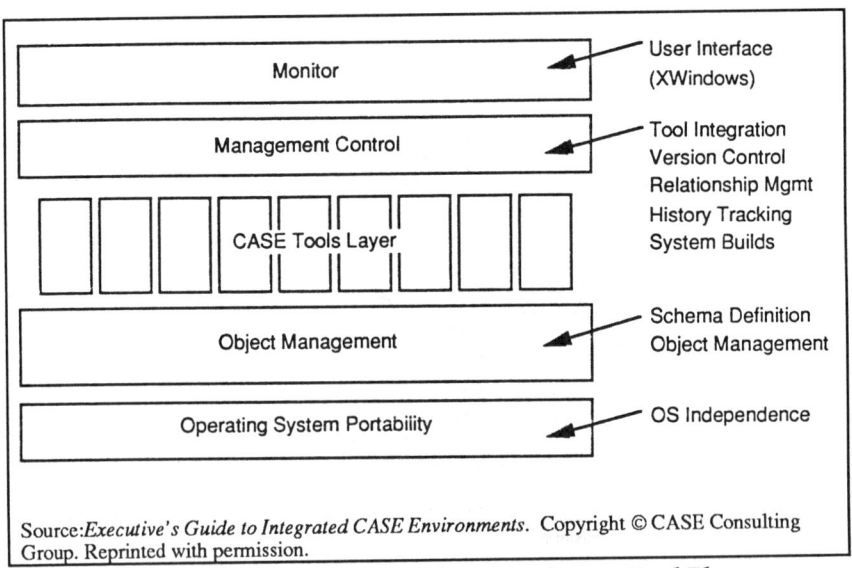

Source:*Executive's Guide to Integrated CASE Environments.* Copyright © CASE Consulting Group. Reprinted with permission.

Figure 20: Atherton Technology's Software BackPlane

Atherton's Software BackPlane

The Software BackPlane was one of the first commercial implementations of a CASE integration framework. Its organization is close to the integration reference model described earlier, with layers for user interface presentation, tool integration and control, object management and operating system portability (see Figure 20). The Software BackPlane goes beyond link management and provides an object-oriented repository facility for tool data integration. It also provides an event notification facility via the data interface, but does not support direct tool-to-tool message transfer.

The tool integrator has a choice of several integration levels when using the Software BackPlane. The easiest alternative, level 1, requires about one day of effort to register a tool in the environment so it can be accessed on common menus. The files created by a tool can be placed under Software BackPlane configuration management with the second level of integration, which requires one to five days of effort per tool. The first two levels require no source code modification within the tool itself. Full data integration at the object level does require tool code modification and typically takes from two to four weeks. In the DEC environment, an object management layer derived from the Software BackPlane is built on top of CDD/Repository to provide tool integration services.

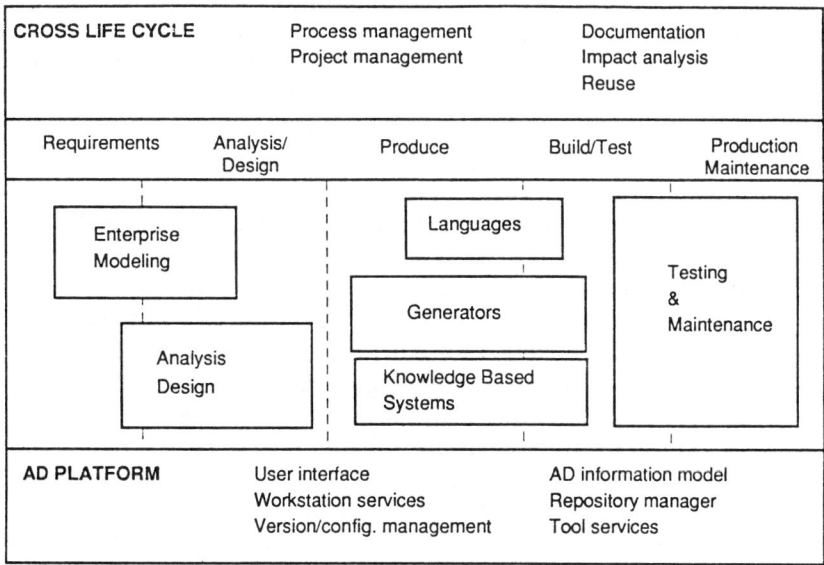

Copyright © IBM Corporation. Reprinted with permission.

Figure 21: IBM's AD/Cycle

46   Forte

IBM's AD/Cycle

AD/Cycle, as originally defined by IBM, also has a layered architecture with a user interface (presentation) layer on top of individual CASE tools (see Figure 21). A process control layer is also placed on top of the tools to monitor and control the software development process and to activate tools in support of the process. Below the tools is a set of common tool services and the repository layer which implements a meta model, object management, and other data integration services. AD/Cycle supports data triggers, global and tool-specific rules, and methods associated with objects and tools.

The data integration mechanism for AD/Cycle is Repository Manager/MVS (RM), an ERA-based development repository built on top of the DB2 relational database manager. RM provides tool integration and design data management facilities, a tool integration interface, facilities for creating new tools, an information model (still in progress) that defines the semantics of design data shared by multiple tools operating from RM, and administrative facilities to manage models in the repository. RM can manage all types of development data, including textual and graphical design documents, and source and object files (which are physically stored outside the repository). RM facilities support the creation of new forms-based tool interfaces that can access the repository via the information (meta) model. It also supports initiation of user-defined procedures (written in the SAA 3GLs) triggered by changes in the state of design data. RM helps enforce user-defined integrity constraints on design data such as mandatory relationships, valid domains and ranges, dependencies, etc.

The RM information model is a published interface, permitting third party tool suppliers to generate RM-compatible versions of their tools. Currently, RM operates only on IBM mainframes in a cooperative processing mode (central data, multiple workstations). PC-DOS and OS/2 workstations can access RM information directly or via interactive CASE tools running on the workstation.

In 1992, IBM announced that it would merge its AD/Cycle and AIX-based software development solutions in a new environment called "AD Platform" internally. AD Platform will integrate Hewlett Packard's Broadcast Message Server with an IBM implementation of PCTE acting as the repository. The Information Model developed for AD/Cycle will be ported to AD Platform and Extended. Both OS/2 and AIX workstations will be able to interoperate on a single Ethernet-TCP/IP network running a variety of software tools and accessing the shared PCTE repository executing initially on RS/6000-AIX servers. IBMs vision is that most of the software tools developed by IBM and its partners for AD/Cycle will be able to run in the AD Platform environment as well. To help achieve this, IBM is providing C++ user interface class libraries for AIX/Motif and OS/2 PM that will enable source code portability between the two window environments. IBM also wants to make its Information Model as an industry standard and has submitted it to ANSI for consideration. Acceptance of an open version of IM could be the "Rosetta Stone" the industry needs to achieve true tool integration, not only among all IBM-provided tools, but on an industry-wide basis.

DEC's Cohesion and ACA

DEC's overall CASE strategy is called Cohesion and is composed of computer system architectural standards (NAS), a CASE integration framework, a variety of Cohesion-compatible tools from DEC and third parties, and a training and consulting program. Integration under Cohesion is accomplished via DECwindows/Motif (presentation integration), CDD/Repository (data integration) and Advanced Communication Architecture Services (control integration).

CDD/Repository Version 5 is comprised of an object-oriented tool interface and object management system (based on the proposed ATIS standard) built on DEC's Rdb multiuser, distributed relational database and NAS network facilities. It is available under both VMS and Ultrix. An object-property-role-relationship (OPRR) model is used to store all development work products (design data and metadata) and their relationships across the life cycle. CDD/Repository is extensible; it supports method encapsulation, inheritance, versioned collections, workflow management, configuration management, dependency tracking, security management and tight integration of third-party tools. It currently works with Rdb, VAX Rally, VAX Cobol Generator, VAX Cobol, VAX Vida and third party tools from Cognos, Information Builders, and Andersen Consulting. DEC plans to eventually integrate most of its software tools with CDD/Repository.

CDD/Administrator provides direct access and administration facilities for an enterprise repository administrator. Based on DECwindows/Motif graphical interface, it provides multiple hierarchical navigators and graphical editors to browse, modify or extend the respository meta model and to examine and display repository contents. CDD/Administrator supports searches on keywords and attributes, produces customized reports, and operates in multiple workspaces showing user-specified subsets of the repository. It also provides a callable interface to allow customized displays, editors and reports, and supports the definition of roles as well as objects and properties enabling role-based access control and behavior.

ACAS provides facilities for integrating independently developed VMS and Ultrix applications and services across a networked, mixed-platform computing environment. ACAS provides services for handling application interaction, communication, and start-up. ACAS can be implemented at three levels, the first two requiring no source code changes to the application. The first level provides support mechanisms for registering and invoking independently developed applications. The second level allows applications to publish their externalized functions across a network. At the third level ACAS calls are used by the application to conduct communications with other ACAS servers and clients.

DEC FUSE for Ultrix is an programmer's workbench similar to HP SoftBench and SPARCworks built on top of a Multicast Message Server which integrates the activities of all DEC FUSE tools. MMS maintains a list of message patterns that each tool can send and receive and routes messages to the appropriate receivers. DEC FUSE provides a uniform DECwindows/Motif user interface across all tools and includes a source editor with breakpoints and trace integrated with a Motif-based dbx debugger. It supports multiple simultaneous debugger sessions with record and playback. A Program Builder supports makefile generation and provides graphical display of dependencies. A Call Graph Browser displays the program calling structure with panning and zooming to aid program navigation and provides mouse-sensitive program flowcharts for code analysis. A Profiler collects timing and performance information from prof, pixie and pixstats and displays it in bar chart form. A Cross-Referencer locates and classifies named program elements with user query capability and a Code Manager provides source code control based on sccs.

Softlab's Maestro II

Maestro II is a software development environment that is methodology, language, and target-platform independent. Maestro II provides communications facilities, a project management and time accounting system, an integrated database and library management system, editing and word processing functions, electronic mail, on-line help and documentation, and other facilities. It supports structured analysis and design methodologies with customizable graphical and pseudocode editors, a dialog design tool, a screen painter, and tools for JCL, 3GL and 4GL code generation. It also provides syntax and consistency checking, version control and audit trails, and workflow controls for implementation of development standards. Future versions of Maestro II will integrate with IBM's CASE platform and follow SAA specifications including Common User Access (CUA) guidelines as implemented in OS/2 and OS/2 EE.

Maestro II is based on a proprietary high-performance, multiuser, object-oriented database, called the Object Management System (OMS) specially designed to support software development. OMS employs an object/attribute/relationship/attribute metamodel with complex objects and object classes. The customizable metamodel can support a variety of tools and methods. All data and metadata associated with projects, including graphical and textual design representations, project plans, requirements, source and binary code, test data, and configurations, are stored in the OMS and are shared by all developers and tools (subject to access rights and rules). OMS supports elementary and user-defined transactions with multi-level access privileges, versions and variants, user roles and distributed data storage. It provides a data entry mask and menu browser, object editor, and query language interfaces to the OMS contents. Prolan II and C interfaces are also supported.

The base Maestro II system (which includes the OMS) provides the platform on which all other Maestro II product components run. It includes a multitasking, window-oriented user interface and desktop with various browsers, remote windowing, and terminal emulation. It also includes a text and document editing system, and a customizable, general-purpose graphics editor with diagram and template editing. A distributed file system (using NFS or RFS) supports electronic mail. There is also a print system with layout formatter and Postscript support, a user interface customizing facility, tool cusomizing facilities to describe unique tool meta models, and direct interfaces to the Object Management System using table editors and the proprietary PROLAN II compiled language. Administration functions are provided for management of security and access protection, configuration management and Maestro update support.

CASE INTEGRATION STANDARDS

Ideally, an open CASE integration framework would be based on industry standards. Unfortunately, there are no universally accepted CASE standards at present. However, there are a few official standards, and a number of standards bodies are continuing to study the problem from different perspectives with demonstration projects underway to assess the usefulness of the proposals. The most significant standards and standards proposals are:

- CAIS/A—Common APSE Interface Specification—a definition to allow independently developed tools to be used in an integrated Ada development environment. CAIS is sponsored by the Ada Joint Program Office, which is also investigating how to merge CAIS with the PCTE effort in Europe (see below).
- CDIF—CASE Data Interchange Format—a standard for exchanging information between two CASE tools proposed by the CDIF Technical Subcommittee of the EIA.
- IEEE-1175—a proposal by the IEEE Task Force on Professional Tools for a CASE tool interconnection standard (similar to CDIF). The proposal defines a way to exchange both syntactic and semantic information and deals with both textual and graphical data types.
- CIS/ATIS—CASE Integration Standard—a joint proposal by Digital and Atherton Technology for an extention to IRDS to make it a full object-oriented integration framework modeled after the Software BackPlane.
- PCTE—Portable Common Tool Environment—is a project which began in 1983 and was funded under the ESPRIT Program by a group of sponsors including Bull, GE, ICL, Nixdorf, Siemens, and Olivetti. A second generation of PCTE, PCTE+, was defined after extensive use and review of the first version. PCTE+ adds a number of additional capabilities beyond those provided by PCTE, including composite entities, definable versioning and security policies, an object-based metabase (meta model), type inheritance, process and activity representations, accounting facilities, new attribute types for reals and enumerations, and event notification. In 1991, ECMA adopted PCTE+ with some revisions as ECMA Standard 149 and also adopted the associated open reference model as Technical Report 55 (ECMA, 1990). In October of 1992, the U.S. National Institute of Standards and Technology (NIST), the U.S. Office of Defense Information and the Object Management Group (OMG) jointly proposed a North American PCTE Initiative (NAPI). The purpose of NAPI would be to build a publicly available reference implementation of PCTE, to establish a validation capability and to support the acquisition of PCTE-based products. Under the proposal, NAPI would be jointly funded by the U.S. Government and private companies. As of this writing, the proposal is still in the discussion stage with open meetings being conducted among interested parties.

Integrated CASE Environments 51

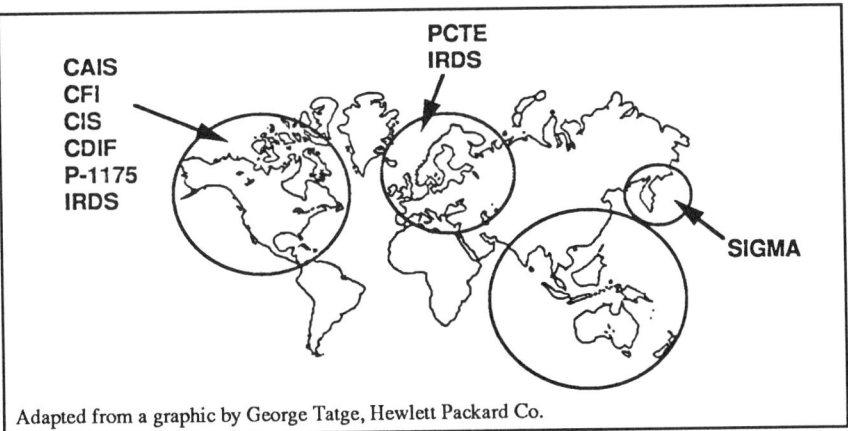

Adapted from a graphic by George Tatge, Hewlett Packard Co.

Figure 22: World Impact of CASE Standards

- IRDS—Information Resource Directory Services—is actually two standards (one from ANSI and a different one from ISO) defining the architecture and services for an information systems repository. Several vendors, including IBM and Pansophic Systems (two driving forces behind IRDS), have stated their intent to remain compatible with IRDS, which is still evolving.
- SIGMA—Software Industrialized Generator & Maintenance Aids—is not really a standard. It is the Japanese software engineering initiative which is primarily focused on how to achieve software reusability through the Software Factory concept. Under this program a consortium of Japanese companies is working to build advanced programming workstations and to build reusable modules for specific industry segments. These modules will be shared by the firms involved.
- OOTIS—Object Oriented Tool Interface Standard—is an IBM-proposed extension to PCTE (ECMA 149) which adds object-oriented features and facilities. It has been submitted to the PCTE standard committee, the Object Management Group and ANSI X3H6 among other public forums. Along with the Information Model, OOTIS represents IBMs attempt to drive the open tool integration standards process.
- CASE Communique—is an industry group initiated by Hewlett Packard, IBM, Control Data Corp. and Informix in order to standardize the messages exchanged among tools using HPs Broadcast Message Server facility. The goal of the group is to define platform-independent "operation specifications" that describe the syntax and functionality of a set of services which may be invoked via messages sent over the BMS. Ultimately the goal is to have the

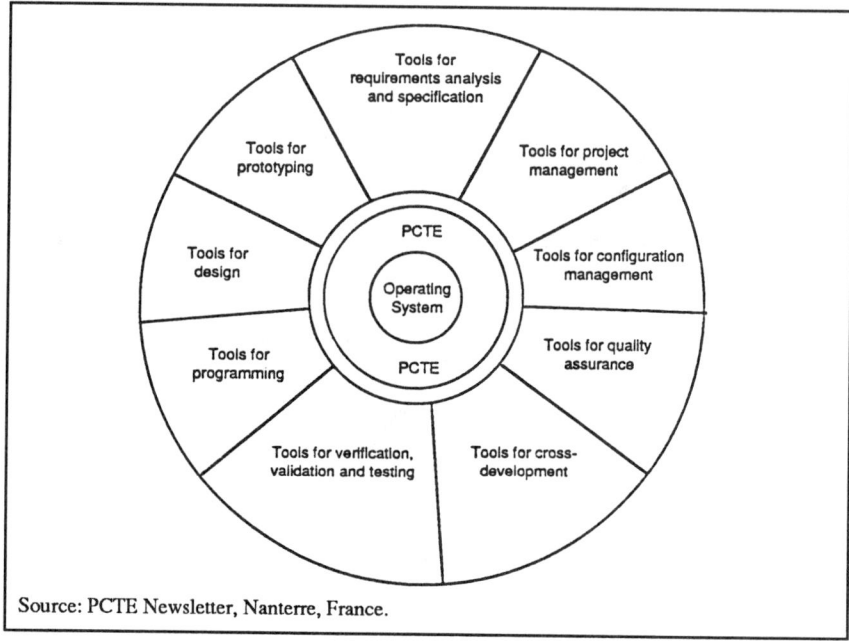

Source: PCTE Newsletter, Nanterre, France.

Figure 23: PCTE Reference Model

services implemented by tools which are integrated into the BMS environment. CASE communique's objective is to make it possible for users to select from a wide variety of CC-compliant tools that can "plus-and-play" in a BMS-based tool integration framework.

- In response to CASE Communique, Digital Equipment Corp., SunSoft and Silicon Graphs have proposed their own set of messages, called the CASE Interoperability Message Sets, to the ANSI X3H6 Committee. Although similar to the CASE Communique messages in philosophy, structure, syntax and functionality, the CIMS are intended for implementation using SunSoft's ToolTalk message service and, in the future, the OMG CORBA (object request broker) services. Although the CIMS sponsors claim that their approach is more open since the specification has been submitted to ANSI, CASE Communique has also responded by placing the results of their effort into the ANSI standard process. The X3H6 committee will have the task of reconciling differences and recommending an industry standard for message-based services.

The geographical areas of influence for currently vying standards for CASE integration are shown in Figure 22. Europe and Japan seem to be taking a more cooperative approach, while U.S.

firms and agencies are still experimenting and negotiating. In addition to PCTE, there some new emerging efforts in Europe, including the Eureka Software Factory. Southeast Asia will most likely adopt the emerging standards from other regions.

Of the vying standards, PCTE has perhaps the most extensive experience base of any integration framework and is being carefully monitored by CASE vendors in North America, Asia and Europe. In a sense it is a kind of generic operating system that hides the details of the underlying platform operating system and hardware, thus promoting CASE tool portability. Tools that run on one implementation of PCTE (on a particular workstation brand and model) will work on any other implementation.

PCTE is not an Integrated Programming Support Environment (IPSE) in and of itself. Rather, ESPRIT approached the integration problem by factoring out all the common features required by virtually all CASE tools, in particular data management and user interface facilities. By placing these common features in a layer above the native operating system, PCTE provides the foundation for building an IPSE from a set of CASE tools.

Current implementations of PCTE contain an object management system (OMS) to store the wide variety of object types needed in a CASE environment, including text, diagrams, code, costs, schedules, tests, requirements, designs, and configuration management records. The OMS is distributed so that information can be located on various workstations around a network and accessed transparently by any node.

A number of IPSE's have been built on PCTE and PCTE+ by various consortiums of European and North American companies. Among these are the Emeraude project and its several implementations, Sapphire, Pave, Aphrodite, the ALF project, Syseca's ENTERPRISE-II, IRENA (in process), PACT, SFGL's EAST, version of PCTE by Verilog (France) and by Heuristix (India) in support of their own toolsets. As of this writing, only the Emeraude and Verilog versions are commercially supported implementations of PCTE. IBM, Sun, and HP have also endorsed PCTE and will provide it on their platforms, although exact schedules have not been announced as of this writing. Efforts are underway in North America by NIST, PCIS, STARS and other groups to review PCTE and other proposed integration standards to see how their capabilities map to requirements. The hope is to be able to choose a commercially-supportable standard or merge several frameworks to establish a dominant integration architecture and tool interface. Descriptions of some of the commercial implementations of IPSEs based on PCTE are included below.

SFGL's EAST

EAST is a LAN-based, distributed Integrated Project Support Environment (IPSE) for large project teams. EAST is based on the PCTE implementation from Emeraude, is workstation independent, and supports heterogeneous networks with team and project support services, as well as tool integration facilities. The PCTE repository has a user-modifiable ERA metamodel and EAST provides repository administration tools, including a browser, schema editor and query language facility. All EAST tools have a common user interface under X-Windows/OSF/Motif which represents repository entities as typed objects.

Process management services include support for process models (including IEEE-STD-1002-1987, MIL-STD-2167A and ESA Software Engineering Standard), individual workloads, task definition, and task state control and monitoring.

Project management services support work breakdown structures, resource allocation, separate draft and valid work plans, work history, effort scheduling, planning, cost estimation and calendar management, and export facilities for Lotus 1-2-3.

Documentation services are based on a WYSIWYG text and graphics editor derived from INRIA's GRIF. It supports structured documents with pre-defined models for DOD-STD-2167A, IEEE-1002-1987 and ESA standards. It also has hypertext facilities with links, navigation and dynamic document update.

Configuration management services support object and collection versioning, version history, and traceability. EAST also includes a generic build facility integrated with documentation services for report generation.

Tools encapsulated under EAST include Cadre's Teamwork, LPS' Key One, Intecs' Ada-Nice and C-Nice, Alsys Ada compiler and host-based C and Fortran compilers. Traditional Unix tools, such as vi, are also accessible under EAST.

Syseca's Enterprise II

Enterprise II is a software development framework, built on the Emeraude implementation of PCTE, that provides tool integration services and facilities common to all phases of the life cycle. Enterprise II includes three data dictionary schemas for methods (meta model), for project and design data (encyclopedia), and for reusable objects. It employs either OSF/Motif or Open Look for presentation integration.

Enterprise II provides context management, tool and work

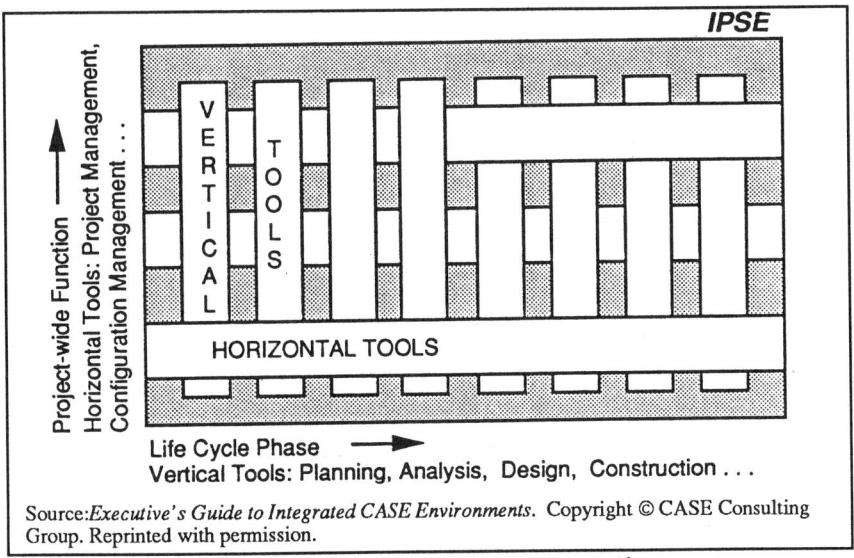

Figure 24: Trend Toward Open Integration

product access control, version and configuration management and IPSE administration facilities. Standard processes include Gam T17 V2, DOD-STD-2167A, and DO 178A, but users may customize the metamodel for other methods.

The Configuration Manager tool supports versioning of objects and collections, version history, archiving, problem reports, evolution requests, change requests and modification sheets. A Tracking Facility provides horizontal (cross life cycle) views of software production.

A Documentation Manager automates production and management of technical documentation using a software breakdown tree. It is integrated with Interleaf's TPS and Frame Technology's FrameMaker.

Project Manager supports structuring, organizing, estimation, planning, scheduling and monitoring. It is interfaced with the Artemis project management tool.

Enterprise II is also integrated with compiler technologies for Ada, C, C++, and LTR3. It supports source object navigation and relationship/dependency management including a generic build facility. It also includes a multi-language syntax editor.

A Reusable Object Dictionary manages objects common to all projects in the environment, organized in a tree structure. This supports archiving, searching, extraction and insertion into a project encyclopedia.

A Communication Manager provides e-mail, report composition, broadcasting, notes, agendas, meeting minutes, etc. It also

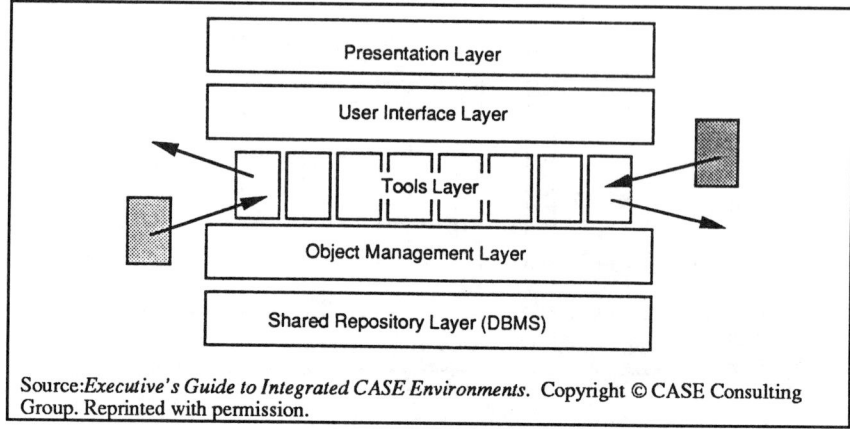

Figure 25: Tool Interchangeability

supports the transfer of objects between remote locations.

Tools may be integrated through encapsulation or full integration with the PCTE tool interface. The environment provides services for development of interactive tool dialogs, including a window manager, dialog manager, repository access services, graphic navigator, and a shell language.

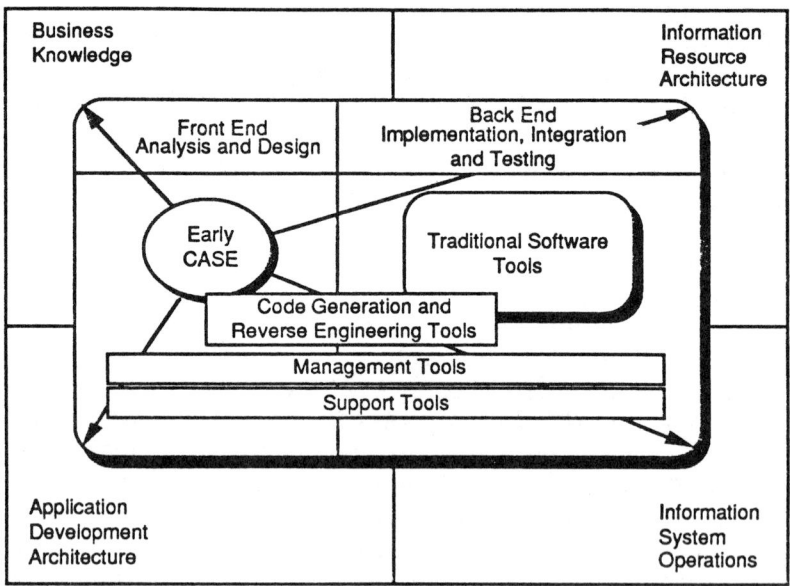

Figure 26: The CASE Enterprise View

FUTURE TRENDS

Early CASE vendors entered the market by serving a particular niche based on a specific phase of the life cycle (vertical tools) or a particular project-wide function (horizontal tools). As the market developed and the vendors sought to expand their market share and their product line, they extended their tool set either by building it outward or by forming alliances with other vendors. Many monolithic environments that evolved through expansion have exhausted the robustness of their original architecture and are facing the eventuality of rebuilding their products on a more flexible base, or integrating the nucleus of their tools into an open framework. Environments that evolved through tool-to-tool bridges, are now becoming too inflexible and cumbersome to support large project teams with a large number of tools.

These technical factors, plus customer demand for more choices in configuring CASE environments, are driving the market toward solutions based on open integration frameworks (see Figure 24). In the future, integrated project support environments will support a wide variety of vertical and horizontal CASE tools. Customers will have the opportunity to select tools based on their specific capabilities and the fit to their application domain and process standards. As conditions change, customers will be able to replace or add to their toolkits without drastically altering the CASE user interface, data management facilities and process control procedures (see Figure 25). In other words, open integration provides maximum value added and more flexibility in response to evolving technology, while preserving the user's investment in training and process management.

Emergence of the Enterprise View

Placing the CASE integration architecture in the larger context of the organization, there are opportunities for integrating and managing information beyond the duration of a development project. For example, the CASE repository becomes the storage facility for models of the business itself, including entities, data, procedures and rules involved in running the business. It might also contain industry-specific models related to key technology, physical or financial processes, product components, etc. These enterprise models may be customizations of generic business models for particular industry sectors developed by other companies, academics or independent consultants.

The CASE environment also is a central facility for documenting and enforcing design methodologies and processes for software development quality assurance employed throughout the company.

A full CASE environment also supports the practice of software reuse by providing information management facilities for reusable code modules, system models, data models, user interface models, classes, system documentation, test suites and results, and other information assets that have value beyond the end of the development project and from one project to another. Exploiting this larger role for CASE technology will be an emerging theme in the 1990's.

REFERENCES

Campbell, Ian, ed. (1991). PCTE Newsletter, (April), (91)6. EC2, 269-287 rue de la Garenne, 92024, Nanterre Cedex, France.

ECMA (1990). Standard ECMA-149, and *A Reference Model for Computer Assited Software Environment Frameworks*, ECMA TR/55. European Computer Manufacturers Associates, Geneva.

Hewett, Julian & Durham, Tony (1989). *CASE: The Next Steps.* Ovum Ltd., London.

Jones, Capers (1987) The Cost and Value of CASE. CASE OUTLOOK *Journal of Software Automation*, (October), (1)4, 1, 9-15.

Nolan, Chris (1988). *An Object-Oriented View of Tool Integration.* Digital Equipment Corp., Nashua, N.H.

Wasserman, Anthony (1990). Tool Integration in Software Engineering Environments. *Software Engineering Environments,* ed. F. W. Long, Springer Verlag Lecture Notes in Computer Science (467), 137-149.

This chapter is based on a manuscript being published simultaneously by *CASE Outlook,* Lake Oswego, Oregon, 1993. Published by reciprocal agreement.

CHAPTER TWO

Integrating CASE Using Existing Tools

Hasan H. Sayani
Advanced Systems Technology Corp., MD

Cyril P. Svoboda
Advanced Systems Technology Corp., MD

This paper examines the requirements for integrating computer-aided software engineering (CASE) tools and suggests a general method to accomplish this objective. CASE tools do not presently communicate with one another because they were built in isolation from one another by individuals who were trying to support one or two phases of the overall information system development life cycle. Each tool keeps its data in its own proprietary dictionary/repository, creating "Islands of CASE." In the absence of a standard data interchange format, individuals who wanted to link these islands were forced to build "bridge tools" that would interpret the data held in the form understood by a "source" CASE tool and translate that data into a form understood by a "target" CASE tool. These bridges were one-way because there is no metamodel common to CASE tools. Instead the bridge builder had to design a program to interpret the data held in the metamodel of the source and translate it into the metamodel of the target. A different program would be required if the CASE tools to be bridged changed source and target roles. The authors suggest a different approach: bridge CASE tools to a central repository the metamodel of which contains all the constructs of the tools linked to it. In this scenario, a bridge tool would interpret the data held in a source CASE tool into a form demanded by the central repository. The repository's report utility could then be used to extract the imported data in the form required by the target CASE tool. The authors describe actual work done to approximate an integrated CASE environment using existing CASE tools, a semantic-based repository, and bridge tools to diagram-drawing tools, spreadsheets, programming languages, and outline generators. They discuss the problems encountered with forming an initial integrated CASE environment and the difficulties that lie ahead.

The CASE Environment

The field of software development, whether of large, complex information systems or of smaller, simpler applications, is on its own odyssey. The trek began with the field being an art form and is progressing toward becoming a recognized engineering science. Though practitioners of software development have covered themselves in the cloak of "software engineering", many would question the validity of such a title, given the present maturity level of most organizations involved in software development.

True, software developers have pieced together what is called a software development environment and academics have studied the components and characteristics of such a construct. Dart et al (1987) offered a taxonomy of environments to explain the "technological trends that have produced state-of-the-art environments" comprised within today's software development environment. Wasserman (1981) suggested a number of "ecological considerations" in the software development environment. However, these individuals are the scouts who ride ahead of the wagon train and send back reports of what lies ahead, rather than identifying where the train is at present.

In the 1980s, a new term was added to the software development lexicon: Computer-aided Software Engineering (CASE), and a bandwagon was created. Almost immediately CASE became the latest panacea causing many software developers to feel that this time Godot had come, the silver bullet was found, and Nirvana was just over the horizon. Yet, not all was sweetness and light. Individuals argued over the very meaning of the term: did CASE stand for Computer-aided *Software* or *System* Engineering? Is a CASE environment the same as a software development environment? If it is, what has been gained with the change of terms?

In this chapter, we are not interested in criticizing CASE or software engineering, nor do we intend to breathlessly assume that answers to these questions do not matter. We pose these questions to advance our understanding of the CASE environment and to increase the payoff we can derive from its several components. When the CASE bandwagon first came trundling down the software development road, it generated a lot of excitement and expectations. A bevy of CASE experts predicted that CASE was destined to be a multi-billion dollar industry. Yet today, voices are being heard questioning the true value and place of CASE. Recently, Jacobs (1992) analyzed many misconceptions about CASE, both from the perspective of the software developer and from that of the business owner. She concludes that "one major obstacle is the lack of clearly define CASE standards, such as repositories and inter-communications among different tools. Sayani (1991) described the current CASE environment, not as an integrated whole, but a jerry-built amalgam of several components, called "CASE Islands".

The Islands of CASE

Large, complex information systems can not be designed on the back of an envelope. Instead, they require the efforts of several different individuals with different kinds of expertise. The information system development life cycle comprises activities ranging from project inception to project deployment and continuing maintenance. These activities are grouped into several different phases, such as planning, requirements analysis, design, implementation, testing, operations and maintenance. Each activity produces work products of different types, e.g.,

- Data
- Activity
- Control

all under the influence of various constraints. While the different work products of any one life cycle phase may be inter-related with one another, they are not so easily related with the work products of subsequent or preceding phases. For instance, the *Processes* of the Analysis phase are not mapped "one-to-one" with the *Modules* of the Design phase.

From a macro-level view, the general direction of development is uni-directionally forward, from Planning to Analysis to Design, etc. However, from a micro-level view, development moves "back and forth", sometimes jumping ahead to consider a sub-system down stream, at other times revisiting a prior stage for the purpose of making modifications before progressing onward.

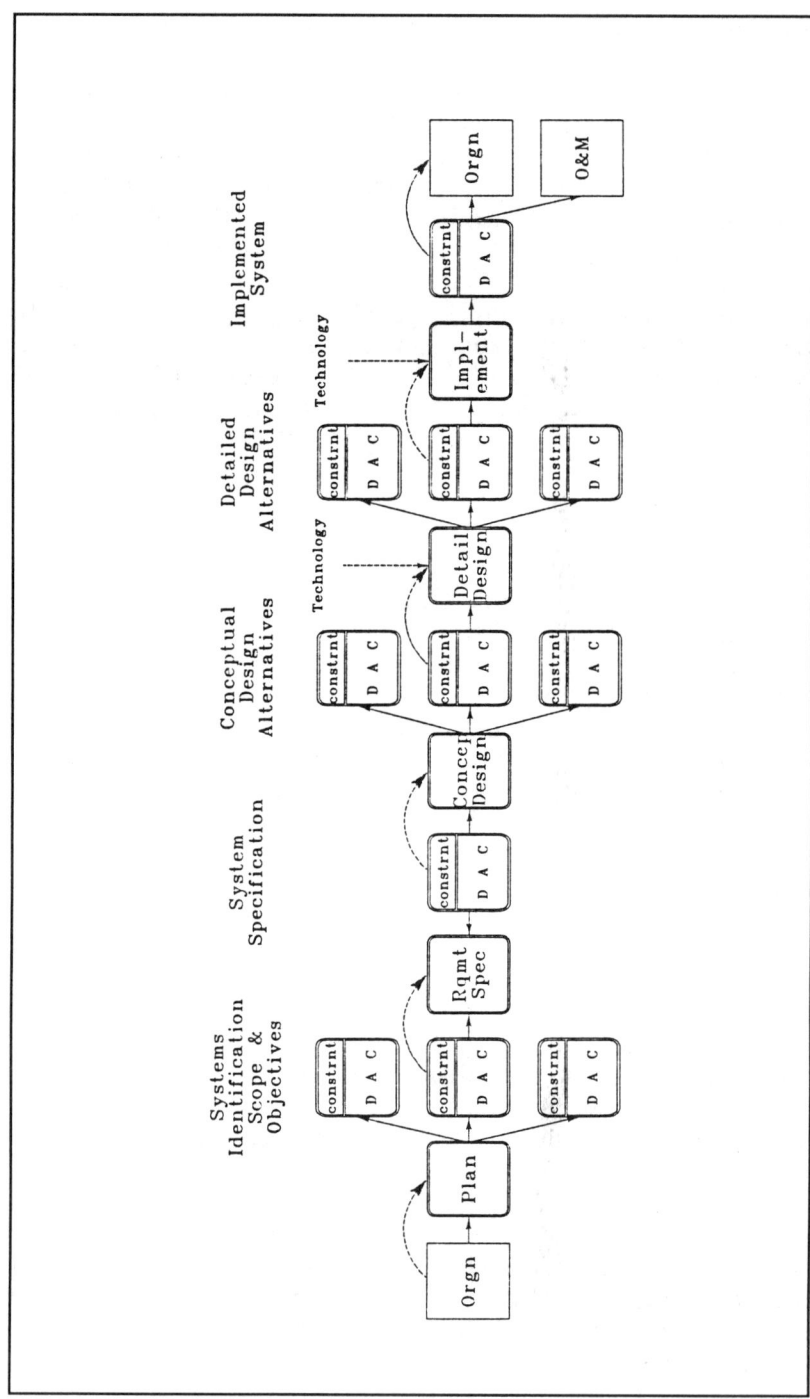

Figure 1: Information Systems Development Life Cycle (Forward Engineering)

Figure 1 depicts the march of life cycle phases, with the delivery of various work products, some of which reside at the phase of origin and others which become the input to the next phase. While this diagram presents an *ideal* state, the outputs of one phase are not always the inputs of the subsequent phase. Anyone who has watched the product of the Planning phase gather dust on a shelf, instead of being a prime ingredient in the Analysis phase, will readily testify to this fact.

Today many experts are promoting a different approach to developing information systems, sometimes pictured as a spiral evolving from a simple production to increasingly more complex versions. Whether this different approach is called "rapid prototyping", "rapid application development (RAD), or "concurrent engineering", it is an attempt to move away from the rigid, waterfall approach toward something that is more flexible, faster, and, hopefully, more in tune with user needs. Rather than concluding that the traditional waterfall approach and the rapid prototyping-RAD-Concurrent Engineering approach are diametrically opposed, Svoboda (1989) suggested that the waterfall model describes the general development of large information systems, while the RAD-Concurrent Engineering approach describes the development of system components (applications).

Whatever the life cycle approach used by developers, CASE vendors originally built tools to support work in one or, often at most, two phases of the life cycle. Some of the earliest CASE tools typically supported work in the Analysis and Design phases. Other vendors built tools that supported work in the Planning phase or the Implementation phase. The result was that, over time, we had many different tools supporting work in different phases. We even learned to group those tools that supported the Planning, Analysis, and Design phases in a category called Upper CASE, while we grouped tools that supported work in the Implementation, Testing, or Maintenance phases in a category called Lower CASE. Despite the variety of CASE tools and the many phases of the life cycle that they support, system development has not become a seamless technology. In fact, as Svoboda (1988) described the situation, using CASE technology across the life cycle is somewhat like making a trip across the country, forced to change modes of transportation from city to city.

Each different CASE tool allows the user to do work in the phase(s) it supports and maintians the information in its own dictionary/repository, since these tools were built in isolation, by developers driven to create tools that supported phase-specific work, according to their own perspectives. To make matters worse, the dictionaries/repositories underlying each tool were proprietary

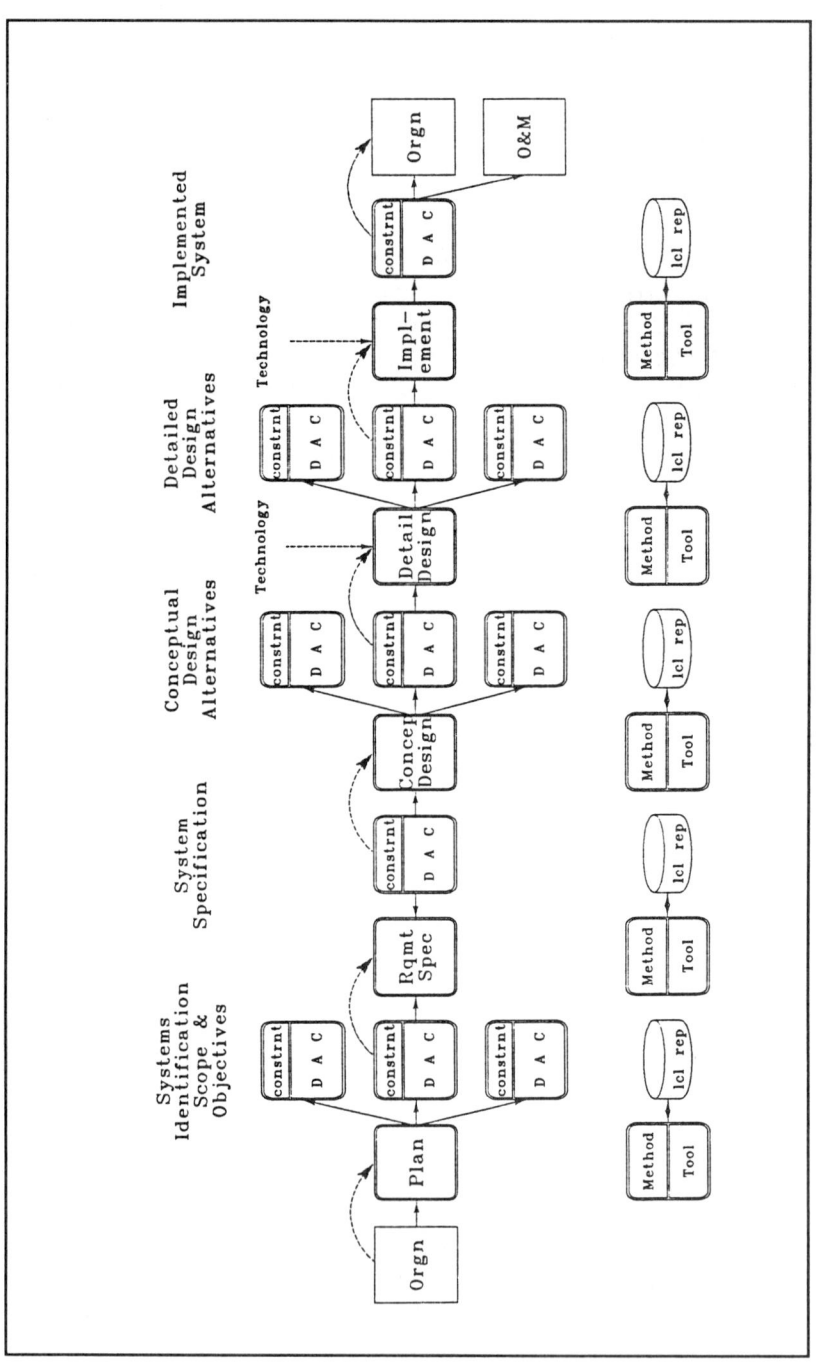

Figure 2: CASE Islands

to each developer. The information entered in each could not be extracted and fed directly to the dictionary of another. Therefore, developing an information system across the life cycle using these tools created many different information islands, as seen in Figure 2.

The Use of Bridge Tools

CASE developers recognized the problem, and eventually most adopted what they called an open architecture. This meant, for the most part, that they incorporated some form of import/export capability in their tools: each published the prescribed form they required for data to be accepted by their tool, as well as the form in which each would make data available. Again, because standards were not yet agreed upon, these forms differed, depending on the dictionary on which each tool was built. (Today CASE vendors are nearing a common standard called CASE Data Interchange Format [CDIF] which, when it is implemented, will allow data to pass from one CASE tool to the next with relative ease. However, CDIF is not implemented yet.) Therefore, if an integrator wants two CASE tools to communicate with one another, that individual would have to build a software package that would *bridge* the two dictionaries. At the outset, bridge tools were most often one way, that is, they interpreted data stored in the dictionary of a source CASE tool and translated it into the form required by a target CASE tool. The flow was only from source to target, it could not be reversed without writing a completely different bridge.

Some software tools already had swapping capabilities, e.g., data in a spreadsheet could be swapped into a word processor or vice versa. Data in one form could be made available in a different form. However, the task in building a bridge between CASE tools is a bit more imposing. The dictionary in each CASE tool handles data in terms of its own metamodel. Therefore, a bridge tool would have to understand the metamodel in the source tool and be able to translate the constructs and their meanings into the constructs and their matching meanings in the metamodel of the *target* tool. In addition to syntactical translation, CASE bridges require semantical translation.

Because the metamodels of different CASE tools are esoteric, if not unique, bridge tools have to interpret the constructs of the source metamodel and translate them into the constructs of the target metamodel. To reverse direction would require a different, but comparable amount of code. Even then, the bridge would be limited to function as a communication link only between the particular set of source and target CASE tools: an altogether different tool would be required to use a different target tool. This means that developers would have to build as many bridge tools as there are possible pairwise combinations of CASE tools, no simple task given the number and variety of CASE tools, not to mention the marginal return on such investments.

One approach to solving this need for a plethora of bridge tools is to build a bridge tool that has the capability to interpret the metamodel of a given source tool and, by referring to a user-modifiable *rules* file, translate the data in terms of any target metamodel the user specifies. In such an arrangement, the bridge would have both the syntax and semantics of the source tool hard-coded and would translate this data into whatever form the user specified in the rules file. The developer of the bridge would only have to deal with the syntax and semantics of the source tool; the user would have to define the mapping between the constructs of both the source and target tools in the rules file. This approach would reduce the number of bridge tools from pair-wise combinations to a bridge for any particular source tool. However, it limits the information exchange only between the source and the specified target tools for which the rules files have been written.

Bridging to a Central Repository

A different, more comprehensive approach would be to bridge various CASE tools to a central repository which contained all the constructs of the tools linked to it. This would still demand the capability to interpret the metamodel of each CASE tool bridged, but would give the very important benefit of making data available for interchange from any phase of the life cycle supported by the tools bridged to the repository. In this approach, the data would be interpreted by the bridge tool and translated into the precise import format demanded by the central repository. The repository's report utility could then be used to extract data from the repository and translate it into the import format required by any CASE tool with which one wanted to share data. This approach is based on a concept similar to the one described above, i.e., rules-driven interpretation.

As can be seen in Figure 3, the data from each bridged CASE tool is taken from its dictionary/repository and is synthesized in a central repository. Separate bridge programs would be necessary to interpret the data in terms of the metamodel of each bridged source tool, but the central repository would be able to express its data in terms of any of the metamodels of the CASE tools bridged to it by means of its reporting mechanism. In this way, information systems develop-

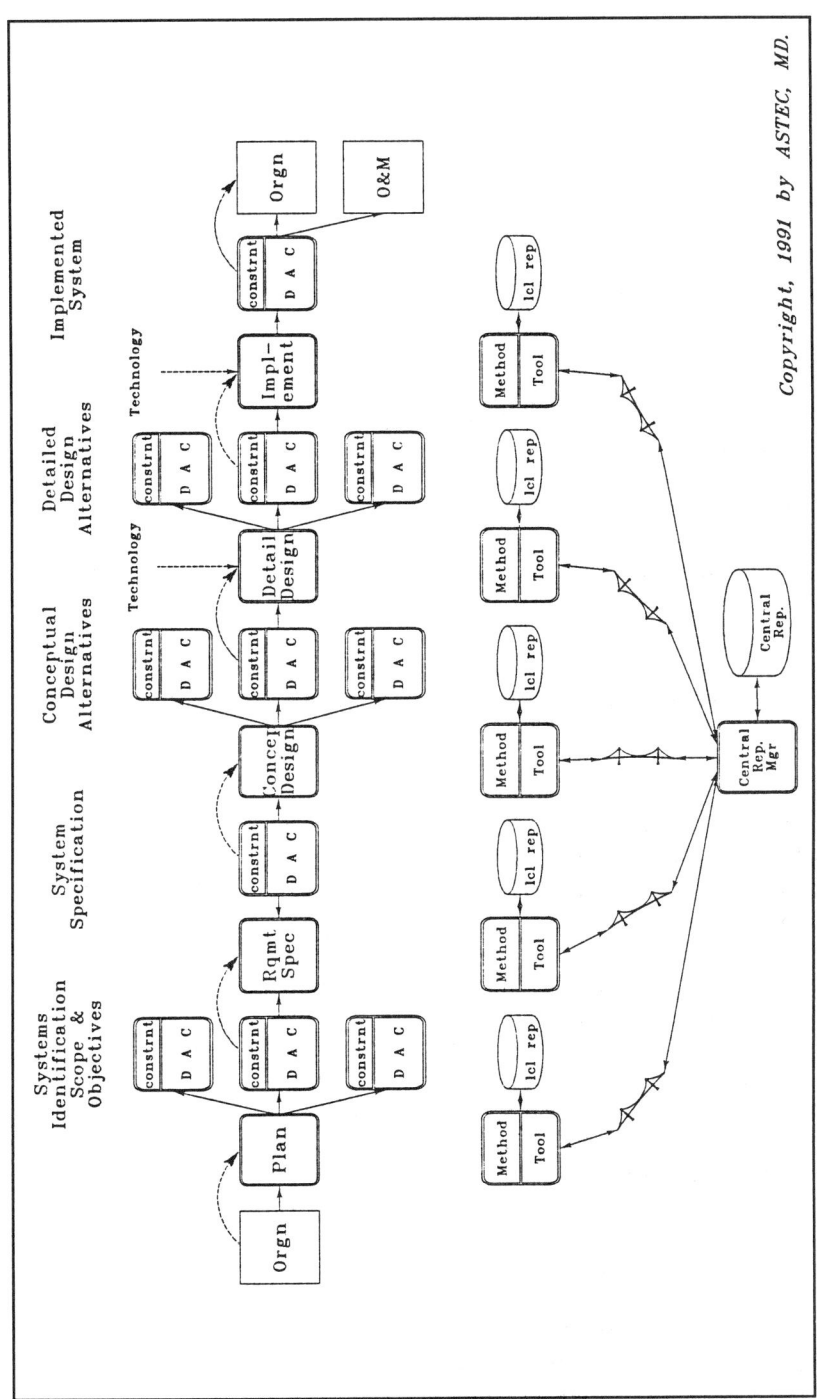

Figure 3: CASE Islands Bridged Together

ers could continue to use their CASE tools for the particular support they provide to activities in one or more life cycle phases. However, the data gathered would then be available to any other tool supporting any other phase of the life cycle, as long as there was some mapping between that information and the constructs of the target tool's metamodel.

In addition to more widespread data availability, the use of a central repository would have the benefit of providing real traceability both across different teams using different CASE tools, and across different phases of the life cycle. To make this possible, the metamodel of the central repository would have the various constructs from the bridged CASE tools, the relationships that link different constructs with one another, and the various properties that would attach to the constructs and their relationships. Traces to former or subsequent constructs could be captured by means of relationships such as *BECOMES* or *EVOLVES-TO*. Properties such as *RESPONSIBLE-DEFINER* or *SOURCE-PHASE* could be used to categorize constructs to the individual or team that originally defined them, or to the phase of the life cycle when they first appeared in the repository.

A Fully Integrated CASE Environment

Currently the term "I-CASE" is used to describe a set of integrated CASE tools or CASE environment. Beyond that, CASE developers are discussing the Integrated Project Support Environment (IPSE), which adds to I-CASE such capabilities as project management, configuration management, etc. I-CASE is intended to provide the very kinds of benefits discussed in the previous section. The main purpose of I-CASE is to provide support to the information system developer across all the phases of the life cycle. It would allow developers to continue to use phase-specific tools with which they are already familiar, but would link these tools to a central repository. Such an environment could be vendor-packaged, linking together tools from one vendor. This would permit the IPSE to be fine tuned for tools from the same family. However, it would probably make assimilation of tools from outside that family extremely difficult, if not impossible. On the other hand, an IPSE could have an open architecture which would make it easier to link to, but would require additional code which translated the constructs of the tool to be linked into the metamodel of the central repository.

Figure 4 depicts the ideal situation for linking several CASE tools to a single, powerful repository. In the rest of this chapter, we will describe actual work done to approximate this ideal using

Integrating CASE 69

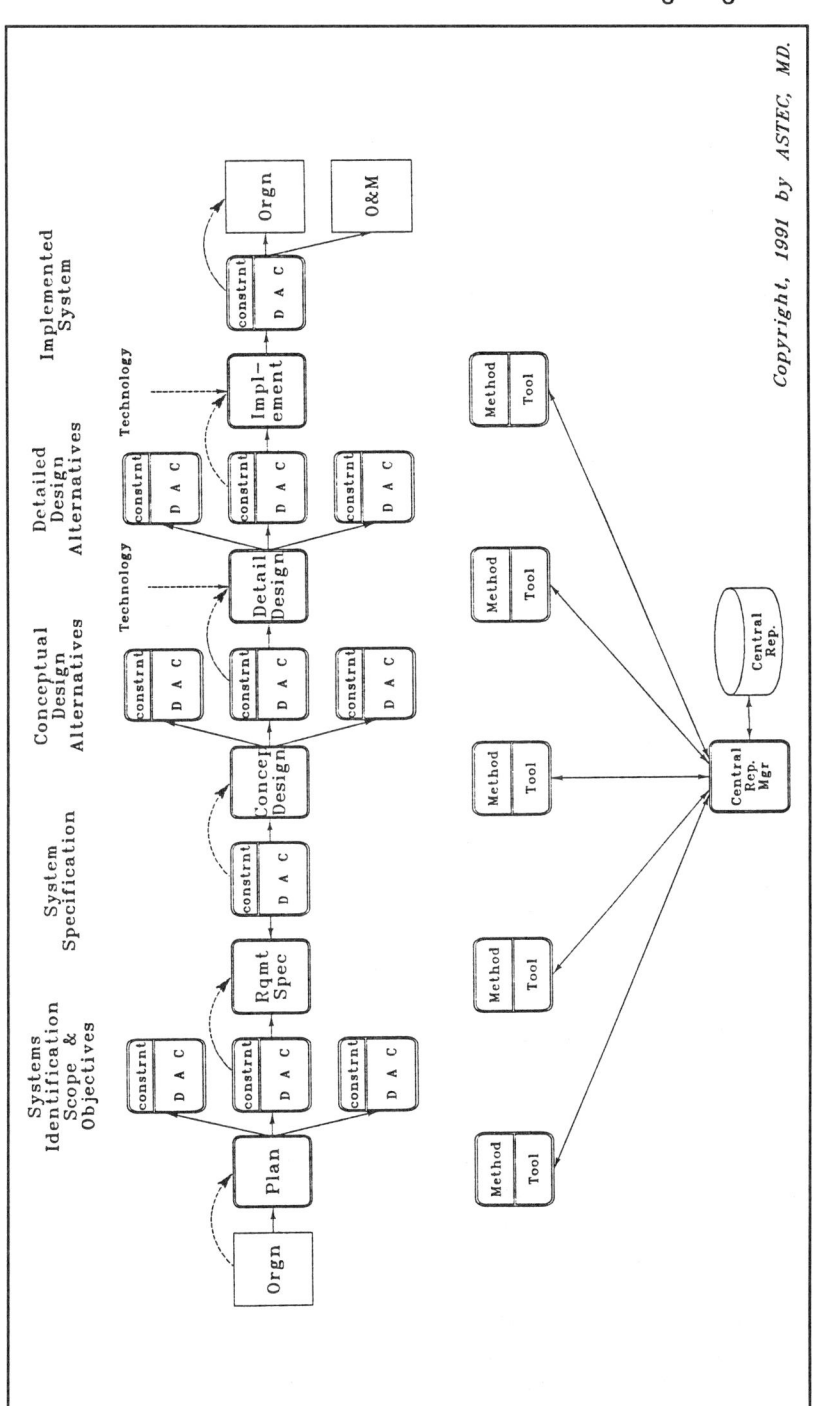

Figure 4: Integrated Project Support Environment

existing CASE tools, a semantic-based repository, and bridge tools to both upper- and lower-CASE tools. We will also provide examples of various types of bridges created to accomplish different types of translations. While the examples shown will be incomplete by design, they are taken from real work done on full-sized systems.

ARCHITECTURES

The Rationale for Bridging

We have already intimated why developers have felt the need to bridge CASE tools. In reality, they have had little choice. In problem-solving, we need to have all the information gathered thus far about the problem, available to us as we advance toward solution. Otherwise, we might end up re-inventing the wheel or running down blind alleys (several times) in the course of problem solution. When we are involved in information system development, which is a form of problem-solving, we need to have all the information about that system gathered in prior phases integrated and available for work in subsequent phases of the development life cycle. This is true because problem-solving, e.g. systems development, is not a single activity, but an amalgam of several different processes, as shown in Figure 5.

Each problem-solving activity can be thought of as a different way to represent the problem. When we first encounter a problem, we immediately try to identify what kind of problem it is, whether we have encountered such a problem before, and the best strategy for solving this problem. If we have not encountered such a problem before, we have to *formulate* the problem, i.e., identify the major components of the problem, how they inter-relate with one another, and any particularly important attributes of the components or the inter-relationships. The process of formulation is one of conceptually re-presenting the problem to ourselves. CASE tools have been designed to support a limited number of formulations or methodologies.

Another approach that we might find helpful is to *graphically* represent the problem to ourselves. We do this by employing some means of visualizing the problem. Irrespective of the diagramming techniques used, we usually find it helpful to reduce the complexity of the problem by a process of *visualization*. We focus our attention on the major components of the problem and represent them by various icons. We use different "connectors" to represent the inter-relationships linking the major components. Usually our visualization techniques are closely related to conceptual model in the methodology we employ, i.e., our formulation of the problem. CASE tools enable the user to draw various kinds of diagrams to visualize the problem.

Information about the problem may be captured not only graphically, but also linguistically. We find that as we give verbal expression to our thoughts, we generally become clearer about them. By means of this process, we represent the problem to ourselves linguistically by writing or speaking out words that express our perception of the problem, i.e., capturing in some formal manner the information we consider important for solving the problem. Any CASE tool that is not just a diagramming tool should give the user the chance to amplify the information about the problem, as represented in the diagrams by describing the different symbols on the diagram to the dictionary.

As we learn more about a problem, we find that we perform the process of *synthesis* almost automatically. New information is integrated with information captured earlier, not just added to it. Our minds work to form a well-knit fabric of the information we uncover about the problem. In fact, the very purpose of the subconscious seems to be to form as many different connections as possible between disparate pieces of information about a topic. Many CASE tools integrate information in their information store (dictionary) and, in some cases, integrate the information in the diagrams with that in the dictionary.

Once we have begun to capture information we need to examine it from time to time to ensure that what we have said, is what we intended to say. This process of *reflection* represents the problem to ourselves objectively, so that we can hear or see it without any kind of interpretation or filtering. In a CASE tool, we usually find the capability of producing various kinds of reports based on information in diagrams, and in the dictionary. We use both the tool's standard or canned reports and its ability to create *ad hoc* reports as we see fit.

In addition, we find it necessary from time to time to evaluate the data that we have captured by means of the CASE tool. We do this by posing queries or deriving various kinds of analyses against the database, generating reports that compare the data against predefined criteria. This process of *analysis* is our way of re-presenting the problem to ourselves critically. CASE tools usually have a set number of analysis reports that we can run against the database to detect inconsistency, incompleteness, or other forms of inadequacy in the data.

From time to time, during any activity, we find the need to *modify* some part of the database, either by adding new data, deleting existing expressions, or replacing parts of them. This process of modification is a way of representing the data about our problem to

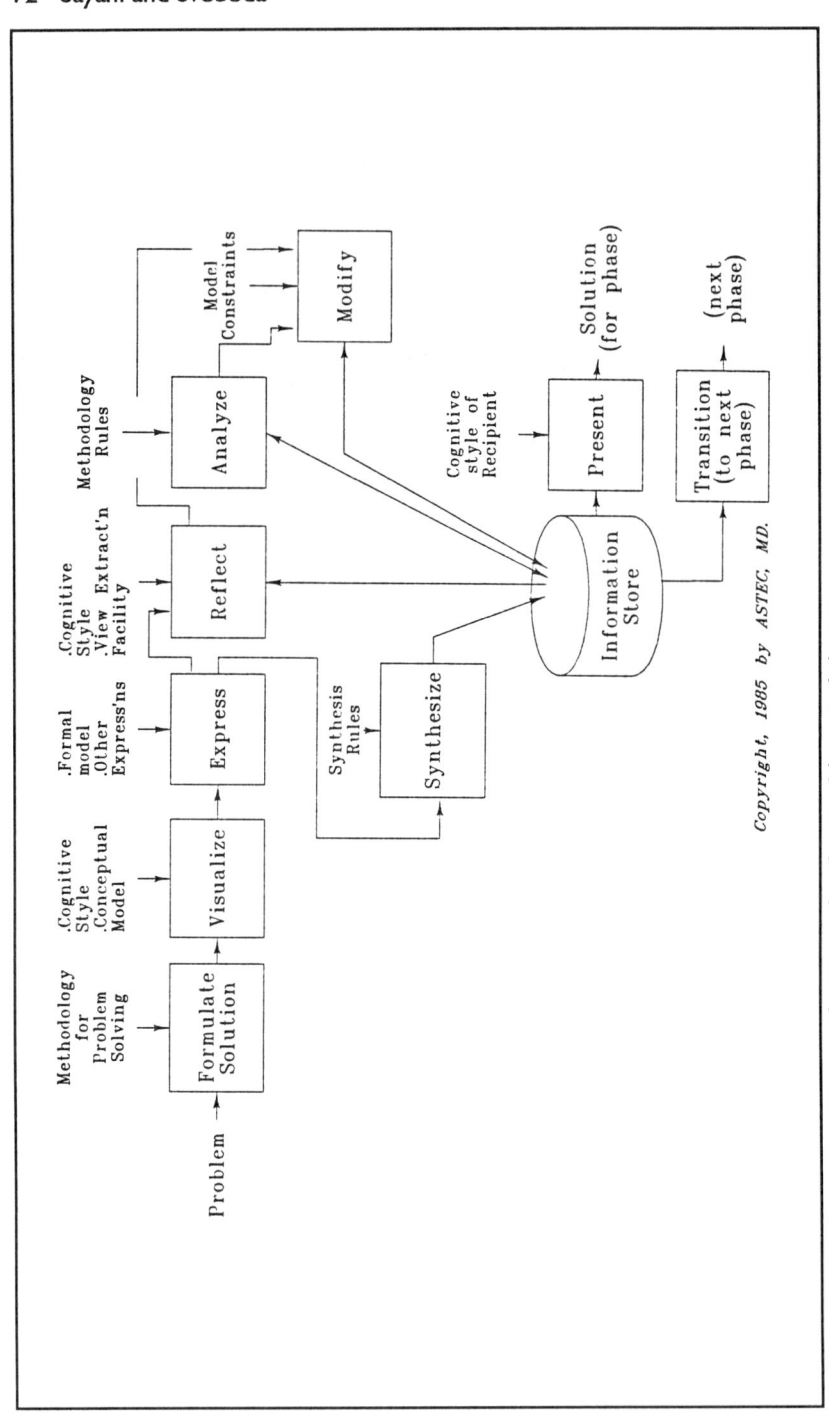

Figure 5: Steps in the Problem-Solving Process

ourselves alternatively. Sometimes our what-if questions help us to realize that our present view of the problem is deficient. All CASE tools allow the user to make modifications to some part of the database or to the diagrams. This is certainly necessary, since we rarely get it right first time out.

The problem-solving process called *presentation* is often relegated to an after-thought, something that has to be done after the interesting work of solving the problem is finished. Anyone who has spent a lot of time and effort on a problem, only to find the solution ignored, has discovered the importance of presenting the solution properly. Indeed, the presentation can be as important as the solution! Some CASE tools do a better job of permitting the user to produce attractive documentation using the ingredients in its database. Developers of CASE tools who do not value this problem-solving process expect you to use some other tool for producing documentation, a stance that has contributed the present problem of islands of CASE.

When dealing with information problems, we use these many processes, though not always in the sequence presented here. Our minds do not keep the data gained through any of these processes separate in distinct stores. Instead, when problem-solving, the human mind works over all the information about the problem under consideration to form an integrated whole. When developing an information system, we have the same need, i.e., for an integrated whole of information about the problem being attacked. CASE tools are merely a means of supporting our problem-solving processes, and as such should communicate with one another to produce a synthesis of information about the problem.

Depending on the sensitivity of their developers, some CASE tools will accommodate different *cognitive styles* or preferences in their users. Depending on the experience of the developers in real-life system development projects, their tools can be used to take data from, say, the information store of a planning tool and produce a financial analysis, or use information from a requirements specification in narrative form and produce formal, traceable requirements, or system documentation that conforms to a standard, such as DoD 2167A.

REQUIRED COMPONENTS OF A BRIDGE

Required Mechanisms

CASE tools are a means of supporting these problem-solving processes throughout the information system development life cycle.

Lest the problem-solver be left with pieces of the puzzle in different stores, someone needs to find a way to integrate the information about the system into a central store, called a repository. Until CASE tools talk the same language, CASE tool users need to build bridges between the tools they are presently using, whether these bridges are one-way and two-way bridges. In either of these two types, certain mechanisms seem absolutely essential.

For instance, a bridge must have some mechanism for acquiring data from the source tool. This may be done by having a program that reads and interprets data in an export file by the source tool. Such an approach requires the user to first produce an export file using the source tool, and then to present this file for interpretation. A different approach would be possible if the source tool had a programmer's interface that would allow the bridge tool access to the source tool's files from which it could then take the data needed. Whether the source tool uses an export file or programmer's interface mechanism, the bridge tool would also require a second mechanism, namely an interpreter program to make sense of the data from the source tool.

Once the information had been interpreted, the bridge would need a third mechanism, to translate the interpreted information into the form required by the target tool. These translation rules could be hard coded in the translator program or could be stored and modified in a rules file which could be edited by a user to accommodate any special conventions for the project. Finally, the target tool would have to have a mechanism by which it would assimilate the information produced by the translator mechanism. If the information was to be produced graphically in the target tool, it would need an "info-draw" facility that could interpret data in linguistic form and translate it into a form that conforms to its own specific graphical syntax.

A Model Translator

An approach that creates a bridge that directly links one CASE tool with another implies that developers will build different bridges for each different pair of CASE tools, as stated above. An alternative approach would be to build a bridge that can interpret the data in any particular CASE tool and provide that interpreted data, either directly or indirectly, to a central repository in its own import form. In such an arrangement, the repository would act as a model integrator in that it would have within itself all the constructs found in the metamodels of the different tools that were to be unified. This would create the basis for an Integrated CASE (I-CASE) Environment.

A key component of a central repository would be an agreed-upon canonical form that comprises objects, relationships between objects, and appropriate properties of both objects and relationships. The canonical form would be a simple, rigorous form of expression that had sufficient richness to express information in any of the bridged tools, yet with a stream format that could be easily parsed. An example of such a canonical form, although limited, is the command language of the Information Resource Dictionary System (IRDS).

In addition to being able to parse information in its canonical form, the central repository would have to have a comprehensive *metamodel* so that it could map its constructs to those in the various tools linked to it. For instance, the central repository would have to accommodate the constructs of Planning, Analysis, Design, Implementation, Testing, and Maintenance across the life cycle and the different constructs of methodologies within a specific phase of the life cycle, e.g., Structured Analysis, IDEF0, or Information Engineering.

The metamodel required of a central repository that could accept and produce data from the several tools linked to it would have to be robust, semantically clean, and precise. In our view, the hierarchical, network, and relational data models found in current database management systems do not possess these characteristics. Instead, the data model that comes closest to natural language sentences and is easiest to grasp (for it mimics the way we think) is the Entity-Relationship-Attribute model (an extended version of what King and McLeod (1985) referred to as the "semantic data model"). Similar to the data model underlying the IRDS, this semantic data model possesses several desirable characteristics.

Because of the need to accommodate the metamodel underlying the various life cycle phases, and the many methodologies that support them, the metamodel of the repository would have to be extendable. In creating over one hundred different metamodels, we have not found any construct that the semantic data model can not accommodate. When you recognize that Entities are expressed in English as nouns, Relationships as verbs, and Attributes as adjectives and adverbs, this is not surprising. If we can think and express the constructs of a problem, their inter-relationships, and their distinctive characteristics in language, we can accommodate them in the semantic data model.

Consider the simple "*subject-verb-object*" (SVO) sentence: "The child hit the ball". Two entities or objects, "child" and "ball" are linked by the relationship (verb) "hit". There is no ambiguity in this statement: we know who did the hitting and what received the action.

No one would wonder if the ball hit the child, because in this statement we know not only what objects are involved, but which object is playing the subject role and which the object or recipient role. The "*simple, active, affirmative, declarative*" (SAAD) statement is the core of our expression in English, but we are not restricted to statements which have only two roles (binary relationship). Instead, we expand the number of roles in such a statement, as when we say, "The child hit the ball with a bat" (if we were dealing with a "baseball metamodel") . Again, this sentence can semantically be enriched by saying, "The child hit the ball with a bat in the park". In this latter expression we have related "child" to "ball" to "bat" to "park" in an "n-ary relationship". In fact, we extend the simple SAAD by having relationships play roles in a relationship, as when we add relative or embedded clauses.

We believe that the central repository must have the capability to capture such complex expressions, if we want to use it in capturing information in a large, complex information system. If, for instance, you wanted to capture the information in a typical *calling sequence*, you would need an "n-ary relationship" to express the simultaneous inter-relationship of the *triggering condition* which stimulates the *invoking module* to call the *invoked module* passing *data down* and receiving *data back*, as well as a *return status*. By means of a six-role relationship, we could express the fact that when "Condition A" reaches a pre-defined critical point, "Module X" invokes "Module Y", passing "Data M" and receiving back "Data N" and a "Status Flag".

The central repository, based on a semantic data model, should also be able to permit declaration of rules governing which *entities* can play which roles or how many entities can play a role in any particular relationship. These rules regarding cardinality and participation should be expressible as meta-definition statements, rather than as procedural code. These characteristics and others make a database management system, based on the semantic data model, powerful enough to accommodate the many constructs and inter-relationships of the many different tools (actually their conceptual models) which are linked to the repository.

We have found that the unifying central repository must permit the extraction of *specialized views* without the necessity of programming in a traditional programming language. One such view extraction should be its own canonical form, which permits easy transfer between various installations of the repository. Other types of views that can be extracted would be those required by the other CASE tools (at least until CDIF becomes a reality) linked to it, whether in the same or adjacent phases of the life cycle. Since information system development must be documented, the central repository should also have the capability to produce system documentation as a by-product, rather than as an after-thought.

The repository must be capable not only of permitting extraction of selected information, but the formulation of that information into a format required by either a CASE tool or a document production facility. Typically, this capability molds the view extracted from the repository into a form usable by a particular tool. For graphic tools, this may imply producing placement information (for objects) and routing information (for connectors/relationships). Similar types of requirements exist for producing diagrams on paper or for producing the information in the form of a spreadsheet.

We have also found that a central repository must permit *ad hoc* queries in a form close to the semantic model of the problem under study. In addition to formal queries, the repository should permit the naive user to easily obtain information about the contents of the repository by means of reports on the contents of the metamodel or the database of instances. This browsing capability could be amplified by a programmer's interface that permits calls to the repository, and composes the returned information in special combinations or formats not presently available in the repository's standard set of reports.

EXAMPLES OF BRIDGES

Lest the reader think that the foregoing is merely blue sky or wishful thinking, we would like to describe actual examples of CASE tools that have been bridged with various repositories. Because of the limitations of space in this chapter, we can not show all the many aspects of bridging that are possible, but we hope that what we do present will convince the reader that I-CASE is possible now, using existing tools. An actual architecture is shown in Figure 6.

Linking Diagram-Drawing Tools

The first bridge tool we created was called *SafeSpan*. Its purpose was to link Nastec's *DesignAid* with the *Problem Statement Language/Problem Statement Analyzer* (PSL/PSA). To get at the data stored in *DesignAid*, we had to rely on an "unload file" that was designed and controlled by *DesignAid*'s developer. When calling *SafeSpan*, the user had to name the "unload file" (that he/she had already asked *DesignAid* to create) as well as the "conventions file" that contained the translation rules *SafeSpan* was to follow when

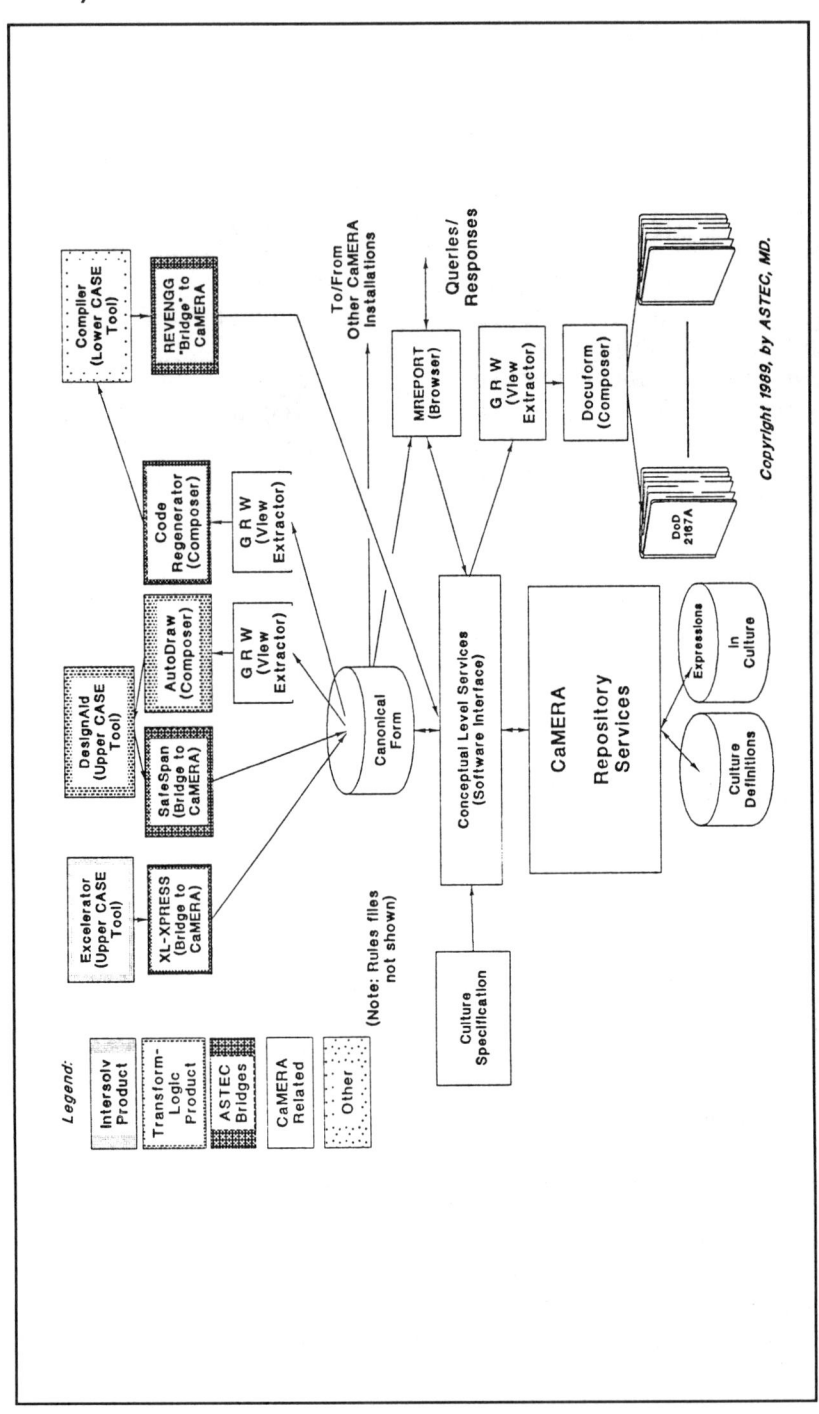

Figure 6: Integrated CASE Environment Using CaMERA, REVENGG, and Bridges

Integrating CASE 79

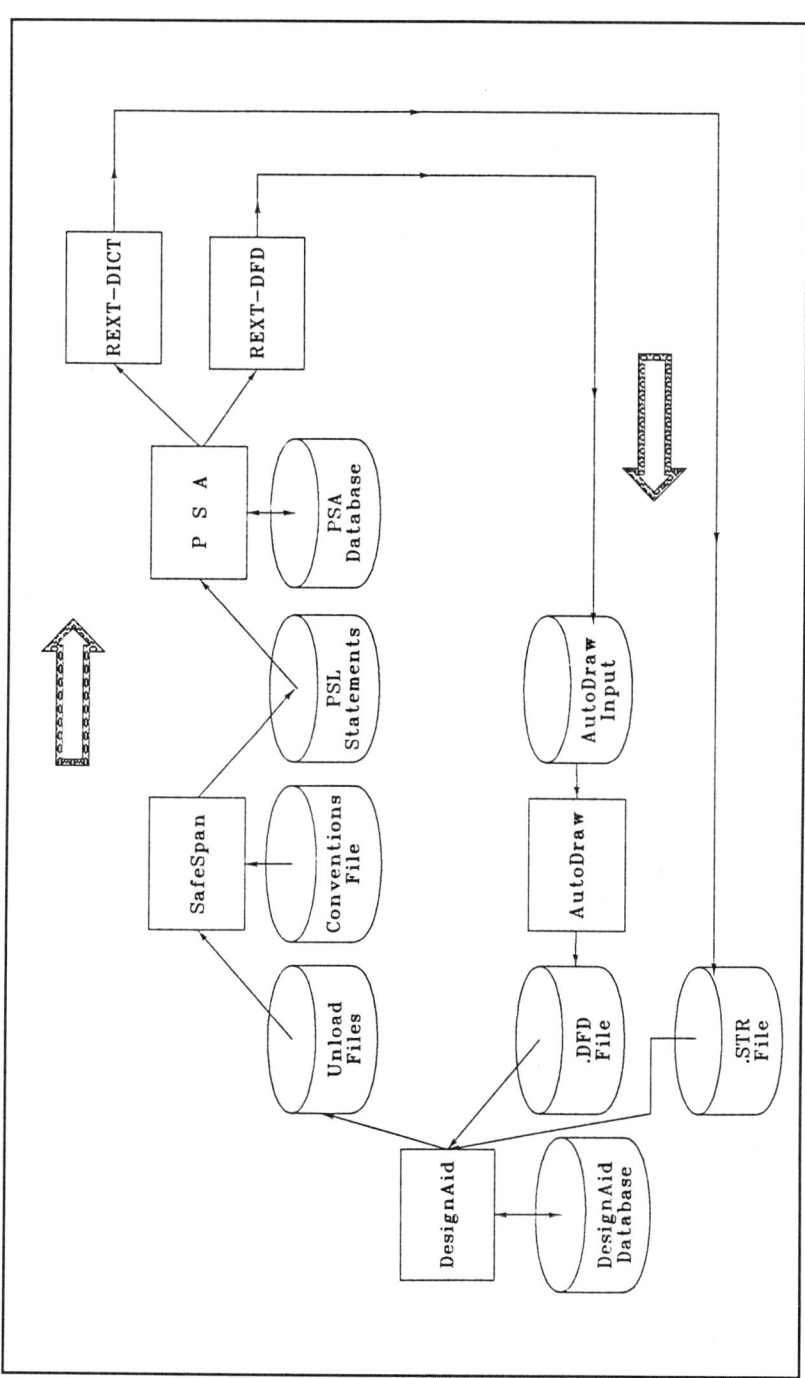

Figure 7: Two-Way Bridge Between DesignAid and PSL/PSA

putting out the translated data. The bridge interpreted the data found in the unload file and translated it into the form mandated in the conventions file, as can be seen in Figure 7.

Because Nastec had designed an *AutoDraw* tool that could take data in linguistic form and convert it into diagrams, we were able to make *SafeSpan* a two-way bridge. Data from the PSA database could be put out into two different files required by *DesignAid*. One file contained data for the constructs that would appear on the diagram *AutoDraw* would produce for *DesignAid*; the other contained information that would go directly into *DesignAid* for entry into its dictionary.

Any user desiring to link-translate data flow diagrams (DFD) drawn by *DesignAid* into *PSL* statements for entry into the *PSA* database would first have to map the DFD constructs and related dictionary information into *PSL* objects, properties, and relationships. This mapping would then be entered into a "conventions file" in the following format:

```
DEFINITION PASS1 %type PROCESS:
    DEFINE PROCESS %name;
        ATTRIBUTE Defined-by '%defineby';
        DESCRITPION%hidesemi %desc;
ALIAS PASS1 %type PROCESS:
        SYNONYM %aliasname:  /* From DA ALIAS*/
```

Such cryptic rules were given for all the different DFD constructs (or any of the other construct types that *DesignAid* permitted) in similar sections. The first line of a definition told *SafeSpan* what to do if it came across data in the "unload file" for an object of type PROCESS. In this case it was to put out the words "DEFINE PROCESS" followed by the actual name of the PROCESS entered into *DesignAid*. Then it was to take the housekeeping information about the name of the analyst who defined this PROCESS from the unload file and put it out in the *PSL* form for an ATTRIBUTE, in this case using "Defined-by" followed by the actual name entered into *DesignAid* by the analyst as a value of that ATTRIBUTE. If the analyst entered narrative text describing this PROCESS, the "conventions file" instructed *SafeSpan* to translate this in the form that *PSL* demanded for a DESCRIPTION. *PSA* expected narrative text, called a comment-entry, to be announced by the text-type that was to follow. This announcement was terminated by a semi-colon and the actual text was put out "as is" and terminated by a semi-colon. The last line of the above instructions told *SafeSpan* how to handle an alias for the PROCESS name, if it encountered one. In such a case, it was to put out the *PSL* term "SYNONYM" followed by the actual alias entered into *DesignAid*.

Other rules were included in the conventions file instructing *SafeSpan* on the desired form for handling such cases as a DATAFLOW moving between two PROCESSES or between a PROCESS and a DATA STORE or the structural relationship between a parent PROCESS and its child PROCESSES. Given these rules, and the name of an "unload file", *SafeSpan* would put out such *PSL* statements as:

DEFINE PROCESS COLLECT_INVENTORY_TRANSACTIONS;
ATTRIBUTE Defined-by 'NASTEC';
DESCRITPION;
System defined during Validation;
SYNONYM COL-INV-TRANS; /* From DA ALIAS*/
•
•
•
DEFINE ENTITY INVENTORY_MASTER_RECORDS;
FLOWS FROM INVENTORY_MASTER_FILE TO
COLLECT_INVENTORY_TRANSACTIONS;
COLLECTED IN INVENTORY_MASTER_FILE;

Another bridge that we were asked to build was to link Index Technology's *Excelerator* and any other repository. In this case, we were not given an "export" file, but instead worked through an utility called the "Programmer's Interface". This tool allowed us to make calls to *Excelerator* and selectively extract data from *Excelerator's* dictionary. As can be seen in Figure 8, a System Manager would be responsible for entering in a "conventions file" the mapping between the constructs in *Excelerator* (whether on Data Flow Diagrams, Structure Charts, Data Model Diagrams, or Entity-Relationship-Attribute Diagrams) and those in the target repository. On this diagram, we show the same System Manager using a tool called *Cultdef* to define the "culture" or metamodel to the *CaMERA* repository. A Librarian for a project might then call on the bridge, called *XL-XPRESS* naming the project files and the conventions file that were to be used. *XL-XPRESS* would work through *Programmer's Interface* to extract the data for the diagram (and its "children" and "grandchildren" if desired) that the Librarian named. Using the conventions file, *XL-XPRESS* would translate the extracted data into the form specified in the conventions file.

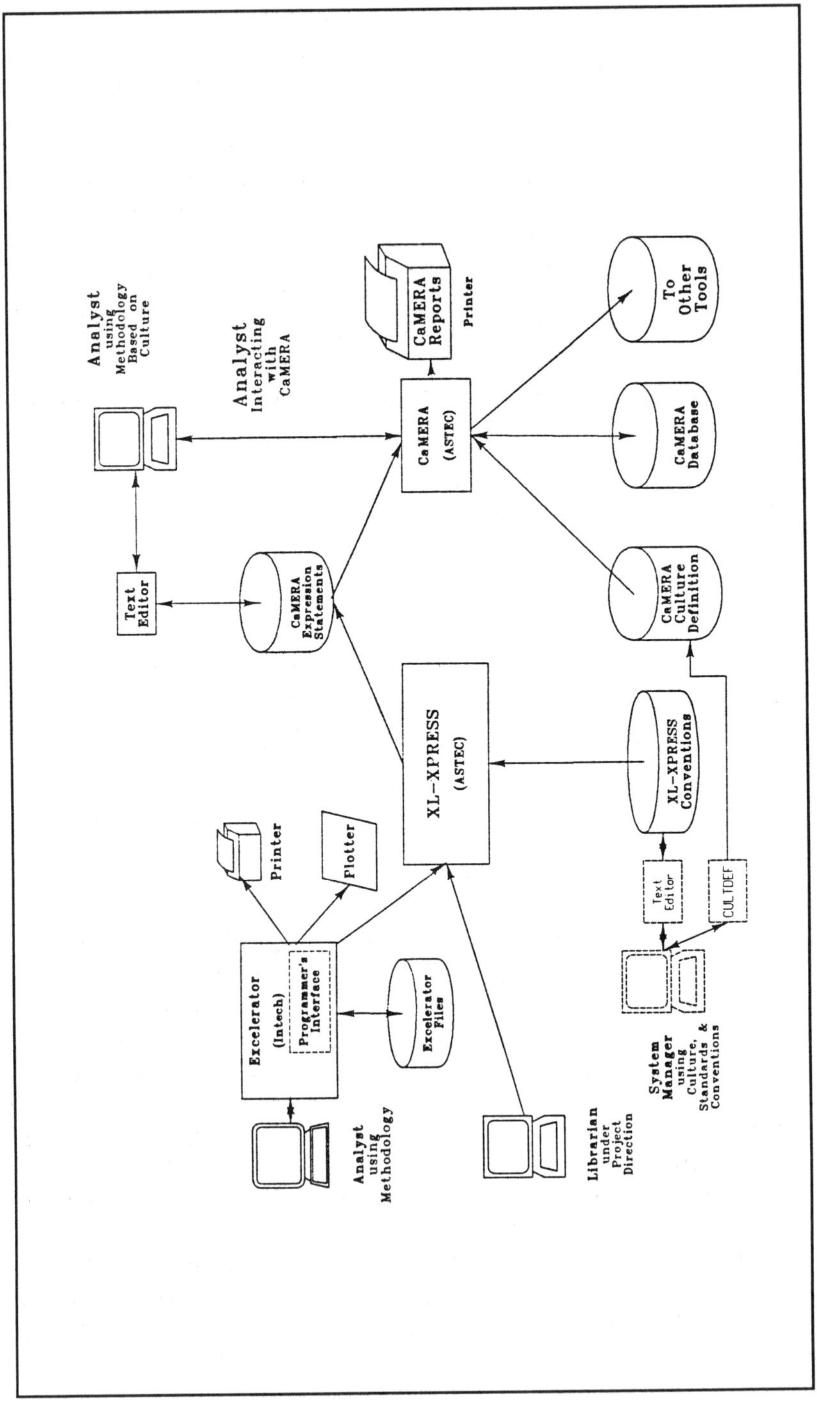

Figure 8: XL-XPRESS System Diagram

Integrating CASE 83

A major reason for building such a bridge was to make possible the creation of a project repository that would merge into one site, all the data captured by many different analysts, each working with his/her own copy of Excelerator. While *Excelerator* does have its own interface capability between distinct projects, it could easily be overwhelmed if the work of twenty analysts needed to be synthesized into a single project. Another reason for such a bridge was to transfer data from *Excelerator* to other CASE tools that a project might be using. As can be seen on Figure 8, once in the repository, (in this case, *CaMERA*), it was possible to have its extraction mechanism put the data out in a form that was demanded by the target tool.

Before using *XL-XPRESS*, the Librarian might use some of the Analysis reports in Excelerator to verify that the diagrams are complete and that all the objects on the diagrams are fully "described" to the dictionary. When ready, the Librarian would invoke *XL-XPRESS*, specifying the project name, the "conventions file", the diagram-type of interest and the scope of the translation desired, i.e., whether only a single diagram and its constructs are to be translated, or a specific diagram and its children or all grandchildren diagrams. The bridge tool will read the conventions file, interact with the *Programmer Interface*, and produce an output file containing statements in the form required by the CaMERA repository.

For instance, a project may be interested in translating the data in *Excelerator* for the following diagram:

If the Librarian (or whoever is using *XL-XPRESS*) had given the

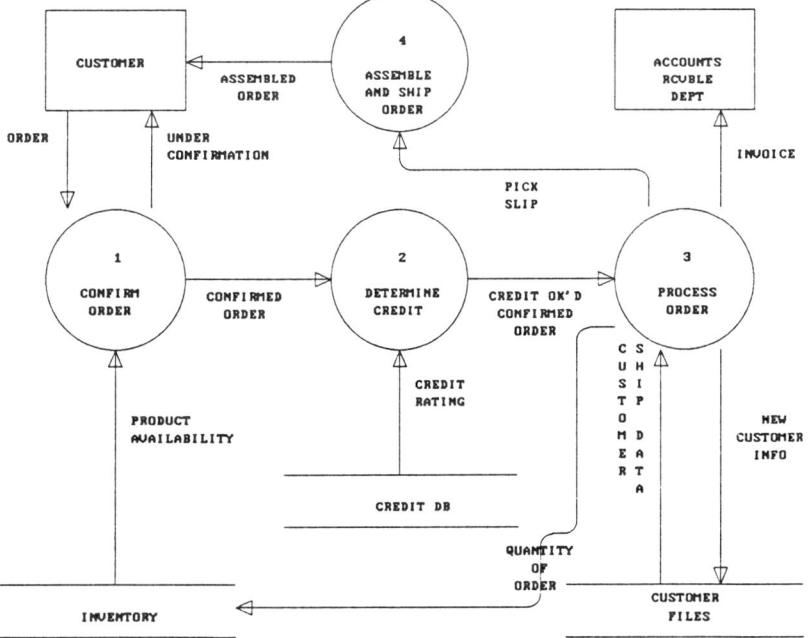

above-required information, *XL-XPRESS* would process such statements as:

Language Statements for "OBJECTS" in dfd "DFD Demo"

ADD OBJ PROCESS "Assemble and Ship Order";
  ADD PROP OF "Assemble and Ship Order" DESCRIPTION
"This process ships the order to the customer.";
ADD PROP OF "Assemble and Ship Order" SOURCE-DIAGRAM
"DFD Demo";

ADD OBJ DATASTORE "Inventory File";
  ADD PROP OF "Inventory File" DESCRIPTION
"This is the file from which product availability is checked.";
  ADD PROP OF "Inventory File" SOURCE-DIAGRAM
  "DFD Demo";

Language Statements for "DATAFLOWS" in dfd "DFD Demo"

ADD OBJ DATAFLOW "Product Availability";

ADD REL FLOW
  RTPART SOURCE "Inventory File"
  RTPART ITEM "Order from Customer"
  RTPART TARGET "Confirm Order";
ADD PROP OF "Product Availability" SOURCE-DIAGRAM "DFD Demo";

A relatively simple set of changes to the "conventions file" would make this same information come out in the form required by the Information Resource Dictionary System (IRDS):

Language Statements for "OBJECTS" in dfd "DFD Demo"

ADD ENTITY 'Assemble and Ship Order'
ENTITY_TYPE=PROCESS
  WITH DESCRIPTION='This process ships the order to the customer.'
  WITH SOURCE-DIAGRAM='DFD Demo';
ADD ENTITY DATASTORE 'Inventory File'
ENTITY_TYPE=DATASTORE
  WITH DESCRIPTION='This is the file from which product availability is checked.'
  WITH SOURCE-DIAGRAM='DFD Demo';

Language Statements for "DATAFLOWS" in dfd "DFD Demo"

ADD ENTITY 'Product Availability' ENTITY_TYPE=DATAFLOW
   WITH SOURCE-DIAGRAM="DFD Demo";
ADD RELATIONSHIP
   'Inventory File' FILE-PROCESSES-RECORD 'Order from Customer'
ADD RELATIONSHIP
   Confirm Order' PROGRAM-PROCESSES-RECORD 'Order from Customer';

Bridging Spreadsheets to a Repository

Many organizations have become accustomed to capturing data on spreadsheets. Spreadsheets are especially helpful when performing mathematical computations on data or when producing various graphs or charts. We were able to use our *GENCAM* bridge linking *Lotus 1-2-3* to our repository, *CaMERA*. As can be seen in Figure 9, we use the *Lotus* utility called *Translate* to convert the spreadsheet (in .wk1 format) to the Lotus Data Interchange Format (.dif). When the user of the bridge gives the command, he/she must also give the name of the DIF file and the name of the file into which it is to be translated. The user can also give an acronym and specific starting number for use in creating unique names for the *CaMERA* relationships that it will create as part of the translation. *GENCAM* translates the data in the DIF file into *CaMERA* statements which the Librarian can then present to *CaMERA* for entry into the repository.

If individuals on a project using these tools wanted to take data from the repository to perform computations or produce charts, they could use the *CaMERA* extraction mechanism to pull out the pertinent data and, by using a conventions file , translate it to a format (.prn) that *Lotus* can import as numbers. By using this bridged environment, we were able to take many hundreds of spreadsheets, synthesize them in the *CaMERA* repository, and later selectively extract data and put it into *Lotus* to create a brand new spreadsheet, with data synthesized from multiple spreadsheets.

For instance, if a project had a number of spreadsheets that contained information somewhat like the following abbreviated version:

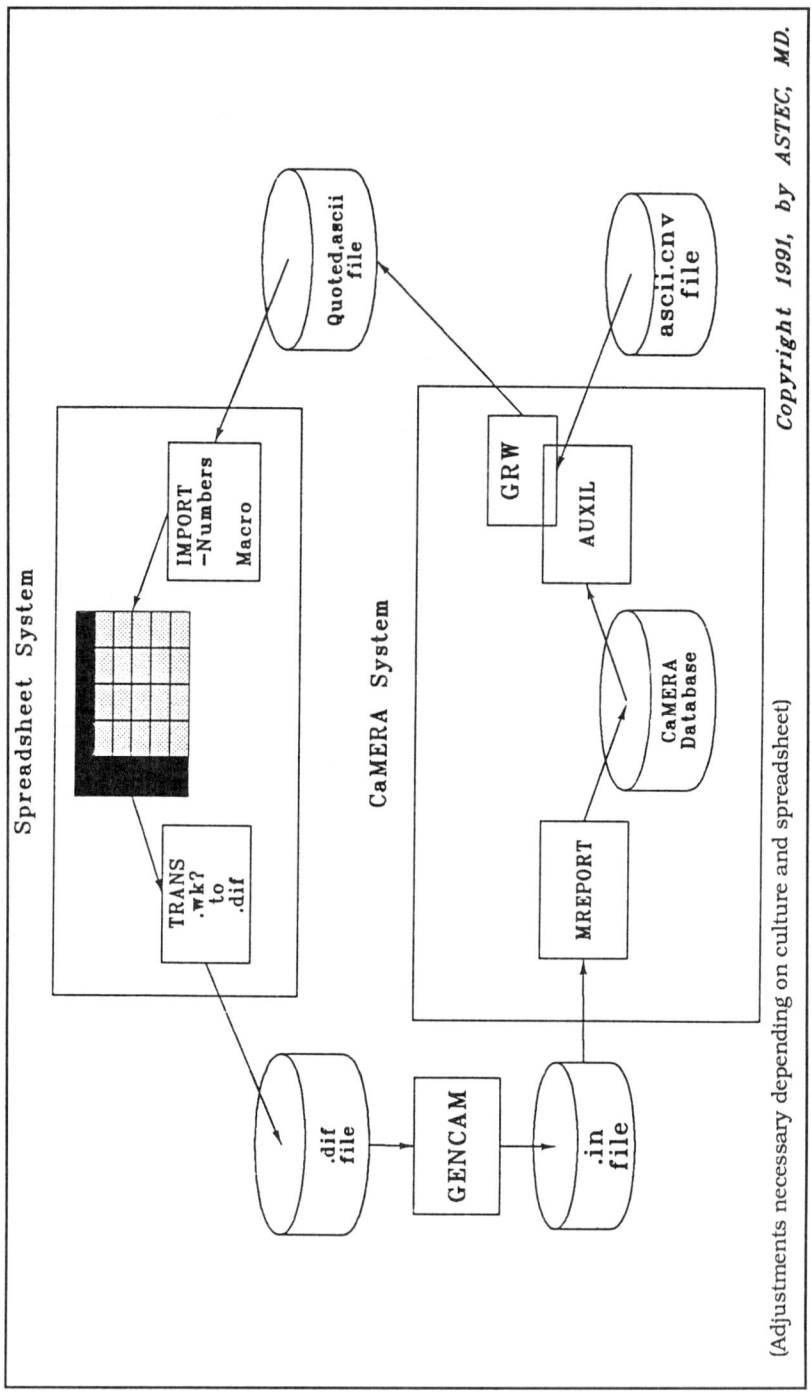

Figure 9: **Architecture of Two-way Bridge between Spreadsheet and CaMERA**

FUNCTION: PROCESS CHECKS
DATE PREPARED: 920114
PREPARER NAME: John Quiqley

TASK NAME:	PCNT-REG-TIME:	OVR-TIME-HRS:
Analyze All Claims	15	5
Clarify Discrepancies	10	5
Give Approval for Check Writing	35	10
Print and Wrap Checks	40	25

it could translate this to DIF format and then translate that file to *CaMERA* statements using *GENCAM*, which would put out statements like the following:

    START TRANS;
  ADD REL PREPARATION "PREP WFC 920112100";
    ADD ROLE TO "PREP WFC 920112100" RTPART ITEM-PREPARED "PROCESS CHECKS";
    ADD ROLE TO "PREP WFC 920112100" RTPART DATE-PREPARED "920112";
    ADD ROLE TO "PREP WFC 920112100" RTPART PREPARER-NAME "John Quiqley";

  ADD REL PERFORMANCE "PERF WFC 920112100";
    ADD ROLE TO "PERF WFC 920112100" RTPART "ITEM-PFMD" "Analyze All Claims";
    ADD ROLE TO "PERF WFC 920112100" RTPART "PCNT-REG-TIME" "15";
    ADD ROLE TO "PERF WFC 920112100" RTPART "OVR-TIME-HRS" "5";

  ADD REL PERFORMANCE "PERF WFC 920112101";
    ADD ROLE TO "PERF WFC 920112100" RTPART "ITEM-PFMD" "Clarify Discrepancies";
    ADD ROLE TO "PERF WFC 920112100" RTPART "PCNT-REG-TIME" "10";
    ADD ROLE TO "PERF WFC 920112100" RTPART "OVR-TIME-HRS" "5";

  ADD REL PERFORMANCE "PERF WFC 920112103";
    ADD ROLE TO "PERF WFC 920112100" RTPART "ITEM-PFMD" "Print and Wrap Checks";
    ADD ROLE TO "PERF WFC 920112100" RTPART "PCNT-REG-TIME" "40";
    ADD ROLE TO "PERF WFC 920112100" RTPART "OVR-TIME-HRS" "25";

Linking Programming Languages

While the foregoing examples dealt with bridges between a repository and "upper-CASE" tools, we have also built bridges to "lower-CASE" tools. In one case we built a "proof of concept"bridge between a code generator and the repository. However, we have had much more interest in building a bridge between code and the repository.

Many organizations have most of their computer programs written in COBOL. These programs have usually been repeatedly patched over the years, and are poorly documented. In fact, in many cases we have encountered organizations that realize that the documentation for many of their programs is hopelessly obsolete because of the number of undocumented changes made to the code. These legacy systems require the expenditure of a lot of resources just to keep them functioning properly. While individual maintenance programmers have learned to understand their parts of the program, they may not feel comfortable tweaking any unfamiliar part of the code. If any of them are absent from work, or leave the organization, their hard-won knowledge goes with them; no one else can easily learn the architecture or function of the code.

To help overcome this situation, we built a reverse-engineering tool, called REVENGG, which takes standard COBOL code and translates it into CaMERA statements for entry into the repository. The maintainer can pose various queries to the database or generate various reports. These queries and reports can be directed to a particular program or to a whole suite of programs, permitting either a micro-view or a macro-view of the legacy system.

Moreover, once in CaMERA, it is possible to make a working copy of the database. Maintainers concerned with making enhancements to the code can examine and analyze it in various ways. Once they come up with a design that seems to embody the enhancements desired, they can make changes to the working copy of the repository and then, using the extraction mechanism, regenerate the code, incorporating the changes. In this way, enhancements could be tried out to verify whether or not they work and satisfy the needs of the system user community.

Figure 10 shows REVENGG as able to take in standard COBOL and FORTRAN code (now in "beta test") and translate it into CaMERA statements. This diagram also shows that maintainers or analysts could use several other "upper-CASE" tools to also produce CaMERA statements, perhaps of the design changes being contemplated. From the CaMERA database, using various other tools, it is possible

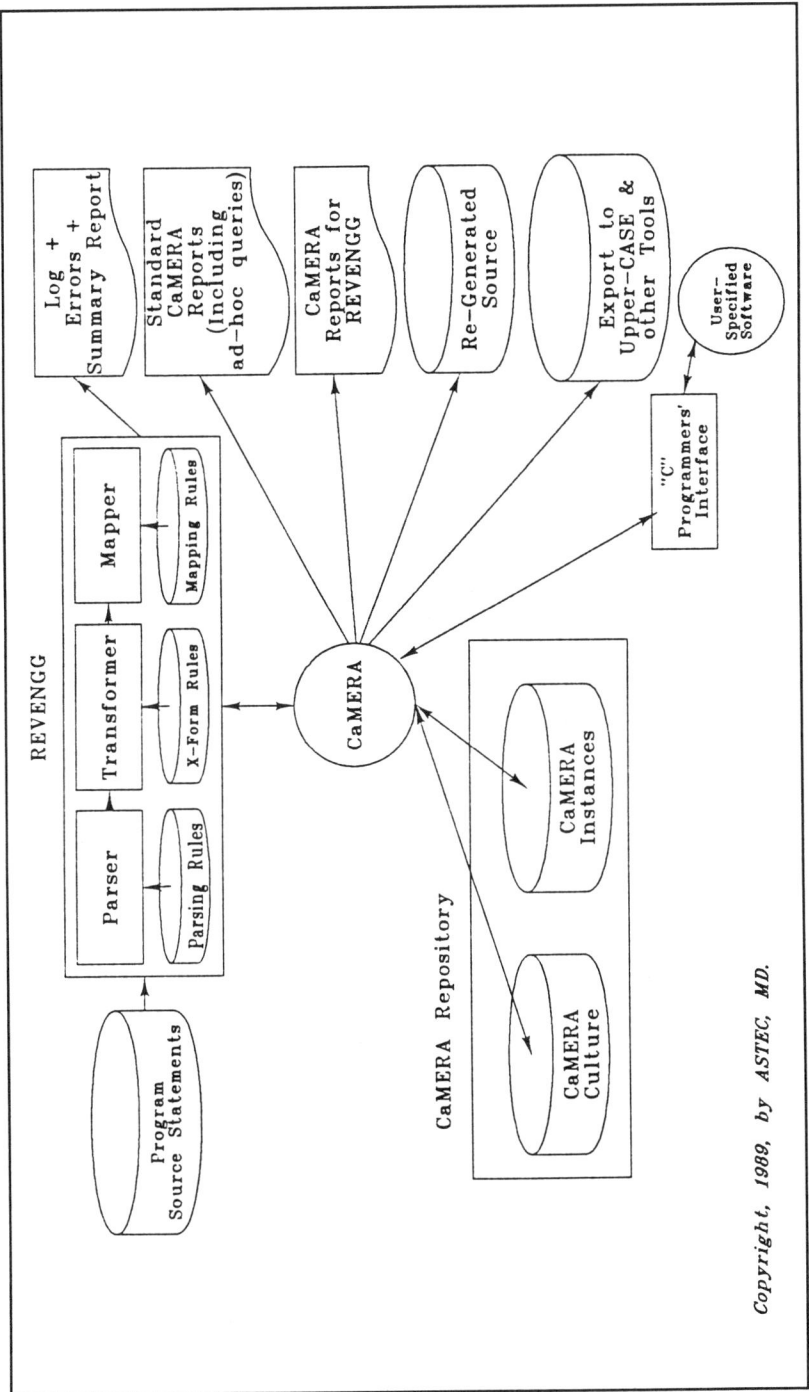

Figure 10: Architecture of Reverse Engineering Environment

Copyright, 1989, by ASTEC, MD.

to produce documentation in forms that adhere to any selected documentation standards. For instance, for the Air Force, we were able to demonstrate the translation of a FORTRAN program and the production of documentation following the Department of Defense Documentation Standard, 2167A.

Figure 10 also implies that it is theoretically possible to take data from the *CaMERA* repository, send it to a code generator, and produce code in any programming language desired. While we have been able to produce code in the same language as the original, we have thus far only been able to produce a proof-of-concept translation from one programming language into another, without producing some mutation like "AdaTRAN" or "FORBOL", which are faithful to neither the source nor target languages. Programming languages do not enjoy a one-to-one mapping to each other. Ada has constructs in it that are not present in COBOL or FORTRAN. Therefore, even if we translate every bit of code in a COBOL program, we could not find material to supply for the missing constructs. Human beings have to intervene and supply the missing information. Obviously, this could be done by adding information to the working repository mentioned above. Then, the enhanced information in the repository could be handed off to a code generator to produce the program in the new programming language.

Other Types of Bridges

In addition to these types of bridges, we are presently working on two other tools: one to translate arbitrary text (expressed in a regular format) into a repository and another to translate data supplied on questionnaires into a repository. The former takes data from an inventory tool's report writer and translates it into *CaMERA* statements for synthesis into the repository. This done, the user will have formal statements about data that was formerly informal or arbitrary. In its informal state, the data can only be reproduced. Once it has become formal, the data can be synthesized with other formal data following the same metamodel. As such, it can be examined, analyzed, and reproduced in any form desired.

The other tool that we are working on takes data scanned from a questionnaire and translates it into *CaMERA* statements for entry into a database. The questionnaire solicits information from employees about their knowledge, skills, and abilities that could be used in a work setting. This data will be integrated with other data already gathered concerning the FUNCTIONS, TASKS, and Sub-TASKS performed in an organization, as well as human resource cost data associated with the TASKS. The purpose of this integration is to enable the organization to cope with changes resulting from the introduction of new automation capabilities. Being able to identify the individuals whose TASKS will be replaced by automation, and the knowledge, skills, and abilities they possess, managers will be better able to transfer these individuals to positions requiring their present skills or provide them with training opportunities for new positions.

CONCLUSIONS

CASE tools were originally developed in isolation from one another. For that reason, there is little wonder that they do not communicate with one another. Each developer was intent on supporting what seemed to be the most important activity in the life cycle. Probably for that reason, requirements analysis received much more attention than did planning. Even when two tools supported the same phase of the life cycle or the same methodology, they did it quite distinctly. The developers provided support that reflected their interpretation of what was supposed to be done in that phase within a specific methodology. Of course, another explanation has to do with expedience: developers probably gave their tools the capabilities that were easiest to implement.

The CASE environment needs to be integrated so that all the information gathered in all life cycle phases is available to developers during all subsequent phases. Information kept in separate locations is of limited use. Information must be made available to different individuals working on a project and it must be made available to more phases of the life cycle than the one in which it was created. Since developing an information system is a form of problem-solving, the information about the system, irrespective of phase or format must be available to everyone working on the problem.

While it could be possible to build bridges between each pair of CASE tools, this does not not seem to be feasible: the number and scope of CASE tools presently available would make this a time-consuming task with little promise of compensatory return for the effort expended. An approach with better promise is one that envisions different CASE tools linked directly to a central repository and indirectly to one another. In this way, different tools in a CASE environment could begin to form an Integrated CASE Environment (I-CASE) and would serve as the base for an Integrated Project Support Environment (IPSE). While the ideal would be an environment in which the product of one phase of the life cycle would be the exact input to the next phase, an interim configuration in which different CASE tools can at least have their data synthesized in a single repository would be acceptable.

In this chapter, we have tried to argue for an integrated CASE environment and to show that such an environment has been successfully created, at least partially. While the information of one phase has not yet automatically become the ingredients for subsequent phases, it has been integrated in a single, semantic data model-based repository. We have tried to show that it has been possible to bridge "upper-CASE" tools and "lower-CASE" tools directly with a repository and indirectly with one another. However, our work has not yet been taken through each phase of the system development life cycle. We have been able to link several different tools, but we have not used this early I-CASE environment on a single project through each phase of the life cycle.

Given our experience to date, we have uncovered two different types of problems:

1) when two tools with the same metamodel are to be linked, and
2) when two tools with different metamodels are to be linked.

In the first case, there are problems with how to handle meaning that is expressed informally. Information exists on different levels of formality, at the highest level, meaning is precise and rule-based. At a lower, less formal level, information is more ambiguous and based on project-determined meanings. On the lowest level of formality, information is devoid of rules and is relatively free-form. The software that manages this data can not subject it to rules for tests of integrity. Words, at this lowest level, mean whatever the user wants them to mean, but that gives no guarantee that the reader/listener will adopt the same meaning.

When dealing with such a problem, it is imperative that a project establish a set of standards and practices. These are conventions that determine such matters as: the phases of the life cycle for a project, individual roles and responsibilities through the life of the project, how project members will refer to entities (naming conventions), the criteria by which members will judge quality, the ownership of the data that is captured in the different phases of the life cycle, who will have the right to change the data, and who will have the responsibility for ensuring that the data is continually backed-up to prevent loss of all project information.

The problem of trying to bridge two tools with different metamodels is even more difficult. Since the tools are based on different metamodels, there is the distinct possibility that any mapping of the constructs will be incomplete. If the information in the two models can not be integrated, they will be merely added together. If there is some mapping, someone has to determine how a construct in the first tool maps to a construct in the second. Because the mapping is not perfectly one-to-one, someone has to decide how the information in the source will be handled, since it is not in the target. Indeed, someone has to decide where information not in the source will come from in order to map the information in the target model.

Presently, there are several different groups trying to resolve these difficult problems. They are not simply solved, because they are not simply stated. Yet they are problems that must be addressed and solved, if CASE is ever to achieve the promise held out for it. We can not ignore these problems because they will not go away. Nor can we hope that they will be simply solved in the short term. There will be no silver bullets. We have to work hard for I-CASE to become a reality.

REFERENCES

Dart, S., Ellison, R, Feiler, P, and Habermann, A. (1987)."Software Development Environments". *Computer*, November, pp. 18-28.

Jacobs, P. (1992). "Is That Upper- or Lower-CASE?". *HP Professional*, August, pp. 24-34.

King, R. and McLeod, D. (1985). "Semantic Data Models". In S. Bing Yao, Ed. *Principles of Database Design*, Vol.1: Logical Organizations. Englewood Cliffs, NJ: Prentice-Hall, 1985.

Sayani, H. H. (1991). "Fitting Reverse Engineering into the Development Cycle". Presented at Reverse Engineering Forum: Capturing Value, April 23 & 24, 1991, Washington University, St. Louis, MO .

Svoboda, C. (1988). "Bridging Between Existing CASE Tools". Presented at CASE Studies, May 15 & 16, Falls Church, VA.

Svoboda, C. (1989). "Manager Exchange," *IEEE Software*, September, p. 38.

Wasserman, A. (1981). "The Ecology of Software Development Environments". *Software Development Environments*, pp.47-52.

CHAPTER THREE

An Integrated CASE Model for Forward and Reverse Software Engineering

Shirley A. Becker, B.J. Gleason and Anita J. LaSalle
The American University

This chapter describes a model for representing and building an integrated CASE environment as well as CASE tool developments that have broad application in the field of software (re)engineering. The model described in this chapter incorporates both traditional approaches to software (re)engineering and new approaches that are based on developments in Expert Systems (ES). The application of ES technology to traditional and evolving CASE methodologies shows promise as an adjunct for "Forward Engineering" and "Reverse Engineering" of both existing software and software under development. ES is also a mechanism for building a platform to support an integrated CASE environment. The integrated CASE environment described in this chapter is based on a "layered" model. Each layer defines a set of specific services available through CASE tools. A particular tool "resides" in the layer that best characterizes the tool's services. Integration of CASE tools is enhanced through precisely defined layer interfaces. A layered model for representing CASE tool capabilities combined with the application of ES to some layer services shows great promise for the integration of existing and evolving CASE technologies.

The repertoire of CASE tools proliferated during the last decade as industry searched for an effective means of minimizing software

Integrated CASE Model 95

defects. The chief proponents of CASE tools were, and still are, organizations that suffer from the long-term impacts of servicing low-quality system applications. The maintenance costs of supporting these systems are uncontrollable and drain corporate resources. Some experts estimate that the support allocated to maintaining the health of aging systems is approximately 50% to 70% of the total system development effort (Kozaczynski & Ning, 1989).

Despite the early promise of CASE technology, many practitioners are disillusioned with CASE as a means of resolving the software maintenance crisis because CASE tools have not delivered on their promise to improve software quality. While the ineffectiveness of CASE tools may be attributed to a number of factors, a primary shortcoming is that existing tools are not integrated. Stand-alone CASE tools force organizations to build software "bridges" to meet specific needs and to permit migration from the use of one tool to another.

Another weakness of existing CASE architectures is an absence of standards for requirements specification, design notation, application code and coding styles, and documentation. System development and maintenance tasks are performed more effectively when there are standard formats for system specification, designs, code structure, and documentation (Hevner, Becker, and Pedowitz, 1992) and all the other phases of the Software Development Life Cycle (SDLC).

Finally, most existing CASE environments focus on a few specific functions that support certain activities in the life-cycle of a system. But to achieve zero-defect, easily-maintainable systems, the CASE environment should be comprised of a comprehensive set of "specific-function" CASE tools so that all activities in the system lifecycle, including system modification, are supported.

These and other shortcomings of CASE emphasize the need for:

- an integrated CASE environment where information is transparently exchanged among CASE tools,
- (flexible) representational and notational standards for all phases of the software development life cycle, and
- transparent transitions from the use of one CASE tool to another (without having to re-implement existing CASE tools.)

The work described in this chapter addresses how the criteria listed above might be satisfied in a unique way. Expert Systems (ES) technology has already shown great potential for being applied to the solution of a broad class of "human-judgment" problems. Much success has been reported in the literature and the commercial availability of ES tools attests to the acceptance of this technology. The use of ES to address the problems of CASE tool development and integration shows promise where other conventional approaches may fail. "Expert" tools can be applied from the stages of system development through maintenance where the output from one tool can transparently become the input to other tools. Figure 1 shows a comprehensive set of CASE tools that are supported by an Expert System CASE Tool Integrator that manages information through a common repository. The CASE tool subdomains overlap the needs of different phases of the software development life cycle and may address both forward and reverse engineering (these terms/concepts will be described in the next section).

An automated SDLC environment is requisite to designing a high-quality system because usually no one practitioner can maintain intellectual control over the design of a complete system. History has shown that the processes of system design, development, and maintenance are wrought with pitfalls. Often a system component is designed in isolation of other system components. As a result, it is possible that system components that have already been developed (but are not recognized as reusable) may be redundantly designed. When making changes to an existing system, it is necessary to comprehend the side-effects of the changes on other

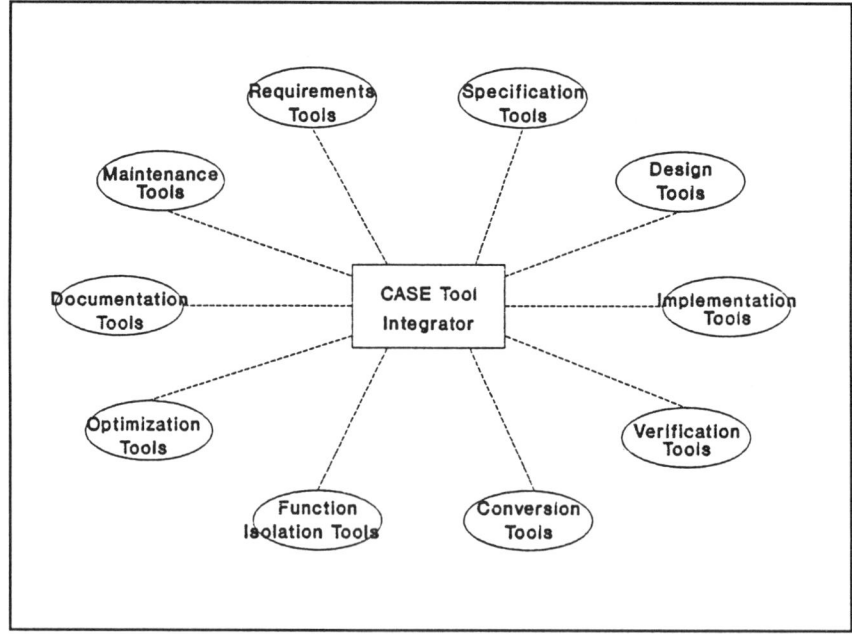

Figure 1: Domain of CASE Tools

system components. As the developer modifies the system to compensate for possible side-effects, the overall system is "perturbed" and in fact more errors may be introduced. Ultimately, the process will stop when a compromise is reached between quality and cost (Levendal, 1991). Because of the complexity of today's systems, intellectual control over the design of a system can only be achieved by CASE tool support for system development and maintenance. In turn, intellectual control over the broad repertoire of CASE tools can be achieved with the introduction of intelligent tools designed for this purpose.

A CLARIFICATION OF SOFTWARE (RE)ENGINEERING TERMINOLOGY

As the title of this chapter implies, both the processes of *forward* and *reverse* engineering are candidates for improvement using CASE tools. Determining which tool is appropriate for a specific task may be complicated because of confusion over terminology related to system (re)engineering. For example, Biggerstaff categorized commercial products that can be "loosely" classified as *reverse* engineering tools in Table 1(Biggerstaff, 1989). This classification demonstrates the lack of a widely-accepted categorization scheme for reverse engineering. Most of the tools listed in Table 1 perform functions such as system testing, conversion, and code structuring. These activities are important in achieving a high quality system design but may not provide capability for other software development functions.

- test coverage analyzers
- debuggers and execution monitors
- source-to-source translators
- cross reference facilities
- code reformatters, pretty printers, restructurers
- structure and metrics analyzers
- file comparators
- CASE-oriented reverse engineering (and re-engineering tools)

Table 1: Classification of Commercial Reverse Engineering Tools

The following terms; forward engineering, reverse engineering, redocumentation, design recovery, restructuring, and reengineering need to be defined in order to gain an understanding of the functions of specific CASE tools in system (re)engineering.[1] Chikofsky recognized the need for standard definitions and proposed the following (Chikofsky, 1990):

- ***forward engineering*** - the process of moving from high level abstractions and logical, implementation-independent designs to the physical implementation of a system.
- ***reverse engineering*** - the process of analyzing a system or system design in terms of system components and their interrelationships, and representations of the system in another form or at a higher level of abstraction.
- ***redocumentation*** - the process of creating or revising a semantically equivalent representation within the same relative abstraction level. The alternate representation can be considered another view (e.g., code is represented in a data flow graph).
- ***restructuring*** - the process of transforming one representation to another form at the same relative abstraction level while preserving the system's external behavior functionally and semantically (e.g., altering code to get rid of GOTO statements).
- ***reengineering -*** the process of examining and altering a system to reconstitute it in a new form and the subsequent implementation of the new form. Generally, reengineering means applying reverse engineering and forward engineering to modify an existing system.

We will use these definitions in the remainder of the chapter.

APPROACHES TO SOFTWARE (RE)ENGINEERING

The improvement of the maintenance phase of the SDLC is one of the primary motivations for reengineering software. There are, however, many other phases that are served by tools that perform program transformations. The software industry is still living with the legacies of the "Software Crisis" of several decades ago as well as the more recent "Software Maintenance Crisis." Poor programming methodologies and the code that resulted from them, little or no documentation of existing software, code developed with prehistoric compilers and development tools, evolutionary systems whose components were developed using different tools and under different organizational policies, are all issues that must be managed when software must be developed, extended or maintained. In the extreme case, developers will rewrite software in an effort to insure some level of maintainability and extendibility. However, much unretrievable knowledge may be embedded in existing software that is obscured by bad coding practices and fragmented logic. To complicate matters, software that is produced by several individuals may reflect different abstraction techniques (Shaw, 1989).

Software transformation methodologies and tools have evolved during the past decade to compensate for many of the problems described above. These methodologies and tools for forward engineering, reverse engineering, redocumentation, restructuring, and reengineering take a variety of forms including: "invasive" tools for program tracing and monitoring, "intelligent" tools for extracting the semantics (contextual meaning) of abstract representations of problem solutions (from the problem definition phase to the coded representation), analytical tools for extracting code structures, data structures, and data dependencies, and transforming tools that rely on one or more of these techniques to alter the form of some version of a problem solution abstraction. Deciding when to apply these different approaches may complicate practitioners' tasks.

The following summarizes some of the better known (re)engineering techniques and the motivations for using them. It is clear that these techniques and motivations are interrelated —one technique may necessarily have to be applied as a precursor to another. A number of these approaches reflect the great deal of attention that has been paid to techniques that result in program code transformations, however, many of the items listed also address earlier phases of the SDLC. While not all of these activities have resulted in formal CASE tools, most of the functional capabilities described here are reflected in various CASE technologies:

- performance improvement/optimization techniques: Program transformations that will result in existing code being made more efficient. Efficiency can be gauged as faster execution (e.g., isolating code segments for parallel execution or recoding array structure operations to reflect compiler/memory interactions) or by other measures such as improved resource utilization (e.g., relying on program execution history to improve memory paging). Performance improvement/optimization techniques may involve static analysis of program structure or dynamic analysis of program behavior.
- software reuse approaches: According to Standish (1984), "Software reuse has ... become a keystone in many current efforts to improve productivity. One impressive way to lower the cost of building software is to pay either nothing at all or a small cost for

retrieval (and perhaps instantiation) by reusing what has been previously built. ... what is needed is an effective method for expressing software abstractions and for generating particular instances by transformation or refinement, suited to many varying concrete settings of use." Some approaches that have been used to either capture code reusability or insure that code will be reusable are:

— use Very High Level Languages (VHLLs) to describe program abstractions that are then realized from a reservoir of available code modules (Matsumoto, 1984),
— extract program segments whose logical structure (in some standard representation such as a flowdiagram) matches or approximates the target logic (Matsumoto, 1984),
— transform programs into languages that support reusability (Cheatham, 1984),
— capture program segment functionality so that it can later be used in rapid prototyping environments or for different applications (Cheatham, 1984).

- *validation/verification methods:* Much attention has been paid to the problem of program verification, ranging from formal mathematical proofs to error detection through testing (Deak, 1981; Arthur & Ramanaayashreethan, 1981; Voges, Gmeiner, & Mayrhauser, 1980). A number of interactive function isolation tools have been developed to discover both static and dynamic program structures and then use those structures for verification, test data design, and behavior evaluation. The "output" of these tools includes:
  — static program relationships generated by compilers (e.g., cross-reference listings, style checkers),
  — identification of potential unwanted side-effects,
  — traces of data dependencies,
  — dynamic relationships traced during program execution (e.g., frequency and sequences of procedures calls, infrequently used segments of code).

One complication that accompanies the use of validation/verification monitors or program transformers is the difficulty of verifying the correctness of the tool.

- *maintenance/extensibility/change improvement approaches:* Software (re)engineering to improve the maintenance phase (to be able to extend the functionality of the software or change it) may take place at several levels. In the early specification phase, it may mean using formal specification techniques that result in maintainable programs (Bersoff & Davis, 1991). In later phases, it may mean transforming unstructured, obscure code into structured, less complex code.

- **decomposition strategies for function isolation:** The trend toward integrated systems and code re-use has led to a number of decomposition techniques that attempt to isolate system/program functionality. Decomposition of operational systems not only leads to more easily maintained components but may also permit new tools to be applied to those components for basic improvements.
- **methods for documentation improvement:** Virtually all of the (re)engineering techniques and CASE tools described in this chapter lead to more easily documented or automatically documented systems.
- **transformations for function identification:** An early example of this (re)engineering technique was reverse-compilation or disassembling. Tools that accomplish this class of transformation attempt to reverse the compilation process to discern higher-level representations of program abstractions.
- **methods for transforming formal notations:** Bersoff (1991) calls this "automated software synthesis," a process that may involve more than one sequence of actions. These actions, typically taken during a phase or sub-phase of the life cycle, can involve focused automated tools that perform transformations such as:

Initial Representation		Final Representation
	tool(s)	
Formal System Specification	——>	Software
	tool(s)	
Formal Requirements Specification	——>	High-Level Design
	tool(s)	
Formal High-Level Design and Specification Algorithms	——>	Low-Level Code

- **transformations to take advantage of new representational paradigms:** As the body of knowledge pertaining to programming formalisms has expanded, new formalisms have evolved that lead to more reliable and maintainable systems. These include, for example: formal specification languages with richness of expression for describing a program's environment, process and structures (Balzer & Cheatham, 1981), techniques for abstracting data structures "to permit local optimization of those structures" (Wile, 1981), and restructuring tools to permit (re)engineering software features such as user interfaces to take advantage of developments

in methodologies and equipment.
- ***decomposition strategies to capture organizational paradigms:*** Software captures not only procedural specifications but also, in many cases, organizational policies and practices. The process of decomposing existing software may be motivated by a need to isolate functions for clarity/classification (for re-application in other systems or to change those functions), or in order to determine which organizational policies were embedded in systems.
- ***decomposition approaches to capture development process(es):*** "...research with experts and novices in various technical domains ... have shown that the former seem to develop chunks that represent functional units in their respective domains, ... (Balzer & Cheatham, 1981)" The expert's knowledge evolves over time, and with experience and, represents logic structures and program structures that are models of practices and conventions that have a high degree of past-use integrity. The intellectual processes that are captured can be formalized and migrated to other systems.
- ***transformations to take advantage of evolving technologies:*** As computing methodologies and technologies evolve, software development processes and software (re)engineering practices are altered to take advantage of enhancements. This was evident in the past with the introduction of Data Base Management Systems and more recently with the development of parallel languages and algorithms, object-oriented languages, and knowledge-based systems. The converse is also true, new technologies and paradigms may permit certain transformations that were not possible in the past. For example, knowledge-based systems can serve as platforms for the transformation process itself.
- ***techniques for isolation of security kernels/safety kernels:*** The application of computers and their software to the solution of problems where there are inherent risks (of human safety, financial loss, or legal liability) has lead to intense interest in isolating functions where risks are focused. This isolation also supports security protection for proprietary or defense applications. Once kernels are isolated, validation/verification techniques can be applied to insure the integrity of those modules.

While this is an extensive list, it is not exhaustive. Intense interest in improving the software development life cycle continues to yield new and novel tools that can be applied to all phases. The CASE environment described in this chapter addresses the integration of these techniques in order to support (re)engineering.

AN INTEGRATED MODEL FOR SOFTWARE (RE)ENGINEERING

The approaches and specific techniques described in the previous section are highly focused. Each was designed to compensate for a problem that originated in one of the phases of the SDLC or because technologies evolved that showed promise of improving some aspect of a software system or the life cycle used to develop that system. While each approach has integrity in a specific area of software (re)engineering, an integrated approach, transparently combining many of these techniques, has greatest potential for impacting on the total quality of software systems.

A Layered Model for Integrating CASE tools

The field of software (re)engineering is not the first technology to suffer from rapid growth, proliferation of disparate methodologies, systems and tools, and incompatibilities resulting from the absence of standards. Telecommunications is an instance of another technology that experienced explosive growth over the last several decades. So many organizations and countries were involved in telecommunications and network development that system integration became a nightmare. The solution to the problem was the gradual universal acceptance of a model for system development called the OSI 7-Layer model. The purpose of this model is the isolation of functional capabilities into well-defined "layers" starting from the level of user applications down to the physical delivery of communication signals. In this model, every layer delivers some service(s) to the layer above, and layer interfaces are precisely defined. The 7-layer model does not address *how* services must be implemented, only the *kinds* of services to be implemented. Another innovative aspect of the 7-layer model is the acceptance of a standardized notational language (ASN.1) for defining protocols that facilitate delivery of layer services at all layers.

A "Layered Model" is a convenient one for specifying structure and capability in many areas, and is particularly useful for attacking the problems involved in building cohesive representations of software (re)engineering methods and tools. Because investment in software and CASE tools is so extensive, it is unlikely that organizations will be willing to abandon existing systems and products in order to comply with new standards. Rather, what is needed is a representational model, and integration standards, that permit organizations to fit their systems into new frameworks.

Layer		
12	Requirements Layer	
11	System Specification Layer	System
10	High-Level Design Layer	Development
9	Low-Level Design Layer	Layers
8	Implementation Layer	
7	Verification Layer	
6	Conversion Layer	System
5	Function Isolation Layer	Reengineering
4	Knowledge Extraction Layer	Layers
3	Performance Improvement Layer	
2	Documentation Layer	
1	Maintenance Layer	

Figure 2: Integrated CASE Tool Layered Model

Figure 2 depicts a layered model for software (re)engineering CASE tools. It is important to emphasize that this is a CASE tool integration model. It does not imply any particular CASE tool application sequence or software development life cycle. The integration model incorporates all of the CASE tool functional subdomains that evolved over time as a consequence of the traditional "waterfall" life cycle. The tools whose functions are included in Figure 2 support any software life cycle model despite the hierarchical nature of the integration model.

We will not dwell on the layer services and layer interfaces, but mainly describe the features of this model that are significant in the context of an integrated CASE tool environment. It is important to note that even though the "Documentation Layer" occurs at Layer 2, this does not imply that all documentation functions are assigned to one isolated layer. Most commercially available tools, regardless of the functions they perform, include documentation capabilities. While twelve layers may seem complicated, each layer represents services that have been or can be offered by CASE tools. Some of these are already incorporated into commercial and research products and were defined in the *Approaches to Software (Re)Engineering* section. The important aspect of such a model is that CASE tools at any one layer can take any form. It is the specification(s) of layer interfaces that defines how tools interact and consequently insure their integration potential. For example, Figure 2 specifies that verification (and validation, testing, and debugging) services be

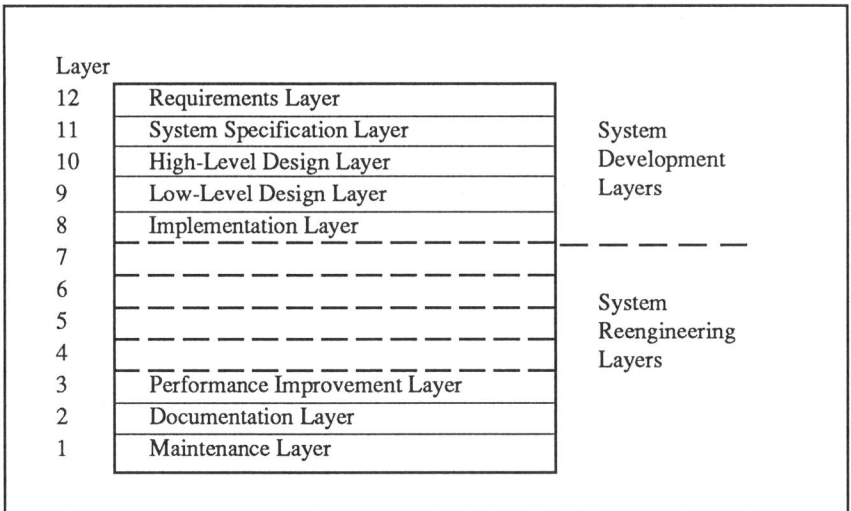

Figure 3: CASE Layered Model With Null Layers

provided at Layer 7. How verification is done within layer 7 is not defined. However, the input ("down" from Layer 8 from a tool such as a compiler) to Layer 7 and its output ("down" to Layer 6 which may include such services as restructuring and beautification) can be well defined. The specification of layer inputs and outputs can be structured to conform to the scope of a particular layer. Just as in the case of the OSI 7-Layer communications model, some layers may be "null" in the context of some tools and problem spaces. Figure 3 could represent two such possible scenarios. In the first case, output from a compiler (layer 8) is input to a performance improvement tool (layer 3). In the second case, layers 8 down to 3 are represented by a single "optimizing" compiler. In both these situations, layers 7 through 4 are null (unless, for example, the performance improvement tool relies on function extraction or the capabilities of other sublayers). Reverse engineering usually takes place from Layers 7 down to 1. In this case, layers 12 to 8 are essentially null. In the context of System Development (forward engineering), not all layers may be significant — Layers 5 and 4, for example, may be null.

The isolation of CASE tool functional capabilities into well-defined layers will not constrain any aspect of CASE tool development, or existing CASE tool enhancement or integration. On the contrary, it provides a framework for ensuring the compatibility of existing and future products. CASE tools "cooperate" through standard interfaces and well-defined interface data structures. However, since it is unlikely that organizations will develop and agree upon large sets of layer interface standards in the near future, there remains the problem of how to achieve integration in the short term. One approach, the application of Expert Systems to the problem of CASE tool integration, holds promise for immediate practical realization.

The Role of Expert Systems in Integrating CASE Tools

An Expert System (ES) captures, automates, and makes available the knowledge of experts. ESs are most suitable where "rule-of-thumb" logic dominates the actions of the expert. The phases of the SDLC and the application of CASE tools to those phases are rich in such expert judgements. Even "mechanical" language-to-language reverse engineering translators have some judgment components associated with them.

Figure 1 depicted the domain of CASE tools with a central "CASE TOOL INTEGRATOR." ES technology presents a unique solution to the problem of implementing the CASE tool integrator. For example, function isolation services necessarily involve "human judgment" about the identification of modules that are abstracted from a program. This process is usually carried on in the context of some previously "understood" functionality. The role of ES at this layer is to (among other tasks) archive knowledge about functions that have been identified in a common (standardized) data base that can be applied to subsequent function isolation tasks.

The remainder of this chapter describes the role of CASE tools at several CASE layers (primarily System Development Layers), current research into specific tools and methodologies, and examples of the role of ES technology in permitting the integration of such tools.

CLEANROOM SYSTEMS ENGINEERING: AN UNDERLYING THEORY FOR CASE INTEGRATION

A synergy is created in systems development when a comprehensive CASE environment and a formal systems development method are combined. A CASE environment is useful in supporting systems development activities only when a rigorous methodology provides the underlying foundation for integrating the CASE tools. A relatively new paradigm, Cleanroom Systems (Software) Engineering, is described here as a means of transparently linking the CASE layers shown in Figure 2. A rigorous methodology such as Cleanroom

Integrated CASE Model 107

becomes much more effective in practice, when a CASE environment is developed to support its activities. An overview of the Cleanroom method is presented, and its role in supporting an integrated CASE model is explained.

Overview of Cleanroom Systems Engineering

The traditional waterfall life cycle (Figure 4) is no longer a viable means of developing high-quality software. It has proven to be ineffective because today's multiprocessing and distributed processing systems are too complex to be successfully developed using a predefined sequence of development activities. Many practical, alternative approaches to the traditional life cycle have been introduced including evolutionary prototyping, operational prototyping, the software reuse model, and automated software synthesis among others (Bersoff & Davis, 1991). Even though these methods are easy to apply, they lack the formal theory that is necessary for correctness verification of software components. Researchers have also developed elegant formalisms to improve our understanding of software and abstract its functionality. These formalisms include predicate calculus, functions, and state machines (based on work by R. Floyd, E. Dijkstra, C. Hoare, and H. Mills, among others)(Basili & Musa, 1991). Unfortunately, many of these formalisms have not been used

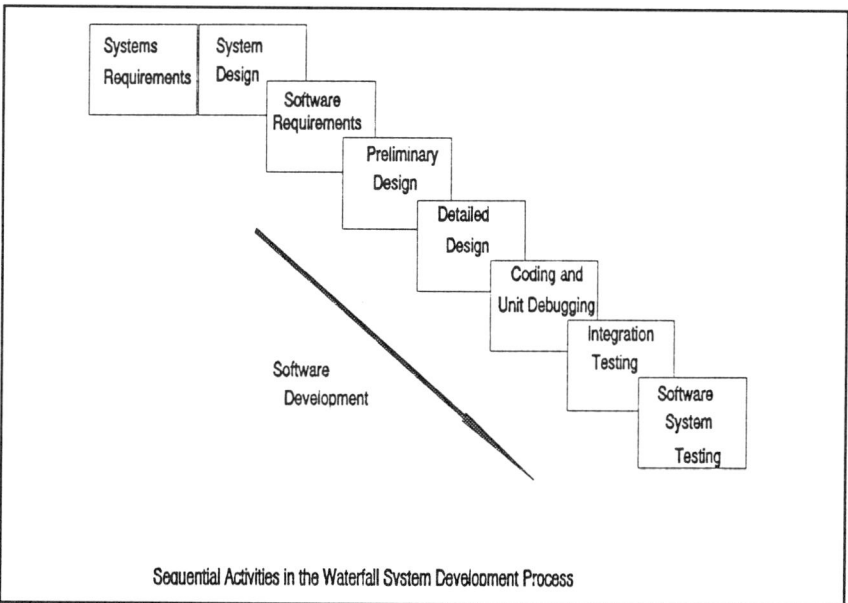

Figure 4: Waterfall Model of the Software Development Life Cycle (Bersoff & Davis, 1991)

in practice because of their complexity.

A recent innovation, the Cleanroom System Development Process (CSDP), has combined theory and practice in a comprehensive development environment. Cleanroom was initially developed and implemented at IBM Corporation and has become increasingly popular because of its success in developing near-zero defect software (Cobb & Mills, 1990). Typical Cleanroom projects that produced robust software included an IBM language product, an Air Force contract helicopter flight program, and a NASA contract space-transportation planning system, among others (Mills, Dyer, & Linger, 1987). Software is engineered with the Cleanroom method under rigorous statistical quality control. The emphasis of the methodology is error prevention rather than error detection (Mills, Dyer, & Linger, 1987).

Unlike the traditional "waterfall" life cycle approach, Cleanroom is a flexible process that allows development teams to perform activities in a dynamic sequence, and as many times as necessary to achieve high-quality software. The Cleanroom Systems Development Process shown in Figure 5 presents an iterative set of systems development activities (Hevner, Becker, & Pedowitz, 1992). Development teams gather customer requirements and produce requirement specification and usage specification documents that become

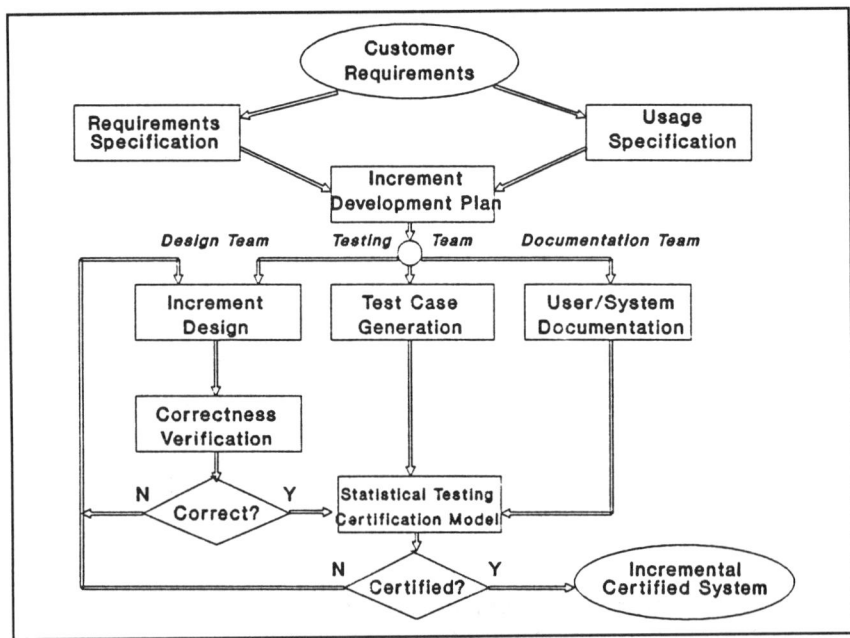

Figure 5: Cleanroom Approach to Software Development

the inputs to the design activities. The overall system design is decomposed into manageable design increments in order to maintain intellectual control over the systems development process. Each design increment adds system functionality to previous design increments.

Cleanroom enforces both mathematic verification of system designs, and statistical testing of design components. A design team applies formal correctness verification techniques to each of the system components that comprise a design increment (correctness verification is discussed in the next section). Once this is accomplished, each design increment is statistically tested using randomly generated test cases. Statistical usage testing is performed by simulating the user's operational environment. It requires the identification of all inputs to the system along with their probability distributions. A test case is defined as the set of inputs comprising a single use of the system, and each test case is randomly selected for execution based on its usage probability. The interfail times experienced in statistical usage testing, form an exponential distribution that can be used to generate the expected Mean Free Time Between Failure and certify the reliability of the system (a comprehensive discussion of Cleanroom testing is found in Cobbs & Mills, 1990).

Each design increment is documented to support various levels of users including operators, managers, and system developers. Documentation consistency is enforced by maintaining a cross-reference list of document changes and design modifications. The Cleanroom approach to systems development has an underlying mathematics-based theory called the Box Structure Methodology (BSM). BSM provides both a formal and informal notation for describing system behavior and enforces management control through its Box Structure Usage Hierarchy (BSUH). Box-structured information can easily be shared among the systems development layers because of its standard representation of information. Initial studies by Hevner et. al. have shown that a set of commercial CASE tools can be transparently linked together when box structure notation is used to analyze and design system components (Hevner, Wilkey, & Becker, 1991; Hevner, Becker, & Pedowitz, 1992). Hevner et. al. have also identified box structure data models for a common CASE repository for supporting the Cleanroom process (Hevner & Becker, 1992). This common repository is essential for the effective integration of the supporting development tools in order to store, organize, and maintain the components of a software application. Box structure representation of information provides a foundation for an Integrated CASE Model to support Cleanroom Systems

Engineering. The box-structured analysis and design method is described in the next section.

Overview of Box Structure Methodology

The Box Structure Methodology is an integral component of the Cleanroom process because it provides both a syntactic as well as a graphic notation for describing system behavior, and it's underlying semantics provides the basis for formal correctness verification of a system design (Mills, 1986). Each system design is described in three levels of increasing detail: a black box, a state box, and a clear box.

A black box is defined by a mathematical function from histories of stimuli (S) to the next response (R). The black box function, f, maps historical sequences of stimuli S*, to responses, R, in the form:

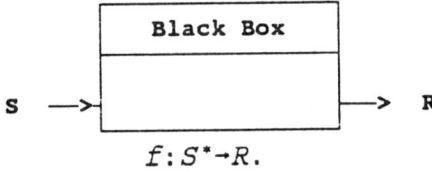

$$f: S^* \rightarrow R.$$

A state box refines a black box by identifying state data (T) to be stored between stimuli so that only a current stimulus is required but not previous history. A state box function, g, is composed of an internal data abstraction (black box) that has a compound stimulus consisting of the external stimulus and the internal state and a compound response consisting of the external response and the new internal state. The state box function, g, takes the form:

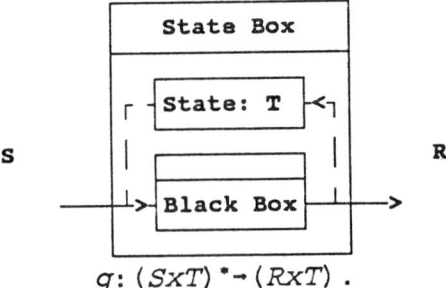

$$g: (S \times T)^* \rightarrow (R \times T).$$

A clear box expands a state box by replacing the internal data abstraction with the procedural behavior of new data abstractions that can be expanded into lower level software designs. Procedural behavior may be described in terms of sequence, alternation, iteration, or concurrency constructs (Mills, Linger, & Hevner, 1986;

Becker & Hevner, 1991). These programming rules specify the functional behavior of the system and will be demonstrated in the next section.

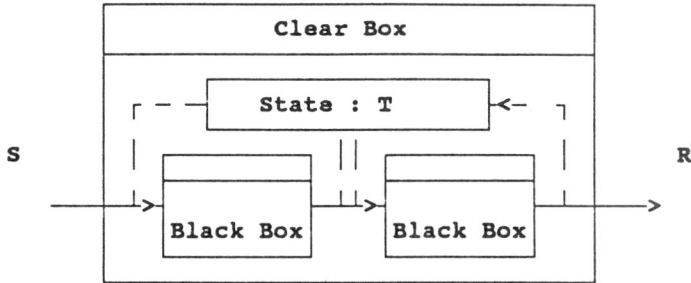

These box structure concepts are illustrated via a small example called the Selling Price System. The Selling Price System is used to calculate a selling price for an item. The item's selling price is determined by multiplying the cost of materials by a constant amount to cover other costs, such as, labor expenses, overhead costs, and research and development. Finally, this amount is increased by a fixed percentage to include a profit. The three box structure views of the Selling Price System can be described graphically as presented in Figure 6.

A box structure can also be described in a formal design language called the box definition language (BDL). The BDL for the Selling Price System is shown below for each of the three box structures.

```
Black Box Selling Price System
    stimulus
       percentage : real;
       constant   : real;
       mat_cost   : real;
    response
       selling_price : real;
    transaction
       selling_price := (constant * mat_cost) +
                       (percentage * (constant * mat_cost));
    end transaction;
end Black Box Selling Price System.

    State Box Selling Price System
    stimulus
       mat_cost   : real;
       percentage : real;
```

```
        constant  : real;
    response
        selling_price : real;
    state
        p : real;
        c : real;
    transaction
        if percentage != p then
                p := percentage;
        if constant != c then
                c := constant;
        selling_price := (c * mat_cost) +
                (p * (c * mat_cost));
    end transaction;
end State Box Selling Price System.

Clear Box Selling Price System
    stimulus
        mat_cost : real;
        percentage: real;
        constant : real;
    response
        selling_price : real;
    state
        p : real;
        c : real;
    transaction
        use update_state(stim percentage, constant);
        use fixed_costs(stim mat_cost; resp tot_cost);
        use profit(stim tot_cost; resp selling_price);
    end transaction;
end Clear Box Selling Price System.
```

The design of the Selling Price System is a creative invention of expanding the black box view into state and clear box views of system behavior. Each expansion step is immediately verified for correctness before continuing the design process. For example, the behavior of the Selling Price System clear box can be verified as consistent with its state box design by a function abstraction process (Mills, Linger, & Hevner, 1986):

Step 1: Derive the state box behavior by eliminating the procedural details of the clear box.
Procedural behavior: tot_cost := c * mat_cost; selling_price := tot_cost + (p * tot_cost);
Substitution: selling_price := (c * mat_cost) + (p * (c * mat_cost));

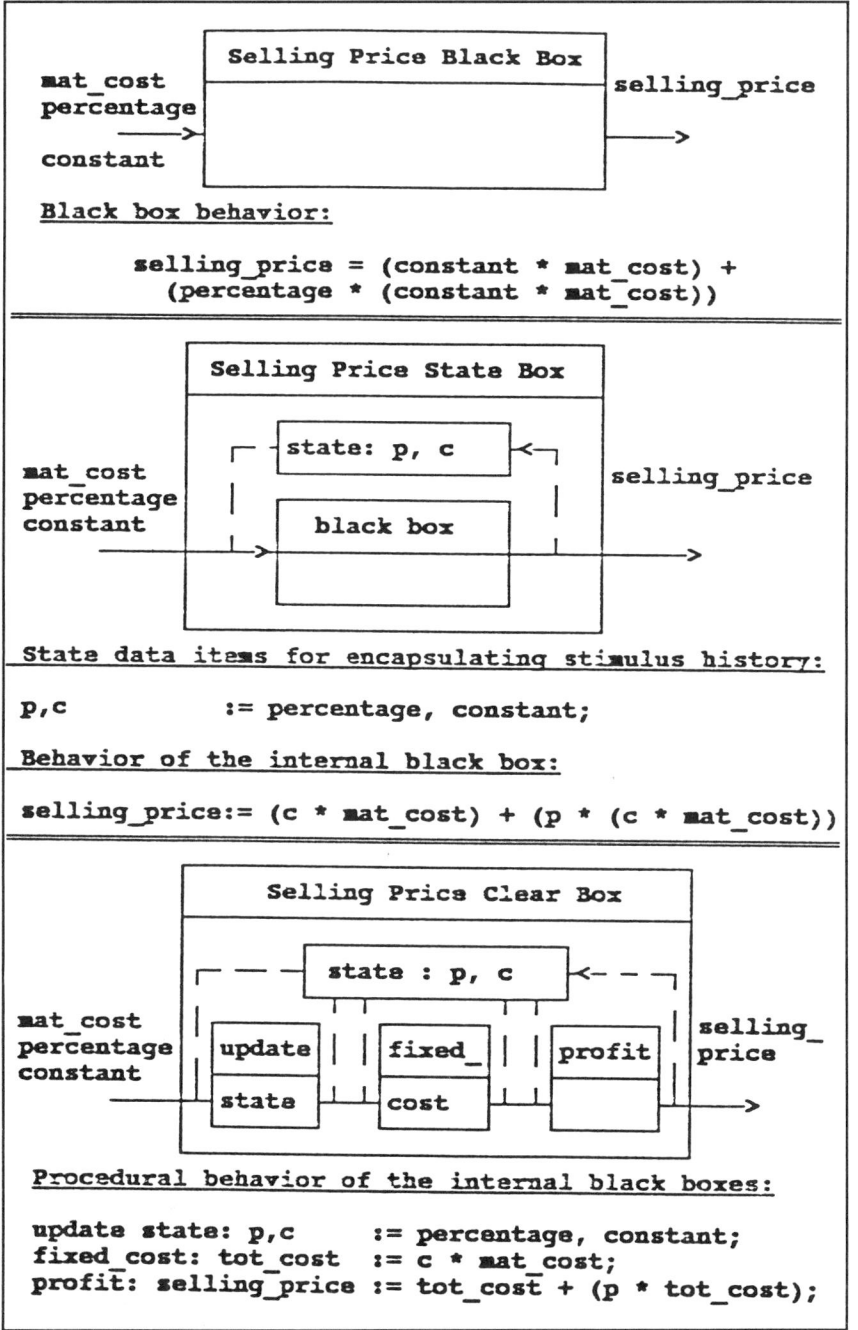

Figure 6: Box Structure Views of "The Selling Price System"

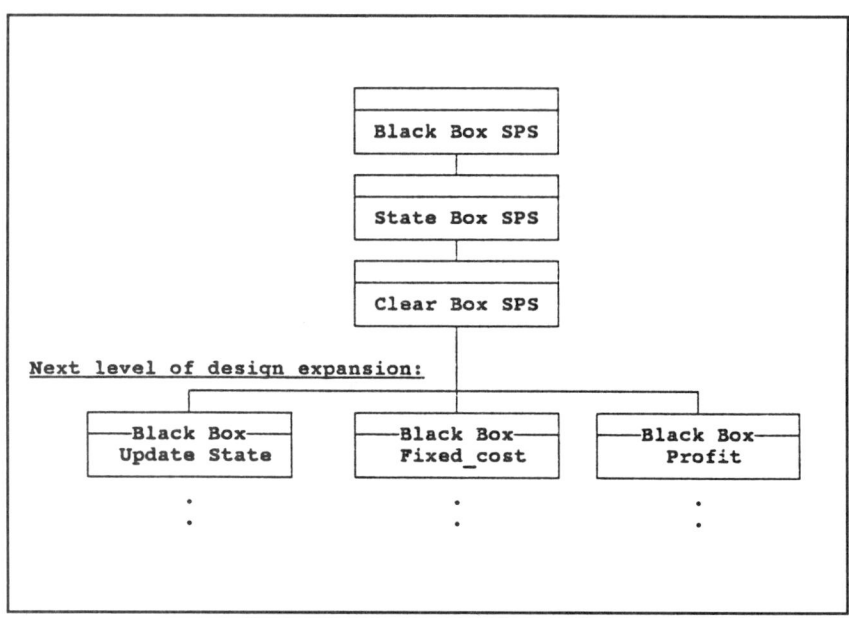

Figure 7: BSUH for the Selling Price System (SPS)

Step 2: Compare the derived function of the clear box to the intended function of the state box for consistency.
Intended State Box Function: selling_price := (c * mat_cost) + (p * (c * mat_cost));
Derived State Box Function: selling_price := (c * mat_cost) + (p * (c * mat_cost));

The consistency verification of the Selling Price System design is a simple demonstration of the formal verification process conducted by Cleanroom development teams to minimize the number of system defects. Once the clear box has been verified for correctness, it is refined into lower level box structure designs that are in turn verified for correctness. All box structure designs are organized in a Box Structure Usage Hierarchy (BSUH) for management control. The BSUH for the Selling Price System is shown in Figure 7.

It is important to note that this function abstraction process is the basis for the Cleanroom forward engineering of a new system design. It can also be applied during the Cleanroom reverse engineering of an existing system in order to abstract the behavior of existing application code or designs. These issues will be addressed in subsequent sections.

Forward Engineering and its Role in The Integrated Layered CASE Model

Automated support of the function abstraction process is currently being researched in order to assist Cleanroom developers in the correctness verification of design components. Widely used CASE tools have not yet evolved to support this process. However, automated support of the function abstraction process will reduce the time and cost of systems development while further increasing the quality of software. The function abstraction process for simple modules such as the Selling Price System is a relatively straightforward process. However, for more complex system components, the manual abstraction of functional behavior may become labor-intensive and may be less formally applied than if automated support were made available.

There are a small number of design primitives that need to be supported by an automated function abstraction tool. These primitives (often referred to as structured primes) can be used to form system designs of any size or complexity (Dyer 1988). For example, The Selling Price System design was comprised of a set of sequence functions (update_state, fixed_costs, and profit sequences), but system designs may be described using any of the prime functions shown in Table 2 (Hausler, Linger, Pleszkoch, & Hevner, 1990).

Dyer summarized correctness criteria used in the verification of the consistency of a system design with its requirements (Dyer, 88). These correctness criteria are listed in Table 3 for each prime

FUNCTION TYPE:	STRUCTURE	EXAMPLE
sequence	P = g;h	MOVE X TO T MOVE Y TO X MOVE T TO Y

alternation	P = If b then g
	else h fi
		IF A > B
		    MOVE X TO T
		ELSE
		    MOVE Y TO T

iteration	P = While b do g od	PERFORM UNTIL NOT (T > 0) ADD Y TO Z SUBTRACT 1 FROM T

Table 2: Basic Prime Functions

structure: sequence, alternation, or iteration. (A comprehensive explanation of the verification process can be found in Hausler, Linger, Plezskoch, & Hevner, 1990; and Linger, Mills, & Witt, 1979).

The function abstraction tool not only provides a mechanism for correctness verification, but also supports reusability by identifying system components by their intended functions. Automated support of re-usable system components is critical to achieving productivity gains in software development. In the past, re-use was relatively limited to application code. But what is needed is a means of identifying re-usable system components at a higher-level in the design activities. Box structure theory supports reusability by identifying system components by their intended functions. The common repository must be able to support the standard representation of these functions so that they can be easily accessed. During subsequent system analysis and design cycles for new or revised applications, the repository would provide "off-the-shelf" functions for reuse.

The discussion thus far on function abstraction may have oversimplified the function abstraction process. This process may become very complex especially when developers are unfamiliar with the basic prime structures and structured programming concepts. The use of Box Structure Description language in the design of a system (as shown in the Selling Price System example) supports the use of structured programming concepts. The BDL syntax guides a developer in maintaining a certain level of structure in high level

Function Type	Correctness Consideration
Sequence	Sum of function parts equals whole.
Alternation	Function equals thenpart when predicate is true and function equals elsepart when predicate is false.
Iteration	Termination for any loop argument and function equals looppart when argument true and function equals identity when argument is false.
(Loopexit variation of iteration)	Termination for any loop argument and function equals looppart when argument true and function equals looppart followed by identity when argument is false.

Table 3: Correctness Criteria (Dyer, 1988)

designs as well as lower level designs. But it is important to note that since the design process is an inventive process, there is nothing to prevent an inexperienced designer from developing a complex design that is difficult to verify when a simpler design could have been chosen. The simplification and abstraction of a system design into a readable and human comprehendible format is an essential topic for future research.

Hausler et. al. have presented an in depth discussion on the usefulness of pattern matching in the function abstraction of iteration constructs (loops). Even though the presentation of their work is beyond the scope of this chapter, it is important to note that their research has provided the foundation for developing an expert system tool to support the function abstraction of alternation patterns (Hausler, Linger, Pleszkoch, & Hevner, 91). This area of research is critical in supporting the various "patterns" associated with programming loops. In order to effectively use an automated function abstraction tool, a set of supporting CASE tools are needed to link the various layers in the Integrated CASE Tools Model. These tools are discussed next.

Supporting CASE Tools for Systems Development in the Integrated CASE Tool Layered Model

The box structure method provides a standard design notation to support system requirements that may be described informally in english text, intermediate system designs that may be described in structured english or mathematic notation, and low level system designs that may be directly translated into application code. These levels of design are represented in the Integrated CASE Tool Layered Model (shown in Figure 2). The application of box structure notation in a CASE environment will provide a standard representation of information so that the system engineering layers can be transparently linked together. Hevner et. al. have categorized the CASE tools necessary for effective support of the Cleanroom Systems Development Process. These CASE tools are listed in Table 4. The CASE tools have been categorized by Cleanroom development activity; these tools support the 12 CASE Tool Layers presented in Figure 2 (a comprehensive overview of these CASE tools is found in (Hevner, Becker, & Pedowitz, 1992)).

Many of the CASE tools listed in Table 4 are commercially available. However, in addition to the function abstraction tool identified previously, there is an essential set of CASE tools that are not currently available that need to be developed to support the Cleanroom process. For example, at the requirements layer, auto-

	CASE Model Layer
Requirements Determination: • Intelligent Editor • Box Structure Graphics • Decomposition Tool • Usage Specification Tool Incremental Development: • Spreadsheets • Statistical Packages • Scheduling Tools • Decision Support Systems Box Structure Analysis and Design Method: • Intelligent Editor • Box Structure Graphics • Box Structure Usage Hierarchy Manager • Prototyping Tool • Decomposition Tool • Data Structuring Tool • Application Generator • Performance Evaluation Tools	7 - 12
Statistical Testing: • Random Case Generator • Statistical Packages	7
Documentation • Intelligent Editor • Graphics Capability • Modification Report Generator	2

Table 4: CASE Tool Support for Cleanroom System Development (Hevner, 1991)

mated support is needed to abstract the system requirements from fuzzy customer requirements. An expert system tool would be useful in identifying common components within the system requirements, and structuring the fuzzy information in a box-structured format. This expert system tool would generate a high level design from the system requirements. The high level system design can be further decomposed with the support of the CASE tools listed for box-structured systems analysis and design in Table 4. A Box Structure Usage Hierarchy Management tool is essential for automated support of top-down development and identifying reusable system components. Many of the CASE tools presented in Table 4 can be used to support the system reengineering layers in the Integrated CASE Tool Layer Model. In the next section, automated support for maintaining existing systems is discussed.

Automated Support of Reverse Engineering Within the CASE Layered Model

In our discussion on the use of a function abstraction tool in forward engineering, it was pointed out that the function abstraction tool could also play a critical role in reverse engineering an existing system. A function abstraction tool and other supporting tools are essential in gaining insight on the functionality of an existing system because the maintainer may not be the same person as the developer, and the software may be poorly documented and poorly structured. A function abstraction tool can be used to guide the maintainer in understanding the functionality of software components, and to assist in structuring existing designs in a comprehensible format. The insight gained by the maintainer will allow for successful software modifications with little likelihood of unwanted or unpredictable side-effects on other software components.

Another automated tool that would support the reverse engineering process is a "data flow analysis" tool that tracks the flow of data in a software application in order to evaluate its usage. This tool supports the identification of data anomalies including overloaded data items that can be corrected before the reverse engineering process is applied (Hevner & Linger, 1989). For example, when a data item is repeatedly written between reads, such usage may indicate an overloaded data item.

In order to effectively apply a function abstraction tool to existing application code, the code needs to be in a structured format. A structuring tool plays an important role in supporting software analysis and maintenance by restructuring code in a top-down structured format. A structuring tool that was developed by a Cleanroom development team for this purpose is called the COBOL

```
        PROCEDURE DIVISION
        MAIN.
            OPEN INPUT ACCOUNT_FILE
                 OUTPUT ADJUSTMENT_FILE.
            READ_NEXT_ACCT. <―
                READ ACCOUNT_FILE
                    AT END GO TO DONE.―
                MOVE CORRESPONDING ACCOUNT_REC TO ADJUST_REC.
                IF BALANCE OF ADJUST_REC < 0.00
                    MOVE 'Y' TO DEFAULT
                ELSE
                    MOVE 'N' TO DEFAULT.
            MORE. <―
                IF (BALANCE OF ADJUST_REC NOT < 0.00) OR
                   (LOAN_OUT OF ADJUST_REC + 100.00 > LOAN_MAX OF ADJUST_REC)
                    GO TO WRAP_UP.―
                ADD 100.00 TO LOAN_OUT OF ADJUST_REC.
                ADD 100.00 TO BALANCE OF ADJUST_REC.
                GO TO MORE.―
            WRAP_UP. <―
                WRITE ADJUST_REC.
                GO TO READ_NEXT_ACCT.―
            DONE. <―
                CLOSE ACCOUNT_FILE
                      ADJUSTMENT_FILE.
                STOP RUN.
```

Figure 8: GOTO "Spaghetti" Code

```
PROCEDURE DIVISION
CSF_MAIN.
   OPEN INPUT ACCOUNT_FILE
        OUTPUT ADJUSTMENT_FILE.
   PERFORM READ_NEXT_ACCT
   PERFORM
      UNTIL CSF_AT_END = 'T'
      MOVE CORRESPONDING ACCOUNT_REC TO ADJUST_REC
      IF BALANCE OF ADJUST_REC < 0.00
         MOVE 'Y' TO DEFAULT
      ELSE
         MOVE 'N' TO DEFAULT
      END IF
      PERFORM
         UNTIL (BALANCE OF ADJUST_REC NOT < 0.00) OR
               (LOAN_OUT OF ADJUST_REC + 100.00 > LOAN_MAX OF ADJUST_REC)
            ADD 100.00 TO LOAN_OUT OF ADJUST_REC
            ADD 100.00 TO BALANCE OF ADJUST_REC
      END_PERFORM
      WRITE ADJUST_REC
      PERFORM READ_NEXT_ACCT
   END_PERFORM
   CLOSE ACCOUNT_FILE
         ADJUSTMENT_FILE
   STOP RUN.
READ_NEXT_ACCT.
   MOVE 'F' TO CSF_AT_END
   READ ACCOUNT_FILE
      AT END
         MOVE 'T' TO CSF_AT_END
   END_READ.
```

Figure 9: Restructured Code

Structuring Facility (COBOL/SF)®[2] COBOL/SF transforms GOTO statements into more effective programming constructs, structures each module with one entry and one exit point, and eliminates or flags sections of "dead code". The restructuring process performed by COBOL/SF is demonstrated on the banking system code in Figure 8 and Figure 9 (Hausler, Linger, Plezskoch, & Hevner, 1990). Figure 8 depicts a portion of existing code with spurious "GOTO" sequences. Figure 9 depicts the same code sequence after using COBOL/SF. Upon inspection of Figure 9, it is clear that the poorly structured code depicted in Figure 8 has been transformed into well-structured code that is made more readable and consequently more easily maintained and may be a candidate for reuse in future applications.

Example of an Expert System-Based Tool for Function Identification

As new computing paradigms and technologies evolve, many are incorporated into CASE tools. One such technology is an expert system. In this section, a unique application of expert systems to the services provided by two layers is demonstrated with an ES-based

```
dim y(10), x(10)

start := 1;
endd := 10;

for ptr = start to endd
        y(ptr) := 0;
next x;

ptr := 1;
while ptr < = endd
        x(ptr) := ptr * 2;
wend;

ptr := 1;
repeat
        t := x(ptr);
        x(ptr) := y(ptr);
        y(ptr) := t;
        ptr := ptr + 1;
until ptr > endd;
```

Figure 10: Test Code Segment for ES Function Extraction CASE Tool

function extraction tool.

While the example shown here is necessarily simplistic, it demonstrates how an ES can be used not only to integrate CASE tools, but also extract "human knowledge" from existing systems. Consider layers 6, 5, and 4 of Figure 2. The input to layer 6 from the tools used in the layers above 6, is a collection of code representing an abstraction of a problem's solution. The specification of layer interfaces is not complicated at this level since the data passed across the layer interface are programming language statements written in some (reasonably) standardized language. The services provided by layer 6 may include, for example, transformations on the code to produce a structured, beautified format. The role of ES at this level is to assist in the production of restructured code in accordance with accepted practices and/or organizational conventions. These structured templates are maintained in a database of past (approved) structuring practices and are used by the ES in making decisions about structure choices.

The purpose of layer 5 is to isolate functions from the data passed to it and, with the aid of the ES front-end, build a database of descriptive phrases (and possibly alternative representations) for certain statements and/or groups of statements. Figures 10 and 11 depict a portion of a session with the function extraction CASE tool. Figure 10 shows a segment of program code before the application of the tool; Figure 11 shows its operation on the code segment.

Figure 11 shows statements classified according to basic type

```
[ 1]    dim y(10),x(10)
[ 3]    start := 1;
                Assignment : Initialization
[ 4]    endd := 10;
                Assignment : Initialization
[ 6]    for ptr = start to endd
                Loop: Start : For #1 : Index = ptr
[ 7]    y(ptr) := 0;
                Assignment : Initialization
[ 8]    next x
                Loop : End : For #1
                *** Array Initialization ***
[10]    ptr := 1;
                Assignment : Initialization
[11]    while ptr < = endd
                Start While Loop #1
[12]    x(ptr) := ptr * 2;
                Assignment : Number of Ops = 1
[13]    wend;
                End While Loop #1
[15]    ptr := 1;
                Assignment : Initialization
[16]    repeat
                Start Repeat Loop #1
[17]    t := x(ptr);
                Assignment : Transfer 1
[18]    x(ptr) := y(ptr);
                Assignment : Transfer 2
[19]    y(ptr) := t;
                Assignment : Transfer 3
                *** Swap *** 17 18 19
[20]    ptr := ptr + 1;
                Assignment : *** Increment
[21]    until ptr > endd;
                End Repeat Loop #1
```

Figure 11: Operation of ES Tool on Program Segment

(e.g., Assignment : Initialization) or a recognized sequence (e.g., Swap). Statement classification is based on both user supplied information and a database of templates of statement types. Likewise, the identification of a series of statements (e.g., [17], [18], and [19]) as matching a recognized pattern (SWAP) is done using the template database, a knowledge base of statement classifications, and the user's interface. While this is a simplistic example, it demonstrates that the application of ES to the problems of code conversion and function extraction is a natural arena for this new technology. Expert systems provide a mechanism for accommodating a layered set of CASE tools for a variety of services and interfaces.

ES-based CASE-Layer Integration

The previous section showed how a particular CASE tool operates in a narrow CASE domain — i.e., simple function extraction within a code segment. The benefits resulting from the successful

Integrated CASE Model 123

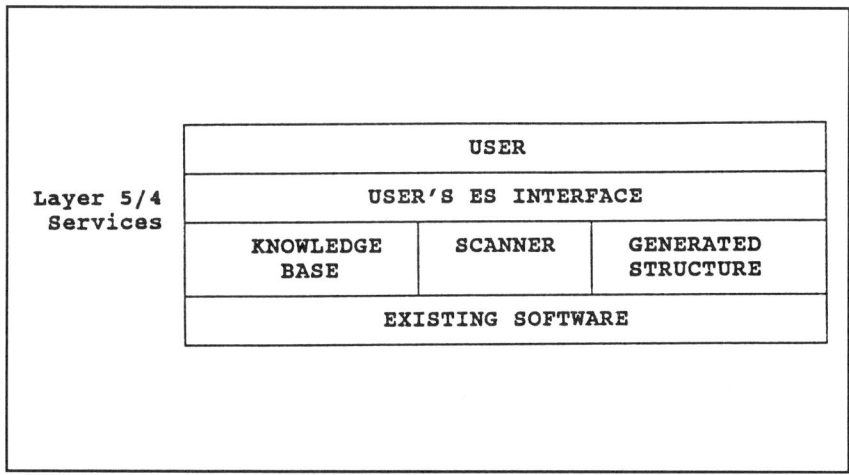

Figure 12: ES-based Layer Services

application of ESs to other CASE layers, and layer interfaces, are considerable. Services provided by CASE layers 3 through 7 are particularly amenable to enhancement through the application of ESs. Figure 12 depicts an ES-based environment that supports both layer 5 and layer 4. The structure shown in Figure 12 is the backbone of the example shown in the section, *Example of an Expert System-Based Tool for Function Identification.*

The identity and purpose of the sub-layers shown in Figure 10 are as follows:

- at the lowest sub-layer is existing software written in a structured higher-level language such as 'C', Pascal, or Ada.
- at the next higher sub-layer are three interacting components:
  —a knowledge base of statement classification templates. This evolutionary knowledge base is specific to the implementation language. As the system is used, the knowledge base expands to recognize new programming practices and organizational procedures imbedded in programs.
  —a parser/scanner analyzes program statements and sequences of statements, interacting with the knowledge base to classify program structures according to templates stored in the (expanding) knowledge base.
  —the parser/scanner produces descriptive statements and/or alternative representations of the program in the form of a new generated structure.
- on top of the scanner sub-layer is the user and ES interface sub-layer that provides interactive access to the scanning/classifica-

tion process.

Once functions are isolated and knowledge extracted about a program's structure (in layers 5 and 4), performance improvement mechanisms can be more easily applied in layer 3 and documentation and maintenance improved using tools available at layers 2 and 1.

Other CASE Tool Support

The first six subsections under *Cleanroom Systems Engineering: An Underlying Theory for CASE Integration*, demonstrated some current activities involving the automation of forward and reverse engineering CASE tools. There are many other CASE tools that support all phases of the SDLC. These tools include sophisticated editors, design language shells, graphic support packages, control flow and data flow analyzers, program dependency analyzers, program change analyzers (to discern ripple effects), program structure graphic generators, program symbolic behavior evaluators, and program/record dependency analyzers, among others. Many of these tools are combined in one package. For example, COBOL/SF® is comprised of a structuring component, and a control flow and data flow analysis component.

A survey of software engineering tools (Holbrook & Thebaut, 1987) reported the availability of the following range of commercially available software tools:

- 22 code analyzers that statically evaluate program structures and program data flow;
- 52 documentation aids to depict program logic;
- 44 cross-referencers that trace data elements and operations on those data elements;
- 5 restructurers that convert unstructured code into a structured format;
- 24 reformatters that "beautify" code by converting it into a uniform, easily maintained style;
- 15 execution monitoring/debugging tools that dynamically monitor a program's execution to examine its behavior;
- 18 test case coverage tools that permit monitoring of a program's behavior when it is executed with different sets of test data; and,
- 17 source comparators that permit programmers to determine exact differences between different program versions.

The number and scope of these tools are strong indicators of the demand for mechanisms for improving program understanding.

CONCLUSIONS

The development and maintenance of complex software requires insight into program structures, the interaction among software components, potential re-use, and the sharing of data. Automated support of these processes will minimize the number of errors introduced into a software design at each level of refinement.

This chapter described a CASE tool classification and integration model, demonstrated some recent activities in CASE tool development, and discussed the role that expert systems can play in improving software (re)engineering. The availability of hundreds of commercial software engineering tools is evidence of the need for mechanisms for improving the quality of both new and existing software. However, as the repertoire of tools expands, the problem of integration is exacerbated. One solution to this problem is the acceptance of a "standard" model for CASE tool classification and integration. Such a model facilitates the integration of CASE tools by focusing on well-defined services provided by tools and interface specifications rather than by implementation specifications. The availability of new technologies, such as expert systems, improve the potential for CASE tool integration, and enhance the services and interfacing capabilities of both existing and new tools that will develop over time.

ENDNOTES

[1] The term (re) engineering is used throughout this chapter to denote any one or all of the terms and processes defined in the second major section of this chapter, A Clarification of Software (Re)Engineering Terminology.

[2] COBOL/SF is a registered trademark of IBM Corporation.

REFERENCES

Arthur, J., & Ramanaayashreethan, J. (1981, January). Design of Analyzers for Selective Program Analysis. *IEEE Transactions on Software Engineering*, Vol. SE-7 (No. 1), pp. 39-51.

Balzer, R. (1981, January). Transformational Implementation: An Example. *IEEE Transactions on Software Engineering*, Vol. SE-7 (No. 1), pp. 3-13.

Balzer, R., & Cheatham, T., E. (1981, January). Editorial: Program Transformations. *IEEE Transactions on Software Engineering*, Vol. SE-7(No. 1), pp. 1-2.

Becker, S. (1990, May). The Analysis and Design of Concurrency Using Box Structures: PhD Thesis. College Park: University of Maryland.

Becker, S., & Hevner, A. (1990, March). A White Box Analysis of Concurrent System Designs. (No.10). Scottsdale: *Proceedings of the 10th Annual International Phoenix Conference on Computers and Communications.*

Bersoff, E., H., & Davis, A., M. (1991, August). Impacts of Life Cycle Models on Software. *Communications of the ACM*, Vol. 34 (No. 8), pp. 104-118.

Biggerstaff, T. (1989, July). Design Recovery for Maintenance and Reuse. *IEEE Computer*, Vol. 22 (No. 7), pp. 36-49.

Bishop, J., M. (1990, April). The Effect of Data Abstraction on Loop Programming Techniques. *IEEE Transactions on Software Engineering*, Vol. 16 (No. 4), pp. 389-402.

Cheatham, T. E. (1984, September). Reusability Through Program Transformations. *IEEE Transactions on Software Engineering*, Vol. SE-10 (No. 5), pp. 589-594.

Chikofsky, E., & Cross II, J.(1990, January). Reverse Engineering and Design Recovery: A Taxonomy. *IEEE Software*, Vol 7(No. 1), pp. 13-17.

Clark, K., L., & van Emden, M. (1981, January). Consequence Verification of Flowcharts. *IEEE Transactions on Software Engineering*, Vol. SE-7 (No. 1), pp. 52-59.

Cobb, R., & Mills, H. (1990, November). Engineering Software Under Statistical Quality Control. *IEEE Software*, Vol. 7 (No. 6), pp. 44-54. IEEE.

Date, C.J. (1990) *An Introduction to Database Systems*, Vol. 1, Fifth Edition, Addison-Wesley Publishing Co.

Deak, E. (1981, January). A Transformational Derivation of a Parsing Algorithm in a High-Level Language. *IEEE Transactions on Software Engineering*, Vol. SE-7 (No. 1), pp. 23-31.

Dyer, M. (1988, July/August). *Designing Software for Provable Correctness Information and Software Technology*, Vol. 30 (No.6), pp. 331-340.

Eisenstadt, M., Domingue, J., Rajan, T., & Motta, E. (1990, October). Visual Knowledge Engineering. *IEEE Transactions on Software Engineering*, Vol. 16 (No. 10), pp. 1164-1177.

Hausler, P., Linger, R., Pleszkoch, M., & Hevner, A. (1990, January). Using Function Abstraction to Understand Program Behavior. *IEEE Software*, Vol. 7 (No. 1), 55-63. IEEE.

Hevner, A., & Becker, S. (1992, January). Central Repository Data Models for Cleanroom Systems Development. *Proceedings of the 25th Annual Hawaii International Conference on System Sciences*, Vol. 2 (No. 25), pp. 459-468. Hawaii.

Hevner, A., Becker, S., & Pedowitz, L. (1992). An Integrated CASE Environment for Cleanroom Systems Engineering. To be published in IEEE Software, March 1992.

Hevner, A., Wilkey, J., & Becker, S. (1991, January). CASE Support for Box Structure System Development: A Case Study. *Proceedings of the 24th Annual Hawaii International Conference on System Sciences*, Vol. 2 (No. 24), pp. 532-542. Hawaii.

Hevner, A., & Linger, R. (1989, January). A Method for Data Re-engineering in Structured Programs. *Proceedings of the 22nd Hawaii International Conference on System Sciences*, Vol. 1 (No. 22), pp. 1025-1034. Hawaii.

Holbrook, H., & Thebaut, S. (1987, September). A Survey of Software Maintenance Tools That Enhance Program Understanding. University of Florida Gainesville Software Engineering Research Center Report No. SERC-TR-9-F.

Huang, J. (1990, August). State Constraints and Pathwise Decomposition of Programs. *IEEE Transactions on Software Engineering*, Vol. 16 (No. 8), pp. 880-896.

Johnson, A., M., & Malek, M. (1988, December). Survey of Software Tools for Evaluating Reliability, Availability, and Serviceability. *ACM Computing Surveys*, Vol. 20 (No. 4), pp. 227-269.

Karimi, J., & Konsynski, B., R. (1988, February). An Automated Software Design Assistant. *IEEE Transactions on Software Engineering*, Vol. 14 (No. 2), pp. 194-210.

Kozaczynski, W., & Ning, J., Q. (1989, May). SRE: A Knowledge-based Environment for Large-Scale Software Re-engineering Activities. *Proceedings of the 11th International Conference on Software Engineering*, 113-122.

Lafue, G. (1989, October). Introduction to Knowledge-Based Reverse Software

Engineering. *Proceedings of the National Communications Forum,* Vol.43, pp. 279-282.

Lazzerini, B., & Lopriore, L. (1989, July). Abstraction Mechanisms for Event Control in Program Debugging. *IEEE Transactions on Software Engineering,* Vol. 15 (No. 7), pp. 890-901.

Levendel, Y. (1991, March). Improving Quality With a Manufacturing Process. *IEEE Software,* Vol. 8 (No. 2), pp. 13-25. IEEE.

Linger, R., Mills, H., & Witt, B. (1979). *Structured Programming: Theory and Practice.* Cambridge: Addison-Wesley.

Matsumoto, Y. (1984, September). Some Experiences in Promoting Reusable Software: Presentation in Higher Abstract Levels. *IEEE Transactions on Software Engineering,* Vol. SE-10 (No. 5), pp. 502-513.

Mills, H. (1988, January). Stepwise Refinement and Verification in Box-Structured Systems. *IEEE Computer,* Vol. 21 (No. 6), pp. xx-xx. IEEE.

Mills, R., Dyer, M.,& Linger, R. (1987, September). Cleanroom Software Engineering. *IEEE Software,* Vol. x, No. x, pp. 19-25.

Mills, H., Linger, R., & Hevner, A. (1986). *Principles of Information Systems Analysis and Design.* New York: Academic Press.

Patel, S., Orr, R., Norris, M., & Bustard, D. (1989, May). Tools to Support Formal Methods. *Proceedings of the 11th International Conference on Software Engineering,* pp. 123-130.

Scheels, A., M. (1989, October). Software Re(Engineering). *Proceedings of the National Communications Forum,* Vol.43, pp. 272.

Shaw, M. (1989, October). Larger Scale Systems Require Higher Level Abstractions. *Proceedings of the National Communications Forum,* Vol. 43, pp. 274-278.

Soloway, E., & Ehrlich, K. (1984, September). Empirical Studies of Programming Knowledge. *IEEE Transactions on Software Engineering,* Vol. SE-10 (No. 5), pp. 595-609.

Standish, T., A. (1984, September). A Essay on Software Reuse. *IEEE Transactions on Software Engineering,* Vol. SE-10 (No. 5), pp. 494-497.

Steinbreugge, J. (1989, October). Changing the Application Development Arena. *Proceedings of the National Communications Forum,* Vol. 43, pp. 272-274.

Voges, U., Gmeiner, L., & von Mayrhauser, A. A. (1980, May). SADAT - An Automated Testing Tool. *IEEE Transactions on Software Engineering,* Vol. SE-6 (No. 3), pp. 286-290.

Wile, D., S. (1981, January). Type Transformation. *IEEE Transactions on Software Engineering,* Vol. SE-7 (No. 1), pp. 32-39.

Section II

Managing the Transition to CASE

CHAPTER FOUR

Factors Influencing the Adoption of CASE

Mary Sumner
Southern Illinois University at Edwardsville

The purpose of this chapter is to describe the organizational, application development, and support factors which are associated with the successful transition to computer-aided software engineering. Understanding these factors may help information systems professionals commit to changes that underlie the adoption of CASE.

A case study approach is used to describe the experiences of project managers in organizations using CASE and to compare their views with managers in non-CASE organizations. In the organizations using CASE tools, there was a slightly greater commitment to structured methods in systems analysis and design. The CASE users reported that CASE was a vehicle which facilitated the use of structured tools in systems design. One of the most important motivations for using CASE was the ability to conform with design standards.

Some of the barriers to CASE included the limited capability of CASE tools, the learning curve, and the high cost of making the transition to CASE. Several organizations felt that it was necessary to re-introduce basic structured methodologies prior to selecting and implementing a CASE tool. Another of the pressing issues with CASE was the inability to gain management support for an innovation without measurable returns on the investment.

For CASE to be successful, an organizational change strategy must accompany the introduction of new technology. Organizational change requires management commitment, training, and integration of a methodology supported by the CASE tool. The chapter concludes by presenting a model for identifying factors that influence the decision to adopt CASE technology.

The concept of computer-assisted software engineering (CASE) is envisioned as a key strategy for improving systems development productivity. CASE is a discipline which can bring about the construction of flexible, maintainable information systems. CASE provides methods of building quality and reliability into software. CASE is also viewed as a way to reduce development time, to cut maintenance costs, and to improve the discipline of information systems development.

Many claims have been made about the benefits of CASE. A number of industry reports show that CASE improves productivity, reduces costs and results in higher-quality software (Perrone, 1988; Orlikowski, 1988). CASE tools allow a systems analyst to document and model an information system from the beginning when user requirements are defined, through to design and implementation (Chikofsky, 1987).

One of the major benefits of CASE is the introduction of engineering-like discipline into the systems development process. Using CASE tools, a software engineer can take advantage of diagramming tools, design checking tools, and a disciplined methodology. CASE brings the same benefits to application development that computer-assisted design and manufacturing brought to the manufacturing process (Abi, November, 1987). CASE tools are used to facilitate greater standardization of work procedures and adherence with design discipline (Orlikowski, 1988).

Yet, even with these benefits, most organizations have found it difficult to implement CASE. A number of issues, including technology issues, economic issues, cultural issues, personnel issues, and systems design issues complicate the transition to CASE. Some of the commonly mentioned obstacles to implementing CASE are cost, resistance by systems developers, and unacceptable learning curve (Yourdon, 1989). Many CASE tools focus on a narrow slice of the software development life cycle, rather than being integrated throughout (Bond, 1987). Since many CASE tools operate in a standalone fashion, there are significant problems in bridging phases of the life cycle.

Resistance by systems developers themselves remains an issue that is much more difficult to address than the quality of the tools themselves (Bouldin, 1987). Experienced designers and programmers feel that highly-structured tools interfere with their job autonomy and creativity (Kull, 1987). Sometimes, resistance has to be counteracted by finding the most creative, ingenious staffers to do the job (Hayley and Lyman, 1990). Successful introduction of CASE may require significant changes in the organization and management of systems development. To get a better understanding of factors which may be associated with the successful adoption of CASE, it is useful to review the literature on the adoption of innovations. Ideas from this literature can then be applied to actual case studies in MIS development.

THE PURPOSE OF THIS CHAPTER

The purpose of this chapter is to describe factors which may be associated with the successful transition to computer-assisted software engineering and to apply these factors to understanding case studies of organizations which are implementing CASE. This chapter includes a comparison of organizational factors, application development factors, and support factors in firms which have introduced CASE and in firms which have not adopted CASE. These case studies provide a basis for identifying factors which influence the successful transition to computer-assisted software engineering.

FACTORS ASSOCIATED WITH ADOPTION OF CASE

The factors which may be associated with the successful transition to CASE include organizational factors, application development factors, policy factors, environmental factors, and support factors. The transition to CASE is an innovation involving organizational change. As such, many of the factors which influence successful innovation within organizations can be considered independent variables influencing adoption of CASE.

Organizational Factors

Organizational structure is frequently linked with innovation. The two types of organizational structures depicted in the literature are mechanistic and organic. The mechanistic structure is depicted by a bureaucratic organization with hierarchical control. Organic structures, which are characterized by flexible communications, internal interaction, and networking, are more likely to foster innovation (Burns and Stalker, 1961).

In their study of the effects of specialization, differentiation, and centralization on the adoption of innovation, Moch and Morse (1977) concluded that specialized, functionally differentiated, and decentralized organizations have more innovations. Independent task forces are conducive to innovation (Madique, 1980).

Integration may be related to the adoption of CASE. Lawrence and Lorsch (1967) define integration as the collaboration between technical specialists and line managers in the achievement of functional goals. Shrivastava and Souder (1987) note that successful management of technological innovation requires high levels of integration across departments and levels. In the context of making the transition to CASE, it would seem that a coalition of users, information systems professionals, and general managers is needed to align information systems priorities with business strategy.

Another organizational factor which should be related to the transition to CASE is the importance of information technology planning to business planning. In organizations in which information technology is used to achieve a competitive edge, the need to integrate business plans and information technology plans is critical (Porter and Millar, 1985). In these organizations, the transition to CASE may become a high priority. This is because CASE builds quality into the software development process and helps to ensure flexibility and maintainability of important business systems.

Finally, a technological innovation must be consistent with the firm's capabilities and skills (Burgleman, 1983). Several researchers have indicated that this compatibility is positively related to the rate of adoption of innovations (Rogers and Shoemaker, 1971; Damanpour and Evans, 1984). Successful innovations cannot take place without an existing technological infrastructure (Madique and Zirger, 1984). In the context of CASE, this infrastructure may translate into the availability of development workstations which provide access to a central data repository and appropriate development tools.

Application Development Factors

Successful use of CASE requires a change in systems design practices. An information engineering approach, which starts with strategic information planning, must be used in conjunction with CASE. Software engineering includes data modeling, process modeling, and event modeling. In data modeling, the construction of a logical data model becomes the basis for designing a database. Once the database is designed, a prototyping approach can be used to generate screens and reports using either procedural or non-procedural languages.

Problems occur when structured methods are plugged into one phase of the systems development life cycle, rather than being integrated throughout the entire development process. Commitment to making CASE work requires a commitment to learning new methods for systems planning, analysis, design, and detailed design. Commitment to new methods requires extensive training of personnel.

An important factor in the diffusion of innovations is compatibility with the beliefs, experiences, and values of potential adopters (Rogers, 1983). Effective introduction of technological innovation depends upon the existence of skills available to use the innovation effectively. It is likely that organizations with a commitment to using structured techniques in systems analysis and design are in an excellent position to introduce CASE tools. This means that internal know-how in structured software development techniques must be developed as a part of the transition to CASE, if this expertise doesn't already exist.

Policy Factors

A number of policy factors influence innovation. Ettlie (1983) found that firms which try to keep technologically ahead of other firms in their industry are likely to introduce innovation. Firms are also likely to introduce a particular innovation if a high proportion of firms in their industry have already done so (Mansfield, 1968). Based upon these findings, a firm with an aggressive technology strategy in an industry in which other firms have introduced CASE is likely to introduce CASE as well.

Organizational factors also influence innovation. Top management vision must be communicated throughout the organization in order for employees to recognize the opportunity (Quinn, 1985).

Management risk propensity is another factor influencing innovation. McFarlan suggests that high technology, low structure, and large-size projects carry considerable risk in information systems development (McFarlan, 1981). Radical innovations such as CASE also introduce risk, partly because of new technologies and partly because of challenges to existing work methods and procedures. When management exhibits a higher propensity to take risks, the likelihood of adopting an innovation is greater.

The justification policy for MIS projects is also a factor influencing innovation. Traditionally, MIS projects have been justified using cost-benefit analysis to demonstrate the return on investment in information systems. However, a cost-benefit strategy limits the kinds of projects that can be justified to those whose outcomes are clear. These projects are typically operational-type projects which cut costs by automating certain business functions. In contrast, projects which are highly innovative and carry potential risk are more difficult to justify using cost-benefit techniques. As such, an investment in CASE tools may not be easy to justify using a return on investment approach. If an organization is willing to pursue innovative technology projects that are driven by a business justification, rather than by expected financial returns, it will be more likely to pursue a CASE approach.

Environmental Factors

The relationship between environmental factors and innovation has been highly researched. A number of studies point out that the higher the competitive intensity of an industry, the higher the rate of innovation (Robertson and Gatignon, 1986; Utterback, 1974). Therefore, it is likely that CASE tools would be introduced in highly competitive environments.

In addition, Utterback (1974) also demonstrates a strong relationship between the rate of adoption of an innovation and the number of firms within an industry which have adopted the innovation. In industries in which CASE tools are being introduced to improve software quality, you will find most firms moving aggressively in this direction.

Support Factors

The final set of factors influencing innovation are support factors. Most researchers conclude that highly enthusiastic individuals that become champions of an innovation play a vital role in influencing the process of innovation (Madique, 1980). The positive role of the champion is related the adoption of the innovation and to its successful implementation (Kimberly and Evanisko, 1981).

Other support factors influencing the success of an innovation are vendor support, top management support, and user involvement. In high-technology innovations, effective vendor support may be critical to success (Ettlie, 1986). Top management commitment and support for an innovation is also critical (Quinn, 1985 and Burgleman, 1983). Overcoming resistance to change is an important strategy in introducing innovation, and user participation not only helps to lessen such resistance but also contributes to the success of the innovation (Madique and Zirger, 1984). User involvement is important to the success of CASE.

Effective marketing of the innovation has also been discussed by researchers as a key factor in success. Robertson and Gatignon (1986), for example, conclude that effective "selling" of an innovation is important in influencing the speed of its diffusion.

A COMPARATIVE STUDY OF CASE AND NON-CASE USERS

To get a better understanding of factors associated with the introduction and implementation of CASE technology, a case study approach is useful. This study reports the experiences of CASE and non-CASE users in a sample of St. Louis based organizations. The intent of this study is to describe and analyze organizational factors, application development environments, and systems development methods in both CASE and non-CASE organizations. Specific objectives are:

1. To describe organizational and environmental factors relevant to the introduction of CASE in the organizations studied.
2. To describe the application development environment and systems development methods used in firms using CASE technology and in the firms not using CASE.
3. To describe the extent of use of CASE tools to support various tasks in the systems development life cycle.
4. To assess the benefits and barriers of CASE, both as experienced by the CASE users and as perceived by the non-CASE users.
5. To follow-up on the experiences of CASE and non-CASE users to determine the current status of CASE.

METHODS FOR CONDUCTING THE STUDY

The study involved two groups: 13 project managers who were using CASE technology and 15 project managers who were non-CASE users. The majority of these firms had under 100 full-time information systems professionals, in Table 1.

The study was accomplished with interviewing teams consisting of MIS graduate students. Each interviewing team used interview results to develop case studies for one CASE firm and for one non-CASE firm. Data for these case studies were gathered from questionnaires.

	CASE Users	# firms	Non-CASE Users	# firms
	Under 100 employees	8	Under 100 employees	11
	100 - 500 employees	3	100 - 500 employees	4
	Over 500 employees	2	Over 500 employees	0
		13		15

Table 1: MIS Professionals in the Organizations Studied

FINDINGS AND ANALYSIS

The findings collected about the CASE and non-CASE firms during the study included organizational factors, application development environment, and systems development portfolio.

Organizational Factors

One of the predominant variables associated with successful innovation is top management commitment. Top management commitment to information systems planning and information technology may be associated with the rank or level of the "chief information officer" within the management reporting structure. Each of the respondents was asked to identify the reporting relationship of the senior-most MIS executive.

In the firms adopting CASE, about 75 percent of the "chief information officers" reported to an executive at the vice-president level. In contrast, in the firms without CASE, 50 percent of the information officers reported to a VP-level executive, and an additional 14 percent reported to "top management." About 36 percent of the MIS executives in non-CASE firms reported to division-level line managers.

Investment in Information Technology

Another indicator of management commitment to MIS is the overall investment in information systems. This overall investment may be indicative of the importance of information technology in achieving business plans. In firms with a commitment to using technology to support competitive strategy, MIS innovation may be a high priority.

The firms studied were partitioned into three groupings: firms spending 3 or less percent of gross sales in information systems,

	CASE Firms	Non-CASE Firms
Greater than 6%	3 (23%)	4 (27%)
Over 3% and less than 6%	2 (15%)	0 (0)
3% or less	5 (39%)	8 (53%)
Uncertain	3 (23%)	3 (20%)
	13	15

Table 2: Investment in Information Systems

firms spending over 3 but less than 6 percent, and firms spending greater than 6 percent of gross sales in information systems. Table 2 shows these findings.

As you can see, the data describing the investment in information systems in both the CASE and non-CASE firms is inconclusive. Approximately one-fourth of the respondents were uncertain about the investment in information technology. About 25 percent of the CASE firms and non-CASE firms noted an investment of greater than 6 percent of gross sales in MIS. About 50 percent of the non-CASE firms reported an investment of 3 percent or less in information systems.

While these data may signify that firms with a greater over-all investment in information technology may be more likely to introduce CASE technology, these results are not conclusive. In addition, the investment in information technology varies from industry to industry. With a broader range of firms in specific industry categories represented, it might be possible to analyze the investments in information technology in CASE and in non-CASE firms.

Organization of Information Systems

The organization of the information systems function within the firms studied was depicted as either centralized, decentralized, or distributed. A centralized form of organization was defined as a central MIS organization employing systems development professionals, including programmers and analysts. A decentralized organization was depicted as one in which systems professionals (programmers and analysts) worked within functional areas of the business. A distributed organization was defined as one in which responsibilities for systems development and operations were shared between a central MIS group and systems professionals within functional areas of the business. As you can see from the data in Table 3, all three types of MIS organization were represented in the firms studied.

	CASE Firms	Non-CASE Firms
Centralized	6	8
Decentralized	5	4
Distributed	2	3
	13	15

Table 3: Organization of Systems Development

	CASE Users	Non-CASE Users
Traditional	69.0%	63.7%
Prototyping with 4GL's	16.3%	18.2%
End-user Development	6.5%	16.3%
Other	8.2%	1.8%

Table 4: Expenditures in Application Development

Application Development Environment

A variety of industry sources report that CASE is an effective strategy for attacking the application development backlog. In both the CASE and non-CASE firms, the average new application backlog ranged from one to two years, and the maintenance backlog averaged six months to one year.

The usefulness of CASE may be influenced by the nature of the application portfolio. The application portfolio in many organizations is changing with a larger emphasis being placed on prototyping and end-user development (Necco, Gordon, Tsai, 1987). The project managers were asked to estimate the approximate percentage of cost expenditures spent on various application development approaches. As you can see from Table 4, the investment in application development was concentrated largely on "traditional" applications being developed using COBOL or other procedural languages. This was true in both the CASE firms and the non-CASE firms. About 20 percent of the cost of application development was attributed to prototyping with 4GL's, and approximately 6 and 16 percent were connected with end-user development in the CASE and in the non-CASE firms respectively. The percentages given for end-user development may be inexact, given the difficulty in assessing the scope of end-user computing.

The relative proportion of new and maintenance projects is also an important feature of the current application environment. According to a recent survey, about 65 percent of systems' staff time is

	CASE Firms	Non-CASE Firms
New Application Development	34.5%	37.9%
Maintenance	46.4%	37.6%
End-user Support	9.9%	22.3%
Research and Development	8.8%	5.5%
Other	.4	2.7%

Table 5: How Programmer/Analysts' Time is Allocated

Type of system	Current Portfolio		Planned Portfolio	
	CASE Users	Non-CASE	CASE Users	Non-CASE
Operational	63.7%	53.4%	51.9%	43.4%
Decision support	13.8%	13.8%	20.0%	17.8%
Inter-organizational	16.7%	15.6%	22.3%	20.0%

Table 6: Investment in Information Systems

spent enhancing existing software (Rinaldi, October 1987). According to the data from both CASE and non-CASE project managers in this study, about 40 percent of programmer/analysts' time was devoted to new application development, and an additional 40 percent was spent on maintaining old systems. In general, the "mix" of application development activities in CASE and non-CASE firms was comparable. These findings are illustrated in Table 5.

CASE tools may have an impact on new application development and on maintenance. At the time of this study, reverse engineering tools, which may be of greatest value in managing the maintenance backlog, were still in their infancy.

When asked to describe the current and planned application development portfolio within their respective firms, both the CASE and non-CASE managers reported a shift away from information systems that support day-to-day business operations (operational systems) to information systems that support management reporting (decision support systems). There was also an increase in the projected investment in information systems that provide links to customers, suppliers, or vendors (inter-organizational systems).

Table 6 reports the current and planned investment in the application portfolio, based upon the approximate percentage of cost expenditures spent on information systems of these various types, including: operational systems, decision support systems, and inter-organizational systems.

As you can see from these data, traditional operational systems supporting day-to-day business activities are a declining percentage of the application portfolio within these firms.

The changing portfolio was true of the organizations with CASE and those without CASE tools. A relevant question is whether CASE technology can facilitate efforts to develop the new portfolio of decision support systems and inter organizational systems. If CASE tools cannot help systems developers build the new portfolio, other application development technologies (4GL's, prototyping tools, packages) may be used to do the job.

Tools and Techniques in Application Development

Most studies describing the transition to using CASE technology show that organizations with an existing systems development life cycle methodology achieve the greatest benefits of CASE (Davis, Winter 1990). If an organization does not have a methodology in place, one has to be established in order to make CASE work (Zagorsky, Summer 1990). One author argues: "Trying to install CASE workstations in an organization where design methods have failed is like providing a sophisticated computer-assisted design (CAD) system to someone who has flunked out of the first year of architecture school" (Highsmith, September 1987).

A number of experts concur with the importance of an underlying methodology in CASE implementation. "CASE tools do nothing," Vaughn Merlyn offers, "unless you understand and apply the underlying principles of software engineering" (Snyders, October 1987). "Those organizations that achieve the biggest productivity gains," McClure notes, "choose the right software development methodology as a foundation upon which to build" (McClure, Sept. 1987). "You need to establish and control a methodology early in the process," argue Hughes and Clark, in order to capitalize on the benefits of CASE (Hughes and Clark, 1990). This means setting and enforcing design standards. "The tools require a methodology, almost a new way of thinking." (Kull, February 1987).

The use of a formal systems development methodology was more prevalent in the CASE firms, with 69 percent of these organizations reporting a methodology as contrasted with only 43 percent of the non-CASE firms. However, the existence of a methodology does not always mean that it is used. A recent *Software News* survey, for example, reported that 67.2 percent of the respondents felt that a software development methodology was important, but 62.2 percent reported that their companies were not planning to standardize on a particular methodology (Rinaldi, October 1987).

Any technological innovation must be consistent with a firm's capabilities and skills. If system analysts currently use structured

	CASE Users	Non-CASE Users
Logical database	3.85	3.06
Structured analysis	3.69	3.30
Fourth generation tools	3.69	1.69
Data dictionary	2.92	2.88
Code generators	1.92	1.25
Screen/report prototyping tools	1.69	2.00

Scale: 5 = active use; 3 = moderate use; 1 = limited use

Table 7: Application Development Tools and Techniques

methods in analysis/design, it may be easier to introduce automated methods. In a study by Necco, Gordon, and Tsai, about 62 percent of the organizations reported using structured approaches. Of those using structured methods, the most frequently used tools were data flow diagrams (80%), data dictionary (97%), and structure charts (75%). A large percentage of these organizations used structured walkthroughs (90%). In another study, progammer/analysts reported that they were familiar with structured tools but often could not justify the additional time and effort to use them effectively because of project time and cost constraints (Sumner and Sitek, 1986).

In addition, new fourth and fifth generation methodologies such as prototyping with 4GL's and rapid application development reduce the relevance of structured tools which support traditional life cycle methodologies. The increasing use of "information engineering" approaches, centered on data-driven methods, also lessens the extensive use of traditional "process-oriented" tools such as data flow diagrams and structure charts. CASE tools which support both the process-oriented and information engineering approaches may be most adaptable to changing systems development methods.

Since the use of a systems development methodology underlies the success of CASE, one of the questions posed in this study was the extent to which structured tools and techniques for systems analysis were being used. Both the CASE and non-CASE project managers reported moderate use of logical database design techniques and structured analysis/design methods, as shown in Table 7.

In general, tools and techniques for structured analysis and design were used to a moderate extent in both the CASE and non-CASE firms. Data flow diagrams and structure charts were used to a greater extent than other structured tools, as shown in Table 8.

Effective introduction of an innovation depends upon the existence of skills available to use the innovation effectively. "The

	CASE Users	Non-CASE Users
Data flow diagrams	3.61	2.75
Structure charts	3.15	2.44
Decision tables	2.08	1.94
E-R diagrams	2.77	1.88
Structured flowcharts	2.62	2.19
Warnier-Orr diagrams	.88	.88

Scale: 5 = active use   3 = moderate use   1 = limited use

Table 8: Extent of Use of Structured Tools and Techniques

	CASE Users	Non-CASE Users
Structured analysis/design	3.54	2.62
4GL's	3.31	2.06
Logical database design	2.85	2.56
CASE tools	2.54	NA
Code generators	1.84	.50
Data dictionary	1.31	.69
Screen/report prototyping tools	1.00	.81

Scale: 5 = frequently offered; 3 = occasionally offered; 1 = seldom offered.

Table 9: Extent of Training in CASE vs. non-CASE Firms

investment in the tools is only about 10 percent of the total money you have to spend before you see productivity improvement," one author notes in making an argument for training in basic systems development methods (Snyders, October 1987).

Formal training in structured methodologies, 4GL's and CASE was occasionally offered in the CASE firms, and less frequently offered in the non-CASE group, as shown in Table 9. As you can see from these data, training was seldom offered in the use of code generators, data dictionary, and screen/report prototyping tools, even though these tools are an integral part of a CASE environment.

The CASE Environment

There is limited data about the extent to which CASE is being used. In one study, automated tools for data flow diagrams and structure charts were used by about one-fourth of the respondents, and code generators by about one-fifth of those surveyed (Necco, Gordon, and Tsai, 1987). Of those using automated tools, extensive use was made of packages for data dictionary (86%), screen design (91%), and report design (75%). In another survey, less than 15

	Current:	A Year from Now:
New Application Development	40.8%	52.9%
Maintenance Projects	21.5%	32.2%

Table 10: Percent of Projects with CASE Support

	# of Firms with Current Uses	A Year from Now
Strategic business planning	3	5
Systems analysis and design	13	11
Physical design (screens, etc)	7	9
Coding	4	8
Project management	4	7
Documentation	10	10

Table 11: Activities Supported by CASE

percent of the firms were using CASE; most were just "testing" the new technology (*Software News*, October 1987).

The thirteen project managers in this study reported using a variety of CASE tools, including ProKit Workbench, Excelerator, and Information Engineering Facility. In the firms studied, CASE was being used in both new application development projects and in maintenance projects. When asked what percentage of all application development projects were being supported by a CASE tool, the project managers responded that approximately 40 percent of new application development projects were being supported, as compared with 21 percent of their maintenance projects. CASE usage was expected to grow in the year ahead.

Although these data indicate that CASE tools were used in 40 percent of the new application development projects, the tools were used to support isolated activities within the systems development life cycle, rather than being integrated throughout the life cycle. As you can see from Table 11, CASE tools were being used primarily to automate specific life cycle activities, including analysis and design specifications (data flow diagrams, etc.) and documentation.

The use of CASE in systems analysis and design showed an adherence with structured methods. As you can see from Table 12, the majority of the CASE users applied the tools for data flow diagrams and data dictionary. To a lesser extent, they used the tools to draw structure charts, to design logical data models, and to

	# of Firms with Current Uses	A Year from Now
Drawing Data Flow Diagrams	10	7
Developing a Data Dictionary	11	10
Drawing Structure Charts	6	5
Data Modeling	7	7
Prototyping Screens and Reports	6	8

Table 12: **Systems Development Tasks Supported by CASE**

prototype screens and reports.

The extensive use of CASE to draw diagrams and to define data dictionary specifications is indicative of the fact that the tools being used (ProKit, Excelerator) are particularly well designed to automate the diagram-drawing aspects of systems analysis and design. This is consistent with many current CASE tools, which focus on a narrow slice of the systems development process (Suydam, 1987).

Training is important in the CASE environment (Hayley and Lynam, 1990). The project managers were asked what kind of training methods were being used to educate analysts in the use of CASE tools. By far the largest percentage of systems designers were learning to use CASE via hands-on experience. In about half of the cases, a vendor training course or an in-house training class was used to provide designers with training in CASE tools and techniques.

The Benefits and Barriers of CASE

The benefits of CASE tools have been described by researchers and practitioners (Martin, 1987; Merlyn, 1987; Orlikowski, 1988). CASE users can improve efficiency by using error-correcting mechanisms for systems design and by using diagramming tools to prevent the re-drawing of diagrams. Systems designers can save time by creating and maintaining a central repository of system design documentation.

The CASE users were asked to describe their motivations for introducing CASE. In three firms, a CASE tool was selected specifically to support a standard systems development methodology. In one of these firms, a CASE tool supporting a central data repository was chosen because the firm had selected a data-driven methodology. Many of the firms opting for CASE viewed CASE as a tool for building quality and reliability into the systems engineering process.

The CASE users were asked to evaluate the benefits of CASE in terms of their relative importance, using a "5" to "1" scale, with "5" connoting a "very important benefit" and "1" meaning a "benefit of limited importance." In addition, the non-CASE users were asked to assess the importance of the benefits of CASE tools from their vantage point.

As you can see from Table 13, two of the important benefits reported by the CASE users were "prevents the re-drawing of diagrams" and "serves as a vehicle for using structured systems design methods."

The non-CASE users also rated "serves as a vehicle for using structured design methods" as one of the most important benefits of CASE tools. In contrast to the CASE users, the non-CASE users perceived a very important benefit of CASE to be "creates a system-wide data dictionary." Other important benefits were "creates a repository of systems design documentation" and "ensures conformance with design standards."

One interesting aspect of these findings was that the non-users perceived different benefits of CASE as compared with the CASE users. The non-users noted creation of a repository and conformance with design standards as important benefits. In contrast, the CASE users mentioned that preventing re-drawing of diagrams and serving as a vehicle for using structured methods were "moderately important" benefits.

One can speculate that the users of CASE tools were experiencing ambivalence about the benefits of CASE. Their experience

	CASE Users	Non-users
Vehicle for using structured design	3.69	4.33
Prevents re-drawing of diagrams	3.61	3.67
Provides improved maintenance	3.38	3.33
Increases user involvement in system design	3.38	3.00
Creates a repository of design documentation	3.38	4.00
Supports prototyping	3.23	3.00
Creates a system-wide data dictionary	3.15	5.00
Provides checks on design errors	2.92	3.67
Ensures conformance with design standards	2.92	4.00
Aids project management and control	2.54	2.83

Scale: 5 = very important benefit; 3 = moderately important benefit; 1 = limited benefit

Table 13: The Benefits of CASE

	CASE	Non-CASE
Limited capability of CASE tools	2.92	3.60
Unacceptable learning curve	2.61	2.50
Lack of fit with current methodology	2.54	2.82
Uncertain benefits	2.54	3.40
Resistance by systems developers	2.23	2.30
High cost	2.07	3.36

Scale= 5 = major barrier; 3 = moderate barrier; 1 = minor barrier

Table 14: Barriers to Using CASE

implementing CASE was largely limited to using isolated tools to automate the development of data flow diagrams, structure charts, and data dictionaries. Since ProKit Workbench was limited to a single-workstation version at the time of the initial interviews, a common repository of systems design documentation was not feasible. It was too soon to determine the maintenance-related impacts of CASE tools, and there was no real evidence of the impact of CASE on user involvement.

Barriers to CASE

Both the CASE users and non-CASE users perceived some barriers to the successful use of CASE. Most of these barriers were characterized as being "moderately significant barriers" by the CASE users. As you can see from Table 14, the CASE users felt that the "limited capability of CASE tools" was the most significant barrier to their successful use. In contrast, the non-CASE users perceived that "high cost," "uncertain benefits," and "limited capability" were barriers.

While these barriers may be relevant, other factors were also associated with the decision not to adopt CASE. The most frequently mentioned reason for not adopting CASE was cost. Eight of the project managers in firms without CASE said that they could not justify the investment in CASE in terms of direct, short-term benefits. Several firms cited the high cost of CASE and its uncertain benefits at a time when MIS resources were tight. To reap the benefits of CASE, one project manager felt, "you need to make a long-term commitment without immediate pay-offs." Yet, "management is looking for immediate payoffs."

Another reason why CASE is not being adopted is the diversity of systems development practices. In the divisionalized firms, project managers found it difficult to introduce a standard systems development methodology. In several organizations, programmers and analysts used their own discretion with respect to the tools and techniques they used in systems development projects. One firm characterized its programmer/analysts as "somewhat undisciplined;" "able to do their own thing." Another firm noted that "everyone can use their own methodology." In another, MIS professionals resisted a "formalized, structured systems development methodology." Without overall acceptance of a standard methodology, CASE is difficult to introduce.

Another reason for not adopting CASE was the limited nature of the tools themselves. One project manager noted that "CASE tools are not sufficiently adaptable to address the wide range of design problems that occur." From management's view, there was no comprehensive CASE product. In one firm, a manager argued that CASE was supposed to increase systems development productivity, but "in reality all it does is automate diagram-drawing." Another respondent noted, "existing CASE tools support isolated functions rather than the entire range of systems development activities."

Finally, a number of firms used different approaches to improve application development productivity. Instead of using CASE, these organizations emphasized prototyping with 4GL's, logical database design, and code generation. The emphasis on prototyping with 4GL's was not reinforced with the use of current CASE products, several respondents felt. Fourth generation tools were being introduced primarily to impact the maintenance backlog.

Success Factors and Obstacles

The experiences of CASE and non-CASE users revealed some "successes" and "obstacles." The two success factors most frequently mentioned by CASE users were "top management commitment" and "adherence to the methodology being supported by the CASE tool." Adherence to the methodology enabled these users to standardize documentation and to create a system-wide repository.

The method of introducing design discipline varied from firm to firm. In some cases, organizations adopted a standard systems development methodology first, and then introduced a CASE tool that supported that methodology. In other cases, firms selected a CASE tool and then introduced a standard methodology supported by that CASE tool. In the former environments, the CASE tool was integrated with existing work methods and procedures. In the latter cases, introducing CASE gave management an opportunity to introduce design discipline. In either scenario, the CASE tool became a vehicle for standardizing systems design practices.

In the firms in which CASE was not implemented, a number of factors were attributed to its lack of success. One of these factors was related to organizational structure. In firms with decentralized systems development groups in which each group used its own application development methodology, it was virtually impossible to superimpose a set of standardized systems development practices supported by CASE.

In highly competitive environments, in which systems had to be implemented quickly, time spent up-front developing analysis and design documentation using CASE could not be justified. CASE tools did not cut the time or cost of systems development, nor did they impact the maintenance backlog.

Some of the firms adopting CASE also had reservations about its value. CASE users did not report productivity gains, and systems development time was not shortened. CASE tools were used primarily to automate certain isolated activities, such as data flow diagrams. Few CASE tools offered a set of integrated tools, and one in particular had poor documentation. Several managers mentioned the limitations of current tools.

Another obstacle was the resistance of current systems development professionals. Without extensive training and a management commitment to changing traditional work methods and procedures, this resistance is difficult to overcome.

FOLLOW-UP DATA

Two years after the original study was conducted, follow-up questionnaires were sent out to the thirteen project managers using CASE tools and to the 15 project managers not using CASE. Of the thirteen CASE users contacted, four were continuing to use CASE tools in systems development projects. Three of the respondents were no longer using CASE because of a management decision to discontinue its use. The other six project managers were no longer with their firms or else had been re-assigned to different functional areas.

The four project managers using CASE were primarily interested in its usefulness in providing systems design documentation. Two mentioned the importance of developing a central data repository. A third user found CASE useful in checking the validity of data elements. From the standpoint of the CASE users, the major limitations of CASE tools were lack of product integration, the volatility of current products, and the limited usefulness of CASE in addressing the backlog of legacy systems.

The three project managers who had discontinued the use of CASE had a variety of reasons for their decision. In one of these firms, CASE represented a very large investment, and top management dropped the project because of the lack of return on their investment. Lack of understanding of the technology and its limits led management to have unrealistic and unfulfilled expectations for its benefits. When these benefits were not realized, the project was "doomed," according to the respondent.

Another firm which made a preliminary commitment to using CASE "dropped it" because the systems developers did not have the underlying knowledge of structured methodology needed to make CASE work. This firm decided to retrench and to introduce a standardized, structured systems development methodology and formalized documentation procedures prior to re-introducing CASE.

Unrealistic expectations, lack of an underlying systems development methodology, non-integrated tools, and lack of measurable benefits were all associated with the decision to delay or to discontinue the use of CASE tools. In one firm attempting to transfer CASE technology into systems development groups, the major challenge ahead was "changing the culture" of systems development from a haphazard set of design methods to a disciplined, standardized set of practices organized around a consistent methodology supported by the CASE tool.

When the project managers in the follow-up survey were asked about their future plans, they were clearly interested in pursuing systems development productivity improvement strategies, including the use of CASE tools. One firm was introducing an interface between a data modeling CASE tool and their mainframe-based data dictionary. Another firm was introducing a standardized set of documentation procedures for systems design projects. Another was focusing in on cultural changes through training and management education. These firms were hoping to move ahead in implementing CASE technology.

However, a larger number of firms "dropped" CASE or else decided not to adopt CASE because of cost, lack of measurable returns, lack of fit with current practices, and the learning curve. None of the non-CASE users in the original study were using CASE at the time of the follow-up study. Most of their reasons were similar to the ones they had originally given for not adopting CASE. These reasons included the large investment, lack of returns, and lack of fit with current systems development practices. Many of the non-CASE firms were using alternative productivity improvement strategies such as prototyping with 4GL's.

SUMMARY AND RECOMMENDATIONS

The study of CASE users and their comparison with non-CASE users reveals some interesting findings.

Lack of Fit Between CASE and Development Methods

In most of the firms studied, CASE was being introduced at the same time as application development portfolios were changing. The growing proportion of decision support systems lent new importance to emerging methodologies like rapid prototyping and joint application design. These approaches lessen the time spent on developing requirements analysis and design specifications, using the diagramming conventions (e.g. data flow diagrams, structure charts) supported best by the CASE tools. Increasing prototyping and end-user systems development call for different tools.

Lack of CASE Support for Critical Activities in Systems Design

A second issue is related to the role of CASE in supporting critical activities in systems analysis and design. One of the strengths of CASE tools is their ability to "automate" the drawing of diagrams, particularly data flow diagrams and structure charts. However, diagramming may not be as important as other systems development activities, such as involving the user in the systems design process and developing an understanding of the users' business.

Evidence of the moderate value of documentation techniques in systems design was included in the study. Both the CASE and non-CASE users reported moderate use of structured systems documentation techniques, particularly data flow diagrams and structure charts. Without question, the CASE tools used in these projects supported these documentation techniques well. But one can argue that these CASE tools supported moderately-important systems design activities, rather than critical tasks.

A more relevant issue is the extent to which the CASE tools support critical factors in systems analysis and design. Such critical factors include the ability to obtain client involvement, the ability to understand the user's business problem, and the ability to establish effective communications with the user. Another critical factor is the ability to organize, manage, and complete project activities on a timely basis and within budget constraints.

From the data collected in this study, users did not report that the use of CASE increased user involvement in the systems design process. They did not indicate that CASE enabled them to accomplish project management tasks more effectively. They did not argue that the use of CASE facilitated more effective communications between the designer and client. They did not note that the use of CASE enabled them to develop a better understanding of the client's business situation. According to these views, CASE tools may not be designed to support the most critical elements of systems analysis and design projects at the current time. Other methods, such as rapid prototyping and the use of project management software, may be more useful for achieving these results.

CASE may provide some benefits that are not critical to the success of information systems design projects. CASE may help provide better design documentation, but better design documentation may not be as critical as client involvement. If CASE is to be successfully adopted and implemented, it must be designed to support critical systems development tasks.

IMPLICATIONS FOR THE ADOPTION OF CASE

The case studies of firms using CASE technology provide some insights into factors which may underlie the successful transition to CASE. These factors include application development factors, organizational factors, and support factors. Data from these case studies did not provide evidence of the policy factors and environmental factors which might underlie the transition to CASE.

Application Development Factors

In the firms using CASE, there was a moderate commitment to using structured methods in analysis and design. Evidence from this study seems to indicate that the skills of systems developers need to be updated and upgraded in order to take advantage of software engineering tools. With increased investments in training, the skill-set of systems developers will be more compatible with CASE. Making a commitment to CASE means making a commitment to a standard systems development methodology.

Organizational Factors

Prior research shows that independent task forces may serve as a catalyst for innovation. In this context, it may be easier to establish a "new culture" for systems development. This new culture entails closer integration and cooperation between information systems professionals and functional area managers. The one organization which was experiencing the greatest success in its use of CASE tools recognized the importance of cultural change and was investing its resources in management education and the development of collaborative work groups.

Support Factors

The case studies also indicated that a number of support factors were critical to the successful transition to CASE. These support factors include top management commitment, user involvement, and the ability to "sell" CASE as an important systems development strategy. In organizations in which top managers were unwilling to support the ongoing investment in CASE because of questionable results, projects tended to die. A number of the respondents noted that effective marketing of computer-assisted software engineering as an overall strategy for systems engineering is critical to gaining management support, and management support is essential for making the transition to CASE.

Another support factor related to CASE is vendor support. In a highly volatile marketplace, the stability of the CASE vendor a firm selects may be critical. The MIS group must attempt to select a CASE vendor which is able to integrate its tools throughout the systems development life cycle and to offer training and support.

Based upon these case studies, a model depicting some of the factors which may influence the successful transition to CASE can be proposed. In Table 15, you will find factors which are a part of the model.

This model might be useful to organizations which are interested in understanding the organizational and people factors which are associated with successful innovation of a new technology. Computer-assisted software engineering cannot succeed without an underlying commitment to a systems engineering process which supports the critical outcomes of systems design. Once this systems engineering process is established and accepted, CASE tools will provide the productivity impacts which are envisioned.

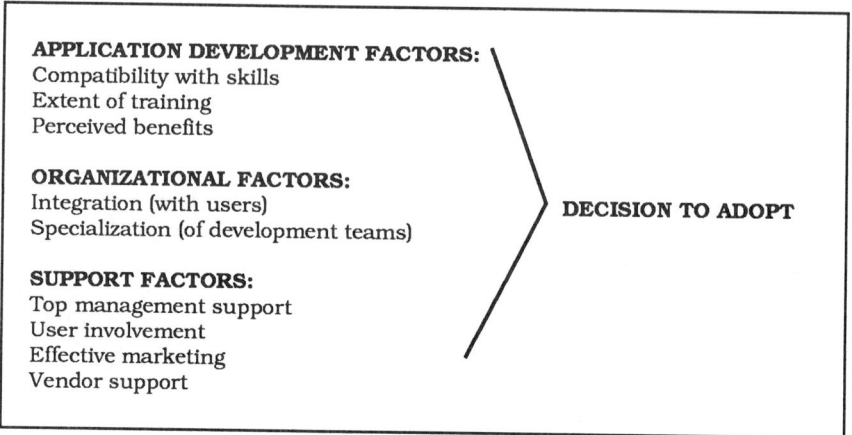

Table 15: Factors Influencing Adoption of CASE

REFERENCES

Bouldin, Barbara, "Implementing CASE: From strategy to reality," COMPUTERWORLD, Nov. 9, 1987, p. 518.

Burgelman, R.A., "Corporate Entrepreneurship and Strategic Management: Insights from a Process Study," Management Science, V. 28, December 1983, pp. 1349-1364.

Burns, T. and Stalker, G. M., The Management of Innovation, Tavistock Publications, London, 1961.

Chikofsky, Elliot J., "Reliability Engineering for Information Systems: The Emerging CASE Technology," Index Technology Corporation, Cambridge, MA, 1987.

Damampour, F. and Even, W. M., "Organizational Innovation and Performance: The Problem of Organizational Lag," Administrative Science Quarterly, V. 29, 1984, pp. 392-409.

Davis, Richard K., "What the real world is saying about CASE," Chief Information Officer Journal, V. 2, No. 3, Winter 1990.

Ein-Dor, P. and Segev, E., "Organizational Context and MIS Structure: Some Empirical Evidence," MIS Quarterly, September, 1982, pp. 55-68.

Ettlie, J.E., "Organizational Policy and Innovation Among Suppliers to the Food Processing Sector," Academy of Management Journal, V. 26, 1983, pp. 27-44.

Hayler, Kathryn and Lyman, H. T., "The Realities of CASE," Journal of Information Systems Management, Summer 1990.

Highsmith, Jim, "Software Design Methodologies in a CASE World," Business Software Review, September 1987, pp. 36-39.

Hughes, Cary T. and Clark, Jon D., "The Stages of CASE Usage," Datamation, V. 36, N. 3, February, 1990.

Kimberly, J.R. and Evanisko, M.J., "Organizational Innovation: The Influence of Individual, Organizational, and Contextual Factors on Hospital Adoption of Technological and Administrative Innovations," Academy of Management Journal, V. 24, 1981, pp. 689-713.

Kull, David, "The Rough Road to Productivity," Computer Decisions, February 23, 1987, pp. 30-41.

Madique, M.A., "Entrepreneurs, Champions, and Technological Innovation,"

Sloan Management Review, Winter, 1980, pp. 59-76.

Madique, M.A. and Zirger, B. J., "A Study of Success and Failure in Product Innovation: The Case of the U.S. Electronics Industry," *IEEE Transactions on Engineering Management*, November, 1984, pp. 192-203.

Mansfield, E. *Industrial Research and Technological Innovation: An Econometric Analysis*, Norton, New York, 1968.

Martin, Charles F., "Second Generation CASE Tools: A Challenge to Vendors, *IEEE Software*, March, 1988, pp. 46-49.

McClure, Carma. "The CASE Experience," *Byte Magazine*, April 1989.

McClure, Carma. "Software Automation," *Business Software Review*, September 1987, pp. 28-34.

McFarlan, E.W., "Portfolio Approach to Information Systems," *Harvard Business Review*, Sept-Oct, 1981, pp. 142-150.

Messenheimer, Susan and Weiszmann, Carol, "Quality Software Quest," *Software Magazine*, February 1988, pp. 29-36.

Moch, M. K. and Morse, E. V., "Size Centralization, and Organizational Adoption of Innovations," *American Sociological Review*, V. 42, October, 1977, pp. 716-725.

Necco, Charles R.; Gordon, Carl L.; and Tsai, Nancy W., "Systems Analysis and Design: Current Practices," *MIS Quarterly*, December 1987, pp 461-475.

Orikowski, Wanda J., "CASE tools and the IS workplace," *Proceedings of The 1988 ACM SIGCPR Conference on the Management of Information Systems Personnel*, College Park, Md, April 7-8, 1988, pp. 88-97.

Parsons, G.L., "Information Technology: A New Competitive Weapon," *Sloan Management Review*, Fall, 1983, pp. 3-14.

Perrone, Giovanni, "Primary Product in the Development Life Cycle," *Software Magazine*, August 1988, pp. 35-41.

Porter, M. and Millar, V., "How Information Technology Gives you Competitive Advantage," *Harvard Business Review*, July-August, 1985, pp. 149-160.

Quinn, J.B., "Managing Innovation: Controlled Chaos," *Harvard Business Review*, July-August, 1985, pp. 149-160.

Rinaldi, Damian, "Software Developers Mired in Maintenance," *Software News*, October 1987, pp. 75-76.

Robertson, T.S. and Gatignon, H., "Competitive Effects on Technology Diffusion," *Journal of Marketing*, V. 50, July, 1988, pp. 1-12.

Rogers, E. M. *Diffusion of Innovations*, Free Press, New York, 1983.

Rogers, E. M. and Shoemaker, F. F., *Communication of Innovations*, Free Press, New York, 1971.

Shrivastava, P. and Souder, W.E., "The Strategic Management of Technological Innovation: A Review and a Model," *Journal of Management Studies*, V. 24, January, 1987, pp. 25-41.

Snyders, Jane, "A CASE of Unknown Identity," *Infosystems*, October 87, pp 55-59.

Strebel, P., "Organizing for Innovation over an Industry Cycle," *Strategic Management Journal*, V. 8, 1987, pp. 117-124.

Sullivan, C.H., "Systems Planning in the Information Age," *Sloan Management Review*, Winter, 1985, pp. 3-11.

Sumner, M. and Sitek, J., "Structured Methodologies: Are They Being Used?" *Journal of Systems Management*, V. 4, No. 2, Spring 1986.

Suydam, William, "CASE makes strides toward automated software development," *Computer Design*, January 1, 1987.

Utterback, J. M., "Innovation in Industry and the Diffusion of Technology," *Science*, V. 183, February, 1974, pp. 620-626.

Yourdon, Edward, "Serious Case" in the 90's; What Do We Do When the Novelty Wears Off?" *Show CASE Conference IV*, October 10, 1989.

Zagorsky, Carol, "Case Study: Managing the Change to CASE," *Journal of Information Systems Management*, Summer 1990.

CHAPTER FIVE

Development Effectiveness: The Quest for Continuous Improvement

Robert Schooley
University of Tulsa

John Parkinson, Roy Youngman and J. Philip Vidrine
Ernst & Young

Most software development organizations experience chronic project cost overruns, schedule delays, scrapped systems, large backlogs, prohibitive maintenance costs, and dissatisfied customers. Empirical, trial-and-error solutions to these problems, implemented serially, have not always added up to real improvement. This chapter focuses on why it is important for an organization to frame its use of CASE within the bounds of an overall "development effectiveness" strategy. Ideas on how to create such a strategy are presented and discussed.

The impact of information technology on organizations today and in the next decade was the subject of a five-year, multidisciplinary research project entitled *Management in the 1990's*. Initiated in 1984 by the Alfred P. Sloan School of Management at the Massachusetts Institute of Technology, the research was co-sponsored by Ernst & Young and eleven other corporate and public-sector participants.

"Effective implementation of information technology is, at its core," the project concluded in its final report, "a task of managing change." Introducing technology into a culture, requires a structured and comprehensive approach, one that views change as a gradual, evolutionary process, not a revolutionary one, and as a process that must be planned for and managed from the onset.

The introduction of Computer Aided Software Engineering (CASE) into an information systems development environment is an excellent example of such a change. Some of the organizations that embraced CASE as the panacea for their development woes have watched their productivity erode due to a lack of planning, a lack of training, and/or a lack of consistency in approach. By introducing CASE without addressing these issues, organizations may be supporting a strategy that speeds up the construction of wrong and defective systems, thereby increasing the maintenance burden, and decreasing overall productivity.

In the face of competing improvement initiatives, a common framework (plan and structure) for effectiveness will make the best use of resources. Such a framework would establish the right priorities for ongoing programs and supporting projects as well as "future-proofing" current development investments. The development of a managerial context for the adoption of CASE and other development environment enhancements (such as an information engineering-based methodology) is just as important, if not more important, than the enhancement itself.

Due to our belief that an overall development environment plan and infrastructure should be an IS group's first order of business, we felt it necessary to first present our views concerning development effectiveness before discussing CASE and its effects.

CURRENT PROBLEMS

Most software development organizations experience chronic project cost overruns, schedule delays, scrapped systems, large backlogs, prohibitive maintenance costs, and dissatisfied customers (Ewusi-Mensah, 1991, Izzo, 1989; Moran, 1992). Empirical, trial-and-error solutions to these problems, implemented serially, have not always added up to real improvement. In many situations, the problems only re-surface elsewhere with further complications (Conner, 1991; Jones, 1991, Pallatto, 1989; Parkinson, 1991).

Many organizations have attempted improvement solely through a piecemeal approach that might include the adoption of automated technologies or advanced development methodologies (Gibson, 1989). The recorded difficulties have been numerous, and some of the common observations (Parkinson, 1991) about improvement experiences include the following:

some pilot success, but limited widespread impact;

progress is slow and products are oversold by automation vendors;

massive technology flux significantly increases overall complexity;

infrastructure to support new environment is inadequate;

mentors to ensure skill development and behavior changes are insufficient;

no process exists to guide the transition to a new environment;

initiatives are tabled, delayed, and entirely forgotten;

momentum fades after the initial impulse to change;

sponsors lose (or fail to demonstrate) commitment; and

measurement data to justify the value of IS and investment in IS improvement is absent.

Experience tells us that these observations are symptoms of a deeper class of problems: insufficient investment in examining core systems development processes; lack of understanding of the significant shift in thinking and behavior required to benefit from new approaches and technologies; the need to build capacity to manage change and recognize its impact; and the need to move from reactive solutions to strategic thinking about solutions.

PREPARING FOR THE FUTURE

Organizations are not only interested in solving today's problems, but in preparing for the future (Champy, 1992). IS executives rank the following at the top of their list of systems development issues:

identifying and developing strategic information systems;

developing an information architecture;

achieving support for cross-functional systems;

increasing developer productivity;

rapidly responding to systems requests; and

dealing with maintenance, obsolescence, and migration to new systems;

An IS infrastructure must be built that can address all of these critical issues in an integrated fashion (Eskow, 1990, Goff, 1989). For example, the issue of developer productivity can not be solved by simply implementing CASE (Jones, 1991). All development effectiveness enhancements should be implemented within the context of a business partnership program, that includes a systems planning effort addressing the identification of strategic, cross-functional systems and the development of a corporate knowledge base (Parkinson, 1991).

DEVELOPMENT ENVIRONMENT OBJECTIVES

Making the leap from today's software environment to that of tomorrow will not be easy (Conner, 1991). Finding the right infrastructure mechanisms and implementing them will not be easy (Barton, 1991). There are no pat answers for what the infrastructure of the development environment of the future should, or will, look like. All development groups have differing levels of experience, but most importantly, they have their own version of what they would like to become (or, more likely, many visions with no consensus).

Regardless of vision, there are a few important and commonly needed elements which should be present when considering development environment investment opportunities. These are:

customer satisfaction through quality;

quality and productivity through continuous improvement;

team learning and the measurement and feedback of results;

enterprise ownership of information through architecture;

assemble-to-order software manufacturing;

resilience to change and capacity to change; and

building on existing IS investment.

Customer satisfaction can no longer be defined by internal standards, or explicitly stated customer "requirements." Customer satisfaction is a tangible and moving target. IS organizations that are skilled at partnering with their customers, understanding the customer's multi-dimensional needs, and constantly monitoring changes to the nature of those needs, will be an asset to their organization. When IS organizations achieve customer satisfaction through quality, the cost of maintenance is reduced because the system will meet the business needs of the customer from the start. To "delight and excite" the customer - a phrase used in Japan for customer satisfaction - is an important part of everyone's job within the IS function.

Without a high quality work process, production of defects, waste, and rework will undermine any attempt to improve productivity. The effectiveness of the work process depends upon the vigilance of those engaged in the work - managers and staff. The objective of continuous pursuit of improvement and excellence applies in the development of information systems as it does in any other process of production. IS organizations that meet this objective reduce the overall cost of quality by shifting their focus to prevention. Moreover, the continuous pursuit of improvement will allow an organization to anticipate and prepare for the future, while making the current operation as efficient and effective as possible.

Improvement is impossible except by accident unless results can be reasonably evaluated. Individuals, teams, and organizations must be able to learn from experience in order to be competitive in the future. Unless teams can learn, the organization cannot learn. Teams capture learning in the form of increased individual competence, but more importantly, as improved work processes. IS endeavors are, by their very nature, team-oriented efforts. An IS organization that can leverage the experience of its individuals and teams will build a strong network - a network focused on continuous improvement.

When organizational barriers are removed and information is accessible to all groups, then enterprise ownership of information is achieved. Without structure, this form of multiple access will bring chaos. With a structure founded on principles of effective development - an architecture - the knowledge base of the enterprise becomes a vital asset. Such an information architecture not only enables IS to build systems that satisfy customers' needs, but also prepares for future needs by enabling separate functional areas to integrate their use of information to achieve strategic advantage in the marketplace.

A major shift in software manufacturing paradigms needs to take place, from a "custom build" or "make-to-order" basis to an "assemble-to-order" basis (Parkinson, 1991). With this new view of software development, the creation of software can be approached from a manufacturing perspective. In other words, deliverables from the software development process, such as data models, business process models, reusable code, and so forth, can be quickly assembled to meet specific customer needs instead of being created entirely from scratch. As more and more reusable objects are created, and the technology matures to manage these objects, software development will become increasingly less expensive, more predictable, more timely, and better match customer needs.

Changes impinge on systems developers from many different directions. The improving technology of software production, the rapidly developing platform for delivery of systems, whole new areas of emerging business technology, and increasing competitive pressure (both external and internal) are only a few of the issues developers must consider. Effective development teams must be responsive to all these sources of change - they must develop "change muscle." Although the development process must be robust and rigorous where stability and consistency are essential, the development environment must also be flexible to shifts in business strategy and proactive in exploiting new technology.

Existing systems embody a rich repository of knowledge of business rules, processes, and information. Eighty percent or more of the systems building effort is typically devoted to maintaining existing systems. These investments must be exploited - captured in an effective form and leveraged into new systems. The development of new systems should start from a platform which already includes valuable knowledge from the past. The means to achieve this exist: formal redevelopment engineering disciplines and effective tools and techniques. These are part of the armory of the effective systems development team. IS organizations that build upon existing investments reduce the cost of going forward and ensure that new technologies (such as CASE) are appropriately applied.

This set of broad objectives reflects a new agenda which we feel nearly all development teams should strive to obtain. The remainder of our chapter will be devoted to implementation and usage issues associated with CASE.

MAKING CASE WORK

Currently the most popular development environment investment is CASE technology. Buying and trying out a CASE tool can be either very cheap or very expensive. There are a number of stand-alone CASE tools which cost less than $1,000 and can be learned in a day or so of "hands on" learning; even more sophisticated workstation tools cost less than $10,000 a copy. If hardware and human resources are factored in, "trying out" CASE on this basis still costs only $20,000 to $25,000 - an insignificant amount for most IS departments. At the other extreme, a fully integrated CASE (I-CASE) toolset may cost upwards of $250,000 to buy and another $250,000 to install and implement. In each situation, however, IS departments need more than just idle curiosity and good intentions if they are to avoid wasting their resources. A plan for the introduction and effective use of CASE tools of any sort must be a subset of the organization's development effectiveness master plan.

Senge (1990) describes the value of systems thinking and the danger of making interventions into a system without a broader, "holistic" perspective. Such interventions, even with well meaning intentions, often produce counter-productive results in the long term. Perhaps no industry illustrates the need for broad systems thinking more than that of systems development. The past few decades have seen many improvement attempts targeted at specific aspects of systems development which have delivered marginal or even negative returns. Why? Because the process of delivering the information resource to the information consumer is a complex interaction of many subsystems, and any attempt to improve one subsystem without understanding how the intervention may impact the system as a whole, will likely yield less than desirable results.

In the following sections, we will look at some of the key issues in adopting CASE, some of the major practical problems with current tools, and some of the factors that have proved critical to the successful adoption of CASE tools in organizations that have made them work effectively. For the remainder of this chapter we have relied heavily on our 50+ years of combined IS consulting experience

GETTING EFFECTIVE COMMITMENT FROM IS AND USER MANAGEMENT

In working with a number of organizations that are in the process of introducing CASE, we have found that analysts, designers, and programmers take to CASE fairly readily, although a proportion of staff at this level do not want to make the change. Senior managers are also reasonably easy to convince in most instances. It is the personnel in the levels between who offer the strongest resistance, and who are often the ones who actually control the selection process.

Given that CASE will more than likely cause massive changes to the development techniques they have spent their working lives getting comfortable with, it's not at all surprising that many middle level IS mangers are reluctant to look at it seriously. Many people outside of the IS group also fear the effects of CASE. In particular, changes that require much more direct user contact and accountability are often strongly resisted.

SETTING REASONABLE EXPECTATIONS

CASE is far from being the answer to all IS development problems; it is important for those directly involved to understand this and to make the point clear to everyone else. In particular, CASE does not:

Remove the need for understanding users' business problems.

Do all the work of information gathering, model building, and option evaluation - it just makes some of these activities less tedious and time consuming.

Speed up the overall process of Analysis or Design. (In many instances, the requirement to correctly use a structured method and the introduction of rigor into the modeling process, actually slows things down - a price of greatly improved quality.)

Make life easier for users during the requirements definition process. (In many instances, users will be required to become more involved (not less) and will be expected to take on a more responsible role in the quality control process for deliverables.)

MAKING THE COST/BENEFIT CASE

The costs of CASE are relatively easy to identify (although they vary considerably from tool to tool) but are usually understated by ignoring or reducing the estimates for training and learning curve effects. Costs associated with integrating new tools into an existing environment, and with tool customization (when this is possible), are also generally forgotten. If you add everything up, it turns out that the cost of the tools themselves is a fairly trivial element in the overall cost benefit process. Nevertheless, it's the one that gets the most attention.

As with all cost/benefit calculations, the value of the exercise depends on how well the current situation is quantified (you can't measure improvements in anything if you don't know how good or bad things currently are), and whether the proposed savings can be realized in cash (or at least budgetary) terms. In IS development environments, the position is usually fairly grim on both counts (Jones, 1991; Parkinson, 1991). Very few departments keep detailed productivity records. Many don't even keep accurate utilization records structured by application development and maintenance, and recorded on the basis of individual applications. Most large scale installations do keep hardware resource usage statistics, but it is often difficult to relate these to individual applications or to the installation's workload. So the baselines for estimating quality improvements, performance enhancements, and cost savings are very weak at best. It follows for this, that very few organizations are able to describe the benefits of CASE in cash terms. There is no easy remedy for this, since, once again, virtually no one keeps records in sufficient detail to calculate any sort of "unit cost" on which to base savings calculations.

CASE LEARNING CURVE

Learning to operate CASE tools is generally simple and quick, learning to use them effectively is not. In addition, CASE tools focus on the need to carry out planning, analysis, and design activities with much greater attention to detail, and with much more awareness of users' requirements than has sometimes been the case in the past. Learning how to do this effectively is not easy for most IS departments, and while they are learning, they are not going to perform as efficiently as usual. They're also going to make mistakes, possibly serious ones, in the early projects, usually due to unfamiliarity with techniques and methods that the tools help to automate. These mistakes will not always be easy to spot or, once spotted, to correct.

Evidence indicates that it takes 12 - 18 months to bring a significant proportion of an IS department's development staff up the

CASE learning curve (Parkinson, 1991). Very few organizations have reached this point so far (Jones, 1991). Given this view, a majority of the cost/benefit analyses concerning CASE would have to be classified as premature.

METHODS OF EVALUATION

Traditional measures of IS effectiveness (user satisfaction with installed systems and IS performance in general) must be adapted for CASE-based development environments. Measures must be developed to capture the following data:

The number of change requests received during the design and construction stages of a project. This measure looks at how well the user requirements specifications reflected actual requirements.

The number of change requests received during the 3, 6, 9, and 12 months following implementation of a new system or application. This is also a measure of how well the system matches user requirements, however, it also provides information on the necessary rate of evolution required to ensure that systems stay in line with business needs.

The elapsed time from project proposal to delivery of functionality to users. This measure sets a baseline for the type of development projects undertaken by the IS department, and provides a means of identifying changes in the size and duration of projects using CASE tools. If the promise of CASE is realized, projects should get smaller, shorter, and better.

It should be made clear that none of these measures will prove anything overnight. However, compensating for the time lag associated with the learning curve, these measures will provide a baseline from which CASE-based development efforts can be measured. The basic principle remains: if you don't try to measure what's going on now, you won't be able to tell what changed after a CASE tool is implemented. If you can't prove what changed, you can't demonstrate that CASE made any difference in the areas of productivity or quality.

CHOOSING A TOOL OR TOOL KIT

The introduction of a CASE tool involves a great many adjustments, some minor and some major, and both types should be identified and documented early in the evaluation process. An important point to remember is that a CASE tool is just that - a tool. It is also only one of the many tools needed to develop systems. Building a development environment around a CASE tool is a very risky strategy.

Very few organizations planning to adopt CASE answer the questions "Why do we want CASE?" and "What do we expect to use CASE for?" If you think this is stating the obvious, you're absolutely right, but our experience is that it needs stating, over and over again. Other key items that should be considered when choosing a CASE tool (not listed in any order) are:

Match the tool to the methodology. Methodology is a key determinant for the success of CASE tools, and determines the type and format of diagrams that users feel comfortable with. Based on our collective experience, we strongly suggest IS groups adopt an Information Engineering-based methodology that assumes the use of automated support. CASE tools can then be selected that match this approach. Cosmetic issues, such as the tools use of color and display fonts, may seem trivial in the selection process, but they will play a significant role in the ease and success of the initial adoption process.

Match the tool to the technology architecture. Many CASE users are unaware that virtually all CASE tools require some additional investment in suitable platform resources such as additional computer memory (increased RAM and external hard drive capacity), networks, and faster processors. The burden, placed on the technology support staff, both from a time and cost perspective, are rarely included in the cost of CASE.

Match the tool to the organizational style and culture. Organizations with a sophisticated IS department that already have a data administration (not just data base administration) or information resource management function in place, are typically able to use more sophisticated tools than organizations that have yet to install a DBMS.

Select tools that match the level of sophistication your organization can achieve, but remember that you will become more sophisticated much faster than the tools will, so don't go for something too basic, which you will outgrow quickly.

STARTING IN THE RIGHT PLACE IN THE DEVELOPMENT LIFE CYCLE

Most organizations start using CASE on an analysis project using analysis support tools. There's nothing really wrong with this -after all, requirements specifications is one area where CASE is supposed to make a big impact - and it's an area that most IS development groups feel that they need support. Unfortunately, our experience indicates that it's often a bad place to start (from the point of view of a successful implementation), because:

Structured methods are often absent or, if present, are used badly or not at all. Analysts don't understand how to use the tools effectively because they don't really understand the techniques the tools support. In particular, data analysis techniques are badly understood and poorly executed, yet the deliverables from these techniques are essential to a high quality specification.

Many of the architectural issues raised by using CASE can't be resolved if there is no Strategic Information Plan in place, so pilot projects get sidetracked into addressing these issues and thus cease to be a reasonable basis for evaluating and learning about the tools themselves.

Scoping an Analysis project is very difficult without corporate models for organization, data, and functions, so pilot projects have to be adjusted as they go along, adding complication, distorting comparisons, and potentially wasting scarce resources.

Good pilot projects are not always available, so inappropriate projects or "make work" exercises get used instead.

There is a significantly reduced opportunity for added value from the first project, if the models built with the CASE tools are limited to one business area and not readily usable in others.

Training often is cursory or overlooked in the rush to get started, resulting in confusion and uncertainty in the project team and low morale during the project. This usually ends up being seen as a bad reflection on the tools.

There is a severe danger of "the blind leading the blind" on the project. Recently trained or even untrained CASE users have to become instant experts, usually unsuccessfully. They make mistakes in their use and understanding of the tools and these mistakes can easily become working practice because there's no one to tell them what they are doing wrong or showing them how to do things correctly or more effectively.

The above situations can make an analysis project a less than optimum place to start the CASE adoption process. The *best* place to start is at the beginning, with a proper Information Strategy Planning exercise on a major operational division, so that the key corporate models (organization, data, and function) are in place and agreed upon, and the essential architectures (data, applications, and technology) are identified, planned, and understood.

Subsequent analysis projects can then work from a common and consistent baseline, with assigned and agreed upon priorities and high added value from the planning models. The information strategy planning process is also less dependent on structured methods skills (although it still requires a basic set of data and process modeling skills to be available to the team) and planning teams usually consist of more experienced staff. The duration of the planning phase also allows time for sensible methods and tools training for analysts and designers who will be involved in later CASE-based development efforts.

Given the above argument (starting a CASE implementation effort with an Information Strategy Planning (ISP) project), why do 8 out of 10 development groups start their use of CASE with an Analysis project? We think that there are a few reasons why this happens:

The choice of CASE tools that support planning is limited. If your favorite vendor's tool doesn't provide support (yet), you won't want to start with a project that will show the tool in a bad light. There's a much wider range of choice of analysis tools, so it's safer to start there and move on to design.

Decisions about "trying out" CASE are made in the IS department, at a level below that which usually initiates or proposes an ISP project. CASE is often brought in without senior management's knowledge or consent, "just to get some experience." Starting with a small low risk analysis project also avoids facing the issue of convincing senior managers that CASE is a good idea.

Not everyone feels confident that an ISP project is necessary or desirable, or the organization already has, or claims to have an Information Systems Plan and doesn't want to repeat the exercise.

If an ISP already exists, a good approach is to use CASE tools to document it thoroughly, and to construct the relevant corporate models. This helps validate the contents of the plan and gives any subsequent Analysis projects a head start with a set of CASE tools based on data and function models.

IMPLEMENTATION APPROACH OPTIONS

Conventional wisdom recommends that you start something new, especially when it's expensive and risky, with a pilot project. The rationale is that pilot projects can fail without doing serious damage to the business, so the risk is contained. They also involve only a small proportion of the IS department's resources, so they're relatively cheap to run and not too difficult to manage. Using a pilot project to introduce CASE is a safe choice, but not always the best choice. Jones (1991) reports that some organizations have accelerated the acceptance of CASE by using high-profile or strategic projects for the initial project. Although this is a high-risk approach (some call it "betting my job"), if it works, it can result in widespread knowledge of the success and an increased rate of acceptance of CASE.

Another alternative is to recognize the strategic role that CASE will play within the IS development environment, and mandate its use on all projects, without going through the pilot stage. This "Big Bang" approach certainly demonstrates commitment but also requires that the tools chosen be suitable for the work to be done and the environment in which they will be used. From that point of view, this is an extremely risky approach. On the other hand, given a sound development environment and a good choice of tools, the benefits will be available that much sooner.

PICKING A GOOD FIRST PROJECT

Picking a good first project can make the difference between getting CASE going successfully and missing the opportunity. Some of the things to consider are:

The project should be one that's going to be done anyway, not something invented for the purpose of the pilot. That means it is a "real" project, the outcome of which matters to the IS department and to the business.

The project should be one that's already been scoped and sized, so some comparison can be made between what was expected without CASE tools, and what actually happened.

The project should be the right size; small enough to allow for the appropriate training of inexperienced staff and large enough so that the results are not dismissed as trivial. The project should last long enough to get the team over the worst of the learning curve effects, but not so long that the benefits assessment and evaluation are delayed. A good guideline to use is a team of 3 to 5 people for 4 to 6 months, with an absolute upper limit of 9 months for the elapsed time. Leadership of the team should come from the IS department, but include at least one user from the business area under investigation.

The project should be in an area that is already well understood by both the business and the IS department, in order to minimize the additional learning effects that might otherwise be present. Try to avoid areas that have serious organizational or managerial problems that will blur the effect of the tools on progress and quality.

The area to be investigated should not be associated with the introduction or use of new or unfamiliar technology or software (such as a new workstation environment, operating system, communications network, or DBMS) apart from the CASE tools. Once again, the idea is to minimize the number of variables that the project team has to cope with.

If possible, the project should provide opportunities to add value to the modeling work by re-using it in subsequent projects. Data and process models developed in this project should be refinements of the enterprise model, and they should serve as the basis for future downstream projects in this business area.

Most medium and large scale installations will have a project that fits a majority of these criteria, although it may be a problem in smaller organizations. And just to prove that all of the above is really only a guideline, the authors have witnessed a successful installation (at a bank) where they changed virtually everything in the IS department all at once (hardware vendor, operating system, DBMS, development location, and departmental location) and still managed a successful implementation project in a critical business area.

GETTING BEYOND GETTING STARTED

All the initial project really does, is confirm that the CASE tool selected works to an acceptable degree in the circumstances in which it was used. There is still the much larger problem of how a successful first project involving only a half-dozen people can be transformed into widespread use of the tools in an IS department that may be hundreds strong.

More than one organization has put so much effort into its initial CASE tools project that it had no energy or enthusiasm left to continue the implementation process once the first project proved successful. Yet CASE implementation is not complete until everyone who could be using a CASE tool, is actually doing so, routinely. So how do we get from the start-up project to complete implementation? There are two main issues to consider once the first project has been successfully completed:

How do we "finish" the application that has just been specified and/or designed? and

What should the second CASE-based project be?

If an organization waits until the first project is over before making these decisions, there will be an inevitable loss of momentum in the CASE tools adoption process, and enthusiasm and interest may be lost. This is another argument for selecting an Information Strategy Planning project as the first CASE project, because the organization will have done most of the work required to plan the development projects for the next two to five year period. In addition, the organization will understand the priorities, project dependencies, and opportunities for added value from one department to another. Under these circumstances, it's easy to answer the "what should we do next" questions, and possibly plan ahead for the additional tools and facilities that will be required for later projects.

When all is said and done, most organizations do not opt for this approach. However, it is critical that they should at least develop a strategy that will get them to the same end, albeit with more effort and risk. The strategy should cover:

Extending the business models produced during the initial project, particularly the data model, to cover the entire business division or the complete organization.

Identification of subsequent development projects and project phases, for which CASE will be used.

Planning the acquisition of any additional tools and training that will be required by these projects.

Continuation of education and training programs for IS department and user management and staff.

The plan should also address the overall migration issues concerned with converting existing systems into the CASE tools environment.

CASE IN THE MAINSTREAM: ISSUES AND CONCERNS

Most IS departments have the beginnings of an architecture for their use of technology (although sometimes this is limited to a list of technology IS managers think is installed). Without an Information Strategy Plan, there probably won't be equivalent architectures for data and applications. These architectures are essential for planning and control of application development, whether or not you use CASE tools. Without the tools, however, they are difficult to construct and impossible to maintain effectively. An Information Strategy Plan project builds them explicitly. An Analysis project doesn't, but does create sufficient "seed corn" models, allowing a separate architecture development project to start once the business area models are available.

Once an IS department has CASE tools established and in routine use, a number of ancillary issues arise that need to be addressed if the full benefits of the tools are to be realized. Addressing them is difficult, not necessarily because the problems are difficult, but because solving them requires action outside of the normal areas of activity of the IS department. This puts IS managers and staff in uncharted territories and acting in new roles that are unfamiliar and often uncomfortable. Nevertheless, these efforts are worth pursuing because they provide the opportunity for the IS department to establish a true strategic role in the business, and get away from the old image of an ineffective service function.

One issue that invariably comes up early, is taking a corporate view of data, and establishing ownership of the main business entities or subject data bases in the corporate data model. The introduction of CASE tools will not resolve the issues around this topic; however, the education and training associated with implementing CASE are excellent opportunities to begin the process of bringing together senior user managers in hopes of facilitating an agreement. This is another opportunity for the IS department to enhance its internal corporate image by providing leadership.

Another issue arises because of the modeling and analysis capabilities of CASE tools. IS departments using CASE have the possibility of using these models to support all kinds of business activities that have critical information related aspects, such as the management of:

mergers and acquisitions: the corporate information model gives a comprehensive picture of an organization's activities, structure, and information assets. Modelling a target business and comparing the models can illustrate all sorts of potential incompatibilities in organizational structure, functional overlap or underlap, and information systems compatibility. This can affect the valuation of the target and/or the desirability of the overall deal.

product development: modelling the information needs of a new product line can influence decisionswith respect to viability and potential profitability, and allow for the examination of the effects new products will have on existing products and services. It's also possible to use the models to investigate possible new product areas and generate new product ideas based on existing information assets.

corporate reorganization: most businesses go through cycles of organizational structure and culture, moving between extremes of centralization and decentralization. Traditionally they do this entirely out of phase with their information systems, with the result that systems were rarely synchronized with organizational structure, or were at best, a compromise solution. CASE tool-based models and development facilities allow the impact of organizational change to be assessed and architectures to be adjusted to match the changes on a reliable and timely basis.

CONCLUSION

To effectively increase their contribution to the achievement of organizational goals and objectives, IS development groups must continuously improve their systems development processes. A broad framework must be developed from which various managerial and technical programs aimed at bringing fresh, new perspectives about the nature of information management can be launched.

Pressing problems of the moment (project cost overruns, schedule delays, scrapped systems, large backlogs, prohibitive maintenance costs, and dissatisfied customers) must be recast into "solutions" which solve not only the immediate problems, but also the larger class of problems they represent (insufficient investment in examining core systems development processes; lack of understanding of the significant shift in thinking and behavior required to benefit from new approaches and technologies; the need to build capacity to manage change and recognize its impact; and the need to move IS from a reactive to proactive, strategic mode). These solutions, such as CASE and IE-based methodology, must be selected and implemented based on an overall framework or structure which details all of the activities required to attain the objectives of a continuously improving effective development environment.

REFERENCES

Andrews, Dorine C., "CASE Users Find Implementation Trail Tough, But Following the Correct Path Results in Gains," *MIS Week*, 2/6/89

Baker, Jerry, "Are You Ready for CASE?" *MIS Week*, 1/8/90, pp. 23

Barton, Richard, "Pardigms for CASE Planning," *Information Week*, AppliCASE White Paper, 11/25/91

Boone, Greg, "CASE Has Not Delivered on Its Promises," *Computerworld*, 7/21/89, pp S12

Champy, James A., "Mission: Critical," *CIO*, January 1992, pp. 18

Conner, Daryl, "How to Manage Change," *Information Week*, AppliCASE White Paper, 11/25/91

Corbit, Gail F. and Norman, Ronald J., "Implementation: The Operational Feasibility Perspective," *Journal of Systems Management*, October 1991, pp 32

Ewusi-Mensah, Kweku and Przasnyski, Zbigniew H., "On Information Systems Project Abandonment: An Exploratory Study of Organizational Practices," *MIS Quarterly*, March 1991, pp.67

Eskow, Dennis, "IS Chiefs Seek to Revamp Business Processes," *PC Week*, 2/12/90, pp. 12

Fink, Carl, "The Case for CASE," *Systems Builder*, April/MAY 1989, pp. 30

Friedlander, Philip, "Project Management and CASE Integration: Technical and Cultural Pitfalls," *DATAPRO*, October 1991, #1083

Gibson, Michael L., "The CASE Philosophy," *Byte*, April 1989, pp. 209

Goff, Leslie, "Business Strategies Misaligned with MIS Resources," *MIS Week*, 11/6/89, pp.38

Izzo, Joseph E., *The Embattled Fortress*, Jossey-Bass Publishers, San Francisco, 1987, 155 pp.

Jones, Kevan, "The Benefits of CASE: Myths and Reality," Bultler Cox PEP Paper 20, November, 1991, 42 pp.

Martin, James, "The Key to Success with CASE is Integration," *PC Week*, 1/9/89, pp. 46

McClure, Carma, "The CASE Experience," *Byte*, April 1989, pp. 235

McConnell, Vicki and Koch, Karl, "Misuses of Power," *Computerworld*, 1/28/91, pp. 67

Moran, Robert, "The Case Against CASE," *Information Week*, 2/17/92, pp. 29

Pallatto, John, "Survey Uncovers the Truths of Real-Life CASE Histories," *PC Week*, 1/23/89, pp. 38

Parkinson, John, *Making CASE Work*, NCC Blackwell Ltd., England, 1991, 300 pp.

Rubin, H. A., "Using 'Readiness' to Guide CASE Implementation," *CASE Trends*, January/February 1991, pp 37

"The Shape of Things: CASE Tool User Profile," *MIS Week*, 3/12/90, pp. 30

Senge, Peter, *The Fifth Discipline, The Art & Practice of the Learning Organization*, Doubleday, New York, 1990

Smithson, Barbara T., "Nutmeg Loses up to $8M in Xmas Sales due to Computer Problems," *MIS Week*, 1/1/90, pp, 17

CHAPTER SIX

Current Limitations in CASE Methodology and Recommendations for Improvement

Oscar Gutierrez
University of Massachusetts at Boston

Increasing organizational demands to deal more effectively with current applications, and growing competitive pressures for newer and more complex systems, are driving organizations to look into CASE technology as a possible solution. This technology, although not yet mature, has contributed to increases in productivity and improved systems quality. However, current limitations of available tools account for an evident mismatch between a dominant technical development perspective, and an emerging business paradigm that poses demands which the current paradigm tends to ignore. The chapter explores this issue and proposes an integrative perspective between product and business views as they relate to CASE. The author concludes that active user involvement will be necessary for effective CASE implementation. The chapter discusses adoption strategies, and elaborates on the idea of End-User CASE.

Over the last fifteen years, Software Engineering has transformed systems development from a craft into an engineering discipline. This transition has formalized the solutions to problems learned from attempts to streamline the programming task. The process has been distilled in the form of techniques, notational conventions, and methodological guidelines. More recently, we have seen the emergence of immensely sophisticated Computer-Aided Software Engineering (CASE) tools and lately Integrated CASE (ICASE) environments that support and reinforce the discipline. Although this technology is, in some respects, still in its infancy, it has already demonstrated its power and technical benefits. These advances are evident in the perceived increased productivity of development staff (Norman and Nunamaker, 1989) and the superior quality of the products developed with these tools (Boone, 1989; Siegel, 1991).

The rapid evolution of this technology has resulted in an abundance of remarkable products in a market that is growing at a rate of between 20% and 30% per year (Forte, 1991). But, even more importantly, there has been a broadening of the subject matter which CASE now covers. The most noteworthy products offer support facilities that extend through the entire systems life cycle. The implications of this should not be taken lightly, because this technology will almost certainly modify the ways in which systems development will be approached in the future: first, by reducing the manual effort during system construction and maintenance, and replacing this with better methods of systems analysis and design, and second, by allowing business analysts to concentrate on enterprise modeling to carry out the development directly from very high levels of abstraction. The requirements to deal with this emerging scenario extend beyond the need to satisfy programs of technical training; they involve organizational commitment and fundamental changes in the way systems developers do their jobs.

Ultimate future developments cannot yet be determined, but it is possible to highlight some areas in the current technology where improvements can be made. By CASE technology, we mean the body of methods and tools to achieve effective software engineering, as well as the organizational initiatives to assimilate it. This chapter discusses two such areas, with particular emphasis on current CASE methodology. The first area involves mechanisms to adopt automated tools, the second area concerns systems methodology aspects that may facilitate end-user involvement in a CASE environment. We shall refer to the latter area as End-User CASE.

In the sections that follow, we discuss the development paradigm to which the current technology applies. We then review an emerging paradigm which is based on the need to adopt evaluative or experimental practices from a broad business perspective. We highlight the difficulties confronting CASE usage in this emerging context. Since effective adoption of this technology by organizations depends upon their own process paradigms and technology adoption strategies, we elaborate on organizational readiness for CASE adoption, discuss methodology management issues, and expound on the idea of end-user CASE. Finally, we provide some conclusions.

CASE AND CURRENT AND EMERGING DEVELOPMENT PARADIGMS: AN EVALUATION

"An organization cannot make effective use of CASE tools unless the software engineering principles on which they are based are understood and applied by their development staff" (Due, 1991).The truth of this statement, and its implications, are widely recognized in the professional literature (Due, 1991; Orr, 1991). An emerging issue is the extent to which the software engineering principles embedded in these tools are sufficient to satisfy the range of problems that organizations are now forced to address. Present software engineering techniques were designed to deal with problems found primarily in operative areas of the organization such as accounting, personnel and sales, areas where these techniques are more effective. These are fairly stable and straightforward formal problems from which the system requirements can be satisfactorily elicited by technical developers. However, current organizational problems, for which computer-based systems support is now expected, are much more complex, interdependent, and farther away from the technical core of the organization. This new environment is more dynamic and uncertain because there are now greater social and organizational contingencies in play. For example, many software engineering principles do not accommodate the complexities of informal organizational life. Consider the functional decomposition principle which is based on the representation of graphical objects arranged hierarchically by level of detail. All the depictions made at various levels of decomposition must be traceable and should be accounted for in the system being analyzed. These depictions are made in a specialized language suitable to the profession that utilizes the supporting techniques. However, users operate under different perspectives and employ different languages, particularly those user groups that operate farther away from technical core areas. These groups frequently develop informal systems that overtake existing formal procedures. Even though these informal systems may be more effective, they are difficult to document and trace, because after all, they are unauthorized (Land, 1982). In hard to specify problems, developers who recognize the limitations of the rationalistic perspective that characterizes software engineering practice today, are forced to engage in experimentation. This is achieved, for example, by developing scaled-down applications to test assumptions about the behavior of the real life system.

Current techniques based on experimentation, however, promote experimental behavior only in the context of low-level systems design. For example, prototyping, now supported in many current CASE tools, can mean anything from screen and report painting to development of limited operational systems used for demonstration and subsequent enlargement into a production system. The rationale for prototyping, essentially an evolutionary one, is adequate to deal with changing conditions because it is the way in which the technology becomes embedded in the social perception and sense-making process of the organization (Hirschheim and Klein, 1989). However, it remains underutilized because it is ingrained within a dominant product-driven perspective (Gutierrez, 1993). For experimental or evolutionary approaches to make a significant advance in automated systems development, their supporting techniques must be placed at the highest level of design and must be driven by an integrated business perspective. The following sections discuss the product and business paradigms. Figure 1 summarizes the primary assumptions of these paradigms.

Product Paradigm

In the product paradigm, the organizational consensus is that systems development is primarily a technical process. The product of design is, therefore, the result of the interplay between the systems expert and a sophisticated set of techniques and tools. The resulting design should satisfy a clear set of objectives. Development is conducted under full responsibility of the developer and with the assumption that organizational depictions can be obtained by purely rational means. Another commonly held assumption is that the representation of organizational phenomena is deterministic, meaning that it can be explained by tracing and mapping means and ends. In this paradigm, the language, symbolism and representations for describing a system are equally rational and objective. As a problem-solving approach, the goal of the product paradigm is to seek optimal solutions. These beliefs are ingrained in most of the current structured techniques (for systems analysis and design) in use today (Gane and Sarson, 1979; DeMarco, 1978; Chen, 1980).

This is a product driven perspective because at the core of the development lies a product view which is a perception of a new or modified system in future operation. It is this view which drives the process. In this paradigm, the role of project management is to oversee this product view and to align resources to respond to

Product Paradigm	Business Paradigm
Systems development is primarily a technical process that draws from highly specialized resources	The process of development is an integrative one involving those who are most familiar with the parts of the organization being analyzed
The description of object systems is based on language & representations that belong in the realm of rational discourse	Organizational depictions are formulated in the context of social discourse
The center of activity focuses on development of independent product views	The activity focuses on responding to changes in an evolving organization-wide system
Organizational phenomena can be explained by mapping means and ends	Organizational phenomena involve a social context which is essentially unpredictable
Development proceeds by prescription based on the specification of a product view	Recognition of social evolution, organizational learning dynamics, and need for experimentation during development
Problem solving is rational, clear-cut, and seeks optimal solutions	Problem solving is heuristic and seeks satisfying solutions

Figure 1: Product and Business Development Paradigms

emerging contingencies. For project management to be effective, the product view must be completely specified so that it can be translated into manageable project components (i.e. deliverables, activities, tasks, etc.). Most CASE tools that include a project management component support this product view. Due to the nature of contractual agreements and resource allocations, a common practice is for management to limit the scope of projects to a single product that is independent and has very little or no direct interface or communication with other systems.

Business Paradigm

A number of factors have been influential in the emergence of the business paradigm in systems development as an alternative perspective to the product view. Some of the factors which help to highlight the primary assumptions underlying the business paradigm are discussed below.

First is the recognition that systems behavior is not deterministic (Land and Kennedy-McGregor, 1987). Basing Information Systems (IS) understanding, and making representations in terms of observable causal mappings, produces partial system views. An increasing body of literature now recognizes and focuses on the organizational and behavioral contexts of the field (Kumar & Bjorn-Andersen, 1990; Keen, 1981; Swanson, 1983). The argument is that with information systems, one must go beyond the normal design activity found in other fields of engineering. Information systems methodology must provide the means of understanding the set of complex and non-specific human behaviors involved, and must represent them consistently (Turner, 1987). Hence, in the business paradigm, organizational phenomena are recognized as involving an important social context which may be inconsistent, and in many cases, unpredictable.

Second, is the acknowledgment that most of the software engineering methodology that supports the latter parts of systems design and implementation has matured. It is now possible to focus on providing support and understanding to user and business information needs. In the business paradigm development activities focus on defining requirements and responding to changes in an evolving organization-wide system. Therefore, systems development in the business paradigm has an integrative perspective in two respects: first, in its perception of systems development as a sociotechnical process involving those who are familiar with the parts of the organization being analyzed (Bostrom and Heinen, 1977; Mumford, 1981; Land and Hirschheim, 1983), and second, in terms of the natural interdependencies between cross-functional business activity. This view may not be easily implemented with further methodology automation only, since expanded or new approaches are needed to accommodate the analysis and representation of organizational depictions in the context of social discourse.

Third, is the need to understand and help solve the problems associated with the dynamic nature of the information systems environment. The emerging issue is how to develop systems with enough flexibility to respond to continuous change (Fitzgerald, 1990). This calls for approaches that allow us to de-emphasize the assumptions that lead to the formulation of product views, in order to accommodate the adoption of multi-disciplinary work process enablers. In this paradigm the process of formulating requirements becomes as important as the requirements themselves. The information management function no longer provides services as a part of any given business process, instead it emerges as a self-contained process entity (Targowski, 1988). Because this paradigm assumes the juxtaposition of partial worlds, (i.e. the views of the enterprise expert with those of the developer), it recognizes the dynamics of organizational learning and supports the allocation of resources for explicit experimentation.

INTEGRATING PRODUCT AND BUSINESS VIEWS

The above discussion highlights assumptions that make the two paradigms different. In doing so we do not imply that they are necessarily opposing perspectives, but rather that they complement one another. The former is the established dominant paradigm founded on sound software engineering practice. The latter is an emerging, broader perspective, based on opportunities and realizations made possible by new technology and the need to understand and avoid the systems failures of the past. The task facing researchers and practitioners in the 1990s, is to find ways to accommodate a growing range of issues in systems development methodology, thereby producing better quality products. The integrative perspective depicted in Figure 2 addresses issues concerning globalization, integration, and development strategy. These are viewed across three dimensions of information systems development: technical, methodological, and work processes.

	Technical	**Methodological**	**Work Processes**
Globalization	Enterprise modeling	Organization-wide planning/ IS architecture	Collaborative process enablers/ Representation
Integration	ICASE	Methodology adoption/ standards	Communication & consensus forming devices
Development Strategy	Experimental systems development tools	Evolutionary development	Evaluative behavior

Figure 2. Integrating Product and Business Perspectives

Globalization

Globalization at a technical level requires support to represent, store and update enterprise-wide information systems architectures. Efforts in this area are in process by major computer manufacturers, notably IBM and DEC. For example, Application Development/Cycle (AD/Cycle) (Mercurio, et al, 1990) is IBM's initiative to provide a comprehensive methodology-independent standard application development platform. One important feature of AD/Cycle is that it offers an enterprise modeling approach supported by a range of tools to create, validate, and analyze, enterprise-wide models. Enterprise modeling is a process whereby business experts identify and define business processes, procedures, and policies, that go beyond functional boundaries and apply to multiple applications. By their very nature these processes have to be consistent across the organization.

From a methodology perspective, globalization means the support of organization-wide planning for global IS architectures. As such, any planning framework must go beyond the conventional applications portfolio supported by current CASE tools. Targowski (1988) refers to this framework as the Information Management Complex (IMC) composed of logically grouped information management systems "federations," such as, management IS, office IS, engineering IS, information service, and operations IS federations. Each federation is composed of more specific systems and subsystems. In this framework, these categories of systems are mapped onto the processes and resources of a business, according to the direction of the flow of goods, services, and information, from input to output, and according to the various levels of management. Targowski (1988) also makes reference to a Systems Planning Technique as a procedural tool for defining enterprise-wide systems requirements. Of particular importance is the fact that the architecture of the information management complex is based on the users' needs, business culture, and methods of operating. At the present time CASE does not provide such support: systems are still defined and developed in isolated product-project contexts.

From a work process perspective, globalization endeavors to understand business needs at a global level. This requires the presence of process enablers to support active representation of multiple user groups not only in business analysis and requirements definition, but also in planning and development. Kay (1991) describes efforts by GTE Data Services (GTEDS) in Temple Terrace Florida to meet this need. GTEDS has formed a CASE Steering Committee, where the director of software productivity and the manager of software engineering tools meet with management from various functional groups to guide the use of CASE technology in keeping up to date with global requirements.

The tasks of a CASE Committee are to:

- Determine feasibilities and priorities for CASE adoption.
- Setup a portfolio of projects aligned with global strategies.
- Make recommendations for major acquisitions pertaining to CASE technology.
- Approve the appointment of key personnel in CASE-intensive projects.
- Monitor CASE technology usage.

By the nature of the tasks, the CASE Committee requires a centralized focus of value judgement and decision-making. Although the formation of a Steering Committee to support the ongoing collaborative work advocated here may be insufficient, it certainly demonstrates the level of commitment and involvement required. Further, formal support for collaborative and representative work processes by methodology and CASE vendors is necessary and urgent. An example of this effort is UNISYS's Advanced Solution Development (ASD) Framework (Williamson, 1991). ASD is based on a set of business oriented principles that focus on enabling end user participation with application developers, in the various facets of a development project. A significant difference in the ASD strategy, is the emphasis on iterative development and user involvement throughout the life cycle tools.

Globalization should not be confused with centralized enterprise computing. On the contrary, globalization represents the resources necessary for the growth of cross-functional applications. These are computer-based systems that integrate different organizational business units by effective distribution and sharing of information resources. Globalization, therefore, is a requisite for integration.

Integration

Technical integration involves automated support of all or most of the work tasks in a systems life cycle under an all-encompassing support architecture. Environments of this kind such as AD/Cycle mentioned above, have been put forward as strategic development frameworks by computer manufacturers, and enable third party CASE vendors to integrate their platforms. Another example is DEC's COHESION (Saad, 1991) environment which is based on a strategy that looks at both full coverage of application development tasks, and deployment across multiple vendor platforms. DEC's COHESION and IBM's AD/Cycle are both repository-centered CASE strategies. At the core of these ICASE environments is the central design repository that addresses the life cycle from planning to code generation. The repository approach provides not only a storage view of a design database, but also conceptual and logical views and mappings. From a business perspective, this approach provides the requisite accessibility, flexibility, and moreover, global view for business experts and systems users to more easily engage in collaborative development.

Various degrees of technical integration have been achieved by some third party CASE vendors, notably Andersen Consulting's FOUNDATION; Intersolv and Deloitte & Touche's 4FRONT; KnowledgWare's ADW; and Texas Instruments' IEF, all of which are regarded as ICASE because they cover the whole systems development life cycle. However, the great majority of tools in the CASE market today are component CASE tools. These tools address certain lifecycle phases more fully than other phases, or target a specific phase. The trend, however, is toward greater integration. Vendors of modeling tools are building bridges to code generators. Similarly, vendors of low-level design and implementation tools are developing CASE front-ends. A number of partnerships are being formed among CASE vendors and also between CASE vendors and computer manufacturers advocating a development tool framework based on a central design repository. As an example of an exception to the repository approach, Hewlett-Packard (1989), does not directly support any repository at this time, but uses a tool integration platform called SoftBench.

It must be said that the full technical integration ideal has not yet been realized. There are concerns about the promise of AD/Cycle, since it is two years in the making with no clear results to date. DEC's vision of a future in which software is developed, deployed and managed across the entire enterprise, has not been fully realized. Although this has been DEC's vision for nearly a decade, it seems that the target date for a complete environment is somewhere in the mid 1990s. The reality today, however, is that third party ICASE and component CASE vendors support systems development in the context of partial, and much narrower product driven, views.

Integration, in the context of methodology and work processes, means the adoption of a specific systemic discipline whose principles, policies, and norms are generally accepted by the organization as a whole. This is evident when the enterprise adopts systems development and representation methods and techniques, as well as operating standards transcending the boundaries of the development organization. These techniques and standards represent how the entire organization has assimilated, or agreed to incorporate, a set of mapping and communication conventions with respect to information technology issues.

CASE tools create an environment that permits the sharing of information relating to software development. Such tools can increase the precision of communications among team members, but may employ a set of symbols and conventions that, for the most part are alien to the average business professional. In fact, these valuable tools are not meant to be used by the business professional, but by the average systems professional. Kumar and Bjorn-Andersen (1990) argue that when particular methodologies are used as standards for systems development, the organization inevitably ascribes to assumptions of what constitutes organizational reality, and also to assumptions of how to conduct the development. For example, the authors argue that if a particular structured method is applied instead of a socio-technical approach, the design objectives are likely to be predominantly technical and economic, instead of socio-political. The system will obviously be described in terms of data dictionaries and data flows, instead of work role descriptions.

CASE technology today supports a predominantly economic and technical paradigm. We argue that to achieve an extent of organizational integration for systems development we must expand our coverage of the subject matter beyond a product driven technical integration. A similar effort must be made to facilitate organizational integration, in support of resolving information technology problems. For example, end-user front-ends must be developed to facilitate communication and consensus not only in the development organization, but also in functional areas of the enterprise. Specific recommendations in this regard are provided later in this chapter.

Development Strategy

Development strategy is the systems methodology dimension where product and business perspectives differ the most. While CASE technology continues to strengthen the formality of software engineering principles, the organizational problems for which computer-based support is now expected, have become exceedingly complex and elusive. Business professionals demand approaches that recognize the partiality of organizational mappings, and by experience, reject the formality and rigor of technically led processes. Often, both business professionals and developers become involved with so much technical detail, that they fail to recognize that they are describing two different worlds with the same notation. Developers are forced to ignore the changing nature of user requirements because there is no single reality that can be depicted with existing techniques, and which satisfies the multiple and sometimes contradictory perceptions of what constitutes "the system." The systems objectives of modern applications cannot be effectively discerned with the clarity assumed by rigorous technology, but emerge as part of a learning process during the development. CASE technology, at present, constrains users' and developers' views to a single set of mapping and representation notations. With these tools, a system design is usually presented as the only objective possibility, and not as one proposed design that must be submitted to critical inspection from alternative frames of reference.

A marriage between product and business perspectives can only be achieved if CASE technology includes within its collection of tools, those that might support experimental systems development. This strategy views projects in terms of unified partial worlds. Procedurally, it represents ongoing analysis and problem reformulation, practice, and gradual implementation (Gilb, 1988). It is a model that supports commitment to inter-disciplinary group work. The requisite technical support must, therefore, satisfy two fundamental requirements: first, to facilitate social interaction for development across functional boundaries; and second, to allow continuous modification of evolving systems.

To benefit from experimentation beyond that which sometimes

is exercised on computational systems through low-level prototyping, there must be a shift in methodology and attitude. This shift calls for a realignment of the development strategy from an approach which is predominantly linear, to an approach based on the concept of continuous systems evolution. In the context of evolutionary methods, projects are based on, and initiated by, an open premise which is to be tested. Because systems requirements change and evolve, users with knowledge of the business and information needs of the application, must be integral participants in the effort. Furthermore, a flexible managerial structure is critical.

It is clear that advances in CASE technology make it possible for developers to support the goals of this evolutionary strategy. For example, the repository approach permits individual users to define processes and data in a way they perceive as natural, while still operating within a common design and data pool. This facility appears to each user as if it were developed specifically in terms of the user's own norms and understanding; each user can proceed accordingly, without affecting other components or systems (Land and Kennedy-McGregor, 1987). Similarly, techniques based on functional decomposition and modularity, make it possible for developers to change a part of the system without serious repercussions to other parts.

To effectively adopt experimental or evolutionary practices, we argue that more in-depth commitment is needed, and that technical and methodological solutions alone are insufficient to assume quality applications (Gutierrez, 1993). The organization must be actively involved in self-evaluative practices, and be supportive of, or engaged in, deliberate pro-active change. Organizations that experiment for practical reasons that result in successful new processes or structural forms, are more likely to adopt evolutionary development strategies. In such organizations, experimental techniques (Gutierrez, 1989) would represent a suitable form of the required innovative organizational technology.

ASSESSING READINESS FOR THE ADOPTION OF CASE TOOLS

There is ample historical evidence to suggest that a major concern in applying systems development methods has been managing the activities of the design and implementation stages of the systems life cycle: assembling the parts to produce the most efficient system with available technical expertise and resources. This is indicative of the relatively small investment on the earlier parts of the systems development process, i.e., requirements analysis and systems definition. This focus on implementation, still current in many organizations, has its roots in the early days of computing where programming was a major systemic concern. However, leading organizations today are entering a new era where the most complex systems are yet to be developed. Such systems will require the creativity and inventiveness of inter-disciplinary groups to formulate credible specifications, where the direction of the development depends on what the parties believe to be sound and true, and, where issues such as deferred judgement and experimentation are not inhibited as they are in the classical systems development paradigm.

The present state of affairs suggests a continuous evolution of how organizations approach computer-based systems development. This evolution reflects a shift in concerns, and marks the beginning and end of different eras of systems development by organizations. A model that outlines the key characteristics of a series of systems development "eras" is offered as a tool to assess readiness to adopt CASE technologies. It offers a range of categories of state-of-the-art tools and environments that may be suitable in each particular developmental stage. These eras are the following:

- The era when computer-based systems development is regarded as a programming problem.

- The era when systems development is regarded as a methodological problem.

- The era when systems development is regarded as primarily an organizational concern.

The model is summarized in Figure 3.

Programming Era

A systems development organization that is going through the programming era is characterized by the presence of a predominant pool of technical experts who are in charge. The investment in human resources is mostly in programming staff, and the time distribution requirements for systems development emphasize construction and maintenance. Work by development teams is generally done in isolation since there is minimum involvement with user groups. There are no clear project standards, and individual project leaders (normally regarded as "the champions" of the development group) define and manage their own development lifecycle stages very effectively. The development process normally proceeds in a linear fashion because systems specifications are conveniently frozen early in the development. This is so, because in this era, the specifications are normally based on authoritative agreements of what the organizational information requirements should be. However, most systems are independent from each other. Suitable tools for organizations in this era include low-end CASE, integrated programming environments, fourth generation languages, and re-engineering tools. This is a natural progression for any systems development organization that relies heavily on the programming staff.

Methodology Era

In the methodology era, attitudes shift from laissez-faire to specialization and management of the development function. Development teams interact more closely with user groups, and a clear distinction is made between technical staff managers and technical champions. Managers are hired by the development organization, or are those technical experts who in the past have demonstrated in-depth knowledge of, and sensitivity to, the needs of the business that they serve. Other role distinctions are more explicit, particularly within development teams. The most obvious example is the one in which the process of analysis is conducted by business-oriented staff and systems construction is performed by technical experts. This process of specialization is made possible by the formalization of project lifecycle stages and, possibly, by the adoption of a specific methodology. Thus, the major efforts in this era are to adopt mechanisms to deal with the increasing applications backlog and also to reduce maintenance costs. In this era, there is a development portfolio and a consistent discipline to manage the overall systems development function. Because of the use of standards, it is possible to develop interdependent applications that share common platforms. With accumulated experience and a growing infrastructure, it is also possible to deal with business needs in a fashion which is consistent with the changing nature of the environment. Systems specifications are, therefore, more loosely defined and development teams begin to explore alternative development strategies to the linear approach identified above. Appropriate tools, in addition to the ones that apply to the previous era include, high-end CASE and Integrated Programming Support Environments (IPSE). The former enforce the standards available in popular methodologies, the latter specialize in project management support.

Current Limitations 191

	PROGRAMMING ERA	METHODOLOGY ERA	ORGANIZATION ERA
Development team	Mainly programming staff	Specialization of development activities within development organization	User groups represented Business analysts
	Work done in isolation	User groups brought in for analysis	Integrated business and developer groups
Lifecycle coverage	Informal project lifecycle stages	Delineated project lifecycle stages	Delineated project lifecycle and cross-functional boundaries
	Majority of effort spent in construction and maintenance	Effort to align resources to satisfy applications backlogs and reduce maintenance costs	Effort to understand business information requirements
Project management	Non-existent or managed by lead programmer	Consistent discipline to coordinate various technical groups	Comprehensive automated support
		Development portfolio	Comprehensive strategic development plans Contractual approach
Type of systems	Independent	Interdependent Storage and reuse of normalized data	Integrated Storage and reuse of normalized data and business rules
	Authoritative specifications	+ Changing requirements	+ Non-specifiable Evolving
Development strategy	Linear	+ Iterative	+ Evolutionary
Computer-aided tools	Low-end CASE Programming environments IPSE Re-engineering tools 4GLs	+ High-end CASE	+ ICASE

Note: the "+" mean that the concepts that apply to previous eras also apply to the era in question.

Figure 3. Characteristics of each developmental era

Organization Era

In the organization era user groups are actively represented in the various facets of the systems development process. Organizations in this era have taken action to resolve the emerging bilateral needs. On one hand, the user has learned and has become familiar with certain aspects of information technology and design methods. On the other hand, the development organization is exploring or developing suitable methods for communicating with users, and has extended its operative base by further specializing its business analysts in the various functional areas. Systems development is highly structured and disciplined, which has allowed teams to interact in the development of cross functional applications. A major effort during systems development is to understand the business information requirements that satisfy specific application needs, and to align solutions with a global perspective. There is comprehensive automated support for project management which operates on a contractual basis, and a comprehensive development agenda. The systems being developed aim at integrating business functions and share not only data platforms but also normalized business rules. The development strategy is primarily an evolutionary one that aims at refining, exploiting and enhancing the wealth of data and code developed in previous developmental eras. The tools to support such an integrative perspective are found in addition to the ones already mentioned above, in Integrated CASE environments.

Technology Adoption Archetypes

The above model attempts to take into account the organization's placement of the information systems function, particularly the progression in systems development practice. It suggests that organizations that reach a level of integration, openness and participation have accumulated experience from previous developmental stages. However, it does not suggest that the organizational era is the ultimate level of maturity. For example, the model does not account for cross-organizational or cross-agency developments in forming strategic alliances (Keen, 1989).

When we speak of an emerging business perspective and of the increasingly dynamic environments where modern systems must fit, the model may suggest that the programming era has been left behind. Although, only a small percentage (15%) of projects consistently use a software development methodology, an even smaller percentage (5%) use formal project management (Shelton, 1989).

Heightened organizational and competitive pressure to update the current IS development infrastructure is an urgent managerial issue in many companies. This is more than a technology-transfer issue that targets business structure and operations. The primary target is the development organization itself. This problem will not be resolved with the acquisition of sophisticated CASE tools alone. The skill requirements to implement the CASE approach are different, and a corporate culture with the disposition to use these new tools must be in place before CASE tools can be successfully used (Due, 1991; Hamilton, 1990).

Individual organizations confront the issue of information technology introduction in diverse ways. In discussing information technology approaches for office automation, Hirschheim (1985a) describes three archetype adoption strategies. These classifications can be used to understand how different companies approach CASE adoption through the various developmental eras.

Hirschheim's first archetype, the procrastinator, represents the conservative and cautious organization that takes a reactive strategy towards information technology adoption. This type responds to technological change only after observing the effect of change in other organizations, or after the technology has become widely used. This type of organization is barely familiar with any CASE tool in use today, and its overall conservatism causes extreme difficulties in making technical transitions. It is therefore likely, that the procrastinator organization is still in the programming era. This type views the adoption of a development methodology as an end in itself, and considers the broader implications of organizational involvement in systems development as non-practicable. Thus, organizations that adopt this strategy are likely to proceed at a lower pace than the industry as a whole, and, if they do not align their strategy, they may gradually loose their technological competitiveness.

The second archetype, the innovator, represents the type of company that considers itself a leading organization in its industry. This type follows a proactive strategy in its approach to information technology adoption. The innovator encourages developers to actively engage in innovative plans by discerning the effectiveness of new programs of activity, and decides which should be modified or discarded on the basis of practical evidence. This type of organization is already committed to an ICASE strategy, and awaits the time when the next component is available. Evolutionary transitions may be difficult, but the difficulty is due to the fact that the organization is trying new forms, structures and procedures. Once out of the programming era, this type of organization quickly adopts and expands its methodological base and views the methodological era as a requisite transitional stage in preparing for broader organizational coverage.

The final archetype, the learner, is an organization that is cautious but receptive to emerging trends. In many respects, the learner organization balances the two other archetypes and as such, adopts technology by following an anticipatory strategy. While a reactive approach represents a delayed response to a need for adaptation, and a proactive strategy represents active influence, this approach is an attempt by the organization not to be left behind. The intention is not the manipulation of the environment as suggested in the innovator strategy, rather it is an attempt to understand current events and possible trends emerging from the imperfect information that is available. The learner organization is actively evaluating CASE technology, and is in the process of preparing its IS infrastructure for CASE. Of the three models, this is the organization that experiences the smoothest technical transitions. By learning from the experience of others, it is quick to respond to the demands for adaptation. The pace, although not as accelerated as that of the innovator, is faster than that of the procrastinator.

These three adoption strategies are based on prototypical models. It is reasonable to suggest that organizations categorized as going through one certain era, may expose characteristics of other developmental stages in certain aspects of their evolving infrastructure. A typical example is the development organization that places major emphasis on customer service and user satisfaction, but has not initiated an overall project management agenda, or has not contemplated the transition from its 3GL-based applications. This type of organization has accelerated its service approach, and may have adopted elements of collaborative development strategies. However, with respect to its technical infrastructure, it has not made a consistent and significant transition.

Organizations must develop a vision of how they want to, and how they are able to, confront the challenges of the ultra-sophisticated technologies of the 1990s. They must then define strategies to update their current development infrastructure. This task involves self-evaluation, and the assessment of technologies that the organization might deem suitable for adoption. The following sections present a set of recommendations for dealing with some of these issues.

A STRATEGY FOR CASE ADOPTION

Making an organizational commitment to CASE technology is a management issue that requires a broader perspective than that gained from the software selection process alone. The following recommendations summarized in Figure 4, focus particularly on methodology management. They are grouped into the following areas:
- Assessment of development infrastructure,
- Selection process,
- Project management.

Assessment of Development Infrastructure

Assessment of the development infrastructure involves two tasks. The first task is a critical examination of the current development organization as it pertains to the practice of methods and standards. The second task is an evaluation of how a proposed CASE strategy fits with current organizational pressures. The first task is internal to the development organization and involves measures of efficiency in terms of productivity and costs. The second task deals with attempts to find an adequate fit between a proposed CASE strategy and its effectiveness in the organizational context. A recommended starting point for the assessment is to begin by forming a CASE Committee to oversee the evaluation and development of a CASE strategic plan and its implementation.

Much of the assessment effort should concentrate on gathering information and concerns from management, business users, and development staff about current development practice. Audits should be applied to recently completed projects to compile information for an overall review. These audits should include an examination of the composition of development teams, proportional project phase cycle times, reviews of past project management practices, identification of any areas of strength or weakness in methodology, and a brief survey of available and applied tools. Because it is expected that the introduction of CASE will occur in an organizational context, it is necessary to establish a perception of what a "good fit" would be between management and users' expectations, and the promises of the new technology.

While the internal assessment should help determine the category of tools and techniques suitable for the current development infrastructure, a major management objective must be to evaluate the organization's readiness to adopt CASE. From an organizational perspective, CASE technology will shift development resources from

Assessment of Development Infrastructure	Selection Process	Project Management
External Form a CASE Committee. Examine current information Technology pressures. Assess the organization's preparedness for active involvement in development activities. *Internal* Examine current development organization with respect to practice of methods and standards.	Identify practices that should be maintained and nurtured. Survey and select development strategies. Survey, select or improve methodology. Survey, select or improve specific lifecycle techniques. Survey and select tools.	Improve project management techniques based on non-traditional roles of: leadership, work breakdown structures, evaluation structures. Introduce flexible project management through: scenario development, continuous verification, explicit evaluation program, autonomous project breakdown.

Figure 4. A Strategy for CASE Adoption

the non-visible phases of the life cycle (i.e. systems construction) to those that are both visible and accessible to members of the organization (i.e. information requirements and analysis). The types of questions that the CASE Committee should be able to answer, therefore, have to do with the extent to which the organization as a whole is prepared and willing to be more actively involved in systems development activities. Similarly, the Committee must elicit the extent of the development organization's willingness or ability to adopt more collaborative approaches to systems development. The results of both the internal and organizational diagnoses should provide some basis for determining an appropriate mixture of needed resources, and a CASE implementation strategy.

The Selection Process

The selection process involves evaluation of a number of major items before the development organization can commit itself to a set of tools. In this recommendation, the issues are: first, that the selection should not aim at replacing existing practices; and second, that the selection must be made with respect to various levels of tool, methodology, and development strategies.

Even if the organization does not yet have a formal and standardized methodology in place, there are probably areas in its development infrastructure that may be worth maintaining. The risks of cut-over replacement are too great because forcing a methodology that does not embed the values and beliefs of the people who will be applying it, may result in the methodology not being accepted by its users (Hirschheim, 1985b). Change should be incremental, following a steady training or actualization program.

A common approach to the selection process in the CASE literature is to present it in the context of tool comparison. Although the selection of tools is an important aspect of the problem, it is not the only one. Other items involved are the selection of work management models that essentially represent the development guidelines embodied in particular methods, and development styles, which represent particular strategies for dealing with different development situations. Some common development styles are linear, others are experimental, and participatory. For example, if a company adopts a prototype systems development method, then it is likely that integrated CASE tools would be appropriate. Integrated CASE tools facilitate prototyping practice because they support all phases of the life cycle.

There are two requirements for the successful application of tool selection criteria. The first requirement is to develop an awareness of the differences between development style, methodology, and tools. The second requirement is to select supporting techniques and guidelines that more closely satisfy the organization's development style, and it's identified methodological strengths. Current tool evaluation procedures (Topper, 1991) suggest that organizations should conduct an initial assessment to reduce the scope of the evaluation. Once a manageable number of products, that are consistent with the current development infrastructure are selected, then a more in-depth evaluation proceeds. Pilot projects are commonly suggested to elicit the fit between the tools and current methodological practice, training needs, and management techniques.

Project Management

Project management must be extended beyond a product perspective. Further developments in this direction should include improved management techniques and flexible project management strategies. Innovative management techniques will be required to improve the productivity of any multi-disciplinary groups working in various lifecycle processes. These techniques should concentrate on developing a nurturing environment for the exercise of creative talent. Techniques that focus on non-traditional roles of leadership, work breakdown, and evaluation structures must be explored. Self-managing groups and participatory techniques are examples that would extend project management coverage.

Flexible project management means the ability to reflect volatility of the product as systems objectives and requirements change. These are disciplined adaptive practices that document and support evolutionary development. Project management must maintain equilibrium between what is necessary to provide control mechanisms, and what is needed to facilitate the requisite flexibility and adaptability (Gutierrez, 1993). The main attributes of this approach are:

- ***Support for the exploration of scenarios.*** Project managers must define project activities with weeks or months in advance. They must prepare for contingencies that may affect the use of limited resources. To be able to produce an overall projection, project managers would need a clear view of invariant requirements and resources. This is sometimes difficult to obtain, since a clear set of systems requirements may not be available at the beginning of the project. Therefore project managers are constrained to make modest projections into the project's future. Scenarios would provide a feeling about the progression of the project given a set of variable assumptions that could be introduced in various stages of

a simulated project, and would allow projections into the future that are more than just one step ahead of time.
- **Continuous verification processes.** Continuous verification processes involve establishing time spans for project milestone tests, testing conditions, and the nature of data collected. A formal continuous verification process forces an ongoing confrontation among the various project alternatives. The evidence collected from available deliverables serves to test the project's viability given present contingencies and resource changes.
- **Support for an explicit evaluation program.** A commitment to a project evaluation program has two objectives. The first objective is to provide a formal mechanism by which user groups are informed of current developments and continue to exert a degree of influence on the process. The second objective is to ensure that any experimental activities are sustained until they are no longer needed.
- **Modular and autonomous project breakdown.** With modern evolutionary development strategies, each project deliverable culminates a process that needs to be managed almost independently of what comes next. Therefore, deliverables must be autonomous, and the duration of atomic tasks should be considerably less than activities defined with a linear strategy.

END-USER CASE

Current trends in CASE technology point in the direction of further integration, globalization, and automatic systems generation. All of these developments place a major emphasis for the role of the systems developer, and provide little support for the role of the business user. The sections that follow present an argument for the development of tools that directly support business professionals in their interaction with systems development groups.

The End-User CASE Concept

The End-User CASE (EU-CASE) concept represents a vision of automated support for systems analysis taking place beyond the development organization. In this concept, systems analysis occurs within the enterprise, during regular analysis meetings where the individuals involved discuss information requirements of a new or evolving system. Automated support is provided for the end-user who interacts with a specific tool and is assisted by the developer. In these roles, the developer acts as facilitator advising the user to follow a process of elicitation. The user, provides the developer with the knowledge and requirements needed for them to develop together a useful representation of the problem which is recorded by the tool. During initial analysis, the representation may be incomplete and any diagram generated is regarded as preliminary. However, the results of these sessions capture essential terminology and important terms of reference applied by the user community.

Architecture of EU-CASE

The EU-CASE model, presented in Figure 5, depicts a generic CASE environment with four major building blocks: first, the cognitive component of systems analysis and design which is embedded in high-end tools; second, the production component for systems construction, re-engineering and maintenance embedded in low-end tools; third, the central repository; and fourth, cross life cycle tools to support project and work management, configuration management and version control, and documentation. The fifth component in Figure 5 represents tools for the end-user. This component is not too dissimilar to those offered by some ICASE vendors (i.e. IBM's DevelopMate, DEC's DECplan, KnowledgeWare's IEW/Planning Workstation, Andersen Consulting's FOUNDATION/PLAN/1), however, these tools are designed to support the business professionals' involvement, primarily during the planning and enter-

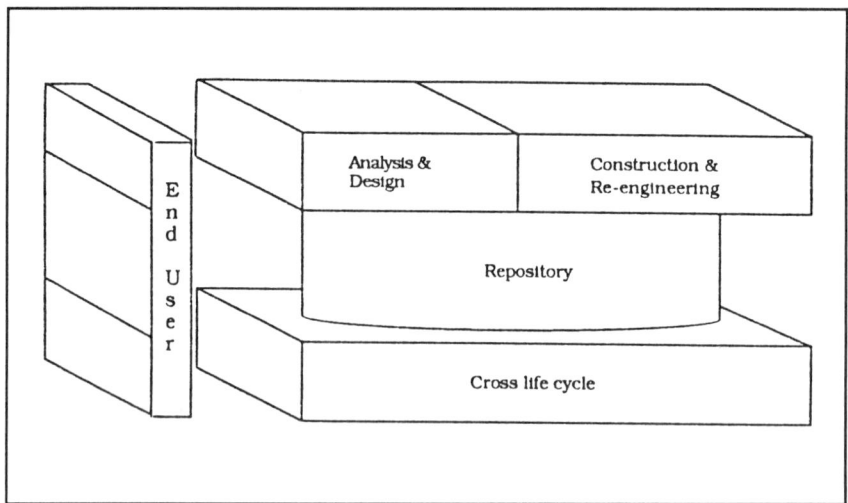

Figure 5. End-User CASE within a generic CASE environment

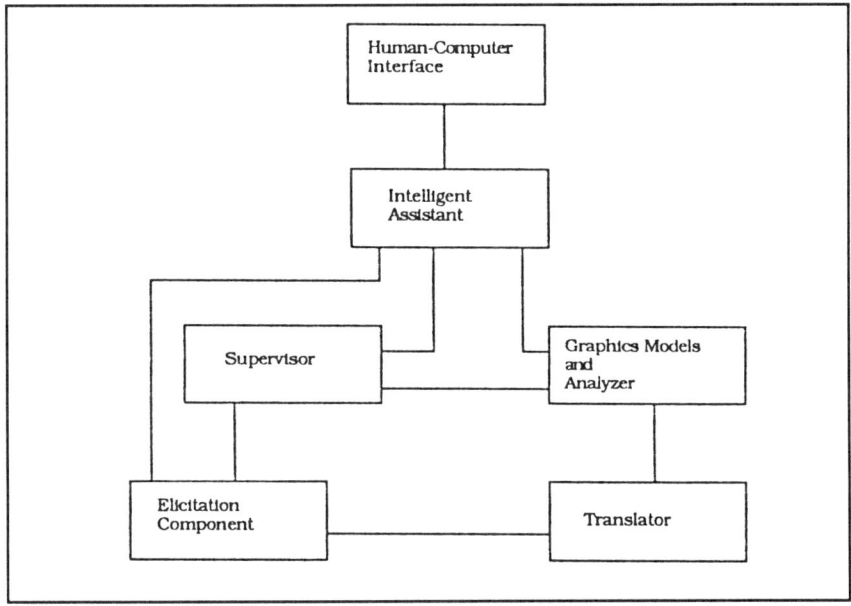

Figure 6. End-User CASE Architecture

prise modeling phases.

The EU-CASE approach is meant to assist user involvement in the early stages of technical systems analysis and design. Figure 6 shows a diagram of a possible EU-CASE component architecture. At the core is the elicitation component. This component supports techniques to assist the end-user through specific conversational dialogs. These dialogs implement an introspective process whereby users identify, classify, and describe specific objects in the system being analyzed. The elicitation component provides the framework for classification and description through a language free of technical jargon. The graphics models and analyzer component takes the output generated from the dialog and produces diagrams, lists, or reports for review by the user. The assistant is a tutoring system and an intelligent help facility that includes complete reference and self-instruction utilities as well as scenario-based examples. The role of the assistant is to support the user with the problem at hand, rather than to provide training, *per se.* The supervisor directs the flow of execution through the various steps of any particular dialog and supports three operational levels: first, a basic level, whereby the user interacts with the assistant; second, the normal operating mode whereby the supervisor directs the user through specific procedural steps; and third, the advanced mode, whereby the user does not follow any particular procedural dialog. He or she may inhibit the conversation and proceed at leisure with the task at hand, utilizing a graphical user interface. The next component, a translator, takes the output generated by EU-CASE and stores it in the host repository for further use by conventional high-end CASE tools. The final component is a human-computer interface that is consistent with the host CASE environment.

Characteristics of EU-CASE

EU-CASE differs from conventional high-end CASE for systems analysis in three respects. First, EU-CASE is user driven. The tools are designed for ease-of-use, are free from technical jargon, follow a conversational format, and include sophisticated intelligent assistants. Conventional high-end CASE tools on the other hand, require detailed knowledge of software engineering principles and a degree of sophistication in the manipulation of graphic-oriented interfaces.

Second, their elicitation methods are diametrically opposite. On the one hand, high-end CASE tools essentially allow the developers to document results of field interviews and observations. EU-CASE tools, on the other hand, take business professionals through an introspective process allowing them to formulate problems or describe aspects of the problem being analyzed.

Third, the representations that EU-CASE tools produce are entirely in the domain of the business professional. High-end CASE tools produce technical mappings. Figure 7 identifies some of the differences in representations between EU-CASE and high-end CASE.

	End-User CASE	High-End CASE
Analysis objects	Activities	Processes
	Document representations	Data flows
	Roles	Data entities
	Responsibilities	Data attributes
	Policies	
	Conditions	
	Rules	
Mapping and notational conventions	Linear responsibility charts	Data flow diagrams
	Mental maps	State transition diagrams
	Issue checklists	Data models
	Role descriptions	Entity-relationship models
	Role maps	
	Functional diagrams	
	Data models	

Figure 7. End-User CASE vs. High-End CASE conventions

Need for Additional Techniques

Techniques are needed to enable end-users to effectively adopt EU-CASE tools. These facilities should assist users in completing intense analysis sessions in their own natural working terminology and atmosphere. Similarly, techniques are needed to enable users to follow conversational dialogs with the computer, resulting in a usable set of factual (i.e. needs) and qualitative (i.e. wants) requirements. Any EU-CASE tool must combine elements of information analysis methods that avoid technical jargon with introspective techniques that guide the elicitation process.

SAMPLE EU-CASE TECHNIQUES

Introspective elicitation techniques are scarce, and the few that can be effectively applied to EU-CASE are likely to be found in the artificial intelligence or psychology literature. In the sections that follow, we describe various user-centered analysis techniques that are combined with an elicitation method based on ideas underlying Personal Construct Psychology (PCT) (Kelly, 1955). PCT suggests that individuals use an implicit theoretical framework to think about, and act with respect to, personal views of events in the world. These events are classified and responded to, according to a dynamic system of appraisal called the personal construct system. This system is used by the individual to construct, evaluate and modify mental models of the individual's immediate environment. It is in terms of these models that information requirements are established at the elicitation level. Further discussion of PCT and its combination with some of the following techniques can be found in Gutierrez, (1987 and 1991) and Gutierrez and Tseng (1991). Figure 8 summarizes a description of the various information analysis techniques discussed here.

Document Analysis

A process that seems natural for business people is the one that individuals follow to describe how they use the specific physical representations involved in their work. These representations are documents, forms, reports, or any physical administrative object whose life cycle can be easily articulated. Document Analysis (DA) is designed to help an individual user think about and describe characteristics, physical attributes and operations performed on

Technique	Description
Document Analysis	A technique to assist individual users to think about and describe characteristics, physical attributes and operations performed on the documents, and reports or forms that are used or will be used in a specific administrative problem.
Role Analysis	Appraisal of specific organizational functions involved in the system being analyzed.
Functional Analysis	Systems analysis technique for systems decomposition in terms of unit operations. Unit operations are small sub-systems of interrelated activities that support a specific business function. Functional analysis is used to identify activities, role characterizations, and the network of activity precedences.
Data Analysis	A technique to allow users to elicit essential data modelling elements, namely, entities and relationships.

Figure 8. User-centered analysis techniques

such representations. The aim of document analysis is to assist in formulating information requirements in terms of how the work is organized, instead of how it is executed. DA is based on a technique for analysis of decision support applications called the ROMC (Representations, Operations, Memory Aids, and Controls) approach (Sprague & Carlson, 1982). ROMC is a non-procedural technique whose outcome is a checklist of design issues based on the four building blocks.

The DA procedure involves four stages. In the first, the system being discussed is decomposed into several areas of analysis, such as the major business functions being looked at or into application sub-systems. Recognizing the limited information processing capacity of individuals, PCT techniques, particularly repertory grids (Stewart & Stewart, 1981), allow the user to manipulate only a limited number of elements and concepts. The areas of analysis, therefore, define the boundaries of the elicitation session.

In the second stage, the actual elicitation process takes place. This stage may involve many forms and variations, but here we highlight the most common procedure.

> The first step in the elicitation process is for the user to identify the documents used in a particular area of analysis. This can be done by asking the user to supply them, by providing a set of

generic examples, or by prompting the user with a set of questions, the answers to which identify the appropriate documents.

The second step involves document characterizations where the user elicits important qualitative traits or properties. This information brings to light some insights into the user's concerns which are difficult to document with conventional face-to-face interviews. The actual process for eliciting document traits and properties is done by comparison and discrimination. A common procedure is to present three documents to the user who is then asked to compare them, and to indicate which document is different with respect to some issue being discussed. The user then discriminates and provides document qualifiers.

In the third step of the elicitation process, a quantitative appraisal of all the documents against all the named properties or characteristics is made through a ranking or rating discipline. These values are used to show how each document is assessed on each characteristic. While the elicitation process continues, the user identifies and describes the operations performed on each document, and describes the documents' data attributes.

The third stage of the DA procedure is analysis of collected data. For example, maps which show concept interrelationships can be graphically produced. This information represents how the user assesses the problem in terms of the whole network of documents. Other outputs are lists of data attributes, lists of operations and manipulations performed on each document, and a checklist of propositions or design issues.

The fourth stage, called prescription, solicits from the user recommendations to improve any administrative aspect related to the handling of new or old documents.

Role Analysis

Role Analysis (RA) assists in the appraisal, by the user, of specific organizational roles or positions involved in the system. This procedure obtains both qualitative job assessments and a description of role functions, i.e., positions that the user is familiar with and can describe comfortably. The goal is to obtain mappings of specific organizational constraints imposed on various groups of people. The

RA procedure, like Document Analysis, is conducted in four stages. In this case, however, the objects of categorization and appraisal are specific organizational positions instead of physical administrative objects.

Output from these analysis sessions may involve role descriptions, representations of the interrelationships of concepts applied by the user in appraising roles, and role maps. Each role in a particular sub-system or major business function carries out a number of activities, some are critical and essential to that role, others less important and able to be performed by others. Role maps and role descriptions represent the user's perception of how the distribution of responsibility is or should be delegated.

Role maps can be used to depict a view of the system showing the connection of process elements from a point of view of a related set of roles.

Functional Analysis

Functional Analysis (FA) provides a framework at a level close to people's natural method of processing data by enabling users to concentrate on specific parts of an application. The primary objective of FA is to identify the essential activities involved in a specific business sub-system. Techniques to allow the business professional to communicate in terms of business activities, responsibilities, business rules, controls and policies are needed. For example, a method which seems suitable for this purpose, called unit operations analysis, helps to describe systems in terms of the necessary activities that support a specific set of interrelated tasks (Land & Kennedy-McGregor, 1987). Unit operations which can be dealt with independently are small sub-systems separated by some kind of spatial or temporal boundary.

FA is also conducted in four procedural stages: first, system decomposition into unit operations; second, elicitation of activities, rules, conditions and precedence; third, analysis of collected data; and fourth, update to graphical mappings. Output from FA is in the form of Functional Diagrams which represent the network of essential activities involved in a unit operation, including inputs, outputs, conditions such as triggers, and rules. Another type of output, the Linear Responsibility Chart, depicts the network of role responsibilities in a unit operation. Functional diagrams can help the user identify omissions and inconsistencies, and linear responsibility charts can assist in identifying coordination issues, and elicit the balance between operational and administrative tasks.

Data Analysis

Data analysis provides abstractions that naturally adapt to the way that users describe enterprises. Data analysis, therefore, provides a natural model structure as well as adequate terms for analysis. This generalization is the construction of set collections of objects and of associations between these objects. More specifically, data analysis allows the user to elicit essential data modeling elements, namely, entities, relationships and data attributes. The procedure focuses on logical data representation.

In contrast with the other techniques, data analysis does not support system decomposition because of the integrated data view required for most modern applications. The elicitation stage consists of three concurrent work sessions: entity identification, relationship identification, and identifier and attribute description. Entity identification may be the most critical and complicated task for users in this procedure. The process can make use of the data collected with other techniques to extend the analysis further. For example, this could be done with data collected in role and document analysis. The analysis and prescription stages involve a graphical representation of a data model for analysis and update.

CONCLUSIONS

This chapter has emphasized the need to balance the orientation of CASE technology adoption between a dominant product perspective and an emerging business view. We have highlighted some limitations in the current product paradigm. The observation is that systems developers can no longer exploit the information technologies of the 1990s without giving serious consideration to the active involvement of the business professional in the development process. The goals, for cross-functional integration and globalization that CASE facilitates, cannot be accomplished without an active organizational commitment.

We have presented an integrative model of both the dominant and emerging paradigms. We have also discussed the issues that suggest that not many organizations have gone beyond the era where systems development is regarded a programming problem. We, therefore, propose a model whereby organizations assess and develop a CASE strategy suitable to their current developmental infrastructure.

To further enhance the support for solving new categories of problems, it is necessary to provide new CASE components that more naturally fit with changing systems conditions. We have discussed the need to develop support for evolutionary and experimental systems development beyond the type that presently exists.

In the latter part of this chapter, we discussed the concept of End-User CASE. An argument was made for the need to adopt and develop introspective techniques to allow business users to interact with computer-assisted elicitation tools. Analysis techniques are also needed that allow business professionals to use the abstractions that naturally arise from the ways they describe the enterprise. The suggestion is made that CASE vendors develop front-end components which are essentially user-driven. We place the use of these tools within the early stages of the analysis and design. An End-User CASE architecture has been proposed and contrasted with High-End CASE services to illustrate the type of facilities that should be provided in this component.

REFERENCES

Boone, G. (1989). *CASE industry trends.* CASE Research Corporation, Bellevue, Washington.

Bostrom, R.P. & Heinen, J. (1977). MIS problems and failures: A socio-technical perspective; Parts I and II. *MIS Quarterly, 2*(3-4).

Chen, P.P. (1980). *Entity-Relationship approach to systems analysis and design.* Amsterdam; North Holland.

DeMarco, T. (1978). *Structured analysis and system specification.* Englewood Cliffs, NJ: Prentice-Hall.

Due, R.T. (1991). The real costs and benefits of CASE. *Journal of Information Systems Management, 8*(3), 63-66.

Fitzgerald, G. (1990). Achieving flexible information systems: the case for improved analysis. *Journal of Information Technology, 5*(1), 5-11.

Forte, G. (1991). CASE industry evolution. *CASE Outlook, 1,* 16-25.

Gane, C. & Sarson, T. (1979). *Structured systems analysis: Tools and techniques.* Englewood Cliffs, NJ: Prentice-Hall.

Gilb, T. (1988). *Principles of software engineering management.* Wokingham, UK: Addison-Wesley.

Gutierrez, O. (1987). Some aspects of information requirements analysis using a repertory grid technique. In R. Galliers (Ed.), *Information Analysis: Selected Readings.* (pp. 347-362). Reading:MA, Addison-Wesley.

Gutierrez, O. (1989). Experimental techniques for information requirements analysis. *Information & Management, 16,* 31-43.

Gutierrez, O. (1991). Facilities to assist end-users in the process of systems analysis with computer-aided software engineering tools. *Proceedings of the 1991 International IEEE Conference: Systems, Man, and Cybernetics.* Charlottesville, VA, pp. 701-706.

Gutierrez, O. (1993). A contingency view on prototyping practice, *Journal of Information Technology, 8*(2), forthcoming..

Gutierrez, O., & Tseng, V. (1991). Problem formulation from analysis of document representations. Working Paper. University of Massachusetts - Boston.

Hamilton, R. (1990). CASE veterans say: Look before you leap. *Computerworld*, 24(27), pp. 27.

Hewlett-Packard. (1989). *Implementing CASE technology today.* Software Engineering Systems Division. CASE Seminar, Burlington, MA.

Hirschheim, R. (1985a). *Office automation: Concepts, technologies and issues.* Wokingham, UK: Addison-Wesley.

Hirschheim, R. (1985b). Office automation: A social and organizational perspective, New York, NY: John Wiley.

Hirschheim, R., & Klein, H.K. (1989). Four paradigms of information systems development. *Communications of the ACM*, 32(10), 1199-1216.

Kay, S. (1991). CASE rolls out at GTEDS. *CASE Trends*, 3(6), 8-10.

Keen, P.G.W. (1981). Information systems and organizational change. *Communications of the ACM*, 24(1), 24-33.

Keen, P.G.W. (1989). Information technology and organizational advantage: The next agenda for research. In P. Gray, W.R. King, E.R. McLean & H.J. Watson (Eds.), *The Management of Information Systems.* (pp. 533-547). Hinsdale:IL, Dryden.

Kelly, G. (1955). The psychology of personal constructs. *A theory of personality.* Vol. 1. New York, NY: W.W. Norton and Co.

Kumar, K., & Bjorn-Andersen, N. (1990). A cross-cultural comparison of IS designer values. *Communications of the ACM*, 33(5), 528-538.

Land, F. (1982). Adapting to changing user requirements. *Information & Management*, 5, 59-75.

Land, F. and Hirschheim, A. (1983). Participative systems design: Rationale, tools and techniques. *Journal of Applied Systems Analysis*, 10, 91-107.

Land F.F. & Kennedy-McGregor, M. (1987). Information and information systems: Concepts and perspectives. In R. Galliers (Ed.), *Information analysis: Selected readings.* (pp. 63-91). Reading, MA: Addison-Wesley.

Mercurio, V.J., Meyers, B.F., Nisbet, A.M., & Radin, G. (1990). AD\Cycle strategy and architecture. *IBM Systems Journal*, 29(2), 170-188.

Mumford, E. (1981). Participative systems design: Structure and methods. Systems, Objectives, *Solutions*, 1(1), 5-19.

Norman, R.J., & Nunamaker, J.F. (1989). CASE productivity perceptions of software engineering professionals. *Communications of the ACM*, 32(9), 1102-1108.

Orr, K. (1991). Understanding software engineering methodologies. *CASE Trends*, 3(6), 20-26.

Saad, D. (1991). COHESION - DEC's CASE Environment, *CASE Trends*, 3(5), 15-19.

Shelton, R.E. (1989). Software construction project management: Matching management and method for successful software projects. *Proceedings STA5. The Mind/Method Interface: Restoring the Balance.* Chicago, IL, pp. 128-142.

Siegel, S. (1991). The quality crisis: manage it or become extinct. *CASE Trends*, 3(6), 24-26.

Sprague, R.H. & Carlson E.D. (1982). *Building effective decision support systems.* Englewood Cliffs, NJ: Prentice-Hall.

Stewart, V. & Stewart, A. (1981). *Business applications of repertory grids.* London: McGraw-Hill.

Swanson, E.B. (1983). Rationality and politics in information System design and implementation: A juxtaposition of two views. *Accounting, Organizations and Society*. 8(2/3), 219-221.

Targowski, A.S. (1988). Systems planning for the enterprise-wide information management complex: the architectural approach. *Journal of Management Information Systems*, 5(2), 23-37.

Topper, A. (1991). Evaluating CASE tools: Guidelines for comparison. *American Programmer*, 4(7), 12-20.

Turner, J.A. (1987). Understanding the elements of system design. In R.J. Boland & R.A. Hirschheim (Eds.), *Critical issues in information systems research.* (pp. 97-111). New York, NY: John Wiley.

Williamson, M. (1991). Alternatives to AD/Cycle. *CASE Strategies, 3*(7), 1-7.

CHAPTER SEVEN

The Adoption and Implementation of CASE Technology

Cyrus H. Azani
University of District of Columbia

Reza Khorramshahgol
The American University

This chapter explains a systematic and comprehensive methodology for effective adoption and implementation of CASE technology. The CASE technology implementation process must begin with a conscious and purposeful search designed to increase the level of understanding and awareness for this technology throughout the organization. CASE technology must also fit within the overall strategy of the organization. A complete technical, economical, and operational assessment must be undertaken before CASE gains acceptance in the organization.

Following justification, the criteria for CASE vendor evaluation should be explicitly defined and utilized. Moreover, the organization's structure, people, and culture must be prepared for acculturation of CASE technology. Also, an implementation plan that deals with both technical and social change needs to be prepared. Finally, a continuous evaluation of progress made during implementation, and periodic monitoring of changes in CASE technology must be undertaken for effective adaptation and implementation of computer-aided-software-engineering.

The successful implementation of CASE in organizations requires far more than just the automation of design, programming, and/or other system development activities. It involves the integration and improvement of all system development life cycle phases, as well as the institutionalization of change, and the continuous improvement of the information systems within the organization. Furthermore, effective application of CASE technology necessitates a complete transformation of the organization. It requires changes in leadership vision and style, a more adaptive organizational structure, the revitalization of the relationship between the organization and its customers, a more progressive organizational culture, and the transformation of the organization's personnel.

This chapter describes a systematic approach to the implementation of CASE technology in the organization. The methodology proposed is a comprehensive approach that takes into consideration the planning, assessment, organizing, adaptation, implementation, evaluation, and control of CASE technology in the organization. It also looks at the implementation of other advanced computer-based technologies and the lessons that could be learned from such experiences in the implementation of CASE technology. Also, the barriers encountered during the introduction of CASE, the strategies used in preparing employees for CASE implementation, and the recommendations of those who have been directly involved with the application and implementation of CASE technology will be discussed.

CASE initially evolved in response to the limitations of the manual application of structured methodologies for software development. The intention during the introduction phase of the technology was to use the computer to automate certain portions of the development methodologies. For example, CASE tools provided automated capabilities for using graphical methods such as data flow diagrams and structure charts. They also enabled programmers to automatically generate high-level language code and automate the conversion of system requirements into program modules.

CASE technology at the present time has the potential to revolutionize the individual's and organizations' capability in the development and utilization of computer systems. It has the potential to become to the 1990's, what personal computers were to the 1980's (Jarvis 1990). The intense competition between the Japanese and U.S. firms working on the development of the advanced CASE tools with integrated capabilities (i.e., workbenches) will most likely result in the automation of most phases of the systems development life cycle (planning, analysis, design, implementation, and maintenance) of a complete system.

Competition may also lead to the full re-structuring of the computer industry throughout the world (Weber 1989). This may explain the hesitance of a lot of CASE users to fully adopt the technology at the present time. According to one estimate, only about 4 percent of potential CASE users have utilized the technology (Burkhard 1989). The situation is perhaps even worse for those who have adopted the technology. For example, one large firm reported that out of nearly 100 CASE toolkits purchased, 80 to 90 percent remain unused (Clark and Hughes 1990). Besides waiting for the industry to mature, many potential CASE users are probably waiting to learn lessons from the success and failure of the organizations which have already adopted the technology. In other words, a lot of firms are concerned about their organization's ability to successfully implement CASE technology.

CASE ADOPTION AND IMPLEMENTATION METHODOLOGY

Numerous approaches and models have been proposed or used to help organizations improve their effectiveness in implementing CASE tools and methodologies. For example, Clark and Hughes (1991) have proposed a stage model approach for implementation of CASE technology.

The five steps in their model are:

- **Stage One: Disenchantment.** Managers become familiar with CASE tools and realize the usefullness of the technology.
- **Stage Two: Resignation.** The initial setbacks are overcome by the promise of future rewards and the realization that, instead of an ad-hoc experimentation, CASE technology requires the adoption and enforcement of a methodology.
- **Stage Three: Commitment.** The organization selects the necessary CASE toolkits and realizes that additional resources are needed in the future.
- **Stage Four: Implementation** Specific CASE tools and methodologies are adopted and managers come to the realization that multiple methodologies are needed for various specific projects.
- **Stage Five: Maturity** The organization becomes mature with respect to the application of alternative CASE methodologies on individual projects.

Development of a successful approach for adoption and implementation of CASE technology requires both a general understanding of the causes of failure and a particular knowledge regarding the barriers experienced by other organizations currently using CASE technology. The following is a list of some important causes of failure in projects implementing a new technology (Azani 1990):

- lack of top management support
- political self-interest of staff and other personnel
- lack of political clout by the implementors of new technology
- lack of participation
- too much reliance on power
- insufficient preparation
- shortsightedness by management
- employees' resistance to change
- existing organization culture

Personal interviews with managers and decision makers as well as a survey of personnel in 41 organizations which have implemented CASE tools and methodologies, resulted in the identification of the following barriers to the introduction and implementation of CASE technology:

1. Existing operators skills.
2. Shortage of suitable manpower.
3. Lack of in-house CASE know-how.
4. Lack of top management support and commitment.
5. Absence of a champion.
6. Lack of participation in the decisions.
7. Employees' resistance to change.
8. Tradition.
9. Existing organization culture.
10. Outdated management philosophy.
11. Cost justification.
12. Financing.
13. Inability to quantify the intangibles.
14. Rapid obsolescence of the technology.
15. Bureaucracy / red tape.
16. Short-term perspective.
17. Lack of an implementation plan.
18. Vague organization.
19. Miscommunication.
20. Protection of ego.
21. Lack of vision.
22. Preoccupation with the present activities.
23. Absence of a structured methodology.
24. Insufficient training.
25. Lack of teamwork and collaboration.

Generally speaking, teaching the use of software tools outside the framework of a methodology may result in weak automation and ineffective development practices (Butler, 1989 et al.). Perhaps more important than a model for implementation, is the need for an integrative, systematic, and structured methodology to guide the organization not only during implementation but also during planning, assessment, justification, selection, and monitoring of CASE technology.

A TECHNOLOGY ADOPTION MODEL

Based on recent research into the successes and failures of organizations with CASE and other advanced computer-based technologies such as CAD/CAM and CIM, a methodology is recommended, as shown in Figure 1.

To successfully implement the proposed methodology, management must first believe in the necessity of using a methodology for the adoption and implementation of CASE technology. Secondly, sufficient attention and efforts must be given to the meaning and requirements of each phase of the methodology. Additionally, the application of Total Quality Management (TQM) principles are highly recommended for the effective implementation of each phase and of the methodology as a whole. During the remainder of this chapter each phase will be defined and the important activities to be done at each phase will be discussed.

Phase One: Saturation

The saturation phase is defined as a conscious and purposeful

---

Eight Stage Methodology

Phase One   : Saturation
Phase Two   : Adaptation
Phase Three : Assessment
Phase Four : Justification
Phase Five : Procurement
Phase Six   : Acculturation
Phase Seven : Implementation
Phase Eight : Monitoring and Control

Figure 1

search designed to increase the level of understanding and awareness of CASE technology by the organization's top management. Management must first understand the position of CASE technology in the overall technology strategy of the organization. Secondly, the potential opportunities and problems that the new technology may create for the organization at the present time and in the future must be analyzed. Finally, the significance of such changes for the sustainability of the organization as a whole needs to be evaluated, and proper strategies and policies to increase the organization's ability to effectively adopt and implement CASE technology must be formulated .

The presence of such an awareness is a very important prerequisite for successful application of CASE technology in the organization. Without the understanding and awareness of top management, there is a very high likelihood that their support in terms of determination, encouragement, and allocation of the necessary resources to CASE projects will not materialize during the planning and implementation of CASE technology. Therefore, during the saturation phase, the management of the organization must become aware of CASE technology, its potential for contributing to the fulfillment of the organization's mission(s), and the opportunities and problems it may bring in the future.

An important requirement for the successful implementation of CASE technology is that top management be actively and continuously involved in the adoption process. CASE technology adoption is a strategic decision that requires sufficient planning and preparation. It necessitates important organizational changes and impacts the expenditure of human and capital resources in the organization. It is a decision that cannot be delegated, unless the top managers are very well versed in the technology and are able to randomly and continuously monitor the process of adoption and implementation of the technology.

Phase Two: Adaptation

Adaptation is the ability of the organization to modify its structure, culture, and behavior in response to changes in the internal and/or external environment. Successful application of CASE technology necessitates a planned adaptation by the organization. In other words, the organization should formulate a Case Adaptation Plan with regard to the adoption and implementation of CASE technology. Some of the important elements and factors to be considered during the development of an adaptation plan are:

- The proper positioning of CASE technology in the overall technology strategy must to be clearly defined in the plan.
- Specific and measurable goals and objectives with regard to the study and implementation of CASE projects must be formulated and agreed upon by all of those being impacted by the adoption.
- Any changes required in the structure, strategies, and policies of the organization as a result of CASE implementation need to be identified in the plan.
- All measures for coordination of business objectives and strategies with the goals and requirement of the CASE project should be an integral part of an adaptation plan.
- A schedule of the (time) duration of the project and the specific milestones regarding the completion of each phase need to be prepared.
- All affected parties and individuals responsible for the study and implementation of the CASE project should be identified in the plan.
- Particular activities and incentives for the involvement of those impacted by the technology, especially top management, must be established in the adaptation plan.

To adopt CASE technology, organizations must have at least one or two CASE specialists on board who are not only familiar with the CASE tools currently available, but are also aware of the trends in the development and advancement of CASE technology in the future.

Phase Three: Assessment

Assessment is defined as a systematic and purposeful evaluation of how CASE technology impacts on the organization and its constituents. The assessment will create guidelines for policy makers and will help make decisions regarding the adoption or non-adoption of CASE tools and technology. CASE technology assessment must be well grounded in facts, create useful information, and be reliable and verifiable.

Similar to the Adaptation Plan, management must also develop an Assessment Plan with specific characteristics and components. Among the components and characteristics to be included in an assessment plan are:

- A list of reasons for the adoption of the CASE technology. For example management needs to know whether the adoption of CASE is required in order to establish distinctive competence,

and/or to improve productivity, and/or to achieve greater customer satisfaction to obtain shorter lead time, and/or to create precision and consistency, and/or to realize greater flexibility, and/or to attain economies of integration, etc.
- CASE technology trends and the direction of the changes as well as the timing of each stage in the technology life cycle (i.e., introduction, growth, maturity, saturation, decline) should be assessed and included in the assessment plan.
- CASE project economic analysis and justification is another important component of the assessment plan. Tangible and intangible costs as well as short term and long term benefits must be determined and analyzed. This is necessary because the bulk of the benefits generated by CASE application are strategic and indirect gains in overhead rather than direct labor saving. These benefits will likely be realized only in the long term and in intangible forms. The intangible benefits include, but are not limited to:

   a. More synergism due to better integration
   b. Improved product / service quality
   c. Ability to respond more quickly to future demands
   d. Increased employee morale
   e. Increased flexibility
   f. More adaptability to adopt other advanced technologies developed in the future
   g. Better customer service
   h. Improved interface between the technology and the users

- Study and identify all parties affected and determine their level of acceptance as well as their influence on the success of the CASE project.
- The technical resources needed for CASE implementation must be also assessed along with any requirements for upgrading the current technical resources. The ability of the organization to absorb additional resources should also be evaluated.
- The positive and negative impacts of CASE technology application on the organizational components, as well as the likelihood and magnitude of each impact, needs to be identified.

Phase Four: Justification

Justification is the rationalization of CASE technology adoption by the top management of the organization. It is the end product of the technical, economic, and operational feasibility done during the adaptation and assessment phases. Top management has to

Adoption and Implementation 219

determine the relationship between CASE technology and the strategic goals and objectives of the organization; and ensure that CASE technology and the firm's strategy are aligned. Top management should also quantify as many of the costs and benefits of the technology as possible. If, for example, the results of net present value analysis or other economic studies are negative, top management should not scrap the CASE project. Instead, they must decide whether the non-quantifiable benefits associated with CASE technology application warrants continuation of the project. Also, top management should not view the application of CASE as a quick fix, nor should they wait too long for a complete and perfect integrated CASE product to reach the market. The justification of CASE technology is not a clear-cut or easy decision. Furthermore, it is not a decision to be made by a single individual in the information systems department, rather, it is one to be made by top management.

Phase Five: Procurement

During the early part of the procurement phase, the specifications of the required CASE technology are determined and placed in a request for proposal (RFP). At the same time, the evaluation criteria for the CASE tool vendor should be identified and weighted. Finally, the vendor proposals are evaluated against the designated criteria and a tool vendor is selected.

To perform the procurement more effectively, a steering committee of computer specialists, the CASE project manager, and other responsible managers should be formed with the following responsibilities:

a. Development of technical specifications for the needed CASE system.
b. Preparation of criteria for evaluation and Request For Proposal (RFP).
c. Identification of the vendors participating in the bid.
d. Evaluating the vendors' proposals.
e. Participating in the site visits and checking the vendors' references.
f. Approving and selecting the finalist(s).

For evaluation and selection of the vendors the following criteria may be considered:

1. The breadth of product offering.
2. The quality of service.
3. Functionality and maturity of the products.
4. Extent of the support provided during installation and utilization of the products.
5. The vendors' track record in developing, updating and modifying their products.
6. The extent of the technological fit between the hardware and software available in the purchasing organization and those offered by the vendors.
7. The financial and technical stability of the vendors.
8. The amount and the extent of vendor experiences.
9. The life cycle costs such as capital costs, installation costs, ongoing operation and maintenance costs, the personnel costs, and the costs of supplies and services must be considered as well. (including training)
10. The ability of the organization to modify the vendors' CASE design and development tools relative to its existing methodology.
11. The capability of the vendors' CASE design and development tools to export portions of the design and development dictionary specifications.
12. The ability of the dictionary software (and DBMS) to share specifications across the functions.
13. The vendors' open architecture philosophy to share file formats and integrate specifications across CASE components.
14. The CASE tools automation capability.
15. The adequacy of the vendors' CASE tool to perform efficient and effective analysis, design, graphics, documentation, and project management functions.

After establishment of the criteria, their relative importance compared to the other criteria need to be determined by some type of weighing system. The vendors should be scored with respect to each criterion and a total weighted score should be computed for each proposer. The vendor(s) with the highest over all weighted score should be selected and notified.

Phase Six: Acculturation

Acculturation is the process by which CASE technology is incorporated into the culture and the specific environment of the organization. CASE technology in its original form may not be appropriately acculturated into the organization system and the organization structure, people, policies, plans, and culture may not be ready for the effective adoption and implementation of the technology. Consequently, an inter-cultural integration between CASE technology and its recipient organization must be created resulting in a blended synergism between the two.

The relationship between the organization and its CASE technology supplier is a very important determinant of the suc-cess or failure of the intercultural integration between the technology and its user organization. The organization is dependant on the CASE vendor for assistance with the installation, training, troubleshooting, and ongoing operation of the CASE tool(s). The CASE technology supplier also relies on the CASE customer for its future product development, business growth, and references. Such a long-lasting relationship should not be based solely on bid price; it must be based on a combination of a lot of other factors such as quality of the product, reputation of the vendor, services given, and the technical and operational characteristics of the technology.

Some of the requirements for making CASE technology an appropriate technology ready for acculturation have been discussed during the saturation, adaptation, assessment, justification, and procurement phases. Integration of CASE technology into the overall business and technology strategy of the organization, sufficient development and understanding of CASE technology technical specifications, and adequacy of the organization in establishing the criteria for vendor evaluation and selection are examples of other activities required for effective CASE technology acculturation. Besides the above, the organization itself needs to become ready for acculturation by changing and developing its own structure, culture, people, policies, and other characteristics.

A. Acculturation of The Organization Structure. Sufficient consideration should be given to the choice of the organizational structure and its synergy with CASE technology. The organizational structure determines the patterns of interaction and coordination that will link CASE technology with tasks and human components. It facilitates the flow of information, specifies the hierarchy of authority and responsibility, and integrates the various organizational subsystems into a cohesive and effective entity suitable for the adoption and continuous upgrading of CASE tools and methodologies. For effective implementation of CASE technology, the organization should adopt an adaptive, open, and flexible structure. A mechanistic organization structure characterized by narrow specialization, autocratic authority, highly standardized rules and procedures, and vertical communication is not conducive to the successful adoption of CASE technology. CASE requires flexible redefined

tasks, sharing of authority and responsibility, and network structure for communication. CASE technology requirements are more effectively met by more advanced organizational structures characterized by terms such as:
- matrix
- adhocracy
- entrepreneurial forms of organization
- organic organizational structure

B. Acculturation of the Organization's People. Preparing the organization for change begins with the alignment of organizational goals with the goals of employees. To be the champion of change, top management and other members of the organization must have sufficient understanding of CASE technology and its contribution toward the fulfillment of the organization's mission. They must know the advantages, limitations, and requirements of the new technology. They also need to have the proper level of training, be ready to face the challenge of the new technology, and be fully committed to effective and efficient implementation of CASE tools and methodology. Training is an essential requirement for the successful adoption of CASE technology. The organization must plan for the training of lower level as well as top level personnel, and should provide training in both CASE concepts as well as products (Duncan 1989).

Without top management determination and commitment, the employees of the organization will be less likely to accept change or become fully committed to its implementation. Additionally, the employees need to be properly rewarded for their change of attitude, efforts toward innovation, risk taking, and self-development. Furthermore, effective acculturation requires that managers, supervisors, operators, and the technical specialists work as a team (Danziger and Haynes 1989). Teamwork is the key to success for implementation of any organizational change and development strategy.

Employee acculturation requires that the need for the CASE technology be effectively communicated to employees of the organization. In addition, proper levels of training must be provided to each user of the new technology. To fulfill the technical requirements of CASE technology, up to date and creative computer science and information systems professionals are needed. Moreover, the employees need to be adequately motivated and rewarded to accept the change and not to resist it. Lack of communication, insufficient training, and absence of effective incentives will likely lead to employee resistance and defensive reactions.

The managers of organizations implementing CASE tools and

methodologies, should identify the reasons for employee resistance and establish proper plans and policies to overcome them. Effective employee acculturation necessitate awareness of employee reasons for resisting CASE technology such as:

1. Protection of status or prerogative.
2. Protection of an existing way of life.
3. Prevention of devaluation of capital invested in the existing facility process.
4. Protection against a reduction of livelihood because CASE tools or methodologies could devalue knowledge or skills presently required.
5. Fear of elimination of a job or profession.
6. Rigidity inherent in large or bureaucratic organizations.
7. Protection of established values, habits, and personalities.
8. Reduction in social satisfaction when the new technology causes the realignment of personnel.
9. Fear of the inability to acquire the necessary skills.
10. Mistrust between the change agents (the initiators of change) and those required to change.
11. Incorrect assumptions and assessments of the possible consequences of the CASE technology.
12. Uncertainty about the future impacts of CASE tools.
13. Excessive work pressure, especially where CASE methodology is seen as intensifying the pressure.
14. Fear of failure.

C. Acculturation of the Organization's Culture. Organizational culture consists of shared ideas, agreements, and beliefs among the members of an organization. Cultivating and adapting a new culture is an important requirement for the success of CASE implementation. Additionally, understanding and recognizing the predominant organizational culture and subcultures will help management overcome resistance to CASE implementation. Research by the authors of forty-one organizations that have successfully adopted various CASE tools and methodologies revealed the following characteristics of organizational culture:

- A belief in the efficacy of confronting interpersonal and interdepartmental problems.
- Emphasis on continuous learning and expansion of ability.
- Open expression of attitudes, feelings, and perceptions throughout the organization.
- A positive attitude toward change and innovation.

- Participative leadership and family culture.
- Systematic search for improvement of performance and customer service.
  - Quality orientation.

Although there is the need to cultivate and adapt to a new culture, the old one still needs to be respected and appreciated. Sufficient time must also be allowed for the transition. The perceptions and expectations generated during the transition will shape the future norms, patterns of behavior, and responsiveness of individuals and groups. Similarly, cultivation and adaptation of a flexible and responsive organizational culture necessitates progressive organizational policies to promote and reward efforts toward innovation, self-development, and risk-taking.

Phase Seven: Implementation

During the implementation phase, the CASE technology will be installed and become operational. An effective implementation necessitates the development of an implementation plan. An implementation plan deals with technical change (i.e., conversion into a new technical system) as well as social change (i., preparation of the organization and its employees for effective adoption and implementation of the CASE technology). Before the installation of CASE tools and methodologies in the organization, an appropriate conversion strategy must be selected and the people in the organization given adequate training, enthusiasm, faith, and trust in themselves and the CASE technology.

Success or failure of an implementation plan is to a large extent determined by the effectiveness of management during the other phases, and the way the unexpected events are managed during the installation and operation of the new system. Management needs to be aware of the causes of failure as well as the critical factors required for success in implementation of a new technology. Additionally, the barriers to the introduction and implementation of CASE technology experienced by other organizations, needs to be identified and studied in the implementation plan.

As discussed at the beginning of the chapter, besides waiting for the industry to mature, many potential CASE users are waiting to learn lessons from the successes and failures of those organizations which have already adopted the technology. A review of the materials related to the success and failure of new technology within an organization, which was mentioned in the introduction, is a very helpful lessons to consider for more effective implementation of CASE technology. Additionally, an important consideration in implementing CASE tools and methodologies, is the adoption of a proactive strategy for identifying barriers and developing plans to surmount them.

Phase Eight: Evaluation and Control

Evaluation and control consists of all the activities performed to measure progress toward the adoption and implementation of CASE technology. It also encompasses appraising the causes of deviations from the various plans (e.g., adaptation and assessment plans) and correcting unfavorable trends.

In order to remain on top of the technology and be able to effectively adopt and implement future generations of CASE technology, evaluation and control must be aimed at not only preventing present and future deviations from the plans, but also on the continuous monitoring of the state of the art of CASE technology. Effective evaluation and control of CASE tools and methodology requires that an individual computer specialist be assigned to continuously monitor CASE technology advances. This person should analyze the opportunities and/or threats such trends may bring to the organization, and report them directly to top management.

CONCLUSION

The adoption and implementation of CASE technology is a strategic decision that requires top management awareness, involvement, and commitment. It demands proper positioning of an overall technology strategy for the organization, and appropriate assessment and justification process. Furthermore, successful adaptation of CASE technology requires changes in organizational structure and culture. Intercultural integration between the technology and its user organization is an important determinant of the success or failure of CASE technology adoption and implementation. Moreover, understanding and recognizing the predominant organization culture and subcultures will be very helpful in overcoming resistance to this advanced technology. Full participation by employees, effective management of unexpected events, and application of total quality management principles are among the other critical factors necessary for successful utilization of CASE tools and technology. Additionally, adoption of a proactive strategy for identifying the barriers and developing plans to overcome them is essential for the effective management of change in the organization. Finally, top management needs to continuously monitor advancements in the state of the art of CASE technology and periodically evaluate the degree to which progress toward the established goals of the organization are being made.

REFERENCES

Azani, C.H. (1990)." Managerial Issues in The Analysis, Design, and Implementation of Computer Integrated Manufacturing" in *Ergonomics of Hybrid Automated Systems II*, Karwowski W. and Rahimi M. (Ed), New York: Elsevier Publication Co.

Burkhard, D.L. (1989). "Implementing CASE Tools". *Journal of Systems Management*, 40(5), 20-25.

Butler, M.C., Corbitt, G.F., McElroy, D.D., & Norman, R.J. (1989). CASE Technology Transfer: a case study of unsuccessful change. *Journal of Systems Management*, 40(5), 33-37.

Clark, J.D. & Hughes, C.T. (1990 February). The Stages of CASE Usage. *DATAMATION*, pp. 41-44.

Duncan, M. (1989 January). Training is CASE Leading Edge. *Computerworld*, pp. 81.

Gibson, M.L. (1989 February). Implementing the Promise. *DATAMATION*, pp. 65-67.

Gibson, M.L., Rainer, R.K., & Snyder, C.A. (1989). CASE: Clarifying Common Misconceptions. *Journal of Systems Management*, 40(5), 92-99.

Hanna, M.A. (1990 January). Move is on to Tie Vision to Information Systems. *Software Magazine*. pp. 39-45.

Holgeson, K.W., Necco, C.R., & Tsai, N.W. (1989). Current Usage of CASE Software. *Journal of Systems Management*, 40(5), 6-11.

Humphrey, W.S. (1989 April). Improving the Software Development Process. *DATAMATION*, pp. 28-30, 52.

Hunt, R. & Rigby, M. (1984 September). Easing the Pain of Change, *Management Review*.

Jarvis, P. (1990 May). Making a Case for CASE. *The Washington Post*, pp. 9, 13.

Loh, M. & Nelson, R.R. (1989 July). Reaping CASE Harvests. *DATAMATION*, pp. 31-34.

Kievet, K. & Martin, M. (1989). Systems Analysis Tools-Who's Using Them? *Journal of Systems Management*, 40(7), 26-29.

Pivnicny, V. & Carmody, J. (1989 August). Criteria Help Hospitals Evaluate Vendor Proposals, *Healthcare Financial Management*.

Moad, J. (1990 February). Maintaining the Competitive Edge. *DATAMATION*, pp. 61-66.

Moad, J. (1990 October). Workstations Win a Big Blue CASE. *DATAMATION*, pp. 37-39.

Statland, N. (1989 April). Payoffs Down the Pike: a CASE Study. *DATAMATION*, pp. 32-33, 52.

Terry, C. (1988 March). Customer Training and Reverse Engineering Promise to Escalate the Acceptance of CASE. *EDN*, pp. 73-78.

Weber, H. (1989 April). From CASE to Software Factories. *DATAMATION*, pp. 34-36, 52.

Welter, T. (1987, November 2). Getting Set For Implementation, *Industry Week*.

CHAPTER EIGHT

Survey of CASE User Experiences

Gordon C. Everest
University of Minnesota

Macedonio Alanis
State of Nuevo Leon, Mexico

This chapter reports on the results of a survey of 19 large organizations in the Twin Cities of Minnesota. An extensive and well tested survey instrument was used to gather information on organizational characteristics, and their use of Information Systems development methodolo-gies and CASE tools. CASE tools are divided into very-front-end for planning and analysis, front-end for design modeling, and back-end for construction. The survey gathered data on the experiences, expectations, realiza-tions, and suggestions regarding the use of CASE tools. It focused on what they considered to be the critical success factors in the introduction and use of CASE. Most organizations had strong management support and a high ranking executive to champion the adoption and use of CASE. More organizations had made a commitment to use construction tools than design, and to use design tools than planning tools. Larger organizations were further along in their commitment to use CASE than smaller organizations. The foremost initial justifications for the use of a methodology were improved system quality and improved communication between end users and designer/developers, both of which were reportedly

---

* Adapted from: Gordon C. Everest & Macedonio Alanis, "Assessing User Experience with CASE Tools: An Exploratory Analysis," *Proceedings of the 25th Hawaii International Conference on System Sciences* (HICSS), Kauai, HI, 1992 January, Copyright © 1992 IEEE Computer Society Press, Los Alamitos, CA, Volume III: Information systems, pages 343-352; reprinted with permission.

realized or partially realized. Reduced system development effort/ cost was the third ranked initial justification and some organizations found the use of a methodology to have a negative impact, that is, to increase the development effort. The top ranked initial justification for the use of CASE tools was reduced development effort, yet only two felt this objective had been achieved. In response to a set of open ended questions at the end of the survey, most organizations indicated that it was too early to determine if the introduction of CASE had been a success. However, factors such as early and abundant training, top management support, managed expectations, and a well-picked pilot project were identified as keys to a better implementation of CASE.

There is a dual imperative behind the need for CASE tools —an imperative in both quantity and quality. The rapid proliferation of personal computer workstations along with the needs of business, government, and industry for information have created an unprecedented demand for information systems software. Yet the supply of skilled systems development personnel falls far short of an ever widening gap. Historically, we have had considerable difficulty building and delivering quality information systems on time and within budget. We must become more efficient and productive in developing and revising our information systems. As organizations become more dependent on computers, systems must become more reliable. Quality control in systems development requires greater discipline, improved consistency and quality standards. CASE offers the hope and promise of developing, delivering, and revising *better* systems, *faster.*

Unfortunately, it is not clear yet whether those hopes and promises will be fulfilled, or what it takes to make them a reality. Researchers consider the first promise, that CASE improves productivity, a controversial issue (Norman & Nunamaker, 1989; Chen, Nunamaker and Weber, 1989). The claim that CASE improves quality also lacks full documentation. Some surveys report *perceived* improvements in productivity [Necco, Tsai & Holgeson, 1989; Statland, 1989]; however, there is no corroboration of this perception by other measurements or research methods. The one effect of CASE tools that researchers and practitioners agree on is that using CASE typically produces change in the organization (Loh & Nelson, 1989). As with any change, there are some social and psychological dynamics in the introduction of CASE that demand attention (Chen, Nunamaker and Weber, 1989; Orlikowski, 1988; Kemerer, 1988). To further complicate matters, products that claim to be CASE tools vary widely in price and features (Alanis & Everest, 1989). As a result, managers are forced to make decisions about selecting and implementing CASE technology with little information and experience about the tools' features, their effects, and the contingencies that influence their implementation process.

To address the issues related to the selection, introduction and implementation of CASE technology in organizations, a discussion group formed by researchers and managers in charge of CASE technology in large organizations met monthly for over three years. The group was sponsored by the Management Information Systems Research Center of the University of Minnesota. Members met in the facilities provided by the participating organizations. During the first year, the group investigated the potential of CASE tools and developed a framework to classify and organize the variety of tools available in the market (for a discussion of the results of the first year see Everest and Alanis, 1991). Later efforts were oriented toward investigating the levels of usage, types of impacts, and specific recommendations for the successful introduction of CASE tools in organizations. To achieve the later goal, the group developed a survey instrument to help identify the general characteristics of organizations using CASE and to share advice on what they considered the critical success factors for the introduction and use of CASE. This initial effort was seen as an exploratory study to assess the environment and to orient further efforts. The survey was administered to a group of large organizations. This chapter reports on the findings of the study.

The next section defines the concepts and terms relating to the survey. Section three discusses the research methodology and instruments used to assess the environment. Section four discusses the findings of the survey. The chapter concludes with a review of the study and suggestions for further research. A copy of the survey document is available from the authors of this chapter (See ed. note at end of chapter).

INFORMATION SYSTEMS, DEVELOPMENT METHODOLOGIES, AND CASE TOOLS

Terms such as "CASE", "information systems" and "systems development methodologies" may have different meanings for different people. The term CASE originated as an acronym for Computer-Aided Software Engineering (Yourdon, 1986]) The original meaning referred to tools that provide computer based support for the methodologies used to develop software. The term has been defined

as:
- "software for developing software" (Henderson and Sifonis, 1989]
- "programs to automate the software development process" (Stamps, 1987)
- "a mechanism for automating structured methodologies" (Glass, et al., 1989)
- "software to aid the systems analyst" (Davis, 1987)
- "a philosophy used as a template to guide the planning and implementation of an environment" (Case, 1985)

Vendors have not agreed on the term either: features of products advertised as CASE tools vary widely. Prices range from under one hundred, to several hundred thousand dollars (Alanis and Everest, 1989). As used today, the term CASE is not limited to the construction of computer programs. CASE tools can provide support to assist in all the stages of the information systems development process, from planning to maintenance (Everest and Alanis, 1991).

To assure a common understanding of the terms that the discussion group was interested in surveying, the first step was to agree on the terminology. An understanding of these terms reduced the possibility of error, or bad responses, due to misinterpretation of the questions. The survey instrument included definitions of these terms:

Information Systems (IS): An integrated user-machine system for providing information to support operations, management, analysis and decision-making functions in an organization [Davis and Olson, 1985]. The information systems department is the organizational unit which encompasses all of the organizational activities associated with information systems and the use of computers — planning, staffing, design, development, operation, maintenance and support.

Methodology: A set of directives or guidelines for designing, developing, maintaining and documenting information systems. The methodology should be considered independently from any particular CASE tool. Questions about methodology recognize that the development methodology chosen is an important consideration in the selection and use of CASE tools. A methodology can range from a full set of guidelines for milestones and deliverables in the entire systems development life cycle to the conventions used in a particular graphical diagramming technique.

CASE tools: Software to support any of the steps of planning, analysis, design, construction, and maintenance of Information Systems; tools which input or use information stored in a IS design database or "repository."

CASE tools are generally divided into two groups: upper-CASE (i.e., planning and design tools) and lower-CASE (i.e., programming tools) (Glass, et al., 1989; Gibson, 1989; McClure, 1989; Everest and Alanis, 1991). By separating the upper-CASE tools into two classes, the survey identified three types of tools:

- very-front-end tools used for planning, analysis, prioritizing, and requirements determination.
- front-end tools used for modeling and design on IS development projects.
- back-end tools for construction and code generation.

Types of CASE tools, as they relate to the systems development life cycle, are shown in Figure 1.

RESEARCH METHODOLOGY

The methodology used to gather information about the status of

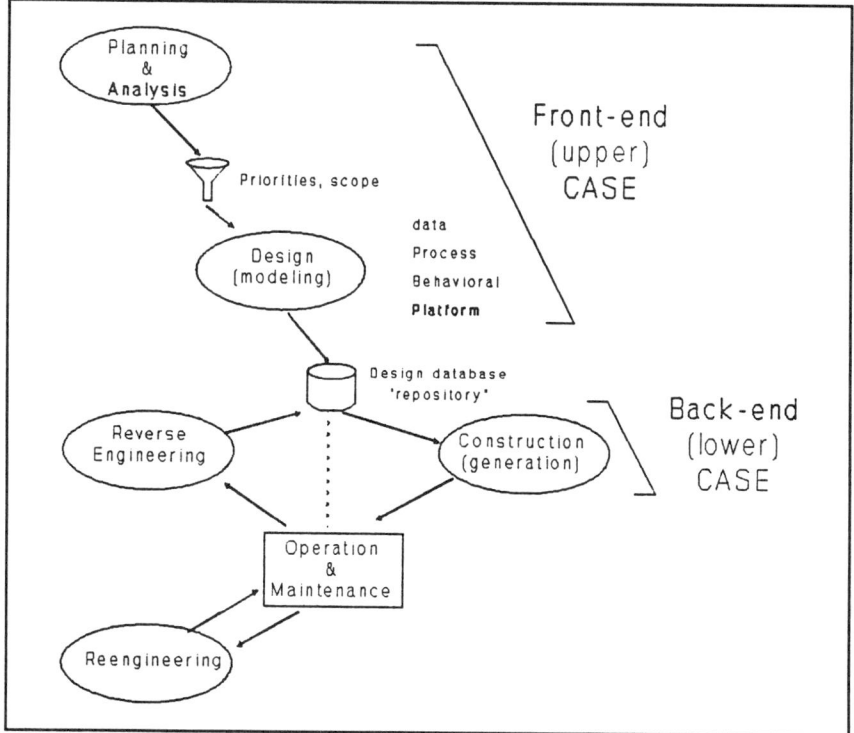

Figure 1: Types of CASE Tools in the Systems Life Cycle

CASE in organizations was a structured questionnaire. This approach is a practical way to obtain new information (Emory, 1980). Questionnaires are good for searching relationships between variables (Davis & Cosenza, 1985), and are useful for the generation of hypotheses (Jenkins, 1984). The instrument was developed with input suggestions and validation from the members of the discussion group. It focused on the information that the group considered necessary to gain an understanding of where the organizations stand in regards to CASE technology and what it took to get there. The instrument was pre-tested by the members of the discussion group and went through several revisions before it was considered ready to send out.

The Survey

The survey was mailed to the respondents with a cover letter that provided the names of the principal researchers who could be contacted for questions or concerns. The survey included a brief description of the objectives of the study, the definition of the terms, and instructions for completing all of the questions.

One copy of the survey was sent to a primary contact person in each organization in the target group, who was responsible for coordinating the completion of the questionnaire. The coordinators would pass the questionnaire on to others within the IS organization who had specialized knowledge concerning the adoption and use of CASE. Seeking out the most knowledgeable person in the organization would ensure a reasonable level of confidence in the overall results. The survey identified functional units which might be able to assist in answering the questions such as: IS Development, IS Planning, IS Development [Support] Center, Data[base] Administration, Information Resource Management, and CASE specialist. The contact person had the option of making additional copies of the questionnaire and sending them to separate IS units if they operated somewhat autonomously within divisions of the organization.

The survey consisted of five major parts. Appendix A contains a copy of the instrument used with tallies of the responses obtained.

The first part (sections zero, one, and two) gathered general information about the respondent, the organization, and the IS department. The information was used to put the rest of the survey in perspective and to determine the environmental characteristics that may have been favorable or unfavorable in the selection and adoption of CASE technology.

Part two, sections three, four, and five, obtained a profile of the organizations' IS development projects and gauged their level of usage of CASE tools.

The third part (section six) included detailed questions about the methodologies used. The survey included multiple copies of this section, and respondents were instructed to respond for each methodology in use. The section included questions about the usage level, the original justification for acquiring the methodology and the selection criteria. The section also inquired as to the extent to which the original goals had been achieved.

Part four (section seven) asked questions about the CASE tools the organization was using or had seriously evaluated. As with section six, the survey contained multiple copies of this section. The respondents were instructed to complete this section once for each tool they had considered for acquisition. The section included questions about the selection or rejection criteria and the extent to which the initial objectives had been achieved. The section also asked respondents to estimate the required training and projected use of the tool.

The last part (section eight) included open ended questions about the overall organizational impact and an overall evaluation of CASE technology. The questions in this section were subjective, but they provided the respondents with the opportunity to express their opinions and provide insight as to what they considered the critical success factors, as well as the impact of CASE technology in their organization.

The Population and Respondent Demographics

The population sampled consisted of large organizations in the Minneapolis/St. Paul area. The organizations selected were associate members of the Management Information Systems Research Center (associate firms pay a fee to the Research Center and obtain access to research results, seminars, speakers, and other events). Although we are not claiming that these firms represent a random sample, associate firms tend to be well motivated towards identifying the latest advances in information systems research and practice, and generally lead other firms in this area. They represent relatively mature and sophisticated IS organizations.

The survey was sent to 25 organizations. There were 19 respondents representing 17 organizations. One organization provided answers from three different divisions. Organizations were generally overall leaders, or leaders in some markets, and had gross revenues of over half a billion dollars and over two thousand employees. Figures 2, 3, and 4 present a profile of the respondents.

The IS departments were generally large: 79% of the respon-

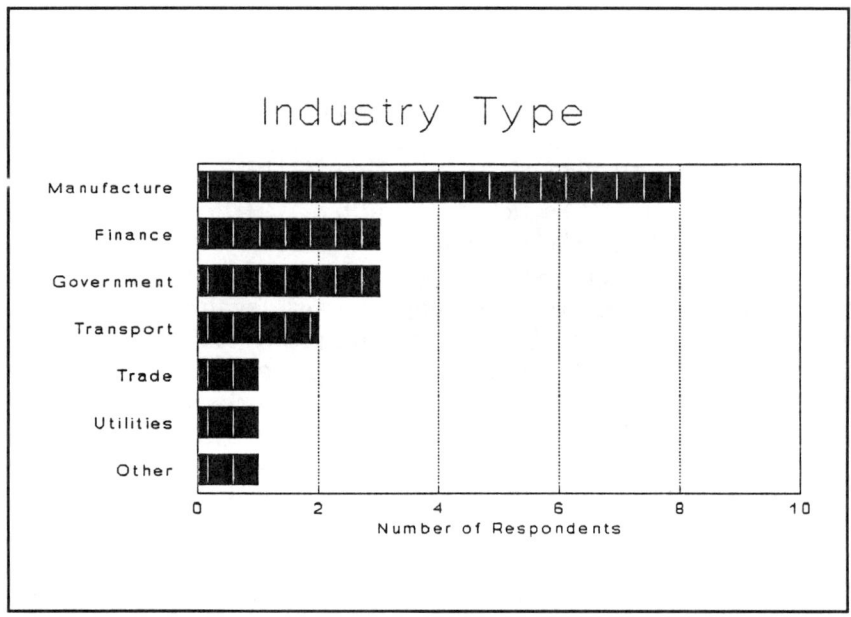

Figure 2: Industry Type of Survey Respondents

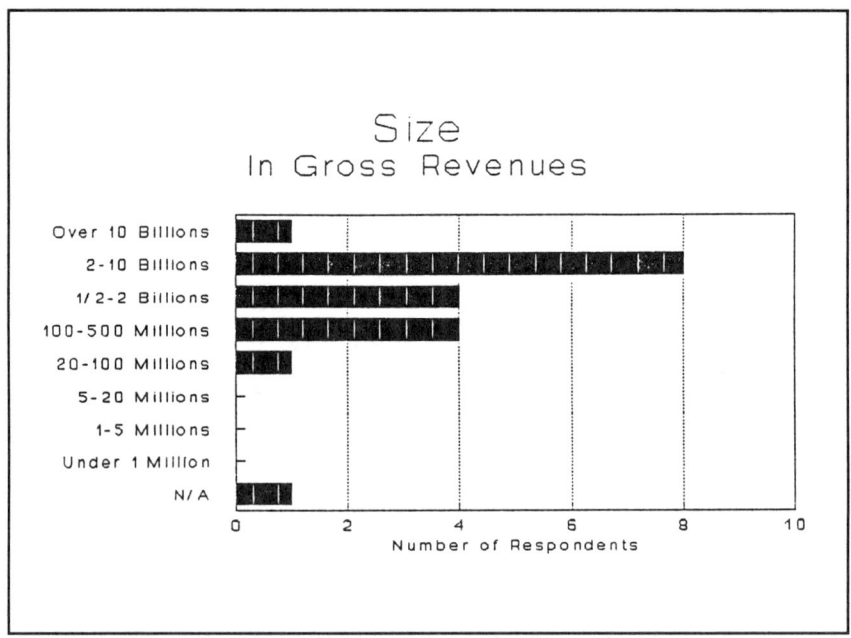

Figure 3: Size of Respondents in Annual Revenues

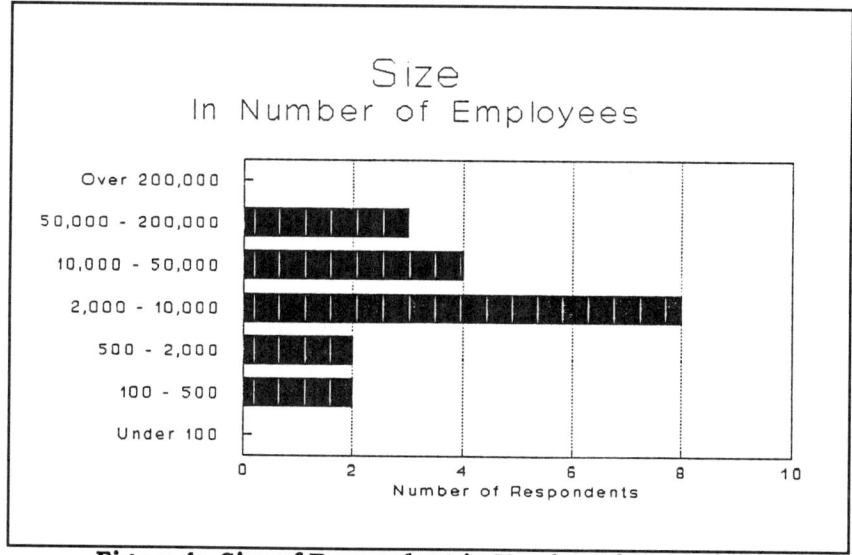

Figure 4: Size of Respondent in Number of Employees

dents had over 20 employees in systems development and maintenance, and over one quarter of the respondents had more than 200 employees in these areas. The development and maintenance staff were all or mostly combined (14 of 19, 74%), and generally centralized (15 of 19, 79%). Most organizations responding (15 of 19, 79%) had developed or were developing an overall or partial global IS architecture (this figure was much higher than expected). Each organization had microcomputers and some kind of mainframe as part of its hardware inventory.

FINDINGS

Profile of IS Development Projects

Respondents were involved in a wide variety of project types and sizes. Typical projects require 2 to 20 employees, with an average of 8.5. However, the respondents reported projects requiring as few as 1 and as many as 190 people. The average time between project initiation and installation was 10.6 months, with typical projects lasting from 2 to 20 months. The effort required by typical projects ranged between 1 and 300 person months, with an average of 83 person months.

The life span of the applications was estimated to range between 1 month and 10 years. The life span of a typical project was estimated between 3 and 15 years, with an average of almost 8 years (95 months). The age of the systems in use ranged from "just installed" to 20 years. Typical systems were 2 to 10 years old, with an average age of 5 and 2/3 years (68 months).

One of the questions asked for the relative proportions of development projects which used (or generated) low-level programming languages versus high-level languages. A low-level programming language is characterized by record-level navigation through a file or database, that is, one record instance at a time. A high-level language is characterized by file-level or set-level operations on files within a database. All respondents were either using a low-level language for most of their development projects, or using a high-level language. Nearly all of the respondents reported using high-level *data* languages for less than 25% of their application development projects. Only two organizations used high-level languages more than low-level languages, and they were in the 80-90% range.

Status of CASE in the Organization

The status of CASE differed for the three levels of CASE tools. The choices for evaluating the status of CASE investigation or commitment were ranked as follows:

[ ] Not using, Not even looking.
[ ] Looking, gathering information on what is available in the marketplace.
[ ] Seriously evaluating available products - no selection yet.
[ ] Piloting/Trial Use - have one (or more) in for evaluation.
[ ] Selection on hold after serious evaluation or trial use.
[ ] Have committed to optional use of (at least) one tool/methodology.
[ ] Organization decrees mandatory use of CASE methodology/tool(s).

While 37% of the respondents (7 of 19 organizations) were not using and not even looking for very-front-end CASE tools, 68% (13 respondents) had committed to optional or mandatory use of a back-end CASE tool. More organizations had gone further in their investigation or commitment to back-end generation CASE tools than design support CASE tools. Figure 5 depicts the current status of CASE within the respondent organizations by tool level.

Comparing the status of CASE with organizational size reveals that larger organizations are further along in the process of adopting CASE. The larger respondents were more committed to optional or mandatory use of CASE in their IS development projects than were the smaller organizations.

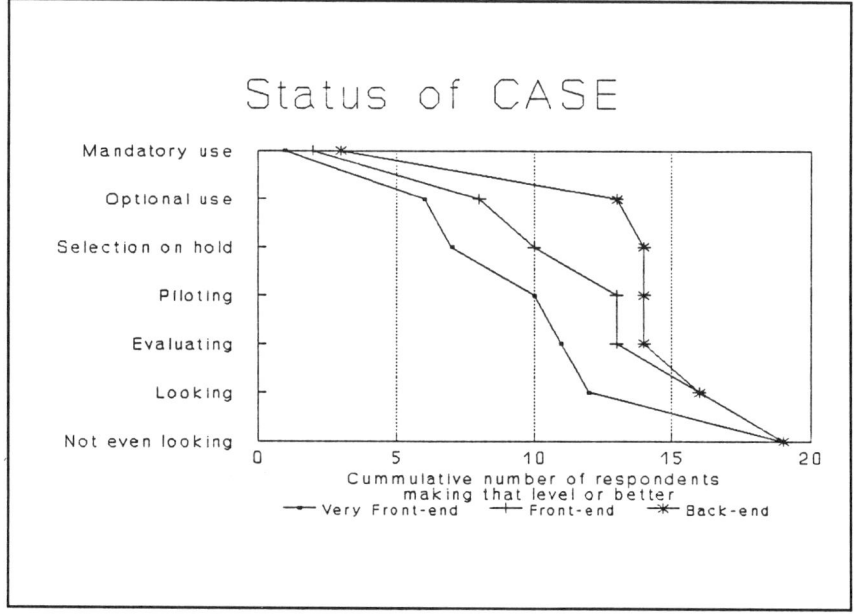

Figure 5: Status of the Different Types of CASE Tools in the Organizations

Focus of Responsibility for CASE

Twelve of the nineteen respondents indicated the points of responsibility for CASE. Of those, eleven identified a champion who was generally within IS. In two cases, the champion was in both the IS and the customer or user side. A champion is a person with substantial peer influence who has the ear and respect of management. This person takes upon him/herself the responsibility for making successful use of CASE technology. The champions identified were generally high ranking officials of the corporation. Figure 6 shows the level of the highest ranking champions for CASE.

The individuals making the decision to adopt or acquire CASE are also high ranking officials. Most of the respondents placed this responsibility with the vice president or head of IS, or with the senior vice president or CIO. Figure 7 shows the position of the person who makes (or made) the decision to adopt CASE.

IS Development Methodologies

The survey respondents identified several methodologies in use

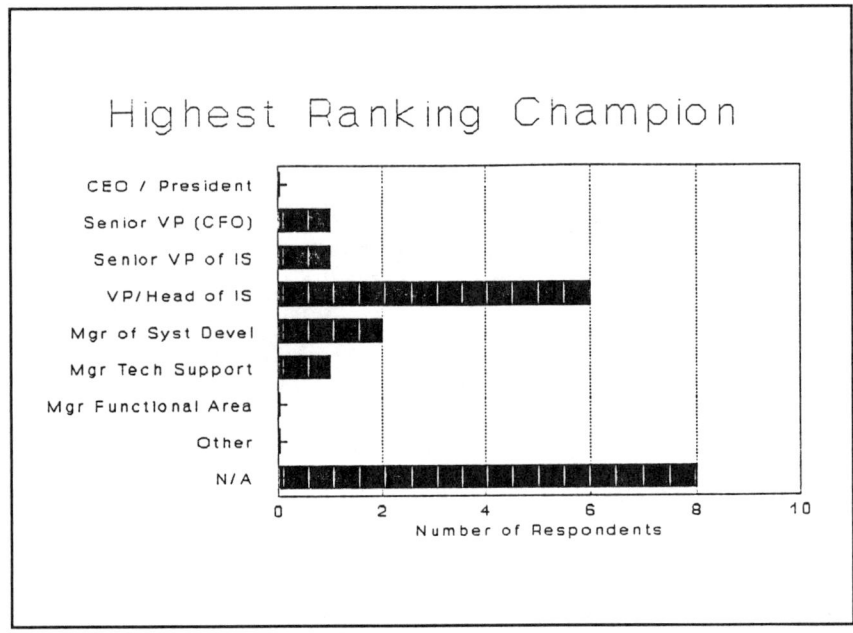

Figure 6: Highest Ranking Champions for CASE

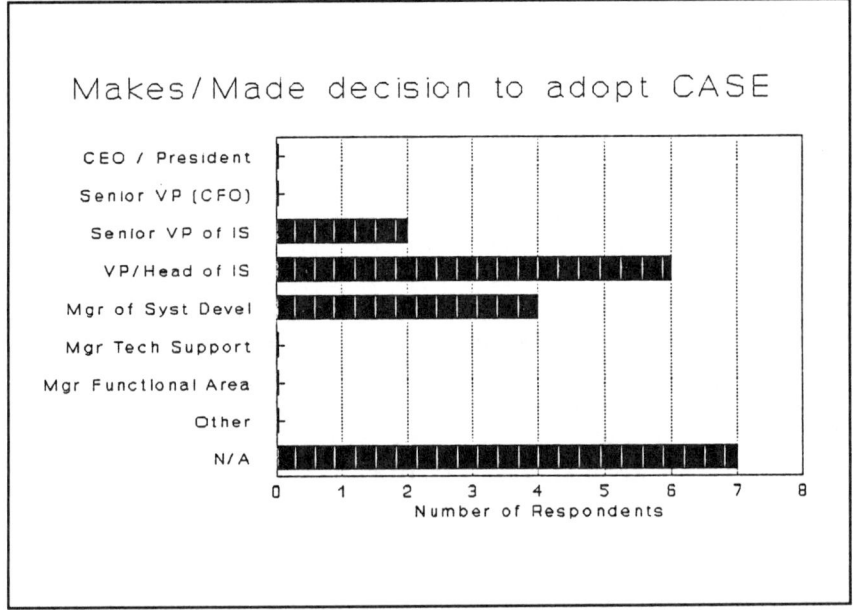

Figure 7: Decision Maker for the Adoption of CASE

			Methodologies		
NUMBER RESP	NAME	% USE	USE	PROJ REQUIRED	TRAINING
4	Info Engnrg	10-50%	++	++/+	
3	SDM	10-90%	==	+	
2	Method/1	20-80%	++/+	+	
2	Dickinson	33-85%	++	++	
4	(internal)	60-100%	==	==	

CODING:
- — Decreasing Much
- - Decreasing
- == Stable
- + Increasing
- ++ Increasing Much

Table 1: IS Development Methodologies in Use

for the development of information systems. Table 1 lists the methodologies reported by the most organizations. The table presents the methodologies' estimated use, expected growth in usage, and training required.

The use of older methodologies appears to have stabilized. They generally require some moderate amount of training. Implementation of newer methodologies requires substantial training, and their use is expected to increase substantially.

The survey suggested 11 reasons or objectives for the initial justification of the methodology, and asked whether those objectives had been achieved. Two objectives stood out from the rest (the number following in parentheses indicates the number of respondents citing that reason in their top five).

- Improved system quality (18).
- Improved communication between end users and designers/developers (17).

Another five were mentioned with about the same frequency:

- Reduced IS development effort/cost (11).
- Reduced maintenance effort/cost (11).
- Introduce discipline and structured methods (10).
- Better documentation (9).
- Better tracking of user requirements (9).

Improved systems quality, improved communication between end users and designers/developers, and better documentation were the only objectives rated by some organizations as having been achieved. Most of the other objectives mentioned were rated as partially or not yet achieved. Only one was rated by some as having a negative impact — reduced IS development effort/cost. That is, the use of the methodology produced the opposite result from what was initially expected or desired, i.e., IS development costs increased. This could best be attributed to the "learning bubble" for the initial year or two in the use of CASE. Most of the surveyed firms had not yet reached a level of experienced mature usage of their CASE tool(s).

Six criteria for the selection of a methodology were mentioned with approximately the same frequency:

- Covered a broad range of the systems development life cycle (12).
- Compatibility with current inhouse practices (12).
- Supported with a CASE tool (11).
- Ability to modify or customize for in-house variations (11).
- Ease of use; Userfriendly forms and documents (10)
- Wide-spread use; Large installed base (8).

Characteristics and Usage of CASE Tools

Although there is a myriad of CASE tools in the market, respondents to the survey identified only 11 tools which they had evaluated or were using (see Table 2). TELON, a back-end tool, is reportedly being used in 75 to 100% of the projects in the organiza-

```
                              CASE Tools

NUMBER                              PROJECTED        TRAINING
RESP    NAME      % PROJECTS        USE             REQUIRED
------  --------  ----------------  ---------       --------
  7     IEW        5 -  60%   ++/+   ++/+
  3     IEF       10 -  40%   ++     ++
  3     TELON     75 - 100%   +      ++
  2     DESIGN/1  20 -  60%   +/==   +/==
  2     BACHMAN    5 -  20%   ++/+   +/==
  1 each PACBASE / EXCELERATOR / PROKIT / APS / SYNON / INSTALL/1

CODING:
  -       Decreasing Much
  .       Decreasing
  = =     Stable
  +       Increasing
  + +     Increasing Much
```

Table 2: CASE Tool in Use or Under Evaluation

tions that have it. The other CASE tools, generally front-end tools, are currently in use in 5 to 60% of the projects. All of the tools require substantial training, but that does not appear to have affected the adoption decision. The tools that reportedly require the most training are also among the ones with the most use and higher projected usage.

We observe that nearly all the firms selected relatively expensive CASE tools, even though many inexpensive tools were available on a PC platform. This indicates a need to survey smaller organizations regarding their use of CASE tools.

Three reasons were cited most often as the initial justification or reason for the acquisition or investigation of the tool:

- Reduced IS development efforts or costs (21).
- Improved systems quality (19).
- Reduced maintenance efforts or costs (16).

Six other factors were mentioned six to eleven times each:

- Improved communication between end-users and developers (11).
- Faster response to changing business needs (9).
- Introduce discipline and structured methods (8).
- Better tracking of user requirements (6).
- Improved system reliability (6).
- Reusable software modules (6).

Several organizations felt that improved quality and reduced maintenance had been achieved or partially achieved. Only two felt that the number one justification, reduced development effort, had been achieved. Of the second level factors that were mentioned, some organizations felt that "improved communication between end users and designer/developers", "introduced discipline", and "reusable software modules" had either been achieved or partially achieved. The top three reasons for selecting a tool were:

- How well it integrated functions and interfaces across modules (14).
- Ease of use; user-friendly graphical interface (13).
- That it covered a broad range of the systems development life cycle (13).

Additional reasons mentioned were:

- That it covered a broad range of modeling support (data, process, realtime) (10).

- Vendor reputation, strength, and support of the product (10).
- Compatibility with other CASE tools (8).
- Widespread use; large installed base (8).

Among the reason for NOT accepting a tool, survey respondents cited:

- Lack of support for management functions(6).
- Difficult to use (4).
- Lack of compatibility with other CASE tools (4).
- High price (4).

The survey also reveals that the acquisition and use of CASE tools tended to be somewhat later than the adoption of system development methodologies.

Overall Organizational Impact and Evaluation

The last part of the survey consisted of a series of open ended questions about the impact of CASE in the organization. Respondents in this section generally agreed that it was too early to determine whether the introduction of CASE technology had been a success. However, factors such as training, top management support, good management of expectations, and a good pilot project were identified as keys to a better implementation of CASE tools.

Most organizations have not yet experienced any significant changes to the organizational structure or operation of the IS department in response to the introduction and use of CASE methodologies and/or tools. Two organizations mentioned, however, that they had set up a development center to support the use of CASE technology.

When asked about the reaction of the systems development staff to CASE, several organizations indicated excitement and positive acceptance among the less experienced personnel. At the same time, they reported a skeptical and apprehensive reaction from seasoned, more experienced systems development personnel. Evidently, less experienced people are searching for assistance in ways to approach the development of information systems and welcome the guidelines of a methodology and the use of a CASE tool. On the other hand, experienced personnel seem to resent and resist being told how to develop information systems. They have become comfortable with their own, sometimes individualized, approaches to systems development and documentation. The message to management is to be cautious in the introduction of CASE tools, so as not to lose their best and most experienced systems development people.

Two thirds of the respondents reported a positive change in the established working relationship with end users. They used phrases like "became full participants", "better communication", and "improved modeling."

When asked what they would do differently, nearly half of the respondents mentioned the importance of a pilot project — doing one at all, selecting it carefully, and picking a small one. Several also mentioned the importance of education and training —doing more of it earlier in the introduction of CASE. Regarding what to do differently, one respondent said they would introduce the methodology first, before introducing the CASE tool.

LIMITATIONS OF THE STUDY

This is an exploratory study. The objective was to identify the general characteristics of organizations using CASE successfully and to share advice on what these companies considered the critical success factors in the introduction and use of CASE. The reduced sample size and the sampling procedure limit the degree to which results can be safely generalized, although the survey was designed to maximize the accuracy and usefulness of the results obtained by directing it to the most qualified person to respond to it in the organization. Further testing of the same instrument with other populations has produced similar results (Everest, 1990). This increases the level of confidence in the findings of this survey.

CONCLUSIONS AND FURTHER RESEARCH

The results of this study indicate that organizations are at different stages of adoption for the different levels of CASE tools; back-end tools are more widely spread than very-front-end tools. Among the possible explanations for this phenomenon is that back-end tools are easier to evaluate and understand, and that tools of this class have been around longer.

Large companies seem to be further along in the process of selecting and adopting CASE tools. This can be attributed to the fact that they have more resources. Other possible explanations are that they may need more complex or accurate information systems, and they may be willing to experiment with possible solutions earlier than smaller companies.

The responses to the initial justification questions and to the selection or rejection criteria indicate that the success of CASE is due more to increases in quality than it is to reductions in development efforts and cost. That is perhaps one of the reasons why although high cost was mentioned as a drawback of CASE tools, the most expensive tools were also among the most popular ones. None of the comparatively inexpensive PC-based CASE tools were even mentioned by any of the respondents, even though some of them may have greater functionality than the more popular and expensive systems running on minicomputer or mainframe platforms.

Although some organizations have had CASE tools for some time, most agree that it is still too early to clearly identify positive results. However, survey respondents identified factors such as having top-management support, conducting a good pilot project, and not over selling the tools as key to the success of CASE. Among the recommendations to tool designers is that tool users value ease of use, compatibility, and integration in a CASE tool.

This study records the experiences of medium to large size corporations, and the results provide a preliminary list of *factors* that the respondents considered important to the successful implementation of CASE technology in an organization. Practitioners can benefit by considering those factors in their implementations. Researchers can find a list of testable hypotheses and researchable issues in the users' experiences.

Editor's Note
A copy of the survey instrument used to collect the data for this chapter is available from: Prof. Gordon C. Everest, University of Minnesota, Carlson School of Management, 271-19 Avenue S., 395 HHH, Minneapolis, MN 55455 VOICE: 612-624-0854, FAX: 612-626-1316 E-Mail: EVEREST@UMNSOM.BITNET.

REFERENCES

Alanis, Macedonio, and Gordon C. Everest (1989), "Factores a Considerar en la Selección de Herramientas de Ingeniería de Software," *Memorias del XIV Simposium Internacional de Sistemas Computacionales*, ITESM, Monterrey, Mexico, 1989 April.

Case, Albert F. Jr. (1986), *Information Systems Development Principles of Computer-Aided Software Engineering*, Prentice-Hall, Englewood Cliffs, NJ, 1986, 238 pages.

Case, Albert F. (1985), "Computer-Aided Software Engineering (CASE): Technology for Improving Software Development Productivity," *Data Base* (17:1), 1985 Fall, pages 35-42.

Chen, M., Jay F. Nunamaker, and Sue Weber (1989), "Computer-Aided Software Engineering: Present Status and Future Directions," *Data Base* (20:3), 1989 Spring, pages 7-13.

Davis, Gordon B. and Margrethe H. Olson (1985), *Management Information*

Systems: Conceptual Foundations, Structure, and Development, McGraw-Hill, 1985.

Davis, Gordon B. (1987), "Evaluation of Computer Aided Software Engineering Packages," Information Technology - *Journal of the Singapore Computer Society* (1:4), 1987 December, pages 51-55.

Davis, D. and R. M. Cosenza (1985), *Business Research for Decision Making*, Kent Publishing Company, Boston, MA, 1985, pages 101-104.

Emory, C. W. (1980), Business Research Methods, Richard D. Irwin, Homewood, IL, 1980, pages 214-256.

Everest, Gordon C. (1990), Presentations for Index Group, Cambridge, MA, 1990 February and May.

Everest, Gordon C. and Macedonio Alanis (1991), "Selecting Computer Aided Software Engineering Tools," MISRC Working Paper Series, MIS Research Center, University of Minnesota, Minneapolis, MN, 1989 February, (revision forthcoming).

Fisher, Alan S. (1988), *CASE — Using Software Development Tools*, John Wiley & Sons, NY, 1988.

Gibson, M. L. (1989), "The CASE Philosophy," *Byte* (14:4), 1989 April, pages 209-218.

Glass, M. C., J. G. Hughes, W. Johnston, and I. McChesney, (1989) "Critical Analysis of Tools for Computer-Aided Software Engineering," *Information and Software Technology* (31:9), 1989 November, pages 486-496.

Henderson, J.C. and Cooprider (1990), "Dimensions of I/S Planning and Design Aids: A Functional Model of CASE Technology," *Information Systems Research* (1:3), 1990.

Henderson, J. C., and J. G. Sifonis (1989), "A Model Predicts Future Use of CASE Technology," *Chief Information Officer Journal*, Fall, pages 5-10.

Hughes, Cary T. and Jon D. Clark (1990), "The Stages of CASE Usage," *Datamation*, 1990 February 1, pages 41-44.

Humphrey, Watts S. (1989), *Managing the Software Process*, Addison-Wesley, Reading, MA, 1989.

Jenkins, Milton (1984), "Research Methodologies and MIS Research," Indiana University Discussion Paper No. 277, Indiana University, 1984.

Kemerer, Chris F. (1988), "An Agenda for Research in the Managerial Evaluation of Computer-Aided Software Engineering (CASE) Tool Impacts," *Proceedings of the 22nd Hawaii International Conference on System Sciences*, 1989 January.

Loh, M. and R. R. Nelson (1989), "Reaping CASE Harvest," *Datamation* (35:13), 1989 July 1, pages 31-34.

McClure, Carma (1989), "The CASE Experience," *Byte* (4:14), 1989 April, pages 235-244.

Moad, Jeff (1990), "The Software Revolution," *Datamation*, 1990 February 15, pages 22-30.

Necco, C.R., N.W. Tsai, & K. W. Holgeson (1989), "Current Usage of CASE Software," *Journal of Systems Management* (40:5), 1989 May, p.6-11

Norman, Ronald J. and Jay F. Nunamaker (1989), "Integrated Development Environments: Technological and Behavioral Productivity Perceptions," *Proceedings of the 22nd Hawaii International Conference on System Sciences*, 1989 January.

Norman, Ronald J. and Jay F. Nunamaker (1988), "An Empirical Study of Information Systems Professionals' Productivity Perceptions of CASE Technology," *Proceedings of the Ninth ICIS Conference*, Minneapolis, MN.

Olle, T. William, et.al. (1991), *Information Systems Methodologies*, second edition, Addison-Wesley.

Orlikowski, Wanda J. (1988), "CASE Tools and the IS Workplace: Some Findings from Empirical Research," *Proceedings of the 1988 ACM SIGCPR Conference on the MIS Personnel*, College Park, MD.

Rochester, Jack B. (1989), "Building More Flexible Systems," *I/S ANALYZER*

(27:10), 1989 October, 16 pages.

Stamps, D. (1987), "CASE: Cranking Out Productivity," Datamation (33:13), July 1, pages 55-58.

Statland, N. (1989), "Payoffs Down the Pike: A CASE Study," *Datamation* (35:7), 1989 April 1, p.32.

Yourdon, E. (1986), "What Ever Happened to Structured Analysis?," *Datamation*, June 1, pps 133-138.

Zachman, John A. (1987), "A Framework for Information Systems Architecture," *IBM Systems Journal* (26:3), 1987.

Section III

Methodology Issues in Existing CASE Tools and Methods

CHAPTER NINE

Flexible CASE Tools for Information Systems Planning

Robert A. Stegwee
University of Groningen

Ria M.C. van Waes
Coopers & Lybrand Management Consultants

Current Computer Aided Systems Engineering (CASE) tools in the area of Information Systems Planning (ISP) are usually specifically designed to support a particular ISP method. Furthermore, these CASE tools usually support only the planning products, not the planning process. However, if we look at an ISP method and compare the prescribed output with the actual planning products in a practical project, we often see substantial differences. From these observations we conclude that current CASE tools for ISP are not successful yet. What causes the differences between method and practice is the evolution of ISP towards a more business oriented planning approach. This changing approach calls for new and different kinds of models to be developed and used in an ISP study. In order to use CASE tools in such an environment, an ISP tool has to be tailored to the specific needs of the situation. The tool itself should provide facilities for introducing new modeling techniques. This can be realized by modifications in the meta-model of the tool. If we do not control such modifications we run the risk that ISP tools will once again become simple drawing assistants. A way in which the modifications of the meta-model can be controlled is by means of a meta-model for the meta-data in the encyclopedia. With an example, based upon current research on ISP tools, we will show that such an approach is feasible.

Information Systems Planning (ISP) is a study leading to the definition of information systems necessary to support (part of) an organization. The deliverables include architectures specifying the information systems that have to be developed or maintained, the organizational layout that coordinates these development and maintenance tasks, and the technical infrastructure that supports the information systems. These architectures are based upon an assessment of, among others, business functions and processes, organizational structure, available data collections, and current information systems.

It can be imagined that a lot of data has to be handled during an ISP project. Therefore, computer based tools can be used to enable the efficient and effective usage of this data. These tools are known as Computer Aided Systems Engineering (CASE) tools. Only a limited number of CASE tools are suited for application within an ISP study, in which case they could be termed ISP tools. The tools commercially available today are often developed for use within a particular ISP method, and hence they are very specific in the kind of data they can handle. Practical experience has shown that such tools are of limited use in an actual ISP study (Brinkkemper, 1990; Wijers, 1991).

Because ISP is a relatively new field, rapid changes are taking place in ISP practice, which gives rise to new requirements for CASE support for ISP. A trend can be observed which includes more business strategic aspects in the ISP process, calling for new and different kinds of models and architectures to be developed and used in an ISP study. An examination of some typical ISP results, produced during practical ISP projects the authors took part in, leads to the conclusion that ISP methods are used creatively. Additions to the method are implemented according to the needs of the particular situation in which the ISP study is carried out. Based upon previous research on the role of architectures within an ISP study (Van Waes, 1991), one can conclude that the type of models that are to be used depends upon the specifics of the organization. Therefore, it can not only be observed, but it is also necessary to amend ISP methods in a practical situation. Such flexible application of ISP methods requires equally flexible support by CASE tools.

This chapter addresses the requirements for future CASE tools for ISP, based upon the changing practice of ISP in the field. The focus will be on the product side of ISP tools, as process support has not yet been implemented by any tool. Process support can be regarded as a necessary component of ISP tools, but little or no reported research addresses this issue. Building upon the product requirements for ISP tools, directions for improvement will be formulated. The discussion is structured along the following lines.

To clarify the topic of this paper, the next section examines current Information Systems Planning practice. Section 3 highlights the necessity of computer based support of ISP, an indication is given of the ISP tools available on the market today, and an assessment is given based upon practical experience in using these tools. Section 4 gives an overview of the changes taking place in the ISP field. These changes are the basis for the formulation of the requirements for future ISP tools. In section 5, a description is given of an approach for the technical implementation of these new requirements.

INFORMATION SYSTEMS PLANNING (ISP)

History of ISP

Over the past few decades, Information Systems Planning (ISP) has become an issue of major importance for many organizations. Reasons for planning and managing the future development of information systems include the need to integrate previously isolated information systems (thus reducing the extent of 'automation islands'), the wish to align information systems with organizational goals and structures, and the ambition of management to come to grips with expenditure on information systems and to acquire the means of controlling the development process. In order to achieve these objectives, both researchers and practitioners started to think about something similar to ISP in the seventies, although they didn't call it ISP at the time. Since then there has been a rapid development of ISP concepts, partly based on practical projects and experiments. A firm step was made with the emergence of methods to support information systems planning: a more or less standard approach to ISP was developed, the desired deliverables were stipulated, and the place of ISP in the organization was discussed. The emergence of this approach, as represented by Business Systems Planning (IBM, 1984) and its derivatives, was a major reason for many organizations to start ISP projects.

A number of well defined stages may be discerned in the growth of information systems planning, e.g. as described by Marchand and Horton (1986). These stages, summarized in Table 1, may be pictured as phases on a learning curve (comparable with that described by Nolan, 1979). Since different organizations formulated ISP methods and implemented ISP at times up to a decade apart, the timing of the various stages shown in Table 1 is merely indicative. The stages are distinguished on the basis of:

- the responsibility for information management (IM),
- the objectives,
- the role of information technology (IT) within the organization,
- the focus of the planning process, and
- the role of business management in the planning process.

ISP started in the mid-sixties, under the name of EDP (electronic data processing) management, as a result of dissatisfaction with the information systems in use and the huge application backlog experienced by most EDP departments. This was stage I, representing the first steps in the development of information systems planning.

Stage II started with the appearance of formal ISP methods such as *Business Systems Planning* (BSP), widening the scope of the information systems planning process to include business functions and goals in addition to purely IT-related factors. Both business and IT trends triggered a profound change in the way organizations looked at their information resources in the course of this stage.

Stage III has seen the impact of IT on business and the evolution of architectures growing to maturity, and information managers aiming at an integrated approach to organizational and IT issues.

Stage IV lies still in the future, but we believe that the principal aim here will be to cope with 'raplexity' (rapid changes in a complex environment) while increasing the potential for practical application.

	Stage I First steps (1965-1975)	Stage II Growth (1975-1985)	Stage III Towards maturity (1985 to date)	Stage IV Maturity (future)
Responsibility for IM	EDP Management	Strategic Information Management	Information Management	Business Information Management
Objectives	Efficiency Effectiveness	Alignment Integration Prioritization	Strategic Impact Business Innovation	Cope with dynamic situation
Role of IT	IT introduction isolated	IT expansion Integrated Re-active	IT exploitation Cross-boundary Pro-active	Interdependencies integral part of business activities
Focus	Technology	Information	Organization Communication	Environment
Role of Business Management	Awareness	Involvement	Responsibility	Use

Table 1: The Evolution of Information Systems Planning

Dynamic models will have to be able to adapt rapidly, and without major problems, to business changes, showing the modified specification for the information supply in a number of consistent architectural models.

ISP Methods

In response to the problems mentioned above, the mid-seventies witnessed the development of methods specifically intended to precede system development. One of the first and best known of these was BSP (Business Systems Planning), and many others were derived from it. The essence of these and other ISP methods is dealt with in the book Strategic Data-Planning Methodologies by James Martin (1982). These methods stress top-down planning of data and localized design of systems in the different user areas. They take the view that information is a corporate asset and should be planned on a corporate basis. Major objectives are: a better alignment of IT applications with business requirements, integration of IS applications, and prioritization of development projects. The methods are strongly data-oriented, and stress the need for top management involvement. For the first time, organized information systems planning was recognized as an indispensable means of controlling an organization's information resources.

Outline of a Classical ISP Methodology. As mentioned above, many ISP methods stem from BSP (IBM, 1984), like Information Engineering (Martin, 1982; Arthur Young, 1988; Hackathorn & Karimi, 1988), Information Systems Study (IBM, 1986) and Strategic Information Management Planning (Gallo, 1988). Some of these add new concepts, such as critical success factors (Rockart, 1979), to the original BSP set of concepts.

In essence, they all follow the main lines shown in Figure 1 (see also Earl, 1989). First, the business strategy derived from the organization's stated mission is formulated in terms of organizational goals and critical success factors. The prevailing IT trends and opportunities are then analyzed to identify new application areas and alternative technical architectures.

Next, an inventory is made of the information systems currently installed in the organization, with comments from both users and (information) technical staff. The information architecture is specified by means of a process model specially developed for the organization, an entity model summarizing the data that has to be stored, and a matrix showing which data is created, retrieved, updated or deleted by which process. The logical information architecture is then manipulated to give the systems architecture specifying individual information systems. The organizational architecture determines the tasks, personnel, and coordinating mechanisms needed to develop and support the information systems. A transition path indicating how to reach the new environment (described by the architectures) from the old, is accompanied by a set of policy statements governing the transition. All these elements form the basis for development of an IT project portfolio and Information Systems Plan.

The rise of ISP methods was accompanied by a growing awareness that information, as one of the principal resources of the organization, had to be planned and managed alongside computers and other EDP resources (see e.g. McFarlan & McKenney, 1983). In particular, the awareness that a long-term information systems plan can only be derived from a stable information base, led to a more data-driven approach and triggered a fundamental look at the information flows throughout the organization. This increased interest in information led to the creation of positions like Information Manager and Data Administrator, and the formulation of an information systems strategy prior to the execution of an ISP project.

All ISP methods stress the need for top-management involvement, especially for determining business objectives and identifying critical success factors. In practice, however, top management still

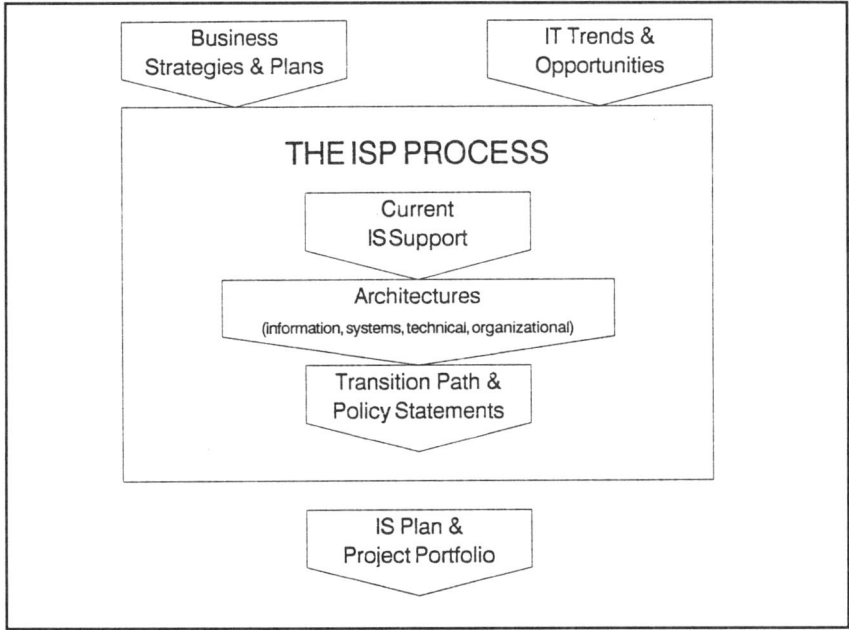

Figure 1: The Basic Elements of a Stage II ISP Method

delegated information matters to subordinates or staff. Apparently, they had not yet recognized the strategic impact information technology can have on the organization (Lederer & Mendelow, 1986 & 1987). This impact was well recognized by those involved in the ISP process, who now were looking for ways of integrating information systems strategy with the strategy for the organization as a whole - a prime characteristic of stage III information systems planning. In fact, a ferment of change ran through the entire second half of stage II. We will discuss this in the next section, as a prologue to our description of the marked methodological changes which began to take effect around 1985.

Prevalent ISP Practice

The original ISP methods described in the previous section were primarily intended as tools for control, planning, and priority setting, which would enable EDP staff to deal with the enormous and still growing backlog in application development and maintenance in the automation field. The approach was data-driven: an integrated map of all the organization's information requirements was made, and served as a basis for the definition of a number of system development projects. The business objectives and strategies formulated by management were then used to set priorities.

But the world was and is changing. IT trends are towards proliferation of a large number of small processing units: the demands concerning flexibility and dynamism are increasing. The changes in the business world are even more important: technology push is giving way to market pull.

Changes in the Content of ISP. It should be clear from the above that the classical approach towards IT, based upon information engineering, is no longer adequate: a more business-oriented, dynamic and flexible approach is needed. This change in paradigm has considerable consequences for the ISP function:

From an isolated to an integrated discipline - Information systems planning needs to become an integral part of business management, and not just a separate discipline as it is nowadays. Every line function comprises some information tasks, and it is a logical consequence for ISP to become an integral part of the responsibility of line managers. The resulting procedures for ISP will then resemble procedures found in other disciplines like personnel or finance: strong integration with other functions, a clear set of rules to organize the activities involved, and a small team to put these rules into practice and fill in the details.

From methods to a toolkit approach - Secondly, the performance of ISP tasks will tend to be supported not by rigid, all embracing methods, but by ISP toolkits, comprising a wide variety of approaches, methods, and techniques. Examples of what might constitute such a toolkit are reference architectures (as analytical tools and road maps for future developments), knowledge and vision of business and IT trends, assessment and auditing techniques, methods and techniques in the fields of brainstorming, workshops and project management, and approaches to business analysis and improvement.

From a static to a dynamic approach - The main function of information systems planning has for a long time been the recognition of IT applications, and the design of (more or less static) working systems to realize them. This function will of course not disappear completely, but it will tend to be largely replaced by a more adaptive, assimilative approach. In line with this, new demands such as open-endedness, future-proofing and transparency (Truijens et al., 1990) will tend to be made on the infrastructure. The visions, methods and tools on both the demand side (business and information systems planning) and the supply side (hardware and software suppliers) will have to adapt to these changed requirements.

The objectives of this new style of information systems planning may be found by consolidating existing objectives and adding a few new ones. The main items in this list are:

- visualizing the contributions IT can make to the business; This visualization can be both reactive and pro-active, i.e. it may consider IT both in a supportive role and as trigger for renewal of business structures.
- identifying IT application areas and setting priorities;
- integrating IT applications;
- controlling IT expenditures;
- providing an infrastructure that responds to the above-mentioned demands.

Characteristics of an ISP Study. The essential elements of a Stage III ISP study are summarized in Figure 2. Such a study starts with an assessment of the current organization and its IT applications, and aims at building a realistic picture of the desired future situation. The assessment of the current situation defines the starting point and estimates the organization's ability to reach the defined goals. The current and future situations are linked by the business strategy and the accompanying IT strategy. The structures (architectures) shown provide the backbone needed to give form to and constrain these strategies. The route is split up into projects that match the strategies and architectures selected.

There are two main lines of entry to such an ISP study, one exploring the business activities to be supported by IT and the other tracing the IT opportunities available. The essence of ISP lies in following these lines in parallel, continuously confronting business and information views and focusing on opportunities for improving one's way of doing business.

The IT trends and opportunities detected indicate which IT tools can support business performance, or even transform the business to yield a competitive advantage in the marketplace. The resulting IT strategy provides a framework for decision-making about priorities for, and use of, IT by the company.

Once ISP has been well established and integrated into the business planning framework, most of the activities indicated above can be carried out following routine procedures. Here, architectures will certainly play a powerful role in IT policy formulation, and in presenting this policy to the organization. However, more is needed to establish a sound basis for a company-wide, integrated, transparent, information systems network. Much of this additional input will come from additional ISP studies, which take a deeper, closer look at the underlying factors. The models used will have a vital, creative

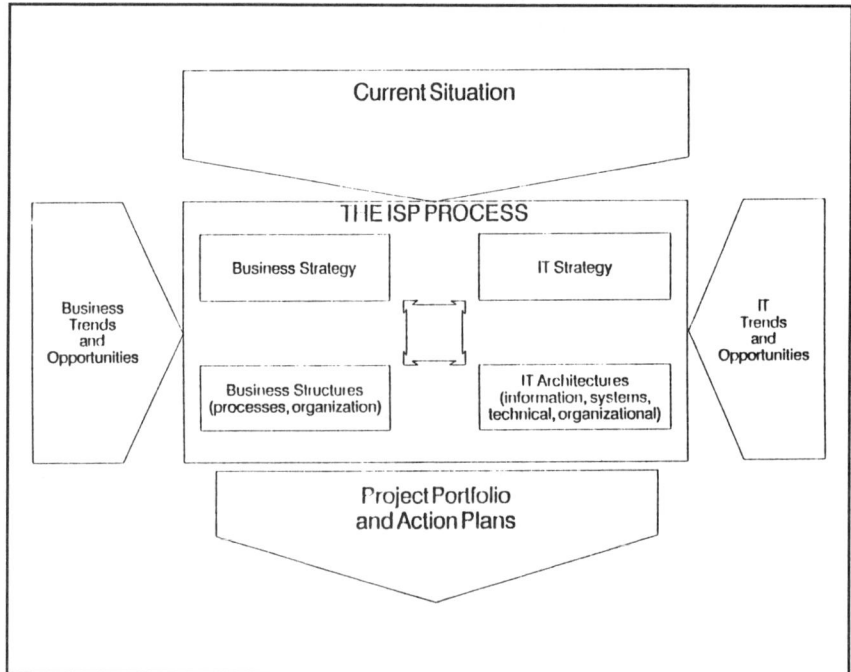

Figure 2: Components of a Stage III ISP Method

role to play here. They will also establish sound action plans for systems development and implementation. CASE tools can be used to support the tasks of creating and maintaining these models.

CURRENT NEED AND USE OF CASE TOOLS IN ISP

The Need for ISP Tools

In order to analyze the need for computer based support for the ISP process, it is helpful to look upon ISP as a modeling activity with respect to information systems support within the organization. Tools for ISP then are supposed to support the different components of modeling. Wijers has arranged these components into a framework for understanding information systems development (Wijers, 1991, p. 14), but they seem to apply to ISP as well. He discerns the following components.

- *Way of thinking.* This reflects the underlying philosophy used to inspect organizations and information systems. It is the set of considerations that influences the process of image construction (see e.g. Bosman, 1977).
- *Way of controlling.* This reflects the managerial activities around a modeling process.
- *Way of modeling.* The product oriented side of information systems development is confusingly called the way of modeling. Way of representing would be a more appropriate term, as it stands for the concepts and terminology used for the models to be produced and their interrelationships.
- *Way of working.* The process oriented side of modeling structures the way in which models are developed.
- *Way of supporting.* A modeling process can be supported by a wide variety of possibly computer based tools. The availability of such tools will influence the modeling process.

A more concise description of the components of a modeling process, and hence of an ISP method, will be used here. As it is our intention to focus on support for information systems planning, the way of supporting, mentioned above, is left out in this context. Including it would suggest that the development of support tools is dependent on currently existing support. Apart from overlap with existing tools, this is not the case. Furthermore, managerial activity is not taken into account separately here. Hence, the components of an ISP method can be given as follows (see also Olle et al., 1988;

Seligmann et al., 1989):

- the philosophy or world view (way of thinking),
- the procedures or steps to be taken (way of working/controlling), and
- the representational conventions (way of representing).

These components do not stand on their own, but are closely related. The philosophy or world view indicates the way in which the procedures are to be carried out. These procedures can not be written down if the representational conventions are not known. However, in order to distinguish the kinds of support an ISP-tool provides, the above distinctions are necessary. Support for a modeling process can be developed in either of the areas mentioned above. However, support for the philosophy or world view is a little hard to imagine, hence the focus will be on the latter two. In current practice, we see a strong accent on the support of operational tasks, especially the representation facilities. The formalized models and designs of one or more methods are then supported by a tool. In this chapter, we will keep the focus on the requirements for ISP tools in the representation area. Other research is addressing CASE tool support for the other aspects of the design environment (see e.g. Wijers & Heijes, 1990).

Several tools have been developed to support the representational aspects needed within the kind of ISP studies described above. One reason for the development of such tools is the overwhelming number of ingredients in the various models and architectures employed in an ISP method. For example, the Business Systems Inventory Model, as employed in *Strategic Information Management Planning* (Gallo, 1988) consists of 17 different items, ranging from organization, function, and process to data structure, hardware, and communication systems. Arthur Young's (1988) planning method specifies a knowledge base consisting of 33 entity types and the various relations between them. When considering the number of occurrences for each entity type, BSP suggests 30-60 business processes and a comparable number of data classes (IBM, 1984). In total, this might lead us to well over a thousand elements to handle. James Martin (1982) advocates an even more fine-grained modeling approach and concludes that computerized tools for ISP are indispensable.

Another basis for the development of ISP tools can be found in the fact that during the ISP process, the various charts have to be revised and updated, which can become quite tedious. Furthermore, consistency checks and version control need to be performed in such a dynamic environment. Manual checking of these consistencies is not feasible.

Finally, the integration of different phases in a systems development environment is mentioned as yet another reason to construct tools for ISP (Parker, Trainor & Benson, 1989). Such integrated CASE tools, or second generation CASE tools, cover all the phases in systems development, from planning to implementation, with usage of design data and checking of consistency across phases (Staring, 1989).

Current CASE Support for ISP

The range of CASE tools offered on the market today is overwhelming. In a recent study Rock-Evans gives an overview of 66 Analyst Workbenches (Rock-Evans, 1989). Some of these workbenches also offer support for ISP. Well-known examples are Excelerator, the Information Engineering Facility, the Information Engineering Workbench, and the System Development Workbench. Other tools have been developed specifically for ISP support, like ISMOD by IBM.

Current tools, as far as they are suited for use within ISP, are strongly oriented towards the modeling support as required in BSP-like methods. Evaluating the currently supported modeling techniques for the ISP stage, we find facilities that support the development of high level models showing: business processes, business functions, subject areas, entities and their relationships, how data is currently stored, how business functions are currently performed, the organizational structure of the enterprise, how the enterprise is distributed geographically, development projects, enterprise information needs, etc.

Apart from these high level models, most tools provide association matrices to perform cross analyses between any two aspects of the strategic plan. For example, the tools help in defining a systems architecture (using association matrices) by grouping data and activities into potential subject databases and applications. Figure 3 visualizes the main model-types as supported by most of the tools mentioned.

Technically speaking, the functionality of ISP modules within CASE tools is usually limited to Decomposition Diagrams, Entity Diagrams, Property Matrices, and Association Matrices. The objects that can be modeled through these tools differ. Some tools, like Excelerator's PC-Prism and the System Development Workbench, leave it to the user to specify which objects should be charted in either the decomposition diagram or the association matrix. This, of

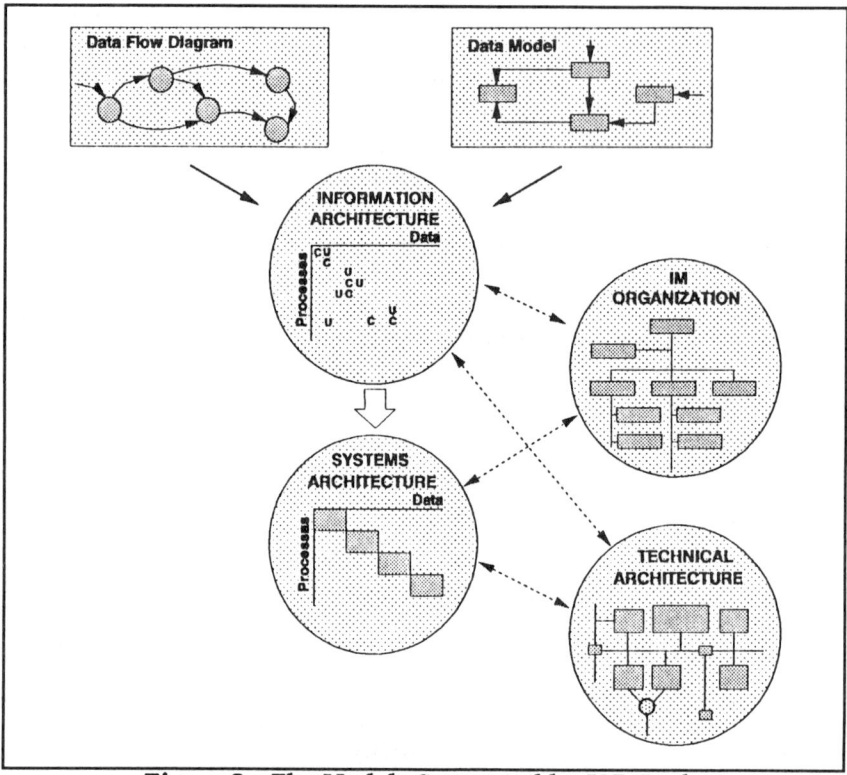

Figure 3: The Models Supported by ISP Tools

course, has severe implications for the validation and consistency checking capabilities of the tool, which are almost absent. Another problem arises with the integration of these objects in the system encyclopedia or repository, and the use of them in other modules of the workbench. Some CASE tools, such as Maestro, offer extensive customization capabilities to overcome these problems. However, in practice the customization process proves to be quite complicated and discussions about the objects, rules, and diagramming techniques that have to be implemented can turn into endless quarrels (Hoogland, 1990).

The Information Engineering Facility (IEF) and Information Engineering Workbench (IEW) take an opposite view. They have predefined objects and associations for the planning phase, strictly following the Information Engineering Methodology. Thus, they provide (very limited) support for the higher levels of the design environment, i.e. the philosophy and the methodology. A comparative study of the two products states that IEW has more extensive support for planning than IEF (Staring, 1989). The differences can

Information Systems Planning   261

mainly be found in the area of information needs identification, where IEW supports the concepts of Management by Objectives and Critical Success Factors. This support, however, is still limited to the definition of objectives or CSFs, assigning properties (e.g. relative importance), and relating them to other objects by means of association matrices. Both products support some kind of affinity analysis within an association matrix for the formation of business areas or information subsystems.

The ISMOD product (IBM, 1986) is more specifically aimed at the analysis of planning data, as gathered through interviews. ISMOD supports the Information Systems Study method, as developed by IBM. However, IBM itself stresses the fact that expert knowledge is needed to use ISMOD and interpret its results. Mainframe based, ISMOD lacks a friendly user interface, and as such is suitable as an analysis tool for the expert information systems planner, but not as an administrative tool for the ISP project team. As ISMOD is not part of an integrated CASE environment and is not geared to the automatic production of ISP deliverables, several advantages of computerized ISP support can not be obtained with ISMOD.

Besides these specific ISP tools, a lot of other tools are being used. These tools support modeling techniques as defined for, and used in, the systems development stage. The most well known are Data Flow diagrams (DeMarco, 1978) Entity Relationship diagrams (Chen, 1976) and ISAC Activity and Information schemata (Lundeberg et al., 1981).

Practical Experience in Using ISP Tools

To give an impression of the use of ISP tools within an ISP project, a short discussion is given of the performance of the Information Engineering Workbench. In the previous paragraph the drawbacks of other tools have been discussed. Various sources indicate the Information Engineering Workbench as one of the leading products, especially with respect to ISP, on the market today (Staring, 1989; Rock-Evans, 1989).

In general, the modeling processes in ISP are not altogether clear-cut; they are cyclic processes in which the subjective impression of the ISP team plays a major role. Therefore, lists and charts are updated a number of times, which gives good grounds for computer based support. The IEW Planning Workstation is extremely useful in updating charts, as used within information systems planning. The chart most frequently used is the association matrix between business processes and entity types, indicating the creation, retrieval, update, and deletion of instances of entity types by processes.

As this matrix forms the substance of the Systems Architecture, it is usually updated several times, when the results of earlier decompositions into information subsystems turn out to be unsatisfactory. For example, when the creation of an entity type does not fall within an information system, it usually indicates that similar entity types have erroneously been combined into one. Another possibility might be that the business processes, creating this entity type, have common components which should be specified separately. Thus, one can see that the modeling process is not an easy and routine task, but rather a creative process requiring a lot of interaction from which the final models slowly evolve.

The entity diagram, representing the company's data model, is another example of a frequently used and updated chart. Finding the proper level of detail for this data model, perhaps triggered by the specification of the Systems Architecture, causes modifications. A major drawback in this area is the impossibility to define sub- or super-entities within the IE Workbench. An aggregation of the data model to a level which is comprehensible for users and management can not be developed on the basis of a complete and detailed entity model.

The documenting capabilities of IEW are good; however, other tools are usually needed for the production of the final deliverables. For example, the decomposition of the company data model into subject areas, as displayed in figure 4, can be most helpful. This data model, drawn from the information systems plan of the CBR (Dutch bureau for certificates of driving proficiency), describes groups of entity types pertaining to theoretical exams, practical exams, external relations, and finance. Other entity types (candidate and medical status) are at a level of detail which does not call for further decomposition. Such a decomposition into subject areas can be achieved using the IEW Planning Workstation. However, a simple graphical presentation, as depicted in Figure 4, cannot be generated. The only way such a decomposition can be displayed, is in the form of a tree-like structure. A simple drawing tool, in this case GEM Draw, had to be used to create Figure 4.

Text handling within IEW proves to be awkward and slows down the workstation's performance considerably. Definitions and comments, as used within IEW, are best documented using a traditional text editor. This, however, gives rise to inconsistencies in the final report, as definitions of obsolete objects, deleted from the graphical presentations, are still in the text document, and comments on newly created objects are missing. To illustrate these kinds of problems, Martin quotes a "bitter practitioner" who commented: "A computerized design tool is a great help. Two computerized design tools are a

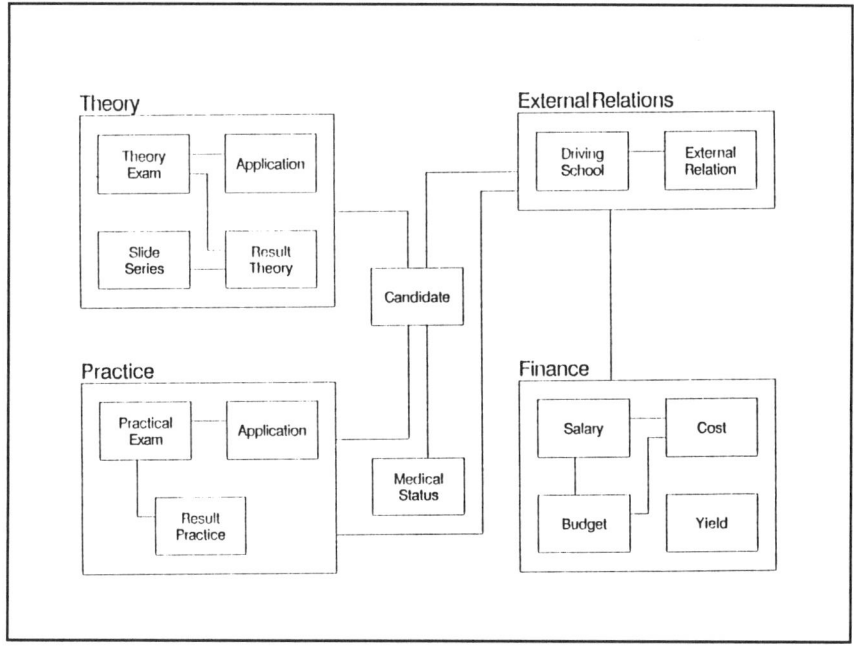

Figure 4: Company Data Model With Subject Areas for the Central Agency for Certificates of Driving Proficiency (Simplified)

disaster!" (Martin, 1982, p. 200).

Usually the ISP project team will not be able to represent all objects within the workstation's encyclopedia. Sometimes one has to use a number of tricks to get things done. For example, an inventory of current information systems has to be entered as objects of the type 'Mechanism'. The items on which the user is asked to score the information systems are usually not the same as the ones implemented in the property matrix for Mechanisms. The same holds for the Data Collections. In general, if one looks at the specification of the knowledge base in the IE method handbook (Arthur Young, 1988) and the modeling components of the IEW (KnowledgeWare, 1989), several discrepancies can be observed which have to be overcome in a practical ISP project.

Another problem exists with respect to storing matrices. In order to save the sequence of objects in a matrix, one has to introduce a dummy object and assign sequential numbers to the relation between the objects and this dummy object. Several other tricks and shortcuts are reported by members of the Dutch IEW users association, in order to fool the system's strict adherence to the Information Engineering Methodology. It seems that, in this manner, the IEW is not an optimally supportive tool for an information systems planning method and has been reduced to one of the less sophisticated administrative documenting tools.

CHANGING REQUIREMENTS FOR ISP TOOLS

The Evolution of Methods

With further elaborations of the methods in current ISP practice (see Stegwee & Van Waes, 1990), the goals and contents of the methods have been modified. Two major reasons for change lie in the increasing importance of IT for organizations and in the belief that each project needs a customized approach instead of using a standardized ISP method.

The increasing importance of IT for organizational performance and competitive edge has increased the need for a close alliance between business and IT, and requires a new emphasis on the (changing) structures of organizations and corresponding IT support. To realize this alignment, business modeling is critical. Business models are tools for business management to use when contemplating strategic changes in the business structure. In these models, the role of IT for the business can be visualized. Examples can be found in the use of IT in customer relations, IT as enabling factor to reduce planning and control levels, and IT promoting integration between business functions along the value chain. Business models are also the basis for deriving the structure of information flows and the IT infrastructure.

With the change in emphasis in ISP, the field of business modeling becomes increasingly important. And although business modeling is not exclusively dedicated to ISP, the lack of business concepts and models forces many ISP project teams to recover or initiate remedial actions. With this changing emphasis, we also find a change in the list of participants: business management is expected to play an increasingly active role.

Given the experience with ISP, we conclude that there is not a single ISP methodology that suits all organizations. A lot of contingency factors (such as size, experience, and the role of IT) influence the way any methodology needs to be customized to changing situations. Depending on the character and context of a project, different approaches and models are needed to visualize the problems and the issues to be tackled.

Information Systems Planning 265

Different Models

Within current ISP projects, IT structures are to be derived from, and attuned to, business structures. Both business structures and IT structures (structures of information, systems, hardware and software) can be represented by models (often also called architectures). Models are, generally speaking, limited representations of reality, which allow one to focus on those aspects that are of interest, given the problem at hand (De Leeuw, 1988). There are many different *types of models*. We have already introduced some of them. Since a given model simplifies reality by showing only some particular aspects of it, it is important to know what kind of model we are dealing with in a particular case; this will allow us to recognize both the limitations and the possibilities of our model.

For each type of problem, we have to choose the type of model that fits best. In this light, the model components, as provided by BSP-like methods, are no longer responsive to the new demands indicated above. For this reason some modifications were made to current ISP practice. This has resulted in a more extensive use of different types of models.

Types of models. Roughly speaking, we find four types of models being used with different functions in ISP projects (derived from Van der Poel & Van Waes, 1989).

- *Business models* make explicit the structure of the business and the way it is controlled. As such they provide communication and design tools for business management to analyze business issues like the location of decoupling points in a flow of goods, control concepts like Material Requirements Planning (MRP2), Computer Aided Manufacturing (CAM) control loops, coordination across functional boundaries etc. The resulting models facilitate management decisions regarding the business structure and indicate information performance requirements (e.g. time resolution for planning, security, etc.) that can be derived from this structure. Figure 5 represents a simplified example of a business model, showing the primary business processes and the planning and control structures.
- *Information models* (often referred to as models that visualize the information architecture) focus on the structure of the information flows and activities in an organization. As such they are further elaborations of the business models dedicated to the information aspect. These models support the users of information as well as IT professionals, and indicate information systems support functions which are usually decomposed into information modules. The

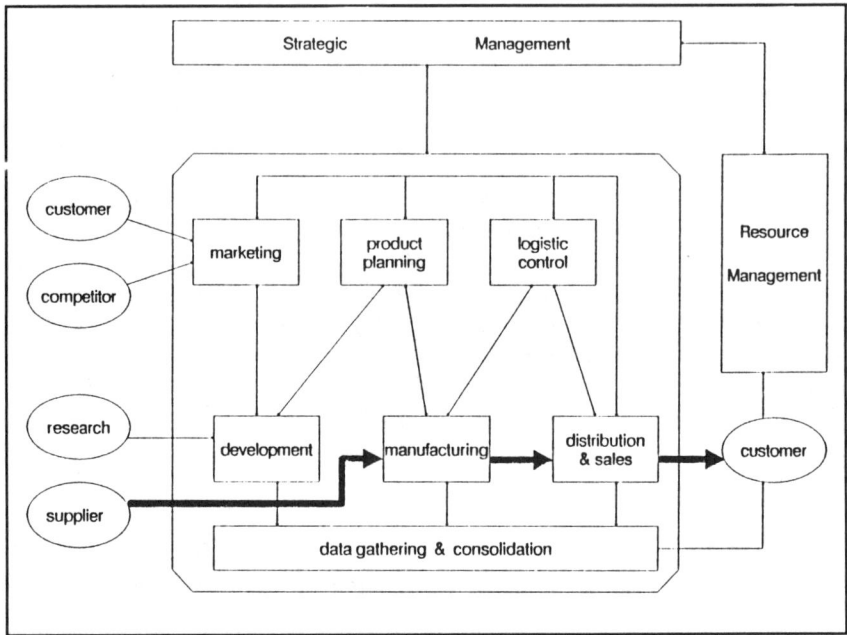

Figure 5: **Example of a Business Model (Simplified)**

relations between these modules in terms of information exchange are also part of these models. The modules should be homogeneous with respect to business oriented criteria like type of information involved and information performance requirements. The Information models serve as reference frameworks for the development of Information Systems models which describe how the former will be implemented.

- *Information Systems models* (visualizing the systems architecture) give a delimitation of information systems and their boundaries, specifying the relationships between systems and their performance requirements. These models are derived from the information models by clustering information modules, taking into account implementation constraints such as minimal data exchange, homogeneity of systems performance requirements, distribution and ownership of information systems, maintainability, etc.. They provide communication tools for business professionals and systems designers to analyze and discuss design decisions concerning things like shared versus application specific databases and monolithic versus networked structures of information systems.
- *Technical models* (representations of the technical architecture) act as blueprints for the physical implementation of information

systems, showing hardware and software facilities. These models are communication tools for business professionals and systems implementors, and may be used to analyze and discuss decisions and actions concerning the technical infrastructure of an organization. This infrastructure comprises more general means like computer hardware and operating systems, database management systems, databases, communication hardware and software, as well as more application specific means like software packages, tailor made software etc. The contents of this architecture are, among others, influenced by the present hardware and software capabilities of the organization, the quality of software packages on the market, and IT standards within the company.

Viewpoints. Within the categories of models described above, there still exists a large variety of specific models. This variety can be explained by looking at the viewpoints or orientations to be modeled. For example, a business can be modeled from an organizational point of view, showing organizational departments and their relationships, or from a data-oriented point of view, showing the major groups of entities and their interrelationships. By means of a differentiation in orientations or viewpoint, it is possible to develop different descriptions of the same organization or process. Still, each of these models is unique and stands on its own, because it serves a distinct purpose. Although lots of viewpoints can be distinguished, we limit ourselves to only the most well known: people (responsibilities), location (geography), process, object and the behavioral perspective.

Roles and Functions of Models in ISP. The roles of models have been addressed by several authors (e.g. Bertels & Nauta, 1974; De Leeuw, 1988; Emory & Cooper, 1991; In 't Veld, 1988). From this body of literature, we have developed the roles of models at different points along the systems development life cycle as follows:

- producing order in chaos, focusing attention on the problem
- guiding problem owners to ask the right questions
- forcing problem owners to explain relationships
- provoking discussion
- providing an unambiguous view of problems and solutions
- structuring the answers to the questions posed
- making decision-making transparent
- providing unambiguous specifications
- supporting use of the systems designed
- providing a tool for system re-design

As was mentioned earlier, a model can be seen as a limited representation of reality, reducing the complexity of the real world. By means of abstraction, certain aspects are left out, in order to focus on those elements that are of interest with regard to the problem at hand (De Leeuw, 1988). The main purpose of a model can be briefly restated as 'the analysis of relationships as an aid to understanding complexities in a design environment'. However, we can define a number of additional roles of models as follows:

- *a means of communication between the various actors in the design process*

Models have to *support and improve the communication process* between problem owners (business management and users) and problem solvers (IT staff/specialists, information managers, systems analysts etc.). Furthermore, they should support communication within the group and assist in arriving at a consensus and an integral view of solutions. Especially in those situations where participants with totally different backgrounds have to discuss and agree on proposals, the lay-out and contents of the models play an important role. An often mentioned example is that you better not confront management with detailed models or matrices if they cannot see the relationship between the models and their own worries or concerns. Instead, you need models that relate to management issues, as described under the 'business model' topic above. Following these lines, it can be stated that for each model, a modeling technique has to be chosen that matches:

(1) the requirements of the participants involved,
(2) the issues to be covered by the model (business concepts up to and including infrastructural issues), and
(3) the dimensions that have to be visualized by the model (control levels, responsibilities etc.).

- *a means of project control during design and realization (documentation, freezing decisions)*

Beside a means of communication, models are developed as a means to design both *business and IT structures*. As mentioned above, design is a problem solving process. Several stages can be distinguished in this process: conceptualization, analysis, choice, and implementation. The models have to answer the demands of the stage they are used in. Models could be developed for the complete route from global business structures up to and including the most detailed structures of the systems solutions. The ISP stage refers only to the global models, which provide an overall insight into the problems. Models are used in this phase to document the design results and, in this way, freeze the decisions made.

- *a means of information supply during use and maintenance of the system.*

Finally, models are used to document the design decisions and results: the models, the definitions of the elements within the models, the decisive criteria used for decisions, and the comments. The documents produced during the design phase serve as an information base during the use and maintenance of the system.

The more dynamic the environment - i.e. the higher the rate of change in the requirements - the more need there is for models. This is especially true in the operation and maintenance phases, where the system will have to be regularly modified to meet the changing requirements of the user environment.

The Need for Flexible CASE Tools

The developments within the field of ISP as described above give rise to new requirements with respect to the automated support needed for such projects. The different types of models and their specific orientation as developed within an ISP study require an ISP tool with an increased amount of flexibility. Since most ISP studies are rather unique in the kind of models they produce, the next generation of CASE tools for ISP should be customizable.

With respect to the communications aspects of ISP models and their supporting tools, we can discern the following areas of requirements. Not all requirements are directly related to flexibility, but influence the way in which flexibility is to be introduced in CASE tools.

Customization to different types of environments. The business environment determines the kinds of objects to be recognized by an ISP tool. For example, logistic decoupling points are essential in industrial environments, but not (yet) in a service environment.

Customization to different types of target groups. The viewpoints or perspectives influence the types of models to be used. In part, this is reflected in the kinds of objects to be modeled. Besides, the (graphical) representation of the objects becomes of crucial importance. Customization with respect to the target groups focuses on the way in which certain objects are to be represented. It is obvious that top management, functional specialists, and information professionals require different representations, since their day-to-day activities vary so much. Yet the objects to be represented are partly the same.

Customization to the level of abstraction. Especially in view of an integrated design environment for planning, development, and implementation of information systems, the issues of aggregation and abstraction have to be tackled. For integration between high level ISP models and detailed designs, distinctions between subject areas, entity types, and sub-entity types, and between business functions and business processes are necessary. These distinctions have not received proper treatment so far.

Accessibility of the contents of the models for all participants involved. Projects are usually not carried out in a strictly linear fashion. The parallel execution of several steps of an ISP method calls for extensive communication. The fact that different models are highly dependent on one another complicates this communication. It is essential that all team members can access the latest versions of the models under construction. The models should also be supported by automated tools to facilitate team and group communication.

Visualization of alternative solutions. Until recently, little attention has been paid within existing ISP methods to the consideration of alternatives. Partly, this is due to the fact that alternatives are not easy to communicate, since the amount of time and effort involved for proper presentation of alternative solutions is very high. This leads to a tendency to optimize certain aspects of the information systems plan, running the risk of arriving at an overall suboptimal solution.

Userfriendliness: simplicity in use and availability (always and everywhere) for the user. To optimize the process described above, the various alternative models should be accessible for the members of the project team, together with tools for the analysis of alternatives. Since this calls for interactive support, the users of ISP tools should not communicate with the tool through an expert operator, but should use the tool themselves. Indirect operation of ISP tools, if any, also introduces noise as a result of doubling the (imperfect) information channels. On the other hand, the users should not have to go through extensive training to master the use of the ISP tool. Therefore, userfriendliness is a prerequisite for successful CASE support for ISP.

The functions of an ISP tool with respect to support of design and documentation may be summarized as follows:

• supporting the design process by building up graphical information

Information Systems Planning 271

interactively;
- supporting the documentation of textual specifications, choices, and comments;
- fixing both formal and informal information; and
- guaranteeing consistency in and between the various models specified.

Furthermore, the ISP tool should be integrated in a total design environment: the tool has to be a part of an integrated toolset that covers the complete life cycle from general business problems to specific IT solutions.

From our discussion above, we can state that each particular project is influenced by:

- the type of business environment;
- the level of abstraction required;
- the types of models to be developed;
- the viewpoints and perspectives to be covered; and
- the target groups for communication.

CASE tools are needed that provide the flexibility to support these differences in circumstances. Depending on the project setting, use may be made of various modeling techniques, which in turn require flexible modeling tools. In order to be able to use CASE tools in such a flexible environment, an ISP tool has to be customizable to the specific needs of the situation. The tool itself should provide facilities for introducing new modeling techniques. In the next section the applicability of meta-modeling for the introduction of this flexibility will be discussed.

IMPLEMENTATION ASPECTS OF FLEXIBLE TOOLS

In order to outline the way in which flexibility can be introduced into CASE tools, we take a more or less formal approach towards the ISP process and its results. This formal approach, called meta-modeling, has been successfully applied in current research in the field of ISP. First a description will be given of how meta-modeling is applied and what its implications are for the design of flexible CASE tools. Next the results of meta-modeling with respect to the representational aspects of an ISP method will be presented. Finally we will show that the meta-modeling approach is feasible, by demonstrating an application of meta-modeling in the design of a decision support system for systems architecture specification.

Meta-modeling and Flexibility

Definition and examples. As information systems planning is a modeling process, support for ISP should lie in either the procedural aspect or the representational aspect of the modeling process, or both. In any case, if one considers computer based support, an information system has to be developed to support a modeling process. The development of such an information system is itself a modeling process. In order to distinguish between the two, the modeling of a modeling process is called meta-modeling. The outcome of meta-modeling is obviously called a meta-model. Meta-models come in two varieties, depending on which aspect of the modeling process they focus on. A meta-data model portrays the representational aspects of the modeling process. On the other hand, the procedural aspects of the modeling process are captured by a meta-activity model.

An example can clarify the concept of meta-modeling. Consider the representation of an everyday transaction in figure 6. This model describes the situation in which an order from a customer is registered. The model is called a data flow diagram. The elements of a data flow diagram are summarized in Figure 7. Let us take a closer look at the diagram in Figure 6. The order information comes from the *external agent* Customer, and enters a *process* called Receive Customer Order. Internal to this process, the customer order is checked against the product inventory by examining a *data store* called Inventory. If all the products ordered are available, the order information is passed on to a process called Accept Order, otherwise it is passed on to the process Reject Order. Both these processes notify the customer of the action taken, while the process Accept Order also saves the information in a data store called Accepted Orders.

The procedures used to develop this model can be found in almost any textbook on information systems analysis (e.g. Gane & Sarson, 1979). The procedural aspect of a method for data flow diagramming can be modeled by means of a meta-activity model, which is not given here. The representational aspect of data flow diagramming can be depicted through a meta-data model. Such a model describes the entity types used in the construction of a data flow diagram, such as Figure 6, and the relationships between these entity types. The meta-data model is shown in Figure 8 in the form of an entity-relationship model. The elements of an entity relationship model are summarized in Figure 9. A closer look into the meta-data model presented in Figure 8 provides us with the following

Information Systems Planning 273

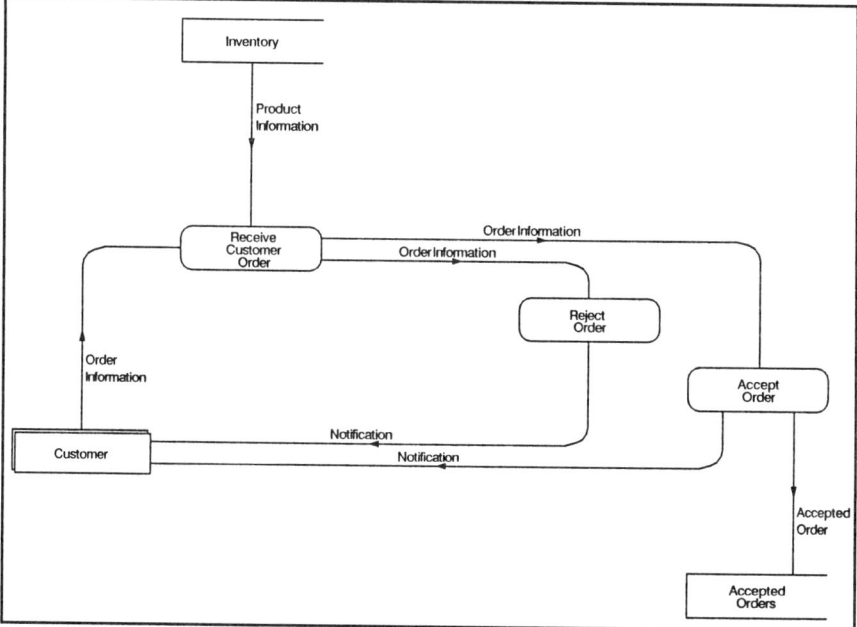

Figure 6: Data Flow Diagram for Order Entry

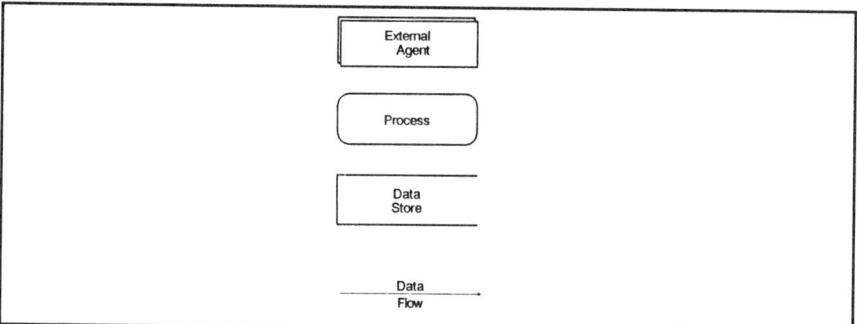

Figure 7: Elements of a Data Flow Diagram

insight into data flow diagramming. As can be derived from the description above, the entity types involved are:

- external agent,
- process,
- data store, and
- data flow.

The latter has not been mentioned in the description above; it refers to the arrows, indicating a 'flow of data' between an external agent and a process, between two processes, or between a process

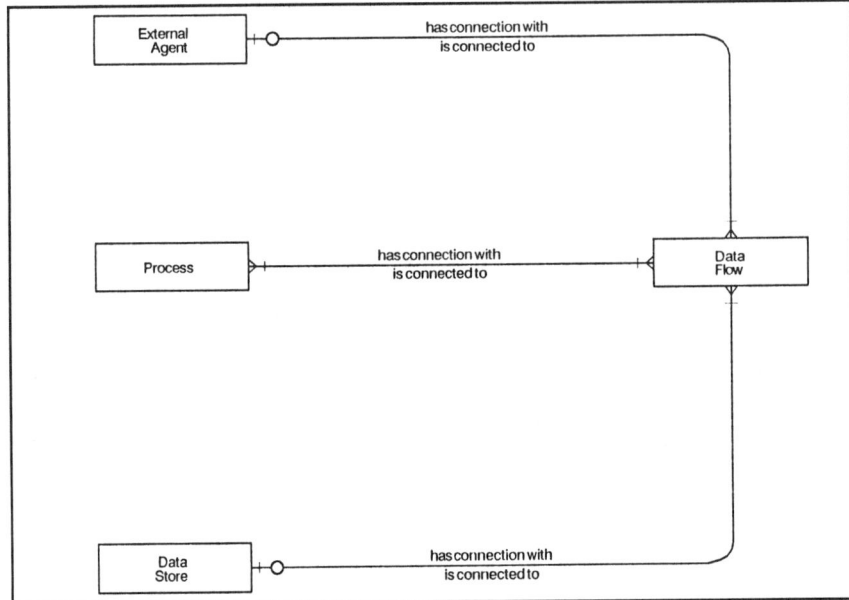

Figure 8: Meta-data Model of Data Flow Diagramming

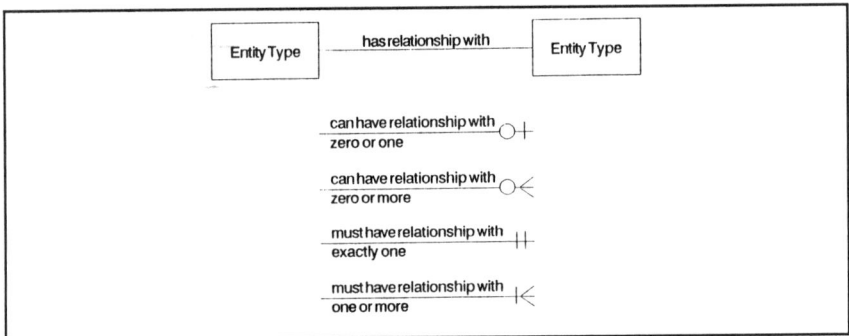

Figure 9: Elements of an Entity-Relationship Diagram

and a data store. This description of data flows gives rise to the relationships depicted in the meta-data model. External agents, processes and data stores can all be connected to one or more data flows. Conversely, data flows can be connected to at most one external agent or data store, and to one or more processes. Even though the representation used for this meta-data model is limited, it conveys the essence of the representational aspects of data flow diagramming, namely the external agents, data stores, and processes, which are connected to one another through data flows.

Meta-modeling serves a lot of purposes in the area of information systems research. Recent uses with which we are familiar include: the comparison of ISP methods and their associated tools (Brinkkemper et al, 1989a), the design of a decision support system for systems architecture specification (Stegwee, 1989), and the determination of 'method companionship', the so-called mapping of the techniques of an information systems development method to a development support tool (Brinkkemper et al, 1989b).

Meta-modeling in ISP

With respect to ISP methods, meta-modeling makes it possible to break up the methods into their building blocks:

- the activities performed within ISP and
- the information gathered and produced.

Meta-activity models are set up to model the activities as prescribed by ISP methods. As an example, let us consider the specification of a systems architecture. A systems architecture is constructed by delineating information systems areas within an information architecture, as shown in Figure 10. An information architecture is usually represented by an association matrix indicating processes and entity types. Processes are usually arranged in order of the business functions they belong to. In the case of Figure 10 the processes belonging to the function 'Education' are listed first, followed by those belonging to the function 'Research'. The cells in the matrix indicate whether a process creates or uses data pertaining to an entity type (indicated with a 'C' and a 'U' respectively). For example, the process 'Develop Curriculum' creates (and uses) data pertaining to the entity type 'Specialization', as the development of a curriculum specifies which fields of specialization are identified. The same process uses data on the entity type 'Course' because it specifies which courses are mandatory for students with a certain specialization, assuming data on the courses themselves are provided by another process. Specification of a systems architecture boils down to drawing non-overlapping boxes within this matrix, the boxes indicating the information systems areas requiring further information systems development.

ISP methods often contain the following rules for forming information systems areas:

- processes that belong to the same function should be supported by one information systems area, and
- entity types should be assigned to the information systems area in

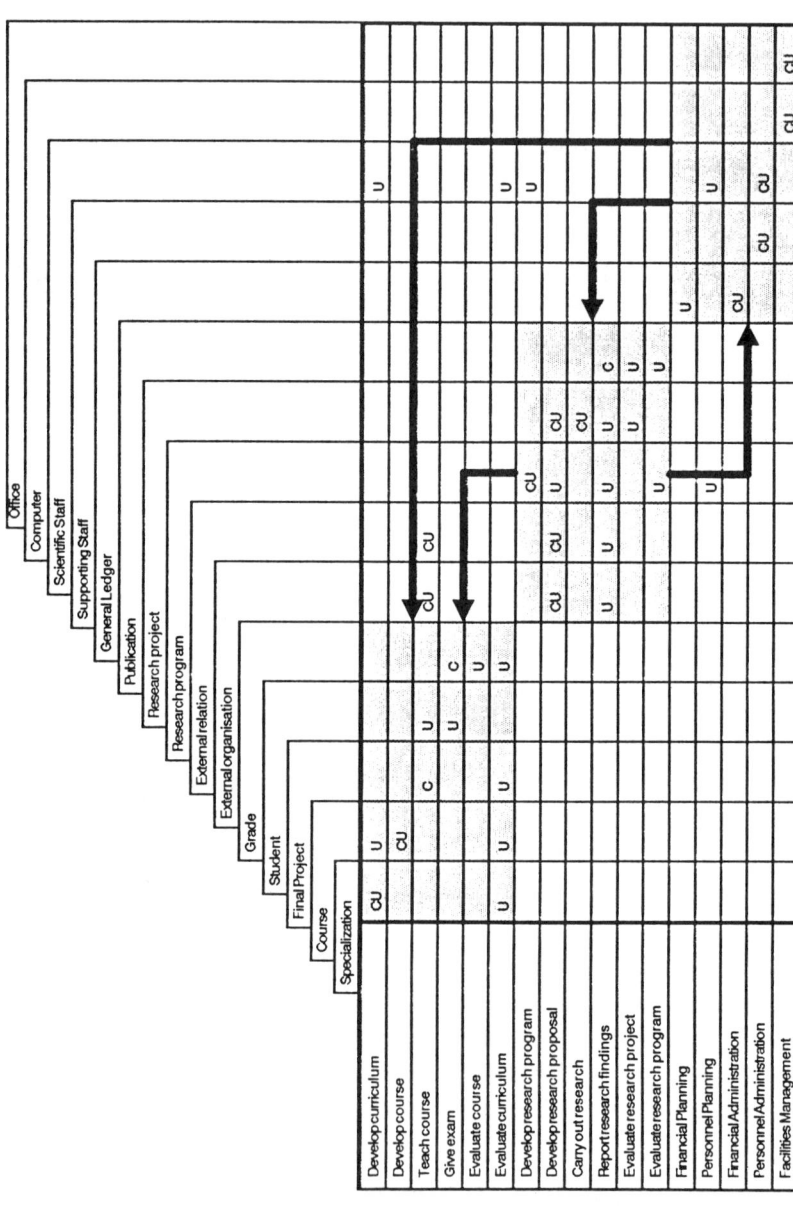

Figure 10: Part of an Information Architecture for a College or University

which data pertaining to the entity type is created.

However, the reason why these rules should be applied is not clear. An alternative approach, which focusses on the responsibility structure, might include different rules, such as:

- processes that are the responsibility of the same organizational unit, should be grouped into one information systems are, and
- entity types should be assigned to the information systems area in which data pertaining to the entity type is created.

Although the two strategies described above produce different systems architectures, they do have the same structure. The rules used in these strategies can be generalized as follows:

- Processes that are in some way similar to one another should be grouped together.
- Entity types that have a certain relation to a business process should be assigned to the group which the business process belongs to.
- A group of processes and entity types forms an information systems area.
- The information systems areas together form a systems architecture.

A meta-activity model representing these generalized rules is presented in Figure 11. Several different strategies can be developed using these generalized rules (Stegwee, 1991). In general, strategies for systems architecture specification use a selection of the available models to arrive at a specific systems architecture. The focus of a particular strategy depends on the selection of the models that are used. It is useful to view the set of models as one overall model, which we will call the Business Information Model. The meta-activity model in figure 11 shows input data (the business information model) and output data (the systems architecture) in the form of data stores. It is possible to specify a data model for these data stores, resulting in the meta-data models for the business information model and the systems architecture. Combining these models into the meta-data model for information systems architecture specification, results in Figure 12. Let us examine this figure in more detail.

The input for systems architecture specification is the business information model. The business information model includes the information architecture, which is based upon processes and entity

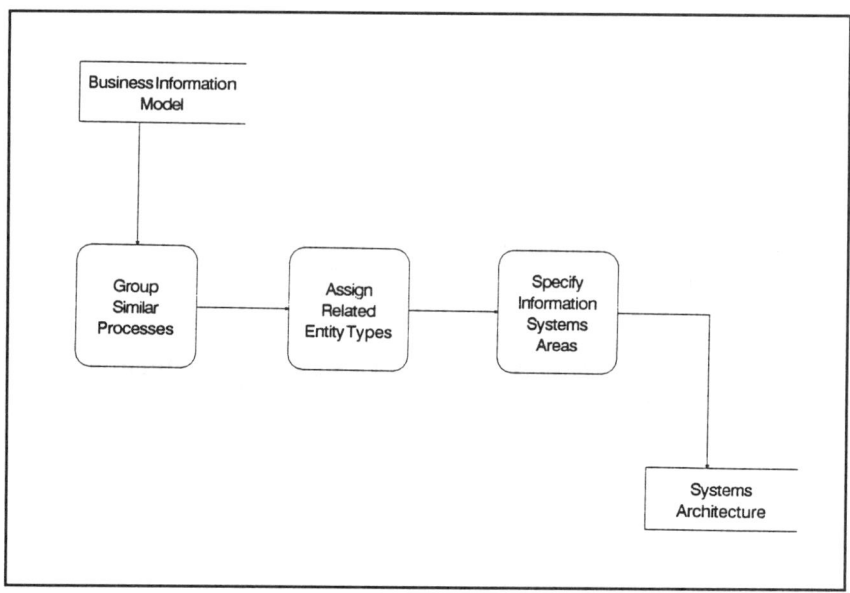

Figure 11: Meta-Activity Model for Systems Architecture Specification

types, and the interactions between them (data creation or usage). A process has interactions with one or more entity types, and an entity type has at least one interaction with a process. A single interaction links exactly one process to exactly one entity type. The fact that processes belong to business functions has been specified by including functions in the meta-data model. Every process belongs to exactly one function. However, not every function has to contain one or more processes, at least not directly. This is due to the fact that usually a functional decomposition is specified in an ISP study. Such a decomposition specifies a tree-structure of functions first, and adds the business processes to the ends of the tree. Hence, a function can contain one or more other functions, instead of processes, when it is not at the end of the initial tree of functions. Conversely, a function can only belong to at most one function. The top level function, i.e. the enterprise, does not belong to any function, hence the relationship 'function belongs to function' is optional.

This leaves one part of Figure 12 open for discussion. The demarcation of information systems areas, as done in the specification of a systems architecture, leads to the introduction of information systems areas in the meta-data model. Relationships have been included to show which processes and which entity types belong to the information systems area. Processes and entity types can, and must, belong to exactly one information systems area. Conversely,

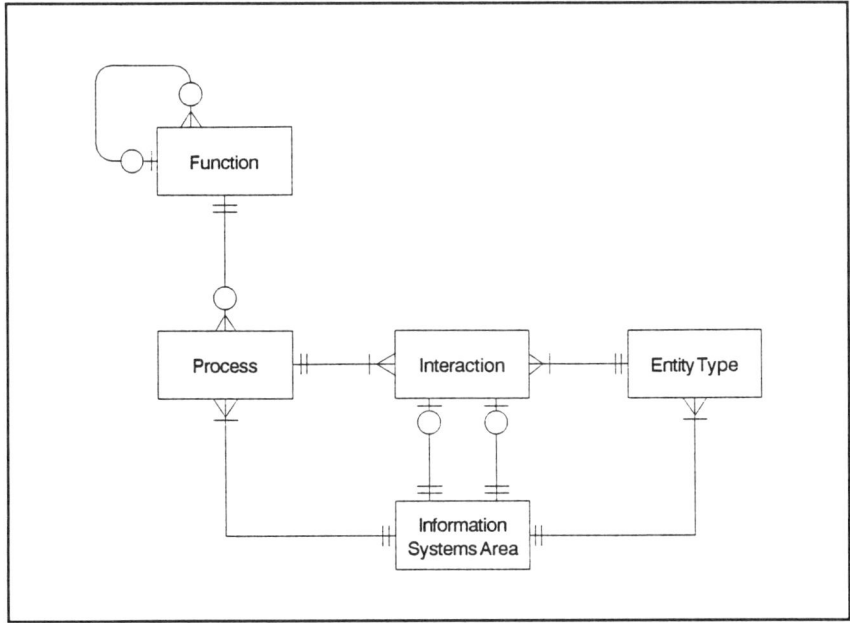

Figure 12: Meta-Data Model for Systems Architecture Specification

an information systems area must contain at least one process and one entity type, otherwise the boxes would be empty. Furthermore, the interactions between processes and entity types belonging to different information systems areas can be aggregated to an interaction between information systems areas. These aggregations are represented by arrows in the system architecture (Figure 10). It is necessary to draw a double relation between information systems area and interaction, because of the double role an information systems area can play. For example, the relation could be: 'Information systems area 1 creates data which are used by information systems area 2'.

In the discussion above, meta-modeling has been applied to the process of specifying a systems architecture, which is part of information systems planning. A similar approach can be followed with respect to CASE tools. Meta-modeling is then used to model the data recording facilities and the functions of the tools. A comparison of the meta-data models of a specific method and a specific ISP tool forms the basis for conclusions with respect to the degree to which the information handled during ISP (carried out according to the method chosen) can be properly recorded using the tool. The amount of support offered by the tool for ISP activities can be established similarly, by comparing the tool's and method's meta-activity models (see Brinkkemper et al., 1989a).

Flexibility. From the discussion of the requirements for CASE tools in the field of ISP, we can distinguish flexibility requirements on the following aspects:

- the objects to be represented,
- the way in which the objects can be represented, and
- the constraints that can be applied to the objects and their interrelationships.

The first aspect has to do with the meta-data model of the ISP tool. By making additions to the meta-data model, the number of types of objects to be represented can be enlarged, since the meta-data model specifies the types of objects that can be represented in the tool. Flexibility with respect to the way in which objects are to be represented can be achieved through a graphical definition language, based upon the contents of the meta-data model. In this way, one or more graphical representations can correspond to a single object type in the meta-data model. This can be a useful feature, especially when using different graphical representations of the same object type for different target groups. Constraints can be specified in the form of a knowledge or rule base, again based on the contents of the meta-data model. Part of these constraints, in particular with respect to internal consistency and conflict resolution within the encyclopedia (the repository of all model data), have been implemented by some of the CASE tools available.

From these observations, the key role of the meta-data model becomes clear. Flexibility with respect to the meta-data model boils down to the ability to change the contents of this meta-model. Preferably, changes within the meta-model are to take place in a well controlled way. One way of achieving this, is to introduce a meta-model of the meta-data (a meta-meta-model), stating the structure of the meta-model for the ISP tool. We have just seen that a meta-model offers opportunities to construct (prespecified classes of) models for a variety of organizations using the same CASE tool. A meta-model is one level of abstraction above a specific organization. This provides us with flexibility in the contents of the models to be developed. However, it does not allow us to change the structure of the models. Such flexibility can be reached by taking the abstraction one step further, to a meta-meta-model for ISP tools.

Within the framework of this meta-meta-model, changes to the meta-model can be specified formally. A few CASE analyst workbenches have already adopted the meta-meta-model approach, for example Oracle's SQL*Design Workstation (Rock-Evans, 1989). An advantage of this approach is, that much of the logic to handle information within the CASE tool can be specified at the meta-meta level, with the individual objects in the meta-model inheriting this logic. The lack of a meta-meta-model in other customizable tools is probably one of the reasons for cumbersome customization processes.

A Meta-Model for Meta-Data

Flexibility of the meta-data model calls for controlled alterations to this meta-model. As mentioned above, alterations to the meta-data model of an ISP tool can be controlled by means of a meta-meta-model, i.e. a meta-model for the meta-data within the tool. In this section such a meta-meta-model will be presented.

In general one can view the set of models to be specified during an ISP study as the Business Information Model (BIM). ISP methods differ in the information they gather, and therefore the structure of the business information model varies over methods. An overall structural specification of the information gathered could be given, by combining the ingredients of the individual ISP methods. However, the interpretation and use of corresponding terms is not consistent between methods. Moreover, individual organizations may have their own terminology and specific issues, that make changes or extensions to the overall model necessary. Therefore, an attempt is made to take the abstraction one step further, formally resulting in a meta-meta-data model for the business information model. The meta-meta-model attempts to capture the generic structure of business information models, as used throughout a multitude of ISP methods. In a schematic form, this model is depicted in Figure 13. Let us take a closer look at the meaning of this model.

The generic structure of models that are used in an ISP study can be described as follows. Each model covers one or more dimensions, which contain a number of elements. Between a pair of dimensions a relationship type can exist, specifying the kind of relationship that elements of these dimensions can have with one another. Furthermore, because it is the intention to specify a systems architecture, groups and group relationships are embodied in the meta-meta-model. A group consists of elements, belonging to certain dimensions. The relationships between elements of different groups give rise to relationships between groups.

A specific method for ISP defines the models to be specified. For example, such a method might call for the development of a functional decomposition, an entity model, and an information architecture. The meta-model, also called model type, used by this

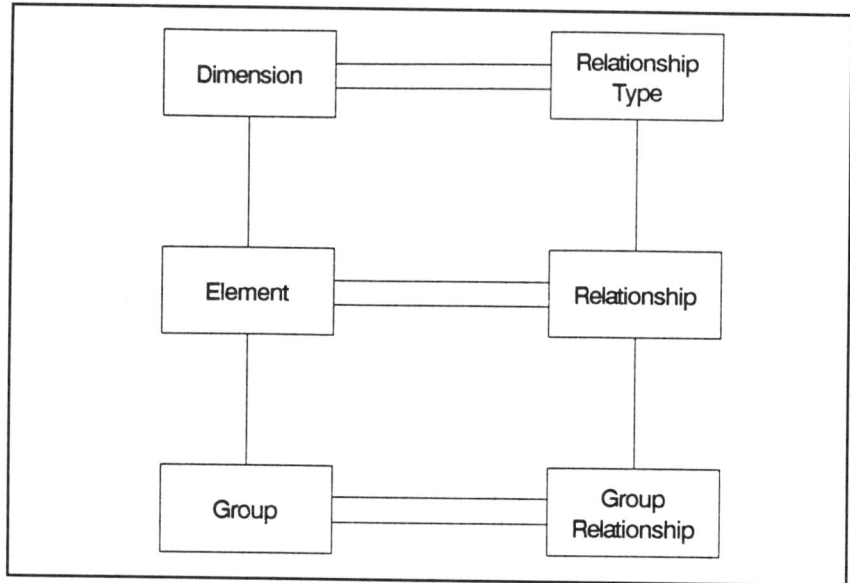

Figure 13: Meta-Meta-Data Model

(simplified) ISP method can be described in terms of dimensions and relationship types, as specified in the meta-meta-model. This description is given in Table 2. It follows that a meta-model can be defined by giving substantial specifications of the dimensions and relationship types that are covered by the prescribed models. Refer to the meta-data model in Figure 12 to see its correspondence with the substantial specifications given in Table 2. The two specifications are very much alike, as both describe the structure of a (simplified) business information model at a meta level.

The Business Information Model itself includes substantial specifications of the elements and relationships present in the models. Examples of elements, as given in the sample systems architecture in Figure 10, are 'Education' (a Business Function), 'Develop Curriculum' (a Business Process), and 'Specialization' (an Entity Type). An example of a relationship is 'Develop Curriculum creates data pertaining to Specialization'. This relationship belongs to the relationship type 'Process involves Entity Type'.

A systems architecture consists of groups of business processes and entity types. Examples of such groups are 'Education', 'Research', and 'Administration', as presented in Figure 10. An example of a group relationship can be found in the sample systems architecture as well, where the information systems area 'Research' uses information from the 'Administration' area.

Dimensions	Relationship Types
Business Function	Function consists of Function
Business Process	Function consists of Process
Entity Type	Process involves Entity Type

Table 2: Description of Model Type Used by a Simplified ISP Method

A Model Hierarchy

It is conceivable that the multitude of models, meta-models, and meta-meta-models leads to confusion. In order to control the complexity of models and the levels at which they are defined, a model hierarchy has been developed. As it is our intention to focus on the information content of the business information model, this model hierarchy will be specified for data models and meta-data models only. If the meta-meta-data model is taken as a starting point, the other models can be specified as instantiations within this model, providing substantial specifications for (part of) the meta-meta-model. The models specified above can be summarized by the model hierarchy depicted in Figure 14. Each model is defined at a different level of abstraction. The meta-meta-model (MMM) only contains structural (generic) specifications. The model type (MT) is defined at a methodological level, where only the ISP method used is known. The business information model (BIM) is specific for a certain organization. Finally, the systems architecture (SA) forms the result of applying strategies for systems architecture specification to the business information model.

Summarizing the previous section, the meta-meta-data model consists of the following elements:

- dimensions,
- elements,
- groups,
- relationship types,
- relationships, and
- group relationships.

The application of a specific method for ISP determines, in combination with the choices of the planning team, the dimensions on which data will be gathered, and the relationship types which will be investigated. Thus, one can discern between types of business information models, depending on the dimensions and relationship types. Once the ISP activities preceding systems architecture specification have been completed, the specific elements of the dimensions are known, along with the relationships between these elements. As follows from our definition of the BIM, this level of instantiation coincides with the business information model. Once the BIM is used for systems architecture specification, the information systems areas will be known, i.e. the groups of elements. Group relationships form the relationships between the information systems areas, which are aggregations of the relationships between their constituent elements.

The Feasibility of the Meta-Modeling Approach

The meta-meta-model, as described in the previous section, has been incorporated in a decision support system (DSS) for systems architecture specification, called GOSSIP, Groningen On-line Simulation Support for Information Planning (Stegwee, 1989; Kiewiet & Stegwee, 1991). The objective of the GOSSIP system has been to support the process of specifying a systems architecture. Based upon a meta-modeling approach, a method for systems architecture specification has been developed, accompanied by a decision support system to make this method feasible. Central to the development of the method and the DSS has been a description of the problem and formulation of objectives. The objectives have been specified as the development of:

- a set of strategies for systems architecture specification, and
- a set of evaluation criteria which render an evaluation of alternative systems architectures on an ordinal scale.

Meta-models of systems architecture specification have been developed, leading to a model hierarchy, as discussed above, and a phased design of decision support. Cluster analysis techniques have been used to provide the necessary functionality of the decision support system. Together these ingredients enabled the construction of a generic decision support system, which is independent of a specific organizational context. In order to show the appropriateness of the method and the generic DSS, a specific DSS has been constructed, based upon a practical situation. A key element in the process of constructing the specific DSS has been the application and interpretation of cluster analysis techniques in terms of their effect on a systems architecture. The practical situation can be modeled by means of a business information model. In one instance, this model has been borrowed from an ISP study carried out at the

CBR, the Dutch bureau for certificates of driving proficiency. Application of the GOSSIP system to the business information model of the CBR organization rendered a set of six strategies for systems architecture specification. The application of these strategies results in truly different systems architectures. In other situations, depending upon the contents of a business information model, different strategies for systems architecture specification can be generated for an organization.

The second part of the objectives concerned the provision of evaluation criteria. The development of the GOSSIP/CBR system rendered a set of seven evaluation criteria, again based upon the contents of the business information model. Application of these seven criteria produced a ranking of systems architectures, in which the systems architecture originally specified during the ISP study, was placed at the high end of the ranking. This means that, at least in this case, the evaluation criteria to some extent coincide with the criteria ISP professionals employ in practice. The generic GOSSIP system provides a means to specify a set of evaluation criteria for other situations as well, again dependent upon the contents of the business information model. A thorough treatment of the development of the GOSSIP system can be found in (Stegwee, 1992).

Due to the use of meta-models and the model hierarchy, described in the previous sections, the GOSSIP system is very flexible. It can be applied to a number of different business information models. As most of the system's functionality has been defined at the meta-meta level, no changes to the system's software are necessary when introducing new objects in the meta-data model. The meta-meta model thus controls the modifications to the meta-data model. Flexibility in the meta-data model of this tool has been achieved without sacrificing the capabilities of the system. Had the system's functionality been specified at the level of the meta-data model, it would have been unable to cope with changes to this meta-data model.

Previously, in our treatment of models for ISP we have argued that the ingredients of a business information model must match a number of specific organizational circumstances, such as the objectives of the ISP study, the target groups for communication, and the participants in the study. The GOSSIP system is able to capture all these different elements. However, it focusses solely on the specification of a systems architecture. Other tools have been used to specify the business information model itself. In the example of the CBR, the Information Engineering Workbench / Planning Workstation had been used to formulate the models. These models had to be converted to a suitable format for application of the GOSSIP system. It turned out to be possible to build a bridge between a conventional ISP tool, in this case the IEW Planning tool, and the GOSSIP system. This, of course, has been achieved by formulating the meta-data model of the IEW Planning tool in terms of the meta-meta-model specified above. Part of this meta-data model, in terms of the GOSSIP MMM, has been given above, in Table 2.

Incidentally, IEW Planning also uses some kind of internal meta-meta-model, as can be derived from their Import/Export Guide (KnowledgeWare, 1989). This meta-meta-model is shown in Figure 15. The figure shows an entity relationship representation of the IEW

			MODEL			
group	element	dimension		relationship type	relationship	group relationship
▲	▲	▲	MMM	▲	▲	▲
▲	▲	■	MT	■	▲	▲
▲	■	■	BIM	■	■	▲
■	■	■	SA	■	■	■

▲ : model includes structural specifications in given category
■ : model includes substantial specifications in given category

Figure 14: Model Hierarchy for Information Architectures

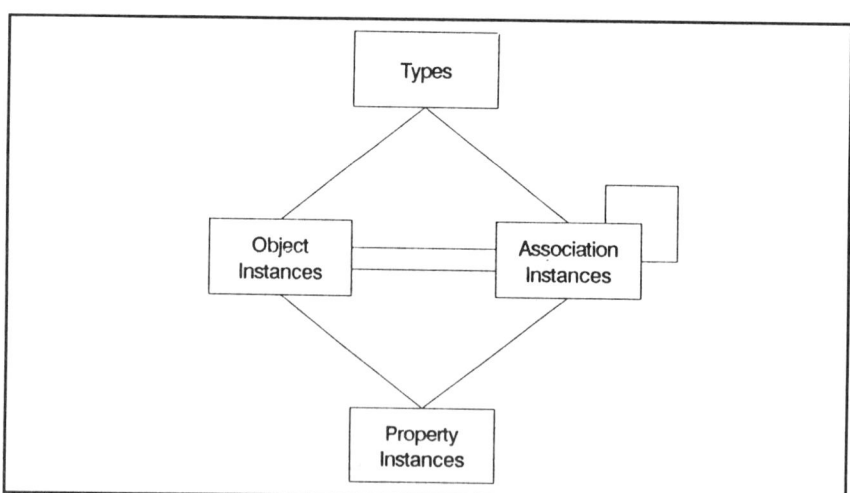

Figure 15: IEW Export Structure Shown as Meta-Meta-Data Model

Information Systems Planning 287

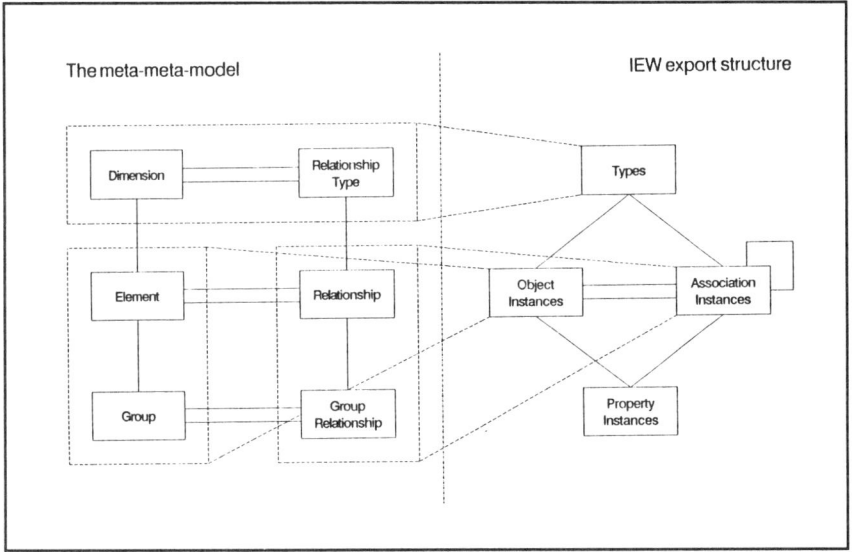

Figure 16: Comparison of the Meta-Meta-Model with the
IEW Export Structure

export structure. The MMM of IEW Planning (Figure 15) discerns *types* of both *object instances* and *association instances*. An object instance could be a business process, such as 'Develop Curriculum', or an entity type, such as 'Specialization'. An association instance in IEW terminology stands for associations such as 'business process Develop Curriculum involves entity type Specialization'. A *property* instance of such an association would be 'Create' or 'Use'. In this way the models described in previous sections can be stored in the IEW Planning workstation. However, even though IEW Planning incorporates an MMM, this does not provide the user with the ability to alter the tool's meta-data model. This is a lack of functionality in IEW, rather than an impossibility. As argued above, the use of an MMM makes such alterations possible and controllable, which are requirements for a flexible ISP tool.

The MMM of IEW Planning is quite similar to the MMM developed for the GOSSIP system, as can be concluded from Figure 16. This figure relates the meta-meta-data models of both the GOSSIP system and IEW Planning, as presented in Figures 13 and 15 respectively. The dotted lines and boxes indicate the way in which parts of the GOSSIP MMM are captured in the IEW Planning MMM. Apart from differences in the specifics of key attributes and numbering conventions, the two models differ only in that IEW takes the types of objects (i.e. dimensions) and the types of associations (i.e.

relationship types) together. Furthermore, the MMM developed for the GOSSIP system has groups and group relations as constituent parts, whereas IEW does not recognize groups as separate entities. It identifies groups as specific types of objects with the association type 'belongs to' to denote group membership. Since the original focus of the GOSSIP MMM was on systems architecture specification, the existence of groups within the MMM is hardly surprising, since the systems architecture consists of groups of business processes and entity types. IEW on the other hand does not support evaluation and analysis of alternative systems architectures, and hence does not need a separate concept of groups or group relations. Finally, IEW has a component called property instance, which is used to store all kinds of information, like the definition and comments for objects, the cardinality of relationships in an ER-chart, the amount of data in a data collection, or the volume of data retrievals by a business process. It is obvious that a similar notion should be incorporated in the MMM of the GOSSIP system, but it has been left out so far for reasons of clarity.

Since it is easy to adapt the GOSSIP system to different meta-data models, this meta-modeling approach can be recommended for use in the construction of ISP tools. Naturally the MMM, as specified above, is not sufficient for commercial application. Some other meta-meta-objects should be added, like properties, and a complete specification of the attributes of the objects should be given. The aim here was to show the feasibility of the meta-modeling approach within the area of ISP tools.

SUMMARY AND CONCLUDING REMARKS

Where information systems planning concentrated on the infological aspects of the integration of information systems in the previous decade, we now find that ISP is rapidly evolving toward a more business-oriented planning approach. This changing approach puts forward new and changing requirements for support by computer based tools. Both qualitative and formal investigations have lead to the conclusion that the tools necessary for these new demands are not commercially available today. Building upon this conclusion we have tried to formulate requirements for future ISP tools and have indicated a promising direction for further development.

The increasing speed of change, both in the possibilities of information technology and the opportunities in business, forms the basis for a more customized approach toward information systems planning. Regularly, changes in business structures have to be evaluated with respect to their consequences for IT structures, such as information flows, hardware, and software. Meanwhile, the potential impact of developments in information technology have to be considered, with respect to both business and IT structures of the organization. In order to control such processes and their ensuing development projects, a large variety of models are being used today. Models are used for evaluation of impact, visualizing alternatives, planning future development, and documenting the choices made.

With respect to the requirements for ISP tool support, it is clear that current tools for ISP only support a limited set of model types, with little flexibility in the way of graphical representation. In this chapter we have stressed the need for flexible tools that can be customized to the specific demands for model support in a given situation. Depending on the participants in the projects and the type of problems tackled, different representations (models) of the same objects should be generated. For example, a business manager needs a different type of model than a systems designer, who in turn needs a different type of model than a technical expert. However, all these models, although dedicated and customized to a specific group, have certain elements in common. In this way various models are related, as they should convey an image of the same business and IT structures to be developed for the organization. Controlling the relationships between these models is one of the possible strengths of ISP tools, which has not been exploited at all, at least until now.

Furthermore, tool support is essential to improve design and documentation activities. The design deliverables from an information systems planning study have to be used as input for the projects following from it. These projects should detail and enrich the ISP models with new elements. Bulky paper deliverables do not lend themselves well to such follow-on activities. To realize such an integrated approach, we need clear and unambiguous models that are well documented by means of the same set of tools. Automated and accessible storage of ISP deliverables can guarantee a consistent and integrated set of models. Such computer based models can greatly enhance the impact of information systems planning projects. Not only can consistency be maintained within each phase of the systems development life cycle, but more importantly across different phases. However, even though current CASE tools are (to a certain extent) able to support this, as evidenced by developments such as AD/Cycle, IBM's Repository, and the Application Development Workbench (ADW), these tools are of limited utility in information systems planning practice.

What is missing in the current development of CASE tools for information systems planning, is the realization that a more business-oriented planning approach requires a large degree of flexibility in the models to be developed. If flexibility is introduced in current CASE tools, it usually reduces the capabilities for integration and consistency checking to almost nothing. In this way, expensive CASE tools provide little more functionality than simple drawing tools.

In this chapter we have introduced another way to introduce flexibility in CASE tools. The use of meta-modeling enables us to change existing models or to specify new types of models, while retaining the ability to control these changes. It is crucial to understand that flexibility in CASE tools means that we should be able to change the contents of the meta-data model of a specific tool. However, as long as the functionality of a CASE tool is defined at this meta-data level, changes to the meta-data model will severely limit the capabilities of these tools with respect to the modified or newly introduced model types. Only when part of the functionality is specified at the level of the meta-model for the meta-data can changes to the meta-model be made without sacrificing the benefits of the CASE tool. The discussion of the GOSSIP system has illustrated these ideas, and has shown their relevance to the development of CASE tools.

Flexibility of the meta-data model itself is not enough. The objects to be modeled form only one (though fundamental) ingredient of flexibility in CASE tools. The other ingredients are the (graphical) representation of objects and their associations, and the automatic maintenance of consistency in the relationships between the various models to be developed, both during a single phase and across all phases of the systems development life cycle. If we do not want ISP tools to become simple drawing or information gathering assistants, proper treatment must be given to these representational and knowledge based aspects in the next generation of ISP tools. Support for the procedural aspect of information systems planning is another area which requires attention. Flexibility seems the most important prerequisite for the success of future tools.

ACKNOWLEDGMENT
The authors wish to thank Tim Bergin (The American University), Sjaak Brinkkemper (University of Nijmegen) and Jacques Boersma (University of Groningen) for their ideas and helpful comments on earlier versions of this chapter.

REFERENCES

Arthur Young (1988), *Information Engineering Computer Systems Methodology: Planning*. Arthur Young International.

Bertels, K. & Nauta, D. (1974), *Inleiding tot het modelbegrip (Introduction to the modeling concept*; in Dutch). Bussum (NL) : De Haan.

Bosman, A. (1977), *Een Metatheorie over het Gedrag van Organisaties (A Meta Theory on the Behavior of Organizations;* in Dutch). Leiden (NL) : Stenfert Kroese.

Brinkkemper, S. (1990), *Formalisation of Information Systems Modelling;* Amsterdam (NL) : Thesis Publishers.

Brinkkemper, S., Geurts, M., Van de Kamp, I. & Acohen, J. (1989a), On a Formal Approach to the Methodology of Information Planning. In: R. Maes (Ed.), *Proceedings of the First Dutch Conference on Information Systems.* Amersfoort (NL), November 1-2.

Brinkkemper, S., De Lange, M., Looman, R. & Van der Steen, F.H.G.C. (1989b), On the Derivation of Method Companionship by Meta-Modelling. In: J. Jenkins (Ed.), *Advance Working Papers, Third International Conference on Computer Aided Software Engineering.* London (UK) : Imperial College

Chen, P.P.-S. (1976), The Entity Relationship Model : Toward a Unified View of Data. *ACM Transactions on Database Systems* (March), 1 (1), 9-36.

De Leeuw, A.C.J. (1988), *Organisaties: management, analyse, ontwerp en verandering : een systeemvisie (Organizations, management, analysis, design, and change : a systems perspective;* in Dutch). Assen (NL) : Van Gorcum.

DeMarco, T. (1978), *Structured Analysis and System Specification.* Englewood Cliffs : Yourdon Press.

Earl, M.J. (1989), *Management Strategies for Information Technology.* Englewood Cliffs : Prentice Hall.

Emory, C.W. & Cooper, D.R. (1991), *Business Research Methods,* 4th edition. Homewood : Irwin.

Gallo, T.E. (1988), *Strategic Information Management Planning.* Englewood Cliffs : Prentice Hall.

Gane, C.P. & Sarson, T. (1979), *Structured Systems Analysis: Tools and Techniques.* Englewood Cliffs : Prentice Hall.

Hackathorn, R.D. & Karimi, J. (1988), A Framework for Comparing Information Engineering Methods. *MIS Quarterly* (June), 12 (2), 203-220.

Hoogland, J. (1990), personal communication on the use of Maestro at a large Dutch bank.

In 't Veld, J. (1988), *Analyse van Organisatieproblemen: Een toepassing van denken in systemen en processen (Analysis of organizational problems : an example of system and process oriented thinking;* in Dutch). Leiden (NL) : Stenfert Kroese.

International Business Machines (1984), *Business Systems Planning - Information Systems Planning Guide.* IBM Publication GE20-0527, Fourth edition.

International Business Machines (1986), *Information System Model and Architecture Generator - Operation Guide.* IBM Publication SB11-5989, Second Edition.

Kiewiet, D.J. & Stegwee, R.A. (1991), Conceptual Modelling and Cluster Analysis: Design Strategies for Information Architectures. In: J. DeGross, I. Benbasat, G. DeSanctis & C.M. Beath (Eds.), *Proceedings of the 12th Annual International Conference on Information Systems,* New York, December 15-18.

KnowledgeWare, Inc. (1989), *Information Engineering Workbench : Planning Workstation;* Atlanta.

Lederer, A.L. & Mendelow, A.L. (1986), Issues in Information System Planning. *Information and Management* (May), 10 (10), 245-254.

Lederer, A.L. & Mendelow, A.L. (1987), Information Resource Planning: Overcoming Difficulties in Identifying Top Management's Objectives. *MIS Quarterly* (September), 11 (3), 389-399.

Lundeberg, M., Goldkuhl, G. & Nilsson, A. (1981), *Systeemontwikkeling volgens ISAC : de ISAC-methodiek (Systems Development according to ISAC : the ISAC methodology;* Dutch translation from Swedish). Alphen a/d Rijn (NL) : Samsom Uitgeverij.

Marchand, D.A., & Horton, F.W. Jr (1986), *Infotrends : Profiting from your Information Resources*. New York : John Wiley & Sons.

Martin, J. (1982), *Strategic Data-Planning Methodologies*. Englewood Cliffs : Prentice Hall.

McFarlan, F.W. & McKenney, J.L. (1983), *Corporate Information Systems Management - The Issues Facing Senior Executives*. Homewood : R.D. Irwin.

Nolan, R.L. (1979), Managing the Crises in Data Processing. *Harvard Business Review* (March-April), 115-126.

Olle, T.W. et al. (1988), *Information Systems Methodologies : A Framework for Understanding*. Reading : Addison Wesley.

Parker, M.M., Trainor, H.E. & Benson, R.J. (1989), *Information Strategy and Economics*. Englewood Cliffs : Prentice Hall.

Rock-Evans, R. (1989), *CASE Analyst Workbenches: a Detailed Product Evaluation*. London (UK) : Ovum Ltd.

Rockart, J.F. (1979), Chief executives define their own data needs. *Harvard Business Review* (March-April), 81-93.

Seligmann, P.S., Wijers, G.M. & Sol, H.G. (1989), Analyzing the structure of IS methodologies : an alternative approach. In: R. Maes (Ed.), *Proceedings of the First Dutch Conference on Information Systems*. Amersfoort (NL), November 1-2.

Staring, W.R. (1989), CASE: vergelijking van Information Engineering Facility (IEF) en Information Engineering Workbench (IEW) (CASE: comparison of IEF and IEW; in Dutch). *Informatie* (May), 31 (5), 344-357.

Stegwee, R.A. (1989), The use of high-level models in the specification of an information architecture. In: R. Maes (Ed.), *Proceedings of the First Dutch Conference on Information Systems*. Amersfoort (NL), November 1-2.

Stegwee, R.A. (1991), Alternative Strategies for Information Architecture Specification. In: A. van Harten and B.G.F. Pol (Eds.), *Bedrijfskundig Onderzoek 1991 : 5e NOBO Onderzoekdag Bedrijfskunde (Research in Management and Organization 1991 : 5th Research Symposium of the Dutch Organization for Research in Management and Organization* (NOBO); partly in Dutch), Enschede (NL), November 29.

Stegwee, R.A. (1992), *Division for Conquest : Decision Support for Information Architecture Specification*. Groningen (NL) : Wolters Noordhof.

Stegwee, R.A. & Van Waes, R.M.C. (1990), The Development of Information Systems Planning towards a Mature Management Tool. *Information Resources Management Journal* (Summer), 3 (3), 8-21.

Truijens, J. et al. (1990), *Informatie-infrastructuur, een instrument voor het management (Information infrastructure, an instrument for management;* in Dutch). Deventer (NL) : Kluwer.

Van der Poel, P.A.M.M. & Van Waes, R.M.C. (1989), Framework for Architectures in Information Planning. In: *Information System Concepts: An In-depth Analysis*. Amsterdam (NL) : North Holland.

Van Waes, R.M.C. (1991), *Architectures for Information Management : A Pragmatic Approach on Architectural Concepts and their Application in Dynamic Environments*. Amsterdam (NL) : Thesis Publishers.

Wijers, G.M. (1991), *Modelling Support for Information Systems Design*. Amsterdam (NL) : Thesis Publishers.

Wijers, G.M. & Heijes, H. (1990), Automated Support of the Modelling Process: A view based on experiments with expert information engineers. In: B. Steinholtz, A. S+lvberg & L. Bergman (Eds.), *Proceedings on Advanced Information Systems Engineering : Second Nordic Conference CAiSE '90*. Stockholm (S), May.

CHAPTER TEN

Integrating Project Planning Tools into the CASE Architecture

Vijay K. Kanabar
University of Winnipeg

One of the key advantages of the CASE architecture is that it lends itself readily to project planning and estimation. This is possible as most CASE tools or systems use a central repository for storing project data. Such a repository could be easily tapped into to obtain various software metrics pertaining to the development process. This chapter describes the CASE architecture as it pertains to the planning function of software project management. It presents our experience with two CASE tools designed at the University of Winnipeg and used by project managers for estimating effort of projects developed using fourth-generation tools or techniques.

CASE technology is defined as "a software technology that provides an automated engineering discipline for software development, maintenance, and project management" (McClure, 1989). CASE systems available in the marketplace today focus largely on the software development and maintenance aspects of projects, and ignore support of the project management function. *Project planning activities* have received hardly any attention from vendors. Regardless, project planning and effort estimation are critical activities that cannot be ignored. This chapter describes our experiences with two tools designed to assist with the task of estimating software development effort. These tools integrate very well with existing CASE tool architecture, and actually depend upon them for input data. Before discussing this, we will first introduce project management.

Project Management

Managing a project involves the use of a project management methodology. Even though there are several project management methodologies, they all involve the three stages of planning, scheduling, and control. During the *planning* stage, a project is broken down into smaller and more manageable components called tasks or activities. Work effort is estimated for each of these activities, using past experience or historical data as a guide. Then, the total work effort is derived for the project. An effort estimation model, as discussed in this chapter, can play a very useful role at this stage by validating the project manager's work effort estimates.

In the *scheduling* stage we allocate resources for each task, map the activities to a calendar, as well as determine the start and finish dates for each task and the total project. Project management tools are available for use at this stage. They range from powerful mainframe based products such as IBM's Application System, to smaller project management tools based on microcomputers such as Microsoft Project, and Time Line (IBM, 1986; Microsoft, 1987; Symantec, 1990) . Such tools contribute significantly to project scheduling, by providing various graphs such as GANTT charts, work-breakdown structures, and CPM or PERT diagrams.

The final stage *control*, ensures that the entire project is completed on time and within budget. Adequate control ensures that the end products are of good quality, within budget, and on schedule. Project management tools can assist us at this stage by providing a wide variety of cost and schedule reports. It is a measure of the newness of CASE, that tools pertaining to project scheduling and control are readily available today, but those relevant to project planning are scarce.

Software Metrics

Software metrics are quantitative measures of various characteristics of projects. They measure the amount of code and documentation, the complexity of the development process and the problem domain, as well as environment characteristics like people, tools, or techniques used (Mills & Dyson, 1990).

Many firms today have adopted a software metrics approach to assist them with various aspects of software development. Such a strategy implies that a database containing various development related metrics such as cost-oriented data and size-oriented data are accumulated for all software development projects. While the project is in progress, but especially on completion, various productivity and quality metrics are generated from such a database. This information is used to improve the quality of future projects, and to evaluate the impact of new tools and techniques.

Grady and Caswell describe Hewlett-Packard's metrics program in detail in their book *Software Metrics: Establishing a Company-Wide Program* (Grady & Caswell, 1987). They indicate that HP had two objectives in mind when they initiated their program - first, an improvement in productivity; and second, the ability to measure tools (developed in-house or purchased) for effectiveness. With regards to the first point, they felt that the very act of measuring the software development process itself would lead to short-term improvements in productivity. They quote from *In Search of Excellence* (Peters & Waterman, 1982) to illustrate their point: People ... like to perform against standards - if the standard is achievable, and especially if it is one they played a role in setting.

Several hundred people were involved in HP's software metrics program. After three years of commitment they were able to achieve several advantages; the most important of these (from the CASE architecture and organizational perspectives) are the:

- ability to measure progress.
- ability to identify practices which lead to the highest quality and productivity.
- ability to estimate and schedule projects better.

When establishing a software metrics program, Grady and Caswell recommend that the following key steps must be performed: assign software metrics responsibility to specific people, convince people of the importance of these metrics and indicate that accuracy depends upon their willingness to take the time to collect data; ,define metrics to be collected (such as size, defects, effort, and cost), try to automate data collection, and, create a metrics database. The last two recommendations can be readily (and elegantly) supported by a CASE system, and indeed, there are such products in the marketplace today. For example, NASTEC's CASE 2000 supports documentation of cost-oriented and size-oriented data pertaining to the software development projects (Nastec, 1986; Case Jr. 1986). Note that when such systems are used for planning purposes, it is usually left up to the project manager to interpret the data recorded in the metric database. It would be advantageous to have CASE tools assist the project manager at this stage.

THE PROBLEM DOMAIN

The importance of estimating the size and time required for software development cannot be over-emphasized. In the foreword to Tom DeMarco's *Controlling Software Projects*, Barry Boehm says the following:

> Better cost estimation methods help us to understand the relative costs and benefits of a proposed future system well enough to be able to reduce its scope or to eliminate portions whose benefits do not justify their estimated costs (De Marco, 1982).

While, progress has been made towards measuring and estimating effort of software applications using 3GLs (Boehm, 1981; Kemerer, 1988), very little research has been done to estimate effort of applications developed using fourth-generation tools or application software generators. In this chapter, we introduce two suitable CASE tools for this domain and describe our experience with them. Definitions, and theoretical aspects of these tools are presented first, followed by experimentation, calibration, and related details.

Effort Estimation and Cost Models

CASE tools designed to support the effort estimation function usually have an underlying cost model. There are several kinds of cost models in existence today. Software engineering and project management books usually describe such models in detail (Pressman, 1992; Pfleeger, 1991; Boehm, 1981; Abdel-Hamid & Madnick, 1991; Dreger, 1989; Jones, 1986; De Marco, 1982; Grady & Caswell, 1987). Cost models estimate software development effort by considering major cost factors such as size and complexity of the application. In principle, such models function by defining a simple relationship between development effort and some early metric of software size and they can be used to forecast project costs with greater accuracy and precision than traditional seat-of-the-pants guestimates (DeMarco & Lister 1990). Cost models are generally very easy to use, and novice project managers or estimators with little or no experience can benefit the most with them. A few cost models such as **Constructive Cost Mo**del (COCOMO), and SPQR/20 (Boehm, 1981; Jones, 1986; Pressman, 1992) are commercially available as full fledged tools.

Existing models are stand-alone products, that is, they do not tap into the CASE metrics database for estimation or planning purposes. However, if such products are tightly coupled with the CASE database, we will realize several benefits of the integration. For instance, we will no longer have to build bridges that import and export data between the estimation model and the CASE product. Also, for the project being estimated, input sizing parameters (required by the cost model for effort estimation purposes) can be directly supplied from the CASE database (which certainly has detailed information, such as the number of files, entities, number of data elements in reports, and screens). The end result is that the estimation process can be automated to a higher degree and we will be able to better estimate future projects. The fact that it is possible and desirable for a cost model to interface with a CASE system is demonstrated by SPQR/20's ability to interface with Excelerator (Whitten & Bentley, 1987).

Fourth Generation Tools

Since this chapter pertains to effort estimation of projects developed using Fourth-Generation Tools (or techniques) (4GTs), it is worthwhile defining this term next. To begin with, a few authors such as Pressman (1992) and Damodaran (1987) prefer to use the term "Fourth Generation Tools'"as opposed to the more common term "Fourth Generation Languages." Damodaran states that "the reason the former is preferred is that the items in question are mostly tools rather than languages" (p. 157). We also prefer to use the term fourth-generation techniques for the same reasons - the products being researched in this chapter are tools not languages. But what are 4GTs? According to Pressman (1987):

> The term fourth generation techniques (4GT) encompasses a broad array of tools that have one thing in common: each enables the software developer to specify some characteristic of software at a high level. The tool then automatically generates source code based on the developer's specification. There is little debate that the higher the level at which the software can be specified to a machine, the faster a program can be built. (p. 24)

4GTs reduce the time and effort required to generate an application by a factor of at least 5 when compared with application development using 3GLs (Martin, 1985; Bate & Vadhia, 1986; Matos & Jalics, 1989) . According to Pressman (1987), "4GTs are likely to become an increasingly important part of software development during the next decade and conventional methods and paradigms are likely to contribute less and less to all software developed" (p. 25).

Within the realm of 4GTs, small to medium business applications, which are developed using tools such as query facilitators, form generators, report generators, application generators, and related specification oriented application packages, are the focus of this chapter.

Project Factors

The project factors (PFs) are a group of project parameters that influence team productivity and project cost. The skill-level or experience of the participants, methods or languages used, etc, are examples of project factors. When planning a project, such factors must be identified and the level of their impact documented. Various PFs that play an important role in effort estimation are described here. Several researchers have identified and documented some of these PFs in their cost models (Albrecht, 1979; Waltson & Felix, 1977; Boehm, 1981; Jones, 1986; Bailey & Basili, 1981; Abdel-Hamid & Madnick; 1991). Our knowledge engineering process (the interviewing of experts) succeeded in revealing some new factors that affect software development costs.

Mode of Development: It is possible for end users today to tackle challenging data processing tasks, and they indeed are doing so in several organizations. When end user based application development is taking place, it is necessary to measure two factors:

1) The extent of support available from various sources such as the Information Center and the extent to which assistance with various aspects of application development is available from the data processing shop. If such support exists, then it serves the purpose of facilitating application development and eventually reducing effort and cost of software development.
2) The type of end user. Six categories of end users have been identified by Rockart & Flannery (1983).
   (a) Data Processing Programmers
   (b) End User Computing Support Personnel (information centre staff members)
   (c) Functional Support Personnel (power users who work in functional departments, outside of IS)
   (d) End User Programmers (who can write code)
   (e) Command Level End Users

(f) Non-Programming End Users

Basically, we can reclassify the above end user categories into three general categories - at the lowest end of the spectrum we have *application users*. Such users are not capable of any end user programming or even executing simple commands, but can operate a menu driven application system. At the upper end, we have *programmer end user* types that are basically full time system developers, highly skilled, and well qualified. The middle category ranges from end users capable of some command level operations (and therefore capable of 4GT programming with adequate training or support), to sophisticated programming types, who are less sophisticated than the professional programmers.

For the purposes of PF correction, end users at the lowest end and the highest end of the spectrum are ignored. The *non-programming end users* probably will never be requested to develop 4GT applications, and the *programmer end user* can very well be classified in the same category as the professional data processing staff member.

Previous Familiarity: Previous familiarity with the application environment identifies attributes such as:

- experience with similar size applications
- experience in the application problem domain (eg, accounting applications)
- previous experience with similar hardware and operating systems
- previous project team experience

Previous experience with 4GT tool: This project factor quantifies previous experience with 4GTs and with the database management system (DBMS). Specifically, it is concerned with the extent of experience with the specific 4GL and DBMS to be used in application development either by the end user or DP staff.

Application Factors: Application factors are concerned with the complexity of the current application being developed. They identify the complexity of attributes such as:

- the reliability required of the new application
- data communications involved
- designing applications that facilitate change, or that facilitate reuse of code
- interface complexity (I/O complexity due to printing on laser printers, or displaying on a VGA monitor).

Methodology Factors: Methodology factors are concerned

with the development rigor of the application development environment. Such factors are concerned with the use of techniques such as:
- top down design
- structured systems analysis techniques
- formal walkthrough's
- acceptance testing
- use of structured programming techniques
- use of automated tools for flowcharting, documentation, testing, etc.
- use of techniques such as JAD and prototyping.

Other Factors: Additional project factors that might affect the overall PF value are: novel applications, staff morale, staff compensation, xeroxing & printing resources, individual workstations, technical education, availability of essential software & hardware, working on a low priority project, staff working on several projects concurrently, etc.

Note that some of the PFs described in this section correlate positively to effort, and some correlate negatively. In addition, some PFs have a more significant impact on the effort estimates than others.

CASE System Architecture

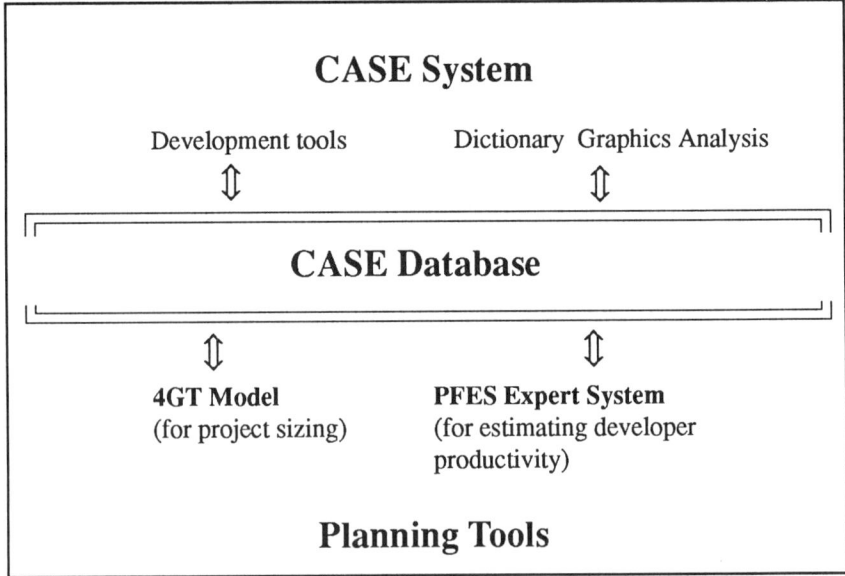

Figure 1: Components of the CASE Planning Architecture

Two sets of factors influence the ultimate cost of a system:

- Application Size Factors, and
- Project Factors (as discussed in the previous section)

The *application size factors* are related to the *size* of the application and the *magnitude* of effort required to implement it. Overall application size is governed by the total number of functions identified for an application. The 4GT Model, identified in Figure 1, is responsible for estimating this component.

The *project factors* are related to project parameters (described earlier). The PFES Expert System, shown in Figure 1, manipulates these factors and determines the productivity level of a project team.

The CASE system architecture involved with estimating a software project, therefore, consists of two planning tools: *4GT Model*, and *PFES Expert System*, and a set of CASE system tools. The planning tools interact with the CASE system tools via the CASE Database. In the next few sections we will describe the above two planning tools in detail. Actual experimentation took place at a large data processing shop in Winnipeg. The results are presented in the concluding section.

The Fourth Generation Tools Estimation Model

The *4GT Estimation Model* was designed and implemented on the basis of interviews with several practitioners, literature research, fourth-generation product study, and project data gathered between 1987 and 1991 (Kanabar, Janzen, Seah & Smith, 1991). The model has been implemented on a personal computer, and is in the public-domain at present. We provide a brief overview of the model below.

In the fourth-generation environment, work effort can be attributed to functions that have to be implemented. In other words information system size can be represented by functions. A function can be classified into one of the following types: *form, report, data,* and *process.* Functions implemented using form generators are called *form* functions, while those implemented with report writers are called *report* functions. The *data* function type represents database tables or files, and these are created using a DBMS. The remaining functions constitute the *process* function type, and include programs coded, if any, using a procedural or non-procedural language. Process function types are not being fully modeled in the present study, therefore only form, report, and data functions are discussed in detail.

A very important characteristic of application development with 4GTs (such as form-generators, report-generators, and application-generators) is that:

a) we generally specify what is to be accomplished, and
b) most of the specification effort is focused on and around screen fields.

The term *screen field* refers to the input and output data elements of forms, reports, and screens including data elements that transfer control such as on *menu screens*. According to Oracle Corporation, the screen field is a very important metric for the specification-oriented programming process used by 4GTs as the default logic is built on screen fields (Oracle, 1988). This aspect holds true for other 4GTs as well, since they are also data oriented, and generate transaction oriented applications.

Like most cost models, the 4GT Model uses a predictor to estimate effort. Predictors play a crucial role in the estimation process. What are predictors? According to DeMarco (1982):

> Every metric falls into one of two categories: either a "result" or a "predictor". A result is a metric of observed cost, scope, or complexity of a completed system. Examples include total cost, total manpower, elapsed time, or cost or manpower.... A predictor is an early-noted metric that has a strong correlation to some later results.

Two predictors are widely used today: lines of code (LOC), and function points (FP) (Boehm, 1981; Albrecht & Gaffney, 1983). But neither are satisfactory predictors for estimating effort of applications developed using fourth-generation tools. The following problems become apparent when we attempt to use LOC as a predictor for 4GT projects.

- There is no standard definition for a line of 4GL code (Verner & Tate, 1988).
- In the case of report, screen, and code generators, it is not practical to use LOC as a predictor since most of the code is generated automatically, and without any substantial programming. Fairly complicated screens and reports are generated by simply specifying the functions.
- 4GLs produce substantially smaller code sizes (LOC) when compared to 3GLs. Consider the fact that while data declarations are almost non-existent in 4GLs they typically constitute more than

half the code for a COBOL program (Misra & Jalics, 1988).

Historically, cost models using LOC as a predictor were designed around data from *third-generation language* (3GL) projects only. Fourth-generation tools, as we know them today, did not exist then. Several limitations have been pointed out with using function points as a predictor as well (Kanabar et al., 1991). For instance, the FP analysis method (Albrecht & Gaffney, 1983) ignores specification effort involving data elements within a report or a screen. But with 4GT-based development, the data elements act as a cost center (for work effort) and therefore cannot be ignored.

To resolve the above difficulties, we use a new predictor called specification element (SE) for estimating effort. The term "specification element" is a hybrid of the two terms specification, and screen- or data-element. An SE can be defined as "a specification task associated with implementing a screen field element or a data element". Examples of an SE are "automatically retrieve name and address when ID is entered", and "convert input data to upper case".

Each SE has an effort value (in person-hours) called a specification element value (SEV) associated with it. This is the work effort required to implement one screen field element or one data element. By using the techniques described in the model one can directly determine this effort value. SEs requiring similar implementation effort are grouped together; this serves to reduce the total number of SEs to a few categories. Nine such SE categories have been identified in the model - four each for form and report function types, and one for the data function type.

Since the total number of data or screen field elements (and hence the development effort) varies from one application to another, we perform a magnitude adjustment. This is accomplished by multiplying the estimated number of screen field elements in a form, report or a data function with the SEV. This gives us the adjusted specification element value (ASEV).

$$ASEV = SE * SEV \tag{1}$$

On summing the ASEVs for i functions ($i = 1..n$) we obtain the total effort due to development.

$$\text{Development Effort} = \sum_{i=1}^{n} ASEV(i) \tag{2}$$

However as Figure 2 indicates, this effort does not include life cycle effort, which accounts for activities such as project manage-

---
Total Project Effort in person-hours

Effort due to Life Cycle includes

- requirements defn.
- analysis and design
- data modelling
- detailed design
- integration testing
- project management
- team meetings
- documentation development

Effort Due to Development includes

- prototyping (if done)
- coding/generation
- data definition & unit testing

Figure 2: Conceptual View of Effort Distribution by 4GT Model

ment, developing user manuals, user interviews, administration, team meeting, as well effort due to requirements definition, analysis and design, etc. In order to obtain the total effort, we multiply the effort due to development by an expansion factor.

Total Effort = Effort due to development * Expansion Factor (3)

The expansion factor is determined by dividing an organization's actual system development effort (available from the CASE database) by the actual effort due to development. The ratio between these two variables accounts for the project management and life cycle effort.

Expansion Factor = Total Effort/Effort due to Development (4)

The expansion factor may differ from one location to another, as every organization uses a different methodology and also practices project management differently.

Categorizing SEs

To facilitate practical use of SEs as a predictor we must first classify them unambiguously. A study of 4GTs, and sample design and development of projects using them, provides us with a basis for categorizing SEs (Corner, 1990; Oracle, 1987; Ingres, 1986; Uniface, 1988). In this section, we classify screen fields and identify various SE categories. The following distinct categories of SEs exist for form and report function types:

Simple SEs. Screens consisting of screen fields have to be created first. Only after the initial skeletal screen structure is implemented can we provide logic to the form. Oracle (1988) describes this activity as the first level of form design where we "create screens consisting of fields without any special validation or enhancement" (page 1-8). SEs in this category, classified as simple SEs, are collectively responsible for creating or altering this initial form. Activities addressed by such SEs include: "re-label fields," "modify field sequence numbers," "cut and paste," and "visual enhancement." All applications require a certain amount of such basic activity.

Basic SEs. While a few screen fields might require no further action once created, several will require some basic validation. Oracle (1988) identifies this as the second of three stages of forms design and describes how one can "... specify field ranges, default values, and help messages, by making a single entry on a SQL*Forms window."(page 1-8). Since SEs in this category involve single action steps or triggers, they are collectively referred to as basic SEs. Examples of such SEs include, "Check fields for valid data", and "Restrict fields to a set of data values".

Detailed SEs. Some screen fields will require additional specification and definition generally by using triggers. Triggers are procedures (like macros) that are activated when certain fields are used. Oracle (1988) describes this as a higher level of form design indicating that at this level we "provide more sophisticated validation and assistance by writing triggers or short sequences of SQL commands" (page 1-8). SEs in this category are classified as detailed SEs in the 4GT Model and include tasks such as "Verify batch totals," or performing a complex data validation.

User Exits. Finally, we describe another distinct category of SEs, the user exits. Some screen field triggers can be implemented in such a way so as to permit a temporary exit to 3GL routines. Languages such as C are commonly used then, to implement the logic required for this particular screen field. This is usually necessary if faster processing speed is required (that is, better user response time is desired), or if the desired functionality cannot be provided using a 4GT, thereby compelling us to use a 3GL.

Data Function Type

The total number of data elements in an application serves to predict effort for the data function type. Several researchers have demonstrated that the number of data elements is a valid predictor for data oriented information systems. For instance, Wrigley & Dexter (1991) use fields in files as a metric in their research model.

They indicate that it correlates very well with application size. Also, Symons (1988) successfully illustrates that data elements are a good measure of system size.

Process Function Type

Screen fields or data elements not addressed in the above categories belong in the *process function* category. For example, almost all applications have menu control screen fields; these are basically responsible for transfer of control from one program to another, and would be classified in this category. At present, the predictors for this category are not fully calibrated, and project managers must directly estimate this function.

4GT Model

So far the following aspects of the 4GT model for project sizing have been characterized:

- An application can be broken down into several functions.
- Each function can be classified into function-types.
- Each function-type has several Specification Elements (SEs) and each of these can be sub-grouped into a few categories. (At present four categories have been identified for each of the form and report functions, and one for the data functions.)
- SEs function as a predictor for development effort (within each function type).
- Each SE category has an associated SE value (SEV). The SEV indicates the amount of time (in person-hours) it would take to implement an SE.

The predictor SE as introduced here can be viewed in terms of Connell & Shafer's (1989) software brick. Their concept of a software brick is explained as follows:

> If a brick wall is to be built, there are metrics available regarding the average amount of time required to lay one brick. Estimating the time required to build a wall then is reduced to simply calculating the number of bricks required from the wall's dimensions and multiplying that number by the current metric for brick laying.

Considering the 4GT Model, the total number of screen fields are equivalent to the "total number of bricks". The nine categories of SEs (four for forms and reports each, and one for data) equates to nine different "sizes of brick." Knowing the total number of screen fields in each category (i.e., total number of bricks required), and their corresponding metric values (i.e., time required to lay each brick), we can obtain an estimate of the total development effort (i.e., time required to build a wall).

AN EXPERT SYSTEM FOR PROJECT FACTOR CORRECTION

In this section, we examine other factors (apart from project size) that affect the cost of software projects. These factors are referred to as project factors (PFs) and acknowledge that the cost of developing an application is affected by variables such as programmer skill, end-user skill, or familiarity with hardware and software. Such factors can influence the ultimate cost of a system and therefore cannot be ignored. Note that the total effort derived above (equation 3), does not take these factors into consideration. The Project Factors Expert System (PFES), developed using expert system technology, accounts for this aspect of software development. Expert system technology is introduced next, followed by details about PFES itself.

Expert Systems Technology

Expert Systems are application systems where domain knowledge is explicit and separate from the rest of the system. Domain knowledge refers to all entities, facts and knowledge related to the application. Expert systems are specialized computer programs that use expert knowledge to attain high levels of performance in a narrow problem area. They mimic the reasoning of experts and are useful for very specific tasks such as medical diagnosis and computer configuration. Waterman (1986) classifies expert systems as a subset of knowledge-based systems. The domain knowledge is contained in the knowledge-base, i.e., all facts and information pertaining to the application are represented in the knowledge-base. In contrast to conventional systems, the data and knowledge are explicit and easily accessible.

Project Factors Manipulated by PFES

The concepts surrounding the expert system design are illustrated in the Figure 3. The detailed flow of reasoning and assumptions are not presented here because it is too technical and prototype specific, but generally speaking, this is what happens. PFES obtains the values of the individual PFs from the estimator, aggregates the values, and gives the overall PF correction factor. Sample rules and PF correction values are presented below:

Sample questions asked by PFES:

- Who is going to develop the application?
  end user, dp staff
- What is the overall experience of the development team?
  very low, low, average, high, very high
- How much familiarity do the developers have with the DBMS and Fourth Generation Tools to be used in implementing the application?
  very low, low, average, high, very high
- What is the level of expertise with the 4GT TOOL?
  very low, low, average, high, very high
- How familiar is the project team with the with the software development project on hand?
  very low, low, average, high, very high

    Sample rules executed by PFES:
    RULE E_U_7
    IF END_USER_IMPACT=SIGNIFICANT AND
        END_USER_SKILL=BASIC
    THEN END_USER_VALUE=1.42
    BECAUSE "End users may range in experience by a fair degree. Some might simply have cursory experience with a 4GL product, others might have more significant experience. ";

    RULE E_U_8
    IF   END_USER_IMPACT=SIGNIFICANT AND
        END_USER_SKILL=COMFORTABLE_USE
    THEN END_USER_VALUE=1.21;

On the basis of input data and execution of rules, a PFES correction value is recommended, such as PFES = 1.25, implying that the total effort estimate needs to be adjusted upwards by 25%.

EXPERIENCE WITH THE CASE TOOLS

Great-West Life is an international corporation with offices

Integrating Project Planning Tools 309

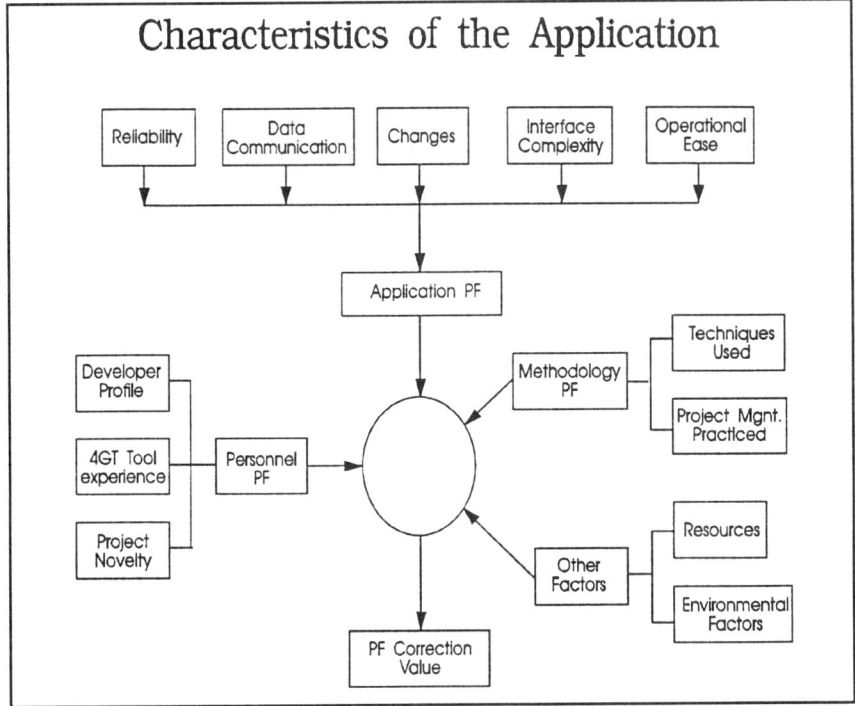

Figure 3: **Conceptual Model of the PFES**

across Canada and the United States. It is headquartered in Winnipeg, and provides a wide range of insurance, retirement and investment products to about six million people. Technology is at the core of their business, and more than 400 systems professionals support their diverse needs in Canada. Great-West Life has very good computing resources. The following are some of the major hardware and software supported: Hardware - IBM 3090 and 286/386 PC's; Software - MVS/ESA, CICS, IMS DB/DC, DB2, TELON, PL/I, COBOL, C, ORACLE, ACCEL and several PC-based software packages.

Since ORACLE was used to experiment with the 4GT CASE tools, we describe this product briefly. Oracle Corporation's ORACLE is a popular relational database management system that supports SQL. The user interface and SQL language are compatible with both IBM's DB2 and SQL/DS. ORACLE comes with a complete set of support tools such as an application generator, report writer, forms generator, and data dictionary. ORACLE is designed for a multi-user environment. The ORACLE environment consists of the following components: a relational database management system, SQL query language, application generator, and report writer. Their CASE system environment consists of the following components: CASE * Dictionary, CASE * Designer, CASE * Generator, and CASE * Method -all fairly standard tools.

Great-West Life was selected as a site for experimentation with the 4GT Model because:

• state of art 4GL development was taking place, and
• data from on-going and historic 4GL projects were readily available.

Several applications using Oracle are being developed at the Great-West Life. One such project called LEGASY was used as a basis for installing the 4GT Model and determining the life cycle expansion factor. Another project, Telephone System, was used to validate the 4GT case tools.

The LEGASY Project

The LEGASY (LEgal SYStem) project was used to calibrate the 4GT Model. The Law Department of Great West Life at Winnipeg was interested in a legal system that met the following requirements:

(1) automated Litigation Management: store information regarding issues, files
(2) automated Calendar of Events: keep track of scheduled events of each file.
(3) automated Time Tracking: record in-house counsel time for each file.
(4) implementing Key Word Document Search: locates document on the system which contains a specific word or a phrase.

Corporate Systems examined the above requirements in April 1990, with a view to implementing the system. The system took 2340 person hours to implement. In May 1991, the process of calibrating the 4GT Model began. The LEGASY project was chosen for this purpose because it was determined that the metrics data gathered from this project was reliable and suitable for cost modeling purposes.

Calibration Procedure

The objective of the calibration procedure was to

Integrating Project Planning Tools 311

- obtain the life cycle expansion factor for Great West Life. (indicated earlier, this expansion factor may differ from one organization to another), and
- create a metrics database consisting of SEs and their SEVs.

The calibration process performed is described in detail in the next section.

Identification of Functions

Identifying form, report, and data functions is a straight forward process with Oracle as they are created using standard tools - SQL*Forms, SQL*Report, and the RDBMS, respectively. Identifying the process functions was also straightforward, as separate files were implemented for each report created using the C language. (Note that C was used to implement some reports since SQL*Report writer was determined to be inadequate for implementing all the reports required by the users.)

Identification of SEs and Determination of the Total SE Count

Next SEs were identified in each of the above functions and classified into SE categories. The following strategy was used to locate SEs.

(a) Form type: count total number of screen fields, and at the same time, classify them as either: basic screen fields, detailed screen fields, and user exit screen fields.
(b) Report type: Count the total number of following report fields - actual report fields, report summaries and related objects, and basic and detailed SEs.
(c) Data type: Count the total number of fields (data elements) in all database tables, views and files.
(d) Process type: In the case of LEGASY, some procedural coding using C programming language occurred. The development effort associated with all process functions was obtained directly as the 4GT Model has no provisions for estimating such code.

Determining the Estimated Development Effort

On multiplying the SEV values of each SE category by a count of the total number of SEs (as determined above) we obtain the estimated effort due to forms and reports using the 4GT Model. By adding the effort due to process functions and we have the estimated development effort due to forms, reports and processes.

4GT MODEL - Calibrated For Legasy

Forms	335.37 person-hours
Reports	197.46 person-hours
Data Type	97.58 person-hours
Process Type	125.00 person-hours
Software Development Effort	755.41 person-hours
Actual Development Effort	2340.00 person-hours
SDLC Ratio For Great West Life	3.10

Estimated Effort =2340.00 person-hours

FORMS

SE Category	SE Value	Magnitude	Total SE Value
Screen Field SE	0.13	185	24.05
Basic SE	0.29	36	10.44
Detailed SE	1.59	32	50.88
User Exit	22.73	11	250.00
Total Effort			335.37 person-hours

REPORTS

SE Category	SE Value	Magnitude	Total SE Value
Screen Field SE	0.13	75	9.75
Basic SE	0.84	14	11.76
Detailed SE	2.55	69	175.95
Total Effort			197.46 person-hours

DATA

SE Category	SE Value	Magnitude	Total SE Value
Field	0.41	238	97.58
Total Effort			97.58 person-hours

Determination of SE Values

A software metrics database listing SEs and corresponding SEVs was created for ORACLE. The average effort values required to implement an SE in each category was documented for several SEs (Kanabar, Janzen, Seah & Smith, 1991). These values were determined to be as follows:

for Form type: 0.13 for simple screen fields (SF); 0.29 for Basic SEs (BSE); 1.59 for Detailed SEs (DSE); and 22.73 for User Exits (UE).

Integrating Project Planning Tools 313

for Report type: 0.13 for simple screen fields (SF), 0.29 for Basic SEs (A), 1.59 for Detailed SEs (B). (Note User Exits are not possible with Oracle's Report Writer.)

for Data type: 0.41 for each data element field.

Determining the Expansion Factor

In order to use the model successfully for future 4GT projects, it is important that we have the actual value of the Expansion Factor for Great-West Life. This factor represents the life cycle effort - activities such as meetings with users, producing user manuals, system documentation, administration effort, team meetings, and project management. The expansion factor needs to be computed at least once for every different organization in which the 4GT Model is to be installed. It would be a useful, however, to revise this number should there be a major change in the life cycle used. The expansion factor is determined by dividing the actual system development effort with the estimated effort due to forms, reports and processes. For the LEGASY project at Great West Life this factor is equal to 3.10 (see above table).

Formulating the 4GT Model

With the calculation of the expansion factor we can now formulate the actual equation of the 4GT Model for estimation projects at Great-West Life.

$$E = 3.10*[(SF*0.13)+(BSE*0.29)+(DSE*1.59)+(UE*22)+ (A*0.84)+(B*2.55)+(DE*0.41] \quad (5)$$

Here SF represents both the form and report screen fields; BSE, DSE, UE are SEVs for the form type; A, and B are SEVs for the report type; and DE for the data type. Note that the effort due to process functions is excluded in the basic equation. If some 3GL coding is to occur, the equation is extended by adding the PRC component (estimated directly by the project manager) as follows:

$$E = 3.10[(SF*0.13)+(BSE*0.29)+(DSE*1.59)+(UE*22)+ (A*0.84)+(B*2.55)+(D\ E*0.41)+(PRC)] \quad (6)$$

Note that E represents raw effort only. This value may have to be adjusted for different project factors such as "skill of programmer", "environment" and "application characteristics".

The above formula is modular and therefore provides more accurate estimates as the project progresses. This is a desirable quality in a cost model as very little information is generally available at the start of a project. Connell and Shafer (1989) describe the advantages of a modular formula concisely as follows:

> We would like the formulas to be modular so actual numbers derived from measured performance can be plugged in at the end of each project phase, thus steadily improving the accuracy of the estimates as the project moves toward completion.

Validation

With the determination of the expansion factor for Great-West Life (using LEGASY) we next proceeded with using the 4GT Model for other projects. The *Telephone System* project developed for the Communications Dept at Great West Life (using ORACLE) was used as a test case. The Telephone Project was suitable for validation purposes for several reasons:

- the project was small and relatively straight forward.
- the essential input data, required for estimation purposes, was readily available.
- it also did not have a 3GL programming component. (Therefore effort due to Process Functions did not have to be estimated.)

The computations relevant to this project are presented below. It reveals that the estimated effort was close to the actual. The estimated effort, after project factor correction, using PFES was 171 person hours. The actual implementation effort for the system was 160 person hours, a difference of +6.8 percent.

Effort Estimation for the Telephone System using the 4GT Model

Form	27.89 person-hours
Report	7.05 person-hours
Data	20.09 person-hours
Process	0.00 person-hours
Total Development Effort (TDE)	55.03 person-hours
Expansion Ratio (SDLC at Great West Life)	3.1
Estimated Effort (TSDE * SDLC)	171 person-hours
Project Factors Correction (PF)	1.024
Adjusted Estimated Effort (Effort * PF)	175 person-hours
Actual Effort (Entered on project completion) =	160 person-hours

FORM

SE Category	SE Value	Magnitude	Total SE Value
Screen Field SE	0.13	101	13.13
Basic SE	0.29	18	5.22
Detailed SE	1.59	6	9.54
User Exit	22.73	0	0.00
Total Effort			27.89 person-hours

REPORT

SE Category	SE Value	Magnitude	Total SE Value
Screen Field SE	0.13	15	1.95
Basic SE	0.84	0	0.00
Detailed SE	2.55	2	5.10
Total Hours			7.05 person-hours

DATA

SE Category	SE Value	Magnitude	Total SE Value
Field	0.41	49	20.09
Total Hours			20.09 person-hours

CONCLUSION

In this chapter we have explained the architecture of two CASE tools — the 4th Generation Tool Model (4GT Model) and the Project Factors Expert System (PFES). Both tools can be used to improve the project planning process. The tools were installed and successfully tested in Winnipeg. The 4GT Model uses software metrics pertaining to the predictor SE as the basis from which future estimates are made. Such a strategy is very useful for cost modeling purposes. According to Pressman (1992), if a metrics baseline consisting of data collected from past software development projects can be established, several benefits can be obtained for cost and effort estimation modeling purposes. In our model, the following input data pertaining to the project being estimated is supplied by the CASE system:

- total number of functions (ie, the total number of database tables, reports, and forms)
- total number of form and report screen fields.
- total number of data elements in a table or file.

We have achieved a degree of software automation here; unnecessary export and import of data is eliminated. The end result is that effort estimates are more accurate.

Limitations and Future Trends

Even though the above tools functioned successfully, we must recognize the following limitations:

- the CASE tools were used for cost modeling ORACLE's 4GTs only; further calibration is required to ensure that the tools can be used for other fourth-generation products.
- using such tools for planning purposes requires a maturity level on several technical fronts: software metrics, cost modeling, expert systems, and use of CASE tools (for systems analysis and design). CASE tools and 4GTs represent new software technology. Cost modeling applications using them is therefore a topic reflecting future trends.

Nevertheless, we have to prepare for the future. Fertuck (1992) describing the importance of such CASE tools, states that "progressive groups are using the most modern support tools in new and innovative ways".

REFERENCES

Abdel-Hamid, T., & Madnick, S. (1991). *Dynamics of Software Project Management*, Englewood Cliffs, NJ: Prentice-Hall.

Albrecht, A. J., & Gaffney, J.E. (1983). Software Function, Source Lines of Code and Development Effort Prediction: A Software Science Validation. *IEEE Trans. Software Engineering*, November, p. 639-648.

Boehm, B. (1981). *Software Engineering Economics*. Englewood-Cliffs, NJ: Prentice-Hall.

Bailey, J, & Basili, V. 1981. A Meta-Model for Software Development and Resource Expenditures. *Proceedings of the 5th International Conference on Software Engineering*. (pp. 107-16). New York: IEEE.

Case, A. Jr. (1986). *Information Systems Development: Principles of Computer-Aided Software Engineering*. Englewood Cliffs, N.J: Prentice-Hall.

Connell, J., & Shafer, B. (1989). *Structured Rapid Prototyping An Evolutionary Approach.* Yourdon Press Computing Series. Englewood Cliffs, N.J: Prentice-Hall.

Corner, R. 1990. *Business Systems Design and Development*. Englewood-Cliffs, NJ: Prentice-Hall.

Damodaran, M. (1987). Fourth Generation Tools - Characteristics, Applications and their Evolution [Summary]. *First International Workshop on Computer-Aided Software Engineering*, Volume I (p. 157-159). Cambridge, MA: Index Technology.

DeMarco, T. (1982). *Controlling Software Projects*. Englewood Cliffs, N.J: Prentice-Hall.

DeMarco, T., & Lister, L. (1990). Software State-of-the-Art: Selected Papers. New York, NY: Dorset House Publishing.

Dredger B. (1989). *Function Point Analysis*. Englewood Cliffs, N.J: Prentice-Hall.

Fertuck, L. (1992). *Systems Analysis and Design with CASE tools*. Dubuque, IA:

Wm C Brown.

Grady, R., & Caswell, D. (1987). *Software Metrics: Establishing a Company-Wide Program.* Englewood-CLiffs, N.J: Prentice-Hall.

Jones C. (1986). *Programming Productivity.* McGraw-Hill.

IBM (1986), *Managing Projects with Application System,* Release 4, Product No. 5767-001, 1986

Ingres. (1986). *Ingres/Applications.* Relational Technology Inc. Alameda: CA.

Kanabar, V., Janzen, T., Seah, E., & Smith, W. (1991). *Installation of a 4GT Model for Effort Estimation of 4GL projects.* Management Library. University of Manitoba, Winnipeg.

Kemerer, C. (1988). Software Cost Estimation Models. Forthcoming in *Software Engineers Reference Book,* Surrey, U.K: Butterworth.

Martin, J. 1982. *Application Development Without Programmers.* N.J: Prentice-Hall.

Martin, J. 1985. *Fourth-Generation Languages.* N.J: Prentice-Hall.

Matos, V.M, & Jalics, P.J. (1989). An Experimental Analysis of the Performance of Fourth Generation Tools on PCs. *Communications ACM,* 32(11), 1340-1351.

McClure, C. (1989). *CASE is Software Automation.* Englewood-Cliffs, N.J: Prentice-Hall.

Mills, H., & Dyson P. (1990). Using Metrics to Quantify Development. *IEEE Software,* March, 15-16.

Microsoft. (1987). *Microsoft Project document: Project Scheduling and Reporting Program,* No. 410720011-400-R00-0887, Part No. 00163.

Misra S., & Jalics, P. (1988). Third Generation versus Fourth-Generation Software Development. *IEEE Software,* July, p. 8-14.

Nastec. (1986). *Nastec CASE 2000,* Nastec Corporation, Southfield, Michigan.

Oracle. (1988). *SQL*FORMS Designer's Reference Version 2.0,* Oracle Corporation, Part No. 3304-V2.0. February.

Peters, T., & Waterman, R. (1982), *In Search of Excellence,* N.Y: Harper & Row, pp. 240.

Pfleeger, S. (1991), *Software Engineering: The Production of Quality Software,* Second Edition, N.Y: Macmillan.

Pressman, R. (1987) *Software Engineering A Practitioners Approach,* 2nd Edition, McGraw-Hill Book Company.

Pressman, R. (1992) *Software Engineering A Practitioners Approach,* 3rd Edition, McGraw-Hill Book Company.

Rockart, J.F, & Flannery, L. (1983). The Management of End User Computing. *Communications of the ACM, Association of Computing Machinery,* Oct., pp. 776-784.

Symantec. (1990). Time Line: The Corporate Choice for Project Management and Presentations, *User Manual,* Part # 03-30-00016.

Symons, C. (1988). Function Point Analysis, Difficulties and Improvements. *IEEE Software Transactions on Software Engineering,* SE-14(1), January, pp. 2-10.

Uniface (1989). *Uniface V. 5.2.* Uniface Corporation. Alameda:CA.

Verner, J., Tate, G. (1988), Estimating Size and Effort in Fourth-Generation Development. *IEEE Software,* July, pp.15-22

Walston, C., & Felix, C. A Method for Programming Measurement and Estimation. *IBM Systems Journal* 16 (1), 54-73.

Waterman, D. (1986). *A Guide to Expert Systems,* Addison Wesley Publishing Co.

Wrigley, C., & Dexter. A. (1991). A Model for Measuring Information System Size. *MIS Quarterly,* June, 245-257.

Whitten, J., & Bentley, L. (1987). *Using Excelerator for Systems Analysis and Design,* Boston: Irwin.

CHAPTER ELEVEN

Object-Oriented Analysis with CASE

Christopher G. Jones
Utah Valley Community College

Object-oriented software development is reported to be growing at 110 percent per year. Much of this growth has been fostered by the advent of object-oriented development environments and languages. The appearance of computerized object-oriented analysis and design tools, however, has lagged. Most CASE tools still center on traditional structured analysis and design methodologies. CASE products with embedded object-oriented analysis and design methodologies are few.

This chapter addresses emerging developments in CASE tools that support object-oriented analysis. After a brief overview of the object-oriented approach to systems analysis, common object-oriented analysis diagramming notations are discussed. This sets the stage for the discussion of available object-oriented analysis CASE tools. Following this, there is an in-depth review of OOATool, one of the first commercial object-oriented analysis CASE tools. A typical business systems analysis project is used to "test drive" OOATool. The chapter concludes with commentary on using OOATool in the classroom and recommendations regarding the direction of object-oriented analysis with CASE.

Although software growth, in general, has slowed to 20 percent annually in the United States, object-oriented software is reported to be growing at 110 percent per year (Blackford, 1990). Much of this growth has been fostered by the emergence of object-oriented development environments and languages. The development of object-oriented analysis and design tools, however, has lagged. Most computer-aided software engineering (CASE) tools still center on traditional structured analysis and design methodologies. CASE products with embedded object-oriented analysis and design methodologies are few. Literature regarding object-oriented CASE tools is almost nonexistent.

With the explosive growth of graphical user interface (GUI) environments and the increasing popularity of C++, object oriented programming is forcing object-oriented design and analysis to the forefront. This chapter addresses emerging developments in CASE tools that support object-oriented analysis.

Since object-oriented analysis is itself an emerging discipline, the chapter begins with a brief overview of the object-oriented approach to systems analysis. A discussion of common object-oriented analysis diagramming notations and available object-oriented analysis CASE tools follows. The balance of the chapter focuses on a "test drive" of an actual object-oriented analysis CASE tool, OOATool, used to develop a typical systems analysis project.

OBJECT-ORIENTED ANALYSIS: SOLUTION FOR THE 90s

In a recent study of several Federal systems projects, the U.S. Army found:

- 47 percent of the systems were delivered but not used
- 29 percent were paid for but not delivered
- 19 percent were abandoned or reworked
- 3 percent were used after making changes
- only 2 percent were used as delivered (QED Information Sciences, Inc. [QED], 1989).

Industry expert T. Capers Jones claims that six generations of programmers maintain a program during its lifetime while up to 25 percent of very large projects are canceled before completion. Further, Jones estimates the average large system is one year late and costs two times the original budget (QED, 1989). This evidence

suggests the software crisis is very real and very much still with us.
The software crisis has often been defined as:

> [T]he problems associated with (1) how we develop software, (2) how we maintain a growing volume of existing software, and (3) how we can expect to keep pace with a growing demand for more software. (Pressman, 1987, p. 13).

The software crisis makes for extraordinary marketing fodder. For years, industry consultants and vendors have hawked products claiming to be the "silver bullet" system engineers were looking for. In the seventies, structured analysis and design promised increased productivity; in the eighties, similar promises were made for CASE tools and fourth-generation languages.

Previous attempts to solve the software crisis once and for all, have seen only modest success. According to object-oriented proponents, the information systems analyst's "worst nightmare" is still with him or her, largely due to an infatuation with system analysis and design based on discrete transformational processes. Object-oriented analysis, design, and implementation is the latest "silver bullet." Advocates claim the object-oriented approach is a major paradigm shift, bringing a whole new way of viewing the systems world—a way that eliminates the maintenance "iceberg" inherited from earlier development approaches.

Analytical Models

An analytical model or paradigm gives the analyst a way of looking at, or viewing, the problem space. This view makes it possible for the analyst to order and structure his or her perception of the problem. The two primary paradigms in use today are the procedural model and the information model. Object-oriented modeling is the latest analytical paradigm to receive widespread attention in the systems community. An outgrowth of object-oriented programming and information modeling, object-oriented analysis is an attempt to comprehend the problem space by building a model of it.

Through the natural mental process of abstraction, the analyst constructs a simplified view of the problem domain by decomposing it into objects and object interactions (Wirfs-Brock, Wilkerson, & Wiener, 1990). The output from object-oriented analysis, then, is a model that maps directly to the problem domain, and the system's responsibility for that domain (Coad & Yourdon, 1991). This approach avoids the indirect mapping of the procedural model and the partial mapping of the information model.

Object-oriented analysis rests on a foundation of essential principles for apprehending reality and managing complexity. These principles include: (1) abstraction, (2) encapsulation, and (3) hierarchical inheritance.

Abstraction

Abstraction allows the analyst to focus on the essential features of real-world objects while ignoring irrelevant details. In an intrinsically complex world, abstraction is a psychological necessity for dealing with overwhelming detail (Wirfs-Brock et al., 1990). Rather than trying to comprehend the entirety, the analyst selects key system details, suppressing all others. The result is a simplified model of reality, much like a scale model of a sailing ship is a simplified version of the real thing.

Choosing which details to feature and which to suppress is guided by fundamental organizing methods. Hoare proposes that "abstraction arises from a recognition of similarities between certain objects, situations, or processes in the real world, and the decision to concentrate upon these similarities and to ignore for the time being the differences" (Booch, 1991, p. 39).

Manfredi and Tortorici (1989) suggest that real world similarities can be grouped using three abstraction mechanisms derived from semantic data modeling—classification, aggregation, and generalization. The classification abstraction mechanism groups real world objects into classes that share common properties. In the semantic data model, these common properties are the object's common data attributes. The object-oriented paradigm extends the classification abstraction to include not only common attributes but also common behavior or operations. The semantic relationship expressed by classification is "has-type/has-instance" and denotes membership in a specific class. Objects, in an object-oriented sense, are instances of a specific class. Classes without objects are referred to as abstract classes.

Aggregation abstraction focuses on an object's composition. Whole objects are grouped with their component parts. Whole-part relationships reduce complexity by making it possible to address the whole without regard to the configuration of the underlying parts. Aggregation classes embody the behavior or operations of the basic whole. The semantic relationship expressed by aggregation is "has-attribute" or "HasA" (Ackroyd & Daum, 1991; Manfredi & Tortorici, 1989).

The generalization abstraction allows the grouping of several classes of objects with common properties into a superclass or general category. Generalization produces a hierarchy of objects and makes possible inheritance, discussed later. The semantic relationship expressed by generalization is "has-subtype" or "IsA" and denotes the generalization-specialization relationship (Ackroyd & Daum, 1991; Manfredi & Tortorici, 1989).

Encapsulation

Encapsulation or information hiding is the principle of packaging the implementation detail of an abstracted object so that it is secret or hidden from the rest of the system. Booch (1991) suggests that:

> Abstraction and encapsulation are complementary concepts: abstraction focuses upon the outside view of an object and encapsulation—also known as information hiding—prevents clients from seeing its inside view, where the behavior of the abstraction is implemented (p. 45).

By hiding implementation detail, volatility is localized inside the object (Coad & Yourdon, 1991). All interaction or communication with the object is through the outside view of the object or interface. Encapsulation makes it possible to make changes to the implementation without affecting the overall system; the interface remains the same. This means that encapsulation "allows program [and analysis and design] changes to be reliably made with limited effort" (Booch, 1991, p. 45).

Hierarchical Inheritance

Generalization abstraction and aggregation abstraction not only allow the analyst to focus on relevant details but also to order objects into natural hierarchies. Generalization produces a "kind of" hierarchy; aggregation, a "part of" hierarchy (Booch, 1991). Generalization hierarchies facilitate inheritance—"the acquisition of properties or attributes from an ancestor [class]" (Chirdon, 1991). A specialization subclass, then, "inherits" or shares the data attributes and behavior of the generalization superclass. Attributes and operations can be inherited unchanged, overridden, or enhanced. As such, inheritance facilitates reuse and system extensibility through the encapsulated commonality of the higher classes in the hierarchy (Korson & McGregor, 1990).

Inheritance provides the leverage in the object-oriented model, making it possible "to state our abstractions with an economy of expression" (Booch, 1991, p. 56). As Cox explains:

> Without inheritance, every class would be a free-standing unit, each developed from the ground up. Different classes would bear no relationship with one another, since the developer of each provides methods in whatever manner he chooses . . . . Inheritance makes it possible to define new software in the same way we introduce any concept to a newcomer, by comparing it with something already familiar (Booch, 1991, p. 56).

Object-Oriented Analysis

Using the principles of abstraction, encapsulation, and hierarchical inheritance, the analyst undertakes a series of analytical activities to develop the problem domain model. The number and order of these activities will vary depending on the practitioner. Object-oriented analysis (OOA) usually includes:

- Investigating the problem domain, which may involve browsing previous object-oriented analysis for reuse possibilities
- Identifying objects
- Identifying object attributes and behaviors (services)
- Classifying objects into hierarchies using aggregation and generalization
- Identifying interaction between objects
- Modeling system responsibilities (Booch, 1991; Coad & Yourdon, 1991; Gibson, 1990; Henderson-Sellers & Edwards, 1990; Manfredi & Tortorici, 1989).

Object-oriented analysis is an iterative process. The activities are not sequential; they "guide the analyst from high levels of abstraction to increasingly lower levels of abstraction" (Coad & Yourdon, 1991, p. 34). As Booch (1991) points out:

> This is an incremental process: the identification of new classes and objects usually causes us to refine and improve upon the semantics of, and relationships among, existing classes and objects. It is also an iterative process: implementing classes and objects often leads us to the discovery or invention of new classes and objects whose presence simplifies and generalizes our design (p. 190).

The outgrowth from the analytical process is a Requirements

Specification composed of object specifications and a possible analysis prototype (Gibson, 1990). Object specifications, again, vary from practitioner to practitioner but usually include:

- A listing of classes and objects in the problem domain
- Class and object descriptions including data attributes and behavior or services
- Class hierarchies showing whole-part and generalization-specialization relationships
- Object relationship charts or tables showing object interaction

DIAGRAMMING METHODOLOGIES AND NOTATIONS

Object-oriented analysis is an emerging analytical paradigm lacking the codification and standards found in more mature approaches to systems analysis such as structured analysis or information modeling. While there have been calls for a uniform object notation (Page-Jones, Constantine, & Weiss, 1990), there are neither *de jure* nor *de facto* standards. As of this writing, popular object-oriented methods and notations include Booch and Coad-Yourdon. Other methods and notations abound, many of which are supported by proprietary CASE tools. Additional object-oriented notations include: OMT (Object Modeling Technique) (Rumbaugh, Blaha, Premerlani, Eddy, & Lorensen, 1991); Wirfs-Brock, Wilkerson, & Weiner (1990) Class-Responsibility-Collaboration (CRC) cards and diagrams adapted from Ward Cunningham; Semaphore Pilot notation (Ackroyd & Daum, 1991); the Uniform Object Notation (Page-Jones et al., 1990); MFD (Message Flow Decomposition) diagramming (Dean, 1991), and Kurtz-Woodfield-Embley notation (Kurtz, Woodfield, & Embley, 1991). Carry overs from object-based design using the Ada language include: HOOD (Hierarchical Object-oriented Design) notation (Schindler, 1990); Buhr diagrams (Buhr, 1984; Buhr, 1990); and, OOSD (Object-oriented Structured Design) notation that "tries to mate the Ward-Mellor methodology with the Booch and Buhr objectives" (Schindler, 1990, p. 270). Finally, there are information modeling notations such as Shlaer/Mellor Information Structure Diagrams (Shlaer & Mellor, 1988). A full discussion of alternative methodologies and notations is beyond the scope of this chapter. However, due to the popularity of Booch and Coad-Yourdon notations examples of each will be provided and discussed.

Booch Diagrams

The Booch methodology is described in detail in *Object Oriented Design with Applications* by Grady Booch (1991). This latest release from Booch updates his earlier work with object-oriented design using the Ada programming language. Both analysis and design modeling are captured in Booch diagrams, which are really a series of views as opposed to a single, monolithic illustration.

A Booch model encompasses Class Structure, Object Structure, Module Architecture, and Process Architecture. These views translate into four diagrams respectively: Class diagrams, Object Diagrams, Module Diagrams, and Process Diagrams that are supported by two additional diagrams—State Transition Diagrams and Timing Diagrams. Since systems analysis focuses on a logical model of the system under consideration, object-oriented analysis under the Booch methodology would produce Class, Object, State Transition, and Timing Diagrams. Figures 1 and 2 show Booch notations for each diagram type including documentation templates for each diagram symbol. Figures 3 and 4 show example diagrams for a hydroponics gardening process control system.

Coad-Yourdon Diagrams

The latest Coad-Yourdon object-oriented analysis methodology and notation is detailed in *Object-Oriented Analysis*, 2nd Ed. by Peter Coad and Ed Yourdon (1991). The first edition (1990) notations have been modified slightly to ensure the distinction between classes and instances. Graham (1991) has suggested further improvements to the revised Coad-Yourdon notation. A separate, companion volume, Object-oriented Design presents the Coad-Yourdon (1991) object-oriented design methodology and notation.

Coad-Yourdon OOA relies on a five-layer model. Figure 5 shows the symbol notation used in the model. As the figure indicates, instantiated classes are referred to as Class-&-Objects, meaning a class and its objects. To further document each Class-&-Object, Coad-Yourdon encourage the use of documentation templates, Object State diagrams, and Service Charts (Figure 6).

Each layer of the five-layer model represents a different view of the problem domain. The Subject layer (Figure 7) shows communities of classes and objects working together, which often translates into something roughly equivalent to a subsystem. The Class-&-Object layer (Figure 8) depicts abstract classes and instantiated classes with objects. Figure 9 shows the Structure layer that depicts class hierarchies—Generalization-Specialization or Whole-Part. The

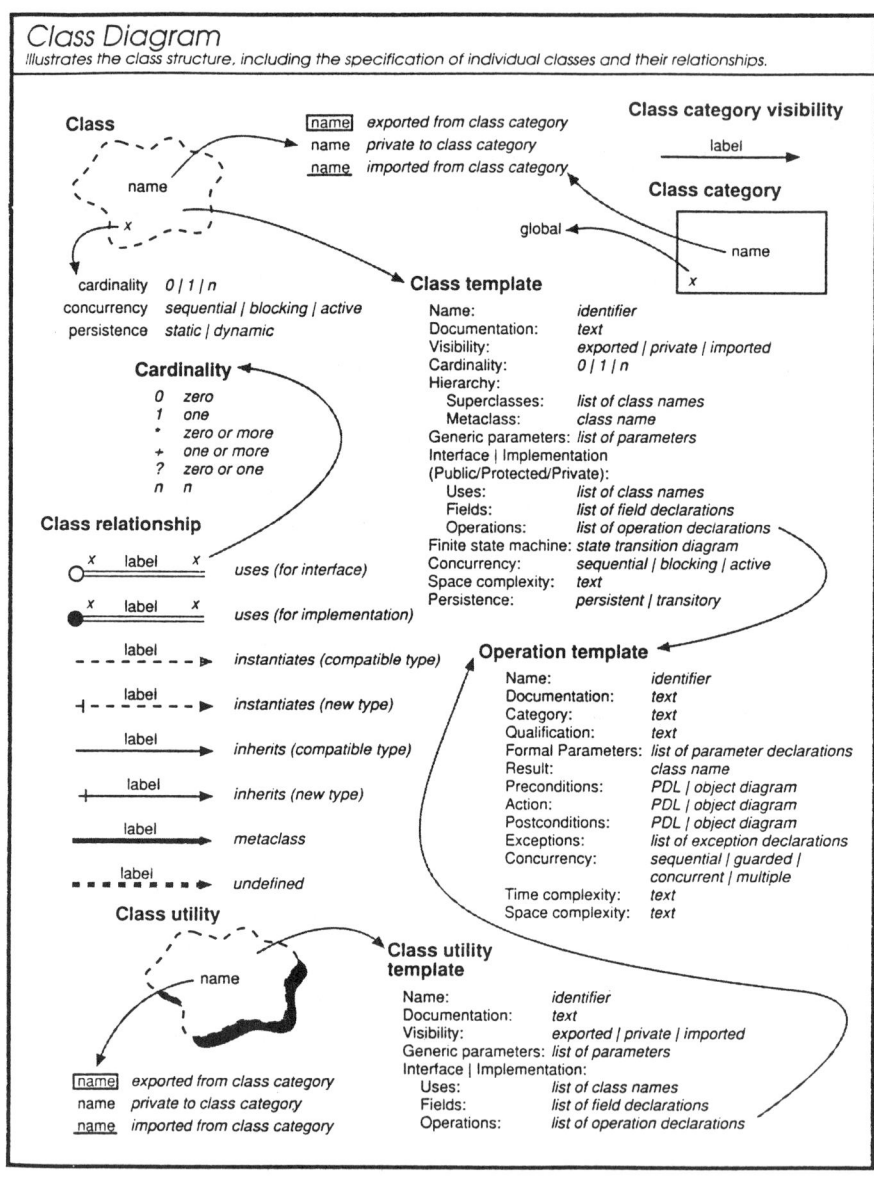

Note: From *Object Oriented Design with Applications* (inside front cover) by G. Booch, 1991, Redwood City, CA: Benjamin/Cummings. Reprinted with permission.

Figure 1: Booch Class Diagram Notation

Object-oriented Analysis 327

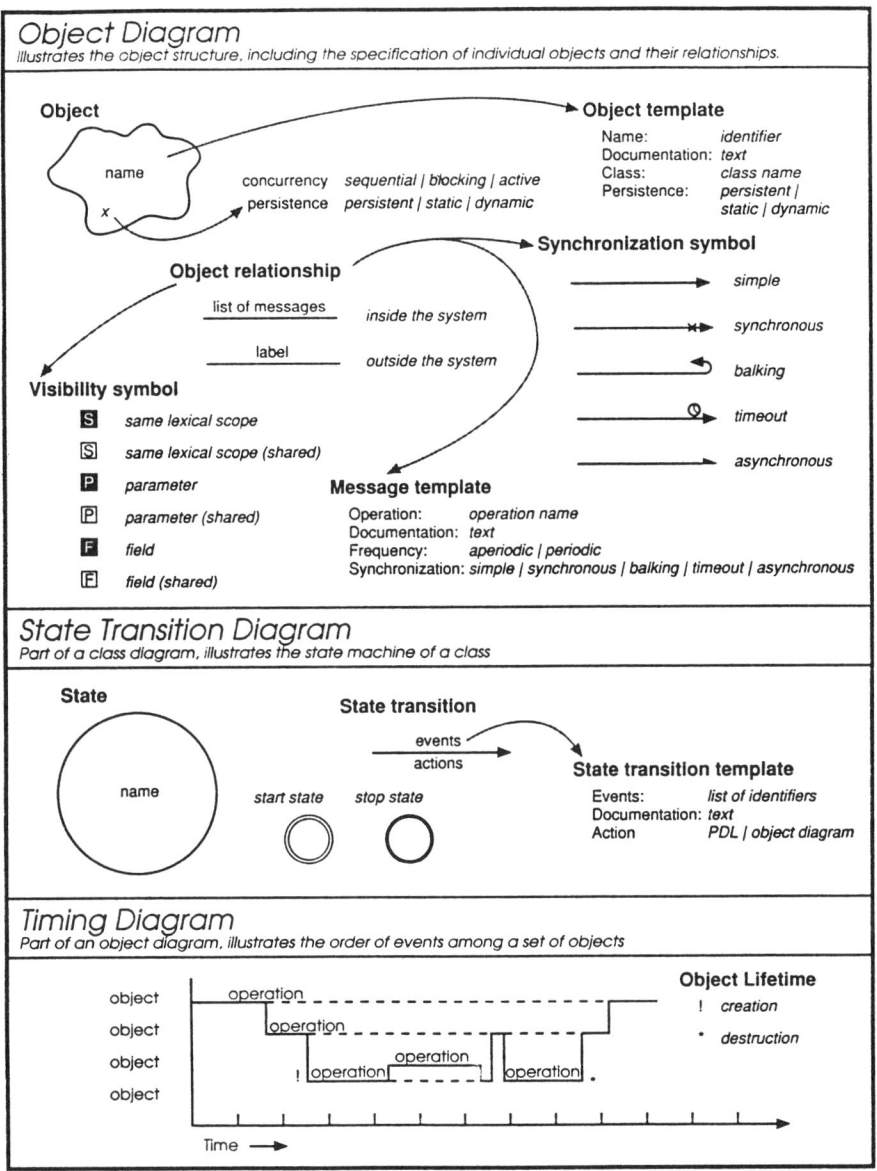

Note: From *Object Oriented Design with Applications* (inside back cover) by G. Booch, 1991, Redwood City, CA: Benjamin/Cummings. Reprinted with permission.

Figure 2: Booch Object, State Transition, and Timing Diagram Notation

328 Jones

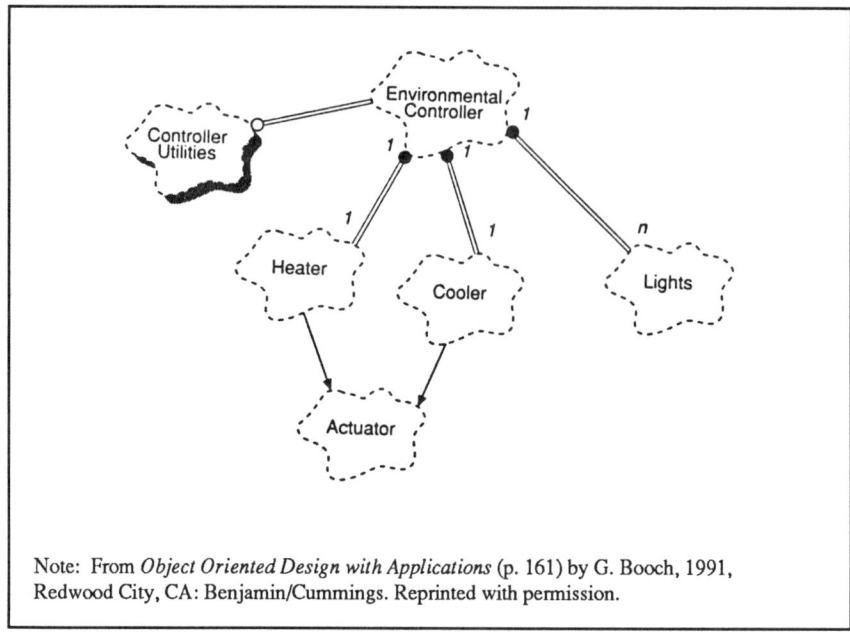

Note: From *Object Oriented Design with Applications* (p. 161) by G. Booch, 1991, Redwood City, CA: Benjamin/Cummings. Reprinted with permission.

Figure 3: Booch Hydroponics System Class Diagram

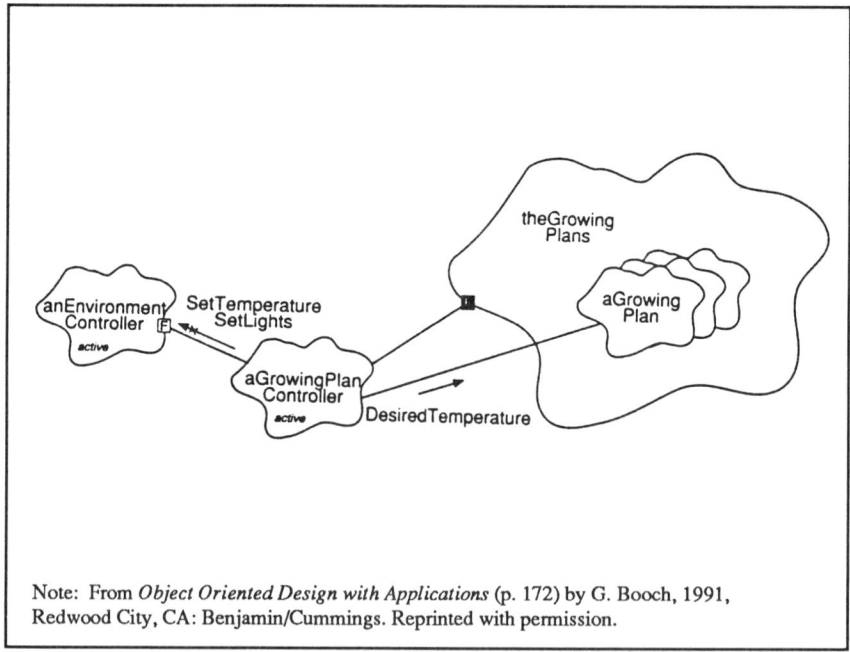

Note: From *Object Oriented Design with Applications* (p. 172) by G. Booch, 1991, Redwood City, CA: Benjamin/Cummings. Reprinted with permission.

Figure 4: Booch Hydroponics Gardening System Object Diagram

Object-oriented Analysis 329

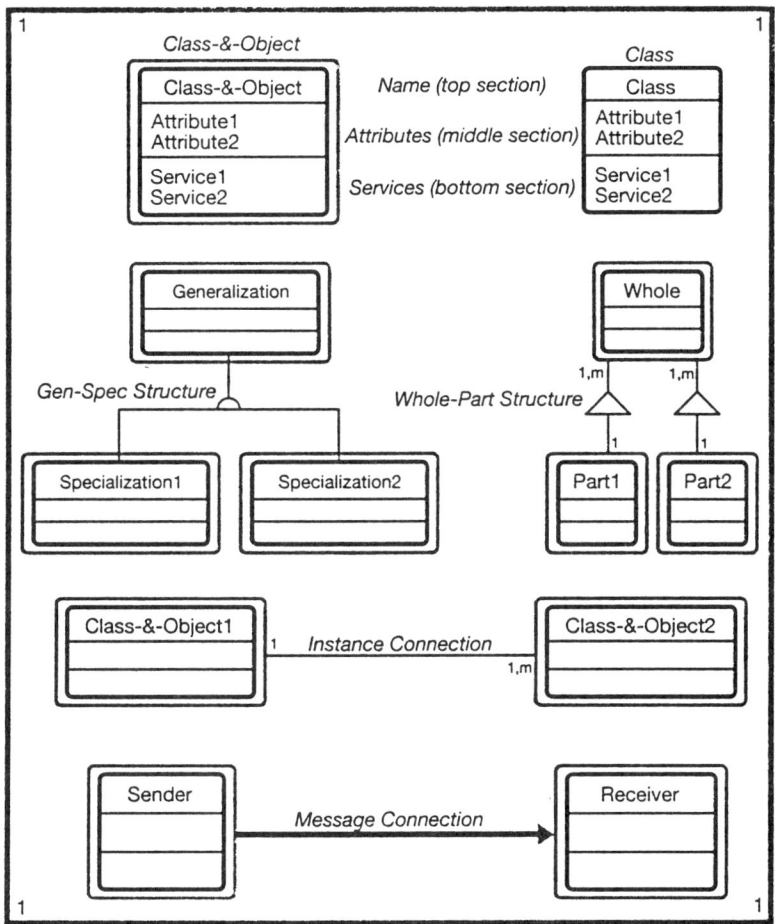

Note: P. Coad/Edward Yourdon, *Object-Oriented Analysis*, (2nd e, © 1991, (p. 196). Reprinted with permission of Prentice Hall, Englewood Cliffs, NJ.

Figure 5: Coad-Yourdon Object-oriented Analysis Notation

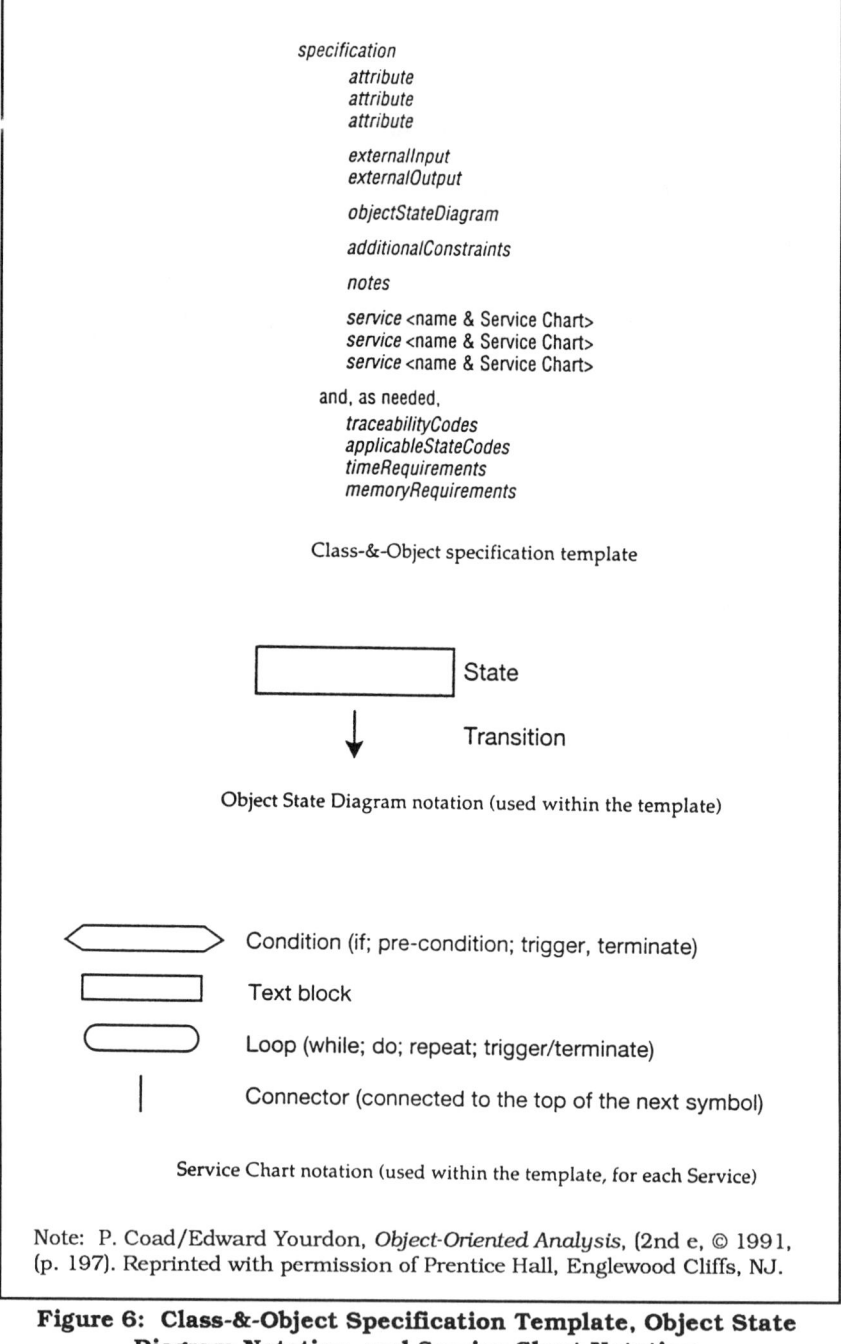

Figure 6: Class-&-Object Specification Template, Object State Diagram Notation, and Service Chart Notation

Object-oriented Analysis 331

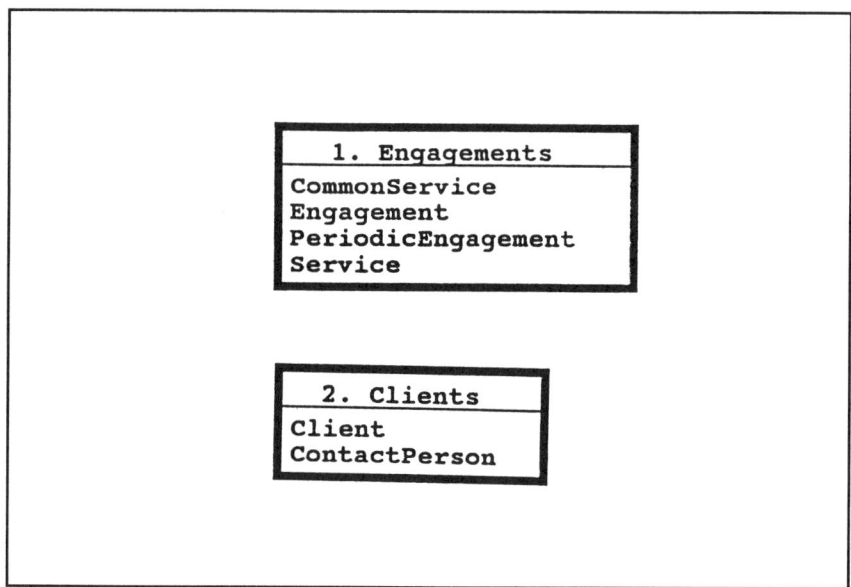

Figure 7: Due Date Monitoring System Subject Layer

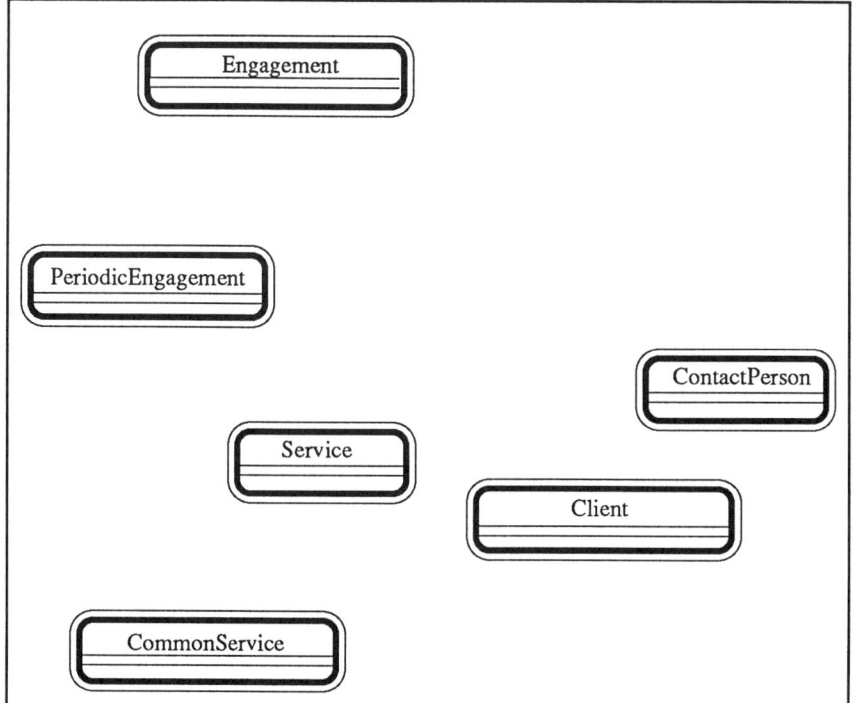

Figure 8: Due Date Monitoring System Class-&-Objects Layer

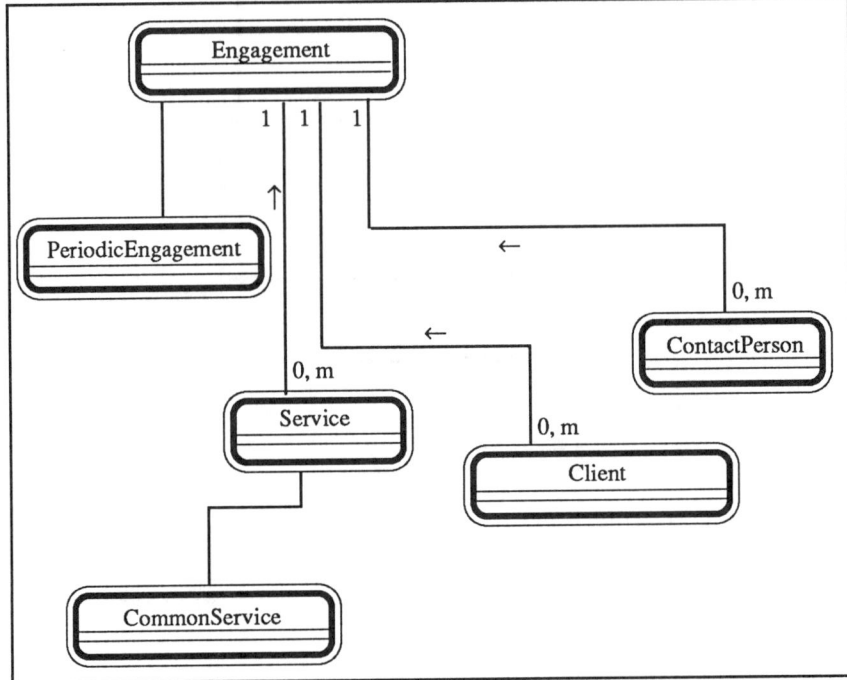

Figure 9: Due Date Monitoring System Structure Layer

Attribute layer (Figure 10) expands the Structure layer to include Class-&-Object attributes and Instance Connections between Class-&-Objects. Instance connections represent associations between independent objects. These associations are needed for an object to fulfill its behavioral responsibility. Association ranges may be 0, 1 or many, as in traditional data modeling. Finally, the Service layer (Figure 11) expands the Class-&-Object to include services and Message Connections between Class-&-Objects. A message connection depicts object communication.

Notational Commonalities

While object-oriented analysis diagramming varies largely from practitioner to practitioner, the concepts being symbolically represented are, for the most part, common. CASE tools used in object-oriented analysis should include, at a minimum, notations for:

- Classes
- Class Attributes
- Class Services (Methods)
- Objects
- Object State Transitions

- Generalization-Specialization (IsA) Relationships
- Whole-Part (HasA) Relationships
- Associative (UsesA) Relationships (Instance Connections)
- Object Communication (Messages, Interface)
- Communities of Objects (Subjects, Subsystems)

AVAILABLE CASE TOOLS FOR OBJECT-ORIENTED ANALYSIS

Until recently, CASE tool support for object-oriented analysis had been virtually nonexistent. Practitioners and instructors alike often used paper methods such as 3x5 cards or their computer counterpart, a HyperCard stack, to annotate class and object specifications (Beck & Cunningham, 1989). Class and object hierarchies, message connections and instance connections were captured in paper drawings. For small projects, paper tools were adequate but cumbersome to modify and maintain.

Early attempts to depict Generalization-Specialization hierarchies using the computer were done with simple drawing tools such as Apple's DrawShapes (Wilson, 1990). Using this approach, all object symbols had to be created and replicated by the analyst. Connections, arrows, and labeling were added by the analyst without automated support. Available tools for this approach include paint programs such as PC Paintbrush™ and MacPaint™ and drawings programs such as Harvard Graphics 3.0™, DrawPerfect 1.1™ or PowerPoint™. Given that many analysts already are familiar with such drawing and painting programs, this a simple way to capture class and object hierarchies, message connections, and instance connections without all the overhead of learning a CASE tool. The drawback is that all drawing elements must be manipulated by the analyst making drawing modification a chore.

In "Designing is Hard: Object-Oriented Software is Different!" Wilf LaLonde and John Pugh (1989) make a case for using the Smalltalk environment as a CASE tool. Smalltalk is a pure object-oriented language often used for prototyping because it is interpreted rather than compiled. The language is packaged as part of a development environment. This environment includes the Smalltalk source interpreter, a graphics development platform, and a class hierarchy browser.

As Smalltalk programs are built, new classes are added to the built-in class library. This repository of classes can be explored using a class hierarchy browser window, as Figure 12 shows. With all previous classes captured as part of the class library, the

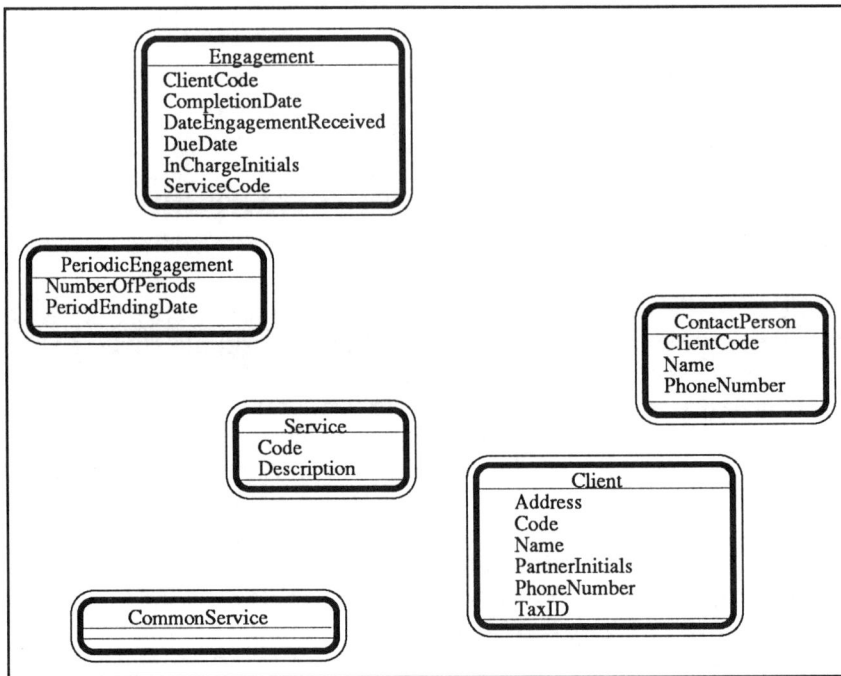

Figure 10: Due Date Monitoring System Attribute Layer

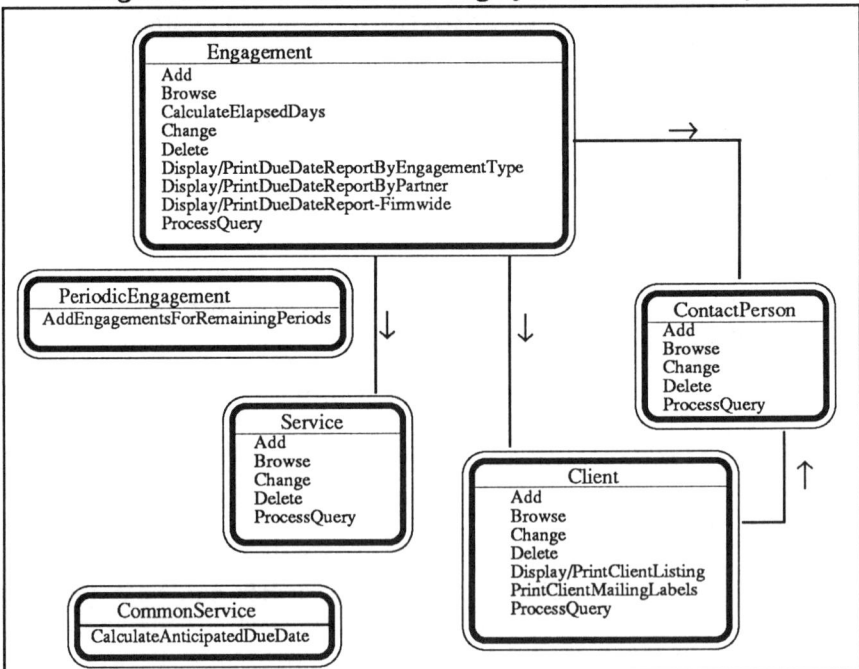

Figure 11: Due Date Monitoring System Service Layer

Smalltalk environment facilitates class reuse. The class hierarchy browser displays the classes in an outline fashion, indicating single inheritance relationships. A class may be selected and examined for its attributes (class and instance variables) and services (methods) using a class browser window (Figure 13). As can be seen, the Smalltalk environment as CASE tool, is text-based with class hierarchies represented by outlines. This approach does not use diagrams with symbolic notations.

More recently, traditional CASE-style support for object-oriented analysis has come to market. This new breed of CASE tools ranges from simple computer-aided drawing and checking tools such as OOATool from Object International to sophisticated CASE tools such as Semaphore with code generation and reverse engineering. The following list highlights some of the major CASE tools for object-oriented analysis:

CASE Tool: ObjectCast
Vendor: Fuji Xerox Information Systems Co., Ltd. 16-6, Nishishinjuku 3 - chome, Shinjuku-ku Tokyo, Japan 160 (81)(3) 3378-8011
Description: ObjectCast is an object-oriented CASE tool supporting system development in the Smalltalk environment. Coad-Yourdon, Rumbaugh OMT, and other notations such as DFD and Petrinet are supported. ObjectCast facilitates human-computer interface development by generating Smalltalk code for screens designed with a built-in interface builder. At the time of this writing, ObjectCast was only available for the clients joining the special project initiated by Fuji Xerox Information Systems Co., Ltd. ObjectCast will be released in Japan at the end of 1992.

CASE Tool: ObjectMaker
Vendor: Mark V Systems Limited 16400 Ventura Blvd., Suite 303 Encino, CA 91436 (818) 995-7671
Description: ObjectMaker is a comprehensive CASE tool supporting over 20 analytical methods and notations including object-oriented notations such as Coad-Yourdon, Booch, and Buhr. Notation and methods are extensible. ObjectMaker provides code generation and reverse engineering in Ada, C, and C++ programming languages. Multiple minicomputer, workstations and, microcomputer hardware platforms are supported as are multiple windowing environments. Class and

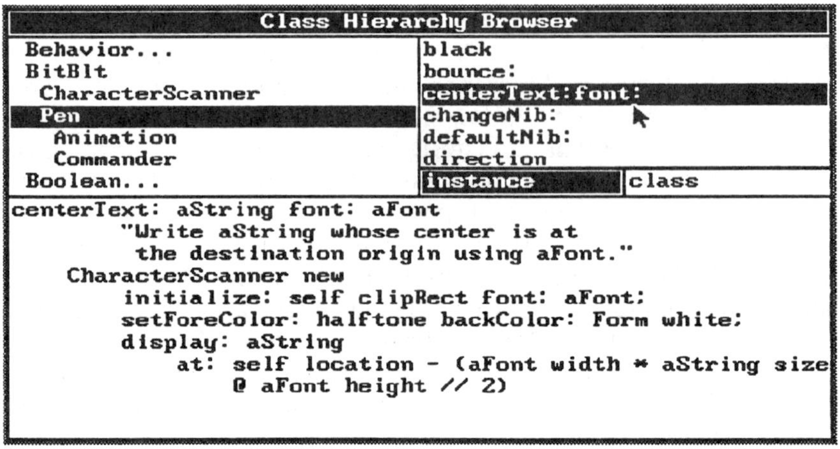

336 Jones

```
╔══════════════ Class Hierarchy Browser ══════════════╗
║ Behavior...              │ black                     ║
║ BitBlt                   │ bounce:                   ║
║   CharacterScanner       │ centerText:font:          ║
║   Pen                    │ changeNib:                ║
║     Animation            │ defaultNib:               ║
║     Commander            │ direction                 ║
║ Boolean...               │ instance      │ class     ║
╠══════════════════════════════════════════════════════╣
║ centerText: aString font: aFont                      ║
║     "Write aString whose center is at                ║
║      the destination origin using aFont."            ║
║     CharacterScanner new                             ║
║         initialize: self clipRect font: aFont;       ║
║         setForeColor: halftone backColor: Form white;║
║         display: aString                             ║
║             at: self location - (aFont width * aString size
║                 @ aFont height // 2)                 ║
╚══════════════════════════════════════════════════════╝
```

Note: From *Smalltalk/V DOS Tutorial and Programming Handbook* (p. 241), 1991, Los Angeles, Digitalk, Inc. copyright 1991 by Digitalk, Inc. Reprinted with permission.

Figure 12: Smalltalk Class Hierarchy Browser

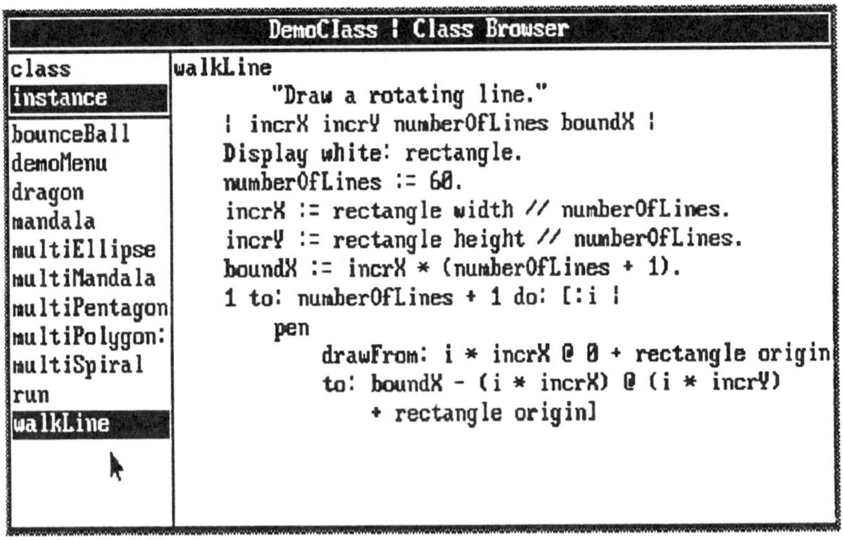

```
╔════════════════ DemoClass | Class Browser ═══════════╗
║ class        │ walkLine                              ║
║ instance     │     "Draw a rotating line."           ║
║ bounceBall   │ | incrX incrY numberOfLines boundX |  ║
║ demoMenu     │ Display white: rectangle.             ║
║ dragon       │ numberOfLines := 60.                  ║
║ mandala      │ incrX := rectangle width // numberOfLines.
║ multiEllipse │ incrY := rectangle height // numberOfLines.
║ multiMandala │ boundX := incrX * (numberOfLines + 1).║
║ multiPentagon│ 1 to: numberOfLines + 1 do: [:i |     ║
║ multiPolygon:│     pen                               ║
║ multiSpiral  │         drawFrom: i * incrX @ 0 + rectangle origin
║ run          │         to: boundX - (i * incrX) @ (i * incrY)
║ walkLine     │             + rectangle origin]       ║
╚══════════════════════════════════════════════════════╝
```

Note: From *Smalltalk/V DOS Tutorial and Programming Handbook* (p. 246), 1991, Los Angeles, Digitalk, Inc. copyright 1991 by Digitalk, Inc. Reprinted with permission.

Figure 13: Smalltalk Class Browser

Object-oriented Analysis 337

hierarchy documentation are provided, as is diagram checking.

CASE Tool: OOWorkbench, consisting of OOATool, OODTool, and OOCodeGen
Vendor: Object International, Inc. 8140 N. MoPac Expressway, 4-200 Austin, TX 78759-8864 (512) 795-0202
Description: OOWorkbench is a comprehensive CASE tool supporting only the Coad-Yourdon method and notation. As of this writing, OODTool and OOCodeGen have not shipped. Target delivery dates are third quarter 1992 for OODTool and six to seven months later for OOCodeGen. Current plans for OOCodeGen include code generation in C++ and Smalltalk. OOATool runs on Apple MacIntosh and IBM compatible hardware. MS-Windows 3.0 or IBM OS/2 is required for IBM compatibles. An upgrade to OOATool that significantly enhances performance is scheduled for early 1992. Class and hierarchy documentation are provided, as is diagram checking.

CASE Tool: ParadigmPlus
Vendor: ProtoSoft, Inc. 17629 El Camino Real, Suite 202 Houston, TX 77058 (713) 480-3233
Description: ParadigmPlus is a comprehensive CASE tool supporting popular object-oriented methods and notations such as Booch, Rumbaugh, and HOOD. Notations and methods are extensible. ParadigmPlus claims code generation in any language from C++ to Structured Query Language (SQL). Reverse engineering is slated for a later release. ParadigmPlus runs under MS-Windows 3.0 on IBM compatibles. Support for Coad-Yourdon, Firesmith, and Shlaer-Mellor (91) is projected for 4th quarter, 1991. Ports to SUN, Apollo, and IBM RS6000 workstations, OS/2 Presentation manager and Apple MacIntosh are projected for the first half of 1992.

CASE Tool: Pilot
Vendor: Semaphore Tools, Inc. 800 Turnpike Street, Suite 200 North Andover, MA 01845 (508) 794-3366
Description: Pilot is a comprehensive CASE tool supporting Coad-Yourdon, Booch, and Semaphore's proprietary object-oriented notation. Notation and methods are

extensible. Pilot provides code generation and reverse engineering in the C++ programming language. Pilot runs under MS-Windows 3.0 on IBM compatible PCs and Unix/Motif on SUN workstations. Class and hierarchy documentation are provided, as is diagram checking.

In addition to pure object-oriented CASE tools, there are several CASE products that support Booch and Buhr notation for the Ada language. These include: ADAFLOW from Iconix Software, Santa Monica, CA; Teamwork/ADA from CADRE Technologies, Providence, RI; and, Object-Oriented Structured Design/ADA from Interactive Development Environment, San Francisco, CA. Many of these CASE tools are extensible and could be configured to support a particular object-oriented methodology and notation. In "Object-Oriented Structured Design and C++" Anthony Wasserman (1991), founder of Interactive Development Environment (IDE), proposes configuration modifications to IDE's OOSD (Object-oriented structured design) CASE tool that would support systems development in a C++ language environment.

USING OOATOOL FOR OBJECT-ORIENTED ANALYSIS

With the background discussion on the object-oriented approach, methodologies, notations, and CASE tools completed, the focus will now shift to using CASE tools to perform object-oriented analysis. This section will provide an evaluation of OOATool from Object International, Inc.

As discussed earlier, CASE tools for object-oriented analysis are just beginning to emerge. OOATool, small project version, was selected because of its ready availability, low price ($95.00 US), and use of Coad/Yourdon notation. *Object-Oriented Analysis* by Coad and Yourdon (1991) is heavily used in the Systems Analysis and Design, Software Engineering, and C++ classes at Utah Valley Community College (UVCC). We wanted a tool that was intuitive, easy-to-use, and that made it possible for our students to have an object-oriented analysis experience without the distraction of having to learn a CASE tool that didn't mirror the classroom discussion.

Throughout *Object Oriented Analysis* and *Object Oriented Design*, Coad and Yourdon, make extensive reference to OOATool, using the analysis and design of this CASE software as a text example. In many respects, OOATool is an extension of the text. The additional detail found in the software complements the text and the discussions in the text make it easier to understand the software, especially the underlying construction of the software design. It is almost as if OOATool were not just designed as a stand-alone analytical tool but as a computer-assisted supplement to *Object-oriented Analysis* and *Object-oriented Design*. Given the pedagogical nature of the software and the easy-to-use MS Windows interface, OOATool appeared to be the best choice for an object-oriented CASE tool at UVCC.

Initial Expectations

Initial expectations of OOATool were influenced to a large extent by two factors, (1) our experience with a variety of traditional CASE tools such as Excelerator from Intersolv (formerly Index Technologies) and EasyCase from Evergreen CASE Tools, and (2) Coad and Yourdon's (1991) comments on CASE tool selection in *Object-Oriented Analysis*.

Excelerator is an integrated CASE tool, with a central repository for all system analysis documentation. Password security, networked files for analytical team access, model critiqueing, and a degree of code generation are all available. Most traditional structured analysis notations are supported along with symbol "explosion" or layering.

EasyCase is a shareware package that can be upgraded to a professional version. Easycase is a stand-alone computer-aided drawing package with no central repository or drawing linkages, such as Data Flow Diagram (DFD) data stores being linked to Entity-Relationship Diagram (ERD) entities. Easycase, then, represents one end of the spectrum in CASE tools, being nothing more than a specialized drawing tool while Excelerator represents the other end of traditional CASE tools touting an integrated package supporting work groups, front-end and back-end CASE.

In Chapter 8 of *Object-Oriented Analysis*, "Selecting CASE for OOA," Coad and Yourdon (1991) downplay today's CASE tools, referring to them as mere "Computer-Aided Drawing and Checking" tools or CADC's. Coad and Yourdon deprecate today's tools by questioning the need to "hard-wire" the CASE tool drawing elements to the notations of a particular methodology, arguing instead for user-defined drawing symbols and connectors.

Criticism aside, Coad and Yourdon (1991) see a "much larger context" for CASE as a valuable "automated assistant" (p. 174) throughout the system development life cycle. Specifically, they propose an object-oriented CASE tool that offers support for their five-layer OOA model. The tool should include notations for Subject, Class-&-Object, Class, Generalization-Specialization Structure, Whole-Part Structure, Class Attributes, Instance Connections, Class Services, and Message Connections. The notations should be supported by a series of documentation templates for describing the model components. The Class-&-Object template should have the capability of displaying Object State Diagrams, Services/States Table, and Service Charts (Figure 6). To facilitate user abstraction, the CASE tool should have the ability to select the visibility of each of the five layers, providing the user with just the view he or she desires. Subjects or communities of objects should be collapsible, partially expandable showing Class-&-Objects, and fully expandable showing all five layers.

Besides the above features, Coad and Yourdon (1991) suggest that an OOA CASE tool should provide drawing checking. The checks "should be project-definable as warnings (rules that can be broken) or as errors (rules that one is not allowed to violate)" (p. 175). Checks for Class-&-Objects would include checking that each Class-&-Object had a unique name within the model, had more than one attribute, had one or more instance connections, had one or more message connections, had unique attribute names, and had unique service names.

Checks for Class-&-Object templates should include whether there is a specification or description for each attribute and service, whether the template content is consistent with the layers of the model, and whether each named input parameter and output result shows usage somewhere in the specification text. For each generalization-specialization structure, the OOA CASE tool should check to make sure that the linked Class-&-Objects have more than one attribute or service per level, that specializations are limited to between one and three levels to minimize complexity, and that attribute and service identifiers are unique between levels. (p. 176)

Beyond these standard features, Coad and Yourdon (1991) suggest several advanced features for OOA CASE tools. These include support for analysis reuse and modeling behavior dynamics. Analysis reuse would be supported by something similar to a class hierarchy browser and class browser such as those found in Smalltalk (Figures 12 and 13). The analyst would be able to search through an organization's Class-&-Object repository that provided support for browsing, classifying, and extracting previous OOA results. A CASE tool that facilitated modeling object behavior dynamics would allow incoming and outgoing message connections to be highlighted based on the service selection. Also, threads of execution could be displayed with graphic distinction that facilitated visualizing the order of execution.

Given Coad and Yourdon's extensive prescription for an OOA CASE tool, we expected as a minimum, OOATool to provide the features identified above. In addition, given our experience with traditional CASE tools, we had hoped for some file security, group file access and record-locking, object explosion or "drill down" by clicking on a Class-&-Object, sample models, a tutorial, some kind of version control, a file backup utility, an attribute and service dictionary (*a la* a database data dictionary), model extensibility, a way to distribute renameable models as starting points for additional analysis, and standardized documentation templates. Additional features that would have been nice, but that we did not expect OOATool to have, include: reverse engineering of traditional structured analysis, design, and programming; code generation; an SQL interface to allow queries of the analysis database; and, project management.

Using OOATool: A Case Study

Object-oriented analysis is billed as a universal model capable of representing diverse problem domains from event-driven systems to traditional information systems. Space limits a full evaluation of the capabilities of OOATool for each of these diverse problem domains. Since traditional information systems account for most systems analysis activity, a typical information system was selected for evaluation purposes.

The Due Date Monitoring System. In addition to teaching responsibilities, the author is a practicing CPA. Certified Public Accounting firms traditionally provide accounting, tax, audit, and consulting services. These services or engagements are provided on a "job-shop" basis with each service produced discretely or in small batches. Usually the service must be provided by some specified due date. Individual tax returns, for example, customarily must be delivered before April 15th. For accounting firms, then, job tracking and due date monitoring are critical.

After exploring the problem domain, we developed the following requirements specification narrative for a custom due date monitoring system for use in the practice. This narrative serves as the foundation for the case study using OOATool.

Requirements Specification Narrative

The Due Date Monitoring System (DDMS) is designed to track each client service or project and provide information whether critical dates are being met. Several reports are available including: Due Date Report - Firmwide, Due Date Report by Partner, Due Date Report by Engagement Type, Client Listing, and Client Mailing Labels.

Main menu options for the DDMS are (1) client maintenance, (2) service maintenance, and (3) engagement maintenance, and (4) reports. Each maintenance menu option provides a submenu with menu selections for adding, changing, deleting, and browsing the respective data table.

Before inputting engagements, users will set up clients and the available services provided by the firm. Client information includes a client code, client name and address, phone numbers, contact person, tax identification numbers, and the initials of the partner responsible for the engagement.

Service information is simply a list of service codes and a description of each service. For example, the code and description for preparing individual returns could be:

Code	Description
1040	U.S. Individual Income Tax Return

Common services codes such as "1040" will be already setup in the DDMS, along with the anticipated due date.

Once available services are cataloged and client information entered, the user adds engagements (jobs) to the DDMS through the engagement maintenance submenu. Each engagement requires the following: client code, service code, initials of the responsible employee, date engagement received, due date, and completion date. Periodic engagements require the following additional information: number of periods and period-ending date

For monthly or quarterly engagements, the DDMS automatically creates an engagement for each remaining period in the year. For example, suppose the firm takes on a quarterly accounting engagement for a company with a July 31st fiscal year-end. The client has requested quarterly financial statements by the 15th of the month following the close of the quarter. The first quarter financial reports would be input as due on November 15th. The DDMS would automatically set up three more engagements for the client with due dates of February 15th, May 15th, and August 15th respectively.

The engagement maintenance submenu is also used to change engagement data, update each engagement for completion, and delete completed engagements.

The report submenu provides many preformatted report

Object-oriented Analysis 343

options and a query option for *ad hoc* inquiries. The Due Date Report -Firmwide lists all incomplete engagements sorted by due date. For each engagement the client name, service description, initials of the responsible firm member, date engagement received, elapsed days, and due date are shown.

The Due Date Report by Partner shows the same information grouped by partner and the Due Date Report by Engagement Type lists the information sorted by service code. The Client Listing Report shows all the information in the client table sorted by last name. Client Mailing Labels provides standard mailing labels for each client.

The query option allows the user to join any of the tables, select any records using standard relational and logical operators (e.g., >, =, and, or), and project or choose any table field in any order. Query results can be displayed or printed.

DDMS: Classes, Attributes, Services and Hierarchies. The process of identifying classes, class objects, class attributes and services is time consuming, iterative in nature, full of false starts, and beyond the scope of this chapter. In order to focus on evaluating OOATool, we have bypassed this process and have simply provided a list of our analytical findings. Readers interested in the object-oriented analytical process should consult *Object-Oriented Analysis* (Coad & Yourdon, 1991), *Designing Object-Oriented Software* (Wirfs-Brock et al., 1990), *Object Oriented Program Design with Examples in C++* (Mullin, 1989), *Object Oriented Design with Applications* (Booch, 1991) and the other publications listed in the extensive bibliographies found in *Object-Oriented Analysis* and *Object-Oriented Design with Applications*.

DDMS Model Elements

CLASS Hierarchy:

  Generalization-Specialization:

    Engagement
      Periodic Engagement

    Service
      Common Tax Service

  Whole-Part Relationships:

Engagement (range 1 for all parts)
    Client (range 0, m)
    ContactPerson (range 0, m)
    Service (range 0, m)
CLASS Listing:

CLASS	ATTRIBUTES	SERVICES

Client	Address
	Code
	Name
	PartnerInitials
	PhoneNumber
	TaxID
		Add
		Browse
		Change
		Delete
		Display/PrintClient
		  Listing
		PrintClientMailing
		  Labels
		ProcessQuery

CommonService		CalculateAnticpated DueDate
ContactPerson	ClientCode Name PhoneNumber	Add Browse Change Delete ProcessQuery

Engagement	ClientCode
	CompletionDate
	DateEngagement
	  Received
	DueDate
	InChargeInitials
	ServiceCode
		Add
		Browse
		CalculateElapsedDays
		Change
		Delete
		Display/PrintDueDate
		  ReportByEngagement
		  Type
		Display/PrintDueDate
		  ReportByPartner
		Display/PrintDueDate
		  Report-Firmwide
		ProcessQuery

Periodic Engagement	NumberOfPeriods PeriodEndingDate	AddEngagmentsFor RemainingPeriods

CLASS	ATTRIBUTES	SERVICES
Service	Code	Add
	Description	Browse
		Change
		Delete
		ProcessQuery

Instance Connections: None

Message Connections:

    Engagement messaged to: Service
        From Engagement object to Service object

    Engagement messaged to: Client
        From Engagement object to Client object

    Engagement messaged to: ContactPerson
        From Engagement object to ContactPerson object

    Client messaged to: ContactPerson
        From Client object to ContactPerson object

Test Drive

    At this point, with a list of DDMS model elements in hand, we were ready to evaluate OOATool against our initial expectations. OOATool uses a Graphic User Interface and is available for Apple MacIntosh, IBM-OS/2, and IBM-Windows platforms. Since the UVCC student labs run IBM-compatible hardware using MS-DOS 5.0 with MS-Windows 3.0, Version 1.3 of OOATool for Microsoft Windows 3.1 was chosen for evaluation. This version requires the following minimum hardware and software configuration:

- MS-DOS or PC-DOS, version 3.1 or later
- For 386 enhanced mode, an Intel 80386 or higher with 8 MB of memory
- For standard mode, an Intel 80236 with 4 MB of memory

- A hard disk with 8 to 10 MB of free disk space
- A 3.5 inch, 1.44 MB floppy drive
- A monitor, printer, and mouse supported by Windows

OOATool was tested on two hardware configurations: (1) an Intel 80386SX-16mhz with 2 MB memory, using a multisync monitor, Logitech serial mouse, and Toshiba P321SL printer, and (2) an Intel 80386DX-33mhz with 4 MB memory using a VGA monitor, Z-nix serial mouse, and a HPLaserjet II, and HPLaserjet III printer. As suggested by the software documentation, 4 MB memory is the minimum acceptable hardware configuration. Running OOATool on the 2 MB machine proved to be frustrating with the program taking close to three minutes to load, and each Class-&-Object one to two minutes to draw itself. While Windows and OOATool will run on an Intel 80286, the user will find him or herself waiting for the screen to refresh between drawing changes. We found the Intel 80386SX with 4 MB to be the minimum practical hardware platform.

Installation. OOATool is supplied on two distribution diskettes. There is not an "Install" program as provided with most commercial software. Rather users are required to set up their own directories and copy the files from the distribution disk to the hard drive. The documentation assumes users are familiar with Microsoft Windows and capable of making directories, copying files, and creating an executable OOATool icon on the Windows desktop.

Operation. OOATool facilitates object-oriented analysis by using several windows. Clicking on the OOATool icon brings up the OOATool Window, which is basically a sign-on screen detailing information about the product, the developer, and how to order. The OOATool Window is the gateway to the other windows that provide the analytical tools for creating an object-oriented model. By the time users get somewhat involved with the OOATool, several windows will have been opened. Navigating through the maze of windows can get confusing at times. It is not always clear how to access nested Windows or how windows are related to each other. Figure 14 shows the relationship between the various windows.

Creating the Five Layer Model. To create the Due Date Monitoring System Model, the user selects New OOA Model/Drawing from the File Menu in the opening OOATool Window. A prompter dialogue box appears, requesting a unique permanent model name. Once the model name is entered, a new model is created and a blank unnamed drawing window appears. Models can have multiple drawings. Each drawing can reflect all layers of the five-layer model or only selected layers.

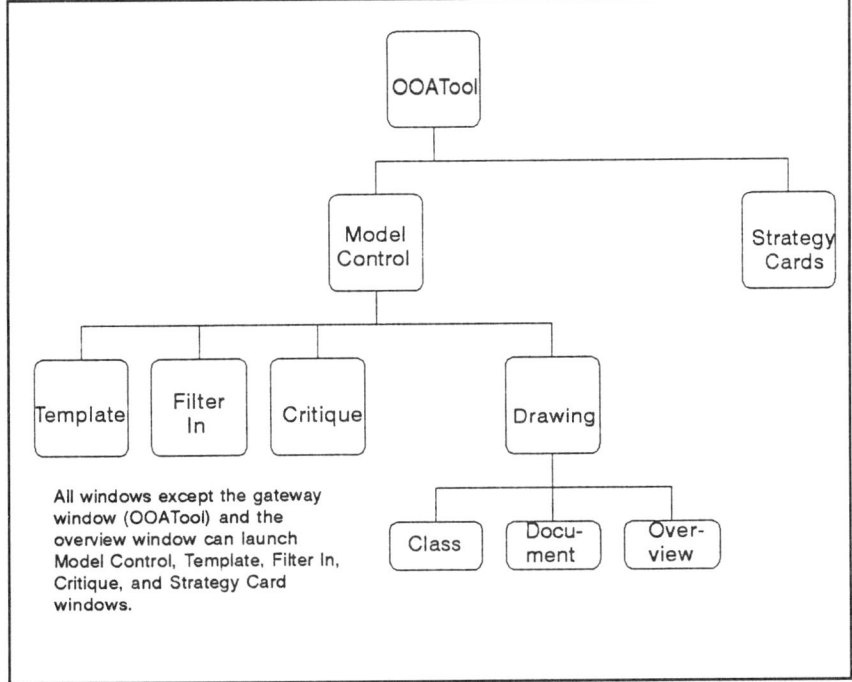

Figure 14: OOATool Window Hierarchy

Sketching the Due Date Monitoring System begins by creating the Class-&-Object rounded rectangles. This is done by clicking on the Create menu option in the Drawing window and by selecting New Class-&-Object. A prompter dialogue box pops up with the default name of New Class for the Class-&-Object symbol. The user simply types in the name of the first object, which for the DDMS is "Client."

As with model names, Class-&-Object names can be any length with spaces allowed. The shape of the rounded rectangle will stretch to accommodate whatever name length is provided. For evaluation purposes only, a Class-&-Object name of 870 characters was entered. The symbol stretched and printed without any problem.

After entering the Class name, a black Class-&-Object symbol appears somewhat to the right of center in the drawing window. From this point on, the creation of the model depends on the analyst's approach. As a simple drawing tool, the analyst can either create all the objects, link them into structures and then add attributes and services, or depending on preference, create each object, fully describe it with attribute and services, etc., and then link these objects through structures, instance and message connections.

If the decision is to just create all the objects first, the program does an interesting thing. It stacks each Class-&-Object behind the previous object. Unscrambling the dogpile of objects can be messy. It seems the original intent was for the analyst to create an object, position it on the drawing surface, add first-pass information, and then create the next object, modeling as he or she goes.

Creating Class-&-Objects can be facilitated with speed keys (e.g., Ctrl-I). All speed keys are identified on the pull down menu bar. Abstract classes can be created by modifying the default Class-&-Objects symbol to the Class only notation, using the Modify menu.

Generalization-Specialization hierarchies. To position the Class-&-Object symbols for placement in a hierarchy, the user selects the object by clicking anywhere inside the rounded rectangle. The rectangle becomes black to indicate it has been selected. Using the mouse, the user drags the symbol to the desired position. Since hierarchies are usually illustrated top to bottom, the parent class should be placed higher in the drawing than the child classes. While OOATool will allow child classes to be spatially above the parents, it is usually easier for the user to follow the diagram using traditional top to bottom placement.

After positioning the parent and child classes, nodes can be connected by selecting the child, clicking on the Create menu and selecting Make Specialization Of.. The parent and child nodes are immediately connected with the semicircle notation indicating inheritance. Generalization-Specialization connecting lines always emanate from the bottom center of the Generalization class and connect at the top of the Specialization class. Unlike mature CASE tools, the analyst lacks control over connecting points; these are program defined.

Whole-Part hierarchies. Like Generalization-Specialization hierarchies, Whole-Part hierarchies are designed to run top to bottom. Whole-Part connecting lines always emanate from the bottom of the Whole class and connect at the top of the Part class. Once highlighted with the mouse, a Part class can be connected to a Whole class by selecting the Create menu, Make Part of.. option. For Whole classes with multiple parts, connection lines from the bottom of the symbol are listed from left to right in the order the connections are made.

Whole-part relationships are similar to traditional associative relationships in terms of cardinality options. When setting up a Whole-Part connection, OOATool defaults to a one-to-one relationship. These default instance ranges are completely modifiable.

Adding attributes and services. Attribute and service identifiers can be added two ways. At the Drawing Window level, the user highlights the appropriate Class-&-Object symbol and then selects

Object-oriented Analysis 349

New Attribute from the Create menu. Service identifiers are added in like fashion. Attribute and Service identifiers can be virtually any length with the symbol automatically expanding to accommodate the length of the attribute and service names.

Expanding symbols can pose problems with hierarchical connections, causing crossing connection lines. It appears, the best approach to creating the five-layer model is to add the Attribute and Service names first, before setting up the hierarchical connections. This way, the final size of the Class-&-Object symbol is known before positioning the symbols on the drawing.

The second approach to adding Attribute and Service identifiers is more involved. After highlighting the Class-&-Object symbol, the user selects Change Class-&-Object from the Edit menu. This brings up a Class window reminiscent of a Smalltalk class window (Figure 15). Given that OOATool is written in Smalltalk V, this isn't surprising.

The Class Window is split into three panes. The upper left quadrant lists Attributes in a scrollable text pane. The upper right quadrant lists Services. The bottom two quadrants form a single text pane. This bottom pane provides an area for documenting the Class, each Attribute, and Service. To add a new Attribute, the user selects New Attribute from the Attribute menu. Adding a new Service is done essentially the same way. Since Attributes and Services are listed in order entered, the Attribute and Service Menus of the Class Window allow the analyst the option to rearrange the order, if desired.

Instance and message connections. Besides attribute names,

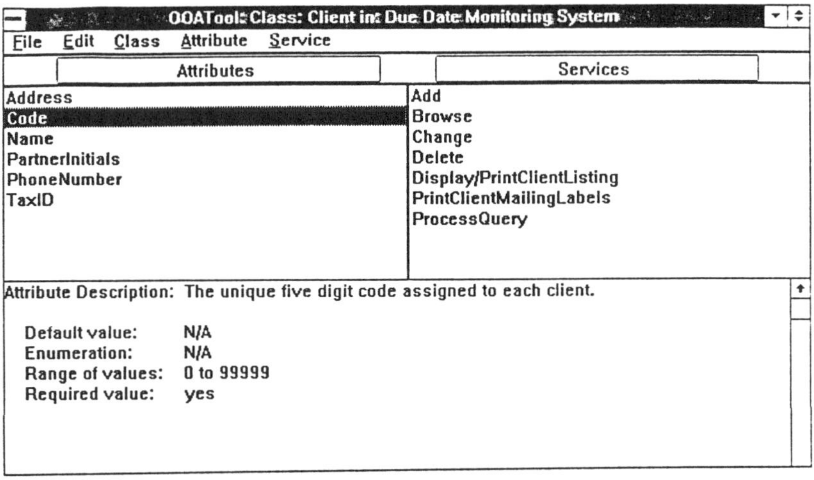

Figure 15: OOATool Class Window for Client Class in Due Date Monitoring System

the Attribute layer also requires the identification of Instance Connections. This is a relatively simple process. After highlighting the Class-&-Object, the user selects Instance Connection To.. from the Create Menu. This allows the user to identify the cardinality between two or more unrelated Class-&-Objects. As with Whole-Part hierarchies, the default relationship is one to one. Again, cardinality ranges are completely modifiable.

The Service layer is completed in a similar fashion, albeit, by creating Message Connections. The user highlights the appropriate Class-&-Object symbol and selects the Message Connection To.. option. A Message Connection arrow appears with the Sender object arrow tail always emanating from the right side of the object near the middle. The Receiver object always connects on the left side near the middle with an arrowhead. Since Message Connections will cross over other drawing lines, this can make the diagram hard to read. The best approach seems to place sender objects on the left and receiver objects on the right in the diagram.

Finishing touches. With Class-&-Objects defined, organized and semantically connected, the Class-&-Objects can be grouped into communities or Subjects. To create a Subject, the user highlights the related Class-&-Object(s) using the mouse and selects the New Subject option. After entering the Subject name, OOATool draws a shaded box around the Subject members.

To add a title to the five-layer model, the user selects New Annotation from the Drawing Window Create menu. This creates a text box in the middle of the screen that the user can drag to the top to give the drawing a title (Figure 16).

Other Features. While OOATool does not offer context-sensitive help, it does provide an on-screen "Strategy Card." OOATool Strategy Cards provide summaries of Coad-Yourdon (1991) methodology for finding Class-&-Objects, identifying Structures and Subjects, and defining Attributes and Services. A hardcopy of these strategy listings can also be found in Appendix A of *Object-Oriented Analysis*.

As drawings become more complicated, Class-&-Objects scroll off the screen. OOATool provides a drawing overview for navigating large drawings.

Critiquing the Model. At any time within OOATool, the five-layer model can be critiqued using a default set of rules derived from Coad & Yourdon's (1991) *Object-Oriented Analysis*. The critique can be printed (Figure 17) or saved to a file for later analysis. While the model critique is not perfect and critique rules are not modifiable or extensible, the critique is helpful in flagging poorly designed classes.

Documenting the Model. OOATool facilitates documentation

Object-oriented Analysis 351

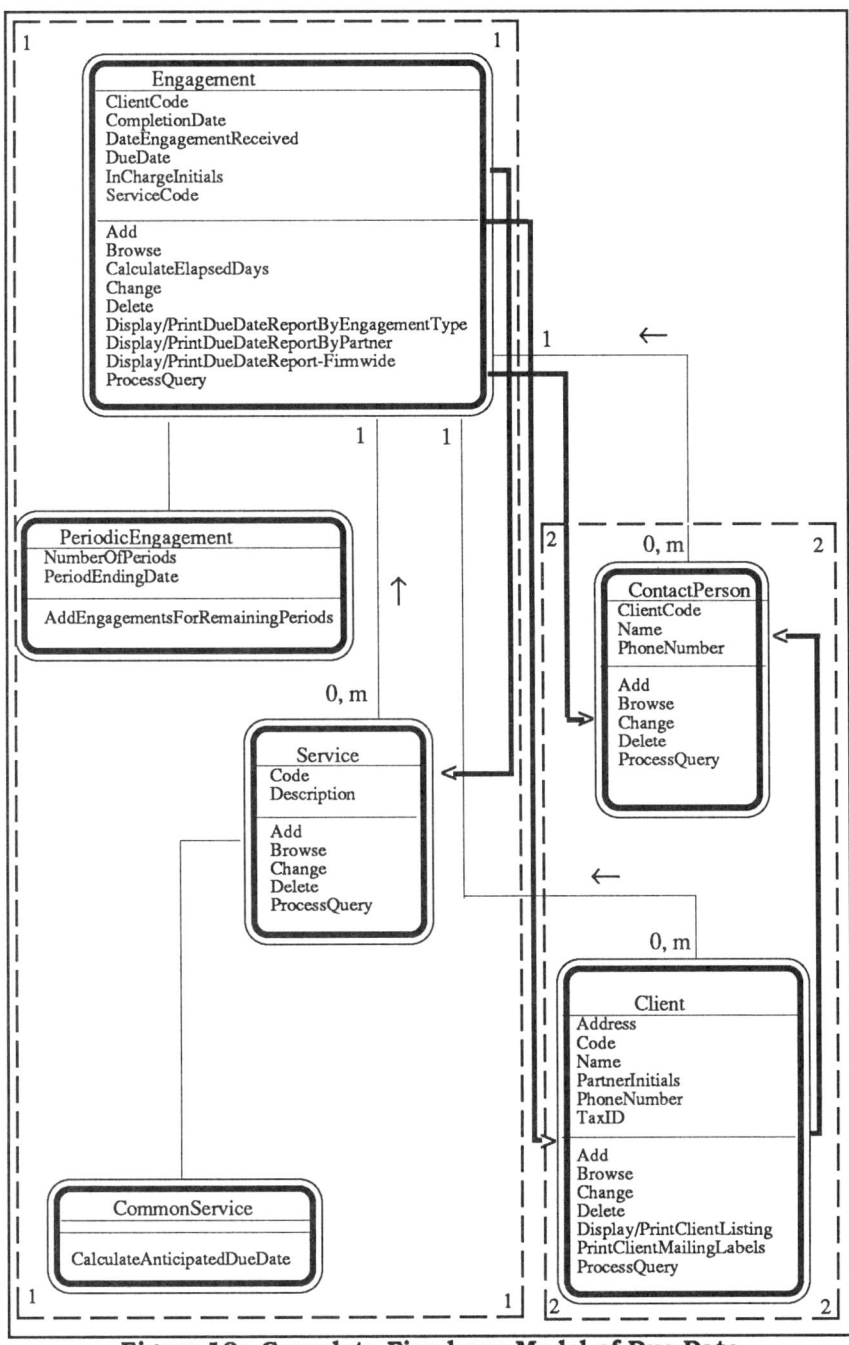

Figure 16: Complete Five-layer Model of Due Date Monitoring System

of object-oriented analysis by providing hardcopy of model drawings and narrative descriptions of model components. A documentation repository or Document Window for each drawing is accessed through the Drawing Window: Document menu option (Figure 18). This Window is split horizontally into two scrollable text panes. The top pane lists the documentation elements for the drawing. The bottom pane displays analyst-provided narrative for each drawing element. Class-&-Objects listed in the top pane are presented in a collapsible outline format.

Much like a Smalltalk class hierarchy browser, the analyst can explore documentation on each Class-&-Object. Documentation includes analyst-provided descriptions of each Class-&-Object attribute and service. User-defined documentation templates can be used to prompt the analyst for the needed documentation of each drawing element. Since the documentation is captured in a text pane, all documentation must be text-based. There is no provision for Object State diagrams or Service Charts (Figure 6) promoted so heavily by Coad and Yourdon (1991). The documentation narrative can be printed (Figure 19) or saved to a file for additional word processing and spell checking. OOATool does not check the spelling of any generated text or model element labels.

Printing. OOATool uses the Windows Print Manager for all printing services. The *OOATool Users Manual* assumes the user is familiar with printer setup, configuration, and selection under Windows.

All OOATool screen displays can be displayed using screen and printer fonts; the default being screen fonts. Fonts can be changed using the Font Menu option from the Drawing Window. Different fonts can be selected for each drawing element, if desired. Page breaks can be viewed by selecting the Page Breaks option from the Drawing Menu.

Before printing, it is best to change to printer fonts as the font size affects the width of all text, which, in turn, determines the final shape of Class-&-Object symbols. What looks quite aesthetic in screen fonts, often radically changes with printer fonts.

For the HPLaserjet II, the best built-in font type was Courier. For the HPLaserjet III, Courier, CG Times Roman, and Universe all worked well; however, 18 points was the smallest available font size for CG Times and Universe, making for rather large text. All OOATool drawings included in this chapter were done with 8 point Courier on an HPLaserjet III.

Backup. OOATool does not provide utilities for version control or backup. Model and drawing backups must be done at the Windows or DOS level using file copy commands.

Object-oriented Analysis 353

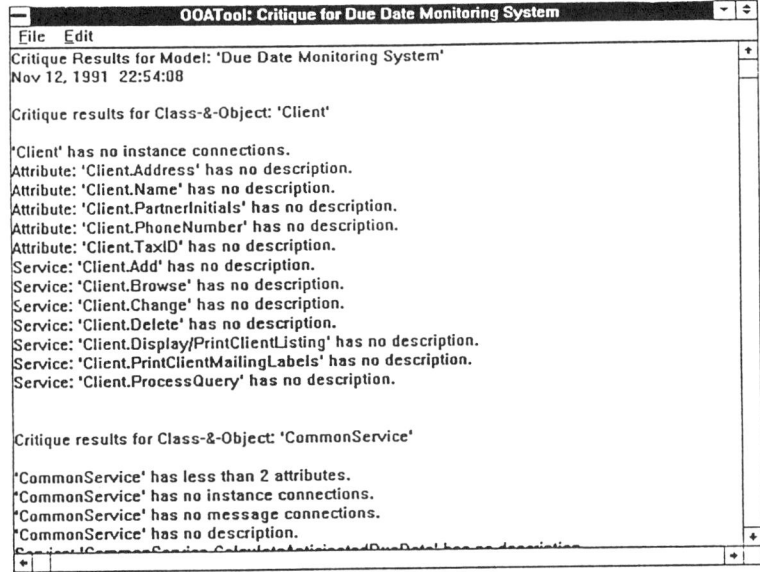

Figure 17: OOATool Critique Window for Due Date Monitoring System

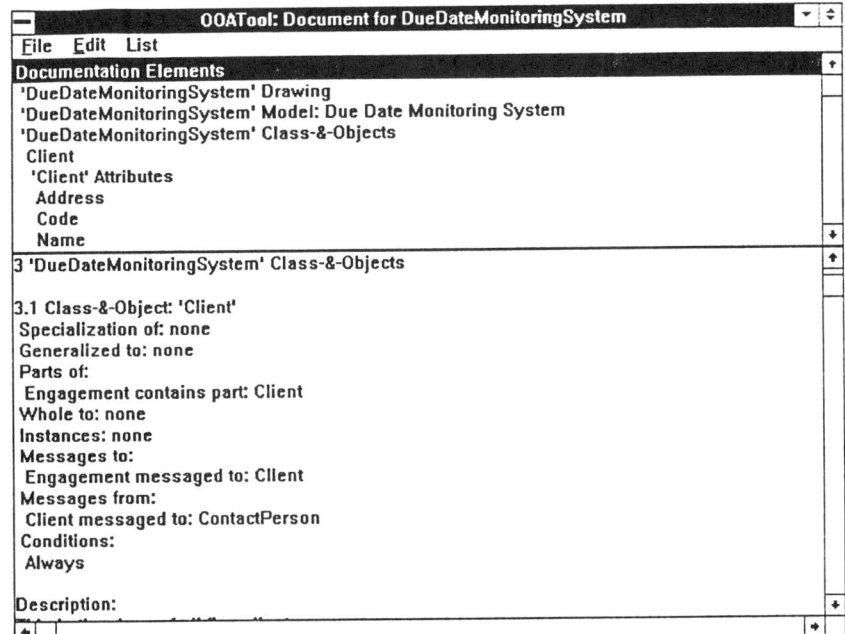

Figure 18: OOATool Document Window for Due Date Monitoring System

```
Documentation from Drawing: 'DueDateMonitoringSystem'
Nov 12, 1991 22:13:10


1 Drawing: 'DueDateMonitoringSystem'
Description:
Version 2.5 of Due Date Monitoring System


2 Model: 'Due Date Monitoring System'
Description:
Due Date Monitoring System Model; Contains only a single drawing:
DDMS.drw


3 'DueDateMonitoringSystem' Class-&-Objects

3.1 Class-&-Object: 'Client'
 Specialization of: none
 Generalized to: none
 Parts of:
  Engagement contains part: Client
 Whole to: none
 Instances: none
 Messages to:
  Engagement messaged to: Client
 Messages from:
  Client messaged to: ContactPerson
 Conditions:
  Always

Description:
This is the class of all firm clients.

3.1.1 'Client' Attributes

3.1.1.1 Address
 Conditions:
  Always

Description:

 none
```

Figure 19: OOATool Sample Documentation Generated for Due Date Monitoring System

Commentary

As a pedagogical tool for reinforcing Coad and Yourdon object-oriented analysis techniques, OOATool is excellent. Object International, Inc. markets a small model version with a 15 Class-&-Object maximum for $95.00 US that is well within most academic budgets. For the most part, students find OOATool to be easy to use and "fun" to work with. Typical student comments include:

> OOATool got put on the computer today so we went down to the lab and played around with it. It was kind of fun. I sat down and figured out how to create all the classes, objects, attributes, and services. We did one diagram of everything on it including the classes, objects, attributes, and services that we have so far on our project.

> When creating the model, we have changed many things, and it is great to be able to make changes without redoing huge amounts of data. OOATool is more than just a way to draw the boxes and put in the information—it really helps you to create the model by giving you cues and doing some of the work automatically.

However, OOATool has some weaknesses that don't go unnoticed by students. The OOATool documentation manual lacks an index, tutorial, or error message listing. The closest thing to a tutorial is the sample model drawings supplied with the program. While the drawings are complete, the accompanying sample documentation is not. Hardcopies of the sample models are not included in the OOATool documentation manual but must be generated separately.

All drawing elements are predetermined. Free-hand modification of drawings is not available. The user lacks control over node connecting points, and OOATool does not support Object State Diagrams or Service Charts. All documentation templates must be user-defined. Default templates patterned after the documentation templates in *Object-oriented Analysis* are not provided.

Contrary to Coad and Yourdon's injunction against "hard-wired" notation, OOATool is, in fact, hard-wired to a single methodology. The notations and critiqueing rules may not be modified nor extended. Work group support, file security, version control, and backup utilities are lacking. More importantly, a comprehensive, multi-model class repository supporting analysis reuse is missing.

When compared to a comprehensive object-oriented CASE tool,

OOATool is as Coad and Yourdon suggest, a CADC—a computer-aided drawing and checking tool. Perhaps, when Object International's complete CASE tool, OOWorkbench, with design support and code generation, is delivered, this situation will change. Until then, OOATool serves admirably as an entry-level CASE product or pedagogical tool, but nothing more.

RECOMMENDATIONS AND CONCLUSIONS

Object-oriented analysis is the "new kid on the block." While object-oriented programming, and to some extent object-oriented design, are fairly well-developed, object-oriented analysis is not. There is considerable debate as to which activities to include in analysis and how to document the results of the analytical effort. Standards do not exist. Each practitioner has his or her own notation. CASE support in such a chaotic environment is difficult. Established CASE vendors with their structured analysis tools have been slow to add object-oriented analysis notation, not knowing which notation to adopt.

Today's object-oriented analysis CASE vendors are largely new players in the CASE arena. Some promote proprietary notations. Others have accommodated the lack of notational standards by offering configurable CASE tools that support multiple symbol sets. Often these pluralistic CASE tools are extensible, providing the ability to adapt to methodological changes as object-oriented analysis matures.

CASE tools genuinely supporting object-oriented analysis are few. For those comprehensive tools such as ObjectMaker, ParadigmPlus, and Pilot, the vendors have largely adopted the best of traditional CASE tools while providing necessary methodological extensions. Thus, these CASE tools as a whole are, as are CASE tools in general, relatively immature.

Common file interchange formats do not exist. User-defined diagram checking rules must be entered through each CASE vendor's proprietary rule language; expert system linkage is missing. Diagramming is tied to the CASE tool as opposed to being managed by an independent user interface management system. Most tools do not provide an interface with IBM's AD/Cycle and Repository or any other standardized analytical repository.

Many object-oriented analysis tools are still geared toward system software development, ignoring the larger class of business application software. This often translates into a lack of form-based

Object-oriented Analysis 357

report and screen design prototyping components often found in traditional CASE products. Class library navigation tools, if they exist, are almost always text-based relying on the collapsible outline metaphor. Alternative navigation tools, on the order of the node-oriented class hierarchy display provided with Borland's C++ 3.1 for Windows, are needed. Dynamic data exchange with external spreadsheet, word processing, and databases is often missing; instead, if linkage is allowed, spreadsheet data, text, and database information are inextricably tied to the proprietary CASE tool. Yet, today's CASE tool support of object-oriented analysis is a far cry from the 3x5 class cards and MacPaint class hierarchy diagrams of just a few years ago.

Trying to be on the "cutting-edge" by jumping into object-oriented analysis CASE tools may result in more of a "bleeding-edge" activity, as organizational resources are consumed in an effort to operationalize a paradigm transitioning to maturity. And yet, as cited earlier, object-oriented software development in the United States is increasing at 110 percent annually (Blackford, 1990) while traditionally software growth has slowed to 20 percent. This is phenomenal, considering serious object-oriented development tools are less than ten years old. Object-oriented analysis may well be the 1990s solution to the software crisis. Yourdon (1990), a primary advocate of the structured systems analysis alternative, claims "Object orientation is the future, and the future is here and now" (p. 263).

Object-oriented analysis offers significant advantages over traditional analytical paradigms such as procedural and information modeling. With its focus on modeling the real world, OOA facilitates the analytical tasks of exploring the problem space, abstracting the problem space, and verifying problem space understanding better than the other methodologies. Where OOA really deserves kudos is in dealing with today's analytical challenges of continual change, increasing complexity, and the push for developmental efficiencies through reuse. As the methodology and notation mature, object-oriented analysis could easily become the dominant analytical model by the turn of the century. Perhaps, Deutsch and Goldberg's (1991) prophesy of the future of object-orientation will come true for object-oriented analysis and supporting CASE tools:

> If we look into our murky crystal ball, how do we see software's use of object technology in the next decade? How do we see it evolving?
> We hope that in 2001, objects will be boring . . . .
> We expect that 10 years from now, the object-oriented approach to software design and implementation will be an accepted,

standard technique used in every language, library, database system, and operating system and will be taught in undergraduate computer science courses at every university (pp. 114-115).

I agree and look forward to an exciting future for object-oriented computer-aided software engineering.

REFERENCES

Ackroyd, M., & Daum, D. (1991, January). Graphical notation for object-oriented design and programming. *Journal of Object-Oriented Programming, 3*(5), 18-28.

Beck, K. & Cunningham, W. (1989). A laboratory for teaching object-oriented thinking. *OOPSLA '89 Proceedings, Association of Computing Machinery,* 1-6.

Blackford, J. (1990, June). The story of "O". *Personal Computing,* pp. 83-85.

Booch, G. (1991). *Object-oriented design with applications.* Redwood City, CA: Benjamin/Cummings.

Buhr, R. (1984). *System design with Ada.* Englewood Cliffs, NJ: Prentice-Hall.

Buhr, R. (1990). *Practical visual techniques in system design with applications to Ada.* Englewood Cliffs, NJ: Prentice-Hall.

Chikofsky, E. J. (1988, March). Software technology people can really use. *IEEE Software,* pp. 8-10.

Chirdon, P. (1991, March). Understanding and applying the object[-]oriented paradigm. *Inside DPMA,* pp. 4-9.

Coad, P., & Yourdon, E. (1990). *Object-oriented analysis.* Englewood Cliffs, NJ: Yourdon Press/Prentice-Hall.

Coad, P., & Yourdon, E. (1991). *Object-oriented analysis* (2nd ed.). Englewood Cliffs, NJ: Yourdon Press/Prentice-Hall.

Coad, P., & Yourdon, E. (1991). *Object-oriented design* Englewood Cliffs, NJ: Yourdon Press/Prentice-Hall.

Dean, H. (1991, May). Object-oriented design using message flow decomposition. *Journal of Object-oriented Programming, 4*(2), 21-31.

Deutsch, L. P., & Goldberg, A. (1991, August). Smalltalk yesterday, today, and tomorrow. *Byte,* pp. 108-115.

Gibson, E. (1990, October). Objects—born and bred. *Byte,* pp. 245-254.

Graham, I. (1991). *Object oriented methods.* Reading, MA: Addison-Wesley.

Henderson-Sellers, B., & Edwards, J. M. (1990, September). The object-oriented systems life cycle. *Communications of the ACM, 33*(9), 142-159.

Korson, T., & McGregor, J. D. (1990, September). Understanding object-oriented: A unifying paradigm. *Communications of the ACM, 33*(9), 40-60.

Kurtz, B., Woodfield, S. & Embley, D. (1991). *Object-oriented systems analysis and specification: A model driven approach.* Englewood Cliffs, NJ: Prentice-Hall.

LaLonde, W., & Pugh, J. (1989, March/April). Designing is hard: Object-oriented software is different! *Journal of Object-Oriented Programming, 1*(6), 46-55.

Manfredi F., & Tortorici, P. (1989). An object-oriented approach to system analysis. In G. Goos & J. Hartmanis (Ed.), *Lecture Notes in Computer Science* (pp. 395-410). Berlin, Germany: Springer-Verlag.

Mullin, M. (1989). *Object oriented program design with examples in C++.* Reading, MA: Addison-Wesley.

Page-Jones, M., Constantine, L., & Weiss, S. (1990, October). Modeling object-oriented systems: The uniform object notation. *Computer Language, 7*(12), 69-87.

Pressman, R. S. (1987). *Software engineering: A practitioner's approach* (2nd ed.). New York: McGraw-Hill.

QED Information Sciences, Inc. (1989). *CASE: The potentials and the pitfalls.* Wellesley, MA: Chantico.

Rumbaugh, J., Blaha, M., Premerlani, W., Eddy, F., & Lorensen, W. (1991). *Object-oriented modeling and design.* Englewood Cliffs, NJ: Prentice-Hall.

Schindler, M. (1990). *Computer-aided software design: Build quality software with CASE.* New York: Wiley & Sons.

Shlaer, S., & Mellor, S. J. (1988). *Object-oriented systems analysis: Modeling the world in data.* Englewood Cliffs, NJ: Yourdon Press/Prentice-Hall.

Wasserman, A. I. & Pircher, P. A. (1991, January). Object-oriented structured design and C++. *Computer Language, 8*(1), 41-52.

Wilson, D. A. (1990, January/February). Class diagrams: A tool for design, documentation, and teaching. *Journal of Object-Oriented Programming, 2*(5), 38-44.

Wirfs-Brock, R., Wilkerson, B., & Wiener, L. (1990). *Designing object-oriented software.* Englewood Cliffs, NJ: Yourdon Press/Prentice-Hall.

Yourdon, E. (1990, October). Auld lang syne. *Byte*, pp. 257.

CHAPTER TWELVE

CASE and Expert Systems Integration Issues

Ludwig Slusky
California State University, Los Angeles

Parviz Partow-Navid
California State University, Los Angeles

Current CASE toolsets are often inadequate for complex software development projects. It is not uncommon that unmanaged use of CASE toolsets is hammered by the lack of conceptual understanding of both business and software engineering methodology. Expert Systems can be useful by defining a navigation path between available methodological instruments for software engineering. An Expert System can identify the necessary CASE functions through a single, consistent interface, and can move from one methodological task to another and back again. This chapter investigates the issues related to the integration of Expert Systems and CASE toolsets. The effectiveness of CASE and Expert Systems integration in five areas is examined: interface through Computer-Aided Instructions, data acquisition through Expert Systems and Voice Recognition, model construction and selection through Expert Systems, and CASE's control logic through machine learning.

This chapter examines the concepts of integration of Computer-Aided Software Engineering (CASE) toolsets and Expert Systems (ES) - in an Integrated Computer-Aided Software Engineering platform (I-CASE/ES platform) - for application software engineering. In

The presented chapter is based on the article "Enhancing CASE Technology with Expert Systems" written by the authors and published in May-June 1992 issue of *Software Engineering Journal*.

this integrated platform, an Expert System serves as a front-end toolset with knowledge representation in the Expert System knowledge base which is linked to the object representation in the CASE encyclopedia. There is a tendency to expand the term repository to the term encyclopedia for CASE toolsets. We shall use the term *encyclopedia* for CASE toolsets and the term *central repository* for a database.

Productivity benefits from the use of CASE toolsets are relative to each software project and the programmers' acceptance of CASE. Current CASE toolsets are often inadequate for complex software development projects. Some major shortcomings of CASE toolsets come from the extensive training required before a developer becomes proficient with the tools and the ever changing methodologies (Loh et al, 1989). Additionally, more and more corporate IS managers are coming to the realization that one CASE-centered methodology is not enough, and that different methodologies for groups of projects may be needed.

It is not uncommon that unmannaged use of CASE toolsets is hampered by the lack of conceptual understanding of both business and software engineering methodology. Developed to bridge the traditional communication gap between user and analyst, CASE technology may have created another one - a methodology gap between designers working on the same project (Slusky, 1987).

Business rules are frequently not defined, stored, analyzed (cross-referenced), or applied properly. Often, the methodology employed does not relate to the available CASE toolsets, and therefore, does not promote the use of these resources. Lack of physical integration between CASE tools, further limits the use of these toolsets, and in some cases hinders the implementation of CASE technology in a project development environment.

CASE toolsets can be distinguished as methodology-dependent or methodology-independent. Methodology-dependent CASE requires a structured software engineering environment in terms of technological resources, necessary human resources (and skills), enforced standards and procedures, and a single methodological approach. Some managers criticize the restrictiveness of these toolsets.

The second category of CASE toolsets, methodology-independent toolsets, have a lesser impact on already formed methodological practices, and therefore, may be easier to implement. On the other hand, the use of a particular CASE toolset supporting multiple methodologies, when coupled with a lack of standards and procedures, may result in disaster. Since methodology-independent CASE tools are designed for different phases of the systems development life cycle, they often do not support the critical transition points between phases.

Expert Systems methods can help solve these problems by defining a navigation path of software engineering tasks between available methodological instruments for software engineering, and can adjust this path according to project requirements as well as a changing engineering environment. Tasks, deliverables, techniques, and methods are stored in the knowledge base, and the inference engine provides advice on possible navigation paths. The systems architect can identify the necessary CASE functions through a single, consistent interface, and can move from one methodological task to another, and back again.

The ultimate objective of integrating Expert Systems and CASE methods is to provide advice to the information systems architects on business needs and methodological solutions. We believe that even though there are problems in the amalgamation of Expert Systems and CASE, there are also the means of eliminating the inconsistencies, thus allowing a compatible union. Only then, will the full power of "expert CASE" become useful as viable software.

The most important part of a software engineering process is defining the specification of the application system: to design complete and clear specifications of the process under consideration. This is possibly the most challenging, time consuming and significant step of all activities in the systems development life cycle. It involves substantial interaction with users. It often amounts to adding necessary information, eliminating contradictions and vagueness, and producing a refined and honed statement of the scope and limitations of the problem.

CASE CONCEPTS AND ARCHITECTURE

CASE ensures that the software engineering process can be controlled and measured. CASE is used for forward engineering (to support development of new applications), re-engineering (to assist with resolution of maintenance problems), reverse engineering (to derive a set of specifications for existing applications), and system integration (to help integrate software packages). Here, we shall concern ourselves primarily with implementation of CASE for forward engineering.

The purpose of CASE is to support the entire System Development Life Cycle (SDLC). However, the objectives and methods of the front-end and back-end phases of the SDLC vary significantly, and for that reason CASE tools are being distinguished as "upper CASE" and "lower CASE" toolsets. (Alternative terms infrequently used for upper CASE and lower CASE are front-end CASE and back-end CASE respectively).

The upper CASE toolsets mostly support phases of application planning, analysis, and design. The results of these three phases are integrated to support the application design solutions. The end results of implementation of these CASE toolsets are process and data models using a wide array of diagramming techniques. Metadata definitions and other project information are stored in an encyclopedia which can be PC or mainframe based. A project and its related encyclopedia can be shared between individual workstations, and multiple encyclopedias can be consolidated, thus supporting a distributed development environment. The toolsets help strengthen and control implementation of design principles and standards.

The lower CASE toolsets support the construction phase. PC-based toolsets generate relational database definitions from data models and data specifications using a data definition language (DDL). Computerized procedures can be automatically packaged for business processes. Application source code for third and fourth generation languages can be constructed from conceptual specifications that were created during process and data modeling. The source code, including on-line dialogues, can be further compiled and run on mainframes. CASE toolsets can also be used for software configuration management, test specifications, and reuse of software components.

Integration

An open architecture is an important feature of CASE toolsets. No existing CASE toolset can be a substitution for the entire development environment, which can include such additional components as Database Management Systems (DBMS), a central repository, software testing facilities, expert systems, etc.

The integration of a specific CASE toolset with other products into a single development platform can be defined on three levels (Wasserman, 1989):

- the integration of graphical presentation capabilities,
- the capability to control integration across the platform, and
- the integration of a specific CASE encyclopedia with the encyclopedia (or central repository, or data dictionary) of another software packages.

Integration of graphical user presentation capabilities, provides a user with a much needed consistency for information presented in graphical form. In AD/Cycle, the unified user presentation is supported by the Common User Access component. CASE integration implies not only interfaces between different types of toolsets (like upper and lower CASE) but also between toolsets which share information over networks.

Control integration is the capability to control information exchange, to coordinate information development tasks in separate CASE toolsets, and to control message communication between individual CASE toolsets. Integration of meta-data stored in an encyclopedia is based on the ability to share information between components of the development platform, and more importantly to control the consistency of logical and physical design descriptions.

Encyclopedia

There are three types of encyclopedias - passive, active, and dynamic. A passive encyclopedia does not interact with the application development process, and is not maintained automatically with metadata created during the application development process. All updates to such an encyclopedia must be made independently and directly by a user. An active encyclopedia is updated automatically (in the background mode) while other system development tasks, e.g., development of the application models, are being performed. Finally, a dynamic encyclopedia is linked to, and updated (in the background mode) during execution of an application.

CASE deals with definitions of diverse objects of project development. In addition to traditional objects such as records, elements, and programs, CASE toolsets operate on, store, and interrelate objects such as data flow diagrams, process models, data models, and screen prototype definitions. CASE toolsets relate these objects to each other, and to the application source code (Slusky, 1991).

The CASE encyclopedia resembles many features found in a relational database management system: meta-data non-redundancy, independence, integrity, concurrency problem handling, security control, on-line queries, and interface to other products.

Architecture

The architecture of CASE toolsets varies widely between different products. With respect to the degree of integration of CASE toolsets, we can describe three levels of functionality. The first generation of CASE can be characterized as "stand-alone" CASE (disintegrated CASE). The new second generation of CASE is evolving toward an integrated CASE (I-CASE) model, dedicated to a specific technological environment and methodology. Often called workbenches, such I-CASE toolsets represent a set of closely coupled facilities which create and exchange planning, analysis, design, and construction information through a dedicated encyclopedia. The next generation of CASE is seen by researchers as based on the concept of interface-compatible CASE components (C-CASE) with open architectures that can work on multiple platforms.

A CASE architecture greatly depends on the central repository architecture. A single, standard, central, repository architecture is not such a remote prospect. Its model is likely to include such features as version management, configuration management, requirements traceability, dependencies tracking, change management, security and access control, naming conventions, and other facilities (Forte, 1989). Configuration management (CM) is a new area being implemented in some CASE toolsets.

CASE toolsets operate with enterprise-wide application environments utilizing multiple platforms. Thus, system integration with CASE toolsets may span the traditional boundaries of individual applications, and link them into an enterprise-wide system. Consequently, the effects of change on application data or application processes may be felt across the entire enterprise.

Both upper and lower CASE toolsets may provide a *requirements traceability* capability. This "cause-effect" analysis can be applied to "forward" and "where-used" tracing. The "forward" tracing identifies all relevant deliverables (e.g., design components in the CASE encyclopedia, various models and software modules) for a specific requirement specification. The "where-used" tracing identifies all requirements that generated a specific deliverable.

In the CASE encyclopedia, some of the stored objects may participate in relationships with other objects. The capability to *track dependencies* across the encyclopedia and to report on all inconsistencies and missing links, is required in order to maintain the integrity of the information in the encyclopedia. Merely reporting on dependencies leaves it up to the user to maintain the dependencies.

Change management helps enforce automated maintenance of dependencies between objects to keep design components synchronized. *Version management* is a further extension of the change management and configuration management concepts, and identifies the set of deliverables for a specific project version by version.

The technological foundation for CASE toolsets today is relational database technology, which unfortunately lacks some needed capabilities (i.e., dependency management). New object-oriented database technology is considered by some vendors as the probable technological foundation for future CASE toolsets.

The *information meta-models* for upper and lower CASE are different. The information meta-model of a generic upper CASE toolset usually consists of seven subject areas: business objects, functions, and business rules; logical data objects and models; process objects and models; software design specifications; database design specifications; project management objects; and system documentation. The information meta-model of a generic lower CASE toolset usually consists of six subject areas: I/O images, application source code, database definitions, configuration management dependencies, dependency tracking and change control data, and software quality parameters. Note, that analysis of graphical models and relational operations on sets of metadata are common to all entity types (e.g., business, data, and functions).

Figure 1 illustrates the architecture of a generic upper CASE toolset. The local encyclopedia contains metadata and other facts and rules that describe a business application or an enterprise. The analyzer contains rules and processing capabilities for verification of metadata, models, and prototypes. The modeling component includes on-line capabilities for building, maintaining, and storing models. The software and database design component includes on-line capabilities for graphical design of application software, and for creating physical data and process specifications. The reports and interface component supports on-line, batch, and communication between a local encyclopedia and the central repository.

The architecture of a generic lower CASE toolset is shown in Figure 2. The local encyclopedia contains metadata and design specifications created by an upper CASE toolset and also includes database definitions and software modules created by the lower CASE toolset. This data includes information on the test and execution environments, packaged software modules, and database definitions. The analyzer applies rules and processing capabilities for verification of source code, database definitions, and prototypes. The code generator helps to construct source code and to package load modules. The screen generator component assists in painting and generating source code for on-line screens. The database generator produces database definitions, and helps in generating and installing a database. The toolset has also interface capabilities, to communicate with other components of the software development platform and with users.

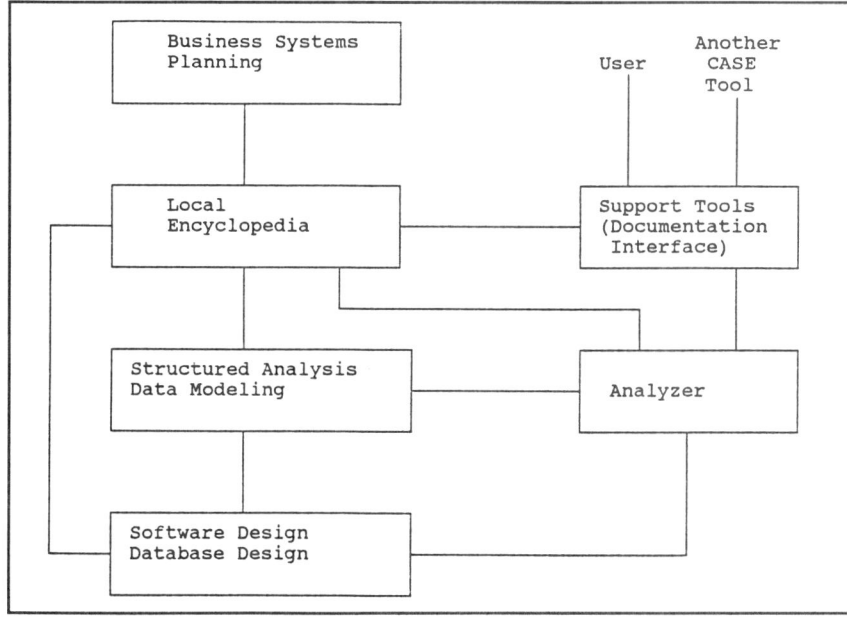

Figure 1: The Architecture of a Generic Upper CASE Toolset

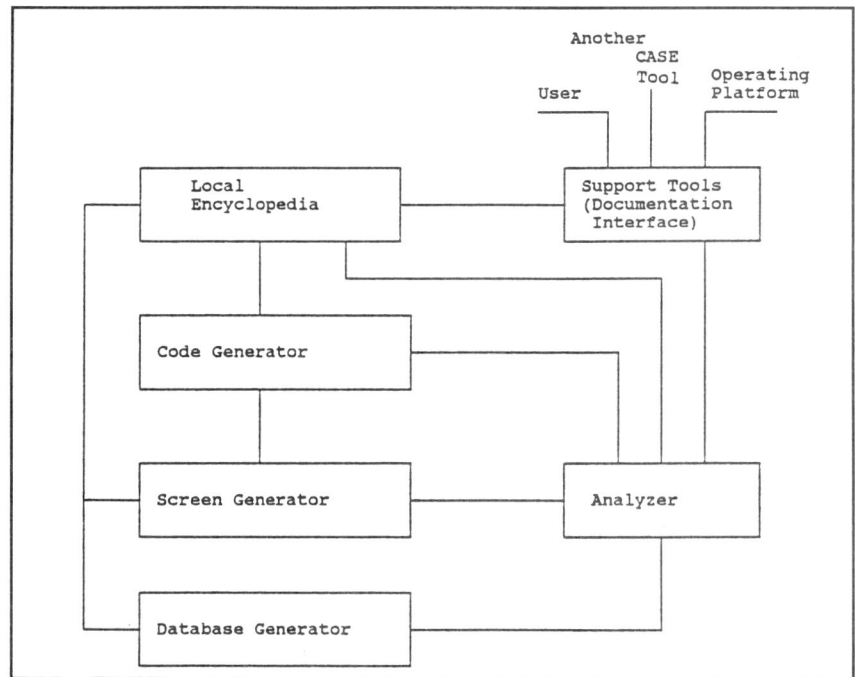

Figure 2: The Architecture of a Generic Lower CASE Toolset

EXPERT SYSTEMS CONCEPTS AND ARCHITECTURE

Of all the commercial developments that resulted from artificial intelligence (AI) research, expert systems have received the most attention. In fact, more than 80% of Fortune 500 companies already use expert systems (Hertz, 1988). These problem-solving techniques were initially called "expert systems" to suggest that they can function as effectively as human experts at their highly sophisticated tasks.

An expert system is a program that manifests some combination of concepts, procedures, and techniques derived from the artificial intelligence field to duplicate, or substitute for, the reasoning processes and knowledge of experts in solving specific types of problems (Turban, 1990). Non-experts can use expert systems to enhance their problem solving skills. Experts can also use them as knowledge assistants. Expert Systems are employed to increase scarce expertise, and to provide improved and consistent solutions.

The knowledge in an expert system consists of facts and heuristics. The "facts" constitute a body of information that is widely shared, publicly available, and generally agreed upon by the experts in a field. The "heuristics" are mostly private, little-discussed rules of good judgment that characterize expert-level decision making in the field. The performance of an expert system is primarily a function of the size and quality of the knowledge base that the system possesses (Miller, 1984).

The functional architecture of expert systems consists of four components which support: knowledge acquisition, knowledge representation, reasoning (inference) engine, and explanation.

The architecture of a generic Expert System is illustrated in Figure 3. The knowledge base contains the facts and rules that constitute the expert's knowledge. The inference engine contains the inference strategies and controls, which an expert employs when manipulating the facts and rules. Knowledge acquisition is the accumulation, storage, and transformation of problem-solving expertise from the expert to a computer program. The interface contains a language processor for friendly communications between the computer program and the user. The working memory is an area of memory responsible for storing intermediate results and recording the description of the current problem, as specified by the input data. The explanation facility is capable of tracing the steps in the process from conclusions to source date, i.e., explaining the expert system's behavior.

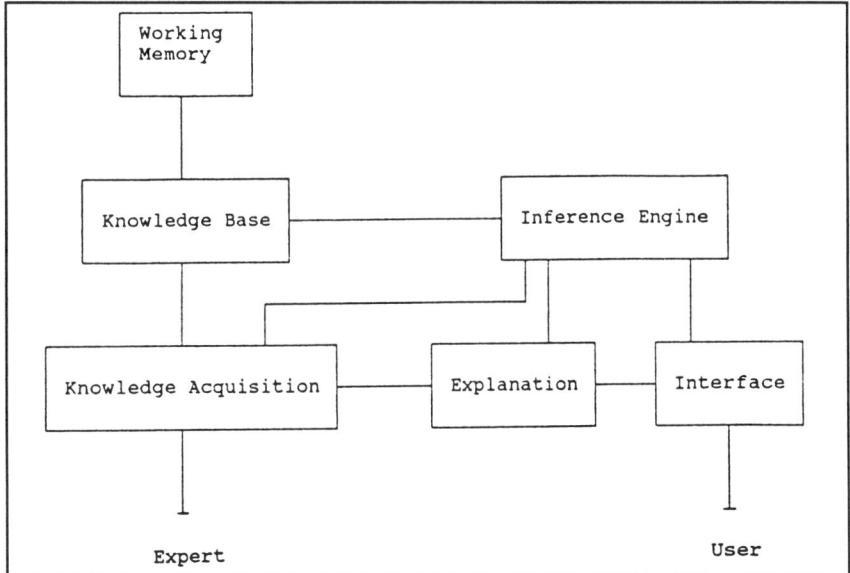

Figure 3: The Architecture of an Expert System

Benefits of Expert Systems

Before examining the role of expert systems in computer-aided software engineering, it is helpful to review the primary benefits of expert systems. Expert systems benefits can be categorized in three primary areas: business planning, application development, and application maintenance.

Business Planning Benefits - With the help of Expert Systems, it is possible to automate critical functions which could not be automated before, or were too costly to develop and maintain. Expert Systems are helping information systems managers to develop applications which encompass rapid, more precise, and consistent decision making; measure the effectiveness of corporate policies; acquire and disseminate knowledge and experience; leverage the organization's investment in computer resources; and support non-technical personnel with applications that include graphical interfaces.

Application Development Benefits - Expert Systems are helpful in increasing programmer productivity, by making it possible to build applications faster. In the application development area expert systems support prototyping capabilities and allow people to pay attention to the problem-solving logic rather than the sequence of applying that logic. Furthermore, expert systems are portable across hardware, operating systems, and windowing environments, making it possible to take advantage of the distinctive characteristics of each platform. Expert systems can also be integrated with existing application software to leverage the organization's software investment and can provide improved access to information in an organization's database. Object-oriented programming techniques may be utilized with an expert system to help reduce the size of the application. Natural language and graphical interfaces will facilitate testing and debugging of application programs.

Application Re-Engineering Benefits - Expert Systems can have a substantial impact on application system re-engineering by supporting maintenance of business logic when the original technology or business setting shifts. Expert systems can help migrate an application design to new implementation platforms—databases, operating systems, window managers, etc. Since expert systems are not procedural languages, re-engineering is not determined by the sequence of the rules that need to be maintained but by the rules themselves. Expert systems employ natural language to gain access to the knowledge base, and as a result, the knowledge base of applications usually requires fewer rules and less maintenance.

Expert Systems Application Areas

Expert systems, similar to databases, store information. Unlike databases, however, they store the kind of information that contains the guidelines, facts, and business rules that comprise the decision-making process. The application areas most suitable for expert systems are applications which emphasize adaptive problem solving.

Information systems organizations have been quite successful in automating tasks that are structured and repetitive. The decision-making methods or activities being automated are the same ones, appliction after application. Automating decision-making processes that demand adaptive problem solving has either been ignored or inadequately implemented with traditional development tools.

Decision making processes suitable for adaptive problem solving are characterized as being semi-structured, and applications to support such processes must be able to modify processing to the specific case at hand. For example, a specific case may only ask for a subset of the guidelines, facts or business rules to be applied. The appropriate policies or rules must be determined according to the data available or according to the goal or objective to be accomplished. Expert systems use artificial intelligence technology to select the rules and the sequence in which to utilize them.

Expert systems can assist in finding solutions to strategic business problems, provide training and help for multiple databases, and support functions in a multi-platform, multi-vendor environment. By automating complex applications that require adaptive problem solving, organizations are achieving more than increased productivity or efficiency.

It is important to realize why developing expert systems applications can be done better with fourth generation languages than with traditional programming languages. Procedural languages are best suited for programming applications which consist of repetitive, well structured, tasks. Application development is a complex and lengthy process, and changes require costly re-coding. This is why expert systems are increasingly viewed as the solution to complex application development needs.

Consistency is a real problem in applications where the rules needed to manage a particular problem can be interpreted differently by users. In such environments, it is important to assure that policies are being implemented consistently, across the many decisions being made everyday. Typical applications in this category include scheduling and production planning, tax calculations, and interpretation of complex laws and codes.

In some applications, identifying the appropriate rules in a short period of time is a difficult task. This is definitely true in the technology driven environment of today's business organizations. Process control and production monitoring are examples of applications in this area.

Another application area exists when expertise or knowledge must be provided to individuals who don't have it. Imagine, for example, a novice user of a large database system who must use the system for making decisions. An expert system could help lead the user through the process of formatting a complex query and provide expert "opinion" whenever it is needed. Applications in this area include: "help desk", training, advisory and decision support.

KNOWLEDGE ACQUISITION IN SYSTEMS DEVELOPMENT

Conceptual integration of CASE and expert system capabilities should support knowledge acquisition and its interpretation. Three categories of knowledge accumulated using expert systems are:

methodology knowledge, business knowledge (application and/or enterprise), and application system knowledge. The scope of this knowledge can be limited to a specific phase of SDLC, an application, or an enterprise.

Building a methodology knowledge base involves knowledge acquisition of methods, techniques, procedures, tasks, deliverables, project categories, required human resources, etc. and representation of methodological components in the knowledge base. The business and application system knowledge is acquired and applied in various phases of SDLC.

The planning and requirements definition phases encompass knowledge acquisition of business rules, knowledge representation in the form of a business rules' knowledge base, and estimation of project development methodology, schedule, etc. The application analysis phase includes knowledge acquisition of business solutions and representation of business solutions (models) in the knowledge base.

The application design phase includes knowledge acquisition of software models (structures) and their references in the knowledge base. The application construction phase also includes knowledge acquisition of software modules and referencing software modules in the knowledge base.

The conceptual integration of CASE toolsets and expert systems (I-CASE/ES platform) can be represented by both informational and functional architectures.

Conceptual integration of CASE and expert systems implies that the informational and functional architectures have related and/or shared components. Physical integration involves hardware, software, and communications components needed to achieve conceptual integration. Several physical integration architectures (schemas) exist: single processor, multiprocessor, networking, and embedded. Physical integration is beyond the scope of this article, and interested readers are encouraged to see (Newman, 1987).

In short, the conceptual integration of CASE and Expert Systems is particularly beneficial in designing systems with a complex architecture in a diverse or methodologically unstructured environment.

USE OF I-CASE/ES

Expert systems support is effective for a range of software engineering tasks, in particular, for activities dealing with business knowledge, models, data evaluation, and planning. Examples include defining the proposed system, cause-effect analysis, and data collection support and interpretation.

In defining the proposed system, expert systems can assist in validating user requirements. A single user view of the proposed system might be incomplete and inaccurate, and expert systems can correct and complete this knowledge. Expert systems can be used to support JAD (Joint Application Design) sessions, assist in validation of system models, and can define design rules for functional specifications, data specifications, and prototyping.

In cause-effect analysis, expert systems can assist in project estimating and planning (tasks, time, costs, and human resources) based on the type of the project and the available pool of expertise. In data collection support and interpretation, expert systems can define templates for data collection, assist in tracing data anomalies, and assist in translation of information to different formats.

Overall, the expert systems functionality can strengthen CASE capabilities in five areas: support the user interface through Natural Language Processing, support tutoring through Computer-Aided Instruction, support data acquisition, support model construction and selection, and optimize CASE's control logic through machine learning (self adaptivity). These five areas are discussed below.

A natural language is any verbal language that humans use to communicate with each other, e.g., English. Natural Language Processors (NLP) are artificially intelligent user interfaces that allow the user to have a conversation with a computer-based system in much the same way as humans converse with each other - without the necessity to learn a strict, inflexible, programming syntax. Thus, with NLP, a manager can retrieve information from a database by typing (or speaking) a query. At the moment, most natural language input to a computer is provided by a user through the keyboard. Future developments, however, will make natural langugage processing more powerful when voice input/output is available. Successful cases in this area are represented by recent systems, which are successful in understanding and interpreting written sentences related to restricted topics such as CLOUT for interfacing with RBase 5000 and HAL for interfacing with Lotus 1-2-3 (Turban, 1990).

There is a need for a two-way interface between the CASE tool and the expert systems. CASE users may use this ES/CASE interface to guide the solution of business and/or methodological problems through expert systems to the CASE toolset. For example, the expert system could be used during the analysis phase to establish the significance of the business problem or to assist in identifying the problem in sufficient detail. Then the problem is forwarded to a CASE tool for possible solution (Courtney, 1987). The end-users of

CASE/ES interface can examine the impact of selected system solutions on the larger scope of business problems. Thus, using a natural language interface, an expert system can offer friendlier user-system interfaces and explanations. Furthermore, they can translate unfamiliar terms to familiar vocabulary for the user.

The second area, tutoring, is an essential component of the overall strategy for implementation of methodology, development toolsets, and application systems. Expert systems can be helpful in building training systems based on computer-aided instruction models for tutoring users on how to use a methodology or a CASE toolsets. Such systems can also assist in strategy formulation for solving business, application system, and methodological problems.

Expert systems may also provide an associative memory containing knowledge of software engineering methodology (phases, tasks, techniques) and inferential rules to assist a system architect in managing a software project. Expert systems offer a user-friendly navigation through methodological activities, and can translate desirable objectives and/or deliverables into methodological tasks, explain methodological steps, and act as a consultant.

The methodology of software engineering requires creativity and judgment. Some project management tasks, based on the accepted methodology (e.g., scheduling, resource requirements evaluation, etc.) already rely on decision support systems. Expert systems can supplement decision support systems (DSS) by providing a built-in associative memory containing knowledge of business and inferential rules (Meador, 1984). A similar approach can be taken with respect to strategy formulation for solving business, application system, and methodological problems.

A third area, Data Acquisition, refers to the earlier activity of the application/system development life cycle (SDLC) and has decisive affect on the subsequent phases of SDLC. System design depends significantly on acquiring high quality information regarding the system under the consideration. System development begins with the requirements definition activity during which analysts and users determine the fundamental requirements of the proposed application system. Errors which occur during this phase, impact the outcome of the system development process significantly. The information gathered during this initial investigation is crucial to the success of the following phases of development.

During the requirement definition stage, the analysts gather information regarding business rules, data objects, business functions, responsibilities of various organizational units, problem areas, and future user needs. One of the main sources for data collection is user interviews. The number of individuals that must be interviewed is usually related to the size of the project. The larger the study boundaries, the more individuals the systems analyst will need to interview. Given the number of users involved and the time required for interviews and discussions, this activity can be lengthy and expensive. In addition, the collected data may not be relevant or accurate.

It is often difficult to determine the kind of data that should be collected from respondents. An expert system can advise the analyst on the type of data needed. With more sophisticated systems that are equipped with a natural language processor and voice recognition, the expert system can ask questions and record the entire interview session.

The data collected from individuals is often contaminated. Some respondents may be unsure, unsettled, nervous and even frightened, or driven by a hidden agenda. Their responses may be guarded, evasive, impulsive, or diversionary. These concerns make it difficult to collect information in the first place, and to trust the dependability of the information gathered. Thus, there is always a need for verification of data. Expert systems can be helpful when trying to verify captured information by accessing the organization data base or utilizing the rules in its knowledge base.

Data could be lost if not maintained systematically. A good filing system is imperative. An expertsystem can act as a "note taker" and record the entire interview session. Data captured by the exert system is saved in an orderly fashion. Another problem that analysts may not be able to "fill in the gaps" where questions were not asked or were not understood. An expert system can act as an advisor by making sure that the captured data, as much as possible, are comprehensive and all the relevant questions are asked.

Sound and understandable conclusions depend on the analyst's skills, experience and awareness. Expert systems could be particularly useful in this regard, making sure that each conclusion be supported by data and phrased in an understandable way.

The fourth area, Model Construction and Selection, is particularly important for user productivity improvements during Analysis and Design phases of SDLC in CASE environment. In a CASE environment, knowledge of an application system is represented through modeling. One of objectives of structured system design is to build and use a library of design models and/or library of software modules. Although building such libraries is not a problem, recognizing patterns and defining the components of the system architecture is a difficult task. Expert systems can help by defining inferential rules and acting as an expert-librarian to relate business needs and problems to system solutions.

The construction of models involves the simplified representation of a real world element or a group of elements with their respective relationships. Identifying the proper degree of simplicity in modeling requires expertise. The proper definition of the problem to be modeled, the required data, and the approximation of parameters and relationships are not easy jobs. An expert system can be helpful in guiding the user in performing the above tasks.

The fifth area is machine learning. The full potential of CASE and expert systems integration will be best served by utilizing sophisticated machine learning capabilities. Machine learning or self adaptivity is a key feature that must be tackled in order to take full advantage of AI technology. In the following paragraphs, we will discuss a number of ways that a machine can learn (Partridge, 1986). They primarily differ in the degree to which the learning process can be guided and manipulated.

Learning General Principles - There are two primary approaches for building knowledge with a machine which is capable of learning the general principles of software engineering: to start with a set of general principles and then restrict usage based on the subsequent occurrences of the counter examples, or to start with a few general principles and generalize usage based on the subsequent examples encountered. Both approaches have been used for machine learning (Bundy & Silver, 1982).

Learning By Being Told - Since expert systems programs are usually large and complex, machine learning of CASE methodological concepts must be treated with caution. If learning is prompted and monitored by the user, then we are in a good position to maintain control over the emerging system. This type of learning process is also the easiest to implement, because most of the teaching responsibilities remain with the human tutor.

Learning By Introspection - This class of machine learning of CASE methodological concepts refers to the prospect of developing new ideas and concepts from old ones. In this process, the expert system reviews previous CASE deliverables and tries to generate improved decision making strategies. The expert system can do this easily during its slack periods. Partridge (1975) has successfully employed this technique within an adaptive FORTRAN translator. The translator has an artificially intelligent module that periodically surveyes the results of previous parsing sessions and then reorganizes its knowledge base. One of the tasks of this module is to delete ill-defined generalizations by identifying the most frequently used unique instances of a general rule and moving them to positions of higher precedence with respect to the general rule itself.

SUMMARY

Use of expert systems will bring the most dramatic changes in CASE toolsets. CASE technology has already demonstrated its effectiveness in the software engineering process. In recent years expert systems have begun to show a promise both for effectively handling ill-defined aspects of businesses (e.g., natural language) and, in particular, for interacting with users as individuals. Hence, expert systems and CASE integration hold a promise of an enriched software engineering environment through economical (compare to human experts) procedures for application development and re-engineering.

However, organizational, methodological and technological problems may deter Information Systems organizations from taking advantage of the integrated I-CASE/ES environment. The next logical step in this research, is to address these issues by developing a prototype of the I-CASE/ES environment to test its capabilities and to better understand implementation problems. When operational, this prototype will help to validate the concepts and principles of CASE/ES integration. Such a prototype will also allow analysis of the effectiveness of the integration in the five areas discussed in this article -interface through Natural Language Interfaces, tutoring through Computer-Aided Instruction modules, data acquisition through the use of expert systems, model construction and selection, and improvement in control logic of CASE tools through machine learning (self adaptivity). Finally, the prototype will help to identify priorities for implementation of I-CASE/ES platforms.

REFERENCES

Bundy, A., & Silver, B. (1982). A critical survey of rule learning programs. *Proceedings of ECAI,* 151-157.

Courtney, J. F. Jr., et al. (Summer, 1987). A Knowledge-based DSS for Managerial Problem Diagnosis. *Decision Sciences.*

Forte, Gene (December 1989). Inside the CASE Repository. *CASE Outlook.*

Hertz, David Bendel (1988). *The Expert Executive.* John Wiley & Sons, Inc., New York.

Loh, Marcus and R.Ryan Nelson (July 1, 1989). Reaping CASE Harvest. *Datamation.*

Meador, C. L., Keem, P. G. W., and Guyote, M. J. (May 7, 1984). Personal "Personal Computer and Distributed Decision Support. *Computerworld.* Vol. 18, No. 19.

Miller, Richard K. (1984). *Artificial Intelligence Applications for Business Management.* SEAI Technical Publications. Madison, CA, 10-11.

Newman, W. M. (1987). *Designing Integrated Systems for the Office Environment.* New York, McGraw Hill.

Partridge, D., (1975). A Dynamic Database which Automatically Removes Unwanted Generalization for the Efficient Analysis of Language features that Exhibit a Disparate Frequency Distribution. *Computer Journal.* Vol. 18, No. 1, pp. 43-48.

Partridge, D., (1986). *Artificial Intelligence: Applications in the future of the software engineering.* Ellis Horwood Limited, Great Britain.

Slusky, Ludwig (September 1987). Integrating Software Modeling and Prototyping Tools. *Information and Software Technology.* Vol 29.

Slusky, Ludwig (October 1991). Modeling of I-CASE Platform. *Information and Software Technology.* Vol 33, No. 8.

Turban, Efraim (1990). *Decision Support and Expert Systems Managerial Perspectives.* 2nd ed., Macmillan Publishing Co., New York.

Wasserman, Anthony (1989). The Architecture of CASE Environments. *CASE Outlook.* No. 2.

CHAPTER THIRTEEN

Using CASE in Expert Systems Design

David Chender Chou
West Texas State University

Most CASE tools are built for assisting analysts during the systems analysis and design phases of a project, but they have a great capacity to be expanded, and one possible area is the expert systems design process. The expert systems design process has features different from the conventional systems analysis and design process. In addition to performing the regular system analysis and design's procedures, the system analysts and designers of expert systems projects need to consult with a field's experts, create suitable knowledge bases, and design the acquisition mechanism, inference engine and presentation systems. These extra expert systems building procedures need to be controlled effectively and efficiently.

The aim of this chapter is to propose incorporating knowledge engineering toolkits into integrated CASE tools, and their use in automating the process of expert systems design and development. This chapter first discusses the processes of the conventional system development life cycle; it then discusses the expert system design life cycle. Each individual phase and the corresponding activities will be briefly discussed, as will the distinguishing features of the expert system life cycle. The concept of using an integrated CASE tool in expert systems design is proposed next, and the toolkits of knowledge engineering are described. Finally, an architecture for incorporating previous toolkits into integrated CASE tool is proposed in the last sections of this chapter.

INFORMATION SYSTEM AND EXPERT SYSTEM DEVELOPMENT LIFE CYCLES

The conventional systems development life cycle (SDLC) consists of the following phases: preliminary investigation, system requirements, system analysis, system design, system development, and implementation and evaluation. (Powers, et al. 1984; Senn, 1989; Kendall & Kendall, 1992) Each phase in the SDLC implements several activities to fulfill its essential objectives. (see Table 1) The iterated phases and activities in the SDLC fulfill the goal of promoting system quality in software engineering.

The expert system development life cycle is different from that used for conventional information systems. This development process may be used to design a new expert system, improve an existing expert system, or add expert system capabilities to an existing information system (to improve the system's functionality). Table 1 also illustrates the various phases and activities of the expert systems development life cycle. The details of these activities are discussed below:

Phase 1: Preliminary Investigation

This phase examines the existing system (conventional information system or expert system) and proposes improvements to management for approval of further study. The preliminary investigation phase consists of the following activities:

1. System performance evaluation: a periodical evaluation of systems performance (to maintain high quality information service) which usually generates a system performance report.
2. Detect system failure: the computer center manager or other personnel work together to detect possible system failure. This study may conclude with a suggestion of an expert system development plan.
3. User request or recommendation: the system user may request some changes to the current system and a possible recommendation of developing an expert system may reach the management level.
4. Needs assessment: the needs from various perspectives will be evaluated by a system development team and a proposal will be

Phases/Activities	CIS	ES	CASE
1. Preliminary Investigation phase			
System performance evaluation	X	X	X
Detect system failure	X	X	X
User request or recommendation	X	X	X
Need assessment	X	X	X
Problem definition	X	X	X
Feasibility study	X	X	X
Management approval	X	X	X
2. System Requirements phase			
Problem domain for new system	X	X	X
New system functions	X	X	X
Data changes (input/output)	X	X	X
Data structure changes	X	X	X
Preliminary software selection	X	X	X
System interfaces	X	X	X
Possible knowledge representation		X	P
3. System Analysis phase			
Current system modelling: physical and logical models.	X	X	X
Organizational charts	X	X	X
Corporate strategies, policies, etc.	X	X	X
Data modelling: inputs, outputs, data structure, etc.	X	X	X
Peripherals and interface analysis	X	X	X
User identification	X	X	X
Expert identification		X	X
Knowledge engineer identification		X	X
4. System Design phase			
Software selection (language/shell)	X	X	X
Programming design: input, output, data structure, file, etc.	X	X	X
Data base design	X	X	X
User interfaces design	X	X	X
Security design	X	X	X
System architecture: on-line/batch	X	X	X
Networking design	X	X	X
Knowledge base design		X	P
Knowledge representation design		X	P
Inference engine design		X	P
Knowledge validation		X	P
Installation and testing planning	X	X	X
5. System Development phase			
Building a prototype	X	X	X
Building data base	X	X	X
Building user interface	X	X	X
Building knowledge base		X	P
Building inference engine		X	P
Knowledge base testing		X	P
System testing	X	X	X

(CONTINUED NEXT PAGE)

Table 1: A Comparison of Systems Development Life Cycles

Phases/Activities	CIS	ES	CASE
6. Implementation and Evaluation phase			
Data conversion	X	X	
System installation	X	X	
System integration	X	X	
User training	X	X	X
System documentations	X	X	X
Development review	X	X	X
Extension of knowledge base		X	P

Note: CIS: in Conventional Information System;
 ES: in Expert System;
 CASE: in Computer-Aided Software Engineering;
 X = Yes/adopted;
 P = Proposed in this chapter.

Table 1: A Comparison of Systems Development Life Cycles

made and submitted to a Steering Committee for further review.
5. Problem definition: the scope, domain and boundaries of proposed expert system development projects will be identified by the system development team.
6. Feasibility study: the system development team conducts various feasibility studies toward the proposed expert system development project in order to measure the possibility of its accomplishment, including the financial feasibility, human factors feasibility, technical feasibility, scheduling feasibility, and so on.
7. Management approval: the computer center manager reviews the proposal and feasibility report and then submits them to the executives or the computer steering committee for final approval.

Phase 2: System's Requirements

The system requirements and specifications are collected after the preliminary investigation. The major goal of this phase is to get the correct specifications for the new system. This phase includes the following activities:

1. Problem domain for the new system: the new system's problem domain must be defined in order to have a complete understanding of the scope of the new system.
2. New system functions: the proposed changes to the existing system usually focus on improving the system's functionality. New system functions are added according to users' requests or as a result of the recommendations made in phase one.
3. Data changes: the new system may change data specifications

such as input and output formats or processing flows. The proposed data changes are identified.
4. Data structure changes: the new system may include the adoption of a new data structure especially if it is an expert system. The possible data structures for the new system are reviewed and evaluated with respect to improving the efficiency of system.
5. Preliminary software selection: the possible expert system shells or languages for the new system are surveyed and a preliminary selection made. The costs and benefits of adopting these software packages are estimated.
6. System interfaces: the changed interfaces in the new system are identified and their hardware and software requirements are analyzed with respect to operational efficiency. The estimated costs and benefits of new system interfaces are carefully evaluated.
7. Possible knowledge representation and rules: the preliminary studies on knowledge representation and inference rules in expert systems are conducted in this phase. The knowledge engineers and field experts communicate with users to get full specifications of the expert system development project.

Phase 3: System Analysis

This phase investigates the scope and functions of the existing system. The major objective of this phase is to collect related information about an existing system's operating environment. The resulting document from this phase is needed for later system design activities. The System Analysis phase consists of the following activities:

1. Current system modelling (physical and logical models): the operation of the existing system can be illustrated through the use of data flow diagrams and other related techniques. These system modelling techniques are frequently implemented in CASE applications. (Martin, 1989; McClure, 1989) The physical model describes the actual system process; the logical models shows the ideal process for the existing system.
2. Organizational charts: the System Analysts need to understand the organizational structure. The structure of the organization is most easily illustrated using an organizational chart, through which the personnel, and functions of the organization and their relationship to the existing system can also be identified.
3. Corporate strategies, policies, etc.: the management's philosophy

affects the behavior of decision-making in the corporation. Corporate strategies, policies, and operation procedures are considered valuable information to incorporate into the expert system design.
4. Data modelling (inputs, output, data structure, etc.): system analysts need to collect the information on data inputs, data outputs, data structure, and various data formats in order to understand the system structure.
5. Peripherals and interface analysis: the system's peripherals and their interfaces with the system are the main source of detecting system errors. Distributed systems usually consist of a large number of peripherals.
6. User identification: the system's main users are identified during this activity. The purpose of identifying system users is to collect detailed information on the system's daily operation and maintenance schedule.
7. Expert identification: Building expert systems requires related field experts to contribute their specialties to knowledge base construction. The various experts in an expert system's application field are identified and invited to contribute to the building of a comprehensive knowledge base.
8. Knowledge engineer identification: Knowledge engineers design the architecture of the knowledge base, the knowledge acquisition process, the inference engine, and the presentation sub-system for the expert system. Suitable knowledge engineers are needed in order to construct a workable expert system. Knowledge engineers should demonstrate communication skills with users, fields experts, programmers, and system analysts.

Phase 4: System Design

This phase transforms the new system requirements into a system's design. The system design phase includes various design activities such as programming design, database design, interface design, security design, and knowledge base design. The system installation and testing plans have to be established before system construction starts in order to control the process and to improve the quality of system building. This phase includes the following activities:

1. Software selection: the selection of an expert system shell or AI language is needed before designing the suitable software for system implementation. The choice between using a programming language or an expert shell is a critical decision prior to

expert system construction.
2. Programming design [if an AI language is used]: the design of software and its inputs, outputs, data structure, and files.
3. Database design: the selection of a suitable database management system is critical. Design of the database structure and its normalization improves the efficiency and effectiveness of the system implementation.
4. User interfaces design: the designs of screens, icons, windows, commands, and various user interface features should meet user's needs and requirements. The major objective of user interface design is to deliver an expert system that is user-friendly.
5. Security design: the design of a security system in the new software is also performed in this phase. The main purpose of adopting a suitable security system is to protect the system and its database.
6. System architecture: the design of system architecture is based on the functions of the new system, i.e., the type of expert system being designed.
7. Networking design: a distributed system necessitates the need to consider the methodology of computer networking. The design of a suitable, inexpensive network protocol is a critical objective.
8. Knowledge base design: the Knowledge base is the heart of the expert system. The domain facts and heuristics of the knowledge base and their relationship to the knowledge representation, knowledge acquisition, inference engine, and presentation system are studied and planned.
9. Knowledge representation design: the design of the structure of representing knowledge in an expert system including the use of predicate calculus, production rules, semantic networks, inference rules, and so on. The selection of the best way to store and implement knowledge in a knowledge base is the major goal of this activity.
10. Inference engine design: the strategies which guide an expert system to draw inferences, show the facts and rules stored in the knowledge base and the information acquired from the user are documented in a design. Also, the control mechanism such as backward and forward chaining, depth-first or breadth-first search, and monotonic or non-monotonic reasoning needs to be evaluated and selected at this stage.
11. Knowledge validation: the facts and rules in the knowledge base need to be validated before a prototype expert system is built. Suitable testing methods must be selected to conduct this validation process.

12. Installation and testing planning: this activity establishes a preliminary plan for the implementation and installation of the new system. It includes all levels of major tasks, working days required, and a schedule for completing the activities. The adoption of a suitable plan for data and system conversions is a major task in installation planning. A testing plan should include criteria of the future system operations. Moreover, this planning should guide the design team in completing the project.

Phase 5: System Development

This phase is where the actual construction of the new expert system occurs. The previous phases create a framework for the new system but the construction of the system begins in this phase. The system development phase consists of the following activities:

1. Building a prototype: a prototype may be considered as a type of system model. A computer system can be developed and expanded based on the prototyped model, and processing alternatives can be evaluated and tested. Achieving this activity is a milestone in expert system construction because of the complexity and difficulty of expert systems.
2. Building the database: the use of database management software (DBMS) in an expert system design enhances the data processing power. Database construction needs to be proceeded by data normalization processes. The interfaces between the DBMS and the expert system need to interact smoothly.
3. Building the user interface: the user-friendliness of system interface improves the efficiency and effectiveness of system processing. The construction of a good user interface is based on the user requirements and software capabiliies.
4. Building a knowledge base: the expert system builder needs to construct the knowledge base, based on the design specifications. A knowledge base prototype can be constructed first, and then expanded later.
5. Building an inference engine: the inference engine is one of the major parts of an expert system. It performs the functions of knowledge inference and control in expert systems. If a shell program is chosen, this step converts to learning how to use the shell.
6. Knowledge base testing: the completeness and correctness of the knowledge base is a critical factor in a successful expert system. The knowledge base should be tested at this stage in order to assure a quality expert system later.

Expert Systems Design 387

7. System testing: system testing activity should cover all subsystems and related software in the environment. The testing process should follow the procedures and plans defined in the systems design phase.

Phase 6: Implementation and Evaluation

During this phase, any data files are converted into the new format and the fully tested system is installed (according to the conversion plan adopted in the system design phase). For implementation of distributed system components, a system integration plan should be followed. In order to support the overall system implementation, user training programs are offered and the system documentation is provided. This phase includes the following activities:

1. Data conversion: a set of data conversion programs are prepared in order to convert the existing data format into the new data format.
2. System installation: the new system must be installed; the end product of this activity is an independent, fully functioning expert system.
3. System integration: the implementation of a distributed system needs to adapt to the standards and protocols of the existing environment. An expert system which operates in the corporate information center has to function well with respect to other corporate processing and applications.
4. User training: new system training courses must be offered in order to assist prospective users in developing their knowledge of the newly installed system. User manuals must be prepared before the training courses are conducted.
5. System documentations: the operational manuals and other system documentation must be prepared for reference. The system documentation must clearly describe the characteristics of the new expert system.
6. Development review: the system development team reviews the system's performance (during a certain period of time) in order to maintain the operational quality of the system. The user will provide feedback on the expert system based on his/her observation and experience.
7. Extension of knowledge base: the expert system's knowledge base needs to be expandable in order to incorporate various aspects of operational needs in the future.

DISTINGUISHING FEATURES IN EXPERT SYSTEM LIFE CYCLE

The expert systems development life cycle has some distinguishing features, when compared to conventional system development acitivities. The differences arise from the various characteristics of expert systems and conventional information systems.

An expert system, or knowledge-based system, is designed to assist users in solving problems based on the information/knowledge gathered from human experts. Two distinguishing features of expert systems are the knowledge acquisition process and inference engine design. The knowledge-base is a database which consists of various types of knowledge about the problem domain, i.e., medicine or chemical engineering. It includes the rules, objects, data, and logic for knowledge representation. The goal of the expert systems development life cycle is to design and develop a structured, logical, and efficent knowledge-base for expert system implementation. The inference engine interacts with the knowledge-base, as well as the knowledge acquisition, presentation, and user interface subsystems. It stores the strategies for inference and control of the expert system.

Other important features of an expert system, are its problem domain and decision characteristics. First of all, expert systems deal with more restricted problems than that of general information systems. This is why expert systems can be used to assist problem solving in a specific area. Sometimes, expert systems face unbounded problems which may not be described or considered in a knowledge base (Liebowitz, 1988). Expert systems can proceed in these situations through the use of fuzzy logic (Zadeh, 1983) and Bayesian inference (Duda et al, 1979; Gibbons, 1982; Nau, 1983). Since the knowledge base serves as the information bank for the expert system, the size of the knowledge base contrains its reasoning capability. Overall, expert systems deal with a more complex problem-solving domain than that of general information systems (Brachman, 1983; Waterman, 1986).

The expert system's design and development processes involve specific personnel. The following personnel participate in the expert system's SDLC: system analyst/designer, programmer, user, knowledge engineer, and knowledge and domain experts. The system analyst/designer, programmer, and user in an expert system life cycle perform the same functions as those in conventional information systems. Knowledge engineers play an important role in an expert system life cycle since their major job is to build the knowledge base. Knowledge experts are the experts of the problem and its related areas. Knowledge engineers acquire knowledge from knowledge experts, design the structure of the knowledge base, set up the strategies for the inference engine, and interact with users and knowledge experts.

CASE TOOLS IN EXPERT SYSTEMS DESIGN

The activities of designing and developing an expert system need refined tools to improve their effectiveness and efficiency. According to Gaines (1990, p. 99), the problems and challenges that face expert systems builders are:

1. *Problems of professionalism:*
   a. Theory: lack of foundations for nature of expertise, knowledge representation, acquisition & processing;
   b. Techniques: lack of well-established techniques for knowledge engineering;
   c. Tools: lack of powerful tools for knowledge acquisition and transfer to expert system shells;
   d. Training: lack of structured training methodologies for developing professional skills in knowledge engineering.
2. *Problems of knowledge acquisition and transfer:*
   a. System specification: lack of formal specification standards for knowledge-based systems;
   b. Access to expertise: difficulties in involvement of experts over time-scales required for development;
   c. Acquisition of skills: difficulties in communication of skilled behavior through verbal channels;
   d. Representation of knowledge: weaknesses in shell capabilities to represent some aspects of expertise.
3. *Problems of system performance:*
   a. Validation: difficulties in establishing objective criteria for the validity of the performance of the system;
   b. Usability: weaknesses in the user interface, language used, and explanation facilities;
   c. Maintainability: effort required to keep systems based on superficial and changing knowledge up to date;
   d. Upgradability: difficulties in improving performance and of integration with other systems.

A number of the identified problems and challenges could be alleviated through the use of automated tools that support the expert systems development life cycle. Some information systems builders considered adopting software engineering techniques for expert systems development without using structured systems analysis techniques (DeSalvo et al, 1987; Liebowitz & DeSalvo, 1989; Agarwal and Tanniru, 1990). Alpar (1990), on the contrary, applied the techniques of structured systems analysis to a real life project for expert systems development and his results encourage further use of these techniques on similar projects. Software engineering techniques also merge prototyping strategies with software development life cycle methodologies, to speed up the process of software design (Dennis et al, 1987, Shoval & Pliskin, 1987). Other tools such as powerful artificial intelligence languages, expert systems shells, and knowledge engineering environments provide further support during the expert systems development life cycle (Sheil, 1984; Alpar, 1990).

Computer-Aided Software Engineering (CASE), according to Carma McClure (1991), includes the following: (1) software automation; (2) a combination of tools and methods; (3) repackaging of structured concepts; (4) re-definition of the software environment: tools, methods, hardware, and management; (5) a change in attitude; (6) rediscovery of software engineering principles; and (7) recognition of the need to automate.

The concept of a repository has been incorporated into CASE implementation (McClure, 1989, 1991; Due, 1991; Gane 1990; Souza, 1990; Martin, 1989). The repository, also known as an encyclopedia, is a database that stores information about organizational and data structures, strategic goals, functional processes and models, implementation procedures, and related computer programs.

Most activities in the information system development life cycle are supported by existing CASE tools (Martin, 1989; McClure, 1989). The CASE tools, along with the repository, provide full software life cycle support to the planning, analysis, design, and construction phases of a project. Integrated CASE, or I-CASE, is used to describe toolkits in which tools for many or all aspects of software development are integrated (Martin, 1989). A critical characteristic of an I-CASE tool is that it generates executable programs, and that its repository stores the knowledge from multiple workbenches in an integrated manner (Martin, 1989).

An I-CASE tool, in addition to supporting all phases of the SDLC in an integrated manner, supports enterprise-wide planning, data modeling, and process modeling to create a framework in support of multiple project life cycles. A detailed listing of the basic characteristics of I-CASE tools can be found in [Martin, 1989].

Expert Systems Design 391

The I-CASE concept can be used to support an automated expert systems life cycle. Moreover, an I-CASE environment could be based on a flexible framework ,that provides a cost-effective tool-integration mechanism, encourages portable tools, facilitates the exchange of development information, adapts to future methods, and extends to other engineering disciplines (Chen & Sibley, 1991; Norman & Chen, 1992). This concept encourages an idea of searching for an automated CASE tool for expert systems development since expert systems have been used and developed in information industries for a long period of time.

Future trends in software development imply that CASE tools will have embedded expert systems (Tanik and Yun, 1988; Luqi, 1988; Czuchry and Harris, 1988; Kant; 1988; Kaiser, et al., 1988; Motoda 1990). The application of expert systems technology to systems design and construction will enhance the power of CASE tools. In like manner the impediments to expert systems development will be diminished with incorporation of CASE tools into the expert system development process.

Table 1 lists the expert system activities which could be supported by I-CASE tools. However, several activities in this SDLC are not supported by existing CASE products; most of these are related to expert system design activities, such as knowledge-base design, representation, validation and testing; and inference engine design and testing.

A valid expert system stems from the correct design and implementation of a knowledge base, a knowledge acquisition process, an inference engine, and a presentation system. This chapter proposes an architecture to fulfill the functionalities of an automated I-CASE tool for expert systems development. The power of this automated tool depends on the degree of data and control integration in the entire system (Chen & Norman, 1992). Data integration functionality offers services that integrate tools with the repository, including: metamodel service, query service, review service, and data-interchange service. Control integration, on the other hand, provides explicit message passing, time- or access-activated triggers, and message servers. These control integration services perform three types of communication: tool-to-tool, tool-to-service, and service-to-service (Wasserman, 1990; Chen & Norman, 1992). The following sections describe the structures and strategies of incorporating four knowledge engineering toolkits in an integrated CASE tool for automating the expert system development life cycle.

INCORPORATING THE KNOWLEDGE BASE

Automated expert system building and development processes need a suitable CASE tool. In order to construct an automated CASE tool, the repository should include knowledge bases, knowledge acquisition mechanisms, rules and strategies for making inferences, and presentation programs.

The knowledge base is the heart of the expert system and stores various facts and rules. Using CASE tools for expert system construction requires a toolkit for knowledge base design and validation. An effective and efficient knowledge base toolkit can design, validate, and create a proper knowledge base for prospective expert system's implementation in a short time.

Knowledge Base Toolkit

The toolkit for knowledge base design and validation should include three components: (1) knowledge identifier, (2) knowledge representation controller, and (3) a knowledge validator. The knowledge base consists of knowledge such as domain facts, rules, heuristics, strategies, terminology definitions, supplementary knowledge for explanation, fuzzy knowledge, and modelling knowledge, etc.

The knowledge identifier tool is used to identify the kinds of knowledge in the knowledge base. This identification assists later processes such as knowledge acquisition, development of inference rules, explanation, and validation. The format of knowledge representation or its storage mechanism will be discussed below.

Knowledge representation methods/media must be manipulated through a knowlege reperesentation controller in order to coordinate and decide the structure of, and relationships between, knowledge in the knowledge base. This controller can also be part of an I-CASE tool. An automated knowledge representation controller can identify a specific knowledge set and represent it through a suitable representation medium. The controller has the ability to identify the following representation methods: predicate logic, production rules, semantic network, frames, neural net, and others.

A knowledge validator tool performs the job of quality assurance by validating, verifying, and testing the knowledge base which is generated through CASE tools. A careful and suitable knowledge validation process can improve the quality of the knowledge base.

Strategies for Knowledge Representation

In order to design the correct knowledge base for an expert

system, several strategies for knowledge representation need to be examined: object-oriented representation, hierarchical representation, and groups representation.

The object-oriented representation method uses a special organization consisting of objects that represent entities capable of exhibiting behavior (Waterman, 1986). The object-oriented approach is more than a structured approach to handle the knowledge representation. An object is something with a set of attributes and features that describe its nature and functionality. An object in a knowledge base consists of related rules and representation methods for future processes. Since objects are self-contained packages of knowledge and media, they are highly reusable. This knowledge reusability is one of the important characteristics of CASE tools (Chen & Norman, 1992).

The usual approach to organizing knowledge in a knowledge base is, according to some predefined hierarchical function. In order to establish a hierarchy, the knowledge engineer reviews the overall knowledge base, and breaks it down into a series of managable parts with proper relationships. This continuous process goes on until the overall knowledge base is defined in understandable forms. This knowledge representation method uses nested subroutines to organize and control program execution (Waterman, 1986). Semantic networks, frames, and neural nets are the major methods which reveal the hierarchy of knowledge.

The concept of modularity in computer software has been widely accepted for a long time. Since a knowledge base consists of a tremendous amount of information, the grouping of the related knowledge in this knowledge base allows it to be intellectually manageable. The methodologies of dividing rules in a knowledge base into groups to make expert systems more understandable, maintainable, and efficient which have been used tools such as ACE (Wright, et al. 1984), PROSPECTOR (Duda, et al. 1978), and a rule grouping method developed by Jacob and Froscher (1990).

INCORPORATING SUPPORT FOR THE KNOWLEDGE ACQUISITION PROCESS

After the objects, problem domains, and possible tasks are selected for the knowledge base, the next step in expert system building is knowledge acquisition. The knowledge for the expert system is acquired from users and field experts by knowledge engineers. The knowledge engineers are the people responsible for design and implementation of the knowledge acquisition sub-system. A suitable knowledge acquisition system facilitates the processes of knowledge base construction, inference engineering, and presentation system operations.

Knowledge Acquisition Toolkit

This knowledge acquisition toolkit should consist of a knowledge interface and a knowledge tool learner. Knowledge engineers need to acquire the knowledge for knowledge base construction. They have to extract the needs and the definition of the problem domain from the users; the facts and heuristics of each task and its environment from the field experts; and the information on business goals and strategies from the CASE repository. In order to interact with these entities to acquire the essential knowledge for the expert system, a knowledge interface toolkit is necessary to handle these operations. This toolkit feeds the functionality of data integration in I-CASE tool (Chen & Norman, 1992).

Knowledge engineers first need to understand the problem domain for a specific expert system. They must complete interviews or questionnaires to collect the essential knowledge. A careful plan must be made before conducting these activities in order to collect complete and appropriate knowledge from the users and field experts. A convenient interface is used to enter the data and modify the knowledge base.

In order to capture the external environment of the problem domain, knowledge engineers need to catch the information about this integrated computer system. A suitable I-CASE interface toolkit would be able to access the repository for retrieving the necessary system information for implementing knowledge acquisition.

The second component in a knowledge acquisition toolkit is the automated knowledge learner. The knowledge in the knowledge base can be acquired through the machine learning process. Machine learning, according to Carbonell et al. (1983, p.5), is the exploration of alternative learning mechanisms, including the discovery of different induction algorithms, the scope and limitations of certain methods, the information that must be available to the learner, the issue of coping with imperfect training data, and the creation of general techniques applicable in many task domains.

An I-CASE tool for expert systems planning, analysis, design, development and maintenance needs an efficient knowledge acquisition system for automated processes. A knowledge learner in I-CASE should assist the knowledge engineers in building and validating the knowledge base easily by supporting various techniques for acquiring knowledge, infering knowledge, and validating knowledge.

Strategies for Knowledge Acquisition

The knowledge acquisition toolkit should assist knowledge engineers in acquiring knowledge for the expert system implementation. In order to create a suitable toolkit for knowledge acquisition, three strategic issues are worth observation: (1) Group knowledge acquisition process, (2) knowledge engineer and expert identification, and (3) an integrated toolkit in I-CASE.

Since biases exist during knowledge acquisition processing, it is possible that the knowledge engineer may acquire imperfect knowledge from the users and field experts. A group knowledge acquisition system, like a group decision support system, allows related personnel to work together to build up the knowledge base. Biases and confusion can be dissolved through an interactive group-based knowledge acquisition process.

One of the common problems in knowledge acquisition is that knowledge engineers have insufficient knowledge about the problem domain and its task environment. In order to remedy this problem, knowledge engineers and field experts have to be identified before starting the requirements analysis phase. Knowledge engineers should participate in the activities of system requirements and specification gathering earlier so they have a complete picture of the overall system and its environment.

A knowledge acquisition toolkit in an I-CASE tool can facilitate access by the knowledge engineers of various information on the external environment such as business goals and strategies, operational definitions, and other system-wide information. An efficient and effective toolkit interface within I-CASE could promote the functionality of the expert system and its overall information system.

INCORPORATING THE INFERENCE ENGINE

Expert systems have the capability of generating a solution by selecting an inference strategy from the inference strategies library and using it to arrive at a conclusion. This inference engine should have two major components: a Strategy Selector, and an Inference Strategies Library.

A Strategy Selector should conduct the job of comparing the prospective problem domain and the available strategies in the library, then selecting a suitable strategy for the problem reasoning process. The selection of a suitable reasoning strategy for a problem is based on the characteristics of the reasoning strategy, properties of facts, size of facts, the possible reasoning direction, uncertainty factors with respect to facts, and the user's processing preference (interactive or justifiable). The inference strategy analyzer should assist the inference engine in adopting a proper and efficient strategy for the reasoning process.

The Inference Strategies Library should store various inference strategies and their reasoning heuristics and algorithms. After the Strategy Selector chooses a proper reasoning strategy for problem solving, the inference engine selects the right module in the Inference Strategies Library for execution of rules and algorithms.

Depending on the characteristics of facts and other related considerations, the following strategies can be included in the Library: (Liebowitz, 1988; Golshani, 1990)

a. forward chaining strategy;
b. backward chaining strategy;
c. forward and backward chaining combined strategy;
d. depth-first strategy;
e. breath-first strategy;
f. conflict resolution mechanism;
g. uncertainty reasoning strategy: Bayesian approach; and
h. inexact reasoning strategies: belief functions, Dempster- Shafer method, and fuzzy logic.

Strategies for Building an Inference Engine

A completed inference engine should store the available strategies for the reasoning process. The information in the Strategy Selector assists the inference engine in choosing a suitable strategy in a short time for later usage. The modular structure (strategy modularization) in the Inference Strategies Library, like knowledge base modularization, should improve the efficiency of processing and promotes reusability and expandability.

INCORPORATING THE PRESENTATION SYSTEM

Expert systems perform a reasoning process to reach a conclusion for a specific problem, which is requested by a user. In addition, a user may request that the expert system explain the logical path it used in reaching such a conclusion. The presentation system tool in I-CASE should assist the user in observing the structured texts, structured graphics, matrices, rules, and logical paths used by the inference engine.

An integrated presentation system in existing CASE environments improves the tool's user-interface. Several integrated presentation tools have been utilized: window-based tools (Wasserman, 1990) and Motif, the presentation standard used by most CASE tools in the open-systems environment (Chen and Norman, 1992). The format for explanation depends on a user's preference: interactive or non-interactive processing, conclusive or non-conclusive explanation, descriptive or diagram or windows displaying, superficial or deep level of explanation, and so on (Waterman, 1986; Wick & Slagle, 1989). The incorporation of these functionalities an I-CASE tool, enhances the power of the expert system and its associated information system design.

CONCLUSION

This chapter identifies the tremendous potential of having integrated CASE tools to assist in the expert systems analysis and design processes. Indeed, one CASE tool (Iconix, 1987) already provides the capability of building expert systems with the PROLOG and LISP languages.

CASE tools for expert systems design and development should include expert systems toolkits in addition to the regular toolkits which have been established for conventional system development activities. This chapter proposes four toolkits to facilitate the process of expert systems development: a knowledge base toolkit, a knowledge acquisition toolkit, an inference engine toolkit, and a presentation toolkit .

As more and more information systems incorporate expert system components and technologies, I-CASE tools as described in this chapter will have even broader applicability. Indeed, when most informaitn systems have expert characteristics, these tools will be a necessity, for users, for designers, and for tool vendors.

REFERENCES

Agarwal, R., & Tanniru, M. (1990). Systems development life-cycle for expert systems. *Knowledge-Based Systems*, 3(3), 170-180.

Alpar, P. (1990). Toward structured expert systems development. *Expert Systems With Applications*, 1(1), 63-70.

Brachman, R., Amarel S., Engelman C., Engelmore R., Feigenbaum E., & Wilkins D. (1983). What are expert systems? In F. Hayes- Roth, D. A. Waterman, and D. Lenat (Eds.), *Building Expert Systems*. Reading, MA: Addison-Wesley.

Carbonell, J. G., Michalski R. S., & Mitchell T. M. (1983). An overview of machine learning. In R. S. Michalski, J. G. Carbonell, and T. M. Mitchell, *Machine Learning* (pp. 3-23). Palo Alto, California: Tioga Publishing Company.

Chen, M., & Sibley, E. H. (1991). Using a CASE-based repository for systems integration. *Proc. Hawaii Int'l Conf. Systems Sciences, Vol. II*, (pp. 578-587). Los Alamitos, CA: IEEE CS Press.

Chen, M., & Norman, R. J. (1992). A framework for integrated CASE. *IEEE Software*, March, 18-22.

Czuchry, A. J. Jr., & Harris D. R. (1988). KBRA: A new paradigm for requirements engineering. *IEEE Expert*, 3(4), 21-35.

Dennis, A. R., Burns, R. N., & Gallupe, R. B. (1987). Phased design: a mixed methodology for application systems development. *Data Base*, 19, 31-37.

DeSalvo, D. A., Glamm, A. E., & Liebowitz, J. (1987). Structured design of an expert system prototype at the National Archives. In B. G. Silverman (Ed.) Expert Systems for Business (pp. 40- 77). Reading, MA: Addison-Wesley.

Duda, R. O., Hart P. E., Nilsson N. J., and Sutherland G. L. (1978). Semantic network representations in rule-based inference systems. In D. A. Waterman & F. Hayes-Roth (Eds.) *Pattern-Directed Inference Systems* (pp. 203-221). New York: Academic.

Duda, R. O., Gaschnig J. G., and Hart P. (1979). Model design in the Prospector consultant system for mineral exploration. In D. H. Michie (Ed.), *Expert Systems in the Micro Electronic Age*. Edinburgh: Edinburgh University Press.

Due, R. T. (1991). The real costs and benefits of CASE. *Journal of Information System Management*. Summer, 63-66.

Gaines, B. R. (1990). Knowledge acquisition systems. In H. Adeli (Ed.) *Knowledge Engineering* (Vol. 1). New York: McGraw-Hill.

Gane, C. (1990). *Computer-Aided Software Engineering*. Englewood Cliffs, NJ: Prentice Hall.

Gibbons, G. D. (1982). *Knowledge-Based Systems*. Berlin Continuing Engineering Education Program, Washington DC: George Washington University.

Golshani, F. (1990) Rule-based Expert Systems. In H. Adeli (Ed.) *Knowledge Engineering* (Vol. 1). New York: McGraw-Hill.

Iconix Software Engineering, Inc. (1987). Product Description of SmartChart. Santa Monica, CA.

Jacob, R. J. K., & Froscher J. N. (1990). A software engineering methodology for rule-based systems. *IEEE Trans. on Knowledge and Data Engineering* 2(2), 173-189.

Kaiser, G. E., Feiler P. H., & Popovich S. S. (1988). Intelligent assistance for software development and maintenance. *IEEE Software* 5(3), 40-49.

Kant, E. (1988). Interactive problem solving using task configuration and control. *IEEE Expert* 3(4), 36-49.

Kendall, K. D. & Kendall J. E. (1992). *Systems Analysis and Design* (2nd Ed.), Englewood Cliffs, NJ: Prentice Hall.

Liebowitz, J. (1988). *Introduction to Expert Systems*, Santa Cruz, CA: Mitchell Publishing.

Liebowitz, J., & DeSalvo, D. A. (Eds.). (1989). *Structured Expert Systems: Domain, Design, and Development*. Englewood Cliffs, NJ: Yourdon Press/Prentice Hall.

Luqi (1988). Knowledge-based support for rapid software prototyping. *IEEE Expert* 3(4), 9-18.

Martin, J. (1989). *Information Engineering: Introduction*, Englewood Cliffs, NJ: Prentice Hall.

McClure, C. (1991). Modeling the enterprise. In *The Consultant Forum*, (Special Ed., pp. 15-19), Digital Equipment Corporation.

McClure, C. (1989). *Case is Software Automation*, Englewood Cliffs, NJ: Prentice Hall.

Motoda, H. (1990). The current status of expert system development and related technologies in Japan. *IEEE Expert* 5(4), 3-11.

Nau, D. S. (1983). Expert Computer Systems. *IEEE Computer 16*(2).

Norman, R. J. & Chen, M. (1992). Working together to integrate CASE. *IEEE Software*, March, 12-16.

Powers, M. J., Adams D. R., & Mills H. D. (1984). *Computer Information Systems Development: Analysis and Design*, Cincinnati: South-Western.

Senn, J. A. (1989). *Analysis and Design of Information Systems* (2nd Ed.), New York: McGraw-Hill.

Sheil, B. A. (1984). Power tools for programmers. In D. Barstow, H. Shrobe, & E. Sanderwall (Eds.), *Interactive Programming Environments* (pp. 19-30). New York: McGraw-Hill.

Shoval, P., & Pliskin, N. (1987). Structured Prototyping: Integrating Prototyping into Structured Systems Development. Working paper, Ben-Gurion University of the Negev.

Souza, E. (1990). Strategies for software engineering implementation. *Journal of Information System Management* (Summer), 33-37.

Tanik, M. M., & Yun D. Y. Y. (1988). Interactions between expert systems and software engineering. *IEEE Expert 3*(4), 5-6.

Wasserman, A. I. (1990). Tool integration in software engineering environment. In F. Long (Ed.) *Software Engineering Environment* (pp. 137-149). Berlin: Springer-Verlag.

Waterman, D. A. (1986). *A Guide to Expert Systems*, Reading MA: Addison-Wesley.

Wick, M. R. & Slagle, J. R. (1989). An explanation facility for today's expert systems. *IEEE Expert 4*(1), 26-36.

Wright, J. B., Miller F. D., Otto G. V. E., Siegfried E. M., Vesonder G. T., & Zielinski J. E. (1984). ACE: Going from prototype to product with an expert system. *Proc. 1984 ACM Annual Conf. 5th Generation Challenge* (pp. 24-28).

Zadeh, L. A. (1983). The role of fuzzy logic in the management of uncertainty in expert systems. In *Fuzzy Sets and Systems*, Amsterdam: North-Holland.

CHAPTER FOURTEEN

CASE in Business and Administrative Information Systems

J. Christopher Westland
University of Southern California

The emergence of computer aided software engineering (CASE) tools over the past decade from curiosity to valuable development tool has changed the manner in which professionals view systems development. The majority of this development, until recently, has taken place on the "software engineering" side — addressing the problems of real-time embedded systems, often in aerospace. CASE tools are typically organized as a set of building blocks each of which supports a discrete methodology. These "building blocks" are not necessarily designed to assure consistency between phases of the systems development life cycle. This chapter shows that current CASE tools when applied to business information systems can be restructured to integrate the products of phases, and provide a seamless methodology that would effectively self-validate. This may be done with minor extensions in underlying methodologies, and slight extensions in the capabilities of the CASE tools. These extensions provide efficient code production and rectify existing problems in development of business information systems. This is possible because business operations and applications of information technology are relatively well structured and repetitive.

BUSINESS SYSTEMS DEVELOPMENT

Information technology assets represent a major investment for corporations. In the U.S. alone, information systems personnel costs through the 1980s averaged 1% of total payroll in the largest corporations. The U.S. may spend as much as $200 billion annually on software, up to $100 billion annually on hardware and perhaps $200 billion annually on the update and maintenance of data (Westland [1990a; 1992a], Schlender [1989], Minton [1990], Scheier [1990]). Peter Keen [1991] estimates that over 50% of recent new capital expenditures in the U.S. have been directed toward information technology, even through periods in which drastic expenditure cuts have occurred throughout the U.S. economy.[1] Surveys indicate that management is disenchanted with excessive costs and poor quality of software investments (see Maglitta [1991]; Westland [1990c]). Roughly half of the U.S.'s software expenditure is directed toward the development of business information systems (Computer Science and Technology Board [1990], Westland [1990a; 1993a; 1992; 1993b], Yourdon [1992], Schlender [1989], Minton [1990]).

Information systems fall roughly into three categories — real-time embedded, business, and information retrieval. BIS are *planned response systems* that record external economic events — typically market exchange transactions of some sort — and provide information about these transactions via reports and screens. In contrast, real time systems respond to external events with an action, which may or may not be preplanned; and information retrieval systems are entirely custodial. Business information systems (BIS) software is distinguished by being data-driven, with relatively simple processing and interfaces, and volatile, complex, voluminous and sometimes ill-structured data requirements. The majority of business information systems (BIS) conform to a common archetype — a central database using on-line or batch programs for database maintenance and reporting. Other features of these classes of systems are presented in Table 1.

Real-time embedded systems initiate and control a system's processing based upon real-world events. Events are data items that are thrown away after use. For example, an automatic teller machine at a bank will ask the customer for their personal identification number in order to authorize the initiation of a bank transaction. After initiation, the personal identification number is discarded.

The focus of *business information systems*, on the other hand, is the recording of real world events for later processing. For example, a credit sales invoice in a retail sales system, describes the

	Real-Time	**BIS**	**Information Retrieval**
Response Time Requirements	Very Fast	Moderate	Slow to Moderate
Event-Driven?	Yes	Generally Not	No
Data Input Volume	Low	Very High	High
Data Storage Requirements	Generally None	Large	Very Large
Data Retrieval Volume	Generally None	Small to Large	Small to Moderate

Table 1: Types of Software and Their Characteristics

"merchandise sale to a customer" event. It needs to be retained in the sales and collection system for billing, collections, and annual financial reporting. In business information systems, the same data item (e.g., an accounting transaction such as a sale) may be processed repeatedly, by a number of different applications.

The focus of *information retrieval systems* is on fast, accurate and complete access to massive amounts of information, typically in the form of documents. They are often associated with library systems, but are commercially important in legal and corporate document tracking. Independent commercial information retrieval systems offer between 50,000 and 100,000 commercial databases in the U.S. alone. DIALOG and Chemical Abstracts are two examples of such commercial databases. Westland [1990d] describes the information retrieval market in depth. This is the fastest growing of the three markets, with sales revenues growing at 35% annually, and current revenues of around $7 billion (Institute for the Future [1986]).

All three types of systems tend to be programmed in languages that are generic, attempting to satisfy the greatest cross-section of end-users in order to establish industry standards. But generic languages may often be too verbose for a specific problem domain such as business. Fourth generation business languages, e.g., Oracle or Focus, tend to be more specific, but they are still incomplete for business process and environment representation. Because BIS must be programmed in generic computer languages — e.g., COBOL or C — these have become *de facto* languages of BIS. Unfortunately they may be inefficient, ignoring fundamental accounting objectives and constraints, and may be ambiguous and have detrimental consequences in decision making and litigation.

This chapter defines extensions to existing methodologies. The existing methodologies are widely implemented in CASE tools. The chapter responds to a need for methodologies specifically oriented toward BIS. The majority of previous CASE and analysis methodology development has been directed toward real-time embedded systems, often in aerospace. But BIS represent an economically significant software business sector that has not received significant attention. CASE tools intended for BIS development often merely transplant methodologies initially designed for database and real-time systems' analysis. A BIS specific methodology is needed, because front-end analysis tasks — if one takes into account reengineering at the coding stage to correct for prior misspecification — now constitute the dominant and increasing portion of development costs (Boehm [1981; 1984; 1975]; Behrens [1977]; Bennington [1956]; Boar [1984]). The methodologies described here have been implemented in CASE tools provided by Synthesis Technologies, Inc. and Iconix Software Engineering, Inc., and reflect theoretical as well as practical requirements and limitations of BIS CASE.

The methodology presented here performs several related functions in systems analysis and development. First, it provides receptacles for recording information learned during the analysis phase. Second, it provides a vehicle for consensus formation and for sharing of decisions, information, and proposals for the system. This is particularly true when implemented as an integral part of a CASE tool. Third, it provides a vehicle for policy implementation as a separable part of the methodology. Finally, the methodology effectively self-validates. This could help eliminate the rewriting and maintenance that causes 99% of systems to be delivered late, averaging twice their original budget (Canning Publications, 1990).

BUSINESS INFORMATION SYSTEMS

Distinguishing Features of Business Information Systems

BIS are distinguished by a particular set of characteristics that both constrain the available design options — thus reducing the decisions made by the analyst — while requiring information not handled by current CASE methodologies. The following design characteristics distinguish BIS.

(1) Representations of real-world economic events, called *transactions*, provide the input data for BIS. BIS are *data centered* in that processing is oriented toward the transformation and storage

of input transactions, rather than initiating processes based on transaction content, as in real-time embedded systems. Stored transactions provide a precise memory for later recall in the form of reports, query responses, and summarizations (as opposed to storing this information in a system "state" as is often done in real-time embedded systems).

(2) BIS are *planned response systems* where the planned response to a given class of transaction input is determined by managerial policy and procedure. This is in contrast to real-time embedded systems that focus on control of a process, or altering the system's state through learning. There is typically no learning that takes place in a BIS (except possibly at the user interface) since this might interfere with policy implementation.

(3) Managerial *policy*, legal precedent, and corporate operating procedures are often primary reasons for investment in a new BIS. Thus their implementation is an important aspect of analysis and design.

(4) BIS *transactions* (i.e., input events) may be unpredictable and unstructured. This translates into longer, more labor intensive acquisition and processing than are found in real-time embedded systems. Over time, the nature and mix of transactions that a BIS is expected to process will change due to changes in the environment and organization.

(5) BIS are typically constrained by data transfer resources — internal busses and device channels, or external telecommunications lines — rather than by processing speed. This is a direct result of the processing and storage conditions placed on BIS transactions noted in (1) above.

Along with these design characteristics, business information systems must be robust to environmental instabilities from four sources: (1) management policy changes, (2) organizational structure changes, (3) hardware life cycles that may be less than one-third as long as software life cycles (Swanson [1988]), and (4) data streams that cannot be fully foreseen. Figure 1 shows the dynamics of this relationship.

Consider each of these in turn. Business information systems are planned response systems, meaning that there should be a prescribed response for each transaction input to the system. The source of this response may be management, responsible for policy and standard operating procedure; regulatory bodies, such as the American Institute of Certified Public Accountants, or the Financial Accounting Standards Board; or may result from legal precedent. Policy and procedures are constantly changing, and the system needs a vehicle for reflecting this.

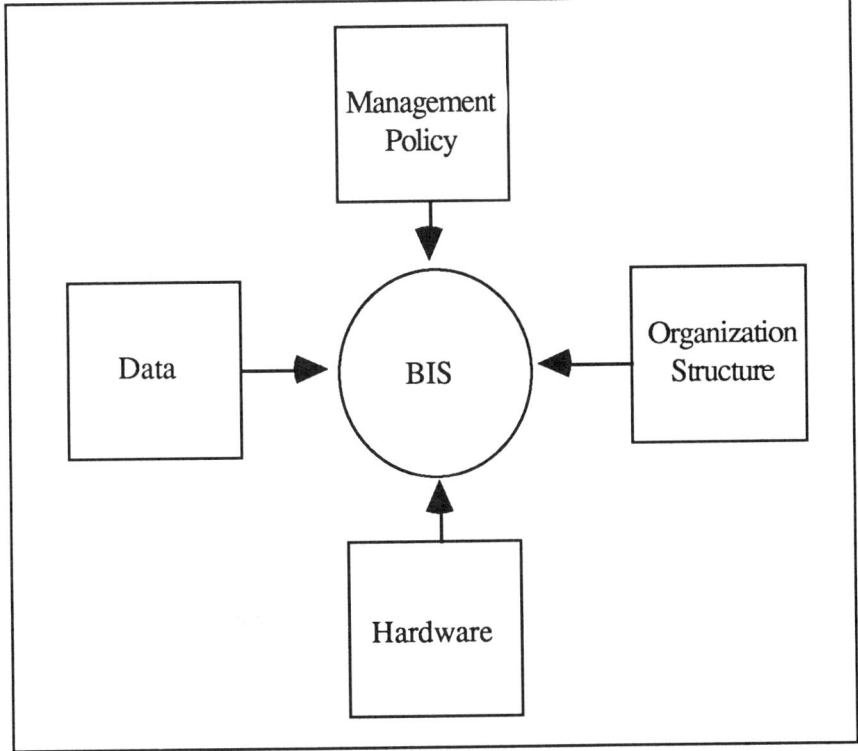

Figure 1: Four unstable components requiring robust BIS analysis & design

Organizational structure changes alter the information requirements, and thus reporting, from the system. This is usually reflected in the demand for new or altered reports — Swanson [1988] notes that roughly 60% of maintenance is dedicated to producing new reports.

BIS must generally be designed for a limited portability onto platforms that do not currently exist. This is because software life cycles average ten years for large systems, while hardware life cycles are, at the time of this writing, around three years or less (Swanson [1988]; Westland [1993a]). In addition, BIS contain data components that endure and are stable over time, remaining essentially stable for 20 to 30 years. As a consequence, software packages must be upwardly compatible, being able to handle both old and new data structures. Hardware is coming to constitute only a minor part of corporate asset investment ($\cong 20\%$) in BIS, with software and databases comprising the larger share (Westland [1993a]).

Prior research has found considerable evidence that these

instabilities span the BIS life-cycle. For example, Merton and Severance [1981] found that "internal control" code may constitute 70% to 80% of the installed code. Much of this is introduced during post-implementation maintenance to correct unforeseen transaction types, or unknown policies *ex post*. Even in a world with no uncertainty about the nature and classification of objects, environments and situations evolve and change. Each change in personnel, and each change in policy results in a large number of secondary and tertiary changes that ripple through, and ultimately impact, existing information systems as unforeseen "surprises." [2]

Classes of Business Information Systems

Inventory control systems, purchasing systems, payroll systems, and billing and accounts receivable systems are examples of *transaction processing systems*. Requirements uncertainty is less of a concern in transaction processing systems, which have a high degree of structure, and a very high volume of activity or transaction processing.

Management information systems generally focus on reporting and control. These have a greater degree of requirements uncertainty, because there may be a wider array of approaches available with which to satisfy the end-user. Typically, these applications are used to track, allocate, and control the use of the organization's resources. Examples of such applications include reports on variables from budgets, identification of inventory cost overruns, and identification of obsolete or excessive inventories. The focus of reporting and control processing is on reporting information from corporate databases in support of particular decision making or problem resolution.

Decision support systems support specific portfolios of decisions and their corresponding action choices. Thus, their reporting tends to be based on the activities of the users who need their reports. These decisions may exhibit a high level of uncertainty. They typically are found where individual analysis and problem solving is important to the solution. Decision support systems often focus on asking "what-if" questions concerning the effects of particular action alternatives in a representative scenario of the end-user's environment.

Executive support systems assist in the enterprise-wide summarization of corporate information. They integrate corporate data across diverse platforms, and make them available on a common platform, e.g., a workstation or microcomputer. Hypertext is actively being pursued as a model for navigation (Westland [1991]).

With all of these system types, there are three sources of events that result in the output of information to an end-user — (1) passage of a time interval, (2) the occurrence of some event within or external to the firm, and (3) the request for information by an end-user. Choice of one approach or another to reporting implicitly involves performance on two statistics — precision and recall (Westland [1989; 1990b]; Kochen [1974]). Precision is the probability of a randomly chosen record being selected conditional upon it being relevant to the question being asked of the database or system. Recall is the probability of a randomly chosen record being relevant conditional upon it being selected and reported to the end-user.

Periodic reports are generated on specific dates, usually at the end of equal intervals, e.g., annually, weekly, and so forth. This is the traditional manner of providing the end-user with information. It involves periodic reporting of particular classes of transactions or database updates. This approach has fallen out of favor because of its high inherent paper and printing costs, the general tendency to overload end-users with information, and the low precision (but moderate to high recall) associated with this approach.

When some event in the internal or external environment causes information to be forwarded to an end-user, the reporting is called *selective dissemination of information*. Executive support systems often rely on selective dissemination of information to keep executives informed. Budget variance, standard cost variance reports and other reports supporting management by exception are often handled via selective dissemination of information. In these cases, the event is an exception about which management wishes to be alerted. Since this sort of reporting provides only types of information that specific end-users have requested (via their user profiles), it is often more cost effective than periodic reporting. Unfortunately, it may overload users with irrelevant data if their information needs are not well specified in the profile. Recall and precision may be very unpredictable in this case.

When timeliness of reporting is imperative, information is generally *disseminated by query*. This approach is useful when the volume of information accessed is small, and is the major approach used in reporting on video display terminal screens. Reports are disseminated by query only when an end-user requests specific information relevant to a query. In this approach, information is disseminated in response to end-user queries. Report volume is usually small with high precision (but perhaps low recall).

EXTENSION OF CASE TO SUPPORT BUSINESS INFORMATION SYSTEMS

Evolution of Programming Languages and Methodologies

Prior to suggesting extensions to CASE, consider the prior evolution of systems development. The first languages consisted of mechanical linkages programmed with wire "patch" boards. A typical program involved thousands of wires connected by hand from point to point on large "patch" boards. John von Neumann proposed a modification to program for new tasks simply by dialing in a new program, consisting of neat, columnar strings of numbers. First generation languages followed, with a one-to-one relationship to a set of switching operations in the computer. Second generation languages (assemblers) still referred directly to hardware instructions, but by a mnemonic language. Third generation languages (procedural languages) such as FORTRAN, COBOL and Pascal were introduced as "automatic programming" tools (Rich and Waters [1988]) with a "natural language" interface to make writing code easier. Fourth generation languages restricted this language to a specific problem domain — most commonly business. This relieved programmers of many tedious and repetitive tasks within the limited problem domain. Fifth generation languages are more concept than implementation in BIS. The concept is to address uncertain transaction input by flexible, learning, sometimes fuzzy systems behavior that generally implements managerial policy. Expert systems and artificial intelligence have been invoked with mixed success. To date, all the languages in which BIS have been implemented on any scale have maintained lines of source code in text format.

There has been a parallel evolution of documentation. Flowcharts have existed since "patch boards," originally being used to program unit record equipment. Up through the 1970s, they usually reflected physical flows of paper or computer media. But starting in the mid-1970's, graphical flowcharting methodologies arose whose focus was the analysis of systems requirements in the abstract. Entity relationship diagrams, Warnier-Orr charts, dataflow diagrams, state-transition diagrams and other graphical methodologies invoked symbols to represent, record, coordinate, and visualize aspects of the real-world that would ultimately influence the design of information systems. Much of this literature arose in response to software engineering requirements of complex military projects — and thus was aimed at real-time embedded systems. In part, CASE implementations reflect market demand. A building block approach satisfies a large market, particularly when that market demands several paradigms. BIS analysis and design methodologies borrowed from this literature, especially when Computer Aided Software Engineering (CASE) tools such as Excelerator were introduced in the mid-1980s. But because these graphical tools were not conceived as integrated tools with business problems in mind, they were applicable to only specific phases of the systems development life cycle, and were, more often than not, viewed as documentation tools.

The concept of providing a graphical programming language is not new — but CASE showed how it could be done. Front-end (analysis and design) CASE methodologies could be used to describe the system, then back-end CASE (code generators) could take the CASE data dictionary as input to generate compilable code. Existing methodologies did not yet fit seamlessly with each other, thus there were difficulties in implementation of this concept — but the direction was clear.

The remainder of this chapter describes extensions of commonly used CASE methodologies to address the specific requirements of BIS as described in section 1. These extensions have been used with CASE tools from Synthesis Technologies, Inc. (Syntek CASE A/P) and with CASE tools from Iconix Software Engineering, Inc. (PowerTools) for BIS analysis and design.

Features of a Business Information System

Section 1 described several features that distinguish a BIS from real-time embedded systems. Figure 2 depicts the interaction between business environment and software life cycle components. The components of the BIS life cycle — scope setting, process and data modeling, software modeling and coding — are in the circles and reflect systems development activities supported by methodologies. The components of the BIS environment are in the boxes and reflect activities that are not explicitly included in current methodologies, except in an *ad hoc* and incomplete manner. The remainder of this chapter describes ways to incorporate these as extensions of currently implemented CASE methodologies.

Business Information Systems Development Life-Cycle

Scope Determination. Scope determination is not typically included in existing CASE tools. Yet well articulated methodologies exist for scope determination, and these should be incorporated as extensions. This section describes an implementation of the critical success factors methodology (Boynton and Zmud [1984]; Rockart

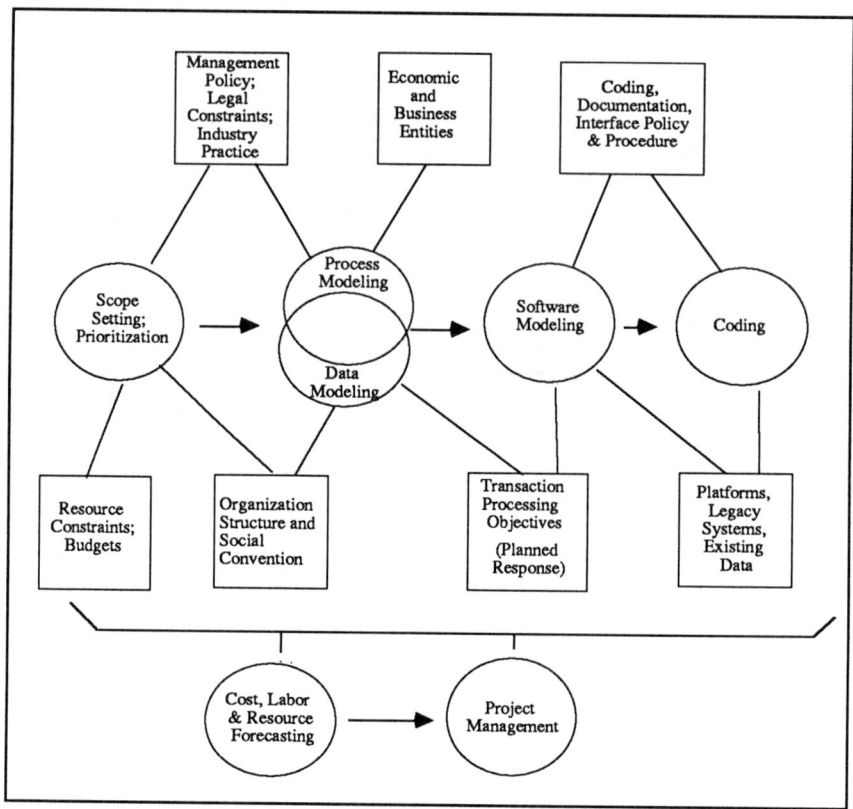

Figure 2: Interaction between environment and BIS life cycle components

[1979]).

Critical success factors (CSF) are a limited set of activities which are crucial for the success of the firm. The CSF task sequence requires:

(1) choosing a business objective (e.g. profit, growth, survival);
(2) defining a specific activity (i.e., the Critical Success Factor) which is important to some constituency in the firm (the proposed system's beneficiaries) who will provide the political and financial support for the system;
(3) defining a metric to determine how well the activity is achieving the objective; and
(4) designing a prototype system.

The use of CSF analysis for scope determination provides

several advantages over other commonly implemented approaches — (1) Enterprise Modeling / Business Systems Planning and (2) political approaches (Kling [1980]). Business Systems Planning views the organization in terms of entities and activities, with the objective of building a portfolio of support systems. Unfortunately, the average IS department has a seven year backlog, and 93% of these departments have more than a three year backlog (Canning [1990]). Since technology is now changing generations in less than three years, strategic system portfolio plans are likely to be out of date prior to even requirements being specified. This alone tends to obviate any benefits from consistency and coordination promised by Business Systems Planning (Arsac [1979]; Balzer and Goldman [1979]; Balzer [1981; 1985]; Rich and Waters [1988]).

Political approaches abdicate systems project choice to functional managers who have the most political influence — even perhaps who complain the most. The choice may be legitimized through use of formal analysis tools such as cash flow and net present value analysis. But the choice ultimately has less to do with the efficient and effective application of technology to corporate decision making, than to the power structure of the firm.

The critical success factors approach is inherently focused and short term. Experience suggests that CSF's are most effective when the CSF — an activity of critical importance to the firm — is important to a single functional manager who can champion the systems project through implementation. CSF's are also more effective when a single CSF results in a single system built around a single database. In terms of systems portfolio structure, this will result in sets of systems that are individually cohesive, and which are more or less loosely coupled, because there will necessarily be some information exchange between databases. Projects defined through CSF analysis are more likely to be implemented due to limited scope and potentially fast implementation. Because political and Business Systems Planning plans do not limit scope, they are much more likely to be postponed or terminated by backlogs and technology changes, to the detriment of the firm.

Resources and Budget Constraints

Any given BIS project will not be the only project competing for scarce resources in a firm. As a consequence, management must be able to prioritize projects by their consumption of constrained resources — money, programmer and analysts' labor, and computer resources — and by time to completion. Project management methodologies (e.g., PERT), and cost estimation approaches (e.g., CoCoMo) address various aspects of resource constrained optimization.

Management Policy, Legal Constraints, and Industry Practice

The critical success factor activity will necessarily be constrained by management policy, the legal environment and industry practice. This additional information is most expediently incorporated at the point that the activity is defined. These constraints comprise refinements in the activity, and may be so extensive as to completely define the activity (as happens with most accounting systems).

Organization Structure

Organizational function and structure define the reporting or querying requirements, as well as information routing imperatives for the system. They may be incorporated in the prototype, and will dictate the design and content of dataflows on the dataflow diagram, and the terminators connected to these dataflows. If the critical success factors approach uses a dataflow diagram context diagram as a prototype, then incorporating these into the analysis is straightforward. The CASE tool should cross-reference the organization chart, annotated for responsibility centers and individuals affected by the proposed system, to determine the full scope of input and output. Prior studies have noted that a large part of post delivery maintenance is dedicated to addition of reports and query screens overlooked in the development process (Lientz and Swanson [1980]; Swanson [1988]).

Analysis and Requirements Specification with Economic and Business Entities

Data Modeling. Because BIS are data-driven, the first step in analysis should define data requirements. The most common approach uses an entity-relationship diagram (Martin and McClure [1985]). This should seamlessly lead to a description of processes involving each entity, which may be perceived as an expansion of the relationship description. Object oriented approaches provide perhaps the best integrated presentation of entities (objects) and their processes (Booch [1986; 1992]; Henderson-Sellers and Edwards [1990]; McGregor and Korson [1990]; McGregor [1990]; Wegner [1987]). Object oriented methodologies are not widely implemented in CASE tools yet. The preferred CASE tool methodology is the dataflow diagram for processes, where entities are represented in the dataflows. This section provides a sketch of the manner in which entity-relationship data can be derived from descriptions of real world processes, and then provide the majority of information needed for the construction of the initial pass of the dataflow diagram. With development, this approach could conceivably allow writing a first-pass dataflow diagram directly from the entity-relationship diagram (Chen [1976; 1983]; Clark and van Emden [1981]; Codd [1970; 1972], Ng [1981]).

The systems analysts should initially, through interviews and deduction, define the major entities and interrelationships between entities that are required in the system. The activities that are required of the system may then be articulated. Entities may be defined through entity-relationship diagrams. The requirements specification is itself capturing a representation of a real world object in its representation of system's memory. Activities may be represented through dataflow diagrams where dataflows are entities or clusters of entities (composite flows), and processes are activities. The entity-relationship diagram should be defined first, and the relationships between entities will attempt to describe processes that will be central to the event level (level 0) dataflow diagram (DeMarco [1979], Gane and Sarson [1979]).

The analyst starts by describing system's data needs via a series of English sentences sketching the details of data and processes by which critical success factors are achieved (see Chen [1976; 1983]). This provides a useful bridge from interview narratives and meeting notes to a valid requirements specification for the database.

Entities are either concepts or tangible entities, either people or groups of people, resources, or events affecting resources. The things that are resources are often described as manpower, money, machines, methods, and materials. The entities that are selected for a database will be ones for which the CSF requires information. Relationships, on the other hand, are intangible, and somehow concisely capture an active or passive interaction between the two entities.

Entities and relationships provide a nexus for clustering data. Individual data items are attributes of the entity or relationship. Attributes are of two types — (1) measurement attributes, e.g., entity "Bob Smith" is "68 inches" tall, and (2) categorical attributes, e.g., entity "Bob Smith" has "red hair." Categories are often coded to preserve expensive computer hardware space. For example, an "integrated circuit with an extensive list of capabilities, made in New York" may be abbreviated as part number "N683".

Most data is recorded in the entity clusters. Data may also be recorded in the data cluster when specifying the active or passive relationship between entities, e.g., Employee "Bob Smith" "Works for" Project "Fixed Assets System" "20% of the time." "20% of the time" clarifies the relationship "Works for."

The following eight guidelines provided by Peter Chen are useful for creating CASE based models for BIS based on interview narratives constructed during the systems analysis process.

Guideline 1: A common noun, e.g., "telephone" or "person," corresponds to an entity type in an ER diagram.

Guideline 2: A transitive verb or transitive verb phrase, i.e., one with both a subject and an object, corresponds to a relationship type in an ER diagram. For example, the sentence "A person uses a telephone" relates "telephone" and "person" with the transitive verb "uses."

Guideline 3: An adjective corresponds to an attribute of an entity in an ER diagram.

Guideline 4: An adverb corresponds to an attribute of a relationship in an ER diagram. For example, consider the sentence "A 39 year old person uses the public telephone for 10% of his calls." "...for 10% of his calls" is an adverbial phrase that modifies the verb "uses." "...39 year old" (a measurement) and "public" (a category) are adjectives modifying entity / nouns.

Guideline 5: If the sentence has the form "There are ... X in Y," where X and Y are clauses, it can be converted into the equivalent form "Y has ... X."

Guideline 6: If the sentence has the form "The X of Y is Z" where X,Y and Z are clauses, and if Z is a proper noun, it is possible to treat X as a relationship between Y and Z.

Guideline 7: If the sentence has the form "The X of Y is Z" where X,Y and Z are clauses, and if Z is not a proper noun, then X is an attribute of Y.

Guideline 8: The entities of algebraic or numeric operations are attributes. For example, consider the sentence "The average age of a person who uses a telephone is 39." "Average" is an algebraic operation, and thus "age" may be assumed to be an attribute.

Process Modeling. Most dataflow diagram processes do not directly benefit end-users, but serve a custodial function for data storage (McMenamin and Palmer [1990]). These custodial functions will fall into four categories:

(1) transportation, coordination and communication related activities and data;
(2) administrative activities and data;
(3) quality control activities; and
(4) activities and data structure which promotes processor efficiency.

The nature of custodial functions largely reflects organization structure and business convention in the firm, thus they are situation specific and difficult to address generically. One class of custodial functions, though, does appear in most BIS and constitutes a significant, if not major portion of the program code. This is data quality control specifically involving security, integrity, accuracy and privacy of data. The majority of implemented business information systems controls involve one or more of six activities[3]:

(1) verification that the transaction input to the system existed in the physical world (existence);
(2) verification that every transaction of this type that existed in the physical world was input to the system (completeness);
(3) verification that the transaction input to the system was recorded in the correct time period (timing);
(4) verification that the transaction input to the system was classified correctly (classification);
(5) verification that the transaction input to the system was authorized (authorization); this control objective is the basis for most privacy and security efforts;
(6) verification that the transaction input to the system is recorded properly in the system (recording).

In practice, much of the quality control code is written as a part of corrective or adaptive maintenance after delivery of the system to the end-user. Accuracy of data for intended use garners most of the attention. Accuracy is the property of information that implies that a particular occurrence of a specific datum correctly reflects the real world phenomenon that it is describing. Different uses of the same data element may require entirely different levels of accuracy. For example, the hourly rate for a factory employee is needed in both the payroll processing system for writing payroll checks, and in the labor distribution system for cost accounting. Calculations supporting the payroll check disbursements must be accurate to the penny. Calculations for the labor distribution, on the other hand, may be accurate to 1% to 2% with little detriment to decision making (Westland [1992b]; Ijiri [1968]; Ijiri and Kriebel [1985]; Leiberman and Whinston [1975]; McCarthy [1979; 1982]).

Software Modeling. Once analysis and requirements specification are complete for a BIS, the next step is software modeling. The standard approaches for software modeling are Yourdon [1982] or Jackson [1983] structure charts. The majority of BIS specific modeling is accounted for in requirements specification, through critical success factors, entity-relationship and dataflow analyses. Two broad areas are specific to BIS — transaction processing objectives, and existing platforms, legacy systems, and databases. In addition, timing requirements and sequence are typically not overriding concerns in BIS as they are in real-time systems (Adams, Michael and Owles [1985]).

Transaction processing objectives reflect the policy, legal constraints and industry practice defined in the analysis and requirements specification stage. In software modeling, they must be interpreted into a specific set of conditional statements which result in specific actions for given conditions. This may not be simple when objectives are subject to complex interpretation or when they are not well defined to begin with. Unfortunately, there is not an easy solution to this. It is essentially the problem which faces rule-based expert systems. Whereas rule-based systems can adequately duplicate the efforts of experts in certain situations, expert decision making may often be based on other modes of analysis (e.g., see Payne [1976], Mintzberg [1976], and Chase and Simon [1973])

The other area of significance is the potential for portions of the systems requirements to already be implemented — albeit not in an ideal form — somewhere else in the firm, through existing hardware platforms, legacy systems, and existing databases. The appropriate way to model software in this circumstance (which is the norm) is to complete the requirements specification, and then consider what systems data already exists within the firm, to process the existing databases (Holley and Rosen, [1981]).

Coding and Documentation: CASE as a Coding Language. CASE tools become particularly interesting when considering the task of coding, testing and debugging. Boehm [1984] estimated that these tasks garner close to 60% of a system's development budget — a surprisingly large figure if one assumes that the majority of design decisions have been made in previous phases of the systems development life cycle. CASE tools are widely accepted as effective documentation, group learning, and consensus forming tools. Why not write machine instructions directly through CASE? This is the concept behind CASE as a coding language.

At the current time, back-end CASE tools (i.e., code generators) allow CASE to be used as a coding language with some success in business applications. There do exist a subset of firms that use the CASE interface as a 4GL, and leave the generated code unmodified. An improvement, though, would be back-end CASE which generated code frames in an interactive debugging environment such as provided in Borland's or Microsoft's C compilers. Where code generation is an integral part of CASE tools in current environments, systems developers are already trying to minimize the amount of direct manipulation of program code, since direct manipulation carries with it the potential for loss of valuable requirements specification and design information. At the same time, program efficiency is typically of concern with only a small proportion of BIS code — typically that involved in on-line, real-time access and manipulation of data. Thus manipulation of code for reasons of efficiency is to be discouraged (Hopcroft and Ullman [1979]; Hunter [1981]).

At this point, a completely seamless integration from front-end to back-end CASE has not been typically implemented. The main problem is lack of a complete specification methodology for all components of the analysis and design process. By suggesting additional constructs for existing CASE methodologies, the current chapter moves toward this sort of methodology integration for BIS. Without complete and comprehensive integration of the information required to define a system into a methodology, there are still decisions to be made at the programming stage, and this must necessarily be made by a human programmer. If you cannot write your machine instructions from the CASE data dictionary, then your CASE documentation methodology is most likely incomplete. If you can write the machine code directly from the documentation, then CASE can effectively be used as the programming language of choice. In this role, BIS oriented CASE would be a graphical language for software coding. Because of the self-documenting character of CASE development, and the inherent advantages of graphics based specification and design, CASE is likely to be the preferred vehicle for BIS development in the not too distant future.

Testing and Debugging

CASE currently provides advantages in testing and debugging in its role as a verification tool, to determine that what is actually programmed is consistent with requirements specification. Were

CASE to be used as the programming language of choice, testing and debugging would be further diminished. This is because language and logic based errors would be significantly easier to avoid or foresee due to the graphic nature of the code representation.

Where errors are the result of unforeseen data types or values in the input transaction stream to which the system is required to provide planned responses, CASE would probably have less impact. Test data has traditionally been used to assure that the code properly meets transaction processing objectives for all "foreseen" data types. Unfortunately, the developers of test data — programmers — are often the least qualified to determine real-world transactions. End-users would be better producers; but the best source of test data is from existing systems, manual or automated, which perform the same tasks. Even this has been shown to be inadequate for testing. For example, Littlewood and Strigini [1992] note that a large study by IBM found that roughly 33% of software errors would occur on average only once every 5000 years, and fully 80% of software errors would occur on average only once in 500 years, following roughly a Zipf [1949] distribution. Since parallel processing is unlikely to proceed for more than six months at a maximum, it is unlikely that most errors will be detected in test. Although the likelihood of *any one* error occurring is low, the likelihood of *an* error occurring is high. The solution is to assure, in the analysis and design phase, that the consequence of an error is limited, and that the time to its detection and correction be made as short as possible. These involve modification of the procedures and systems surrounding the system under development.

CASE tools might be extended in two ways to better allow testing of systems. First, transaction streams from the real-world could be "bootstrapped" to artificially expand the time period tested. "Bootstrapping" is used in statistics, meaning the expansion of a dataset by creating artificial data with the same statistical characteristics as the real data. BIS transactions may, in many cases, arrive slowly in comparison to real-time systems, e.g., a particular department may average one sale every minute, whereas a real-time system may be updated many times a minute. "Bootstrapping" could process many years worth of artificial data through the system in a relatively short time, making it more likely to detect Littlewood and Strigini's [1992] 5000-year errors.

Second, CASE tools could keep detailed logs of transaction processing, similar to current debuggers in interactive programming environments, allowing resolution and correction of transaction processing errors as they are encountered. Figure 3 depicts a parallel processing arrangement that might be implemented in

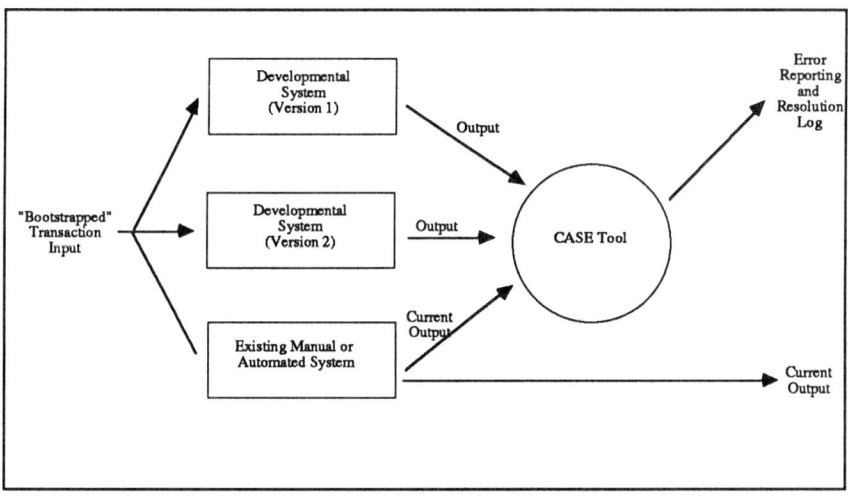

Figure 3: Parallel Processing

CASE to allow existing data streams to be used as test data for a new system.

Forecasting and Project Management

Project management — as it is supported by specific software tools — is the process of tracking costs and labor utilization, as well as assignment of resources to specific phases of the life cycle, in order to assure that the project is completed within time, labor and cost budgets. Budgets themselves are the products of contracting with management and end-users based on forecasts of time, labor and cost to produce the required software.

Project management, estimation and tracking must occur throughout the systems development life cycle. These functions become most important during the increase in staff and activity that occurs at the time of design and coding. In an extended CASE methodology, traditional estimation tools such as CoCoMo (Boehm [1984]) and traditional scheduling and tracking tools, such as PERT or CPM, can take code modules from structure diagrams, or alternatively Dataflow diagram primitive processes as fundamental units for cost and labor estimation and control. Current CASE tools typically do not incorporate estimation and tracking as an integral part of their tools, reserving these for specialized packages. As these are integral tasks of analysis, design and programming, they should also be incorporated in CASE (Mohanty [1981]; Kemerer [1987]).

Maintenance

Each time maintenance is performed on an operating BIS, analysts and programmers proceed through the analysis and design steps. Thus CASE methodologies appropriate for development should be adequate for maintenance. Minor modifications can be suggested to account for distinguishing features of maintenance. Maintenance effort is categorized into three major classes—corrective, adaptive and perfective maintenance. *Corrective* maintenance is work performed in response to recognized systems failures. A system may fail: (1) by producing incorrect output or by failing to operate at all; (2) through poor performance, such as in turnaround or response time; or (3) through poor quality of implementation. *Adaptive* maintenance is performed in response to anticipated changes in the data programming environments, such as a restructuring of the data base, the installation of new hardware, or a new version of the operating system. Such work is undertaken to avoid subsequent corrective maintenance when either the operating environment or the end-users information needs have changed significantly. As such, they reflect changes in the firm's organizational structure. *Perfective* maintenance consists of work performed to optimize the performance of the system, to improve maintainability of the system, or to provide the end-user with functional support that is an extension of the original requirements specification, e.g., new reports or screens. It may also arise through an opportunistic extension of existing requirements specifications. The reformatting of a report or screen, adding data types to a database, and so forth are examples of perfective maintenance. Perfective maintenance adds end-user benefits to an existing system.

In a study conducted by IBM on how maintenance programmers spend their time, it was determined that 47 percent or nearly half of the maintenance personnel's time is spent on code analysis (Hamilton [1990]); i.e., determining what the code is doing so that logic can be added to support some new business requirement. This is a time-consuming task because of the variety of styles and approaches that programmers use to write code. CASE tools can support code analysis through limited reverse engineering as currently implemented in CASE such as the McCabe tool (see also McCabe [1976]), Bachman tool or the Canonizer tool (Inmon [1987]). These provide structure charts detailing the calling sequence and parameters passed in code modules, and may provide some detailing of program logic. Where CASE tools are used for maintenance analysis and design, limited reengineering should be an option supported.

CONCLUSIONS

This chapter presented some suggestions for extensions to existing CASE tools to address BIS analysis and design. A recent addition to BIS is telecommunications networks. This was not incorporated in the chapter recommendations because widely used telecommunications analysis and requirements specification methodologies have yet to appear in CASE. The growth of telecommunications in BIS has been facilitated by two developments — (1) the availability of low cost, efficient local area network hardware and software; and (2) the availability of cost effective data services from major telecommunications carriers arising, at least indirectly, from deregulation in the early 1980's. Local area networks have made steady inroads into the traditional turf of mainframe computers, largely through the client server model that depends on local area networking for implementation. Local area network software has yet to reach a point where transaction integrity, accuracy and tracking are commensurate with mainframes, but new software is steadily closing the gap. Future CASE must to incorporate both the requirements and design aspects of telecommunications. The most likely focal point for this inclusion is into dataflows, or similar constructs, by identifying the "topology / geography" of transmission of data from one physical point to another.

This chapter showed that BIS are distinguished by a particular set of characteristics which both constrain the available design options — thus reducing the decisions made by the analyst — while requiring information not handled by current CASE methodologies. Specifically, (1) BIS development centered on transactions, representing unpredictable and unstructured real world events, which where stored for later reporting, (2) BIS were planned response systems, (3) BIS design and requirements might be largely determined by managerial policy, legal precedent, and corporate operating procedures; and (5) BIS operations and efficiencies were constrained by data transfer resources — internal busses and device channels, or external telecommunications lines — rather than by processing speed. Additionally, BIS need to be robust to environmental instabilities from four sources: (1) management policy changes, (2) organizational structure changes, (3) hardware life cycles that may be less than one-third as long as software life cycles, and (4) data streams that cannot be fully foreseen. The inclusion in the analyst's set of tools of methodologies to address these specifics holds forth the possibility of integrated CASE specifically oriented toward business systems problems perhaps within the next several years.

ENDNOTES

1 Precise figures are difficult to find since no single agency tracks information technology investments, and financial reporting does not require the segregation of information technology expenditures on financial statements.

2 Other statistics on BIS provide more insight into the nature of the problem
- Annual maintenance costs typically run about 10% to 20% of the total development cost for a corporate information system (Swanson [1988]; Boehm [1984])
- Business information systems operate for an average of ten years from delivery to retirement (Swanson [1988], Lientz and Swanson [1980])
- An average of 75% of delivered systems source code is dedicated to internal controls and edit verification of input data (Merton and Severance [1981], System Builder [1989])
- One half of an information systems department's budget is allocated to new systems development, and one half to ongoing maintenance (Swanson [1988], Lientz and Swanson [1980])
- The average backlog of unstarted new systems projects is equivalent to 7 years worth of specification and programming effort (Schlender [1989], Hamilton [1990])
- Maintenance effort is proportional to (Age of system in years)$^{1.5}$, and thus accelerates as a system ages (Swanson [1988])
- 99% of systems are delivered late and over budget. On average, systems are delivered one year later than originally contracted with the end user, and at twice the contracted budget (Canning Publications [1990], Hamilton [1990], Bunnel [1987])
- An average of 50% of the code in a ten year old system is "dead" code, i.e., it is never run and currently does not support a needed business function (Merton and Severance [1981])
- The cost of correcting a specification error increases by a factor of about 10 if that error is discovered in the coding phase instead of the requirements specification phase, and similarly increases by a factor of about 10 if that error is discovered after system's release to production rather than in the coding phase. The cost of undetected errors in operating systems may be without limit (Boehm [1984], Rubin [1987])

3 Adapted from the American Institute of Certified Public Accountant's Statements on Auditing Procedures No. 31

REFERENCES

Adams, David R., Michael J. Powers and V. Arthur Owles, *Computer Information Systems Development: Design and Implementation*, South-Western Publishing Co., 1985.

AICPA (American Institute of Certified Public Accountants), *Statements on Auditing Standards*, New York:AICPA, 1991

Arsac, J., Syntactic source to source transforms and program manipulations,

Communications of the ACM, v. 22, January 1979

Balzer, R. and N. Goldman Principles of good software specification and their implications for specification languages, *Proceedings of the Conference on Specifications of Reliable Software*, Boston, MA, p. 58, 1979

Balzer, R. A 15 Year Perspective on Automatic Programming, *IEEE Transactions on Software Engineering*, November, 1257-67, 1985

Balzer, R. Transformational Implementation: An Example, *IEEE Transactions on Software Engineering*, v. SE—7(1), January 1981

Behrens, C.A. Measuring the Productivity of Computer Systems Development Activities with Function Points, *IEEE Transactions on Software Engineering*, SE-9(6), 648-652, 1977

Bennington, H.D., Production of Large Computer Programs, *Proceedings ONR symposium on Advanced Programming Methods for Digital Computers*, June, pp. 15-27, 1956

Boehm, B.W., *Software Engineering Economics*, Englewood Cliffs:Prentice-Hall, 1981

Boehm, B.W., Software Engineering Economics, *IEEE Transactions on Software Engineering*, Volume SE-10, Number 1, January 1984.

Boehm, B.W., *The High Cost of Software*, in Practical Strategies for Developing Large Software Systems, Ellis Horowitz (ed.) Reading: Addison-Wesley, 3-14, 1975

Boehm, B.W., *A Spiral Model of Software Development and Enhancement*, August, V.11(4), 21-42, 1986

Bohm, C. and G. Jacopini, Flow Diagrams, Turing Machines and Languages with Only Two Formation Rules, *Communications of the ACM*, May 1966, pp. 366—371

Booch, G. *Object-Oriented Analysis and Design*, Englewood Cliffs: Prentice-Hall, 1992

Booch, G. Object-Oriented Development, *IEEE Transactions on Software Engineering*, v. SE12(2), 1986

Boynton, D.C. and R. Zmud critical success factors, *Sloan Management Review*, Summer 1984

Brooks, F.P., Jr. *The Mythical Man-Month*, Reading:MA: Addison-Wesley, 1975

Broy, M. and P. Pepper Program Development as a Formal Activity, *IEEE Transactions on Software Engineering*, v. SE—7(1), January 1981

Bunnell, D. The Challenge of Hypermedia, *.PC World.*, November 1987, 17-26.1987

Bureau of Economic Analysis. The National Income and Product Accounts of the United States, Washington, D.C.1989

Byers, T.J. Built by Association, *.PC World.*, April 1987

Canning Publications, *EDP In-Depth Reports*, v. 12(4), p. 11, 1990

Chase, W.G. and H.A. Simon,The Mind's Eye in Chess, in W.G. Chase (ed.) *Visual Information Processing*, New York:Academic Press, 215—281, 1973

Chen, P.P., The Entity—Relationship Model Toward a Unified View of Data, *ACM Transactions on Database Systems*, March 1976

Chen, P.P.,English Sentence Structure and Entity-Relationship Diagrams, *Information Sciences* v.29, 127-149, 1983

Clark, K.L. and M.H. van Emden,Consequence Verification of Flowcharts, *IEEE Transactions on Software Engineering*, v. SE—7(1), January 1981

Codd, E. 1972. Relational Completeness of Database Sublanguages and Further Normalization of the Data Base Relational Model, in Rustin (ed.) *Database Systems*, Englewood Cliffs: Prentice Hall

Codd, E., A Relational Model for Large Shared Data Banks, *Communications of the ACM*, v. 13(6), June 1970

Colantoni, C.S., R.P.Manus, and A.B. Whinston (1971) A Unified Approach to the Theory of Accounting and Information Systems, *Accounting Review*, January

Computer Science and Technology Board, National Research Council, *Keeping the US Computer Industry Competitive*, National Academy Press, Washington, D.C., 1990

Cooper, R. and R.S. Kaplin, *The Design of Cost Management Systems*, Englewood Cliffs: Prentice-Hall, 1992

De Marco, Tom, *Structured Analysis and System Specification*, Yourdon Press, 1979.

DeMarco, T., *Structure Analysis and Systems Specification*, New York:Yourdon Press, 1980

Dewan, S, and H. Mendelson, User Delay Costs and Internal Pricing for a Service Facility, *Management Science*, v. 36(12), 1502-17, 1991

Dolan, Kathleen A., *Business Computer Systems Design*, Mitchell Publishing Inc., 1984.

Embley, D., NFQL: the Natural Forms Query Language, *ACM/TODS*, v. 14 (2) June 1989

Everest, G.C. and R. Weber, A Relational Approach to Accounting Models, *The Accounting Review*, 1983

Fisher, I., *The Theory of Interest*, Macmillan, New York, 1930

Flynn, M.K., Oracle Unveils OLTP Version of its Relational DBMS. *Datamation*, September 1, p. 93, 1988

Foster G., and C.T. Horngren, *Cost accounting: a managerial emphasis* (6th ed.), Englewood Cliffs: Prentice-Hall, 1987

Gane, Chris and Trish Sarson, *Structured Systems Analysis: Tools and Techniques*, Prentice-Hall, 1979.

Geers, J., A New Generation of Benchmarking, *MIPS*, v. 1(2), 92-98, 1989

Halstead, M., *Elements of Software Science*, New York: Elsevier/North Holland, 1977

Hamilton, D., Application Development Stars. *System Builder*, April/May 1990

Henderson-Sellers, B. and Edwards, J.M., The object-oriented systems life cycle, *Communications of the ACM*, September, v. 33(9), 1990

Hinnant, D.F., What Makes a Good Benchmark?, *MIPS*, v. 1(9), p. 100-104, 1989

Holley, L.H. and B.K. Rosen, Qualified Data Flow Problems, *IEEE Transactions on Software Engineering*, v. SE—7(1), January 1981

Hopcroft, J.E. and J.D. Ullman. . *Introduction to Automata Theory, Languages and Computation*, Reading, MA: Addison—Wesley, 1979

Hunter, R. *The Design and Construction of Compilers.* Chichester, NY: John Wiley, 1981

Ijiri, Y. and C.H.Kriebel, "Data Collection and Information Technology in the Accounting Curriculum" in D.L.Jensen (ed.), *Information Systems in Accounting*, Ohio State University, 1985

Ijiri, Y. *The Foundations of Accounting Measurement*, New York:Prentice—Hall, 1968

Inmon, W.H., Denormalize for Efficiency. *Computerworld*, (March 16), v. 21(11), 19-21, 1987

Institute for the Future Electronic Information Services, Report R-71, Park, 1986

Jackson, Michael A., *System Development*, Prentice-Hall, 1983.

Jenkins, A.M. "Prototyping: A Methodology for the Design and Development of Application Systems," *Sim Spectrum*, v.2(2), April 1985, pp. 1-8

Keen, P. G.W., *Shaping the Future: Business Design Through Information Technology;* Boston:Harvard Business School Press, 1991

Kemerer, C.F., An Empirical Validation of Software Cost Estimation Models, *Communications of the ACM* v. 30(5), 416-429, 1987

Kling, R., Social analyses of computing: theoretical perspectives in recent empirical research, *Computing Surveys*, v. 12, 61-110, 1980

Kochen, M., *Principles of Information Retrieval*. Los Angeles: Melville, 1974

Leiberman, A.Z. and A.B. Whinston, A Structuring of an Events—Accounting Information System, *Accounting Review*, April 1975

Levitt, J. Better Benchmarks Are Brewing, *UNIX Today!*, January 20, 1992, 47-50, 1992

Lientz, B.P. and E.B. Swanson,*Software Maintenance Management: A Study of the Maintained of Computer Application Software in 487 Data Processing Organizations*, Reading, MA:Addison-Wesley, 1980

Littlewood, B. and L. Strigini, The Risks of Software, *Scientific American*, November 1992

Maglitta, J., It's Reality Time, *Computerworld*, April 29, 1991, 81-4, 1991

Martin, James, and Carma McClure, *Diagraming Techniques for Analysts and Programmers*, Prentice-Hall, 1985.

McCabe, T.J., A Complexity Measure, *IEEE Transactions on Software Engineering*, SE-8(4), 308-320, 1976

McCarthy, W.E., An Entity—Relationship View of Accounting Models, *Accounting Review*, October 1979

McCarthy, W.E., The REA Model: A Generalized Framework for Accounting Systems in a Shared Data Environment, *Accounting Review*, July 1982

McGregor, J.D. and Korson, T., Object-Oriented Design, *Communications of the ACM*, September, v. 33(9), 1990

McGregor, *Object-Oriented Design and Development*, New York: Van Nostrand Reinhold, 1990

McMenamin, C. and Y. Palmer, *Essential Systems Analysis*, New York:Yourdon, 1990

Merten, A. and D.G. Severance, Data Processing Control: A State—of—the—Art Survey of Attitudes and Concerns of DP Executives, *MIS Quarterly*, v. 5(2), pp. 11—32, 1981

Minton, C. , What's the question again?, *Midrange Systems,* July 10, p. 22, 1990

Mintzberg, H. Planning on the Left Side and Managing on the Right, *Harvard Business Review*, July—August, p. 49, 1976

Mohanty, W.N. , Software Cost Estimation: Present and Future, *Softw. Pract. Exper.*, v. 11, 103-121, 1981

Ng, P. A., Further Analysis of the Entity—Relationship Approach to Database Design, *IEEE Transactions on Software Engineering*, v. SE—7(1), January 1981

Norden, P. , *Using Tools for Project Management, Management of Production*, M.K. Starr, Baltimore: Penguin Books (ed.), 1970

Orr, K. *Structured Requirements Definition*, Ken Orr and Associates, Inc.,1981.

Payne, J.W. Task Complexity and Contingent Processing in Decision Making: An Information Search and Protocol Analysis, *Organization Behavior and Human Performance*, 16 (December), 366—387, 1976

Peters, Lawrence, *Advanced Structured Analysis and Design*, Prentice-Hall,1987.

Putnam, L.H. , A General Empirical Solution to the Macrosoftware Sizing and Estimating Problem, *IEEE Transactions on Software Engineering*, SE-4(4), 345-361, 1978

Rich, C. and R.C. Waters, Automatic Programming: Myths and Prospects, *IEEE Computer*, August, 40-50, 1988

Robey D. and M.L. Markus, Rituals in Information Systems Design, *MIS Quarterly*, March, 5-15, 1984

Rockart, J., Chief executives define their own data needs, *Harvard Business Review*, March-April, 1979

Royce W.W., Managing the Development of Large Software Systems: Concepts and Techniques, *Proceedings of WESCON*, August 1970

Rubin, H. A., "Measure for Measure" *Computerworld*, April 15, 1991, 77-79, 1991

Rubin, H.A. , *A Comparison of Software Cost Estimation Tools*, System Development v. 7(5), 1987

Scheier, R.L., Kodak Unit Overhauls IS and the Business Process, *PC Week*, April 1990, p. 127

Schlender, B.R. 1989. How to Break the Software Logjam, *Fortune*, September 25, 1989, 100—112

Steward, Donald V., *Software Engineering with Systems Analysis and Design*, Brooks/Cole Publishing Co., 1987.

Swanson, D.R. ,Information Retrieval as a Trial-and-Error Process. *Library Quarterly*, v.47(2), 129-48, 1977

Swanson, E.B. , *Information System Implementation*, Homewood, IL:Irwin, 58-73, 1988

System Builder, *The Peoples Choice Awards*, June/July, 27-34, 1989

Wegner, P. Dimensions of object-based language design, in Proceedings of the Conference on Object-Oriented systems, Languages and applications, 1987.

Westland, J.C., a Net Benefits Approach to Measuring Retrieval Performance, Information Processing and Management, v.25(5), 479-581, 1989.

Westland, J.C. Competing in the World's Computer Market, Scientific American, November, 152, 1990a.

Westland, J.C., Scaling Up Output Volumes Predicted by Information Systems Prototypes, Association for Computing Machinery/TODS, v. 15(3), 3341-358.

Westland, J.C., Assessing the Economic Benefits of Information Systems Auditing, *Information Systems Research*, v.1(3), 309-24, 1990c

Westland, J.C. , Topic Specific Monopolies in the Information Services Industry: Evidence from the DIALOG Group of Databases, *The Information Society*, v. 6, 127-138, 1990d

Westland, J.C. , Self-Organizing Executive Information Networks, *Decision Support Systems*, v.8 (1991), 41-53, 1991

Westland, J.C., The Marginal Analysis of Investments in Information Technology, in *Strategic and Economic Impacts of Information Technology Investment: Perspectives on Organizational Growth and Competitive Advantage*, Mahmood, Banker and Kaufman (eds.), Harrisburg, PA: Idea Group Publishing, 1993a

Westland, J.C. , Congestion and Network Externalities in the Short Run Pricing of Information Systems Services, *Management Science*, v. 38(6) July 1992a

Westland, J.C. , Economics and Global Information Technology Education , in *Global Information Technology Education: Issues and Trends*, K. Loch (ed.), Middletown, PA: Idea Group Publishing, 1993b.

Westland, J.C. , Reporting Strategies for 'Events' Accounting, *Journal of Information Systems*, in press, 1992b

Yourdon, E ., *Decline & Fall of the American Programmer*, New York: Yourdon Press, 1992

Yourdon, E ., *Structured Analysis and Design*, New York: Yourdon Press, 1982

Zipf, G.K., *Human Behavior and the Principle of Least Effort*, New York:Hafner 1949 (facsimile 1965)

CHAPTER FIFTEEN

Simulation for CASE:
Use of a Prototype and Experimentation to Assess the Effectiveness of a CASE Method

James R. Warren
The American University

Many fundamental decisions in information system (IS) design are influenced by how quickly work must be done — where to provide computer support, and the choice of hardware platform and database management system — yet modeling the overall dynamics of designs is not a routine part of IS development. This chapter describes an effort to make design performance modeling more accessible to IS developers by allowing the specification of performance models via conventional data flow diagrams (DFDs) annotated with information on the performance of the DFD components. A prototype simulation environment has been developed which produces stochastic (i.e., random-number based) simulation results automatically from annotated DFDs. The prototype reads DFDs as input and formulates a corresponding simulation model. The prototype provides model-based expert advice in the use of the simulation model and in the interpretation of its output. The effectiveness of the prototype is evaluated in an experimental context where twenty-one IS professionals answer batteries of questions about the performance characteristics of several IS design cases. The prototype's simulation capability has a significant positive effect on the accuracy with which IS professionals answer questions about waiting times, system times, and queue (i.e., waiting line) lengths of jobs or customers. The experimental findings support the intuitive notion that DFD-based simulation is a valuable aid to *decision-making about performance issues in IS design. Embedding simulation capabilities in computer-aided software engineering (CASE) workbenches should result in better-designed information systems.*

This chapter presents a method for IS analysts to assess the performance-related (i.e., dynamic) aspects of IS designs without resorting to writing simulation programs. A prototype CASE-tool implementing the features of the proposed method (called CASE/simulation) is described, and the results of laboratory experimentation testing the effectiveness of the prototype are reported.

IS developers frequently benchmark the performance of the hardware and software components of proposed IS designs, but modeling the overall dynamics of the IS design is not a normal part of the system development process. The analysis of overall IS design dynamics entails modeling the extent to which a set of system components in a design (computer-based systems, people, and non-information-processing machinery interacting with the IS) satisfies its performance requirements. It is unfortunate that this variety of analysis is neglected, because IS dynamics are an important consideration in many design decisions. For example:

1. The choice of hardware platform is largely determined on the basis of dynamics. Organizations invest in mainframe computers because they believe they need the capacity and speed. A microcomputer attached to re-writable optical technology may offer the same on-line storage capacity as a mainframe system at far lower cost (one can even purchase products to attach numerous terminals to the microcomputer), but the microcomputer-based system lacks the speed of the mainframe system for most real-world applications.
2. The choice of database management system (DBMS) architecture can be driven by dynamics. When first introduced, there was a great deal of concern that relational DBMSs such as DB2 were too slow for production systems (Inmon, 1983). The first release of DB2 performed 1.65 to 2.35 times slower than the hierarchical IMS DBMS on IMS-type workloads (Loosely, 1985). A DB2-based IS is qualitatively different from an IMS-based system, possessing greater flexibility in modification of the DBMS schema and offering "ad hoc query" capability (Date, 1986). These advantages must be foregone, however, if the IS requires the performance of a hierarchical DBMS. These qualitative trade-offs are increasingly common with the proliferation of DBMS products and fourth-generation languages that offer new advantages and capabilities for developers and end-users.

Simulation for CASE 429

3. IS dynamics influences the focus of automation: what to automate, and to what extent. If a service-oriented company is too slow in attending to customers, the organization's objectives will not be best met by doubling the speed of the employee payroll system. The example application later in this chapter illustrates an operation where a single data-entry process is critical to the dynamics of the system.

A prototype system has been developed which automatically produces stochastic discrete-event-based simulation models from data flow diagrams (DFDs) and additional information regarding the performance of system components. That is, DFDs, a traditional notation used to express the direction and content of normal information flows in proposed and existing systems, are given a new, non-traditional role via annotation with the dynamics of flow among system components. The goal is to provide IS design performance evaluation as an integral part of system development by allowing the production of simulation results directly from CASE-workbench data dictionaries. The prototype demonstrates the feasibility of this goal, because the drawing and annotation of DFDs are already standard CASE features.

A vast array of tools has been developed under the rubric of CASE to aid in the development of information systems (see McClure [1989] or the numerous examples in other chapters in this book). Scientific evaluation of their effectiveness, however, is rarely seen. Sharda, Barr, and McDonnell (1988) note a conspicuous absence of laboratory experiments in the evaluation of the effectiveness of decision support systems (DSS). In favor of controlled experiments, DSS researchers have used case studies and field studies to show the effectiveness of novel tools. These non-experimental methods do a poor job of quantifying the benefits of the tools being studied with measurable levels of certainty. The situation with software engineering tool evaluation is similar to that for DSS. As an exception to the general lack of controlled experimentation in software engineering, Subrimanian, et al. (1992) compare the effectiveness of decision trees versus decision tables in the context of an investment game. They found that users make more correct decisions using trees than tables. They also observed that cognitive style and academic ability are significantly correlated with performance with either tool, but that academic background (computer science versus business) is significant only with the use of decision trees. Thus, through experimentation, Subrimanian, et al. demonstrate the superiority of one tool over another, show that certain individual characteristics affect the ability to use these tools, and show differences in which characteristics are important to specific tools. This chapter presents a laboratory experiment to evaluate the effectiveness of the prototype CASE/simulation system. As was the case in Subrimanian, et al., the results of the experiment help to quantify and qualify the effectiveness of the tool.

The next section reviews some of the technologies and issues influential in the design of the prototype CASE/simulation system, including currently available fourth-generation languages (4GLs) and tools for the production of computer simulations, and the difficulties in using stochastic simulation to make decisions. Section 3 describes the design of the prototype environment, and illustrates the features of the prototype through application to the quality assurance sub-system of an electronic component manufacturing operation. Section 4 presents an experiment to determine the impact of CASE/simulation on the accuracy of IS professionals' assessment of the performance of IS designs. The objective of the experiment is to test the hypothesis that CASE/simulation leads to more accurate assessment of IS design dynamics, and to point the way for further prototype developments and experiments, leading to deepening understanding of the methods of decision support in this domain. The chapter concludes with discussion of the experimental results and the importance of experimentation to CASE in general.

BACKGROUND

Several trends relevant to the design of a CASE/simulation system can be seen in the literature: (a) the use of graphically oriented and integrated environments for IS dynamics modeling, as well as modeling and simulation in general, (b) the delivery of performance modeling capability to IS analysts with models tailored to the specific needs of IS dynamics modeling, (c) increasing integration of dynamics modeling tools with other CASE tools, and (d) the codifying of simulation modeling knowledge into computer-based systems.

Stochastic discrete-event-based simulation of IS designs can be implemented using simulation 4GLs such as GPSS/H (Schriber, 1991) and SIMSCRIPT II.5 (CACI, 1987), but most IS developers lack the time and expertise to write a simulation program every time a question arises about the dynamics of an IS design. The simulation modeling process can be supported by a simulation environment. TESS by Pritsker and Associates, a simulation environment that supports the development of models in the SLAM II 4GL, allows specification of experimental conditions, and automatically stores results in a database for report generation, graphical presentation, and animation (Watson & Blackstone, 1989). The simulation model development environment (SMDE) (Balci & Nance, 1987) exemplifies, general-purpose, graphical, and integrated simulation environments.

Simulation 4GLs, even when encapsulated in simulation environments, are not designed specifically to support IS dynamic modeling. QASE RT by Advanced Systems Technologies (Gore, 1990) supports modeling of wide-area and local-area networks, where the application code size, type of hardware, and operating system of each computer in the network is considered. QASE RT allows the graphical depiction of software running on hardware so developers can study the performance of proposed systems. NEST (Schwartz, Yemini, & Bacon, 1990) is a graphically-oriented communications network and protocol simulator supporting the linkage of actual protocol code (written in C) with the simulation, and "what-if" analysis of situations such as the malfunction of a node or link in the network. A prototype system has been developed which allows developers to consider the performance impact of implementational considera-tions in high-performance software in a machine-independent manner prior to the writing of code (Ammar, 1991). A generic performance modeling shell has also been developed for database architectures (Eich, et al., 1989). These systems offer an improvement over general-purpose simulation 4GLs for the IS developer, because they contain a great deal of knowledge about the dynamics of IS components.

IS developers could make more use of dynamic modeling if no diversion from the IS development task was required. All of the above tools require the developer to examine the proposed IS design in question, and re-code the elements of that design relevant to a dynamic analysis in an environment separate from the developer's CASE workbench. One effort to integrate dynamic analysis with the IS development environment pre-dates CASE (Boydstun, et al., 1980). A variant on the problem statement language (PSL; Teichroew & Hershey, 1977) was used to produce SIMSCRIPT programs directly from the system description. Cadre Technologies is now introducing CASE tools such as Teamwork/SIM (Pallatto, 1990) with dynamic analysis capabilities via system simulation. These capabilities are distinct from diagram-completeness and static requirements analysis functions offered by numerous CASE vendors.

Stochastic (i.e., pseudo-random-number-based) simulation has been widely used for system performance evaluation, but is often presented without attention to the statistical nature of simulation output (Pawlikowski, 1990). The results of a single stochastic simulation run represent merely an observation from a population of possible simulation results. Stochastic simulation can never yield the outcome that a given parameter of the simulated system is exactly x. One must be content with a *confidence interval*; that is, "We are p% confident that the true value lies between $x - \delta$ and $x + \delta$." One of the simplest methods of generating confidence intervals is the method of independent replications, where a simulation run is repeated a number of times to obtain a set of independent observations. For an unknown parameter μ_x of the simulated system,

$$P(\mu_x = \overline{X}(n) \pm t_{n-1, 1-\alpha/2} \, s \sqrt{n}) = 1 - \alpha,$$

where $\overline{X}(n)$ and s are the mean and standard deviation of the independent observations of μ_x, respectively, n is the number of replications, and t represents the t-distribution function (Hoover & Perry, 1989, pp. 313-314). The important simulation run parameters in the method of replications are the *simulation duration*, the *warm-up period* (the amount of time the simulation is run and observations are discarded on the suspicion that the system has not yet reached a steady-state), and, of course, the *number of replications*.

Expert systems have been developed to aid simulationists in the statistical issues of simulation (Park & Mellichamp, 1990). Expert system support can include aid in determining simulation duration and number of replications, assessing the impact of initial conditions, constructing confidence intervals, comparing output from alternative designs, and estimating response/input variable relationships. Knowledge-based support can also be provided through on-line help embedded in a simulation environment. The help system for the SMDE (Frankel & Balci, 1989) includes: (a) a general assistance manager, offering an introduction to the SMDE, tutorials on usage of the tools in the environment, and a glossary of terms; and (b) help routines for specific tools.

A PROTOTYPE CASE/SIMULATION SYSTEM

A prototype CASE/simulation system has been developed which automatically produces stochastic discrete-event-based simulation models from data flow diagrams (DFDs) and additional information regarding the performance of system components (Warren & Stott, 1992; Warren, Stott, & Norcio, 1992a). DFDs are selected because they are graphical, supported by current CASE technology, and familiar to IS analysts. Additionally, there is precedent for the use of semantically extended DFDs in advanced systems analysis approaches (Babin, Lustman, & Shoval, 1991; France, 1992). Each DFD process is viewed as a server/queue in a queuing network. The prototype provides simulation in the context of an integrated simulation environment under the X Window System[1] graphical user interface on Hewlett-Packard HP 9000 workstations. Intelligent help is provided in the formulation of simulation run parameters for the method of replications, and in interpretation of stochastic simulation output. The prototype is oriented towards the analysis of mean performance, as distinct from the emphasis on worst-case performance common in the analysis of real-time systems (Stonyenko, Hamacher, & Holt, 1991).

Figure 1 illustrates major features of the prototype. In the upper-left, a DFD-drawing utility is shown. This allows the specification of system structure and dynamic attributes. A pop-up window allowing the annotation of dynamic attributes to a DFD process appears in the lower-left. In a true integrated-CASE environment, DFD-drawing should be performed using a middle-level CASE tool, where the DFD-components are integrated with the IS-design's data dictionary[2]. In the lower-center portion of the screen is a simulation run parameter input window. This window allows the user to input the parameters to specify a method-of-replications simulation experiment. The prototype automatically interprets the DFD as a network of queues and conducts a simulation under the specified parameters. The user can receive help in formulating the simulation run parameters by clicking on the parameter for which assistance is desired. The upper-right window presents the results of the most recent simulation run. Standard performance statistics (utilization, throughput, waiting time, etc.) are reported for each DFD process and for DFD data stores that are central to the dynamics of the IS design. The user can receive help in understanding the simulation output, confidence interval generation, and heuristic recommendations regarding potential processing bottlenecks from the simulation results window. A pop-up simulation-output help window is shown in the lower-right.

Automatic Simulation from Data Flow Diagrams

The prototype IS simulator produces simulation results directly from DFDs drawn using an augmented DFD-drawing utility. The mapping from DFDs to simulation is accomplished using the model that each DFD process represents a server/queue system; that is, each DFD process represents a line of "jobs" and someone/something that accomplishes those jobs, sending them on to whatever process, data store, or external entity is the output of the process.

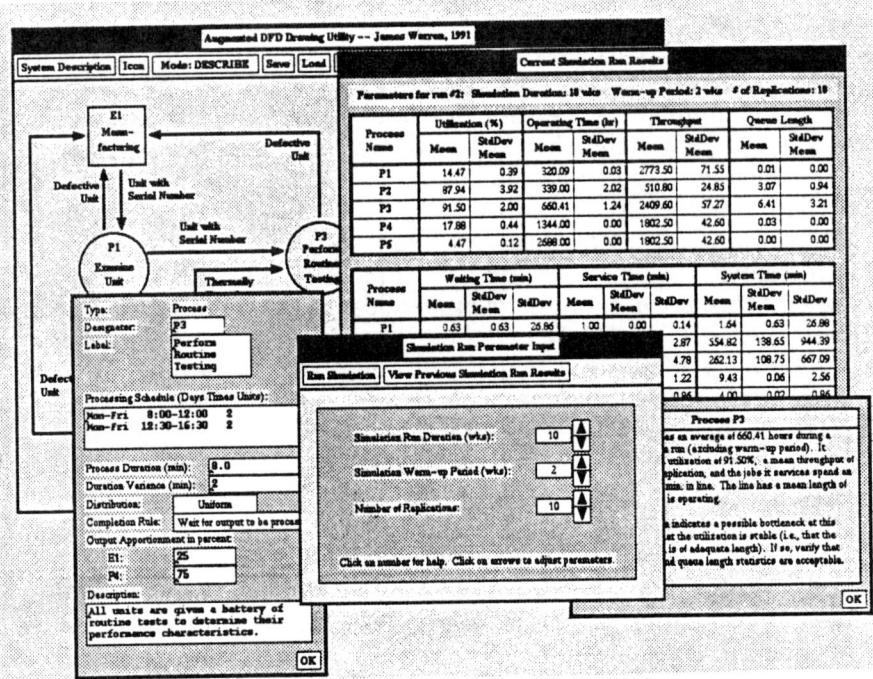

Figure 1: The prototype IS design dynamics simulator runs under X11 on an HP 9000 workstation. The environment presents three main windows: (a) a DFD-drawing utility with pop-up windows to specify attributes of DFD components, (b) a simulation parameter input window with parameter-specificaiton help, and (c) a simulation results window that explains the output, generates confidence intervals, and provides heuristic warnings of processing bottlenecks.

The conventional DFD notation shows the direction and content of flows through the system, but lacks several items relevant to an IS design simulation. Ordinarily, DFDs do not indicate the rate at which jobs are processed, nor do they indicate the amount of time that servers are available to process jobs. The augmentation of DFDs with such dynamics attributes is straight-forward. Figure 2 shows the pop-up editing window associated with a DFD process in the augmented DFD-drawing utility. The window in figure 2 allows the user to specify:

1. A designator and label for the process, as normally appears on a DFD.
2. A processing schedule (indicating that the process functions on Mondays through Fridays, from 8AM until noon and 12:30PM

until 4:30PM, with 1 server available at those times). Schedules may include an "and idle" clause (e.g., "12:30 - 16:30 and idle") to indicate that processing does not conclude until the queue is empty. An end-of-day process can be modeled with clauses such as "P1 off - idle" instead of a time range, which indicates that processing begins at the process when processing stops at P1, and continues until the job queue is empty. The time range may also be replaced with "always" to indicate a resource that is continually available.

3. A processing duration, variance, and distribution (an average of 1 minute per job, uniformly distributed between 0.75 and 1.25 minutes).
4. A processing completion rule (which could indicate that the process server should wait for a completed job to be received, or completed, at a subsequent process before continuing to the next job in the queue).
5. Apportionment of output jobs between the possible destinations (18% to P2, 10% to E1, and 72% to P3).
6. A textual description of the process.

When the developer selects the "Run Simulation" button on the simulation run parameter input window, the discrete event-based simulator of the prototype reads the internal representation of the augmented DFD. The simulator maps the DFD to a network of queues, where the DFD attributes define the service rates and distributions for the queuing systems. Note that it would constitute a minor modification to a middle-level CASE tool such as InterSolve's Excelerator to allow attachment of attributes to the DFD components, allowing the tool to serve as the front-end for a simulation environment such as this prototype.[3]

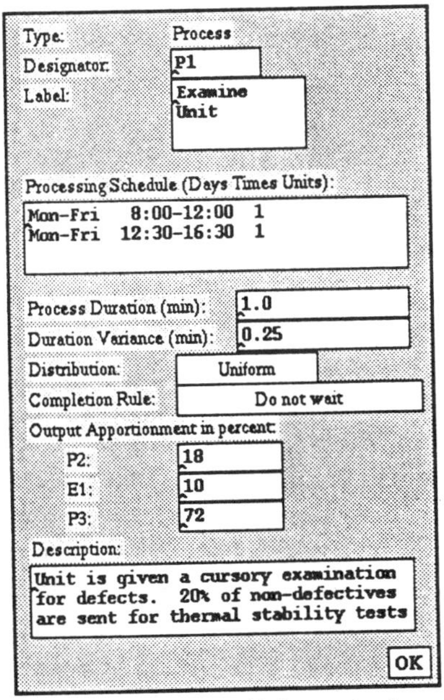

Figure 2: Pop-up editing window for DFD process attributes

Simulation Usage Support

The simulation usage support of the prototype is implemented as an on-line help system rather than in a more obtrusive format. The objective is not to impose a model on the developer's decision-making style, but only to offer assistance in the proper use and interpretation of simulation when the developer requests assistance (by clicking the mouse on the object of interest). Assistance takes the forms of: (a) definitions, (b) explanations and calculations, and (c) recommendations.

On the simulation run parameter input window, the developer indicates the need for help by clicking on a parameter. The prototype will offer a definition of the indicated parameter and give the developer the option of asking for a recommendation. When the developer requests a recommendation, the prototype analyzes the current simulation results to ensure that they are in keeping with its model of proper simulation usage. (If no simulation run has yet been conducted, the prototype offers a heuristic default recommendation, and advises that it will be able formulate a more precise recommendation once a simulation has been run.) The simulation usage model contains three major principles:

1. The difference between the simulation duration and the warm-up period should be adequate to allow a sufficiently high number of observations per simulation run to secure normality of the replication means (based on analysis of process throughput).
2. The warm-up period should not end until the running mean utilization of each process approaches a constant level with a given accuracy δ (Pawlikowski, 1990).
3. An increase in the number of replications or the simulation duration should narrow the confidence intervals of output parameters, but lengthening of the simulation duration is the more efficient of the two methods.

The prototype uses the first two of these principles when making recommendations about simulation duration and warm-up period. Either the parameter is indicated to be adequate or a larger value is recommended for one or both of the parameters. The third principle is implemented in the prototype by responding to the developer's request for a recommendation on number of replications with an explanation of the relationship between confidence intervals and the simulation run parameters.

The simulation run results window offers output-interpretation help in three forms, depending on the area of the simulation output indicated by the developer:

1. Column headers provide a definition of the indicated output parameter.
2. Row headers provide a summary explanation of the all the output shown for the indicated process or data store. A heuristic recommendation is made if the process utilization is sufficiently close to 100% to indicate a possible bottleneck.
3. Cells in the table body provide a confidence interval of the mean of the indicated parameter.

Example Use of the Prototype

Use of the prototype is now illustrated via application to the quality assurance sub-system of an electronic component manufacturing operation[4]. The IS component of the quality assurance sub-system involves the recording of product testing results into a finished goods inventory database and collecting thermal stability testing results for a sample of components. Figure 3 shows the DFD of the quality assurance sub-system of an electronic component manufacturing operation.

Manufacturing produces untested units at an average rate of one every 7 minutes (following the negative exponential distribution). A cursory examination of entering units by the shop supervisor (requiring only 45 to 75 seconds per unit) results in 10% of them being returned as defective, 18% being selected for thermal stability testing, and the remaining 72% going to the routine testing stations. Thermal stability testing requires from 30 to 40 minutes, and results in 20% of components being returned as defective; the remainder go to routine testing. Two routine testing stations, staffed by testers, are available. Routine testing requires 6 to 10 minutes per unit (uniformly distributed across that range) and results in 25% of the units being returned as defective. For components that pass routine testing, their performance characteristics are entered into the finished goods inventory database by the testers. Data entry, requiring 2.5 to 6.5 minutes, is performed at one data entry terminal that pivots between the two stations, and must be performed before testing instruments are cleared to test another unit. Data entry concludes with the printing of a data sheet. After data entry, units are packaged with their data sheet for inventory by the testers, requiring 2.5 to 6.5 minutes, and sent to finished goods inventory. Manufacturing and all quality assurance processes operate from 8 am to noon and 12:30 PM to 4:30 PM, Monday through Friday.

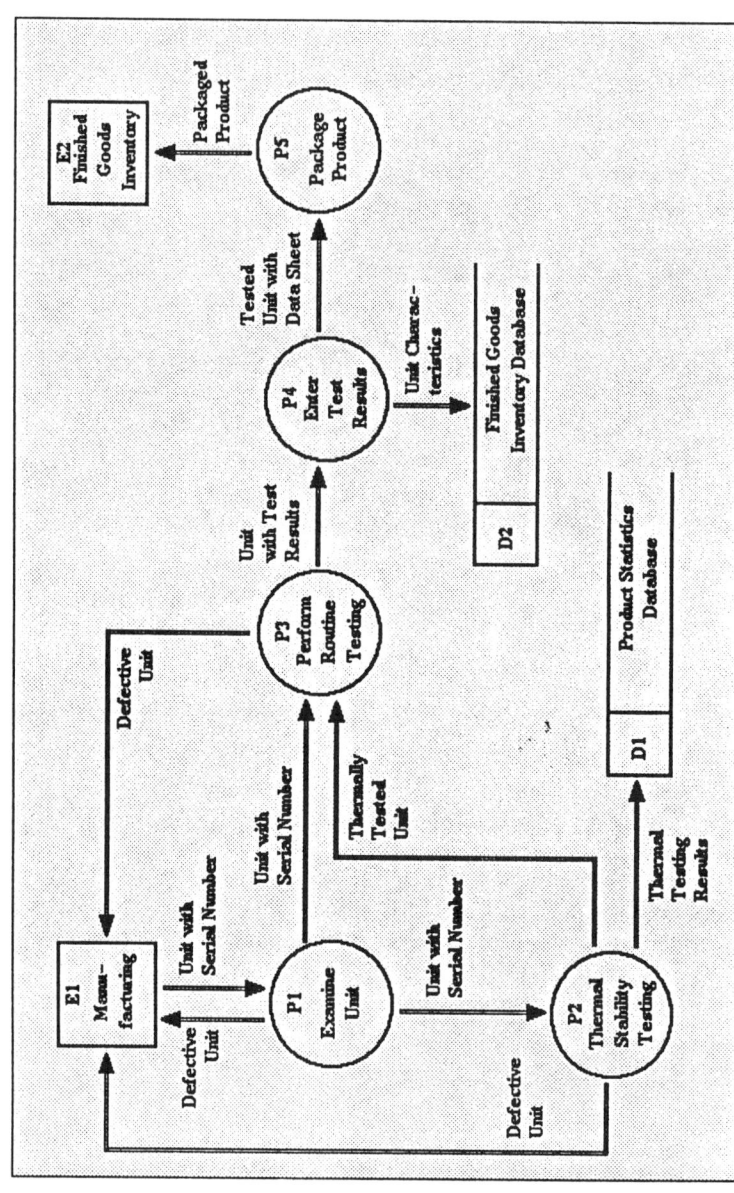

Figure 3: Data flow diagram of the quality assurance sub-system of an electronic component manufacturing operation

Simulation for CASE 439

The system dynamics are encoded in the attributes of the DFD components using the augmented DFD-drawing utility of the prototype. For example, figure 4 shows the annotation for external entity E1, manufacturing. The window specifies the times, rates, and mathematical distributions for jobs entering the system from E1 (one unit every 7 minutes, distributed exponentially, Monday through Friday, during hours of operation). Figure 5 shows the annotation for process P3, "Perform Routine Testing." The processing schedule indicates that two processing units (the testers) are available Monday through Friday, from 8AM to noon and 12:30PM to 4:30PM. Fields indicate that the processing rate is 6 to 10 minutes, distributed uniformly, and that 75% of output jobs proceed to P4 (the "Enter Test Results" process) while the remainder go to E1 (the "Manufacturing" external entity). The completion rule "Wait for output to be processed" directs the simulator to wait for a job to be processed at P4, before continuing to process the next job in those cases where output proceeds to a process. Processing proceeds immediately to the next job in the 25% of cases where output is to external entity E1.

Figure 6 shows the simulation output results for the quality assurance sub-system with a simulation duration of 10 weeks, warm-up period of 2 weeks, and 10 replications. This simulation requires about 50 seconds of processing time on an HP 9000 series 425 workstation with a 25MHz 68040 processor and 16MB RAM.

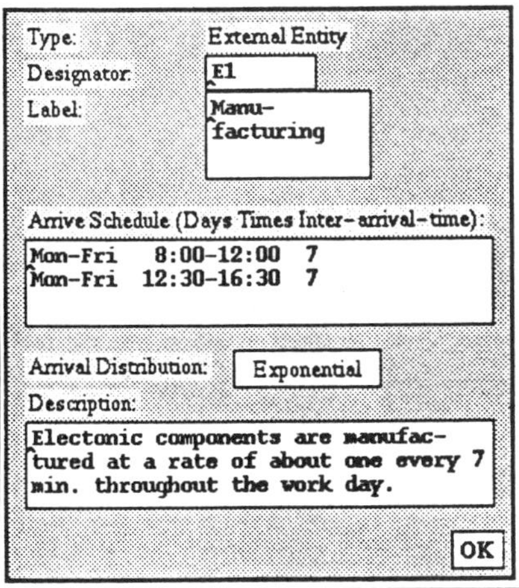

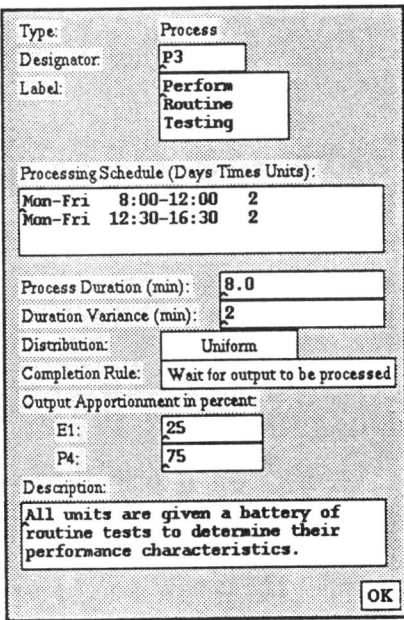

Figure 4: Annotation for process P3 of the quality assurance sub-system

Figure 5: Annotation for external entity E1 of the quality assurance sub-system

Current Simulation Run Results								
Parameters for run #1: Simulation Duration: 10 wks Warm-up Period: 2 wks # of Replications: 10								
Process Name	Utilization (%)		Operating Time (hr)		Throughput		Queue Length	
	Mean	StdDev Mean	Mean	StdDev Mean	Mean	StdDev Mean	Mean	StdDev Mean
P1	14.47	0.39	320.09	0.03	2773.50	71.55	0.01	0.00
P2	87.94	3.92	339.00	2.02	510.80	24.85	3.07	0.94
P3	91.50	2.00	660.41	1.24	2409.60	57.27	6.41	3.21
P4	17.88	0.44	1344.00	0.00	1802.50	42.60	0.03	0.00
P5	4.47	0.12	2688.00	0.00	1802.50	42.60	0.00	0.00

Process Name	Waiting Time (min)			Service Time (min)			System Time (min)		
	Mean	StdDev Mean	StdDev	Mean	StdDev Mean	StdDev	Mean	StdDev Mean	StdDev
P1	0.63	0.63	26.86	1.00	0.00	0.14	1.64	0.63	26.88
P2	519.79	138.67	944.40	35.02	0.14	2.87	554.82	138.65	944.39
P3	247.08	108.72	667.01	15.05	0.12	4.78	262.13	108.75	667.09
P4	1.43	0.04	2.25	8.00	0.02	1.22	9.43	0.06	2.56
P5	0.00	0.00	0.00	4.00	0.02	0.86	4.00	0.02	0.86

Click on table header for definitions. Click on cells for specific help.

Figure 6: Simulation output for the quality assurance sub-system

A cursory view of the utilization figures indicates that the system dynamics are not out of control. While the 91% utilization at P3 may be suspiciously close to a bottleneck, the average queue length of around 6 jobs indicates reasonably smooth operation. Average waiting times of several hours for jobs at the thermal-stability and routine testing stations are due to jobs waiting in queue over night and over the weekend. The relatively low utilizations and large number of hours of operation for P4 and P5 are due to these processes being modeled as continually available to the testers at P3 who perform the data entry and packaging tasks.

One potentially unsatisfactory aspect of the performance profile seen in figure 6 is the average waiting time at process P4; that is, the time testers spend waiting for access to a data entry terminal. Clicking on the "Mean Waiting Time" cell of process P4 causes the prototype to pop-up the window shown in figure 7. We are 95% confident that testers wait an average of 1.401 to 1.463 minutes for access to a data entry terminal before proceeding to packaging. This is completely wasted time, because the testers cannot clear their instruments to test another unit until the results are recorded. Note that the simulation environment merely describes the scenario; it is up to the developer to assess the acceptability of the design dynamics and to formulate alternatives to unacceptable outcomes.

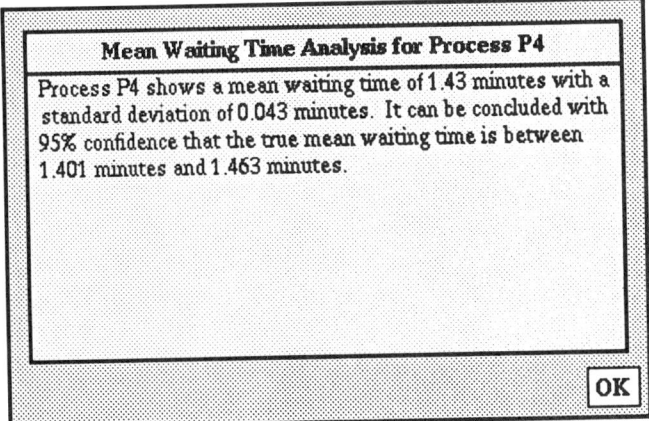

Figure 7: Confidence interval generation for mean waiting time at process P4 ("Enter Test Results") of the quality assurance sub-system

In fact, having testers wait an average of 1.4 minutes to perform data entry may be unacceptable. By modifying the annotation to external entity E1 (figure 4) and re-running the simulation, one can assess that a bottleneck would develop at P3 if manufacturing upped the rate of production from one unit every 7 minutes to one unit every 6 minutes. The developer investigated two classes of candidate design modifications that offered solutions to this problem:

1. Eliminate queuing for data entry. This could be solved simply by increasing the number of terminals to two. This reduces utilization at P3 to around 85%. Even with one unit coming from manufacturing every 6 minutes, there would be no bottleneck at P3. Alternatively, the system could be redesigned as shown in figure 8. An in-house data sheet could be filled out by testers who then proceed immediately to the next unit. In an independent processing sequence, these in-house data sheets could be entered into the finished goods inventory database and customer data sheets printed. These data sheets are packaged with the tested units. This arrangement may not result in any real saving of labor, because testers are likely to spend at least as much time filling out in-house data sheets as they had spent waiting for the data entry terminal. The design does, however, promote specialization of labor, in that testers need not perform data entry and packaging tasks[5].
2. Reduce the amount of data entry time. Halving the data entry time to be uniformly distributed between 1.25 and 2.75 minutes per job lowers the utilization at P3 to about 80% by reducing queuing

time to an average of about 0.75 minutes and, obviously, reducing the data entry time by 2 minutes per job. If entry of routine test results into the finished goods inventory database was completely automatic, allowing packaging to immediately follow routine testing, then utilization at P3 would be only 67%. Even if manufacturing upped the rate of production to one unit every 5 minutes, utilization at P3 reaches only 90%[6].

The dynamics of each of these design modifications is easily investigated with the prototype by modifying the annotation to DFD processes (or slightly re-drawing the system structure for the alternative shown in figure 8) and re-running the simulation. The implementation of these modifications, however, is a more difficult matter. Can a system with two terminals be delivered within budgetary constraints? Is creating a division of labor between testers and data-entry/packaging personnel considered advantageous or disadvantageous by management? Can data entry time be halved? This may be possible by judicious selection of the information that must be entered and/or through good human-computer interface design. Can data entry be completely automated? While the benefits of automatic data entry are large, so are the costs. All testing equipment must be interfaced with a computer that coordinates the testing process and monitors results. The testing software (most likely developed in a conventional programming language such as FORTRAN, Pascal, or C) will need to interface with the finished goods inventory database application (more easily developed in a database 4GL). The hardware requirement will be at least a microcomputer with networking and instrumentation interface capability, rather than a "dumb" terminal.

Summary of Prototype Benefits

The prototype supports the IS developer in determining the most important focus of automation in a proposed IS design. In the example application above, it was found that testers wasted time waiting for a data entry terminal. For many designs, improved performance may be accomplished through buying faster computers, or DBMSs better-suited to high-volume processing. For the quality assurance sub-system, solutions included buying another terminal, altering the work flow, re-designing the data entry task, and developing integrated testing and data entry software. The simulation environment allows the developer to quickly quantify the value of design modifications to the system dynamics, but the developer must assess the value of the alternatives within the context of the syst em requirements, available resources, and organization strategy. The tool promotes the use of system dynamics simulation as an integral part of the IS development process; assessing designs, considering modifications, assessing the modifications. Once the developer has specified the dynamics of system components, the prototype can be asked, "If the components perform like this, what is the overall state of the system dynamics?" This provides evidence for the confirmation (or denial) of the acceptability of the dynamics of the IS design. It also produces a powerful set of dynamics requirements for the IS-component designers; if each component performs as well as specified, then the dynamic performance of the IS should be as good as the simulation results indicate.

EXPERIMENTAL EVALUATION

In our culture, there is a widely-held (and, in the author's opinion, well-founded) belief that a clever person can bend numbers and statistics to say just about anything they wish. The basis of this belief (outside of erroneous, or intentionally false reporting of statistics) lies in imprecise definition of seemingly-precise claims. For example, a claim that a software tool leads to "a 20% improvement in the quality of decision-making" is essentially meaningless without addressing at least:

1. Was a legitimate experiment conducted (i.e., were systematic observations made to support the claim)?
2. Who were the subjects (i.e., who participated in the experiment)?
3. Did all the subjects follow a consistent procedure (i.e., set of activities)?
4. What were the decision-making tasks?
5. How was the quality of decisions measured?
6. What was the experimental control (i.e., to what was the software tool compared)?
7. What was the statistical significance level (i.e., what is the likelihood that the results were not due to simple chance)?

The answers to these questions describe the method employed in an experiment. Through withholding a clear answer to any one of the aspects of the experimental method, the importance and meaning of the findings can be presented in a highly-distorted light.

This section presents an experiment to support the claim that DFD-based simulation is a valuable IS design tool. Twenty-one IS professionals answered batteries of questions about the performance characteristics of several IS design cases. The prototype's simulation capability was found to have a significant positive effect on the accuracy with which the professionals answered questions about waiting times, system times, and queue (i.e., waiting line) lengths of jobs or customers. The "Method" sub-section describes the experimental method in detail, and the subsequent "Results" sub-section gives the experimental findings in the context of terms defined in the "Method" sub-section. The language of this section assumes a non-trivial knowledge of statistics, which can be obtained through the references. The reader may skim or skip this section, but two warnings apply:

1. The reader will have to take "on faith" that the experiment truly supports the claims given in the "Conclusions" section, and
2. One must consider the lack of supportable claims in CASE an impediment to progress. Scientific progress is difficult, if not impossible, without a method by which researchers can assess and verify one another's findings. Statistical inference based on rigorous experimentation is an accepted method of supporting claims in more mature social sciences, such as psychology — and, since the purpose of CASE tools is to aid people in producing software, CASE is a social science.

Research Questions

Several questions can be asked of a system intended to deliver design performance modeling technology to IS analysts:

Q1. Does the system model all necessary aspects of IS design dynamics to support the analysts' decision-making?
Q2. Does the system improve the convenience with which IS design dynamics can be evaluated?
Q3. Does the system improve the accuracy of IS design dynamics evaluation?

Q1 can best be answered by application of CASE/simulation system to a broad spectrum of IS problems. The prototype has been applied to a variety of fairly standard IS designs (Warren & Stott, 1992; Warren, Stott, & Norcio, 1992a and 1992b), providing some demonstration of the feasibility of the approach. With respect to Q2, the prototype provides automated simulation from DFDs annotated with component-performance information. Since the drawing of DFDs is a normal part of IS development, a model of IS dynamics that utilizes the information in DFDs should be more convenient to the IS analyst, than a model that requires re-coding of that information in a simulation 4GL or a specialized notation. Q3 seems especially amenable to being addressed directly via controlled experimentation.

Rather than simply answering Q3 for a given software system, it would be of greater theoretical interest to determine what models are most useful in improving the accuracy with which analysts evaluate the dynamics of IS designs. In practice, however, it is not realistic to deliver models to a decision-maker without some mode of presentation, such as a particular software environment. Additionally, in a software environment providing access to a simulation model (i.e., a simulation environment), it is difficult to draw a sharp distinction between aspects of the environment that are providing the simulation model and aspects of the environment that are providing help in the use of the model and interpretation of its output.

In light of the theoretical and practical considerations, the following two research questions are posed as questions about a software environment such as the prototype CASE/simulation system:

Q4. Does a software environment providing queuing network simulation generated automatically from DFDs augmented with dynamics attributes, including expert help on simulation experiment design and output analysis, allow IS analysts to evaluate more accurately the dynamic performance of IS designs?

Q5. Which, if any, features of a software environment providing queuing network simulation generated automatically from DFDs augmented with dynamics attributes are associated with more accurate evaluation of the dynamic performance of IS designs?

This section describes experimentation addressing questions Q4 and Q5.

Method

Overview of Method. An important feature of the prototype CASE/simulation system is that its software environment can be invoked in one of two modes: (1) a mode that allows viewing of DFDs augmented with dynamics attributes, but provides no simulation capability; or, (2) a mode that, in addition to the DFD-viewing of mode 1, provides queuing network-based simulation of IS designs, including expert help on simulation experiment design and output analysis. From this feature of the prototype, we can define two experimental treatment levels.

Level A. Subjects answer questions about IS designs using the prototype in mode 1, where they are provided with DFDs annotated with dynamics information, but have no simulation capability.

Level B. Subjects answer questions about IS designs using the prototype in mode 2, where they are provided with DFDs annotated with dynamics information, queuing network-based simulation of the IS design represented in the DFD, and expert help on simulation experiment design and output analysis.

Subjects from a population of IS professionals answered a series of questions about the dynamics of IS designs. The subjects attempted to address various sets of questions at the two treatment levels. The observed mean difference in accuracy between treatment levels was expected to lead to the rejection of the null hypothesis that IS-dynamics evaluation accuracy measures are equal for treatment levels A and B. The usage of the software environment was also observed to support analysis of the association of aspects of tool usage with accuracy.

A repeated-measures design was used where each subject responds to each treatment level. Each subject analyzed and answered dynamics questions on four IS design cases, two cases at each level. A pilot version of this study has been conducted using IS graduate students as subjects (Warren, et al., 1992). Pilot study results are used as the basis for various assumptions in method[7].

Dependent Measures. The dependent measure for accuracy in assessment of IS dynamics is determined via subject responses to questions regarding the dynamics of IS designs. Each response receives an evaluation accuracy measure between 0 (poorest accuracy) and 1 (perfect accuracy). Eight questions are asked regarding each of four cases, resulting in a score between 0 and 8 for each case. One of the four cases and its associated dynamics questions is given in appendix A.

As subjects work to answer dynamics question, usage variables are collected to characterize the manner in which the software system is utilized. These variables include: (a) the number of simulation runs conducted, (b) the total duration of the simulation runs (in simulated weeks), (c) the total warm-up period duration (in simulated weeks), (d) the total number of replications, (e) the number of times the simulation run parameter help is consulted, (f) the number of times the simulation output help is consulted, (g) and the number of times the DFD viewer annotation is consulted. After each case, subjects rate their confidence in the accuracy of their responses to the dynamics questions on a seven-point scale.

The dynamics cases are evenly balanced between service and manufacturing. The first two dynamics cases (including the case given in appendix A) are based on illustrated cases in the IS textbook by Saldarini (1989). These cases concern a video-tape rental store and are representative of service-oriented systems. The second pair of cases concern a small high-tech manufacturing operation and are drawn from the authors' own experiences. All of the cases are somewhat modified from their original forms. In particular, the cases are simplified to make the assessment of their dynamics more feasible within the limiting time constraints given to the experimental subjects.

Eight dynamics questions are formulated for each case. The questions can be separated into four categories along two dimensions (see table 1). These dimensions are based upon the type of information required to answer the questions. A first dimension of dynamics question is *expected* versus *emergent*. *Expected* questions are concerned with issues of throughput, service times, utilizations, and operating times of processors, where processing dependencies are straightforward. *Expected* questions can be addressed using straight-forward analysis of the expected values of parameters of the queuing systems. *Emergent* questions are concerned with features of systems performance related to queuing: waiting times and queue lengths of jobs and customers, and system times, especially threads of processing (i.e., the amount of time needed for a job to traverse several connected processes). These questions require the information gathered during a simulation experiment (or in-depth analytic analysis) in order to formulate an answer. The second dimension is *simple* versus *composite*. A *simple* question requires the analysis of only a single server/queue system, whereas a *composite* question requires consideration of multiple server/queues. Each dynamics question can be categorized as *expected-simple, expected-composite, emergent-simple*, or *emergent-composite*. Two questions of each type are presented for each dynamics case.

In the illustrative case in appendix A, the return component of a video tape rental system, the first dynamics question concerns throughput. This is *expected-simple*, because the question can be answered through simple multiplication (arrival-rate times time-period) and requires only the consideration of one queuing system.

	Single Queuing system	Multiple Queuing systems
Simple analytic reasoning	Expected-simple	Expected-composite
Simulation results	Emergent-simple	Emergent-composite

Table 1. Four types of dynamics questions along two dimensions.

Question 3, concerning utilization, is *expected-composite*, because, although it can be solved using a simple set of multiplications and additions, it requires consideration of multiple server/queues (P2.1 and P2.2). The fifth and seventh questions involve the system times of jobs. These are both emergent, because the system time is effectively intractable to calculate analytically, requiring use of simulation results. Question 5 is *emergent-simple*, because only process P2.1 (a single server/queue system) must be considered once simulation results are utilized. The seventh question concerns the processing sequence of customer files; information from multiple server/queue systems must be considered, and therefore it is *emergent-composite*.

Dynamics questions are chosen to relate to concerns likely to arise due to the performance requirements of the analyzed system. For example, in the video tape return case, the questions focus on how long customers wait, how the clerk's time is spent, and how quickly inventory is returned to stock shelves. The responses to these questions characterize the system dynamics relevant to the adequacy of the design and the potential value of introducing further automation.

The response to a dynamics question is transformed to obtain an accuracy measure between zero and one. The accuracy measure is:

$$score = \left(1 - \left(\frac{\varepsilon}{\varepsilon + min(\Re, \hat{\mu})}\right)\right)^2 \qquad (1)$$

where ε is a measure of the error in the subject's response, $\Re$ is the subject's response, and $\hat{\mu}$ is an estimate of the true value. For emergent-type questions, any response within the 95% confidence interval offered by the simulation environment for 10 replications of a 10-week simulation run[8] is considered perfectly accurate (assigned an accuracy measure of unity). For these questions:

$$\varepsilon = \begin{cases} 0 & |\Re - \hat{\mu}| \le \delta_{95} \\ |\Re - \hat{\mu}| & else \end{cases} \qquad (2)$$

where δ_{95} is the half-width of the 95% confidence interval of the estimated actual value and $\hat{\mu}$ is the best estimate of the actual value (the center of the confidence interval). For expected-type questions, ε is simply $|\Re - \hat{\mu}|$ where $\hat{\mu}$ is the exact analytically-determined correct response.

Subjects. Twenty-one IS professionals from the Baltimore-Washington area participated in the present study. Participants are required to have at least three years professional experience. The volunteers had a mean of 8.5 years professional experience with information systems, were employed in various private companies, as well as state and federal government, and had jobs spanning all phases of the system development life-cycle (with systems analyst being the modal job title). Seventeen of the participant had at least a Bachelor's degree, and seven had at least a Master's degree.

Apparatus. The primary experimental apparatus is the prototype CASE/simulation system software and associated hardware. The experiment is conducted using six HP 9000 series workstations with 16-inch color screens running X11. At each experimental level, subjects are provided with two windows: (1) a DFD augmented with dynamics information describing the IS-dynamics case, and (2) a question-asking window querying the user about the dynamics of the IS design. Subjects are also provided with xcalc (a standard X11 utility that emulates a pocket-calculator), and paper and pencil. These two windows provide the subjects with the IS dynamics cases. In treatment level B subjects also receive the "Simulation Run Parameter Input" window (see figure 1), which provides access to IS design simulation and expert help in simulation usage and interpretation.

Procedure. Participation in the study took the form of an all-day workshop where subjects participate in a two-and-one-half-hour introductory session and two ninety-minute problem-solving sessions. During the introductory session, subjects develop a common baseline level of knowledge of modeling and simulation concepts, and work with the prototype on an introductory IS case. The two problem-solving sessions are completed during the day of the introductory session (one before, and one after lunch).

In each problem-solving session, subjects are presented with a description of an organization, and DFDs and corresponding data dictionary entries for two component systems of that organization (video tape rental in session 1, and manufacturing in session 2). Subjects are given up to 15 minutes to peruse these materials. After reading about the organization, subjects are presented with an IS design-dynamics case set in that organization. Subjects spend 30 minutes analyzing the case with the tools available (randomly treatment level A, no simulation, or B, simulation) to answer the dynamics questions on screen. The responses to the dynamics questions and the usage variables are recorded at the end of the session. Subjects are then given 5 minutes to fill out a "Problems & Suggestions" form. After a five-minute break, subjects are presented with another case (set in the same organization), given 30 minutes to answer the dynamics questions, and 5 minutes to fill out another

	Time ——>	
Ordering Group	Problem-solving Session 1	Problem-solving Session 2
	t_1 t_2	t_3 t_4
Group 0	A B	A B
Group 1	B A	B A

Table 2: Treatment Levels by Time for the Study

"Problems & Suggestions" form. At the end of each ninety-minute problem-solving session, subjects are given the worked solutions to the cases they had been analyzing.

Experimental Design. Learning effects over time are to be expected in this study, so the experimental design must address the order of presentation of the treatment levels. Table 2 shows the layout of a design that accounts for the carry-over effects of one treatment on the next (Stevens, 1986). Subjects are randomly assigned to one of two ordering groups. At time t_1, subjects randomly receive either case 1 or case 2 to analyze using either the treatment A environment (if they are in ordering group 0) or the treatment B environment (if they are in ordering group 1). At time t_2 (the second part of the first problem solving session), subjects receive either case 1 or 2, whichever they have not yet analyzed, using the treatment level A (if they are in ordering group 1) or B (if they are in ordering group 0) environment. In problem-solving session 2 (times t_3 and t_4) subjects analyze cases 3 and 4 in random order using treatment level A and B environments in the order determined by their ordering-group membership. In this design, the treatment effect is measured as the interaction of the ordering group membership and time.

One particular mode of analysis is to consider two effects:

γ_1: the improvement in accuracy from the first case of a problem-solving session to the second, the intra-session learning effect.
γ_2: the improvement in accuracy from treatment level A to level B.

We develop a single score for each participant by adding the scores in those cases where the subject experienced treatment level B and subtracting from that sum the scores achieved in the cases performed at level A. That is, for a subject in ordering group 0, their score α_0 is:

$$\alpha_0 = s(t_2) + s(t_4) - s(t_1) - s(t_3), \qquad (3)$$

where $s(t_i)$ is the sum of the accuracy scores achieved at time i.

The theoretical range for α_0 is from -16 to 16 if scores from all eight questions of each case are used, or from -8 to 8 if only the four emergent-type questions of each case are considered (i.e., the emergent-simple and emergent-composite questions). α_0 can be thought to measure the combined effect of learning and treatment, $\gamma_1 + \gamma_2$.

For a subject in ordering group 1, their score α_1 is:
$$\alpha_1 = s(t_1) + s(t_3) - s(t_2) - s(t_4). \qquad (4)$$

α_1 can be thought to measure the treatment effect minus the learning effect, $\gamma_1 - \gamma_2$. This leads to the following statistical null hypothesis:
$$H_0: \gamma_2 = (\alpha_0 + \alpha_1) / 2 = 0. \qquad (5)$$

This hypothesis is tested for: (a) the case where the $s(t_i)$'s are based on all eight dynamics questions, ranging from 0 to 8; and (b) the case where only the emergent-type dynamics question are considered in the $s(t_i)$'s, thereby giving a range from 0 to 4.

In the pilot study, H0 is not rejected using all dynamics questions. H_0 is rejected at the 1.63% level[9], however, for the emergent-type scores only. This is not a surprising result in that emergent-type questions are harder to address without simulation. Due to differences in procedure and population between the present study and the pilot (not to mention limited statistical power in the pilot), it is considered premature to dispose of the hypothesis regarding a treatment effect on all scores combined, expected and emergent. Both hypotheses are tested in the present study, with appropriate multiple-comparison adjustments to significance levels.

Note that, theoretically, the scores α_0 and α_1 are not normally distributed, because they have a limited possible range of values. In the pilot study, however, no observation approaches the limits of the range, and the statistical null hypothesis of normality is not rejected.

The above model is exactly equivalent to testing the interaction between ordering group and time, where time has two levels: (a) beginning of session, and (b) end of session. In other words, for each subject there are two scores, S_1 and S_2, where:
$$S_1 = s(t_1) + s(t_3), \text{ and } S_2 = s(t_2) + s(t_4). \qquad (6)$$

The interpretation of this model requires the assumption that the beginning-of-session versus end-of-session dimension is meaningful. A multivariate model that uses all four levels of time would be based upon less assumptions about the time dimension, in the sense that the two-levels-of-time model discards some information about the correlations among the $s(t_i)$'s. The four-levels-of-time model, however, requires more statistical assumptions than the two-levels-of-time model, which reduces to a simple 2-by-2 design[10]. The pilot study results show both the two-and four-levels-of-time models yielding better than 5% significance for the treatment effect on accuracy scores of emergent-type questions, although the two-level-of-time model appears more powerful (giving a 1.63% level of significance versus a 2.63% significance with the four-levels-of-time model). Both the two-and four-levels-of-times models are considered in the "Results" sub-section.

In the pilot study, subjects that perform a total of more than two simulation runs during the procedure have higher scores on emergent-type questions (summed over the two cases where simulation was available) than those who perform two or less simulation runs. This, *multiple simulation-run effect*, effect is significant in the pilot study at the 5% level and is tested on the current study's observations. Multiple regression is used to analyze the relationship between accuracy scores and usage variables in greater detail. Note that, except for testing of the multiple simulation-run effect, the usage-variable analysis is exploratory in nature. The intention is to build models for future experimental verification, rather than to test the statistical significance with which particular null hypotheses can be rejected.

Results

Treatment Effect on Response Accuracy. Figures 9 and 10 show the overall accuracy scores (i.e., accuracy scores summed over all eight questions of a case) for the subjects in ordering groups 0 and 1, respectively. The heights of the bars indicate the general trends within ordering groups (i.e., aggregated over all the subjects). Table 3 shows the means and standard deviations of overall scores at times 1 through 4, and for the sum of the scores at times 1 and 3 (beginning-of-session), and times 2 and 4 (end-of-session), by ordering group. It can be seen that the overall trend is as predicted, subjects score higher at treatment level B (times 2 and 4 for ordering group 0, and times 1 and 3 for ordering group 1). Specific scores are not always in the direction of the trend. For instance, case 1 shows a decrease in score from time 3 (treatment level A) to time 4 (level B). This is counter to the expected positive sign of both the treatment and learning effects. Note that the decrease in mean scores between times 1 and 2 (session 1) versus times 3 and 4 (session 2) is not counter to an expected learning effect, because cases are not randomized between sessions 1 and 2.

Two modes of analysis of the treatment significance are considered: the two-levels-of-time, and four-levels-of-time approaches (as defined in the "Method" sub-section). For the two-levels-of-time approach, the statistical assumptions of independence of observa-

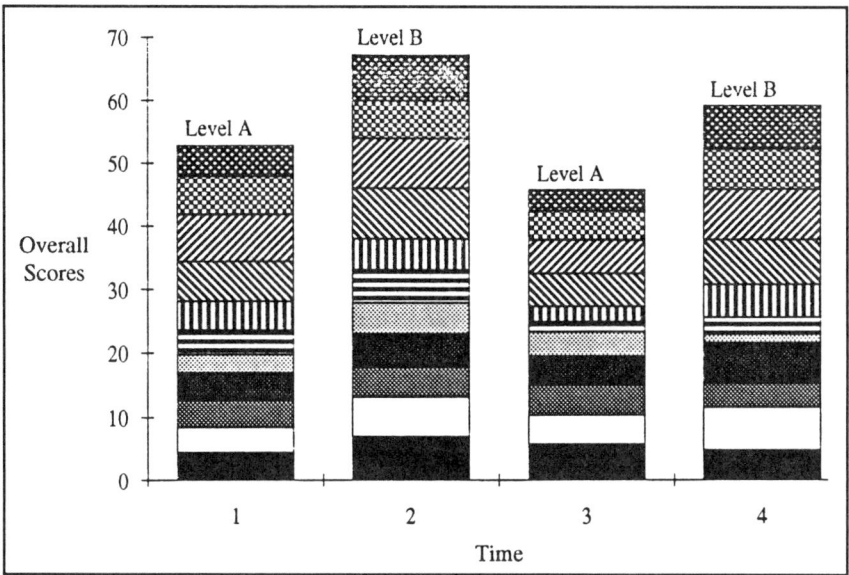

Figure 9: Overall accuracy scores for the 11 subjects in ordering group 0. Individual scores are indicated by different shading patterns.

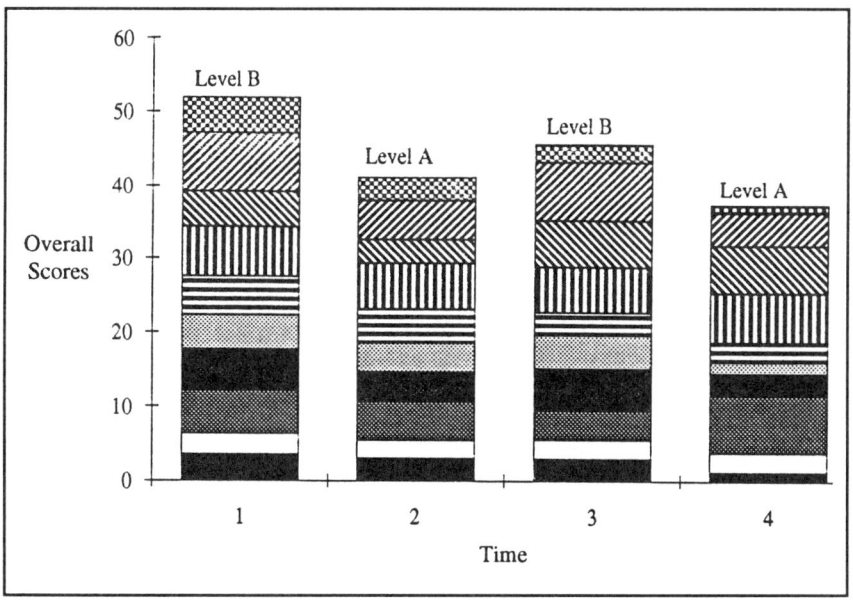

Figure 10: Overall accuracy scores for the 10 subjects in ordering group 1. Individual scores are indicated by different shading patterns.

Ordering Group	Time	Mean	Standard Deviation
0	t_1	4.81	1.30
	t_2	6.11	1.26
	t_3	4.16	1.26
	t_4	5.35	2.06
	$t_1 + t_3$	8.96	2.16
	$t_2 + t_4$	11.45	3.11
1	t_1	5.19	1.49
	t_2	4.12	1.24
	t_3	4.56	1.88
	t_4	3.74	2.45
	$t_1 + t_3$	9.75	3.19
	$t_2 + t_4$	7.86	3.36

Table 3: Observed means and standard deviations of overall accuracy scores by ordering group and time.

tions, multivariate normality, and homogeneity of variance must be addressed. Independence of observations is satisfied by the random assignment of participants to ordering groups. Testing the normality of the marginal distributions over time (beginning-of-session versus end-of-session) and ordering group with the Shapiro-Wilks test (SAS Institute Inc., 1989) reveals no significant violations of normality. Note that non-graphical tests of normality are favored due to the small sample size. Homogeneity of variance in each of the four cells (2 levels of time by 2 ordering groups) is tested using Bartlett's test (Walpole & Myers, 1985), and the homogeneity of variance hypothesis is not rejected.

With assumptions verified, the null hypothesis of no treatment effect on accuracy scores can be tested. This test can take the form of the probability of a true value of zero for the estimated effect, g2, or, equivalently, as the significance of the interaction of two-level time (within subjects) by ordering group. The null hypothesis of no treatment effect is rejected with an F of 19.72 with 1 numerator and 19 denominator degrees of freedom, which is significant at the 0.03% level. The estimate for γ_2 is 2.195, amounting to an effect half that size for overall accuracy scores per case (range 0 to 8).

For the four-levels-of-time approach, treatment significance is assessed with a univariate repeated measures model[11]. Testing the normality of the marginal distributions reveals no significant violations of normality. Heterogeneity of variance is observed (see table 3); however, Maxwell and Delaney (1990) note that ANOVA is robust to moderate violations of homogeneity of variance if group sizes are equal and not less than 5^{12}. Sphericity is violated by Mauchly's criterion (1.19% significance), therefore e-adjustment of the F statistic of the univariate repeated measures ANOVA is appropriate (Maxwell & Delaney; SAS Institute Inc.) . The null hypothesis of no four-level-time by order interaction is rejected with an F of 7.28 with 3 numerator and 57 denominator degrees of freedom, adjusted by a Huynh-Feldt ε of 0.8318, which is significant at the 0.08% level.

Figures 11 and 12 show the emergent-type accuracy scores (i.e., accuracy scores summed over questions 5 through 8 of a case) for the subjects in ordering groups 0 and 1, respectively. The heights of the bars indicate the general trends within ordering groups. Table 4 shows the means and standard deviations of emergent scores at times 1 through 4, and for the sum of the scores at times 1 and 3 (beginning-of-session), and times 2 and 4 (end-of-session), by ordering group. It can be seen that the trend is the same as with the overall scores: subjects score higher at treatment level B. The treatment level B advantage is more acute for ordering group 0 than ordering group 1, particularly for session 2. This is to be expected, because the learning effect, γ_1, complements the treatment effect in ordering group 0, but runs counter to it in ordering group 1.

The two-levels-of-time and four-levels-of-time approaches are considered for assessment of the treatment effect on emergent-type

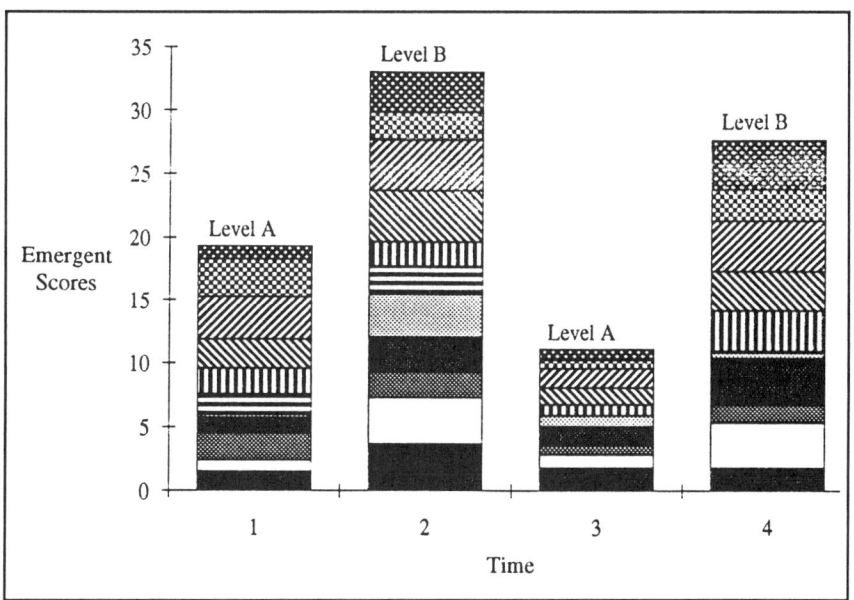

Figure 11: Accuracy scores on emergent-type questions for the 11 subjects in ordering group 0. Individual scores are indicated by different shading patterns.

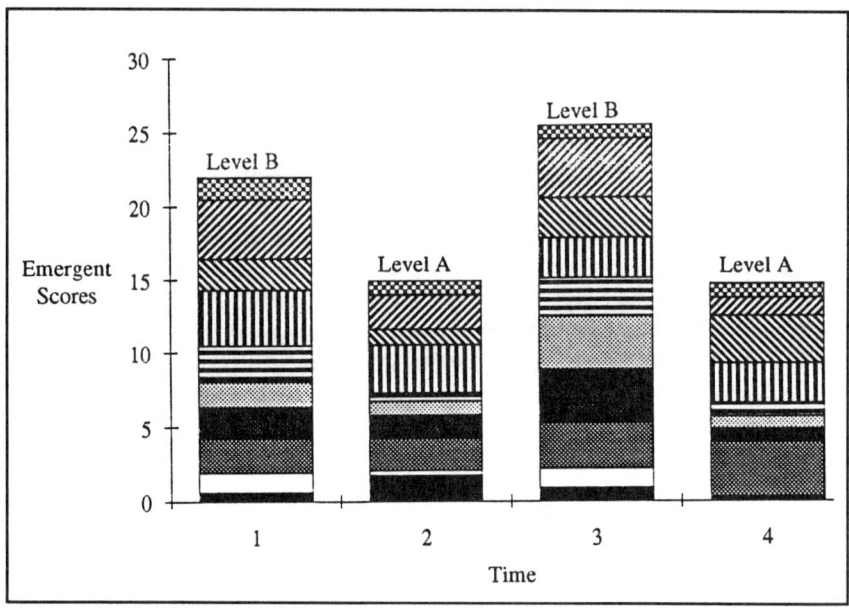

Figure 12: Accuracy scores on emergent-type questions for the 10 subjects in ordering group 1. Individual scores are indicated by different shading patterns.

Ordering Group	Time	Mean	Standard Deviation
0	t_1	1.75	0.92
	t_2	3.01	0.80
	t_3	1.01	0.49
	t_4	2.49	1.37
	$t_1 + t_3$	2.77	1.08
	$t_2 + t_4$	5.50	1.81
1	t_1	2.20	1.05
	t_2	1.49	0.90
	t_3	2.54	1.14
	t_4	1.47	1.28
	$t_1 + t_3$	4.74	2.01
	$t_2 + t_4$	2.96	1.90

Table 4. Observed means and standard deviations of emergent-type accuracy scores by ordering group and time.

accuracy scores. For the two-levels-of-time approach, statistical assumptions are not violated. The null hypothesis of no treatment effect on emergent-type accuracy scores, formulated as a test of the interaction of two-level time with ordering group, is rejected with an F of 36.17 with 1 numerator and 19 denominator degrees of freedom, which is significant at the 0.01% level. The estimate for γ_2 is 2.255, amounting to an effect half that size for emergent-type accuracy scores per case (range 0 to 4).

For the four-levels-of-time approach, treatment significance is assessed with a univariate repeated measures model. Testing of the multivariate normality assumption results in the null hypothesis of normality being rejected in most of the marginal distributions. Distributional transforms suggested in Stevens (p. 211) lead to the use of the arcsine-of-the-square-root transform to bring the emergent-type scores to normality. That is, for each subject i at time j, their emergent score E_{ij} is transformed to E^*_{ij}, where:

$$E^*_{ij} = \sin^{-1}(E_{ij}/4)^{1/2} \qquad (8)$$

The transform brings the scores into compliance with the normality assumption. The homogeneity of variance among the eight cells (4 levels of time by 2 ordering groups) is not rejected. Sphericity is not violated by Mauchly's criterion (57.49% significance), therefore ε-adjustment of the F statistic of the univariate repeated measures ANOVA is not necessary. The null hypothesis of no four-level-time by order interaction is rejected with an F of 15.48 with 3 numerator and 57 denominator degrees of freedom, which is significant at the 0.01% level[13].

To summarize the treatment effect on accuracy, the null hypothesis of no treatment effect on overall accuracy scores is rejected at better than the 1% level, and the null hypothesis of no treatment effect on emergent-type accuracy scores is rejected at better than the 0.05% level. Using the more conservative 4-level-of-time model, multiplying the test significance by two for each of (a) moderate violation of homogeneity of variance, (b) use of two models (two-levels and four-level of time), and (c) multiple comparison (overall and emergent-type scores), yields rejection of the null hypothesis of no treatment effect on overall accuracy scores at the 0.64% level. The estimated treatment effect size on overall accuracy scores is 1.10 on an eight-point accuracy scale. Multiplying the test significance by two for each of (a) use of two models (two-levels and four-level of time), and (b) multiple comparison (overall and emergent-type scores), yields rejection of the null hypothesis of no treatment effect on emergent-type scores at the 0.04% level. The estimated treatment effect size on emergent-type accuracy scores is 1.13 on a four-point accuracy scale, apparently accounting for all of the treatment effect on overall scores. There is no significant observed treatment effect on expected-type accuracy scores.

The accuracy scores are defined in terms of subjects' responses to dynamics questions as shown in equations 1 and 2. Three alternative formulations of accuracy scores are:

$$score_1 = \left(1 - \left(\frac{\varepsilon}{\varepsilon + min(\Re, \hat{\mu})}\right)\right) \tag{9}$$

$$score_2 = e^{-\varepsilon / min(\Re, \hat{\mu})} \tag{10}$$

$$score_3 = e^{-2\varepsilon / min(\Re, \hat{\mu})} \tag{11}$$

Score types 1 and 2 are more "lenient" than the definition from equations 1 and 2 (hereafter, score0); that is, these formulae return higher values for errors of equal magnitude (except for zero errors or zero responses, which result in accuracy scores of 1 and 0, respectively, for all four scoring methods). $Score_3$ is less lenient than $score_0$. Table 5 shows the results of testing the significance of the treatment effect for overall and emergent-type scores using the two-levels-of-time model with each of the four accuracy definitions. The significance of the treatment effect appears relatively tolerant to alternative accuracy definitions, although the F's are noticeably higher under

Accuracy Scoring Method (from most lenient to least lenient)	F (significance of F) for Treatment Effect (two-levels-of-time model)	
	Overall	Emergent
$score_1 = \left(1 - \left(\frac{\varepsilon}{\varepsilon + min(\Re, \hat{\mu})}\right)\right)$	23.78 (0.01%)	39.14 (0.01%)
$score_2 = e^{-\varepsilon / min(\Re, \hat{\mu})}$	20.97 (0.02%)	35.27 (0.01%)
$score_0 = \left(1 - \left(\frac{\varepsilon}{\varepsilon + min(\Re, \hat{\mu})}\right)\right)^2$	19.56 (0.03%)	36.17 (0.01%)
$score_3 = e^{-2\varepsilon / min(\Re, \hat{\mu})}$	17.27 (0.05%)	31.86 (0.01%)

Table 5. F's (and significances) of treatment effects on overall and emergent-type accuracy scores tested with the two-levels-of-time model using four definitions of accuracy.

the most lenient accuracy formula and lower under the least lenient.

Software System Usage Analysis. Figure 13 graphs mean expected, emergent, and overall accuracy scores summed over the 2 cases performed at treatment level B by total number of simulation runs conducted, NRUN. Performing ANOVA on the difference on emergent-type accuracy scores between the group that performs more than 2 simulation runs at treatment level B versus the group that performs a total of 2 or less simulation runs yields an F of 4.74 with 1 denominator and 19 numerator degrees of freedom, which is significant at the 4.23% level. The same ANOVA on overall scores is not significant at the 5% level.

Performing linear regression of the total number of simulation runs conducted at treatment level B on accuracy scores yields significant regression lines. Regression on overall scores gives an estimated slope of 0.92 points per simulation run conducted with an intercept of 7.02. The regression is significant at the 0.36% level (F = 11.039 with 1 and 19 degrees of freedom), and explains 33.42% of the variance in overall scores. Figure 14 plots the regression line against the observations. Regression on emergent scores gives a slope of 0.56 points per simulation run with an intercept of 2.92. This regression is significant at the 0.26% level (F = 12.035), explains 35.56% of the variance in emergent accuracy scores, and is plotted against the observations in figure 15.

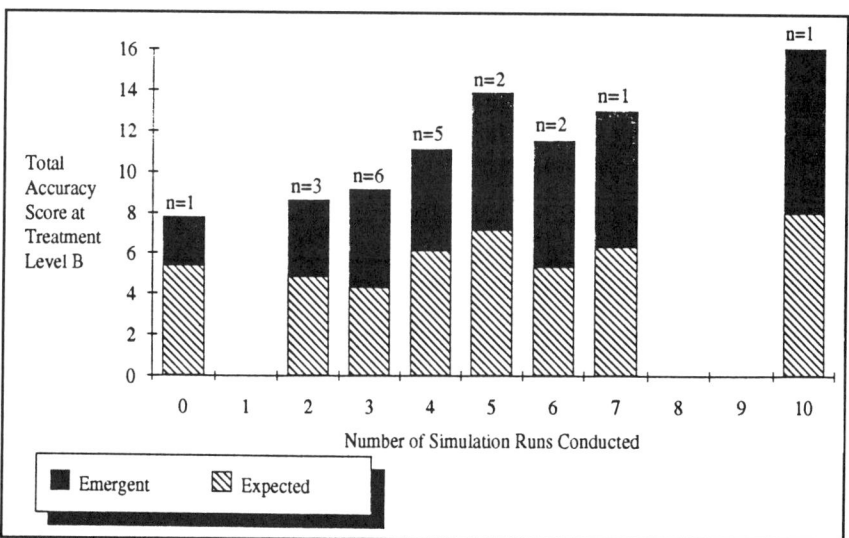

Figure 13: Mean expected, emergent, and overall (as sum of expected and emergent) accuracy scores summed over the 2 cases performed at treatment level B by number of simulation runs conducted.

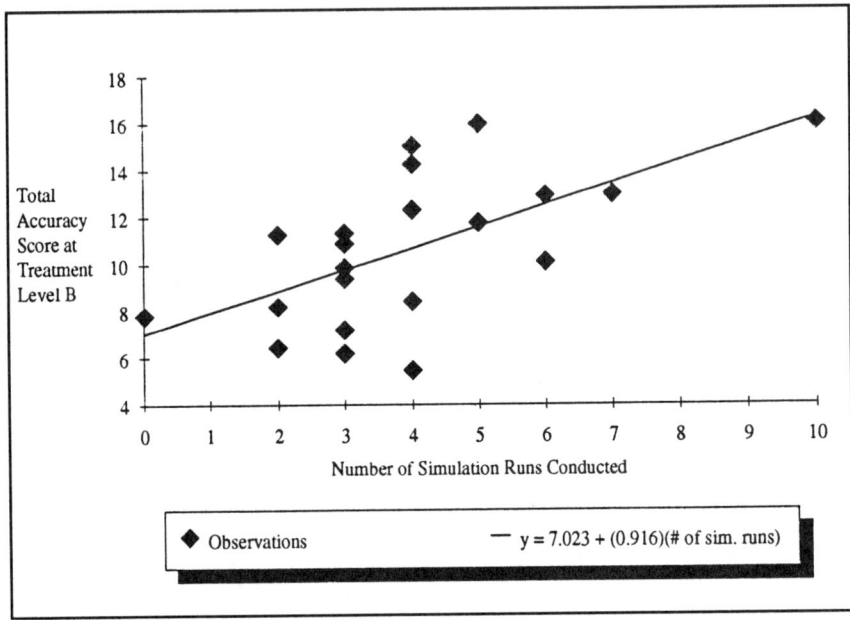

Figure 14: Linear regression of number of simulation runs conducted at treatment level B on overall accuracy scores.

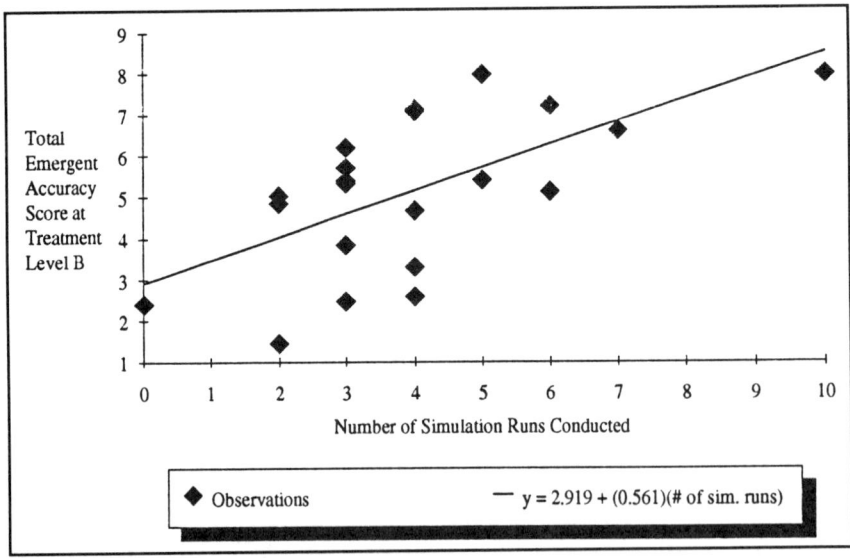

Figure 15: Linear regression of number of simulation runbs conducted at treatment level B on emergent-type accuracy scores.

The total number of weeks simulation, SIMTOT, is highly correlated with NRUN. SIMTOT is a more informative variable, because subsequent simulation runs tend to be longer than initial runs (to achieve narrower confidence intervals). Modeling emergent-type scores in session 2 as a linear function of SIMTOT results in a regression R^2 of 0.3914 with a nominal significance of 0.14%. The residual errors from the regression show a marked heterogeneity of variance in that the lower predicted values have greater error variance. This situation is improved by regressing on the log or square-root of SIMTOT. The cube-root is found to be slightly superior to the log or square-root for this case, yielding an R^2 of 0.5987, nominal significance 0.01%.

Survey Results. Responses to the multiple choice question on the "Problems & Suggestions" form regarding confidence in accuracy of responses are coded as integers in the range 1 to 7. The confidence ratings data significantly violate normality, and analysis of correlations using Kendall's tau-b (a non-parametric measure of association based on numbers of concordant and discordant pairs of observations) is used instead of ANOVA. Table 6 shows correlation of confidence ratings with ordering group. The signs of all eight coefficients favor treatment level B as increasing confidence (positive at t_1 and t_3 when ordering group 1 has simulation capability, and negative at t_2 and t_4 when ordering group 0 has simulation capability). The correlation of treatment with confidence is significant (5% level) at t_1, t_3, and t_4, but not t_2.

Summary of Experimental Findings

The primary experimental objective was to assess the effect of the features of the prototype (simulation capability and intelligent help) on the accuracy with which IS professionals could assess performance-related characteristics of IS designs. Twenty-one IS professionals answered eight questions about each of four IS design

Variable	Time	Correlation Coefficient	Significance
Confidence in	1	0.437	3.66%
Accuracy	2	-0.220	32.53%
	3	0.594	0.67%
	4	-0.455	4.47%

Table 6. Correlation (Kendall's tau b and its two-tailed significance) of confidence ratings with ordering group.

cases. The questions were of two types: (a) expected-type questions are concerned with issues of throughput, service times, utilizations, and operating times of processors; whereas (b) emergent-type questions are concerned with aspects of systems performance related to queuing, waiting times and queue lengths of jobs and customers, system times (especially threads of processing, such as the amount of time needed for a job to traverse several connected processes), and operating times of processes where processing dependencies are complex. The observed treatment effect (i.e., the effect of the simulation and help features of the prototype) is to improve accuracy of responses to emergent-type questions about IS designs, while the accuracy of responses to expected-type questions was unchanged. The observed treatment effect on emergent-type scores is 1.13 points out of a possible 4 points per case. To exemplify the meaning of this effect size, an improvement of 1.13 points would result if one response that is in error by a factor of 2, and a second response in error by a factor of 1.27 are both corrected to perfectly accurate responses. Thus, the observed benefit of the availability of the prototype's capabilities can be characterized as equivalent to one major correction and one minor correction on a battery of four questions concerning queuing-related dynamics. The effect is stable over a variety of possible methods of scoring accuracy of responses and is statistically significant at better than the 1% level. The findings strongly support the assertion that the prototype allows IS professionals to achieve more accurate assessment of IS design performance characteristics.

A secondary experimental objective was to observe specific features of the prototype whose use was correlated with better assessment of IS design dynamics. The intention was to provide support for future prototype developments and fuel further research hypotheses. The number of simulation runs conducted (subjects had the ability to run as many simulations as time permitted, if they wished) is positively correlated with accuracy of responses. Linear regression on accuracy as a function of the number of simulation runs conducted shows scores to improve by almost one point (on a 16 point scale) per simulation run[14]. The regression line explains one-third of the variance in individual accuracy scores and is significant at better than the 1% level. The findings suggest that the prototype should be enhanced to encourage users to use simulation more-extensively.

CONCLUSIONS

Direct production of IS design dynamics simulations from annotated DFDs allows the developer to gain the benefits of simulation without side-tracking to code a simulation in a 4GL or to re-encode the design structure in a specialized notation. This chapter describes a prototype simulation environment to support the dynamic modeling of information systems designs from DFD-based system descriptions. In addition to producing stochastic (i.e., random-number based) simulations automatically from DFDs, the prototype provides a model for simulation usage, and aids in the interpretation of simulation results. The prototype uses a custom DFD-drawing utility to demonstrate the feasibility of the approach. The most beneficial configuration would be one in which the DFD-drawing capability and data dictionary of an integrated CASE workbench are used to supply the system structure for simulation, allowing immediate assessment of the dynamics of proposed designs directly from conventional IS design tools. Application to IS designs, such as the example in section 3, shows that the prototype greatly facilitates testing of a set of component processes' ability to meet overall performance requirements. Furthermore, the prototype provides a powerful "what-if" capability, enabling analysts to consider the benefits and feasibility of variations in an IS design.

A first criterion of success of the prototype is that IS developers make more accurate assessments of the dynamics of IS designs than they would without access to the features of the environment. If this is not accomplished, then there is no mechanism to accomplish the higher goal of the prototype design effort: to support IS developers in the design of systems that better meet their performance-related requirements. The simulation capability of the prototype, including its knowledge-based help features, was manipulated in an experimental context to determine its impact on the accuracy of responses to questions about the dynamics of IS designs. The experimental treatment (i.e., the effect of the manipulated features of the prototype) was observed to improve accuracy of responses to emergent-type questions (questions concerned with queuing of jobs or customers). The observed effect of the prototype can be characterized as equivalent to one major correction and one minor correction on a battery of four quantitative questions concerning queuing-related dynamics of an IS design.

The experimental findings provide a basis for claiming that embedding the prototype's capabilities in a CASE workbench would result in better-designed systems. Simulation capability as delivered by the prototype will lead to more accurate assessment of the dynamics of IS designs where queuing is a factor. The IS cases used in this study illustrate well the variety of ways in which queuing is relevant to service and manufacturing sector systems[15]. Queuing statistics are central to quantifying customer waiting times, manufacturing lead times, numbers of jobs in progress, the time for detection of errors and defects, the time for processing a request, and the time merchandise lays idle before being made available to customers — quantities critical to the acceptability of modern, non-batch information systems. A factor-of-two error in the assessment of one of these quantities for an IS design can easily lead to an unacceptable system. Correcting such an assessment error early in the design phase is a highly desirable goal.

The findings substantiate the importance of vendor's overcoming the barriers to implementation of a full-scale (i.e., non-prototype) CASE/simulation system; that is, by creating a CASE workbench with features that include automatic simulation of design performance from the CASE-tool data dictionary. Boehm (1976) showed (based on experiences at TRW) the cost of correcting a software error at the acceptance testing phase of the system development life-cycle (SDLC) is 10 times as high as correcting an error in the design phase. The goal of early error correction, as a means of achieving low-cost and reliable software development, is central to software engineering (and computer-aided software engineering). The experimental results provide clear evidence that the prototype's simulation capability prevents errors in the assessment of system dynamics that are made in the absence of this ability. Simulation allows the study of system dynamics in the design phase, rather than (at best) in the acceptance testing phase via benchmarking and observation. CASE/simulation accomplishes fundamental software engineering goals by moving the detection of errors in system performance assessment forward in the SDLC.

A second facet of the findings is that more extensive use of simulation is strongly correlated with the accuracy of decisions. The results favor the idea that stochastic simulation environments should support an iterative use of simulation. This result is suggestive for all applications of computer simulation to decision support. Unfortunately, the level of simulation use (beyond the availability of simulation versus its absence) is not manipulated in the present study. For example, the results do not rule out that the subjects which use simulation more actively and score higher, would score higher even if simulation use is limited to a single simulation run. Related open questions are whether there would be benefit in encouraging subjects to use simulation more actively (beyond the encouragement already provided by the prototype's relatively passive on-line help system); whether the availability of on-line help affects accuracy; and whether an automated algorithm for conducting simulation runs of an appropriate length (as dictated by heuristics) would yield results as good as, or better than, manual specification of simulation run parameters. Experimental results explicitly addressing these questions would give a clear design directive to CASE/simulation developers, and would be a factor for consideration by implementors of simulation environments in all application areas. The investigation of hypotheses regarding the decision-support impact of simulation usage is a promising direction for future research.

The method pursued in this study illustrates the importance, the benefits, and the difficulties of using laboratory experiments to validate the utility of CASE tools. CASE tools are used by people; and, lacking a complete mathematical model of human behavior, experimentation (in a laboratory or field setting) is the only method by which the effectiveness of the interaction of people (i.e., IS developers) and novel tools can be measured. The prototype CASE/simulation system was designed in accordance with trends found in the literature and practice, yet the prototype's effectiveness varies dramatically depending on the particular variety of dynamics question (expected versus emergent, as defined in section 4) the user is attempting to answer. Through experimentation, the usefulness of the tool was verified, and the particular types of problems for which it is more or less effective were identified. Additionally, experimentation can point out features of tools, and ways of using tools, which are associated with success. This can lead to theories about how to reliably design good tools, and moreover, how to design better tools.

Laboratory experiments have several drawbacks. Conducting an experiment in CASE requires the effort of numerous participants. For an experiment to be valid, the participants must be representative of the population for which the results are presumed to hold. Therefore, experiments in CASE should be conducted using high-caliber IS professionals, and this is an expensive proposition. Experiments can test only a limited number of hypotheses at a time (the number of participants needed expand rapidly as the number of hypotheses expands). Also, one must be very cautious in generalizing the results of experimentation to contexts and tasks outside those used in the study. For example, in the pilot study, the prototype users were given less time per case (20 minutes instead of 30 minutes), and the observed treatment effect (i.e., the benefit from simulation) was substantially less significant. Due to these limitations of the method, developing theories that reliably predict the benefits of tools over a reasonably broad range of users, tasks, and task durations requires a series of experiments. Additionally, experimentation requires the development of measures of success. Measures of software productivity, error rates, or number of correct decisions are some possible measures. For the present study, accuracy was used as a measure of success, requiring the proposal of an accuracy measure and verification that the results are insensitive over a variety of reasonable definitions of the accuracy metric. Finally, designing an experiment to test a theory about CASE tools and correctly interpreting its results requires a non-trivial knowledge of statistics. For all of these reasons, laboratory studies are very rare in CASE; however, the author believes that the benefits outweigh the costs for the long-term growth of the field.

The two major directions for future CASE/simulation research relate to: (a) making the technology applicable for widespread real-world use, and (b) gaining deeper understanding of how to use stochastic simulation as a decision aid for IS professionals. The barriers to real-world CASE/simulation include: (a) extending the DFD-based notation (as described in section 3) to express all relevant dynamics of a broad class of full-scale IS designs, (b) the automatic mapping of this extended notation to a simulation model, and (c) expanding the output functions to include currently unavailable features such as queuing statistics for specific times of day, graphics, and animation. Deeper research into stochastic simulation as an IS design aid entails: (a) further experiments to determine the interaction of simulation capability with the IS design process (i.e., beyond the evaluation of single designs), (b) investigation of the invariance of the present study's results for larger IS design problems, (c) experiments to identify the value of specific features of a simulation environment (such as knowledge-based help in the forms of confidence interval generation, on-line definitions, and warnings of possible processing bottlenecks), and (d) application of further simulation and operations research principles to achieve higher levels of automation in the IS design process. Of particular interest to the author is the use of goal programming to automatically identify satisfactory IS designs from a large set of possible designs.

APPENDIX A: A SAMPLE CASE

For each cases, subjects are presented with a textual description of the system, a DFD, and an associated data dictionary. After perusing these materials, they are presented with eight dynamics questions to answer to the best of their ability.

System Description

The video tape rental store currently uses a primarily manual information system in its dealings with customers. For each member, a membership envelope is maintained in a customer file. Whenever a member rents or returns video tapes, their membership envelope is pulled from the customer file and updated with information regarding the transaction. When customers rent tapes, the rental clerk fills out a rental agreement form. Copies of the form are given to the customer, placed in the order book, and placed in the customer's membership envelope. When the customer returns the rented inventory, the customer presents their copy of the rental agreement and pays for the rental. The return clerk removes the copy of the rental agreement from the membership envelope and disposes of it, initials the copy in the order book, and initials and returns the customer's copy of the agreement to act as a receipt.

You should have a DFD and data dictionary entries for the return component of the video tape rental system. All entities in the return component are numbered 2.x. Customers arrive to the return desk randomly (inter-arrival times following the ex-ponential distribution) at an average rate of 1 every 4 minutes during the operating hours, noon to 8 PM weekdays. Customers present the return clerk with their pink customer copy of the rental agreement and payment along with the rental inventory. The rental clerk accepts these items and pulls the customer's membership envelope from the customer file (requiring a total of one minute, distributed exponentially). The clerk then performs the return processing, removing the gold copy of the rental agreement from the membership envelope and disposing of it, placing the payment in the cash drawer, returning the inventory to the shelving bin, pulling the appropriate white copy of the rental agreement from the order book, initialing it, and returning it to the order book, and initialing and returning the customer's pink copy. This return processing requires a mean of 1.75 minutes, distributed normally with a standard deviation of 0.5 minutes. At the end of the day, the return clerk re-shelves the inventory in the shelving bin, returning it to the stock shelves (requiring 0.3 to 0.7 minutes per customer return). After re-shelving inventory, the clerk re-files the membership envelopes in the customer file (requiring 30 seconds per job, distributed exponentially).

Data Dictionary

Data dictionary entries annotated with dynamics information,

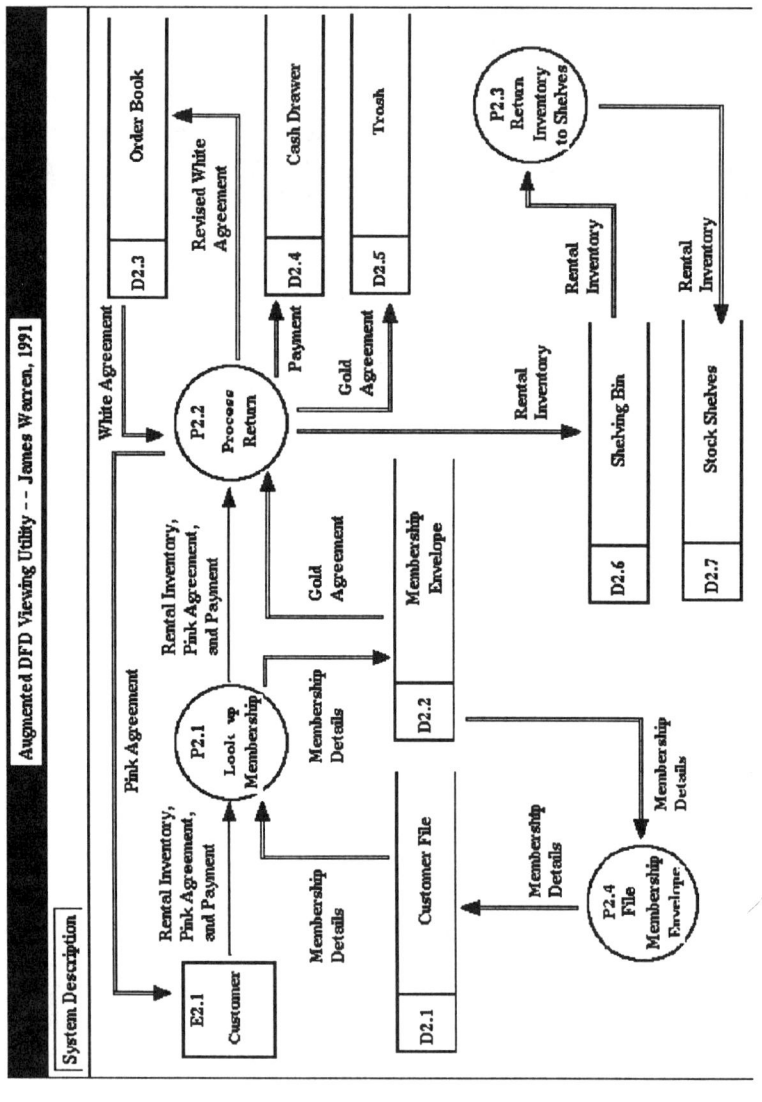

Figure A.1: DFD of the return component of a video tape rental system.

such as this entry for process P2.1, are given for each DFD process, external entity, data store, and data flow corresponding to the elements shown in the DFD in figure A.1.

```
NAME:            P2.1: Look-up Membership
INPUT:           E2.1: Customer
                 D2.1: Customer File
OUTPUT:          P2.2: Process Return
                 D2.2: Membership Envelope
JOB DURATION:    1.00 minutes/job, distributed exponentially.
                 Processor waits for completion of job at output
                 process before continuing to next job.
PROCESSORS:      1 unit: Mon-Fri  12:00-20:00 and idle
DESCRIPTION:     Return clerk accepts inventory, form, and payment
                 from customer and pulls their membership
                 envelope from the customer file.
```

Dynamics Questions

1. How many membership envelopes does the clerk re-file at the end of each day?
2. How long does the clerk work each week at placing returned inventory on the stock shelves?
3. What is the utilization (in percent) of the return clerk at P2.1?
4. How long does a customer spend being serviced at the return desk (excluding time waiting in line)?
5. How long does a customer spend at the return desk (including time waiting in line)?
6. How long is the line at the return desk (excluding the customer being serviced)?
7. How much time elapses between the time a customer's membership envelope is pulled from the customer file (at the beginning of customer service at P2.1) and the re-filing of the envelope in the customer file?
8. How much time elapses between the time a customer begins service at the return desk (P2.1) and the placement of the returned inventory on the stock shelves?

ACKNOWLEDGMENT
Special thanks are owed to those who volunteered their valuable time to participate in this study, to my doctoral dissertation advisor, Dr. A. F. Norcio, to my dissertation committee members, to Dr. N. Nagaraj for patient discussion of experimental design alternatives, and to the University of Maryland Baltimore County Academic Computing Services for their excellent support, including provision of facilities for the primary experiment.

ENDNOTES

1 X Window System and X11 are trademarks of the Massachusetts Institute of Technology.

2 The implementation of a custom DFD-drawing utility is expedient for creating an integrated environment. Further, a highly-controllable DFD editor is desirable for suporting the laboratory experimentation described in this chapter

3 Such a modification could be accomplished with the Excelerator "Customizer" application.

4 This example was originally shown in Warren, Stott, and Norcio (1992a); and, although inspired by a real manufacturer, is contrived for illustrative purposes.

5 Note that labor expenses can be assessed by multiplying hourly personnel costs by the operating time figures provided in the simulation output.

6 As currently specified, however, a bottleneck would develop at P2 if manufacturing produced one unit every 5 minutes.

7 The results of the experimentaiton reported here are also reported by Warren, Norcio, Stott, and Canfield (to appear). The method (including all dynamics cases and quesitons, and handouts to subjects) and results (including individual responses to questions) are described completely in Warren (1992).

8 An arbitrary standard for an extensive simulation experiment.

9 Note that the pilot study was exploratory in nature. The significance level of a test in the pilot study is merely a numerical indicator, and is not intended to be presented as proof of any theory.

10 See the "method" section of Warren (1992) for more on comparison of the technical merits of the two- and four-levels-of-time models.

11 Either a univariate or multivariate repeated measures model could be used. Stevens discusses the relative merits of the univariate and multivariatpproaches and concludes: (a) whev e-adjustment of the degrees of freedom is used in the univariate approach, there is no difference in the ability of the approaches to control the type I error rate; and (b) which method may be more powerful varies with subtleties in the data, and using both approaches (with appropriate adjustment of the significance level) may be advisable in exploratory studies. For simplicity, the univariate approach is ued.

12 When the groups with smaller variances have larger samples, the actual type I error rate is higher than the nominal rate. For the present data, the group sizes are nearly equal (10 versus 11) and the degree of heterogeneity is moderate. From examples given in Maxwell and Delaney, the type I error rate should be inflated by much less than a factor of 2. Thus, univariate analysis proceeds with a cautious eye toward the type I error rate, buth without transforming the data into a less interpretable form.

13 It is interesting to note that if the untransformed emergent scores are used in this analysis: (a) homogeneity of variance is not rejected, (b) sphericity is not violated (53.76% significance for Mauchly's criterion), and (c) the null hypothesis of no four-level-time by order interaction is rejected with an F of 15.70 with 3 numerator and 57 denominator degrees of freedom, which is significant at the 0.01% level. The results are essentially identical to those found with the transformed scores, and cast doubt on the necessity of using a transform.

14 Equivalent to correcting one factor-of-two error and one factor-of-1.15 error to perfect accuracy in response to a battery of sixteen quantitative questions regarding two IS design cases.

15 Excerpts of one of the four IS design cases are given in Appendix A. All four cases are given in complete detail in Warren (1992).

REFERENCES

Ammar, R. (1991). A computer aided design system to develop high performance software. *J. Systems & Software*, 15, 139-147.

Babin, G., Lustman, F., & Shoval, P. (1991). Specification and design of transactions in information systems: A formal approach. *IEEE Trans. Software Engineering*, SE-17, 814-829.

Balci, O., & Nance, R. (1987). Simulation model development environments: A research prototype. *J. Operational Research Soc.*, 38, 753-763.

Boehm, B. (1976). Software engineering. IEEE Trans. Computer, Dec., 225-240. Boydstun, L., Teichroew, D., Spewak, S., Yamamoto, Y., & Starner, G. (1980). Computer aided modeling of information systems. In, *Proc. IEEE COMPSAC 80* (pp. 37-41).

CACI. (1987). *SIMSCRIPT II.5 programming language*. Los Angeles: CACI.

Date, C. (1986). On the performance of relational database systems. In, *Relational DataBase: Selected Readings*. Addison-Wesley.

Eich, M., Fan, C., Sun, W., & Rafiqi, S. (1989). A methodology for simulation of database systems. Simulation, June, 241-254.

France, R. (1992). Semantically extended data flow diagrams: A formal specification tool. *IEEE Trans. Software Engineering*, SE-18, 329-345. F

rankel, V., & Balci, O. (1989). An on-line assistance system for the simulation model development environment. *International J. Man-Machine Studies*, 31, 699-716.

Gore, A. (1990). QASE to configure huge systems. MACWEEK, Nov. 13, p. 20. Hoover, S., & Perry, R. (1989). *Simulation: A Problem-Solving Approach*. Reading, MA: Addison-Wesley. Inmon, W. (1983). What price relational? Computerworld, Nov. 28.

Loosely, C. (1985). IBM Database 2 performance measurements. *InfoIMS*, 5.

Maxwell, S., & Delaney, H. (1990). *Designing Experiments and Analyzing Data: A Model Comparison Perspective*. Belmont, CA: Wadsworth Publishing.

McClure, C. (1989). The CASE experience. *Byte*, April, 235-241.

Pallatto, J. (1990). Cadre to expand suite of CASE workstation tools. *PC Week*, Nov. 26.

Park, Y., & Mellichamp, J. (1990). A statistical expert system for simulation analysis. In, *Proc. Summer Computer Simulation Conf.* (pp. 611-616).

Pawlikowski, K. (1990). Steady-state simulation of queuing processes: A survey of problems and solutions. *ACM Computing Surveys*, 22, June, 123-170.

Saldarini, R. (1989). *Analysis and Design of Business Information Systems*. Macmillan.

SAS Institute Inc. (1989). *SAS/STAT User's Guide*, Version 6 (4th ed.). Cary, NC: SAS Institute.

Schriber, T. (1991). *An Introduction to Simulation Using GPSS/H*. New York: Wiley.

Schwartz, A., Yemini, Y., & Bacon, D. (1990). NEST: A network prototyping testbed. *Comm. ACM*, 33(10), 63-74.

Sharda, R., Barr, S., & McDonnell, J. (1988). Decision support system effectiveness: A review and an empirical test. *Management Science*, 34(2), 139-159.

Stevens, J. (1986). *Applied Multivariate Statistics for the Social Sciences*. Hillsdale, NJ: Lawrence Erlbaum Associates. Stonyenko, A., Hamacher, V., & Holt, R. (1991). Analyzing hard-real-time programs for guaranteed schedulability. *IEEE Trans. Software Engineering*, SE-17, 737-753.

Subrimanian, G., Nosek, J., Raghunathan, S., & Kanitkar, S. (1992). A comparison of the decision table and tree. *Comm. ACM*, 35(1), 89-94.

Teichroew, D., & Hershey, E. (1977). PSL/PSA: A computer-aided technique for structured documentation and analysis of information processing systems. IEEE

Transactions on Software Engineering, 3(1), 41-48.

Walpole, R., & Myers, R. (1985). Probability and Statistics for Engineers and Scientists. Macmillan: New York. Warren, J. (1992). CASE/Simulation Systems. Doctoral dissertation at Dept. of Information Systems, University of Maryland Graduate School, Baltimore.

Warren, J., Norcio, A., Stott, J., & Canfield, G. (1992). Experimental evaluation of a simulation environment for information systems design. Submitted to IEEE Trans. Software Engineering.

Warren, J., Norcio, A., Stott, J., Canfield, G., & Freedman, R. (1992). The decision-support effectiveness of a simulation environment for information systems analysts: An exploratory study. In, *Proc. Third International Working Conf. on Dynamic Modelling of Information Systems* (pp. 419-438).

Warren, J., & Stott, J. (1992). CASE/simulation: Making performance evaluation a normal part of IS development. In H. G. Sol & R. L. Crosslin (Eds.), *Dynamic Modelling of Information Systems, II* (pp. 219-250). Amsterdam: North-Holland/Elsevier Science Publishers.

Warren, J. Stott, J., & Norcio, A. (1992a). Stochastic simulation of information systems designs from data flow diagrams. *J. Systems & Software,* 18(2), 191-199.

Warren, J, Stott, J., & Norcio, A. (1992b). A prototype for including simulation of IS dynamics in CASE environments. In, *Proc. Twenty-Fifth Hawaii International Conf. on System Sciences.*

Watson, H., & Blackstone, J. (1989). *Computer Simulation,* 2nd ed. New York: John Wiley & Sons.

CHAPTER SIXTEEN

The Impact of Computer-Aided Software Engineering on Software Development: An Experiment

Mary J. Granger
George Washington University

Roger Alan Pick
Louisiana Tech University

Increased demand for larger and more complex application software systems has forced organizations to look for new development environments. Many software developers perceive CASE as the answer to their software problems and the software crisis that has plagued the computer industry. With CASE, computers enhance the requirements analysis, design, coding, implementation and maintenance phases of the software development life cycle. Since one of the major objects of CASE technology is improving the quality of the software system being developed, this experimental study evaluates the impact of CASE on software system quality in the design phase of the life cycle. This belief, increased system quality when CASE technologies are used, was partially supported.

Increased demand for larger and more complex application software systems has forced organizations to look for new development environments. Complexity has increased because the application systems of today are larger, deal with more difficult tasks and process more data. CASE (Computer-Aided Software Engineering) is the automation of software development (McClure 1989, p. 4) It is a set of tools or an environment that supports software engineering methodologies (Burkhard, 1989; Norman, 1989). CASE encompasses many products which support the design and development of computer-based information systems.

The term "software crisis" describes the current state of software development: systems that do not meet the client's specifications, systems that are over budget, systems that are late, systems that are unused and systems that are difficult to maintain (Shemer 1987). Many software developers perceive CASE as the answer to their software problems and the software crisis that has plagued the computer industry (Chikofsky 1988; Martin C. 1988b; Nejmeh 1988). With CASE, computers enhance the requirements analysis, design, coding, implementation and maintenance phases of the software development life cycle. CASE technologies support one or more software development methodologies during one or more phases of the life cycle. Structured methods help analysts master the complexity of problems and are the basis for problem solving with or without the computer. Many experts contend that in order to be effective, CASE must have a foundation in structured methods (Martin, C. 1988a; Wallace 1988; Hausen 1981).

This research evaluates the effectiveness of the use of CASE tools during the design phase of software system development. The phased or waterfall model of the software development life cycle consists of requirements analysis, design, implementation or coding, testing and maintenance (Fairley 1985, p. 38; Pressman 1982, p. 129). The primary activities during the design phase are the identification of the software modules or functions, data streams and data stores, and the definition of their relationships and connections (Yourdon 1979, p. 7). Freeman (1983) considers the design phase the central activity of the software development life cycle.

One of the major objectives of CASE technology is improving the quality of the software system being developed (Chikofsky 1989; McClure 1989 p.6). Quality implies a dependable system and includes checks on completeness, consistency, accuracy and redundancy (Chikofsky 1989; McClure 1989; de la Torre 1988). The final system should meet the users' needs. According to advocates of CASE technologies (Acly 1988, Frenkel 1985, Gibson 1989, Lewis 1988), the final design should take less time to develop, have fewer errors and internally be more consistent than a design created without the use of CASE technologies. Therefore, it may be inferred that the system resulting from a design developed with CASE tools also should be less complex than a system developed from a design developed without CASE tools. But this perceived benefit of CASE use may or may not be real. The research question to be answered is, "Are there significant measurable differences in the final product?"

RESEARCH GOALS

The primary goal of this research was to quantitatively support or reject claims of increased software quality when CASE is used to develop the system. There are no studies that quantitatively evaluate the influence of CASE technologies on system quality. In this study, benchmarks for systems developed without the use of CASE technologies were established. The same system was developed using CASE technologies and the data collected was compared to the benchmarks. Statistical tests determined whether there is an increase in system quality. This research addressed the question: when CASE technologies are used to develop software is system quality increased?

LITERATURE REVIEW

Software Quality

Card (1988, p. 82) suggests a two-part definition of software quality: satisfying product requirements effectively and system efficiency. A good or high quality system fulfills all of the initial requirements; it is a complete system because the original specifications are satisfied. An incomplete system does not satisfy some or all of the original specifications; the quality of the system is considered 'poor' because the systems is incomplete. Poor quality means "errors and discrepancies with the requirements." (Card 1988) Efficiency implies a method of system production that "minimizes development costs and rework while maximizing maintainability." (Card 1988) CASE usage should foster better project control and enforcement of standards (Statland 1989), creating a system with increased quality. Inconsistencies and omissions should be detected earlier in the life cycle so that requests for change can be incorporated with less effort (Misra 1988).

A more complex situation requires greater problem solving effort and has a greater possibility that the problem will be solved incorrectly; an incorrect problem solution is one with poor quality. Therefore, the complexity level of a software system affects the quality of that system. Software complexity is difficult to quantify. Software Science (Halstead 1977) was an initial attempt to measure software complexity. Halstead proposed measures of the complexity levels of both the algorithm needed to solve the problem and the computer program written to implement the algorithm. Additional research on software metrics (Gordon 1979a; Elshoff 1984) built on Halstead's metrics. Two characteristics of software quality are maintainability and correctness; the more complex the software the more difficult it is to develop and maintain correct software. Halstead's effort metric has been used to predict the psychological complexity of maintaining a computer system (Curtis, 1979). Improved design techniques reduce the complexity of the product; if software complexity is reduced, less effort is required to build the product, the probability of an incorrect solution is reduced and system quality is improved.

Software Metrics

Software metrics (Halstead 1977) were used to determine whether there were significant differences in the finished projects; one aspect of system quality was evaluated by examining the complexity level of the finished system. The product was evaluated using several different programs that collect data about the finished product and which compute software metrics.

Most of the seminal research on software metrics has been performed by Maurice Halstead (1977) and Thomas McCabe (1976) (Curtis 1983); both Halstead's and McCabe's metrics attempt to define and measure the complexity of a software task. Halstead proposes a set of metrics that apply to both the product and the amount of effort required to produce the product (Mills, 1988). The software metrics used do not depend on any specific type of development methodology (Grady 1987). One of the major results of a study done by Basili, Selby and Hutchens (1986) was that some metrics could differentiate between systems developed using different methodologies. It has been shown that metrics can also differentiate between systems developed using different development technologies while keeping the development methodologies constant. In the present research, the comparison was between a software system developed without CASE technologies and one developed using CASE technologies.

The complexity of a program is of interest because it affects the development time, the number of defects and the ease of modification (Weyuker 1988). As complexity is reduced, development time is reduced, the number of defects decreases and maintenance effort is reduced. However, it is not always easy to determine what to measure. As previously stated, an improved design should reduce the complexity of the product. The number of lines of source code is the most often used and most intuitive indicator of complexity (Boehm 1987). However, there are often questions about the composition of "lines of source code." In this study, separate counts of actual "action" lines and comment lines were taken. As long as we are consistent in our definition of "source code" and are comparing size within the same language and for the same application, size does measure complexity and productivity (Humphrey 1989, p. 317).

Other measures of complexity involve counting the number of operators and operands in a program. Halstead defines operators as any symbols or combinations of symbols that affect the value or ordering of an operand (Ibid.): they may be function calls, mathematical symbols, delimiters or keywords. Operands are constants and variables (Halstead p. 5). Jones (1986, p. 108) suggests a data complexity measure that uses the number of comparison operators as a complexity indicator. Elshoff (1984) studied 20 candidate measures of program complexity and located a set of four measures (using a measurement system developed by Elshoff) that would define program complexity and could be used to classify programs. His four measures are: length of the program, number of unique operators, data difficulty and the number of unique operands (Elshoff 1984). Stevens, Constantine and Meyers (1974) studied the structural complexity of programs. They define absolute structural complexity as the number of modules in the system, and relative structural complexity as the ratio of the number of linkages to the number of modules.

A measure of program clarity is proposed by Gordon (1979a): the measure of program clarity is Halstead's program volume divided by Halstead's estimated program level in units of elementary mental discriminations; the number of individual mental calculations needed to solve or understand a problem. Gordon (1979b) measures the amount of mental effort needed to understand a program and supports his claim that effort is a measure of clarity. Fitzsimmons and Love (1978) concluded that "software science is a possible tool for answering" questions about properties of software development projects and the difficulties of programming.

This research attempts to generate measurable data that can be used to evaluate the improvements in the quality of systems developed with CASE. System quality is evaluated by measuring the completeness and complexity of the final product. No attempt is made to evaluate software quality during the software development life cycle.

THE EMPIRICAL STUDY - USAGE OF CASE TECHNOLOGIES

The Experiment

An experimental study with a control group (non-CASE) and a treatment group (CASE) was designed to investigate the effects of CASE usage. System quality was measured using the differences in the complexity and the levels of completeness of the final systems. The control group designed the system without CASE technologies and the treatment group designed the system with CASE technologies.

This research was a replicated project study; its purpose was to study the effect of different technologies, CASE versus non-CASE, when used to develop a software system. "Replicated project studies examine objective(s) across a set of teams and a single project." (Basili 1986, p. 735).

This study is also a controlled experiment using student subjects implementing a classroom project. Controlled experiments in an organizational environment are too costly and time consuming (Myers, 1978). Real-world projects will not be replicated by software developers because of financial and practical considerations; neither the system nor the programming teams are the same. Due to variations in task complexity caused by product differentiation, two commercial projects are rarely comparable (Humphrey 1988; Eliot 1986; Haas 1989; Basili 1981). This means it is often difficult to isolate and evaluate the effect of the technology being studied (Boehm 1981; Glass 1982; Attewell 1984). For these reasons, student subjects allow experiments with less confounding than is possible in a field setting.

The Task

The project consisted of designing, coding, testing, debugging and documenting a "pretty printer" for Pascal programs. The pretty printer was coded in Pascal; almost all of the subjects were familiar with Pascal. The project is of moderate difficulty and length; it is a non-trivial problem, resulting in an average of 1500-2000 lines of code.

A pretty printer is a computer program that reformats computer programs in a consistent style to improve readability (Cameron 1988; Oppen 1980; Rubin 1983). The new reformatted version of a computer program should be easier to understand and read. The pretty printer may assume that the input is a text file containing a syntactically correct Pascal Program; the code has already been compiled successfully. The output must also be a syntactically correct program with the same execution behavior as the input.

The Subjects

The two groups of subjects were students in the same course, in different quarters, in a near lock-step curriculum. Consequently, the subjects had similar individual characteristics and teams were chosen to try to insure team similarity. The same instructor conducted both sections of the course in order to maintain consistency for the presentation of the course material. The experiment did not interfere with the quality of the instruction given to the students. The main objective of the course was to gain knowledge of structured methodologies and to become familiar with "programming in the large" by working in a programming team environment while implementing a small (600-2,000 line) system. Although 600-2,000 lines would not be considered "programming in the large" in the real world, this is the size that was appropriate for the limited amount of time in a ten week quarter. The students used structured methodologies to implement and complete the project.

All students had the same computer resources available, the same programming language, the same debugging tools and were constrained by the 10-week-quarter time period. Participants in the study were junior level Information Systems majors enrolled in the Software Engineering course in the College of Business Administration, University of Cincinnati. Since these students were majoring in Information Systems they will be the systems analysts of tomorrow. Therefore, it is assumed that the results are likely to generalize to the population of novice, entry-level professional systems analysts and may generalize to the entire population of professional systems analysts. All students enrolled in the two sections participated. Almost all of the students were familiar with the computer system and the implementation language. The students were not familiar with a team concept of programming nor formal structured software development methodologies.

In a previous study using student teams, Rombach (1987) ranked students on their educational performance (grades), experience (industry) and relative programming talent. In this study, educational performance and programming talents were combined as a measure of the students' programming ability and were used in conjunction with work experience in determining team composition. In the spring quarter there were seven three-person teams and in the autumn quarter there were three three-person teams and one four-person team.

Data Collection

In this study metrics were obtained using a program that used the actual finished project procedures (Pascal code) as input character strings and counted the number of unique tokens and the total number of occurrences for each token. Sammet (1969, p. 70) defines the term tokens as "the basic elements in the programming language." Tokens are either defined by the system (key words and punctuation) or user-defined (identifiers, constants, literals and comments). Counts were obtained for each module in a project; these counts were then summed for a total project count for each metric for the team project. This was done for each of the eleven projects, not for each individual student. The student teams handed in a single project and in most cases the authors of individual modules were not identified.

This research used seventeen variables to measure quality. The completeness level is a single variable giving the number of requirements met by each of the systems. Although size is an additional indicator of the complexity of a system, for the sake of clarity, size measures are discussed separately from complexity measures. Size is an indicator of complexity; intuitively, the larger the system the greater the potential for increased complexity. There were eleven variables in the complexity category and six in the size category. The number of lines of code are included in both categories. Completeness is a category by itself. A higher quality system should be less complex and more complete than a system of lower quality. The hypotheses were tested using a difference of means test for variables in the control group (non-CASE) and the treatment group (CASE). The six size variables and eleven complexity variables are listed in Table 1 and are defined in detail in Table 2 and Table 3 respectively.

Initially, each group of students were given the specifications for the pretty printer. There were 24 specific functional tasks that their final projects had to accomplish. The specifications were identical for both the control group and the treatment group. Each group started with the same requirements, thereby controlling for a possible variance in the type and number of specifications that might have developed if each team had written their own requirements. A senior in Information Systems evaluated the projects for completeness, that is, how well the projects fulfilled each of the 24 requirements. He was given all eleven projects to evaluate, but did not know which projects were developed using CASE and which were devel-

VARIABLES USED TO DEFINE SIZE
Number of Lines Of Code (LOC)
Number of Comments (CMMNTS)
Number of Modules (MODULES)
Halstead's Estimated Length (LENGTHN)
Halstead's Volume (VOLUME)
Halstead's Vocabulary (VOCAB)

VARIABLES USED TO DEFINE COMPLEXITY
Number of Lines of Code(LOC)
Number of Unique Operands (n_2)
Number of Procedures and Functions (CALLS)
Number of Iteration Statements (LOOPS)
Number of Selections Statements (SELECTS)
Number of Separate Blocks of Code (BLOCKS)
Number of Unique Operators (n_1)
Halstead's Mental Effort for Comprehension of a
    Computer Program (CLARITY)
Halstead's Mental Activity Required to Convert an Algorithm
    to a Computer Program (EFFORT)
Average Number of Variable Appearances (DATADIFF)
Number of Errors Due to Level of Program Difficulty (DIFF)

Table 1

oped without CASE. The projects were shuffled and the seven without CASE were randomly merged with the four that used CASE. The instructor kept a key to the projects. The original specifications were used to determine the completeness of each project. Once the scales were returned to the instructor, they were re-connected with the appropriate product.

RESEARCH MODEL

Hypothesis

The following belief was tested: Use of CASE technologies increases the quality of the system/program being developed.
The formal hypothesis that tests this belief is:

(H)
H_0: There is no difference in the quality of the system/program developed using CASE technologies and the quality of the system/program developed without CASE technologies.
H_1: System quality is greater when CASE technologies are used than when CASE technologies are not used.

This hypothesis is made operational with the following hypotheses:

(H1)

$H1_0$: There is no difference in the complexity of a system produced with CASE technologies and the complexity of a system produced without CASE technologies.

$H1_1$: A system produced with CASE technologies is less complex than a system produced without CASE technologies.

(H2)

$H2_0$: There is no difference in the completeness of a system produced with CASE technologies and the completeness of a system produced without CASE technologies.

$H2_1$: A system produced with CASE technologies is more complete than a system produced without CASE technologies.

Operational Hypothesis 1
There is no Difference in System Complexity

The first operational hypothesis (H1) was tested by comparing the complexity and size of the systems developed without CASE technology and the complexity and size of the systems developed with CASE technology.

Six variables were used to define size. The number of lines of code (LOC), the number of comments (CMMNTS) and the number of modules (MODULES) were directly counted in the final systems. Program length (LENGTHN), program volume (VOLUME) and program vocabulary (VOCABULARY) are Halstead's (1977) Software Science measures and were all calculated from values that were counted in the final systems. They were included in the size category because they are different ways of expressing the length or volume of a project. See Table 2 for further definitions and calculation formulas.

Eleven variables were used to define complexity. Although these metrics were also calculated from values that were counted in the final systems, they comprise a set of metrics that measure the amount the inherent complexity in the task. The number of lines of code (LOC), the number of procedures and functions invoked (CALLS), the number of iterations statements (LOOPS), the number of selections statements (SELECTS) and the total number of separate blocks within the code (BLOCKS) were counted in the final systems. LOC, BLOCKS and CALLS are direct indicators of length; the longer the project the greater the potential for complexity. LOOPS and SE-

NAME	DESCRIPTION/DEFINITION
LOC	Number of lines of code (excluding comment lines and blank lines)
CMMNTS	Number of lines of comments
MODULES	Number of unique procedures and unique functions
LENGTHN	Sum of the number of operators and operands $N = N_1 + N_2$ N_1 - the total number of operator occurrences N_2 - the total number of operand occurrences
VOCAB	Sum of number of unique operators and unique operands $n = n_1 + n_2$
VOLUME	Program volume - the size of any implementation of any algorithm $N * \log_2 n$

Table 2: Variables Used to Define Size

LECTS are indicators of the number of decisions made to accomplish the task; the more decisions and iterations, the greater the complexity of the system. Halstead's number of unique operators (n_2) and number of unique operands (n_1) are also directly counted in the final project. Halstead's (1977) basic metrics, n_1 and n_2, are also two of Elshoff's (1984) set of complexity measures, the other two being data difficulty (DATADIFF) and length (LENGTHN). Gordon's (1979b) CLARITY and Halstead's (1977) EFFORT are calculated from values counted in the final system. CLARITY is the amount of effort required to understand a computer program and EFFORT is the amount of mental activity necessary to convert an algorithm to a computer program; a more complex program should require more effort to understand and code. Elshoff's data difficulty (DATADIFF) and difficulty (DIFF) were also calculated from values counted in the final system. Data difficulty is the average number of variables, constants or literals; the more variables are used, the more chance for additional complexity. Difficulty measures the number of errors in a program due to problems in understanding the program; a less complex program should have fewer errors in comprehension and therefore a lower level of difficulty. See Table 3 for definitions and calculation formulas.

In order to reject the first operational hypothesis, the values for all or most of the complexity variables should be significantly different between the treatment group (CASE) and the control group (non-CASE). If the systems have a given functionality, we can claim

NAME	DESCRIPTION/DEFINITION
LOC	Number of lines of code (excluding comment lines and blank lines)
n_2	Number of unique operands - the sum of the number of unique constants, unique variables and unique literals
CALLS	Number of procedures and functions invoked
LOOPS	Number of REPEAT, WHILE and FOR loops used
SELECTS	Number of CASE, IF and ELSE statements used
BLOCKS	The total number of PROCEDURE, FUNCTION, BEGIN, IF, WHILE, CASE, FOR, REPEAT statements
EFFORT	The mental activity required to reduce an algorithm to an actual computer program $$\frac{((n_1 + n_2) * \log_2 n)}{(2 * n_2)/(n_1 * N_2)}$$
n_1	Number of unique operators - the sum of the unique number of iteration statements (REPEAT, WHILE, FOR), selection statements (CASE, IF, THEN, ELSE), symbols (mathematical and Boolean), delimiters, sets, records, read statements, write statements, function and procedure calls, the number of begin and end statements, and the number of open and close statements.
DATADIFF	The average number of variable appearances N_2/n_2
CLARITY	The amount of mental effort required to comprehend a computer program $$\frac{((n_1 * \log_2 n_1 + n_2 * \log_2 n_2) * \log_2 n)}{(N * \log_2 n)}$$ $(n = n_1 + n_2; N = N_1 + N_2)$ n is the vocabulary of a computer program N is the length (amount of source code) of a computer program
DIFF	One half of the product of the unique operators and the data difficulty. Corresponds to the number of errors in a program due to the level of effort required to understand the program $(n_1 * DATADIFF)/2$

Table 3: Variable Used to Define Complexity

increased system quality if the complexity of the system developed using CASE technology is significantly less than the complexity of the system developed using non-CASE technology.

Operational Hypothesis 2
   No Difference in System Completeness

The second operational hypothesis was tested using a level of system completeness. A system was more complete if it met a greater number of the requirements than another system. In order to reject the second operational hypothesis for system quality, the levels of completeness of the CASE developed systems and the non-CASE developed systems should be significantly different. We can claim increased quality if the level of completeness of the CASE developed systems were higher than the level of completeness of the non-Case developed systems.

The systems were also rated on the level of completeness of twenty-four logical functions, specified in the original requirements. On each of the different specifications, a "0 - 1 - 2" scale was used to record the completeness. A score of "0" indicates that no attempt was made to accomplish that specification. A score of "1" indicates that some attempt was made, but it was not a totally successful attempt. A score of "2" indicates a totally successful attempt at a particular specification. There were 24 requirements and a totally complete system, one that completely met all the requirements for all the functions, had a rating of 48.

If the null hypotheses can be rejected, then the research will support the original beliefs. The above hypotheses were tested at a 0.10 level using statistical analyses to compare the control group (non-CASE) and the treatment group (CASE).

DATA ANALYSIS

Discriminant analysis is a statistical technique that can be used to classify subjects into groups based on a series of variables and is often used to determine whether a single variable maximizes the difference between two groups. If a single variable determines the difference between the groups, that variable is removed from the analysis and the rest of the variables are re-evaluated. This process is repeated until none of the remaining variables maximize the separation between the two groups. Since none of the variables maximized the difference between the two groups, as determined by the discriminate analysis technique, the analysis was a two group univariate test. Because of the small sample size, "t" tests were an appropriate measure of the difference between the means of the two groups. The levels of significance (p values) were then calculated for each of the individual variables.

Each system was rated on the 24 original requirements and a single value (0-48) is calculated; this variable is the sum of the functional ratings for each of the 24 requirements. Each requirement was either totally functional (rated 2), partially functional (rated 1), or not at all function (rated 0). Using the "t" tests, the level of significance (p values) were then calculated for the single completeness value.

RESULTS OF DATA ANALYSIS

The values, means and levels of significance (p values) are reported for each of the variables within the two categories: size and complexity. Then the results of the evaluation of the level of completeness are described.

Figures 1 through 11 report the values and the levels of significance (p values) for the difference in means and the means for each of the eleven variables for the complexity category. The values, means and levels of significance (p values) for the difference in means for each of the six variables for the size category are reported in Figures 1 (LOC) and 12 through 16. Figure 17 indicates the level of completeness for the eleven projects; Figure 18 the percentage of completeness. The level of significance (p value) was calculated using the mean ratings for both groups.

Results of Data Analysis - Complexity Variables

As previously mentioned, the number of executable lines of code is an indicator of the system's complexity level. Intuitively, the complexity of a system increases as the number of lines of executable code increases. The number of lines of executable code is also an indicator of the size of the system. Comments and blank lines are not executable lines of code. Examining the individual team counts, there is no clear distinction between the control group and the treatment group counts (Figure 1). Five teams (4 non-CASE teams and 1 CASE team) needed between 2,000 and 2,500 lines of code to implement the system. Six teams (3 non-CASE teams and 3 CASE teams) needed between 1,000 and 1,500 lines of code to implement the system. There is no statistical significance between the means for the control group (non-CASE) and the treatment group (CASE), however, the average number of lines of code required to solve the problem by the CASE group is less then the average number of lines

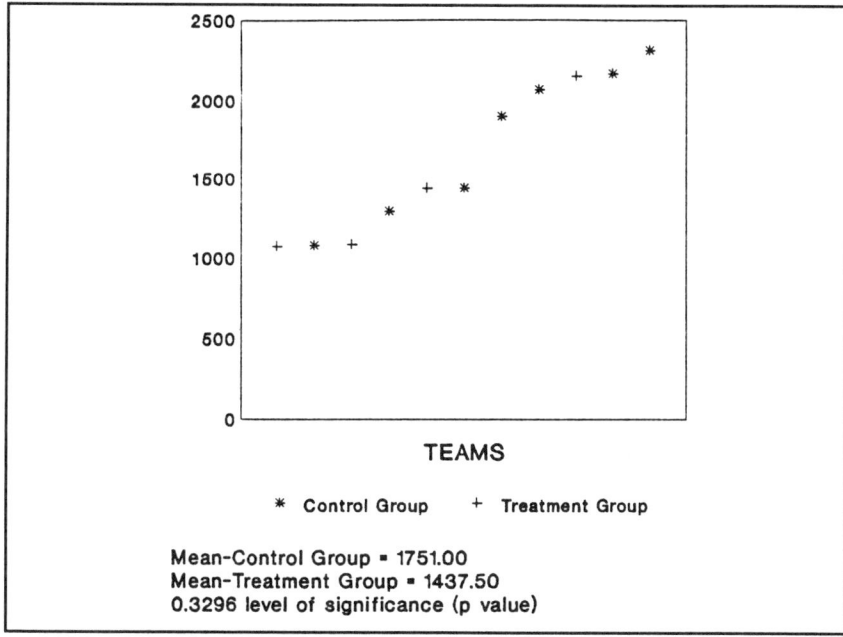

Figure 1: Number of Lines of Code—Group Totals

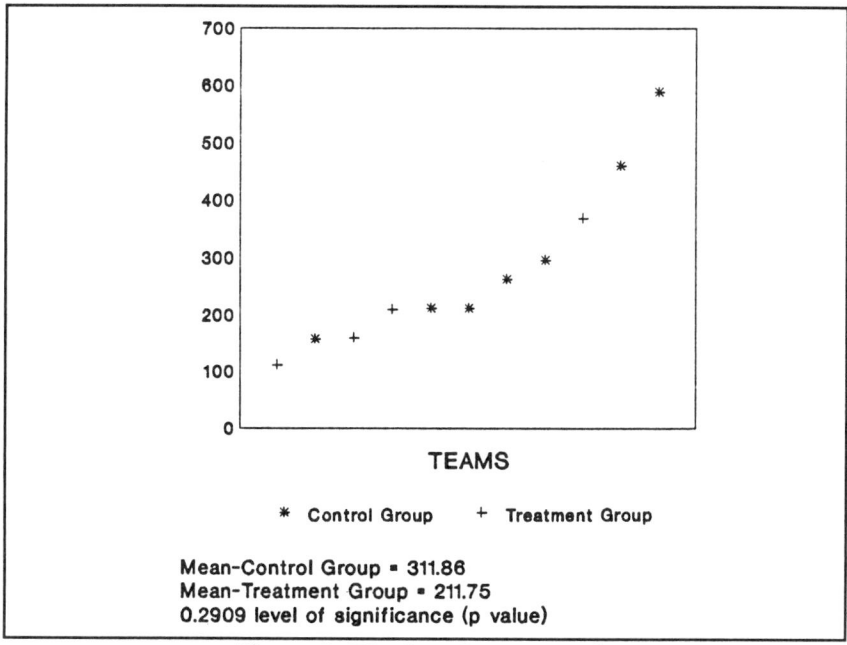

Figure 2: Blocks—Group Totals

of code required by the non-CASE group.

The number of BLOCKS is the total number of groups of code or BLOCKS of code that execute in sequence. These BLOCKS of code are identified by the Pascal reserved words BEGIN, FUNCTION, PROCEDURE, IF, WHILE, CASE, FOR or REPEAT. These values are actual counts from the final projects and indicate the flow of control within the system. As the amount of control required to solve the algorithm increases, both the number of blocks needed for implementation and the complexity of a system increases. Examining the number of BLOCKS for individual teams, there is no clear distinction between the control group (non-CASE) and the treatment group (CASE) counts (Figure 2). There is no statistical significance between the means for the control group (non-CASE) and the treatment group (CASE), however, on the average, the treatment group coded fewer BLOCKS than the control group.

LOOPS (Figure 3), the first subset of BLOCKS (Figure 2), consists of the number of WHILE, FOR and REPEAT statements in each of the final systems. These reserved Pascal words control iteration within a computer program; iteration involves decisions and the greater the number of decisions required to solve a problem, the greater the complexity.

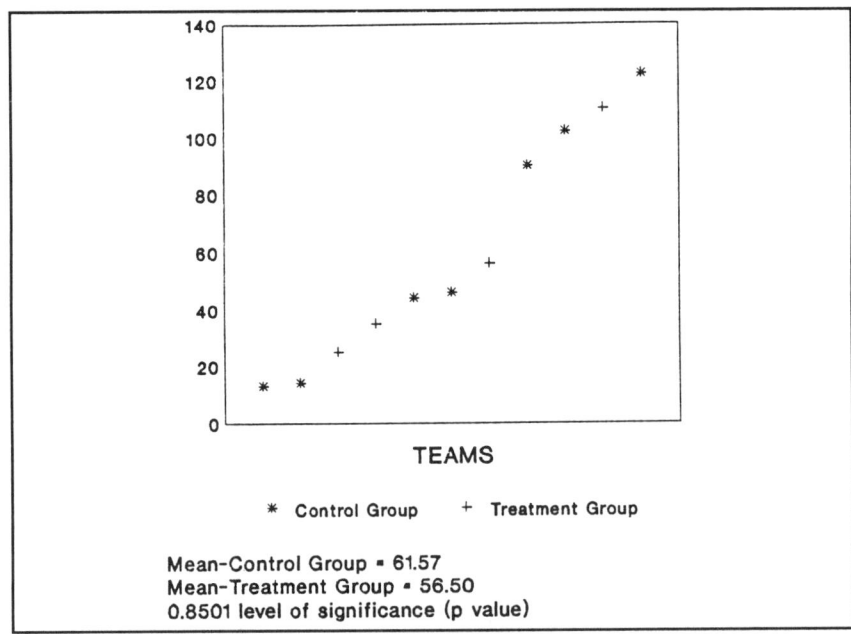

Figure 3: Loops—Group Totals

SELECTS (Figure 4), the second subset of BLOCKS (Figure 2), are the number of IF and CASE statements in each of the final systems. These reserved Pascal words control selection (decisions) within a computer program.

CALLS (Figure 5), the third subset of BLOCKS (Figure 2), are the number of times a function or procedure is invoked. This should not be confused with the number of unique functions and procedures; it is the total number of occurrences in the code where functions and procedures are invoked.

LOOPS (Figure 3), SELECTS (Figure 4) and CALLS (Figure 5) are subsets of BLOCKS (Figure 2). LOOPS, SELECTS and CALLS imply complexity. The greater the number of possible choices within an algorithm, the greater the complexity of the algorithm. If the same problem can be solved with fewer paths, the complexity of the solution can be reduced. Examining the number of LOOPS, SELECTS and CALLS for individual teams, there are no clear distinctions between the control group (non-CASE) and the treatment group (CASE), however, on the average, the treatment group coded less LOOPS, SELECTS and CALLS than the control group.

Gordon's (1979a) measure of clarity is intended to suggest the amount of mental effort required to comprehend a computer program. Intuitively, if less mental effort is required to understand a

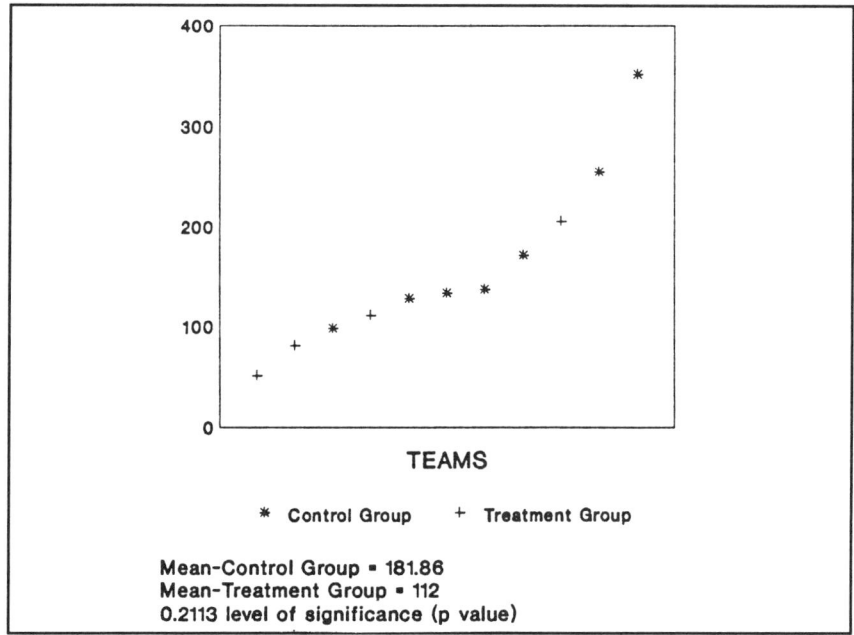

Figure 4: Selects—Group Totals

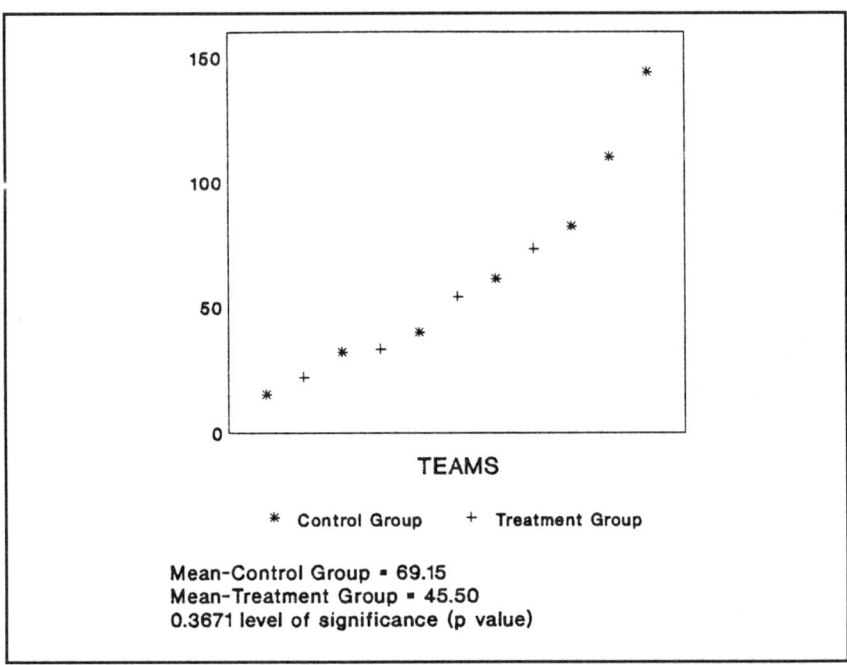

Figure 5: Number of Calls—Group Totals

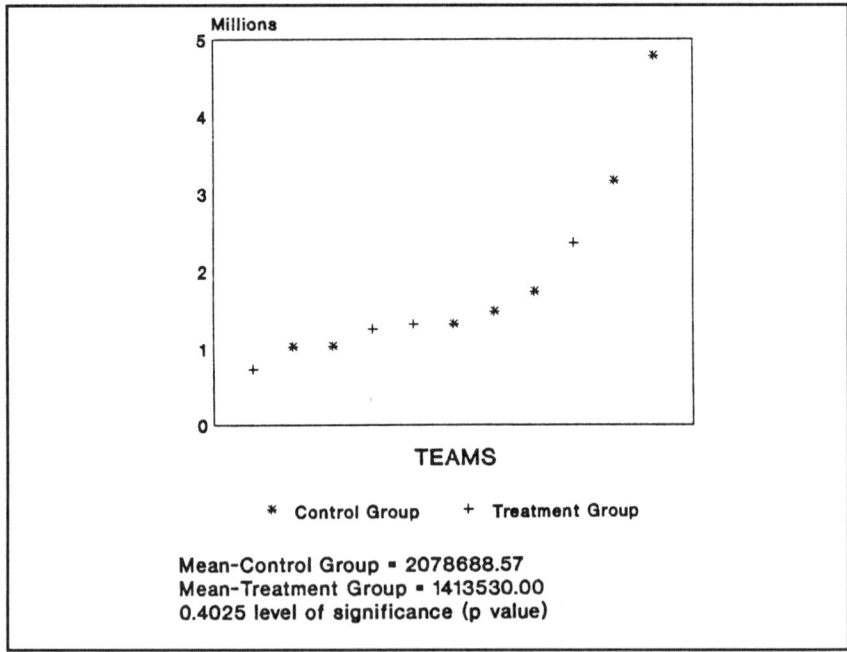

Figure 6: Clarity—Group Totals

program, the program is less complex. Examining the individual team clarity values, there is no clear distinction between the control group (non-CASE) and the treatment group (CASE) values (Figure 6). There is no statistical significance between the means for the control group (non-CASE) and the treatment group (CASE), however, the average clarity value of the treatment group system is less than the average clarity value of control group system. The systems produced with CASE, on the average, required less mental effort to understand the program than the non-CASE systems.

EFFORT (Halstead 1977) is intended to suggest the amount of mental effort required to comprehend a computer program. If less mental effort is required to comprehend one program compared to another, the program requiring less effort should therefore be less complex. Examining the effort values calculated for individual teams, there is no clear distinction between the control group (non-CASE) and the treatment group (CASE) values (Figure 7). There is no statistical significance between the means for the control group (non-CASE) and the treatment group (CASE), however, on the average, programs developed with CASE required less effort for comprehension than those developed without CASE.

The number of unique operands (n_2), the sum of all the unique

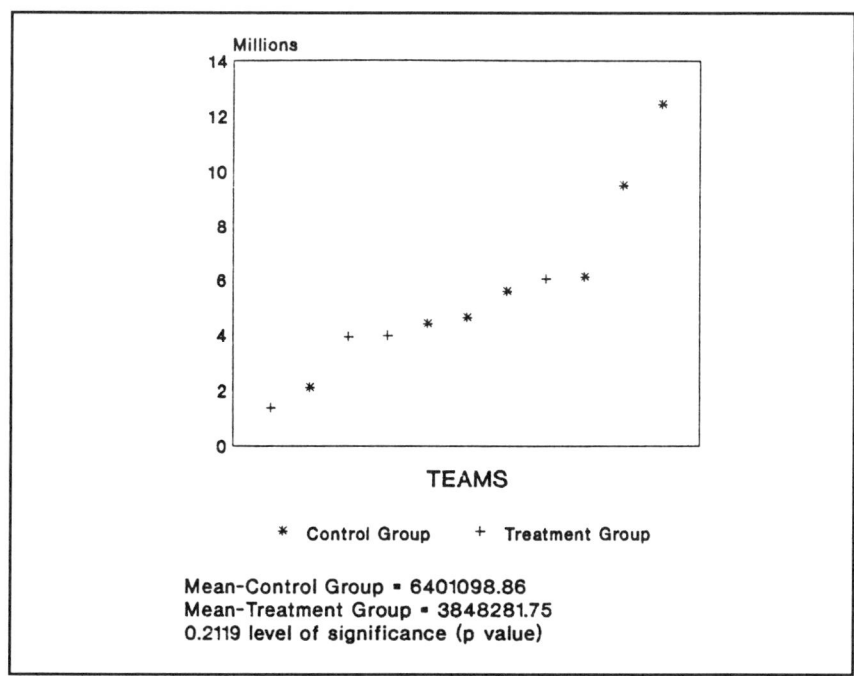

Figure 7: Effort—Group Totals

variables, unique constants and unique literals, varies more than the number of unique operators. These operands are user defined; they are specified by the individual programmer or, in this case, programming team. Different versions of algorithms may require different numbers of operators (Halstead 1977). Given the various levels of operator usage for the same system, it may be that different algorithms were used to solve the same problem or that the same algorithm was implemented in a more complex manner, thereby requiring more operands. Although there is a variance among the individual teams, there are no apparent trends and there is no statistical significance between the means for the control group (non-CASE) and the treatment group (CASE).

The number of unique operators (n_1), the sum of the unique number of iteration statements (REPEAT, WHILE, FOR), selection statements (CASE, IF, THEN, ELSE), symbols (mathematical and Boolean), delimiters, sets, records, read statements, write statements, function and procedure calls, the number of begin and end statements, and the number of open and close statements, is fairly consistent across all the teams. Halstead (1977, p. 5) defines operand as "symbols or combinations of symbols that affect the value or ordering of an operand." An implementation language, in this case Pascal, has a limited number of operators available for use and in a 2,000 line system almost all of them are needed.

Data difficulty (Elshoff 1984) is the average number of variable appearances within a system. It is the total number of operands divided by the number of unique operands. A high level of data difficulty may imply incorrect usage of variables and constants: there may be multiple uses within a program or some expressions should be factored. By introducing ambiguity into the system, misuse of operands can increase system complexity. This value is fairly consistent across the teams and the difference between the means for the control group (non-CASE) and the treatment group (CASE) is not statistically significant.

Difficulty (Elshoff 1984) is one half of the product of the unique operators and the data difficulty. It corresponds to the number of possible errors in a program due to the level of effort required to understand the program. The greater the level of effort required to understand the program, both the potential for errors and the complexity of the program increases. Ten of the teams are fairly consistent in the data difficulty measure; the difference between the means for the control group (non-CASE) and the treatment group (CASE) is not statistically significant.

Statistically, none of the differences in the complexity variables were significant. Therefore, the null hypothesis that there is no

Software Development 493

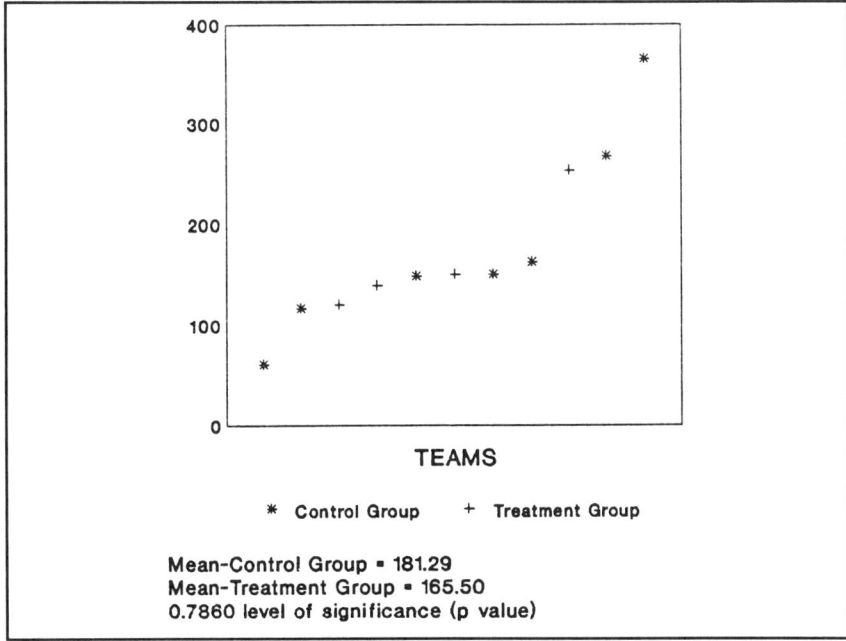

Figure 8: Number of Unique Operands (n2)—Group Totals

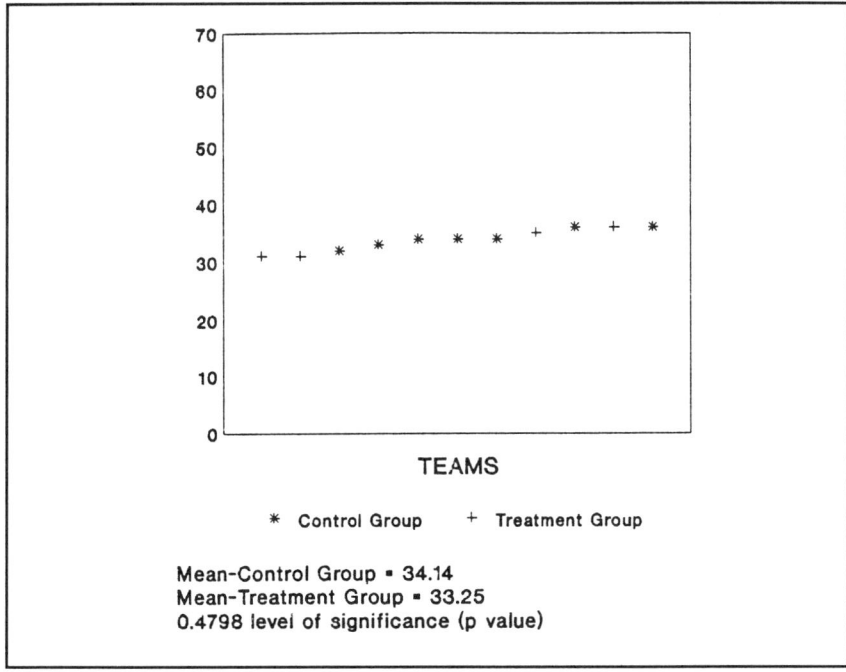

Figure 9: Number of Unique Operators (n1)—Group Totals

difference in the complexities of the two systems could not be rejected. However, some observations from the data concerning complexity can be made.

In Figures 2, 3, 4, 6 and 7 the majority of control teams (non-CASE) tend to cluster at the higher end of each of the scales, with the majority of treatment teams (CASE) clustering at the lower end of each of the scales. While this is interesting, since there is no statistical significance, definite conclusions about the complexity of the systems cannot be drawn. At best, it can be said that with respect to BLOCKS, LOOPS, SELECTS, CLARITY and EFFORT, the majority of the CASE systems appear to be less complex than the majority of the non-CASE systems, but that further study is required as this pattern might be reversed with different subjects.

Values for the Number of Operators (Figure 9) and Data Difficulty (Figure 10) are fairly consistent. Based on the nature of the programming language, these results are not unexpected.

Data for the remainder of the selected complexity variables, Lines of Code (Figure 1), CALLS (Figure 5), Number of Unique Operands (Figure 8) and DIFF (Figure 11), do not indicate any trends and are not statistically significant. These also require further study.

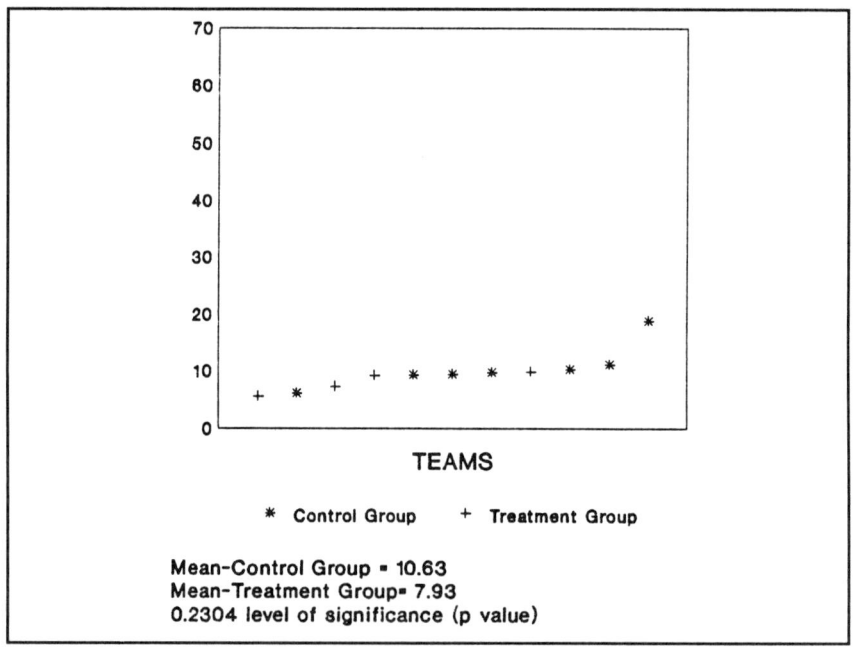

Figure 10: Data Difficulty—Group Totals

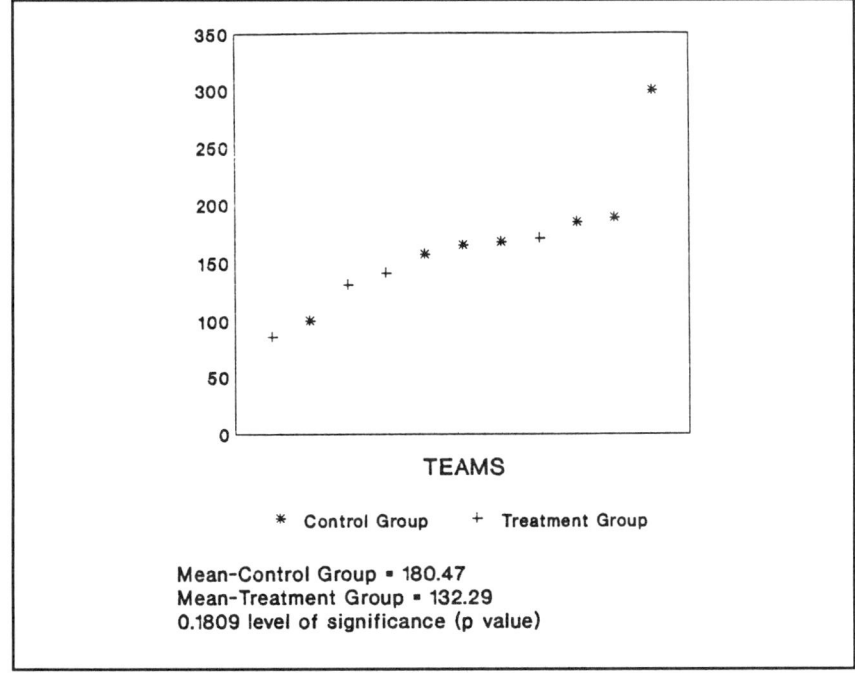

Figure 11: Difficulty—Group Totals

Results of Data Analysis - Size Variables

The number of MODULES is the total number of unique external functions or procedures. A greater number of procedures and functions increases the size of the system. Again, intuitively, as the size of the system increases, the amount of complexity increases. Examining the number of MODULES for individual teams, there is no clear distinction between the control group (non-CASE) and the treatment group (CASE) counts (Figure 12). There is no statistical significance between the means for the control group (non-CASE) and the treatment group (CASE), however, on the average, the treatment group coded fewer MODULES than the control group.

VOLUME (Figure 13) is the size of implementation of any algorithm and is dependent upon the chosen programming language. If an algorithm is implemented in another programming language, the volume may change. In this study, all the systems were coded using Pascal, therefore, it was expected that the volume would be consistent across the teams. On the average, the volume for the treatment group (CASE) was less than the volume for the control group (non-CASE), but there was no statistical significance between the difference of the means.

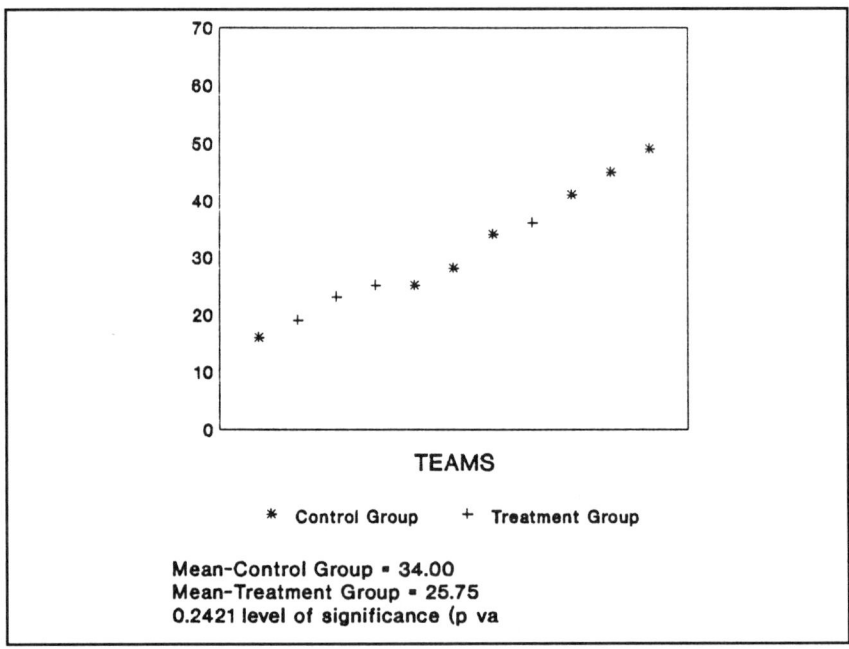

Figure 12: Number of Modules—Group Totals

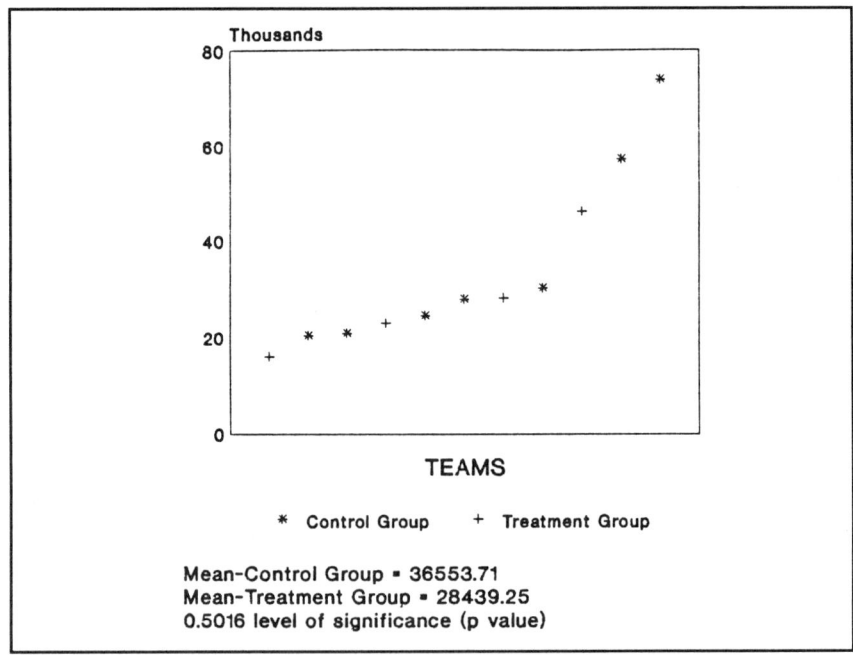

Figure 13: Volume—Group Totals

VOCABULARY (Figure 14) is the sum of the number of unique operands and unique operators and is a measure of the size of the implementation of an algorithm. Since the number of unique operators (Figure 9) was fairly consistent and the number of unique operands (Figure 8) varied with only a slight trend, data points for VOCABULARY should follow path similar to the data points for the number of unique operands, and they do. The average VOCABULARY for the treatment group (CASE) was slightly lower than that for the control group (non-CASE).

LENGTH N (Halstead 1977) is the sum of all the occurrences of the operators and all the occurrences of the operands of a system. This is the actual length of a program expressed in terms of the operators and operands, which were calculated from the actual systems. Previously the Number of Lines of Code (Figure 1) was used convey the length or size of a program. Similar to Lines of Code, the average of LENGTHN for the treatment group (CASE) is lower than the average for the control group (non-CASE).

In Figures 13, 14 and 15, two control teams (non-CASE) and 1 treatment team (CASE) tend to cluster at the higher end of each of the scales, with 3 treatment teams (CASE) and 5 control teams (non-CASE) clustering at the lower end of each of the scales. While this is interesting, since there is no statistical significance, definite conclusions about the size of the systems cannot be drawn.

Number of Comments is the amount of lines in a system that are documentation about the program; they are not executable lines. The more comments, the longer the physical program. The treatment group (CASE), on the average, used more comments than the control group (non-CASE) (Figure 16). While this increases the size of the system, if comments are relevant, they should also aid in the understanding of the program and reduce the complexity of the system.

None of the differences in the means for the size variables were statistically significant. The size of the system developed by CASE users could not be proved different from the sizes of the system developed by non-CASE users. This result was expected. The same task, a Pretty Printer, was performed using the same programming language, Pascal. Unless an extremely efficient or inefficient algorithm was designed, the sizes of the implementation should be fairly consistent. If another programming language was used for all the teams, the size may have changed. It would be expected that it would have changed for all the teams.

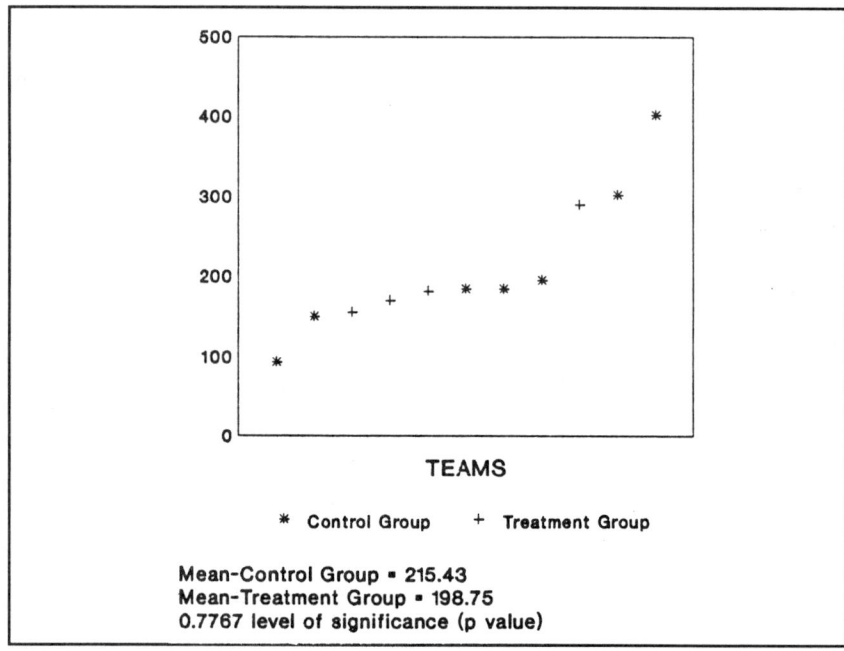

Figure 14: Vocabulary—Group Totals

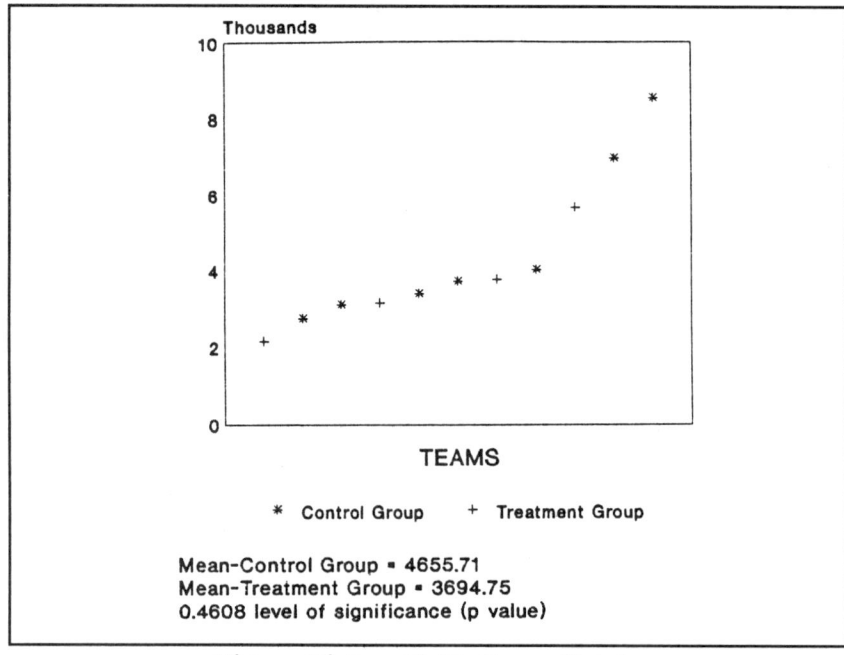

Figure 15: Length N—Group Totals

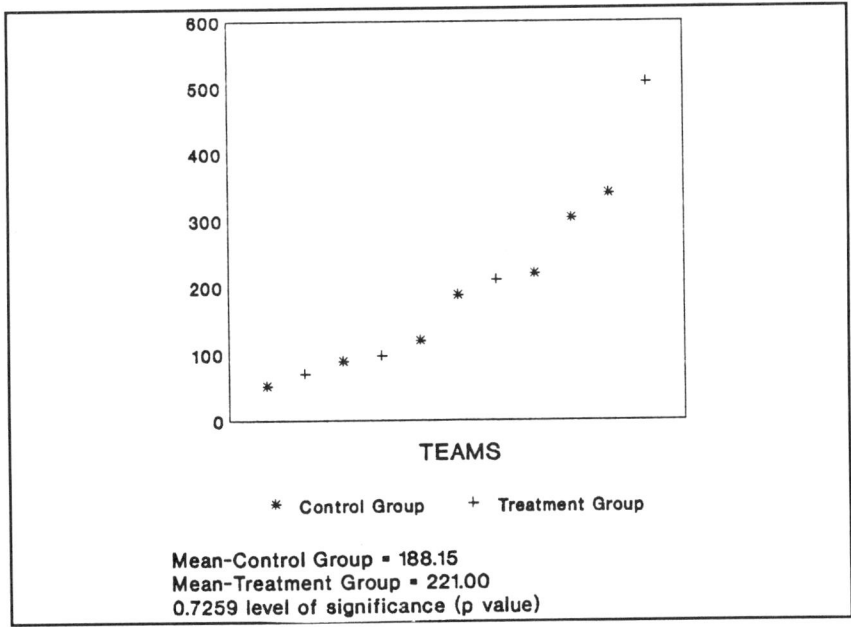

Figure 16: Number of Comments—Group Totals

Results of Data Analysis - Completeness

Figure 17 indicates the level of completeness for the eleven projects; Figure 18 the percentage of completeness. The four projects, all from the control group (non-CASE), that received a '0' rating for all 24 specifications had run time errors caused by either a stack dump or an access violation error; none of the projects had compile errors. Some attempt was made to fix the systems, however, that was not the task of the evaluator. Unfortunately, the documentation, users' manuals and programmers' manuals were of little or no help for the implementation of any of the projects, and they were not a factor in either the maintenance attempts or evaluation of the projects.

The levels of completeness for all the treatment teams (CASE) were higher than the levels of completeness for all the control teams (non-CASE). The 3 projects from the control group that accomplished some of the 24 specification were approximately 33% complete. The four treatment group projects ranged from 44% to 75% complete. The level of significance (p value) was calculated using the mean ratings for both groups. Then the level of significance (p value) was calculated omitting those teams that had run time errors. Both values were significant at the 0.05 level (Table 4). Therefore, the null

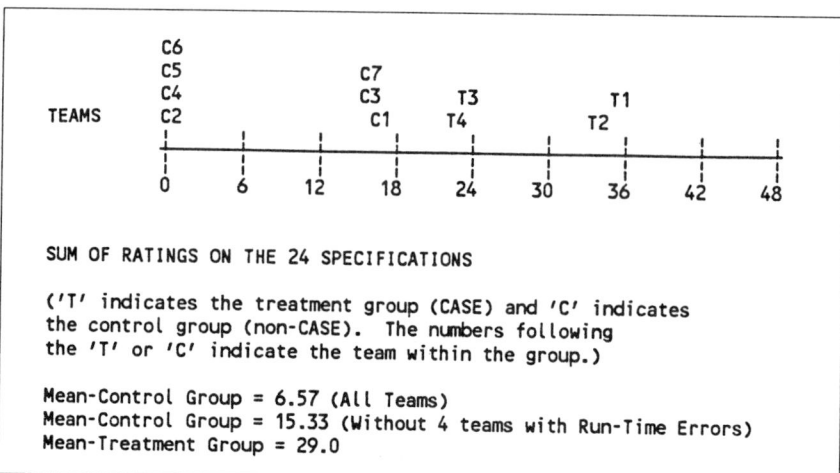

Figure 17: Level of Completeness

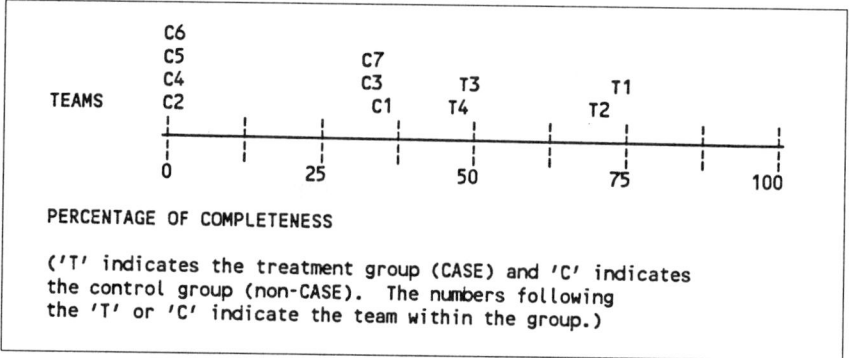

Figure 18: Percentage of Completeness

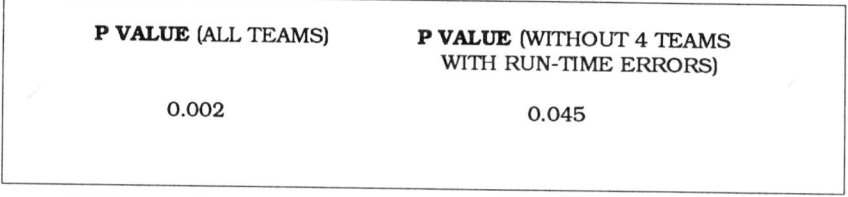

Table 4: Significance (P Values) for System Completeness

hypothesis that there is no difference in the completeness of the two systems could be rejected. *The system developed by CASE users was more complete that the systems developed by non-CASE users.*

CONCLUSIONS

Complexity and completeness measure the quality of the final system. A difference in the complexity of the final systems was not rejected, however there was a difference in the level of completeness of the final systems. The quality of the systems with respect to completeness increased when CASE technologies were used. The treatment group (CASE) produced more complete systems. The CASE-developed systems fulfilled more of the initial requirements, therefore, there was a higher system quality. There was not a significant difference in complexity between CASE developed and non-CASE developed systems. If quality was judged solely on that one aspect, no conclusions could be drawn with respect to quality. The hypothesis was partially supported; there was an increase in one aspect of the quality of the CASE developed system over the non-CASE developed system. The CASE developed systems were better able to meet the specifications than the non-CASE developed systems.

SUMMARY

The original belief, there is increased software system quality when CASE technologies are used, was partially supported. With regard to completeness, there was an increase in the quality of the systems developed using CASE technologies. All of the final projects designed with CASE were more complete than the projects designed without CASE. With regard to complexity, there was no confirmable increase in the quality of the systems developed using CASE technologies. There was a difference in the means for all the variables used to measure complexity; there was less complexity in the systems that were developed using CASE than in the systems developed without CASE, however, it cannot be said with any certainty that this difference would be found again in another sample.

Although the sample sizes in this research were small, the quality of the systems with respect to completeness improved when CASE technologies were used. We argue furthermore that the magnitude of the difference with respect to complexity is large enough to be of practical significance, even if it is not statistically significant. The increase in one aspect of the quality of the systems produced by the CASE users was shown because the level of completeness of the CASE produced systems was greater than the non-CASE produced systems. The analysis supported the original research belief about system quality.

The major contributions of this research are the quantitative measures to the claims of increased system quality when CASE technologies are used. The quality of the systems improved; more complete systems were developed by the teams that used CASE technologies for system design. We can infer that the designs developed with CASE technologies were better than the designs developed without CASE technologies. They fulfilled the requirements specifications and the finished system was more complete.

There was a significant difference in the levels of completeness of the systems. Since increased system quality was defined as being less complex and more complete, it can be concluded that system quality was increased with respect to the level of system completeness, but that more research is needed to make any statements about system complexity. It seems likely that had the non-CASE groups produced systems as complete as the CASE groups, their software would have been more complex. Our original belief about improved system quality was partially supported by the significant difference in completeness and may have been totally supported if the non-CASE groups produced systems with the same level of completeness as the CASE groups.

Results from this research on the complexity measures were inconclusive; further research is required. The metrics appeared to be measuring similar aspects of complexity, and overall the variables selected were consistent. More studies similar to Elshoff (1984) need to be conducted in order to determine the most significant complexity measures and to determine which metrics measure similar components of complexity. The complexity aspect of quality of a system is difficult to define, evaluate and measure.

MANAGERIAL IMPLICATIONS

Information technology managers should be encouraged in their quest for increased system quality. A major component of the software crisis is the inability to measure, estimate, and improve system quality. This study indicates that use of CASE tools could improve system quality and offers some measures of system quality.

Many of the students currently majoring in Information Systems will be the applications-systems analysts of tomorrow. Therefore, the results of this study may be generalized to the entire population of professional system analysts. It should be noted that students in the Autumn 1989 quarter were novices in CASE and in software engineering. Since they were not experienced systems analysts or programmers, they might have been more receptive to the new CASE technology than system analysts or programmers with years of design or programming experience without CASE technology. Programmers with several years of experience are often reluctant to change their style of programming or designing, often claiming that their work is creative and that automation of the process will stifle creativity. Other studies involving students learning new technologies (Misra 1989; Mynatt 1989) also report a learning curve far shorter than expected or experienced in a commercial setting. The learning period might be longer for the entire population of expert analysts than for the subjects in this study. Gains in this study should be attainable in a commercial setting but may take longer because students are more adaptable. On the other hand, professionals already know how to plan well, students do not. It is possible that Excelerator provided a disciplined environment for students that would not be needed by professionals.

Nonetheless, information technology managers should be mindful when applying these findings to a commercial setting that the subjects were novices with CASE technologies, the sample size was small and the project was not a true "programming in the large" project.

FUTURE RESEARCH

Only one CASE tool, Excelerator, was used and we would like to repeat the experiment using different CASE products. Excelerator, a product of Index Technology Corporation, was the first commercial "widely available" IBM PC-based CASE product and currently is the most widely used microcomputer CASE tool. Excelerator is a upper CASE tool used to aid in the requirements analysis and design phases of the system development life cycle and is built around an integrated data dictionary. Excelerator supports several different structured design methodologies; the subjects in this research used Gane/Sarson data flow diagrams, Yourdon/Constantine structure charts, and an integrated data dictionary. There is extensive verification checking against the structured methodologies' rules. Can the results of this research be generalized to other upper CASE tools, or lower CASE tools (code generators)? It appears that similar results would be obtained if a different upper CASE tool was used and the study repeated. Use of a lower CASE tool would require redefinition of data collection methods and evaluation criteria.

This study reported on the results from only one task. Future research and analysis is planned to include the data from additional projects and additional CASE tools. Future research also should include direct investigation of the design process and the design documentation. Data could be collected about the length of time required to design a project and the design itself could be evaluated (Haas 1988). In this study the effects of the design were evaluated using the final software systems and the coding process. This research was an indirect measure of the design and further research should focus on the direct measurement of the design activities.

This study should be viewed as a beginning for establishing some metrics about the product. More research is needed on both CASE and software metrics. Studies in commercial settings are difficult, but once some standards for evaluating the process and the product are established, this type of research should be conducted in a commercial environment.

Although there were no significant differences between the complexity of the two systems, there were significant differences in the completeness of the two systems. It is probable that if the level of completeness for the CASE and non-CASE systems was the same that there would have been differences in the complexity of the two systems. Future research needs to be done in the area of software quality and the relationship between completeness and complexity.

REFERENCES

Acly, E. (1988) "Looking Beyond CASE." *IEEE Software*, March 1988, 39-43.

Attewell, P. and Rule, J. (1984) "Computing and Organizations: What We Know and What We Don't Know." *Communications of the ACM*, Vol 27, No. 12, December 1984, 1184-1192.

Basili, V. R. and Reiter, R. W. (1981) "A Controlled Experiment Quantitatively Comparing Software Development Approaches." *IEEE Transactions on Software Engineering*, Vol. SE-7, No.3, May 1981, 299-320.

Basili, V. R., Selby, R. W. and Hutchens, D. H. (1986) "Experimentation in Software Engineering." *IEEE Transactions on Software Engineering*, Vol. SE-12. No. 7, July 1986, 733-743.

Boehm, B. W. (1981) *Software Engineering Economics*. Englewood Cliffs, New Jersey: Prentice-Hall Inc., 1981.

Boehm, B. W. (1987) "Improving Software Productivity." *IEEE Computer*, September 1987, 43-57.

Burkhard, D. L. (1989) "Implementing CASE Tools." *Journal of Systems Management*, May 1989, Vol. 40, No. 5, 20-25.

Cameron, R. D. (1988) "An Abstract Pretty Printer." *IEEE Software*, Vol. 5, No. 6, November 1988, 61-67.

Card, D. (1988) "Major Obstacles Hinder Successful Measurement." *IEEE Software*, Vol. 5, No. 6, November 1988, 82-86.

Chikofsky, E. J. (1988) "Software Technology People Can Really Use." *IEEE Software*, Vol. 5, No. 2, March 1988, 8-10.

Chikofsky, E. J. (1989) "Making CASE Pay Off." *CIO*, February 1989, Vol. 2, No. 5, 12-16.

Curtis, B., Sheppard, S.B., Milliman, P., Borst, M.A. and Love, T. (1978) "Measuring the Psychological Complexity of Software Maintenance Tasks with the Halstead and McCabe Metrics." *IEEE Transactions on Software Engineering*, Vol. SE-5, No. 2, March 1979, 96-104.

Curtis, B. (1983) "Software Metrics: Guest Editor's Introduction." *IEEE Transactions on Software Engineering*, Vol. SE-9, No. 6, November 1983, 637-638.

de la Torre, J. (1988) "Quality-assured Software in 4GL/CASE." *Business Software Review*, March 1988, Vol. 7, No. 3, 30-33.

Eliot, L. B. and Scacchi, W. (1986) "Towards a Knowledge-Based System Factory: Issues and Implementations." *IEEE Expert*, Vol. 1, No. 4, Winter 1986, 51-58.

Elshoff, J. L. (1984) "Characteristic Program Complexity Measures." *Proceedings of the 7th International Conference on Software Engineering*, March 1984, Orlando, Florida, 288-293 IEEE Computer Society Press, Los Angeles, California.

Fairley, R. E. (1985) *Software Engineering Concepts*. New York: McGraw-Hill Company, 1985.

Fitzsimmons, A. and Love, T. (1979) "A Review And Evaluation of Software Science." *Computing Surveys*, Vol. 10, No. 1, March 1978, 3-18.

Frenkel, K. A. (1985) "Toward Automating the Software-Development Cycle." *Communications of the ACM*, Vol. 28, No. 6, June 1985, 578-589.

Freeman, P. (1983) "Fundamentals of Design." in *Tutorial on Software Design Techniques*, Fourth Edition, ed. Peter Freeman, Silver Spring, Maryland: IEEE Computer Society Press, 1983, 2-22.

Gibson, M. L. (1989) "The CASE Philosophy." *BYTE*. April 1989, 209-218.

Glass, R. L. (1982) "Modern Programming Practices: A Report from Industry." New Jersey: Prentice-Hall, Inc., 1982 as cited in Abdel-Hamid, T. K. Understanding the 90% Syndrome in Software Project Management: A Simulation-Based Case Study, *The Journal of Systems and Software*, Vol. 8, No. 4, August 1988, 319-330.

Gordon, R. D. (1979a) "Measuring Improvements in Program Clarity." *IEEE Transactions on Software Engineering*, SE-5, No.2, March 1979, 79-90.

Gordon, R. D. (1979b) "A Qualitative Justification for a Measure of Program Clarity." *IEEE Transactions on Software Engineering*, SE-5, No.2, March 1979, 121-128.

Grady, R. B. (1987) "Measuring and Managing Software Maintenance." *IEEE Software*, Vol. 4, No. 5, September 1987, 35-45.

Haas, D. F. and Waguespack, L. J. (1989) "Sizing Assignments: A Contribution From Software Engineering to Computer Science Education." *Proceedings of the Twentieth SIGCSE Technical Symposium on Computer Science Education*, Louisville, Kentucky, February 23-25, 1989, eds. Barrett, Robert A. and Mansfield, Maynard J., 190-194, SIGCSE Bulletin, Vol. 21, No. 1, The Association for Computing Machinery, New York, New York.

Halstead, M. H. (1977) *Elements of Software Science*. New York: Elsevier, 1977.

Hausen, H. and Mullerburg, M. (1981) "Conspectus of Software Engineering Environments." *Proceedings of 5th International Conference on Software Engineering*, 34-43, 1981.

Humphrey, W. S. (1988) "Characterizing the Software Process: A Maturity Framework." *IEEE Software*, Vol. 5, No. 2, March 1988, 73-79.

Humphrey, W. S. (1989) *Managing The Software Process*. Reading, Massachusetts: Addison-Wesley Publishing Company, 1989.

Index (1987). *Excelerator*. Cambridge, Mass: Index Technology Corporation.

Jones, C. (1986) *Programming Productivity*. New York: McGraw-Hill Book Company, 1986.

Lewis, T. G. (1988) "Software and The Single Programmer." *Dr. Dobbs Software*

Engineering Sourcebook, Winter 1988, 18-27.

Martin, C. F. (1988a) "Getting CASE in Place." *Business Software Review*, Vol. 7, No. 5, April 1988, 20-25.

Martin, C. F. (1988b) "Second-Generation CASE Tools: A Challenge to Vendors." *IEEE Software*, Vol. 5, No. 2, March 1988, 46-49.

McClure, C. (1989) *CASE is Software Automation*. New Jersey: Prentice-Hall, 1989.

Mills, E. E. (1987) "Software Metrics." *SEI Curriculum Module* SEI-CM-12-1.0, October 1987.

Misra, S. K. and Subramanian, V. (1988) "An Assessment of CASE Technology for Software Design." *Information and Management*, Vol. 15, No. 4, November 1988, 213-228.

Myers, G. J. (1978) "A Controlled Experiment in Program Testing and Code Walkthroughs/Inspections." *Communications of the ACM*, Vol. 21, No. 9, September 1978, 760-768.

Mynatt, Barbee T. and Leventhall, Laura Marie (1989) "A CASE Primer for Computer Science Educators." *Proceedings of the Twentieth SIGCSE Technical Symposium on Computer Science Education*, Louisville, Kentucky, February 23-25, 1989, eds. Barrett, Robert A. and Mansfield, Maynard, J., 122-126.

Nejmeh, B. A. (1988) "Designs on Case." *UNIX Review*, Vol. 6, No. 11, November 1988, 45-50.

Norman, R. J. and Nunamaker, J. F. (1989) "CASE Productivity Perceptions of Software Engineering Professionals." *Communications of the ACM*, Vol. 32, no. 9, September 1989, 1102-1108.

Oppen, D. C. (1980) "Prettyprinting." *ACM Transactions on Programming Languages and Systems*, Vol. 2, No. 4, October 1980, 465-483.

Pressman, R. S. (1982) *Software Engineering: A Practitioner's Approach*. New York: McGraw-Hill Company, 1982.

Rombach, H. D. (1987) "A Controlled Experiment on the Impact of Software Structure on Maintainability." *IEEE Transactions on Software Engineering*, Vol. SE-13, No. 3, March 1987, 344-354.

Rubin, Lisa F. (1983) Syntax-Directed Pretty Printing - A First Step Towards a Syntax-Directed Editor. *IEEE Transactions on Software Engineering*, Vol. SE-9, No. 2, March 1983, 119-127.

Sammet, Jean E. (1969) *Programming Languages: History and Fundamentals*. Englewood Cliffs, N.J., Prentice-Hall, Inc. 1969.

Shemer, I. (1987) "Systems Analysis: A Systematic Analysis of a Conceptual Model." *Communications of the ACM*, Vol. 30, No. 6, June 1987, 506-512.

Stevens, W. P., Constantine, L. L., and Myers, G. J. (1974) "Structured Design." IBM Systems Journal, Vol. 13, No. 2, 115-139.

Statland, N. (1989) "Payoffs Down the Pike: A CASE Study." *Datamation*, Vol. 35, No. 7, April 1, 1989, 32-33,52.

Wallace, S. (1988) "Methodology: CASE's Critical Cornerstone." *Business Software Review*, Vol. 7, No. 5, April 1988, 17-20.

Weyuker, E. J. (1988) "Evaluating Software Complexity Measures." *IEEE Transactions on Software Engineering*, Vol. SE-14, No. 9, September 1988, 1357-1365

Yourdon, E. N. and Constantine, L. L. (1979) *Structured Design*. Prentice-Hall, Englewood Cliffs, New Jersey: Prentice-Hall, 1979.

Section IV

Case Studies of CASE Usage

CHAPTER SEVENTEEN

COBOL-to-Ada Transition: A System Re-Engineering Case Study

Reginald L. Hobbs
Army Research Laboratory

In this study we investigated several issues, methods, and tools that impact the software life cycle development that the Army uses to design, implement, test, and maintain application software. The purpose of this project was not only the evaluation of these methods, but the identification of problems affecting the success of software development within the constraints of current development policy. This chapter outlines a process for transitioning older systems using current software engineering methodologies.

Objective

The main objective of this project was to describe a re-engineering strategy for converting Army Management Information System (MIS) applications from COBOL to Ada. The Department of Defense (DoD) must recover $35 billion in savings, through efficiency and productivity improvements, by fiscal year 1997 (Strassmann, 1991). To realize these savings, the DoD is focusing on new methodologies and tools for creating, modifying, and maintaining systems. Reusability, portability, and maintainability of software applications have

This research was performed as an in-house project at the ARL Software Technology Branch. The information described in this chapter is not to be construed as an official Army position, unless so designated by other authorized documents.

taken priority in the overall life cycle development process. Both government and private industry organizations are facing similar challenges in overhauling outdated systems by implementing software engineering and information systems re-engineering strategies.

The U.S. Army maintains a large inventory of MIS applications in the major functional areas of logistics, personnel, finance, and communications. Many of these are COBOL systems and some have been operational for more than twenty years. Because of the current state of these systems, it is difficult to modernize and merge them with new technology.

Several objectives were established at the beginning of the project to focus the effort on improving the re-engineering process. First, we wanted to automate the design process in order to reduce the errors brought on by poor design. Second, we wanted to gauge the impact of automated tools on the design process. Third, we wanted to select appropriate tools that would assist the developer while minimizing the learning curve necessary to make them effective.

A critical portion of the proposed transition effort was devoted to reverse engineering. The accuracy and completeness of the documentation for the selected MIS system was unreliable since it had not been kept current. Furthermore, software modifications were often performed without regard to their impact on the overall program design. This situation reflects a similar pattern of maintenance for many of the systems in the Army inventory. Reverse engineering techniques were used to construct a high-level representation of the existing system. The results of the reverse engineering analysis could then be used to define the base functional requirements for the new system. We wanted to re-engineer and enhance the system while maintaining most of the original functionality.

System Description

AIRMICS (Army Institute for Research in Management Information, Communications, and Computer Sciences) in conjunction with SDC-A (Software Development Center-Atlanta) selected the Installation Material Condition Status Reporting System (IMCSRS) to re-engineer, using both functional decomposition and object-oriented design methods. The system consisted of 10,000 lines of code in 15 programs. This system appeared to be representative of the typical MIS application being used by the Army (i.e. batch-oriented, report generation, COBOL source code, etc.), but was smaller than average in size.

An important question addressed at the beginning of the project concerned the selection of an appropriate system. What are the factors for deciding which system to re-engineer? We wished to illustrate that CASE (Computer-Aided Software Engineering) tools and structured methodologies could be utilized to effectively transition systems from COBOL to Ada.

Choosing an application that was currently being used by the Army would make the results of the effort more meaningful, as opposed to using a system developed just for this study. Many development problems were avoided by selecting a system that was not extremely complex, involved few interfaces, had a reasonable number of lines of code, decent documentation, etc.. The knowledge and confidence acquired during this pilot project can be used for future systems development.

IMCSRS was designed to consolidate equipment status information submitted by Army installations. IMCSRS formats the information into reports needed by managers to assess the status and condition of selected items of equipment. It produces printed reports on the readiness and maintenance status of items of equipment at installation/division level. It also formats reports for transmission across a wide area network to several major Army Command headquarters. Reports were consolidated at the command level to provide trends analysis and decision support information (U.S. Army, 1991).

IMCSRS was written in the early 1970s. The COBOL version of IMCSRS was run as a remote batch process on a regional data center. The processing platform being used at the regional centers was an Amdahl mainframe.

RE-ENGINEERING ENVIRONMENT

The hardware selection decision for this transition effort was based in part on the software tools selected. Another consideration in the selection of hardware is that most CASE tools have extensive memory requirements. In addition, a multi-tasking windows environment is normally required, especially for the more complex CASE tools.

The analysis and redesign work during the project was done using 2 SUN 386i workstations that were networked together. The network capability allowed for the sharing of the data dictionary, databases, and other software tools while making it possible to do design concurrently on the separate CPUs. The SUN machines were chosen for their compatibility with the existing operating environment and the support for the graphical user interface necessary for diagramming using the selected CASE tools.

The SUN OS 3.5 operating system (BSD UNIX 4.2) was installed on the machines.

CASE/Development Tools.

CASE includes various tools that automate portions of the software development life cycle. Initially, the tools were primarily software aids to assist in the generation of graphical representations of a system. Current tools incorporate other features such as project management, requirements tracking, code generation, etc. CASE tools are sometimes characterized as "Upper" or "Lower" CASE. Upper CASE tools support front-end developmental activities such as business modeling, requirements analysis, entity relationship modeling, etc., while lower CASE tools support back-end stages such as code restructuring and re-engineering (Jones, 1992).

Because of the multitude of CASE products on the market (each with competitive strengths and weakness), the key in selection is to determine at the beginning of the project what characteristics are critical to the tasks to be accomplished (whether the project involves design of a new system, redesign, code maintenance, etc.). Once this is determined, the various tools can be compared against these critical success factors until the tool meeting most, if not all, factors is selected (Jones, 1992).

During the reverse engineering phase of the project, IDE's *Software Through Pictures* CASE tool was used to create the diagrams that mapped the existing system. We selected the CASE tool suite by Cadre Technologies called *Teamwork* for the forward engineering portion of the project. The structured analysis and structured design was done using *Teamwork/SA* and *Teamwork/SD* tools, respectively. The object-oriented design (OOD) was performed with the aid of the *Teamwork/Ada* tool to design the necessary Ada Structure Graphs (ASGs). The primary reasons the Teamwork tools were selected was because they supported both object-oriented and functional decomposition design methods, generation of template Ada code, and support for the DoD documentation standard. This was also a fairly mature product, well supported, and one of the most popular CASE tools on the market.

The *Teamwork* CASE tools include modules for system analysis, information modeling, real-time system analysis, and system design, as well as a utility called *Teamwork/ACCESS* which controls access to other software development packages, project management systems, and document production systems. The user interface consists of a mouse-driven windowing environment containing pop-up and pull-down menus. Multiple windows can be edited simultaneously. All *Teamwork* products access a project database that collects project models and their model objects (Structure Charts, Data Flow Diagrams, module specifications, etc.). This database creates a development environment to completely support the analysis and design phases of the software life cycle by furnishing a common interface to model objects.

RE-ENGINEERING DEVELOPMENT STRATEGY

The term re-engineering is now being widely used to describe any type of redevelopment effort. There are several related terms that are sometimes incorrectly used to describe the entire re-engineering process: forward engineering, reverse engineering, redesign (or design recovery), and restructuring. The definition for these terms and their relationship to re-engineering is based on the underlying engineering process, not the level of automation being used. The concept of re-engineering as it is being used here is based on the taxonomy of software engineering terms defined by IEEE (Chikofsky and Cross, 1990). Forward Engineering can be describe as the traditional software development process that follows the life cycle from requirements analysis, design, and implementation. Reverse engineering is a process of working from the code backwards to uncover design decisions and functional requirements. Redesign (design recovery) involves a technical redesign of the software to reduce complexity. Restructuring is concerned with improving code structure to aid comprehension (i.e. reformatting, pretty printing, etc.). Figure 1 shows the taxonomy of these terms and their relationships (Chikofsky and Cross, 1990).

Re-engineering can be defined as the examination and alteration of a subject system to reconstitute it in a new form and the subsequent implementation of that form. Re-engineering involves a reverse engineering phase (to achieve a description of the old system) and a forward engineering phase. Re-engineering the project involved both phases.

Another objective was to compare alternate design methodologies - object-oriented or functional decomposition. Object-oriented design is a fairly new and unproven method for the design of MIS applications. Functional decomposition is the more traditional and accepted design method. To explore this issue, project members were divided into two teams - one re-designed IMCSRS using the object-oriented approach and one used functional decomposition.

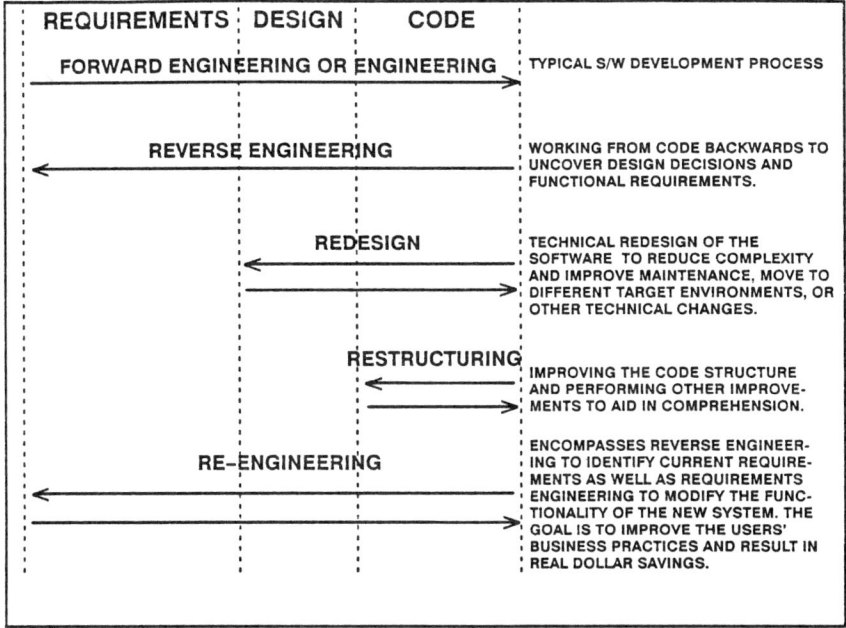

Figure 1: Re-engineering Taxonomy

REVERSE ENGINEERING

Reverse engineering is the process of analyzing a subject system to find the system components and their interrelationships. The components are then mapped into representations of the system in a different form or at a higher level of abstraction. Reverse engineering is not just creating abstract representations of a system; it is also analyzing and interpreting those abstractions to acquire a better understanding of a system's actual functionality.

In the absence of an automated tool to perform an analysis of the source code, a task was undertaken to investigate/develop a method to reverse engineer IMCSRS. The reverse engineering methodology used was a process called *Synchronized Refinement* (Rugaber and Kamper, 1990). Synchronized refinement relates the execution of the program with the program's functional requirements. This is done by simultaneously performing a bottom-up analysis of the source code with a top-down synthesis of the application model. Synchronized refinement should be applied only in situations where a detailed, line-by-line analysis of the source code is required. The analysis is controlled by the determination of design decisions.

Design decisions are data structures and coding practices intended to accomplish the functional goals of the designer. Before a program is written, the original designer makes a series of decisions about the form of the solution to a problem, by decomposing it into pieces and then indicating how the pieces work together to solve the problem. There are 4 categories of design decisions defined using the synchronized refinement methodology (Rugaber and Kamper, 1990):

- Composition/decomposition - Programs are built up from separate modules. This is usually implemented in the code using separate procedures to divide the program into parts.
- Encapsulation/interleaving - Sub-components interact with each other. If the interactions are limited and occur through explicit interfaces, the component is said to be encapsulated. If two or more components use the same section of code or the same data structure, they are considered to be interleaved.
- Generalization/specialization - A program data structure performs a similar function or is coded similar to another component.
- Data/Procedure - The designation of program variables and procedures is a design decision that may give information as to program function, if the designer chooses appropriate names for the application. The data element naming convention is examined to infer functionality.

The result of reverse engineering the IMCSRS system was a set of diagrams, figures, and textual descriptions that defined the functionality of the existing system.

Input into the creation of the functional description included system user manuals, a programmers guide, a maintenance guide, and relevant regulations governing the system, as well as interviews with the system maintainer(s), and source code. A key to understanding a system's functioning is to concentrate on inputs and outputs. Most Army MIS applications are primarily concerned with data collection and report generation. If intermediate or output information is derived from input data, the relevant code must be located and examined in detail.

During the reverse engineering process it is important not to go into great detail with the existing code - if you do you will simply be re-implementing. The key is to discover the basic functions (how the system currently runs), then add new desired features (interactivity, etc.). By applying a synchronized refinement method for code analysis, functionality should be extracted based on implementation of the current system.

The methodology used relied on a variety of representation techniques. Although the CASE tools used during the reverse engineering phase did not perform the actual analysis, they were critical in depicting the information we discovered. IDE's Software Through Pictures CASE tool was used to draw the diagrams created during the analysis. The were 4 main steps involved in reverse engineering IMCSRS (Rugaber and Kamper, 1990):

1. The construction of a textual description of the application. Concurrently, we devise and revise a system's requirements summary. The textual description was written to obtain an initial understanding of the application domain and was derived from information external to the actual system source code. At the textual description level, references were not made to the program internal structure or to the programming language used in order to maintain a high-level of abstraction. The process of deriving the description was repeated at the subprogram and program levels. Each process was described in terms of the requirements placed on it by the system. A summary was produced from the textual descirption that consolidated the overall functional system requirements in a list format.

2. The next step was the construction of Data Flow Diagrams (DFDs). DFDs are used to characterize the major functional activities and files contained in a system. Beginning with a context diagram that described the overall system behavior, multiple layers of DFDs were constructed in a nested, hierarchical structure.

3. After the DFDs were constructed, the input/output structure of each program was developed to give a more detailed description of the files. Jackson diagrams were used to represent this information. Software Through Pictures provided an editor to construct the Jackson Diagrams. Jackson diagrams are a method of graphically depicting the relationships between files, records, and other pieces of data. The editor was integrated with a data dictionary and performed consistency checks on the constructed diagrams.

4. Finally, the analyst identified the algorithmic structure of the system using Synchronized Refinement. Synchronized Refine-

ment was accomplished to some extent by the use of the multiple-window environment provided on the SUN workstation. It was basically a line-by-line analysis process. Code sections were searched for the occurrence of design decisions. Each time a decision was discovered, the entire code section would be replaced by a stub that acted as a place marker in the code. At the same time, the functional description document was revised to reflect where the decision occurred. Since the code was processed bottom-up, each stub removed a level of detail from the implementation of the system to a more abstract view. The functional description document was created from the top down. From the initial high-level expectations, the document was revised with greater details of how the system actually operated, based on the identified design decisions.

Additional information on the reverse engineering methodology used in this project may be found in (Rugaber and Kamper, 1990).

FORWARD ENGINEERING

As previously stated, forward engineering encompasses the traditional software development life cycle. Now that the reverse engineering phase was completed, we had a model on which the new system could be designed. The reverse engineering phase basically takes you up to the point in the normal development life cycle where the requirements analysis is completed.

The following sections will give a description of the actual redesign efforts, beginning with a general overview of each methodology and then a description of the design process.

Object-Oriented Design (OOD)

Object-oriented design has been described as a cognitive process for capturing, organizing, and communicating the essential knowledge of the system's "problem space." The focus is on mapping real world resources and constraints into a system model that can then be mapped to some "solution space" (Buhr, 1984). The method centers on the concept of abstraction - illuminating important system attributes/entities/objects and suppressing implementation considerations. Terms such as information hiding, "black box" design, or encapsulation have also been associated with OOD. Information concerning detailed design or implementation features need not be known by multiple developers implementing a system designed in this manner - only the interface specification between objects. Systems are decomposed based on the principle of making implementation details transparent to the developer using objects to build systems.

Overview of the OOD Methodology

In the object-oriented environment, data are primary, procedures are secondary, functions are associated with related data, and a bottom-up approach is used for development. The major impediment to acceptance of the OOD method is that it involves a paradigm shift for most system designers (from a functional perspective to data perspective).

An object is defined as an entity (file, device, organizational unit, events, physical locations, etc.) that is itself defined by a set of common attributes and services or operations associated with it (sort, retrieve_value, read, write, etc.).

Perhaps the strongest features of this design approach include increased reusability, maintainability, understandability, and partitioning of the problem so that several programmers can implement the system concurrently and with little communication if the interfaces have been well defined.

The strategy within OOD involves the following steps (Buhr, 1984) :
1. identify the objects and their attributes,
2. identify the operations within each object,
3. establish the interfaces to the objects, and
4. implement the operations within each object.

Identifying the objects is the most difficult step in the design methodology. Each object has associated with it attributes that define the object. For example, an object called HUMAN might have defined attributes of sex, height, weight and age. An EMPLOYEE object could use social security number, employee number and salary as attributes.

Each object has operations that act on it. Some of the operations are active, others passive. The active operations alter the object's state and the value of it's attributes. The passive operations do not alter the object but usually return the values of the object's attributes. The operations are established either as visible operations which are accessible by other objects or local operations that can only be used by the object itself. Buhr notation represents an object graphically as a labeled rectangle (1990). The object's attributes are

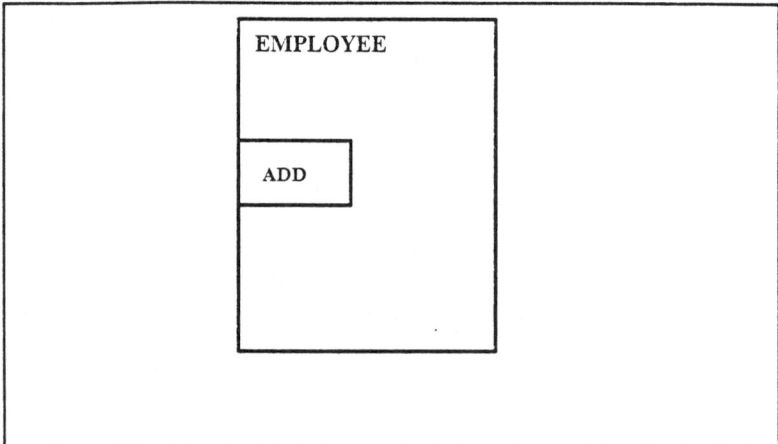

Figure 2: Employee Object with visible ADD operation

not graphically represented but are stored within a data dictionary that describes the object. Each operation is displayed as a smaller rectangle inside the object. Buhr diagrams identify visible operations by "binding" them to the object. The binding is represented by attaching the operation to the side of the object. Figure 2 is an example of an EMPLOYEE object with a visible ADD operation.

Local (hidden) operations with an object are illustrated by separating the operation from the side of the object (Figure 3).

Once all of the objects, their attributes and operations have been defined, the visibility between objects must be established. The visibility will determine if one object "sees" or has access to the

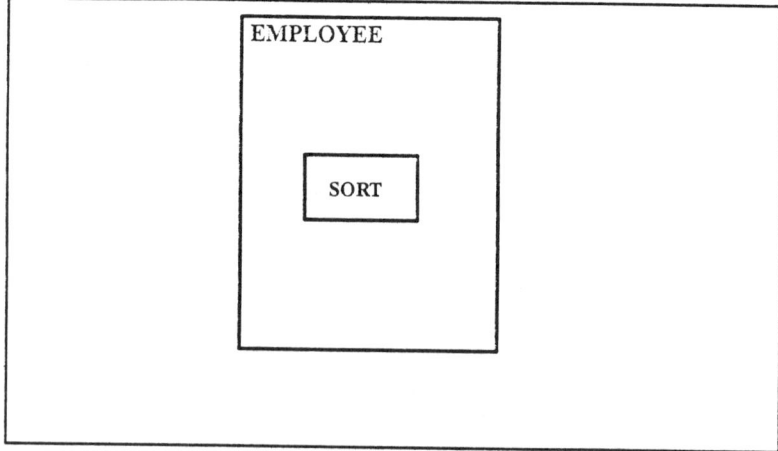

Figure 3: EMPLOYEE object with local SORT operation

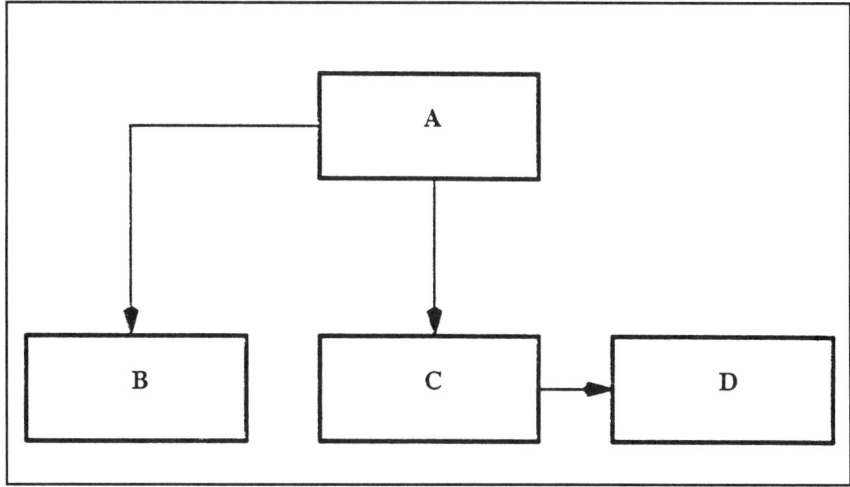

Figure 4: Visibility between objects

operations or attributes of another object. It is imperative for good software engineering to limit the visibility as much as possible. Buhr diagrams illustrate visibility by a directional arrow.

In Figure 4, objects B and object C are visible to object A. Object D is visible only to object C. Object A is not visible to any other object. By limiting visibility to objects that require the services of a receiving object, the ripple effect from software changes is minimized. If object D's implementation is changed there would be no effect on object A (as long as all the interfaces between the objects remained consistent).

The next design step is to establish the interfaces between objects. An interface consists of the allowable parameters to be passed between the initiating object and the receiving object. The parameters can be passed using in , out , or in-out mode. The in parameters are sent into an operation. The out parameters are received from an operation as return values. The in-out parameters are sent in to an operation, modified and sent back out of the operation.

In Figure 5, the in-out parameter ALL_EMPLOYEES of type EMPLOYEES is being passed to the SORT object for modification; it is then returned to the originating object. The in parameter THE_EMPLOYEE_FILE of type EMPLOYEE_FILE is being passed to the LOAD object in order to initiate a process, in this case, the loading of the file to be manipulated. The contents of the parameter are not modified and are not returned to the originating object. The parameter attributes and types are stored in a data dictionary and must be consistent when interfacing objects (i.e. the type of param-

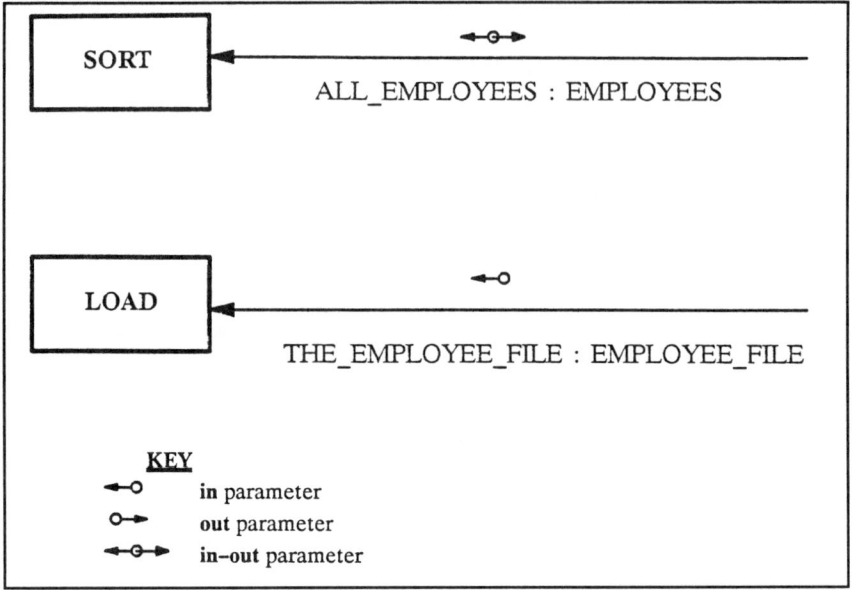

Figure 5: Example object interface representation

eter must agree between objects). The final step in the design is to implement each object. The data structures representing the object will primarily be based on the object attributes. The bodies of the operations must then be developed.

Project-specific Approach

The following sections describes the design process for the OOD version of IMCSRS (Hobbs, et al., 1990). The *Cadre Teamwork/Ada* CASE tool was used to develop the object-oriented design for IMCSRS. *Teamwork/Ada* is a design capture, navigation, and documentation tool. It supports the OOD methodology and Buhr ASG notation.

The *Teamwork/Ada* ASG editor interpreted the ASG structure. All design specifications, including the most detailed interfaces, were be derived from these graphs. These system specifications were in Ada specification format. Body "stubs" were generated for each package and subprogram. The developer was able to use the Ada PDL (Process Definition Language) to annotate each ASG. These notes were inserted into the generated code as exceptions, data structures, and program logic. This code was then processed with a simple compiler that checked the design logic for completeness. It generated errors specifying the location of incorrect design structures. The template Ada code was used as the framework for the new IMCSRS. The actual functionality of the system was added during implementation of the design by replacing the stubs with algorithms to perform specific tasks.

An initial system/user chart was created for the system (Figure 6). This chart represents the overall system behavior of IMCSRS by describing the operational context. The information to create the chart was taken from the reverse engineering functional description, system maintenance manuals, and available user guides.

The COBOL version of IMCSRS was used at the installation level, division level and regimental level. The system was processed through remote connection to an Amdahl mainframe at the installation level. Some installations also used a Honeywell mainframe at the division/regiment level for local processing of IMCSRS. Branches of the the secured Army network originating in the telecommunications centers (TCC) were used to transfer data to Forces Command (FORSCOM), Training and Doctrinal Command (TRADOC) and Materiel Readiness Support Activity (MRSA). The hard copy input data was submitted by individual army units at each installation using a standard army form, DA Form 2406. A pre-processed file of 2406 information could also be submitted from those sub-units that ran local copies of IMCSRS.

Reports went to the DOL (Directorate of Logistics) which had overall responsibility for running the system. Because the system was at the Regional Data Center (RDC), personnel in the Office of Director of Information Management (DOIM) at each installation input the data, executed the remote process, and received the output reports which were then delivered to the DOL.

Once the new System/User chart was developed, it was easy to identify the system objects. These high level "real world" objects were divided into four classes:

1. Reportable Units - the Army units that were required to report their equipment status using the DA Form 2406.
2. Reportable Equipment - the equipment identified as reportable items.
3. Unit 2406s - the hard copy DA Form 2406.
4. Reports - report files generated by the system.

Other objects were defined during design refinement. These objects, often referred to as abstract objects, were used to supplement the real-world objects. Five abstract objects were defined:

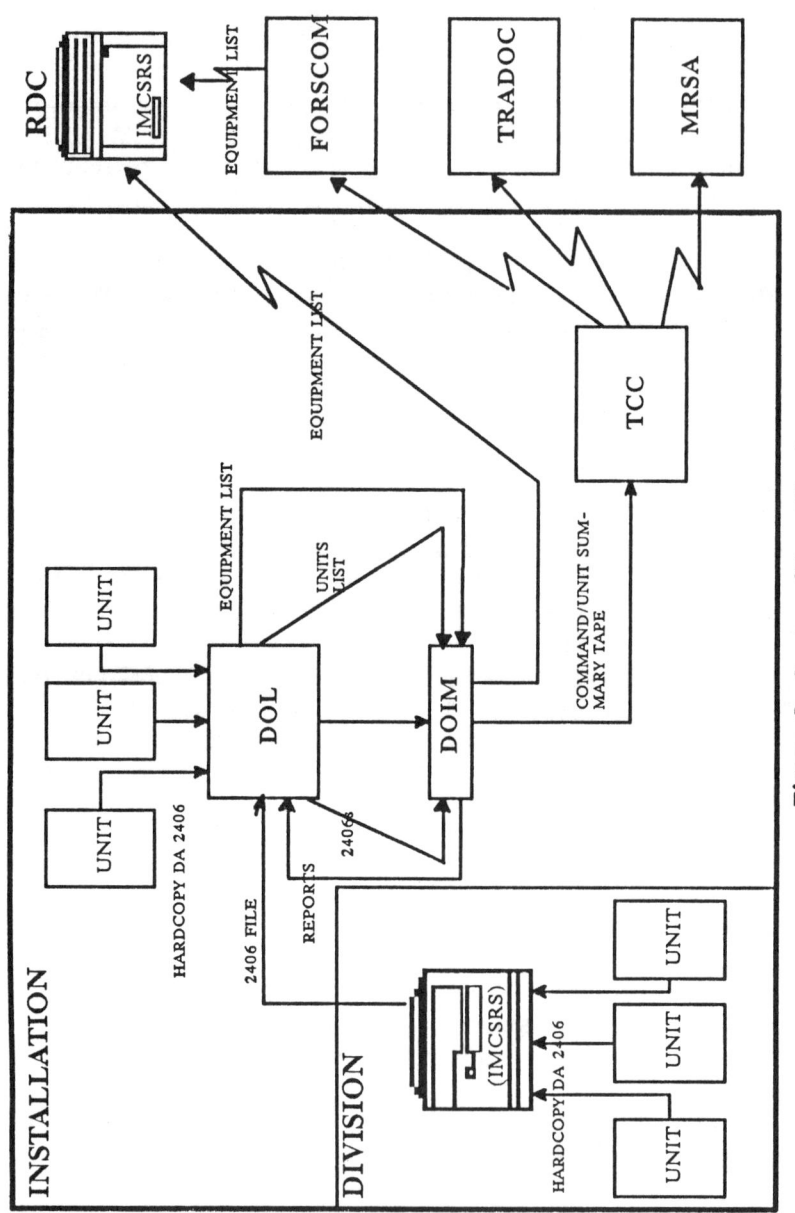

Figure 6: System/User Chart

1. Synchronizer - to manage the data bases.
2. Unit Retriever - control access to the unit list file
3. Equipment Retriever - control access to the equipment list
4. 2406 Retriever - control access to the 2406 information
5. Command I/O - to control all high level menu display and selection operations.

Attributes were then selected to define each object using the header information from the top of the 2406 form. Army units responsible for reporting equipment status are identified using attributes such as UIC (Unit Identification Code), Station Code, Utilization Code, etc. The attributes for Reportable Equipment were limited to items defining a general piece of equipment. Only items of information that were common to all models of Army equipment were included. Reportable Equipment was defined by the line item number (ECC/LIN), model, nomenclature, and average readiness rate.

The Unit 2406 attributes were defined by the fields on the actual 2406 form. The information was unique to the equipment status of a particular Army unit. All general information was captured in the Reportable Unit and Reportable Equipment objects. The 2406 form is divided into two parts, the header and equipment status (line items). The Unit 2406 object was divided in the same two parts to parallel the form. The outermost object defined the overall DA Form 2406.

A Line Item object was created as a smaller object within the Unit 2406 object. Line Item objects were instantiated to depict specific occurrences of an item of equipment on a 2406 form. For example, if an Army unit had 3 personnel carrier vehicles then 3 instances of a Line Item object with the appropriate attributes were created for the unit's 2406 object. During implementation the attributes became fields of the records representing these various objects.

Once each object was clearly defined, the operations that affected the object had to be identified. The basic operations were the same for each object: add an object, delete an object, modify the attributes of an object, and get the value of an attribute. The operations for retrieving for each attribute had to be defined (ie: Get_ECC, Get_NOUN etc). They also had to be Sorted and Searched. When the physical representation of an object was a file, additional operations (such as Open, Close, Save, Load, etc.) had to be implemented.

Figure 7 is an ASG diagram of an INSTALLATION object that was created using the CASE tool. On the diagram, the operations, interfaces (parameters), and visibilities are represented using the

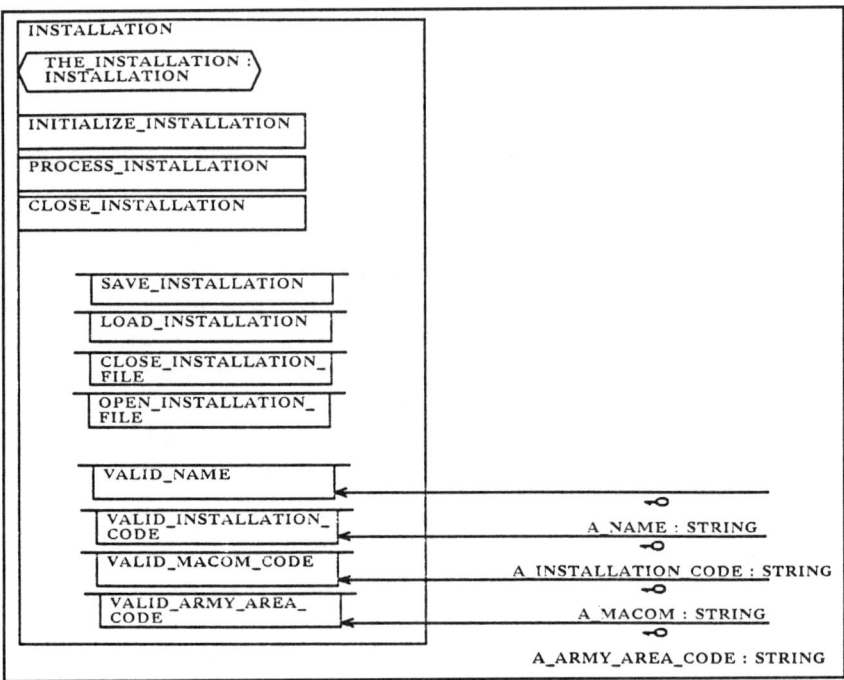

Figure 7: INSTALLATION Object

Buhr notation. The information on the ASG, coupled with the data dictionary entries that specifically described the attributes for the object, were sufficient to generate Ada Packages that contained all the specifications.

Figure 8 is an excerpt of the Ada source code generated for the INSTALLATION object based on its ASG. Note that a "null" statement has been inserted between the "begin" and "end" keywords in one of the function bodies. The algorithm to implement the necessary operation would be coded by the programmer and inserted here. All interface specifications and visibilities are already defined. The generated code was compilable and could be executed to test all the interfaces. However, since all the operation bodies consisted of nulls, the system would not actually perform any function.

Minimizing the interfaces with other objects was a primary concern. By grouping all operations to be performed on an object within that object, the system is more modular and resistant to the affect of software changes. This concept is known as encapsulation.

Figure 9 shows the ASG context diagram for the redesigned system. The main procedure, IMCSRS, was assigned visibility to the Reports, Reportable Units, Reportable Equipment and Unit 2406s objects. This visibility was necessary to add, delete and modify the specific objects within each class.

```
--$$model name: IMCSRS_L1B-00-00
--$$context title: IMCSRS_context
--$$title: No Title
--$$owner: wassmuth
--$$last accessed: Thu Jul 25 09:45:26 1991
--$$last modified: Thu Jul 25 09:44:36 1991
--$$code generated: Thu Jul 25 10:28:46 1991
--$$Teamwork Ada Source Builder Version 3.1/2.12

package body INSTALLATION is

  function VALID_ARMY_AREA_CODE(A_ARMY_AREA_CODE : in STRING) return boolean;

  function VALID_MACOM_CODE(A_MACOM : in STRING) return boolean;

  function VALID_INSTALLATION_CODE(A_INSTALLATION_CODE : in STRING) return boolean;

  function VALID_NAME(A_NAME : in STRING) return boolean;

  procedure OPEN_INSTALLATION_FILE;

  procedure CLOSE_INSTALLATION_FILE;

  procedure LOAD_INSTALLATION;

  procedure SAVE_INSTALLATION;
  function VALID_ARMY_AREA_CODE(A_ARMY_AREA_CODE : in STRING) return boolean is
    TBD : boolean;
  begin -- VALID_ARMY_AREA_CODE
    null;
    return TBD;
  end VALID_ARMY_AREA_CODE;
```

Figure 8: INSTALLATION Object Ada Source Code

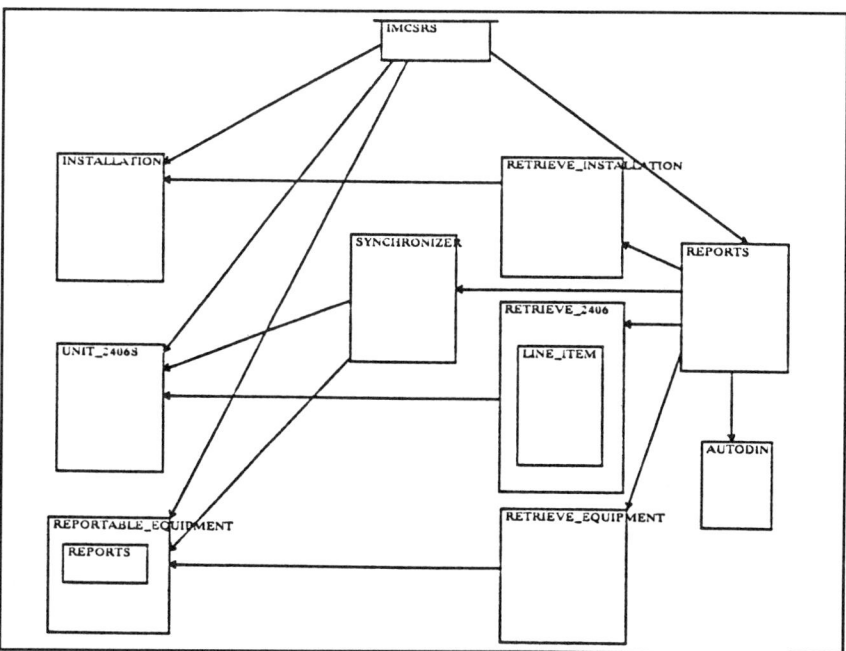

Figure 9: ASG Context Diagram

The high level components of the system were completed with the establishment of the object interfaces. The operations required for each object had been identified and the visibility between objects and interfaces to allow the operations to be accessed had been established. The design was now ready for implementation. To implement the design, the data structures used to represent the objects and the bodies of each operation had to be written.

FUNCTIONAL DECOMPOSITION (STRUCTURED ANALYSIS AND DESIGN)

This phase of the project redesigned the IMCSRS using a functional decomposition methodology. In this approach, the system was analyzed from a functional perspective. The functions and procedural nature of the system were of primary interest; the data is considered during the later stages of development. Functional decomposition is made up of two distinct phases: Structured Analysis and Structured Design (Top-down design). Structured Analysis can be described as the activity of deriving a structural model and the accompanying structured specifications to give a clear "definition of the problem". Structured Design is the development of a computer system solution to a data processing problem, creating a new system containing the same components and process relationships outlined during the analysis of the system (Stevens, et al., 1974).

Overview of the Functional Decomposition Methodology

The structured development techniques used during the project were those outlined by DeMarco (1979) and Stevens, et al., (1974). The CASE tools chosen to implement the analysis and design of the system were based on the techniques described by these methodologies.

The structured analysis of a system precedes its design; structured specifications act as direct input for the design phase. By developing a structured specification that is graphical using the CASE tools, we obtained a model of the system that is very concise and easy to interpret.

The main building block of the structured analysis of a system is the Data Flow Diagram (DFD). A DFD is a graphical representation of a system that depicts the active processes and their interrelationships. DFDs consist of 4 basic elements: Data Flows (directional arrows) , Processes (circles) , Data Stores (2 parallel lines), and Sources/Sinks (rectangles).

Data Flows represent the movement of data. They are represented as directional arrows. This symbol depicts the interface relationships between components on a DFD. Data Flows are basically the media through which data are transmitted. They are labeled with names that described the composition of the data.

A process bubble is placed on a DFD when some transformation of data occurs. Data can be manipulated within a process either of 2 ways: (1) the structure of the data can change, producing as output a reformatted version of the original data or (2) the information in the data can be transformed, generating new data. One of the most difficult tasks during the structured analysis phase is reducing system activities to processes that transform data. Each process should receive a descriptive name that gives a clear picture of the type of transformation occurring within the function.

A data store is where some temporary storage of data occurs. Data stores can represent files, information on magnetic tape, card indexes, entire databases, etc.

The Source/Sink symbol (represented by a rectangular box) represents where the data required by the system originates and where the output of the system ends up. A source/sink can be a person or organization external to the system that is the originator or recipient of data (a source is a data originator; a sink receives data). These symbols are only present on the context diagram for a system using the DeMarco notation for DFDs (DeMarco, 1979). What sources/sinks do with the data of the system cannot affect it in unexpected ways, so they are considered outside the context of the actual system function. For example, what a manager does with a report generated by a system does not affect how the system works. A Context Diagram is a DFD at the highest-level of abstraction for a system; it is usually shown as a single process bubble containing the name of the system with data flows to and from sources and sinks. The context diagram should show the interface between the outside world and the system being developed.

The DFDs within the structured specification were developed using top-down partitioning. Top-down partitioning allows the system to be decomposed into a multidimensional arrangement with differing levels of detail so that there is a smooth progression from the most abstract (top) to the most detailed (bottom). By assigning functions in the system to unique elements within a DFD, redundancy is eliminated. The structured specification also has to be disassociated with the hardware, vendor, or operating procedures of the current environment. It should focus only on how the system functions. Unlike conventional flowcharts, DFDs don't show flow of control or procedure sequences. The system specification should only be concerned with the pieces of a system and how those pieces relate to one another, not the sequence in which they occur or the number of iterations. The main emphasis in a DFD is the flow of data. The structured specification is organized from the viewpoint of data, i.e. the processing that a piece of data goes through from beginning to end of the system.

In the structured design portion of functional decomposition, the structured specification generated during in the analysis phase is utilized as a roadmap for the new design. By using the structured specification as a well-defined statement of the problem, structured design allows the form of the problem to guide the solution. The design is a plan for implementing the new system. Structured design derives a simplified, graphical representation of a system by partitioning the functionality and organizing hierarchical relationships. Partitioning systems modularizes function, effectively isolating functions from updates and changes in different portions of a system. The main tool within structured design is the structure chart (Page-Jones, 1988; Stevens, et al., 1974). Like a DFD, the structure chart is a multidimensional arrangement of a system. A structure chart depicts the partitioning of a system into modules, the organization and hierarchy between the modules, communication interfaces between the modules, and the labels for the modules. The basic elements within a structure chart are: modules, invocations, and couples.

A module is represented by a rectangular box. The contents of a module (the module specifications) are not shown on the structure chart, but can be considered as a continuous set of program statements that have in common input/output, function, mechanics and internal data. A module could be a subroutine, a function, or system call. System or library modules are called pre-defined modules since their development is not part of the design; they perform a function that can be accessed without having to be coded. The modules on a structure chart serve the purpose of "black boxes" in that the actual implementation of the function is transparent to the designer. This allows the programmer flexibility in coding a particular function as long as the module's input and output follows the design. Functions within a module may be further decomposed into sub-functions by invoking subordinate modules at a lower level of the hierarchy. This is consistent with the structured design concept of "one function per module" but allows subtasks to execute specific portions of a function.

The connection between modules (invocation), depicted as an arrow from one module to another, shows module calls. Invocations do not show calling sequence for module communication nor do they show the number of iterations. They just show that a module can potentially invoke a particular subordinate module. The details of module access are handled during actual implementation of a function.

The communication between modules is handled through coupling. Couples show data items moving from one module to the next. Graphically, couples are drawn as an arrow with a circular tail. The amount of coupling between modules determines the measure of independence between them. The level of coupling can also be examined by the designer to ascertain the overall quality of a design. The higher the coupling (and therefore, the more data dependence) between modules,the higher the probability that a change in one module will affectanother module. Minimizing the amount of coupling minimizes the ripple effect of program changes and leads to a system that is more robust. Coupling within a system can be reduced by eliminating unnecessary relationships between modules.

Another method of designing a more robust system and ensuring proper partitioning of a structure chart is determining the level of cohesion within a module. Cohesion is a measure of how the activities within a single module relate to one another. Coupling and cohesion are interdependent, however, in that the cohesion of a module directly affects the level of coupling between it and other modules. Constantine and Yourdon's methodology of structured design delineates 7 levels of possible cohesion between modules(Page-Hones, 1988; Stevens, et al., 1974):

- FUNCTIONAL: A functionally cohesive module limits itself to the performance of one and only one task. This level of cohesion within a structure chart ensures the highest level of maintainability within a system and is the most desirable level.
- SEQUENTIAL: Sequential cohesion occurs when a module outputs information to be used as input by another module within a system. This type of cohesion is maintainable, but the amount of independence between modules is increased.
- COMMUNICATIONAL: Communicatively cohesive modules contain elements that share input/output data from a common activity. Because of the interrelation between these modules that share access to global data, there is a tendency towards redundant coupling or duplication of function.

- PROCEDURAL: Procedural cohesion is distinguished by control flows between activities that are possibly unrelated and execute different functions with a module. This type of cohesion is characterized by flags or switches transmitted as data between modules.
- TEMPORAL: Temporally cohesive modules are made of elements that are connected to each other only by a time sequence of events. These elements in the module do not necessarily share functionality. This type of cohesion can also lead to redundant coupling since there may be a tendency to reproduce code in other modules that have the same type of time dependence.
- LOGICAL: Logical cohesion describes modules that contribute to a similar category of functions to be executed external to the module. In this instance, a module is used to perform several functions depending upon how it is invoked. The activities within the module are forced to share a single interface.
- COINCIDENTAL: The final type of cohesion, coincidental cohesion, is the least desirable in that it exhibits the worst level of coupling and maintainability. A coincidentally cohesive module performs activities that have very little relation to one another. They lack well-defined functions, and the calling module is often tasked with sending a control flag to the receiving module to decide what is to be done. This requires the calling module to be aware of the internals of the called module, which violates the "black box" concept.

The DFDs of the structured analysis phase are converted into structure charts in the design phase through transform analysis. Transform Analysis is a strategy for deriving a first-cut structure chart from the analysis of a system. The initial design is then taken through several iterations of refinement using the methods of determining cohesion and coupling. The main difference between a DFD and a structure chart is the hierarchical nature of a structure chart. Names of a resulting structure chart do not necessarily relate directly to names of processes on the original DFD. The beginning of the transform analysis process involves determining the portion of a DFD that contains the essential functions of a system. This central transform will outline the basic functions that must be accomplished within a system and lead directly to the development of a structure chart.

Project-specific Approach

The functional decomposition portion of the project was accomplished using the *Teamwork/SA* and *Teamwork/SD CASE* tools. *Teamwork/SA* is an environment for systems analysts, which supports the creation and verification of functional systems specifications. *Teamwork/SA* consists of tools for the rapid creation and editing of DFDs, process specifications, and data dictionary entries. Built-in Model Configuration Management tools organized models into leveled sets and helped establish relationships between DFDs and their corresponding process specifications. A versioning facility provided an audit trail during project development by tracking the history of project updates for review. *Teamwork/SA* also maintained a consistency check function with detailed knowledge of structured analysis that gauged system quality for correctness.

Teamwork/SD is an integrated set of design aids for employing a structured systems design methodology. This tool for creating structure charts, module specifications, and other graphic symbols contained within the design process provided a rapid graphical user interface for planning a system. There was also an embedded design rule checker in *Teamwork/SD* that verified the proposed design's overall validity.

Structured Analysis

The initial problem in developing a new design for IMCSRS using functional decomposition was to analyze the functional requirements of the new system. The data flow diagrams (DFDs) developed during the reverse-engineering of IMCSRS were helpful in understanding how the processes within the current COBOL version of IMCSRS interacted, but if we wished to take advantage of a structured methodology within the new system, it would be necessary to come up with DFDs for the new design.

We needed to begin our analysis by determining the overall context of the new system. The context of the system basically describes how the system interfaces with the real world; it outlines the boundary between the outside world and the internal functions of the system. The context diagram for the system is a very simple diagram depicting the external processes that interact with IMCSRS as sources/sinks (Figure 10). On this diagram, we are only concerned with 3 interfaces: 1) Operating system, 2) Data entry operator, and 3) Reporting units.

— The operating system communicates with IMCSRS by not only controlling program execution, but also by supplying the UIC_MASTER and ECCLIN_MASTER files as input. These files

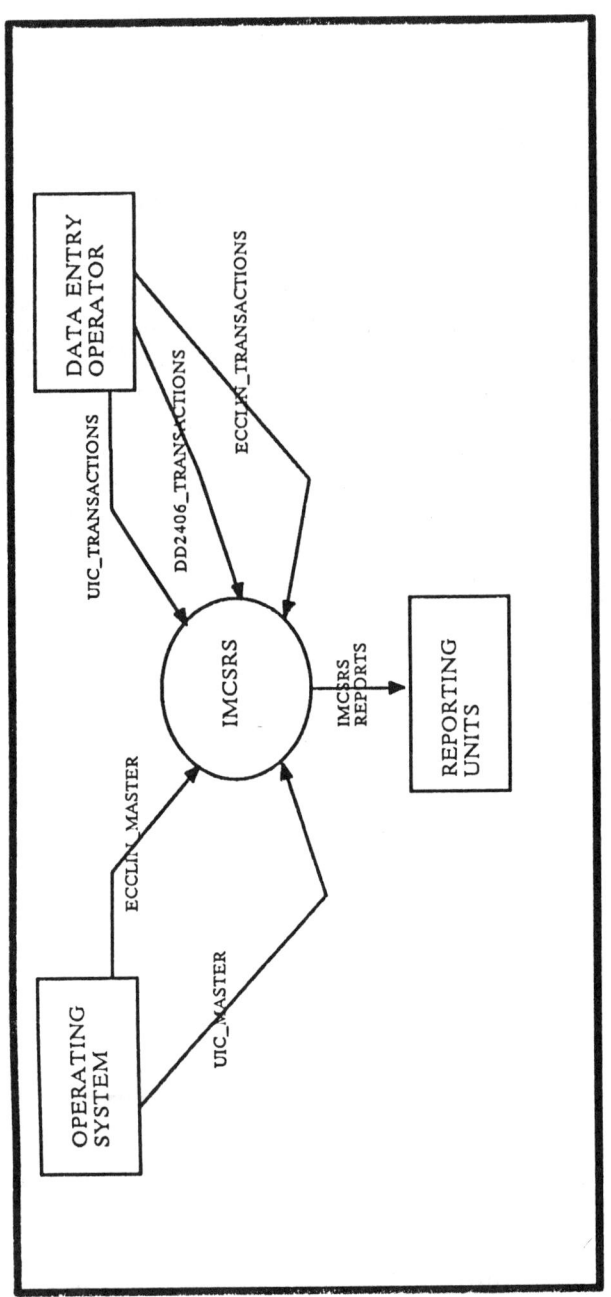

Figure 10: DFD Context Diagram

are updated by IMCSRS.
— The data entry operator is the person or persons within the DOL (Directorate of Logistics) that supply the information from the DD 2406 used to generate the 2406 transaction file. On the current version of IMCSRS, the information exists as card input that the data operators run through the system in batch mode. In the new system, the 2406 will be entered through a menu-driven screen interface. The operator also enters any requests for updating the ECCLIN_MASTER and UIC_MASTER files
— The reporting units include the installation, division, and major command recipients of the output reports. MRSA, FORSCOM, and TRANSCOM receive their output via AUTODIN.

How the sources/sinks receive the output data or produce the input data is not important at this level of abstraction during the analysis of the system. They only appear on the context diagram to represent the external view of IMCSRS.

The next level within the DFD hierarchy, level 0, outlines the major processes that take place within the system (Figure 11). IMCSRS performs 4 different functions:

1. updating the UIC_MASTER file
2. updating the ECCLIN_MASTER file
3. creating, editing the 2406_TRANSACTION file
4. generating output reports

The process bubbles were labeled accordingly. Data flows that enter a process bubble without an originating process are considered to enter the diagram from one level higher in the hierarchy. For example, the UIC_TRANSACTIONS data flow is a component of information obtained from the data entry operator at the context diagram level. By the same token, data flows that have no termination process extend to the parent DFD. The child DFD is a breakdown of the inputs/outputs from its corresponding parent process. All data flows leading away from the GENERATE_2406_REPORTS process bubble would appear in a data dictionary as components of the IMCSRS_REPORTS data flow entering the REPORTING UNITS sink on the context diagram.

The files that are being used at this level are represented as data stores. When a data flow enters or leaves a data store and is not labeled, all the data items contained in the data store are being passed as one unit. The data flow leading from the UIC_MASTER data store to the UPDATE_UIC_MASTER passes the entire UIC_MASTER_RECORD for processing. The non-labeled incoming

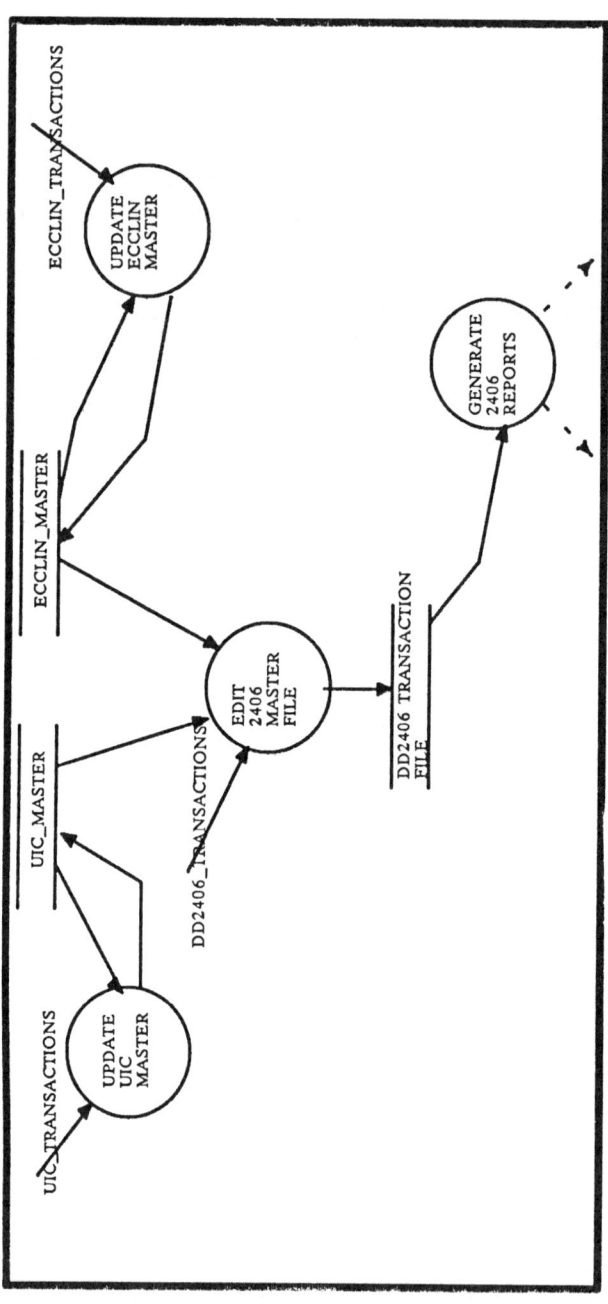

Figure 11: Level 0 DFD

arrow for the UIC_MASTER store indicates that the entire updated record is being sent to the master file for storage.

So far, we are still only identifying the processes that take place within IMCSRS, not how they execute their functions. As an illustration of how the decomposition of the processes takes place, look at the level 0 DFD. Process bubble 1, UPDATE_UIC_MASTER, is not in its primitive (i.e. lowest-level) state. To go down one level in the hierarchy under UPDATE_UIC_MASTER, we had to determine what sub-processes need to happen in order to perform the function. There are 3 possibilities during an update to the master file: new records may be added, current records may be deleted, and current records can be modified. Then we had to determine what data was necessary to accomplish these tasks. In each case, a transaction request was issued to the processes to get them to perform the function (ormally, depicting flow control information on a DFD is avoided except when it is necessary to clarify how processes interact).

On the level 1 diagram (Figure 12), which is the "child" DFD to the UPDATE_UIC_MASTER "parent" process, all data flows originate and terminate at the upper level. This indicates that there is no further decomposition of the parent process below this level.

The other processes on the level 0 DFD are decomposed in a similar fashion, by determining what sub-functions have to happen to support the overall execution of a process. When the analysis is complete, you have a set of diagrams that explain the complete function of the system and can be used to describe the system's functional requirements.

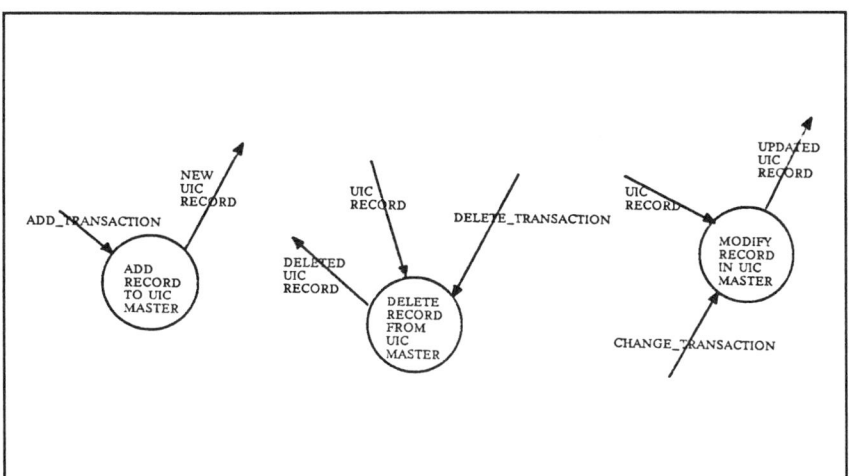

Figure 12: Level 1 DFD — UPDATE_UIC_MASTER

Structured Design

In the system design phase of the IMCSRS functional decomposition, the DFDs developed during the analysis phase are taken through a process of transform analysis to create a multi-layer arrangement of structure charts (Hobbs, et al., 1990). The structure charts serve to partition the system into modules that represent subroutines, functions, or system calls. It is at this stage of the system development that we determine individual functions for the system as opposed to processes that happen within the system. The emphasis is on the modules as functional data structures; we still do not care about the actual implementation of the code. By defining what has to happen, and leaving out details concerning implementation, we may formulate a good design for the system while leaving room for programmer creativity as to choice of algorithm. A clean, concise design will force the programmer to use structured techniques for interaction between the modules.

The main level structure chart (Figure 13) delineates the major functions within the system. Each module may invoke several other modules or be invoked by other modules. The main goal is to have a the proper level of cohesion in the design. The ideal design, one considered functionally cohesive, has modules that perform one and only one function within the system. It doesn't matter that the function is accomplished by invoking a cascading level of submodules, as long as the final result is the performance of a single, specific task.

As an example of how the structure chart determines the design of the new system, we can trace the path of a particular function through the system. On the main structure chart, there is a module called IMCSRS MAIN. This is the main calling procedure for the system. The call (invocation) is represented by the arrow leading to the module. The GET_IMCSRS_TRANSACTION_FROM_SCREEN accepts input from the operator as to the task is to be performed by the system. The information is then passed back to the calling routine as shown by the data couple called IMCSRS_TRANSACTION. The transfer of data is always represented by an arrow with an open circle on the end. When IMCSRS MAIN receives the information it must decide which path to follow to perform the required function. This decision-making process is illustrated on the structure chart by the diamond-shaped "transaction center" at the bottom of the module rectangle. In this example, we need to invoke the module UPDATE_UIC_MASTER_FILE because we want to add a new UIC record. The UPDATE_UIC_MASTER_FILE has to call a subroutine to

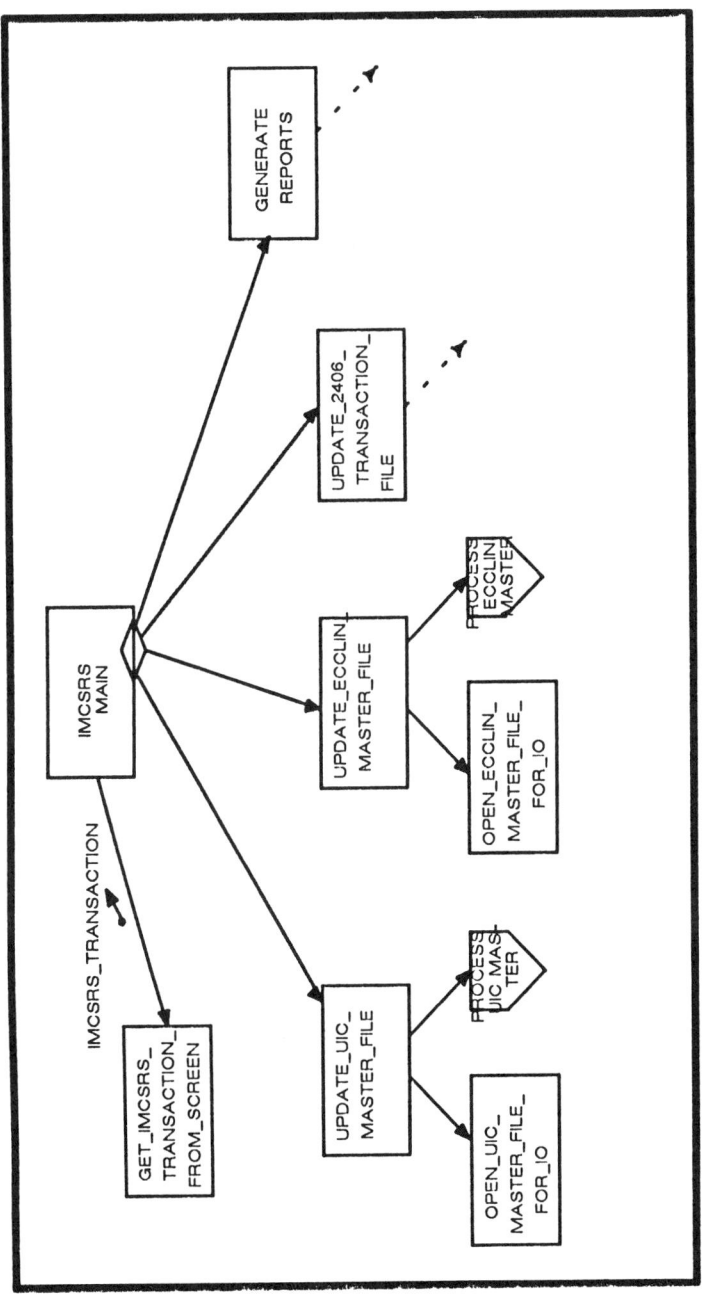

Figure 13: MAIN Structure Chart

open the file for I/O before it can be processed. The calling sequence is not depicted on a structure chart, so the ordering of events is left to the programmer's implementation. On this diagram, UPDATE_UIC_MASTER_FILE calls PROCESS_UIC_MASTER to initiate the transaction. The off-page connector symbol (inverted pentagon) indicates that the module information is external to this structure chart. Although it is acceptable to continue the subordinate levels of the structure chart on one diagram, readability and flow are best maintained by drawing separate charts for major sub-modules.

On the PROCESS_UIC_MASTER structure chart (Figure 14), there is an off-page connector at the top of the diagram showing where the processing continues. The PROCESS_UIC_MASTER_TRANSACTIONS module performs a similar decision-making process as the IMCSRS MAIN module; through its transaction center it decides if records are to be added, deleted, or modified. Following the invocation path to the ADD_UIC_RECORDS module, we can see a further decomposition of the task into subtasks. The iteration

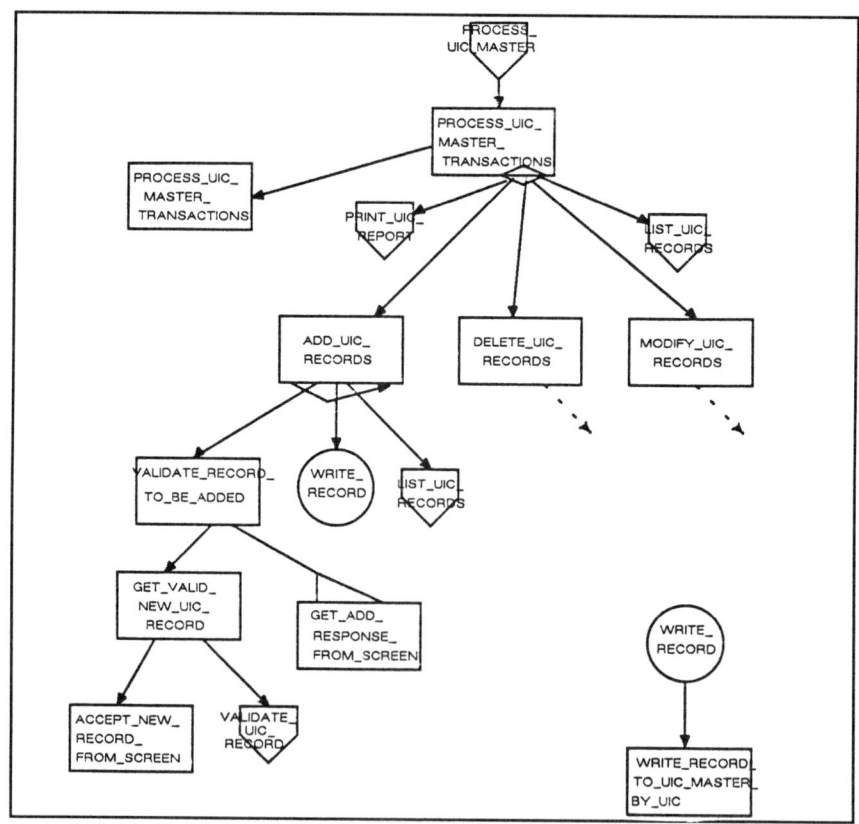

Figure 14: PROCESS_UIC_MASTER Structure Chart

symbol (represented as a bent arrow) underneath the ADD_UIC_RECORDS module means that multiple repetitions can occur, i.e., more than one record may be added at a time.

Unlike the older version of IMCSRS, the new design allows for input validation of the information during data entry. The new record for the UIC_MASTER file is taken directly from a screen interface and validated for correctness prior to being added. The validation process is in two parts: the system validates the record as to syntactic correctness, and the data entry operator is given the opportunity to visually inspect the data. Some possible validation criteria could include checking for integer values within certain ranges, date-time verification, and data format.

Deriving an acceptable level of cohesion was of primary importance in this development effort. We went through several versions of the design before coming up with one that limited the activities of each module to a specific task. The modularity of the design allowed the programmer to work on individual pieces of the problem, or to modify the implementation of a module, while being able to gauge the effect of these changes on the overall system using the structure charts.

IMPLEMENTATION

Detailed Design Refinement

The object-oriented design documentation, consisting of Buhr Diagrams and associated Ada template code, was used to perform a final validation of the system requirements with the functional users. A formal request was submitted and granted to develop the new system from the re-engineered design.

When the coding began, a few functional changes to the application had to be added. The designers were required to integrate this new functionality into the object oriented design. One of the new programmers, after one week of review in OOD concepts, was able to modify the design to meet the new requirements in only four hours.

Code Development

The programmers at SDC-A were tasked with implementing the design for the new system. Because of the modular nature of the design, each major system object could be coded separately as long as the programmers followed the defined interface specifications. As objects were written in Ada, and the source code was compiled, it was inserted into a shareable system library. The library contained all module specifications for the entire application with each parameter and type that would interface between objects. These specifications could be accessed by each programmer on the IMCSRS development team. Library routines could be included in objects being developed because the attributes and operations of all the modules were predefined.

The programmers did not require high-level knowledge of the overall function of the system or how their assigned objects were to be used in the system, they concentrated on the implementation of the operations defined by their particular package specifications. Information hiding ensured design integrity throughout the development. Only after an object was completely coded and thoroughly tested was it placed in the shareable library for access by other programmers. Any time an object was added to the library it was bound and linked to the current version of the system to create an updated executable file. This enabled the system to be incrementally tested as it evolved. Intermodule testing was also conducted prior to an object being placed into the library.

The coding was done using the Ada library procedures available with the Alsys Ada compiler and locally written Ada packages. Reusable, generic modules that were developed by SDC-A programmers were submitted as candidates for inclusion into the Army reuse library. The generated Ada package specifications furnished by the CASE tool described all the interfaces and data necessary for each component, allowing a great deal of programmer flexibility in coding the procedures. The final system consisted of 15,000 lines of Ada code.

CONCLUSION

This project is an example of using the Ada programming language to develop an MIS application. Ada is generally known for the implementation of real-time or embedded systems. The same software engineering principles used for creating those systems, such as encapsulation, information hiding, coupling, and cohesion, can be used to create well designed management information systems. Ada MIS applications can be developed using traditional functional decomposition methods and/or object-oriented techniques. Ada packages allow a software designer to build a system in a modular fashion using either functional decomposition or an object-oriented method. However, the advantages of object-oriented systems often cited in the areas of maintenance, extensibility, software re-use and software cost reduction will only be confirmed after many more large and complex systems have been built using this methodology.

Neither structured analysis nor structured design techniques create representations that lead directly to object-oriented design, but the majority of the basic principles still apply: problem partitioning, component integrity (cohesion), independence (coupling), etc. It is not necessary to unlearn structured analysis and design in order to learn OOD (Keuffel, 1991).

CASE tools, such as those used in the reverse and forward engineering phases of this project, are critical to enhance developer productivity and assure the use of sound software engineering methods. The choice of the proper CASE tools based on the methodology used, organizational software development life cycle, and resource constraints, is one of the most important decisions which should be made prior to beginning this type of re-engineering effort.

The use of a re-engineering strategy such as outlined in this paper can be a cost-effective way to improve organizational productivity and save money in information system development costs. These re-engineering concepts apply both to government and private sector organizations that are concerned with ways to modernize their current base of information system applications.

REFERENCES

Booch, G. (1986). *Software engineering with Ada.* Menlo Park, CA: Benjamin-Cummings.

Buhr, R. J. (1984). *System Design with Ada.* Englewood Cliffs, NJ: Prentice-Hall.

Chikofsky, E. J., Cross, J. H. (1990). Reverse engineering and design recovery: a taxonomy. *IEEE Software, 7*(1), 13-17.

DeMarco, T. (1979). *Structured Analysis and System Specification.* New York, NY: Yourdon Press.

Hobbs, R.L., Nealon, J.J., & Wassmuth, R. (1990). *Ada Transition Research Project (Phase I): Final Report* (AIRMICS ASQB-GI-91-005).

Jones, C. (1992). CASE's missing elements. *IEEE Spectrum, 29*(6), 38-41.

Keuffel, W. (1991). House of structure. *UNIX Review, 9*(2), 28-36.

Page-Jones, M. (1988). *The practical guide to structured systems design.* New York: Yourdon Press.

Rugaber, S.,Kamper, K. (1990). *Design Decision Analysis Research Project - Final Report,* GIT-SERC-90/01, Georgia Institute of Technology, Software Engineering Research Center.

Stevens, W. G., Myers, G. J., & Constantine, L. L., (1974). Structured design. *IBM Systems Journal, 13*(2), 115-139.

Strassmann, P. A. (1991). DoD Goals and Technology. Remarks to the Armed Forces Communications-Electronics Association (AFCEA).

U.S Army Software Development Center-Atlanta (1991). *Installation material condition status reporting system (IMCSRS) end users manual.* FORSCOM Pam 700-138.

CHAPTER EIGHTEEN

Measuring the Effects of CASE

Raoul J. Freeman
California State University

An empirical study that tries to measure the effect of the use of CASE (as compared to its lack of use) in systems development is described. The basic premise tested is that systems projects developed with the aid of CASE will show a smaller percentage change (increase) in total function points between certain phases of the systems development lifecycle than will "similar" projects developed without the use of CASE. The rationale for the use of function points as a measure is given, and a comprehensive data gathering effort is outlined. Various background factors are discussed that may need to be held in parity in order to develop meaningful findings. Some preliminary results are included.

The rationale for CASE has heretofore been best made in informal fashion, and there seems to be a paucity of scientific, systematic evaluation of CASE vs non-CASE in systems development. This paper describes a research effort that has been started in order to fill this gap. Function point methodology is employed as the underlying metric. The basic premise that is being tested is that systems developed with the aid of CASE will show a smaller percentage change (increase) in total function points between selected phases of the systems development lifecycle than will systems developed without CASE.

Contributing to the rationale of the proposal is the fact that function points are based on the user's external views of a system and are closely related to design specifications. CASE lays claim to contributing to well designed specifications and ease of change. Thus, it seems reasonable to conjecture that projects developed with CASE will harden into final form earlier than their non-CASE counterparts, and therefore a smaller change (increase) in total function points should result as the systems development life cycle progresses. It is being postulated that there is greater stability of workload in CASE-assisted design.

The chapter discusses the derivation of the rationale for the study, other factors to be considered, current status of the study and possible future work. A short description of function point methodology is given in the Appendix to this chapter.

STUDY RATIONALE

The ideal empirical environment for a study of this kind would consist of two sets of data on the same systems development projects done at the same time by the same people under the same conditions. One data set would represent the projects done without the aid of CASE, and the second set would represent the projects done with the aid of CASE. The two sets would then be compared for cost, elapsed time, quality of output, etc. Since the only difference between these data sets would be related to the use of CASE, the net difference in the outcome measurements could then be attributed to the use of CASE. Clearly, such an ideal environment will never be found. Thus a substitute, meaningful surrogate needs to be constructed.

In order to derive valid comparisons of "similar" projects, it is necessary to find an appropriate measure of "workload". This refers to the requisite workload inherent in a system's specifications. If a methodology is found that adequately measures workload, then for a given value of workload (with all other relevant factors in relative parity) any marked difference in evaluation attributes could be attributed to the use of CASE. The relevant factors that need to be held in parity are discussed in the next section of this chapter.

As far as evaluation attributes are concerned, elapsed time and cost have previously been mentioned. However, these attributes are influenced by staffing patterns and local overhead practices. Thus, they are not ideal measures. Freeman (1990) indicates that an ideal candidate for such a measure would be function points, because the latter measure the functions performed by a system from the user's external viewpoint and can be viewed independently of time and cost. More specifically, the approach entails looking at the change in total function points during the course of a project. Most systems development projects increase in scope during the systems development life cycle. However, it seems likely that the use of CASE leads to a lesser increase by providing a more stable initial analysis or design. Use of the absolute change in function points could be misleading because the scale of the project would enter the picture. However, use of percentage change in function points eliminates this incongruity. Thus, it was decided to use percentage change in function points between various phases in the systems development lifecycle as the principal measure in the empirical investigation. The candidate phases include systems analysis, systems design, and systems implementation.

OTHER FACTORS TO BE CONSIDERED

In order to make the percentage change in function points truly meaningful, certain other background factors may have to be in relative parity in regard to both the CASE and non-CASE projects. These background factors could include, but are not limited to, experience of staff, use of structured methods, and employment of the same or similar programming languages. Jones (1991) provides a list of factors that may need to be considered. If these factors are allowed to vary, then the influence of one or more of them could possibly overwhelm the influence of the use of CASE. For example, a project done with CASE and an inexperienced staff might not evaluate as "well" as a "similar" project done by an experienced staff without CASE.

At first glance, it is tempting to merely take a population of CASE projects (selected at random) and a population of non-CASE projects (also selected at random) and compare function point percentage changes without paying attention to the background variables. However, even if the function point measure rules in favor of the CASE projects, further research would have to be undertaken to establish that no bias has been caused by the values of the background factors. On the other hand, if the function point measure on the random samples rules against CASE, then it would be of interest to probe further by finding projects with comparable values for the background factors and looking at the results of CASE versus non-CASE for those subsets of projects. Should a subset be found that rules in favor of CASE, then the basic proposition can be taken to be verified but with the caveat that certain specific background factors have to be in parity. Also it would be of interest to be able to show that within such a subset, the "quality" of output, from the user's viewpoint, favored CASE-assisted projects. It should be noted that since function points are used for both the CASE and non-CASE sets, it seems likely that background factors such as the experience of the staff will likely have comparable values. Inexperienced staff usually do not install sophisticated measuring methods such as functions points.

CURRENT STATUS OF THE RESEARCH AND FUTURE WORK

A preliminary design of a data questionnaire has been undertaken and is being tested. The primary requested data is function point totals at various phases of the systems development lifecycle for both CASE assisted and non-CASE projects. A list of background factors has been developed, and information regarding the most important of them is requested in the questionnaire. Broad-scale solicitation of data is contemplated via professional organizations as well as on a direct basis to major corporations. The information that is being requested cannot be deemed to be confidential as the data required about various projects is quite general in nature. In order to ease the task of supplying data, we have tried to avoid asking for extensive detail. The questionnaire for each project is only one page in length. Whether this design is detailed enough remains to be determined. If not, then a supplementary questionnaire will be issued.

Several major entities have already agreed to supply information, and some preliminary data has been received and analyzed. Table 1 shows a tabulation of sample data from some of the initial input that has been received. The number of projects included in Table 1 is far too few from which to draw definitive conclusions. However, it is reassuring to be able to report that for this small sample of twenty projects, the average percent of growth in function points for CASE assisted projects is 2.1 percent vs 11.7 percent for non-CASE assisted projects. Although not tabulated here, the measure of function points per person hour is also quite favorable to the CASE set. Data from some additional projects, not included above, has reinforced the favorable trend in the function point comparison. Some firms that are beginning to set up function point measurement programs have agreed to collect the type of data

Prj	FP1	FP2	% Growth	CA	Exp
1	781	994	27.27	N	4
2	190	200	5.20	N	4
3	528	623	17.99	N	8
4	303	321	5.94	N	5
5	132	138	4.55	N	4
6	1000	1214	21.40	N	5
7	200	227	13.50	N	8
8	172	185	7.56	N	5
9	91	91	0.00	N	4
10	66	75	13.64	N	4
		AVN	11.71		
11	4545	4998	9.97	Y	8
12	995	995	0.00	Y	8
13	192	200	4.17	Y	8
14	152	152	0.00	Y	8
15	244	234	-4.10	Y	8
16	459	459	0.00	Y	7
17	200	204	2.00	Y	8
18	41	41	0.00	Y	4
19	60	60	0.00	Y	4
20	190	207	8.95	Y	8
		AVY	2.10		

Prj	-	Project Identifier
FP1	-	Function Points at end of Systems Analysis Phase
FP2	-	Function Points at and of Systems Implementation
% Growth	-	% Difference between FP1 and FP2
CA	-	Use of CASE tool : Y = Yes; N = No.
Exp	-	Number of Years of Experience of Staff
AVN	-	Average % of Growth of Non-CASE Projects
AVY	-	Average % of Growth of CASE Projects

Table 1: Sample Data Results

needed by this research effort and to make it available in the future. This may be deemed to be significant because quite a few firms are contemplating software measurement programs as part of TQM (total quality management) efforts, and the research data needs of this study could influence the measurement programs that are being established.

Future research could assess the hypothesis that the maintenance of systems constructed with the use of CASE tools require less effort that those developed without CASE. Also, if the database is rich enough, comparisons between various CASE tools could possibly be made. Other avenues for research include attempting to isolate the effects of certain of the background variables as well as the size of projects.

It is anticipated that this study will be continuing for several years. On the broadest level, the results will have to do with the effectiveness of CASE in systems development. Possible adjunct results may deal with some of the future research topics mentioned above. Furthermore, the database of function point histories that will be gathered should be of interest and value to researchers, software developers, and managers for years to come, both for comparative studies and the development of standards.

APPENDIX - FUNCTION POINTS

This section is largely based on Sprouls (1990) and also appears in Freeman (1991). Since the early 70's, substantial research into function points has been carried out. Various individuals have analyzed hundreds of programs to isolate the critical variables which determine programming productivity. Their effort was aimed at the measurement of the value of functions delivered by a program as opposed to using the volume or complexity of the program code as the basis of the evaluation.

Function points are based on the user's external view of a system and are therefore closely related to requirement specifications. This allows the function point technique to be used to estimate development effort. The end user can also better understand and scrutinize such a measurement. The technique is based on the inspection of an application design. Function points are determined by means of steps 1-4, and associated Figures 1-4, as described in the following:

1. Identify the function points contained in an application and classify them by the five types listed in Figure 1.

2. Attach a complexity factor to each function point of a particular type that has been identified, by determining the number of data elements and the number of logical files the function point is related to. Figure 2 shows the complexity matrix for the external input type of function point. An analogous matrix exists for each of the other function point types. Employment of these matrices will lead to development of a total number of function points of each type at each level of complexity.
3. The numbers developed in Step (2) above are then multiplied by the numerical factors listed in Figure 3. When all the various categories in Figure 3 are added together, the unadjusted function point total for the application has been established.
4. This function point total is then adjusted by the level of influence of the factors listed in Figure 4. Each of these factors, which is related to the application as a whole rather than at the individual function point level, is rated between 0 and 5, and then their sum is calculated. This is multiplied by .01, and the result is added to 0.65. The latter total is then multiplied by the raw function point count from Figure 3, and the result is an adjusted function point

Internal Logical File	An Internal Logical File is a user identified group of logically related data or control information maintained and utilized within the boundary of the application.
External Interface File	An External Interface File is a user identifiable group of logically related data or control information utilized by the applications, but maintained by another application.
External Input	An External Input processes data or control information which enters the application's external boundary, and through a unique logical process, maintains an Internal Logical File.
External Output	An External Output processes data or control information that exits the application's external boundary.
External Inquiry	An External Inquiry is a unique input/output combination where an input causes an output and an Internal Logical File is not updated.

Figure 1: Function Point Types

No. of Elements	No. of Logical Files Referenced	Complexity
0 to 1	1 to 4	LOW
0 to 1	5 to 15	LOW
0 to 1	over 15	AVERAGE
2	1 to 4	LOW
2	5 to 15	AVERAGE
2	over 15	HIGH
3 or more	1 to 4	AVERAGE
3 or more	5 to 15	HIGH
3 or more	over 15	HIGH

Figure 2: Complexity Matrix for External Input Type Function PT

TYPE	LEVEL OF COMPLEXITY			TOTAL
	LOW	AVERAGE	HIGH	
LOGICAL INTERNAL FILE	x 7 =	x 10 =	X 15 =	
EXTERNAL INTERFACE FILE	X 5 =	X 7 =	X 10 =	
INPUT	X 3 =	X 4 =	X 6 =	
OUTPUT	X 4 =	X 5 =	X 7 =	
INQUIRY	X 3 =	X 4 =	X 6 =	
TOTAL UNADJUSTED FUNCTION POINTS				

Figure 3: Function Point Summary

	COMPLEXITY FACTOR	VALUE		COMPLEXITY FACTOR	VALUE
1	DATA COMMUNICATIONS		8	ONLINE UPDATE	
2	DISTRIBUTED FUNCTIONS		9	COMPLEX PROCESSING	
3	PERFORMANCE		10	REUSABILITY	
4	HEAVILY USED CONFIG		11	INSTALLATION EASE	
5	TRANSACTION RATE		12	OPERATION EASE	
6	ONLINE DATA ENTRY		13	MULTIPLE SITES	
7	END USER EFFICIENCY		14	FACILITATE CHANGE	
	TOTAL APPLICATION COMPLEXITY FACTOR				

TOTAL APPLICATION COMPLEXITY		APPLICATION COMPLEXITY ADJUSTMENT	UNADJUSTED FUNCTION POINTS		ADJUSTED FUNCTION POINTS
____ * .01 =	____ + .65 =	____	* ____	=	____

Figure 4: Application Complexity Factor Summary

count for the application. The effect of the factors in Figure 4 can change the unadjusted total function points by up to plus or minus 35%.

Logical data flow diagrams are a good starting point for function point analysis. By going over these, the various types and numbers of function points in an application can be found. Then the individual function points, as well as the application as a whole, are evaluated for complexity. This provides the data from which to make the function point calculation. The methodology is rich enough to allow for complex function points in a simple application, as well as simple function points in a complex application. As far as the study is concerned, adjusted function points would be determined at various points in the systems development lifecycle and the percentage change between them calculated.

REFERENCES

Freeman, R. J. (1991, July). CASE Validation - The New Challenge. *CASE and Systems Development Education*, R. Freeman, editor. Cambridge, MA., Intersolv Corporation Press.

Freeman, R. J. (1990, December 5-8). A Methodology for CASE Cost Effectiveness Validation. *CASE-90 Advance Working Papers of the 4th International Workshop on Computer-Aided Software Engineering,* R. Norman & R. Van Ghent, editors. Los Alamitos, CA., IEEE Computer Society Press.

Jones, C. (1991, July). *Applied Software Measurement.* McGraw Hill. New York, N.Y.

Sprouls, J. (ed.). (1990). *Function Point Counting Practices Manual -Release 3.0.* International Function Point Users Group (IFPUG). Westerville, Ohio.

CHAPTER NINETEEN

A Case Study with MicroSTEP

Ismail Bayraktar
Agent Systems, Inc.

Murat M. Tanik
Southern Methodist University

MicroSTEP is a Computer Aided Software Engineering tool, which enables developers to define user requirement specifications through a graphical user interface (SYSCORP, 1991a; SYSCORP, 1991b; SYSCORP, 1991c). The most important characteristic of MicroSTEP is the capacity of working with specifications during the software development process. Using flow diagrams, MicroSTEP allows the developer to define a user's specifications graphically. It provides the means to enter necessary information such as data structures, user interfaces, and process definitions. It also generates executable programs in C language from these graphical specifications. To demonstrate some important features of MicroSTEP, we will use a real-life Insurance Tracking System example throughout the chapter. The Insurance Tracking System that we are using as an example has the following requirements: keeping track of information about customers, policies, loans, vendors, and transactions; printing daily transactions (policies and refund claims); writing notices to customers whose policies are about to expire; and printing several monthly and yearly reports for management and vendors. This chapter introduces MicroSTEP, its characteristics, and traces the step-by-step creation of the Insurance Tracking System application.

The lessons learned in application development since the late 1960's have paved the way for the introduction of numerous computational and environmental aids. Among the tools for application development, are Computer Aided Software Engineering (CASE) tools which address the problems associated with various phases of software development. CASE tools are helpful in the production of software engineering artifacts such as programs and documentation, as well as in the incorporation and enforcement of a software engineering process model during the software production activity.

MicroSTEP is a CASE tool which provides the capability for efficient production of business applications and associated documentation. The software engineering model which MicroSTEP adheres to, is a rapid prototyping process model in which incomplete specifications are allowed and, rapid and iterative feedback is encouraged (Tanik & Yeh, 1989; Tanik & Chan, 1991). A factor which differentiates MicroSTEP from other tools, is its emphasis on rapid prototyping and the spiral model of software production (Tanik & Yeh, 1989; Boehm, 1988).

In the rest of this chapter we will introduce MicroSTEP and the MicroSTEP software development methodology. In addition, we will describe a real-life application developed with MicroSTEP.

MICROSTEP

MicroSTEP allows software developers to specify a user's requirements through a graphical user interface, and generates C language programs from these specifications (SYSCORP, 1991a; SYSCORP, 1991b; SYSCORP, 1991c; Yeh, 1990). MicroSTEP is built upon the rapid prototyping and spiral model paradigms (Tanik & Yeh, 1989; Boehm, 1988). As such, MicroSTEP has the capability to create executable code and handle incomplete specifications. One of the problems in software development is that users usually cannot define their needs precisely and may eventually change their mind about what they really want. By using successive prototypes, a system developer gains a better insight into the user's needs. MicroSTEP uses flow diagrams as a user interface for building specifications. Graphical icons help the developer construct specifications with relative ease. The MicroSTEP system consists of three components:

- a graphical specification language,
- an application generation facility, and

- an application run-time environment.

The graphical specification language serves as the starting point for developing specifications. The first step is to draw a data flow diagram. Next, all the data fields, i.e., variables, are defined. This step is called the "data structure definition." User interfaces in the form of screen views and report layouts are created next. This step is called "format definition." Finally, process definitions are entered during a step called "activity definition."

The application generation facility creates programs in C after checking the specifications for consistency and completeness. This component supports the lower level stages of classical software development - coding and testing, whereas the graphical specification language supports the higher level stages of specification and design.

The application run-time environment provides several features such as automatic range checking for user input (e.g., validation of date), highlighting menus, scrolling windows, context-sensitive help, and report generation.

Software development using MicroSTEP has several advantages over the traditional approaches. First of all, coding, one of the most labor-intensive activities of software development, is eliminated. Because of this, system developers can spend more time on the requirements analysis and specification activities. Lower CASE tools in general, and MicroSTEP in particular, aim at improving programmer productivity. MicroSTEP strongly encourages reusability which is considered as one of the keys to increased productivity (Biggerstaff & Perlis, 1989a; Biggerstaff & Perlis, 1989b). One can easily reuse data definitions and user interface definitions from one project to another (as well as within the same project) by the use of the data dictionary.

Maintenance is one of the most costly activities of the software development life-cycle (Yeh, 1978). Since understanding code is difficult and finding errors in the code is even more difficult, the ability to maintain the application at the specification level in MicroSTEP is a significant advantage.

Documentation of software products is another problem in the software industry (Yeh, 1978). MicroSTEP prints easy-to-understand standard documents for each application. In this way, documentation is always up-to-date (with the application) which is a rare case in traditional software development systems.

MicroSTEP has some shortcomings as well. It is designed primarily for business applications. In fact, it is sometimes called "business definition language." (Yeh, 1990)

We will describe a software development methodology for MicroSTEP in the next section.

MicroSTEP's SOFTWARE DEVELOPMENT METHODOLOGY

An application is developed with MicroSTEP in five stages: requirements analysis, database design, specification definition, application generation, and maintenance. Figure 1 shows MicroSTEP's software development methodology together with MicroSTEP components (right side). The data dictionary and four "builders" (flow diagram builder, format builder, activity builder, data structure builder) are parts of the graphical specification language. The Application Generation System is used for consistency checking and executable code production. An application runtime environment is used to install the application on the target system.

Requirements Analysis

Requirements analysis is the starting point and the most important stage of software development (Yeh, 1978). Understanding user needs in their entirety tends to reduce the time required to complete a software project. MicroSTEP encourages the developer to produce a requirements document that is as complete as possible. Requirements can be written either by the end-user or by the system developer. Regardless of the source of the requirements, the system developer should collect additional information on the current system and environment through interviews and observations.

Database Design

MicroSTEP has a component called the "Data Dictionary" which stores data structures and formats. Since large applications are usually produced by a team, communication among developers is essential. For example, defining a field as integer in one part of the software and as a decimal in another part may cause problems. The best way to avoid this kind of inconsistency is to define and standardize the data structures to be used by all developers at the beginning of the development process. Reusing properly standardized data, in this way, provides consistency when the elements are

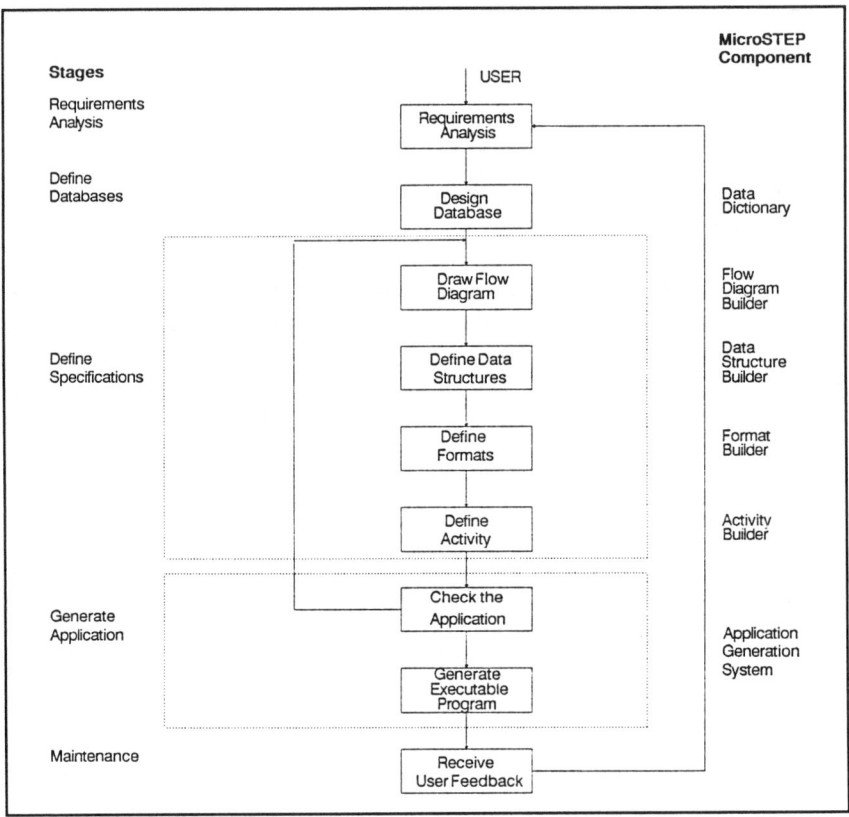

Figure 1. MicroSTEP Software Development Methodology

incorporated in other parts of the application.

Specification Definition

MicroSTEP specifications are defined in four steps: drawing flow diagrams, defining data structures (data fields), defining formats (user intefaces), and defining processes (activities). MicroSTEP's specification language is graphical and based on data flow diagramming. The "Specification Editor" is composed of four "builders", each corresponding to a step mentioned above. The "Flow Diagram Builder" helps to draw flow diagrams using graphical icons. Data fields are defined using "Data Structure Builder." Defining a user interface is called a format and can be done by using the "Format Builder." Lastly, one needs to show how the data is to be processed. The "Activity Builder" provides the means for this purpose.

Application Generation

After the application is created, MicroSTEP tools can be invoked to check the application for consistency and completeness. If there is any missing information, or if two definitions conflict with one another, the Application Generation Component will issue warning messages. If a specification contains multiple sub-specifications, then all the related sub-specificationsare also checked. The final step is to create the executable program. MicroSTEP generates programs in the "C" language, performs linking functions, and delivers executable code.

Maintenance After executable code is generated, the program must be installed on the target system. At this time, the user tests and validates the system,and may come up with modifications or additions to the system. Any necessary modification or corrections are made to the "Specification Editor"

INSURANCE TRACKING SYSTEM USING MicroSTEP (An Example)

Insurance Tracking System

A real-life insurance tracking system is used as an example to demonstrate software development with MicroSTEP. This system was developed to enable a bank to store insurance information. The entire application consists of over 20 MicroSTEP specifications. Only one of them is introduced in this section (Bayraktar & Tanik, 1991).

The bank works with several insurance vendors. Each one may issue insurance policies to customers. From time to time, customers may cancel their insurance which requires the calculation of refund amounts. Also, the bank needs a daily update of all new policies (credit transactions) and cancellations (debit transactions). In addition, customers must be notified if their policy is to expire within ten days. The are printed reports are categorized into three classes: daily, monthly, and upon demand. Transaction and customer notices are printed daily. Management Reports and vendor reports are printed monthly. Listings of all policies for a customer, all policies grouped by customer or loan, vendor information, and year-to-date statistical summary report are printed upon demand.

The user's requirements can be summarized as follows:

- Keep customer, loan, vendor, policy, and transaction information

in databases
- Insertion, modification and deletion of records in databases should be efficiently handled
- New policies should be inserted as credits and cancellations as debits (into the transaction database)
- Print all transactions for the day
- Mail daily warning notices about expiration dates to the customer (according to the policy database)
- Print a report of various policies for a customer (from the policy database)
- Print a report for all policies sorted by customer or loan number (from policy database)
- Print a report reflecting totals for insurance amount (by type), the bank's share, and the vendor's share of the gross amount derived from the transaction and vendor databases
- Print a report of total credit and debit amounts, total and average ages of insured and refunded policyholders, and net income and refund for each vendor on a year-to-date basis

We applied the software development methodology for MicroSTEP shown in Figure 1 to the Insurance Tracking System. The following sections summarize our approach. A more detailed treatment is described in (Bayraktar & Tanik, 1991; Bayraktar, 1991).

Database Design

The MicroSTEP Data Dictionary (a repository) is provided to store and reuse data structures and formats. Menus, data entry screens, and report layouts are designed with the active participation of the user and stored in data dictionary.

We realized that five databases would be the core of this system. Therefore, all five databases in the application were defined in the Data Dictionary. We used at least one of these databases in each specification. During the course of systems development, we copied these data structures from the Data Dictionary about 75 times. Since four people worked together on the project, early definition of databases helped to reduce potential communication errors.

Flow Diagram

MicroSTEP's data-flow-diagramming-based approach lets systems developers define problems graphically. Processes accept data objects as input and produce output data objects.

Top-down and bottom-up design approaches can be applied in

software development. One can define high-level menus and add low-level programs later. Alternatively, one can first develop program parts that perform a particular task and group them by function later. We will describe how to define "printing daily transactions" of the Insurance Tracking System. This printing process is grouped under the "reports" menu.

Since MicroSTEP allows incomplete specifications, we may specify a menu without necessarily completing the necessary subspecifications. This is important because we can create all the menus with limited functionality, and show this prototype of the proposed system to the user.

Figure 2 illustrates the flow diagram for the specification of the menu. It consists of a screen activity, which has two rectangular and one circular object in dashed lines, and four subspecifications (circles with objects in it). Circular objects represent processes and rectangular objects represent data objects. Links between a data object and a process are straight lines, and lines between two processes are dashed lines and indicate conditional branching.

The top line in the Flow Diagram Builder provides feedback information to the user in the form of short messages. The second line is the menu bar which contains all possible options, in this case: view, edit, define, and dictionary. All of them are pull-down menus; on-line help screens guide the developer to the next step. The column on the left is called an icon bar. This user interface is also consistent in all builders. The first icon is called select. The other icons from top to bottom are: text (for documentation), screen activity, database, report, sequential file, temporary data area, process, subspecification,

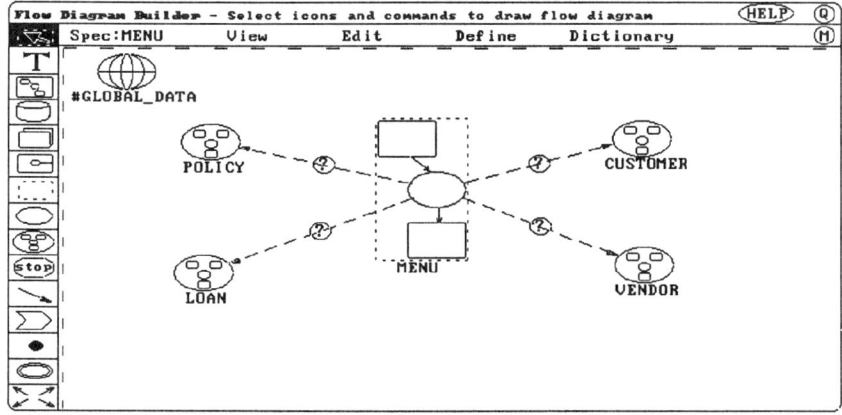

Figure 2. Flow Diagram for MENU

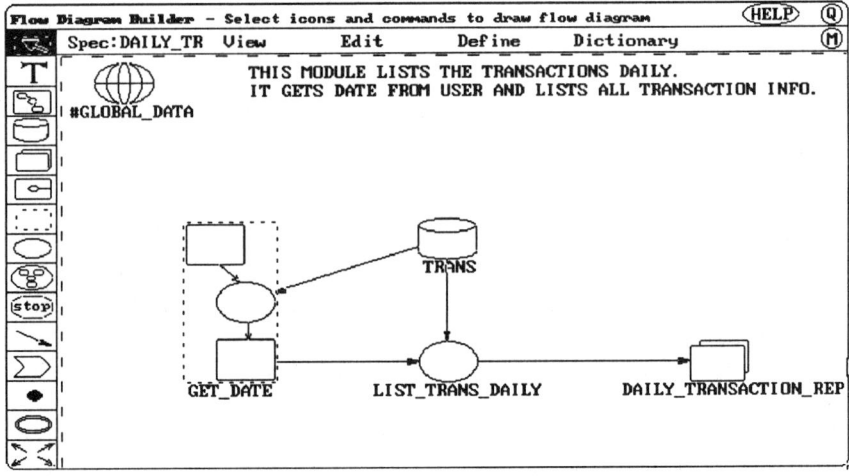

Figure 3. Flow Diagram for Daily Transaction Report

stop, and flow link.

The construction of a menu involves the following steps:

- displaying of all options
- creating the specification based on these options.

To achieve the first step, we need a screen activity which has two data objects within dashed lines. One of them serves as the keyboard and the other as the monitor. The next step is achieved by conditionally branching; sub-specifications are analogous to sub-programs.

The flow diagram for "Printing Daily Transactions" specification is given in Figure 3. The construction of this specification involves the following steps:

• get the date from user
• find the records in the transaction database which has the same date as the one entered by the user
• list the records in the proper format

This requirement implies that we need a screen activity, database, and a report as well as a process to make computations. To get the date from the user we need a screen activity. Next, a process finds all the records in the database and produces the desired report. Structure After completing the flow diagram, we need to define data fields. The Data Structure Builder is where we define all the data

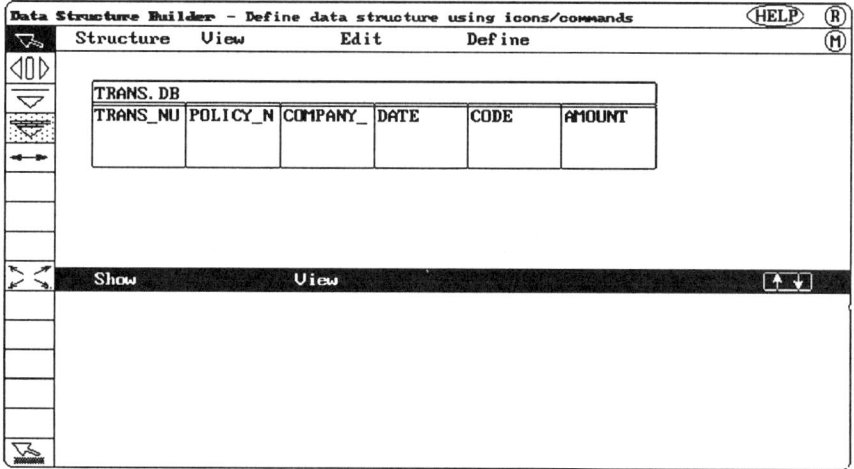

Figure 4: TRANS data structure

fields for a data object. The Data Structure Builder has two windows (see Figure 4).

In the upper window, called the active window, the structure is defined for the selected data object. In the lower window, the reference window, either the flow diagram or another data structure (possibly from the Data Dictionary) can be viewed.

Since we have the structure of the transaction database in the Data Dictionary, we can simply copy it into the current application. Screen activity has a simple structure which consists of only one data field for date.

Format

Format, in MicroSTEP terminology, is the definition of user interfaces. MicroSTEP has the necessary tools to create user interface easily and rapidly. Since screen and report layouts differ, MicroSTEP has two slightly different Format Builders. Screen Format Builder contains features such as pop-up menus, context-sensitive help screens and the ability to control attributes like reverse video. The Report Format Builder functions by dividing a page into three parts: the page header, body, and page footer.

The MicroSTEP specification shown in Figure 3 contains a screen activity icon and a report icon. In the screen activity, a user will enter the date for the transactions to be printed. A helpful prompt can be displayed using the T (text) icon. The MicroSTEP Data Structure Builder divides the screen into two windows: a lower

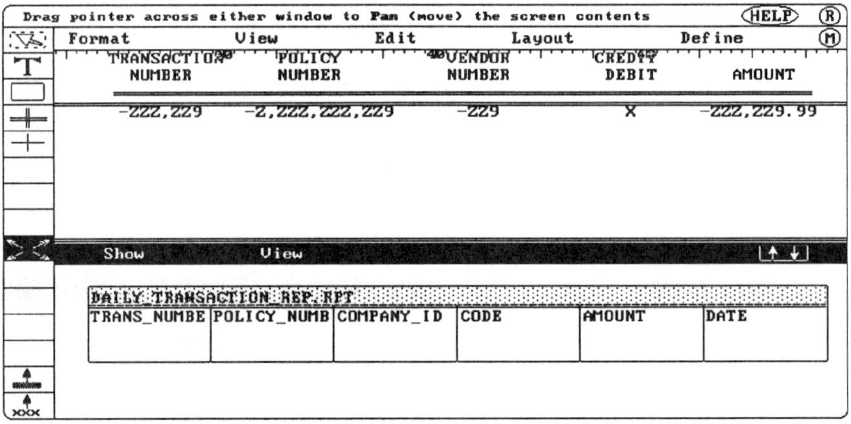

562   Bayraktar and Tanik

Figure 5. Screen Format for GET_DATE

window which displays the data structure of the screen activity, and an upper window illustrating the user's screen. The date field to be displayed, must be copied to the active window. Other features such as a blinking and reverse video can be added using an edit option via pull-down menus on the menu bar. A sample format is shown in Figure 5.

In the report, we need to print all selected transactions. The page header contains a heading like "DAILY TRANSACTION REPORT" together with the date of transactions in the header. We can write the header by selecting T (Text icon). The system date can be retrieved from "Global Data" which contains general data available to all specifications. The footer consists of the page number, which is increased by MicroSTEP automatically. In the report body, we list all transactions under appropriate headings. The Report body consists of all the fields in the report data structure, also contains also contains the a header and footer. The report body footer is usually used for totals. Figure 6 illustrates this report.

Activity

Activities are defined to show how the processing occurs. This includes the following:

- how logical input is defined
- how output is derived
- how filtering is done if one wants to restrict the data as it flows from input to output.

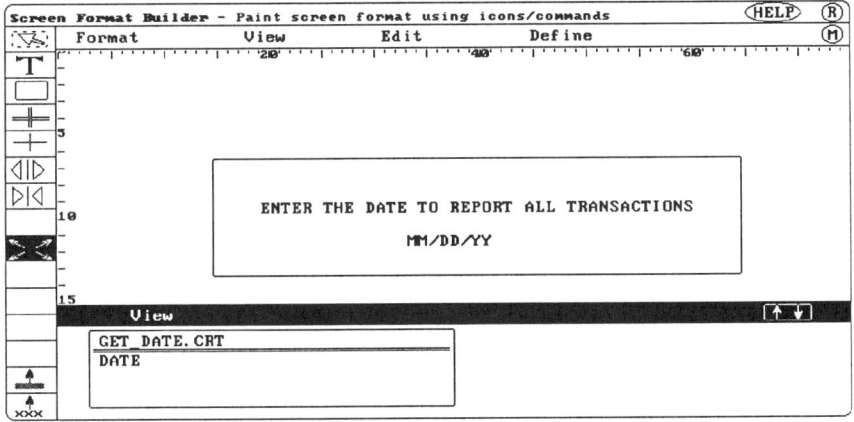

Figure 6. Report Body of Daily Transactions Report

There are two kinds of activities in MicroSTEP, namely: screen activity and regular processing. Screen activity is dedicated to handles all keyboard and monitor related functions. MicroSTEP automatically displays associated formats with the screen activity and then waits for user input. If user input is required, we indicate this to MicroSTEP by copying these fields to the user screen in the format definition. Type checking (e.g., correctness of month within date) is also performed.

The screen activity in this specification is depicted in Figure 7. This actity contains a validation check for existence, that is, it makes sure that there is at least one record for that day in the database before printing. This is called a "lookup."

Lookups can be defined unconditionally and conditionally. In the unconditional case, all data from a lookup are copied to a screen activity. Four options can be selected: bringing the first record (when the condition evaluates true) to the working environment (memory), or bringing all the data satisfying the condition. The third and fourth options do not bring the data to the memory, but only test the condition. Since we are not interested in bringing data, for modifying or working on it, we will select the option, "TEST FOR SUCCESS OF CONDITION."

The next step is to define the condition which specifies that the date in the screen activity and the date in the database are the same (equal). If there is no record in the database satisfying this condition, we will warn the user with the message like the example appearing

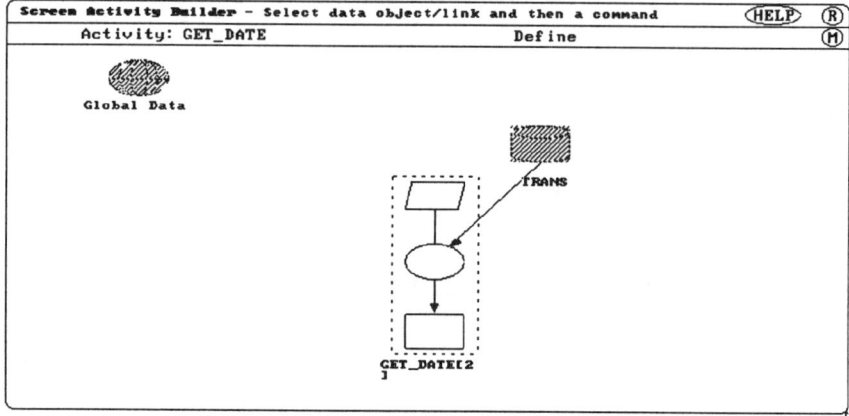

Figure 7. Screen Activity

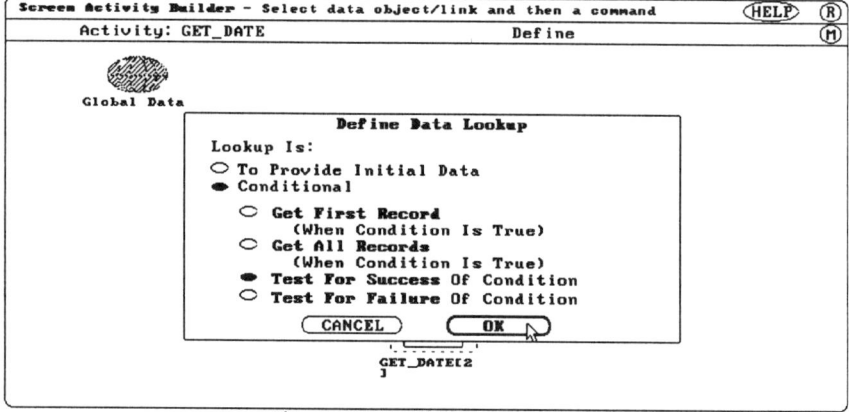

Figure 8. Defining Lookups

at the top of Figure 9. The builder in Figure 9 is called the "Expression Builder" since it helps to define formulas and expressions.

The regular processing has logical input and logical output. Logical input finds records in the database with a date field equal to the user entered date. Every regular process can have at most two inputs. If the logical input is straightforward, as in the case of one input, MicroSTEP determines the input and you do not have to worry about it. Since we have two inputs in this example, we need to define it (Figure 10). One of the inputs is primary (the screen activity) and the other one is secondary (the database in this case). A match condition should be defined to identify the data we want to work on.

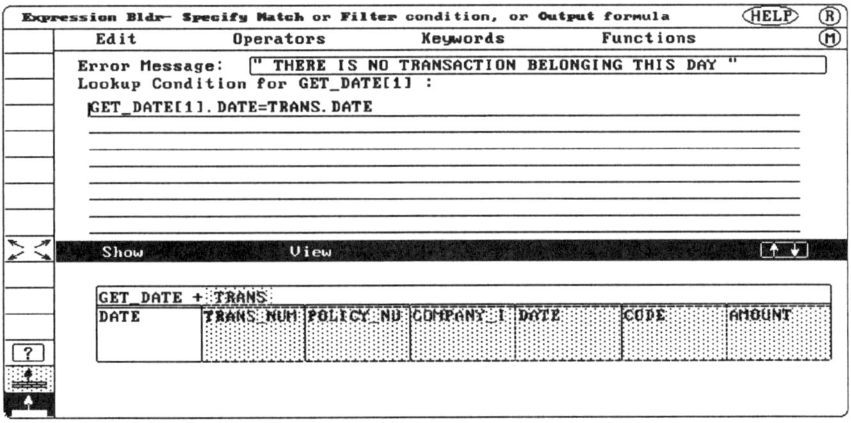

A Case Study With MicroSTEP

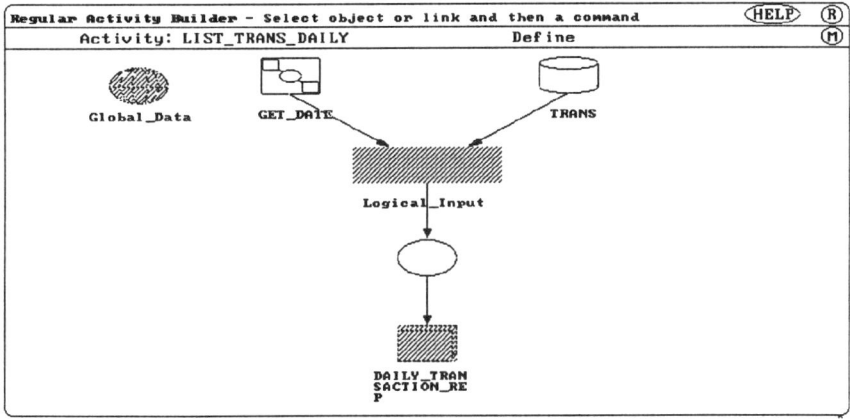

Figure 9. Lookup Condition for TRANS

Figure 10. Regular Process' Activity

Since we want to find the records which match the date in the screen activity, the match condition is "MATCH ALL SECONDARY RECORDS TO EACH PRIMARY RECORD" (Figure 11).

The definition of logical output is defined as either a mapping or a source formula. Mapping is equivalent to an assignment in a procedural language and a source formula is equivalent to calculations. We need to map fields from the database to the report, as shown in Figure 12. Source formulas are defined in the Expression Builder.

Even though we have not used "filters" in the specification, we

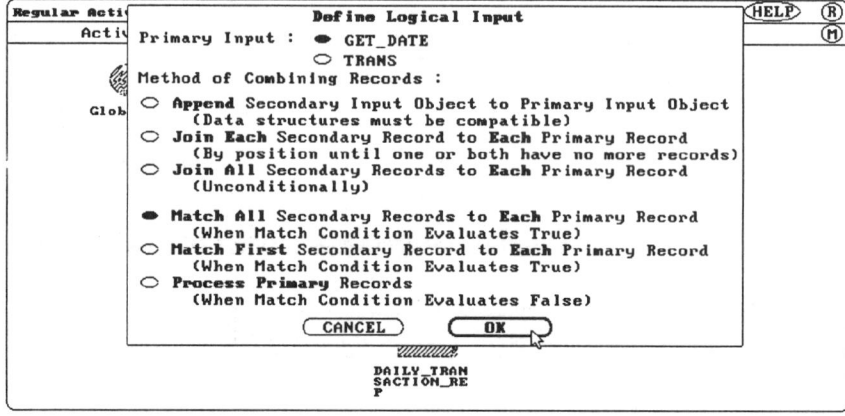

Figure 11. Definition of Logical Input

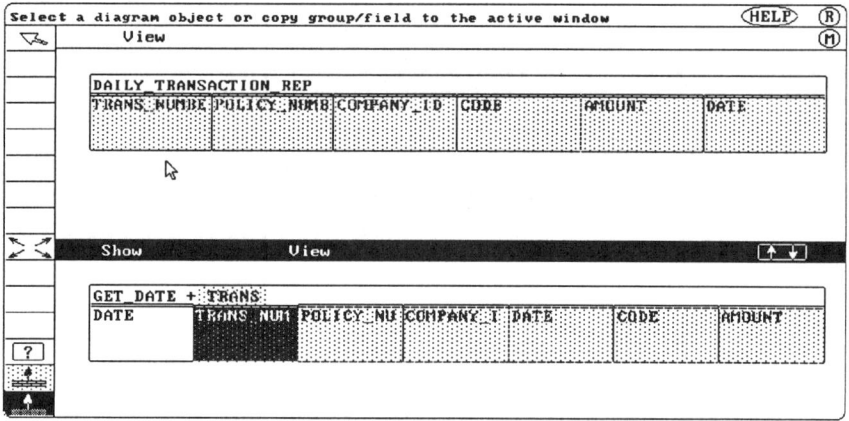

Figure 12. Mapping Fields

can modify it slightly to show how filters might help. Assume that one wants to print only credit transactions. We would simply add a filter between the database and the logical input. The filter condition would be "TRANSACTION CODE IS EQUAL TO CREDIT TYPE" which can be defined in the Expression Builder.

LESSONS LEARNED

Four people worked on the development of this project which

was completed in two months. None of the developers had more than four months experience with MicroSTEP. As a matter of fact, real-life software development was a new concept for most of the team members. The capability of creating prototypes significantly enhanced the developers' ability to better understand the user needs. Our final product was exactly what the user wanted. We believe that this goal would be almost impossible to achieve using classical software development systems. It was easy to modify the user's specifications and rapidly deliver the new application.

SUMMARY AND CONCLUSIONS

We presented the construction of a real-life application, an Insurance Tracking System, by using MicroSTEP CASE tool. A brief introduction to MicroSTEP was given and the software development methodology for MicroSTEP was described. During our two years of working experience with MicroSTEP, we produced other case studies which we recommend to the reader (Bender et al, 1991; Halverson et al, 1991; Key, 1991; Key & Tanik, 1991; Shekhdar et al, 1991). We found specification development with MicroSTEP a rewarding process, especially on small to medium scale business applications. The insurance tracking system was completed in four man-months (four people, half-time for two months) by developers with limited software development and MicroSTEP experience. We anticipate that it would take as long as one man-year with conventional methods and procedural languages to build a comparable system.

ACKNOWLEDGMENTS
MicroSTEP is a registered trademark of Syscorp International, Inc. We would like to thank Kyle L. Townsend for providing us with the original problem for the Insurance Tracking System. Mark A. Halverson, David J. Key, Scott Grissen, and Ron Glover contributed to the development of the Insurance Tracking System. We are thankful to Suzanne N. Delcambre, Onur Demirors, Y.T. Chen, and Ali Dogru for their valuable reviews.

REFERENCES

Bayraktar, I. (1991). *Software Reusability with Specifications.* Master's Thesis, Southern Methodist University, Dallas, Texas.

Bayraktar, I., & Tanik M.M. (1991). *Implementing Specifications with Building Blocks: Insurance Tracking System* (Technical Report 91-CSE-18). Dallas, Texas: Dept. of Computer Science and Engineering, Southern Methodist University.

Bender, R.M., & Reeck, T.L., & Bayraktar, I., & Tanik, M.M. (1991). *A Case Study in MicroSTEP: Hospital Inventory Tracking System* (Technical Report 91-CSE-32). Dallas, Texas: Dept. of Computer Science and Engineering, Southern Methodist University.

Biggerstaff, T.J., & Perlis, A.J. (Eds.) (1989a). *Software Reusability: Concepts and Models* (Vol. 1). Reading, MA: Addison-Wesley Publishing.

Biggerstaff, T.J., & Perlis, A.J. (Eds.) (1989b). *Software Reusability: Applications and Experience* (Vol. 2). Reading, MA: Addison-Wesley Publishing.

Boehm, B.W. (1988). A Spiral Model of Software Development and Enhancement. *IEEE Computer, 21*(3), 61-72.

Halverson, M.A., Bayraktar, I., & Tanik M.M. (1991). *MicroSTEP with Single Concept Cumulative Teaching Method* (Technical Report 90-CSE-28). Dallas, Texas: Dept. of Computer Science and Engineering, Southern Methodist University.

Key, D.J. (1991). *Software Development Life Cycle Issues with the Specification Compiler MicroSTEP*. Master's Thesis, Southern Methodist University, Dallas, Texas.

Key, D.J., & Tanik M.M. (1991). *A Specification Experience: Dual Drilling Supply System with MicroSTEP* (Technical Report 91-CSE-9). Dallas, Texas: Dept. of Computer Science and Engineering, Southern Methodist University.

Shekhdar, K.D., Bayraktar, I., & Tanik, M.M. (1991). *Application Development with MicroSTEP: Member Information System* (Technical Report 91-CSE-10). Dallas, Texas: Dept. of Computer Science and Engineering, Southern Methodist University.

SYSCORP International Inc. (1991a). *MicroSTEP Reference Manual Version 1.5.*

SYSCORP International Inc. (1991b). *MicroSTEP Tutorial Manual Version 1.5.*

SYSCORP International Inc. (1991c). *MicroSTEP Building Blocks Manual: Sample MicroSTEP Specifications Version 1.5.*

Tanik, M.M., & Chan, E.S. (1991). *Fundamentals of Computing for Software Engineers.* New York: Van Nostrand Reinhold.

Tanik, M.M., & Yeh, R.T. (1989). Rapid Prototyping in Software Development. *IEEE Computer, 22*(5), 9-10.

Yeh, R.T. (1978). *Current Trends in Programming Methodology* (Vol. 1-4). Englewood Cliffs, N.J.: Prentice-Hall.

Yeh, R.T. (1990). MicroSTEP: A Business Definition Language. In R.T. Yeh & P.A. Ng (Eds.), *Modern Software Engineering* (pp. 502-536). New York: Van Nostrand Reinhold.

CHAPTER TWENTY

A Methodology for MicroSTEP Based on the Rapid Prototyping Paradigm

David J. Key
U.S. Military Academy, West Point

Murat M. Tanik
Southern Methodist University

As the computer age matures, new hardware with greater capabilities is introduced at an almost exponential rate. The ability to produce sufficient quality software to take advantage of the equipment has lagged further behind with each new development. Techniques, methods, and tools to enhance programmer productivity are being explored frantically. Every day it becomes increasingly evident that companies require a wider variety of more complex tools to stay competitive in today's marketplace. It is also evident that traditional software development methods are not keeping pace with the increasing demand for larger, more complex programs. This work examines one such tool (MicroSTEP), and its inherent paradigm.

In order to effectively produce software, the tool must be used with a design methodology. One such methodology, based on the Rapid Prototyping paradigm, is particularly effective when employed with MicroSTEP. This methodology, the MicroSTEP Rapid Prototyping Methodology (MRPM), is described in detail. The MRPM provides MicroSTEP users with a structured software development technique which can be used to develop a wide range of software applications (Key, 1991).

We begin with a CASE tools review, where data is presented about the characteristics needed for a tool to be classified as a CASE tool. The next section focuses on MicroSTEP, how the tool functions and what capabilities it possesses, including a simple example to follow the MicroSTEP building process. The MRPM is examined in the following section as it was applied to the development of a real-world software application, the Dual Drilling Supply System (DDSS). This section also contains the actual DDSS specifications with their structures, formats and data flows, and the usage information for the executable program, Dual. The final section is a detailed description of the MRPM and how to use it to develop software. It also summarizes the lessons learned during the development of the DDSS (Tanik & Yeh, 1989).

CASE Tools

It is an accepted fact that the increasing demand for bigger and faster software in every facet of society has outstripped the ability of software professionals to produce it (Stamps, 1989). There is a software crisis in the computing world. An average programmer writes only four to ten lines of error-free code per day after counting the time required for designing, coding, testing and maintaining software (Fisher, 1988; Halverson, Bayraktar & Tanik, 1990; Stamps, 1989). Since projects are becoming larger and larger, sometimes into millions of lines of code, supply is not keeping up with demand. Solutions for this problem are constantly being examined by many in the computer industry. There is general agreement (Lewis, Ted & Oman, 1990) that the two best ways to make programmers more productive is through the reuse of software components and greater use of tools. These tools cover a broad range of software development techniques and paradigms. Most of them are called CASE tools.

What is a CASE Tool?

There is no agreement in the industry as to what characteristics a tool must have to be considered a CASE tool. However, a CASE tool is not merely a better programming tool. A true CASE tool supports, ideally, the entire life cycle from requirements analysis to maintenance, and is a tool for engineering software (Oman, 1990). Realistically, the majority of CASE tools on the market support only a portion of the life cycle. However, they are becoming more comprehensive daily. There are "front-end" CASE tools which support design and analysis. Some are focused on a specific application domain or are language-oriented. Others support the later stages, or "back-end", of the life cycle. Other related products are reverse engineering tools which take existing applications and transform them into data flow diagrams and data structures (Watterson, 1989). Typically, each tool is associated with one or more software development methodologies such as Yourdan/Demarco, Warnier/Orr, or Jackson (Norman & Nunamaker, 1989; Oman, 1990; Pressman, 1987). Although MicroSTEP appears to be a back-end CASE tool, through the use of the Rapid Prototyping software development paradigm, it handles the front-end quite well. It is the tool which was used to develop the program presented in later sections. MicroSTEP and its methodology will be explored in greater detail in the next section.

CASE Tool Surveys

Recent surveys of Unix and PC-based CASE tools (Case Trends, 1990; Case Trends, 1991) revealed a variety of capabilities. Out of the 86 tools in the survey, 45 supported analysis/design, 47 supported prototyping, and 44 generated code. Generally, tools which supported one of the preceding capabilities supported them all. Other capabilities supported by fewer tools were planning, reverse engineering, and testing. Some were special purpose tools which only had one or two functionalities. The diversity presented in the surveys substantiates the observation that there is no agreement on an exact definition of what capabilities a tool must possess to be classified as a CASE tool. Therefore, for the purposes of this discussion, a CASE tool is one which supports a software development paradigm and offers facilities for software development.

Software Evolution Paradigm

As depicted in Figure 1, several ingredients are required in order to effectively develop software. Beginning with a main idea, or paradigm, we then implement it with tools, languages, and a methodology. The paradigm with its process model, tools, and languages are described in the sections which follow. The purpose of this paper is to define a methodology to use to complete the recipe. MicroSTEP is primarily a business application tool, so that will be in the scope of the process model described by the inner box in Figure 1. Although the paradigm may well apply to other problem sets, that is not within the scope of this discussion.

MICROSTEP SPECIFICATION COMPILER

MicroSTEP is a CASE tool which encapsulates the later parts of the software development life cycle (Stanford, Allen, Wszola, Joch,

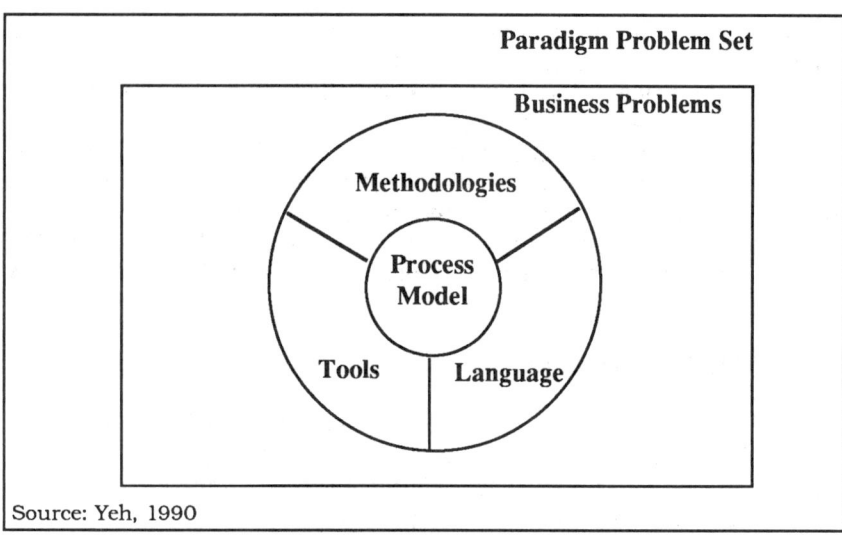

Figure 1: Components of a Software Evolution Paradigm

Apiki & Grehan, 1989). Produced by SYSCORP International, Inc. located in Austin, Texas, MicroSTEP attempts to alleviate those portions of the software development life cycle which have been the most labor-intensive: the coding, testing, modifying, and maintaining (Halverson, Bayraktar & Tanik, 1991). Through the use of a Data Flow Diagram which uses icons to depict the application, the developer can see what the objects look like, then define the characteristics for each object as desired. The data control process is also defined, and the developer may implement a checking mechanism at any time to insure the design's correctness. The letters STEP are an acronym for Specification To Executable Program. MicroSTEP is an applications generator which takes user specifications, and creates C code. It uses a model of software development which borrows heavily from prototyping. This tool is comprised of three basic components (Yeh 1990):

1. a graphics based specification language;
2. a complete application generation system; and,
3. a sophisticated application run-time environment.

MicroSTEP allows the user to build a specification by manipulating graphic icons. It also checks for consistency and completeness, and then generates, compiles, and links the source code. Documentation is facilitated by easy to use, mouse-driven, menus which can incorporate text into the specification.

A Methodology for MicroSTEP 573

This tool encourages software component reuse and eliminates errors by allowing data structures, reports and screen layouts to be stored in data dictionaries. The built-in modularity of a MicroSTEP specification allows the user to specify a change without disrupting other, running modules. This same characteristic also makes these types of programs easy to maintain. Primarily a business tool, it is ideal for the systems analyst or applications programmer. It takes less time to learn and become proficient in using MicroSTEP than a traditional programming language. MicroSTEP speeds up application development because of its iterative approach. The following section examines the inner workings of MicroSTEP in greater detail.

How MicroSTEP Works

The following portions of this section will deal speci-fically with how MicroSTEP works by demonstrating how to build an application. From creating a MicroSTEP specification through installation of a finished program, each step in forming an executable file from the application's requirements will be covered.

TopSTEP

The first screen encountered when entering MicroSTEP is the TopSTEP screen (Figure 2), complete with pulldown menus similar to those in every portion of the program. The menu options shown allow the developer to perform a variety of functions.

The main menu has four options. EXIT quits MicroSTEP and returns to DOS. CHANGE PATH allows you to switch directories to access other MicroSTEP files. CONFIGURE is used to set up the system to recognize peripherals. DOS FUNCTNS enables users to accomplish some DOS functions without leaving MicroSTEP. The SHOW menu has only two choices, SPECS and DDs. SPECS allows viewing of all specifications which have been created in the current directory. Data dictionaries allow the user to store structures (database, report, and screen activities) for future use. This feature promotes efficiency and lower error rates through the reuse of data structures. The EDIT menu permits the user to perform editing functions on data dictionaries and specifications.

The DEFINE menu lets the user create a specification or data dictionary and open them after they are created. The Import DB command is an advanced command which is used to import DBase IV or Btrieve files and use them in MicroSTEP specifications. Finally, the PROGRAM menu is used when the specification is complete and ready to be converted into an executable program. The first five

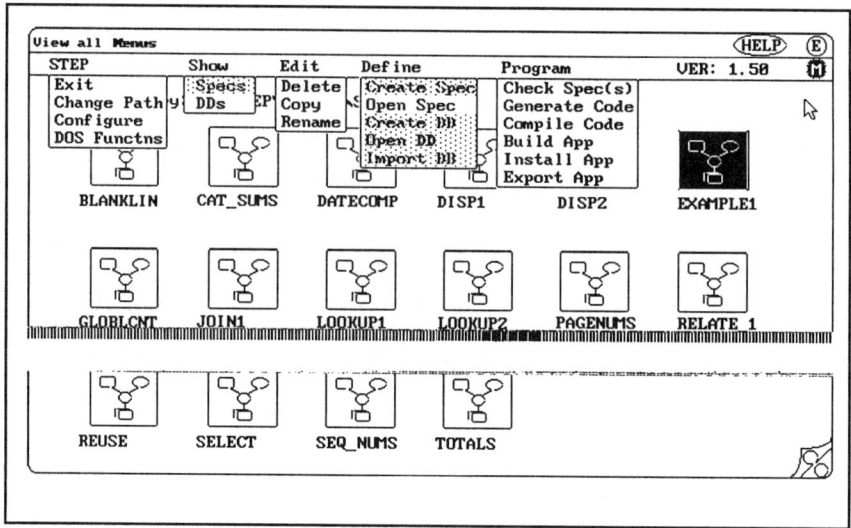

Figure 2: TopSTEP Menu

commands (Check Spec(s), Generate Code, Compile Code, Build App, and Install App) need to be completed in order for a specification to be translated into executable code. The Export App command allows completed applications to be taken to other computers.

Flow Diagram Builder

The next step is to begin the design of the application in MicroSTEP. By choosing DEFINE: Create Spec, an empty screen appears called a Flow Diagram Builder. As shown in Figure 3, there are fifteen icons down the left side of the screen. These icons are used to build the flow diagram of the application to be constructed. Application EXAMPLE1 is displayed in Figure 3. The application accepts addresses, stores them in the database ADDRESS_DB, and prints a list of all the addresses in ADDRESS_DB.

The example application, EXAMPLE1, was built by high-lighting the icons on the left as needed. First, by using the database icon, ADDRESS_DB was placed. Then, the screen activity SCREEN ACTIVITY, followed by report ADDRESS_REPORT, and processes ADD_ADDRESS and PRINT_ADDRESSES were placed on the screen. The database was then duplicated to provide input for the report. Finally, the data flow links were added in the appropriate directions. Once all the icons were on the screen and named, the database, screen activityies, and reports were structured.

The menus across the top of Figure 3 are explained as follows.

A Methodology for MicroSTEP 575

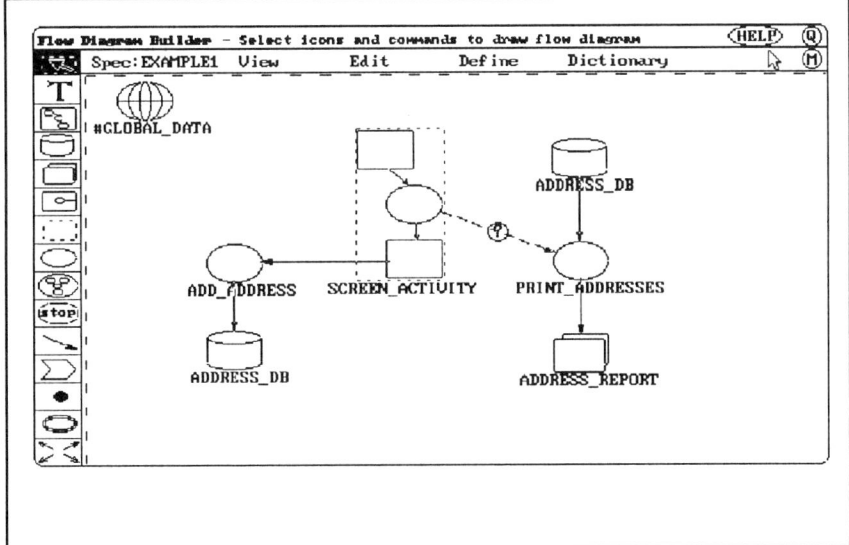

Figure 3: Flow Diagram Builder

The Spec:EXAMPLE1 menu is administrative, providing the capability to save, print, change default values, etc. The View menu changes the scale of the flow diagram to allow the user to see the flow diagram from different scales. The Edit menu enables the Undo, Delete, Copy, Duplicate, Rename, Object Type, Extract and Import Spec commands. The user can Define an object's Structure, Format, Activity and Flow Control. Not all objects on the screen can be defined with all four of these commands, however. Shaded objects are unavailable. The Dictionary, as discussed earlier, is available to copy objects, to or from, in order to reduce repetitive building and reduce errors.

Data Structure Builder

By using the Define Structure command, we can begin defining the structure of the database. The screen which appears is displayed in Figure 4. The environment consists of two windows. The active window is on top, while the reference window is below. This screen, the Data Structure Builder, has only seven icons on the left. The structure is built one field at a time by naming the field, designating it as a key field (or not), then choosing the type of data this field will contain (integer, real, text, date, time, decimal, long integer, or long real).

After the database structure is defined, the structures for the

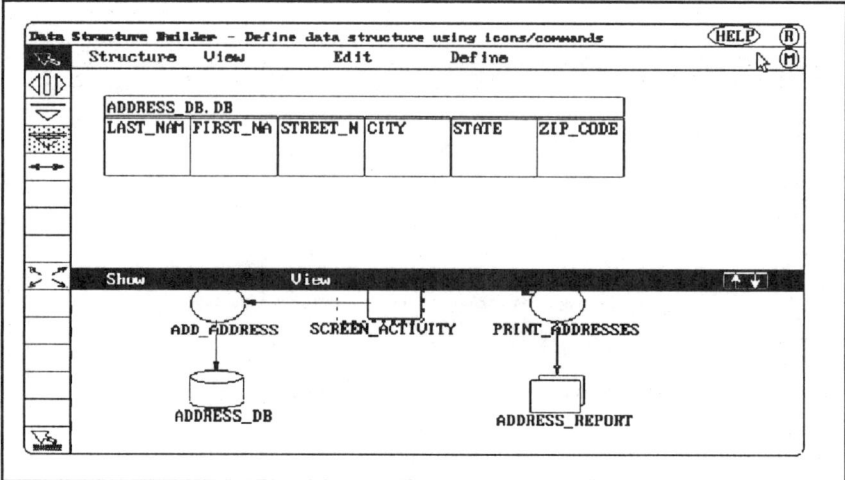

Figure 4: Data Structure Builder

screen activity and the report must be constructed in the Flow Diagram Builder. The database structure is now mapped onto the object in the active window. Finally, a field must be added to the global data corresponding to the PRINT_ADDRESS field in SCREEN_ACTIVITY's structure so that control can be passed to the portion of the application which prints the report.

Format Builder

The next step is to define the screen and report formats. As pictured in Figure 5, the structure appears in the reference window. Initially, the active window is blank. Using the icons on the left, the screen can be formatted rapidly. The final screen is the one users will see when the application is compiled.

Activity Builder

Figure 6 shows the Regular Activity Builder. This builder is reached through the Define Activity commands on process ADD_ADDRESS. Since there is only a simple example with one input, the main requirement is to map the fields from SCREEN_ACTIVITY in the reference window to the appropriate field in ADDRESS_DB in the active window. The shaded area seen immediately below SCREEN_ACTIVITY in Figure 6 is a filter. This filter prevents the user from storing empty records in the database inadvertently.

A Methodology for MicroSTEP 577

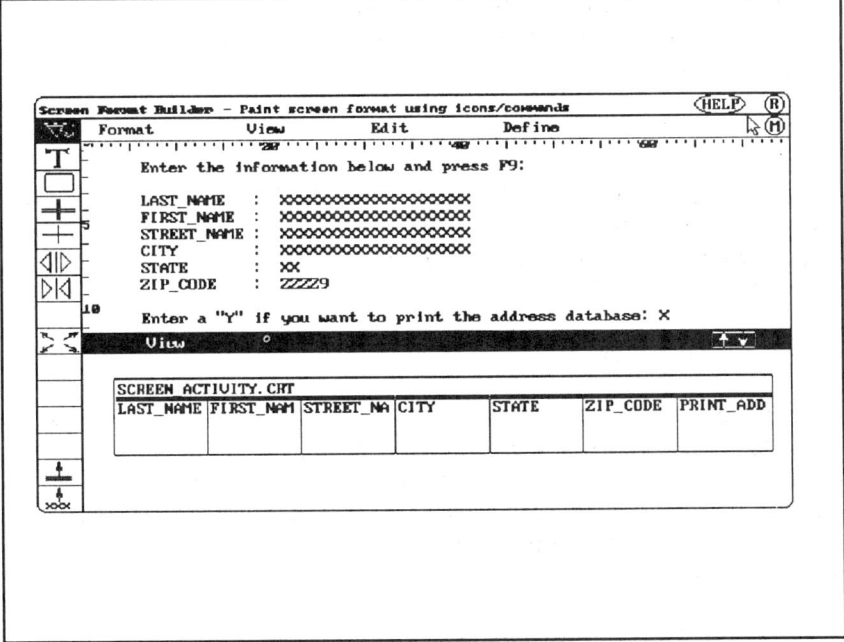

Figure 5: Screen Format Builder

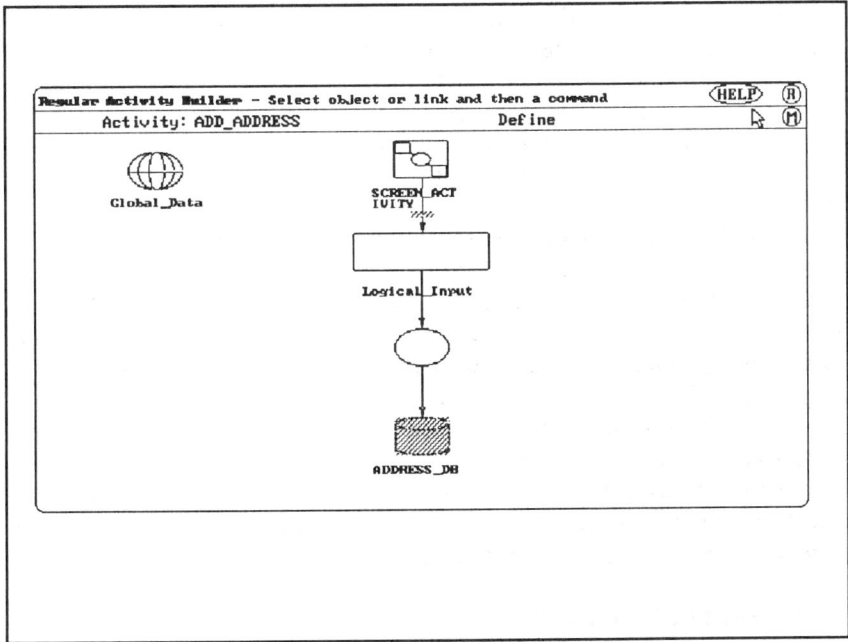

Figure 6: Regular Activity Builder

Lastly, the control field referred to earlier, PRINT_ADDRESS, should be mapped to Global_Data. This action makes that field a global variable.

Flow Control

The dashed line between SCREEN_ACTIVITY and PRINT_ADDRESSES in Figure 3 represents the transfer of control. This flow control is defined by checking to see if the PRINT field of Global_Data equals "Y".

Report Builder

Figure 7 is the Report Builder screen. The active window is where the user screen (shown in Figure 8) is constructed using the report structure from the reference window. Note that the only difference in the structure is that the fields are assembled into a repeating group. This allows all the addresses in the database to be mapped into the report.

MicroSTEP Capabilities

The example, EXAMPLE1 merely touches on some of the capabilities MicroSTEP possesses. There are good and bad aspects to every tool and MicroSTEP is no exception. For instance, although it is aimed at non-programmers, MicroSTEP does require some technical expertise and knowledge to become proficient. The learning curve is somewhat shorter than that of a high level computer language (i.e. Pascal), although how much shorter is dependent on the individual. An advantage is that applications can be generated very quickly with MicroSTEP, thus it supports the Rapid Prototyping paradigm very well. However, the executable code generated by MicroSTEP will likely not be optimized as much as programs generated by more traditional development methods with a high level language. Although SYSCORP is making progress with later versions of the software, the executable portion of an application generated by MicroSTEP typically requires at least 400KB of memory because of overhead. Large applications (more than 50 objects) can take as much as 30-45 minutes to generate code and the application must be recompiled after any change.

Increased Productivity

Using MicroSTEP combines two of the steps (coding and testing)

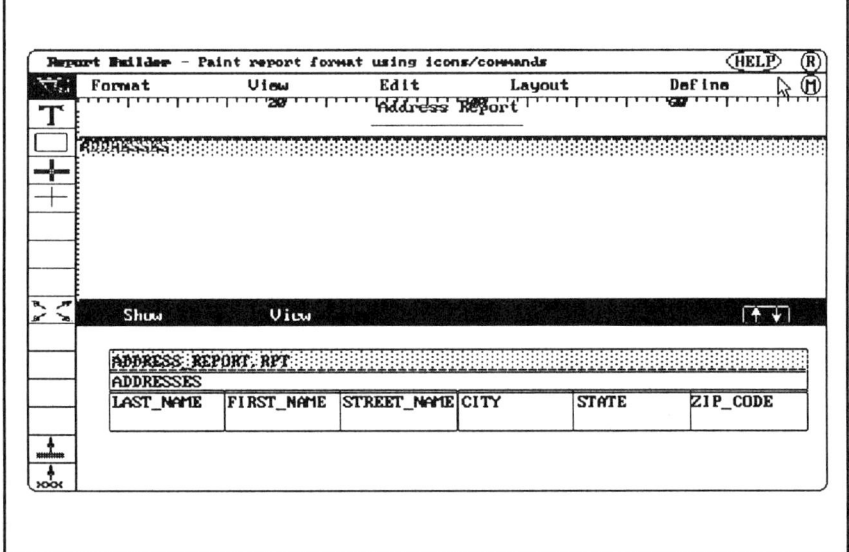

Figure 7: Report Builder

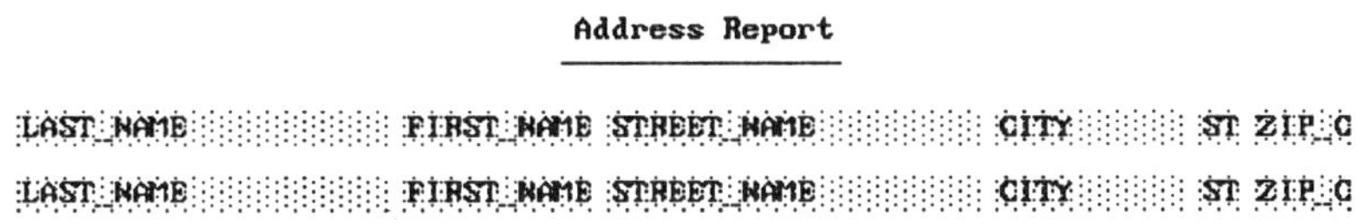

Figure 8: User's Address Report

of the classic "waterfall model" of software development (Stamps, 1989) into one and makes the last step (maintenance) easier for software developed with MicroSTEP. The reusability of pieces of an application ranging in size from an object to entire specifications which can be imported into applications easily, is a plus which makes the most of the software developer's time and energy. Another reusability aspect of MicroSTEP is that of common operations, or reuse of design. These "common" operations are used frequently in many applications. It is useful to maintain them in a library. This library enhances productivity by making reuse easier. The following section deals with the issue of reusability and the use of MicroSTEP, with respect to a common operations example.

A REAL LIFE EXPERIMENT WITH MICROSTEP

The Dual Drilling Supply System (DDSS) was developed using MicroSTEP with our MRPM methodology. By using the tool with the methodology, the project grew incrementally, as better versions of the working model were devised and the specification approached the user's true needs.

Software Development Life Cycle

The traditional "waterfall" software development life cycle is the most widely used paradigm for software engineering. The six steps of the life cycle (Boar, 1984; Fisher, 1988; Pressman, 1987) are as follows:

1. System engineering and analysis
2. Software requirements analysis
3. Design
4. Coding
5. Testing
6. Maintenance

These steps are thorough, and can produce quality results, but this software development paradigm is inevitably cumbersome and time-consuming for large projects. The development method discussed here is the MicroSTEP Rapid Prototyping methodology. This methodology involves an iteration of (1) requirement definition, (2) specification/design, and (3) coding/testing. The cycle goes 1-2-3-1. Since the complete requirement specification is extremely rare, prototyping delivers incrementally what the user said they wanted. Then when additional requirements are identified (and they will be), the next version of the prototype will be able to encompass them.

Rapid prototyping is a variant of the Rapid Application Development (RAD) methods which have received much attention in the industry press (Carey, 1990; Lea & Chung, 1990; Lewis & Oman 1990; Martin, 1989; PC Week, 1989; Tanik & Yeh, 1989; Tate, 1990; Tate & Verner 1990; Whitten, Bentley & Barlow, 1989). Upon analysis, this model is both evolutionary, and iterative, and it heavily involves the user in the development process. The remainder of this chapter traces the MRPM as it was applied using MicroSTEP through the development of the DDSS.

Current Operations at Dual Drilling

Dual Drilling Company is a company primarily engaged in leasing oil rights and operating offshore oil drilling platforms in several locations outside the United States. These include Indonesia, Malaysia, the Philippines, South Korea and Brazil. Headquartered in Dallas, Texas, the company employs no personnel trained to write computer software. As automation problems occur, they either buy an off-the-shelf solution, or hire a consultant.

The supply system used by the Dual Drilling Company was selected as the test implementation system. Although it is adequate for current needs, the company's planned growth will overtake the supply system's capacity within a year. One employee runs the system at the headquarters, and she has other duties. An explanation of the present manual supply system is detailed below.

A graphical representation of the Dual Drilling supply system is seen in Figure 9. The system begins when the supply clerk on an offshore oil rig sends a Material Request (MR) by mail or fax to the company headquarters(HQ). These MR's have several data items on them:

1. MR number (identifying number by date and rig)
2. Date
3. Description of major equipment or category the parts are for
4. Item number
5. Quantity
6. Part number (if available from a catalog)
7. Description of part
8. Comments

There can be multiple categories or major pieces of equipment as well as multiple parts under each MR. Each week, the HQ supply supervisor consolidates the MR's into a Quote Request (QR) which will be sent to all vendors which supply equipment to Dual Drilling. At present, this involves typing all the information on the MR's received.

The QR's are sent by fax to the vendors. When vendors get a QR, they see the description of each item, the quantity required, part numbers, what the item is a component of (if any), and the date by which the vendors must return their bids to Dual Drilling. As the vendors return their bids, the lowest prices are noted for each item.

When all the bids are returned, all items for which a particular vendor was low bidder are consolidated into a Purchase Order (PO).

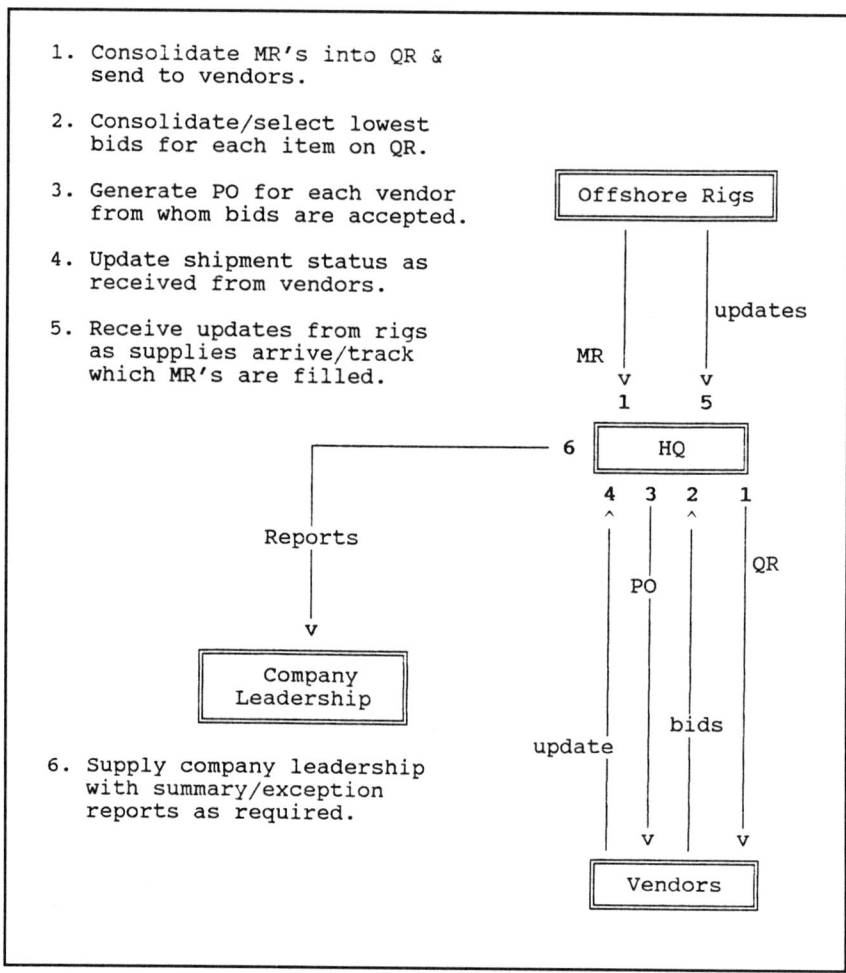

Figure 9: How the System Works

This is done for each vendor who was the lowest bidder for an item. The same data is typed again onto the company PO forms. If there are multiple items under a major category, they can be supplied by multiple vendors. The PO forms also have columns for unit price and total price. As the vendors ship the merchandise, they send a shipment status to the company which includes data such as method of shipment, whether it was shipped on time, and if any items were back ordered. The supply supervisor also receives updates from the offshore rigs as the shipments arrive. This information allows for follow-up on late orders and checking on which MR's are complete.

Finally, two reports are produced for company management. The Summary Report lists all MR's which are still incomplete. To prepare this report the supply supervisor once again types much of the same information, and since it may be a period of several months from the time an MR is received, until the items all reach the offshore rig, that data could be repeated many, many times. The second report identifies all the items which have not reached their destination by the date promised by the vendor when the bid was submitted. Creating this report involves a search of all outstanding orders to find the ones which are late. This report is done infrequently because it is very time consuming.

The bottom line is that the current system is not as responsive as it needs to be for the company leadership to make decisions. The information is there, but not in a form which is easily manipulated. The next section deals with the approach taken in automating this supply system.

Approach to Automation

There are many opportunities in the manual supply system used by Dual Drilling for automation. The approach used was to interview the supply personnel at the headquarters to determine the specifications desired for the system. Since they had not worked with an automated system, they did not know exactly how to specify requirements. Thus, several prototype systems were presented over a period of months to refine the specifications to the desired functionality.

Project Specifications

Later sections of this chapter detail the exact structure, format and functions of the automated system, however, the specifications evolved as follows. There was a definite need to create and maintain a database for the Material Requests (MR). (The structure of this database is also discussed below.) It was convenient and efficient to add additional data to the MR database form, which was not on the original MR's when they arrived, i.e. dates, identifying numbers and comments. Since the data from the MR's are turned into Quote Requests (QR) to send to vendors, the logical route was to take the MR database, search it for new MR's, add an identifying number, and then print this in a report to send to vendors.

Information about the vendors was needed, so a procedure to create and maintain a vendor database was included. Like the MR database, there are provisions to add, modify and delete vendor records as necessary. When bids are returned, the MR database is modified. After the lowest bids are determined and entered into the MR database, supply personnel generates Purchase Orders (PO) to send to the appropriate vendors.

Headquarters receives information about shipments from both vendors and the offshore oil rigs which ordered the supplies originally. These updates provide information on how the order is being shipped, comments, and other specifics. This data allows the supply supervisor to monitor the shipments in order to assist with problems which occur regularly in international transportation.

Finally, the data contained in the MR and PO databases are manipulated to provide two reports for company executives. A summary of all active MR's is provided bi-weekly which contains identifying PO and MR numbers, plus much of the update information provided by the vendors and oil rigs. The late report shows which items have not been delivered to the rigs by the promised date as well as the vendor, the item, and when it was supposed to be there.

Iteration

Once the initial specification and design was done, the next step was to enter the design into MicroSTEP. Despite that, the cycle of specifying the requirements; designing any necessary changes; testing and debugging the MicroSTEP program; and installing/testing the new prototype produced positive results. There is no doubt that the developer of this application learned to "code" proficiently in MicroSTEP and developed the DDSS in considerably less time than it would have taken using another method. The amount of time saved by using MicroSTEP with the MPRM, versus more traditional software development methods, is a question which needs more research before a conclusive answer can be given.

User's View of the Dual Drilling Supply System: DUAL

In the following pages, the user view is presented. The first screen of the DDSS is shown in Figure 10. The program is asking for user input at this time. In order to give a flavor of the program, we will discuss a portion of the first entry (Change MR/Vendor databases) of the initial screen (Figure 10). This program is fully menu driven and the user can return to the previous screen at any time by pressing the Escape key. The structure of the menus was a developer choice. MicroSTEP supports hierarchical or flat menu structures. An entry is chosen by placing the dark scroll bar on top of the entry and then pressing the Return key.

A Methodology for MicroSTEP 585

```
This program has several functions. You can
change databases, generate/manipulate Quote
Requests, make Purchase Orders, and print
reports. Please choose the one you want.

     Change MR/Vendor databases
     Make/Change QR's
     Make PO's/Print Reports
```

Figure 10: Initial Screen for Dual Drilling Supply System

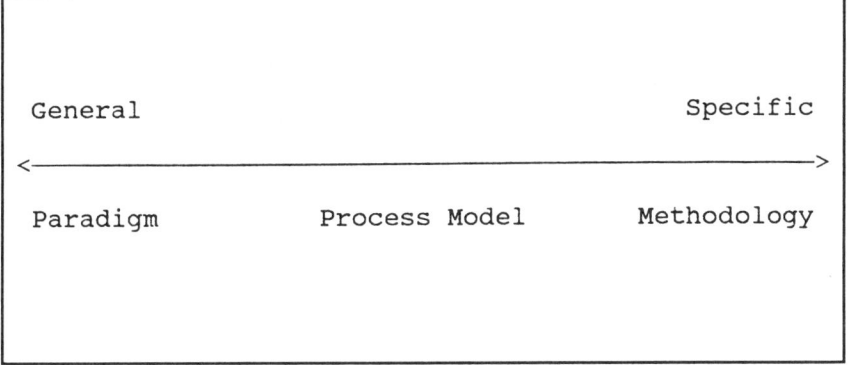

Figure 11: Process Model Specificity Continuum

Dual Drilling Supply System Specification Implementation

The functionality of this program completely automates the manual supply system described before. Here we examined some of the individual parts which comprise the program DUAL. There are twelve individual specifications which are contained in the overall specification DUAL. The rest of this section looks at several of them in turn.

A METHODOLOGY FOR MicroSTEP-MicroSTEP RAPID PROTOTYPING METHODOLOGY (MRPM)

The MRPM software development methodology, when used with MicroSTEP, is an effective software development method. In order to develop a methodology, there must be an underlying paradigm.

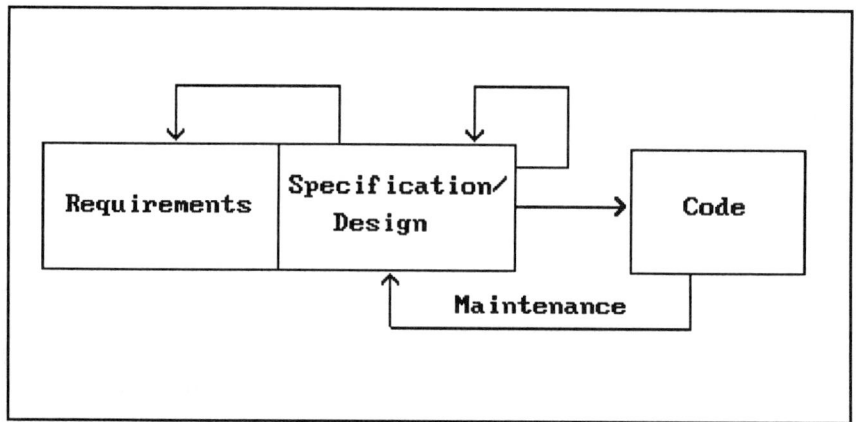

Figure 12: Rapid Prototyping Paradigm

Figure 11 shows a continuum from "how-to-do-it" on one end to "what-should-be-done" on the other end. The process model is shown as being between a paradigm and a methodology. A methodology is a step-by-step "recipe" for accomplishing a generic task. In this case, the task is developing software.

The paradigm underlying the MicroSTEP Rapid Prototyping methodology has three axioms. The first is that humans cannot specify accurately all the requirements of a software project before they see it in operation. The second axiom is that quick feedback from the end-user to the software developer is desirable. The third axiom is that automated means are needed to support rapid feedback by the analyst. The paradigm of Rapid Prototyping focuses on the requirements, specification, and design aspects of the software development life cycle (SDLC) as shown in Figure 12.

Another definition of prototyping is that it is a process by which a scaled-down version of a system is built to model the full-scale system (Microstep, 1991). Rapid prototyping uses automated means, like MicroSTEP, to develop the prototype more quickly than with conventional (waterfall-type) approaches. Prototyping provides feedback efficiently and quickly, as the user evaluates the latest version of the system.

Used with MicroSTEP, the MRPM is an iterative process where design decisions are made gradually. MicroSTEP is the environment on which these decisions are implemented. A model which depicts the structure of MicroSTEP in its role as a design environment is shown in Figure 13.

The next section describes the MRPM as it applies to MicroSTEP in detail. This will allow others to produce software using the same method by following the enumerated steps.

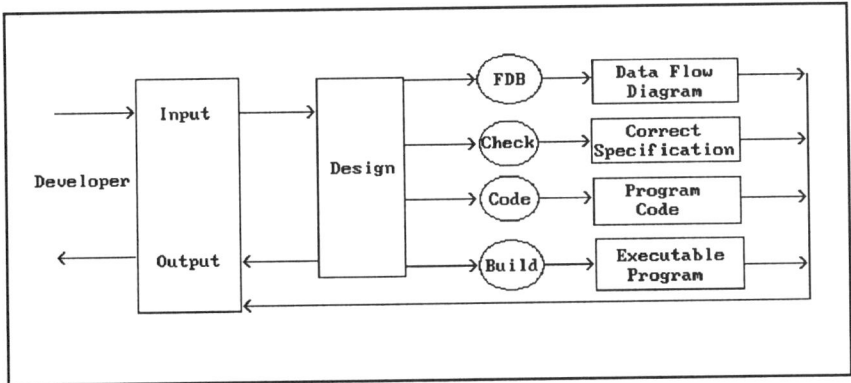

Figure 13: MicroSTEP Design Environment

The Structure of MicroSTEP Rapid Prototyping Methodology

In order to produce quality software using the MRPM with MicroSTEP, specific steps are necessary. These steps are shown in Figure 14, and detail the necessary actions to develop software with end-user contributions at every stage. Each step has an input and output component, as well as a feedback loop to correspond with the Rapid Prototyping Paradigm. In figure 14, the five major steps of the methodology are shown in capitals.

Step One: Develop Requirements. First, like any other software development methodology, developers must spend sufficient time defining requirements. Although the requirements specification will not be complete, we knew from experience that making it as complete as possible at the beginning, would reduce the number of radical changes which would be required later in the life cycle. This step was done for the DDSS project by examining the present system in detail (Figure 9) and interviewing the individuals responsible (the end-user) for the system. The initial interview with the end-user obtained representative data to test the prototype. The interviews and observations of the present system served as the input for this step. The test data for the "Dual" application was in the form of old Material Requests which formed the basis of an MR database. The specific manner in which the software developer determines the initial requirements may vary with the situation, but it is imperative that good communications are established with the end-user at the beginning of the project. By communicating with the end-user, the developer achieves the feedback part of Step One. Output from Step One are written requirements for the proposed system's functionality, formats, and data flows , as well as the test data to be used in Step Four.

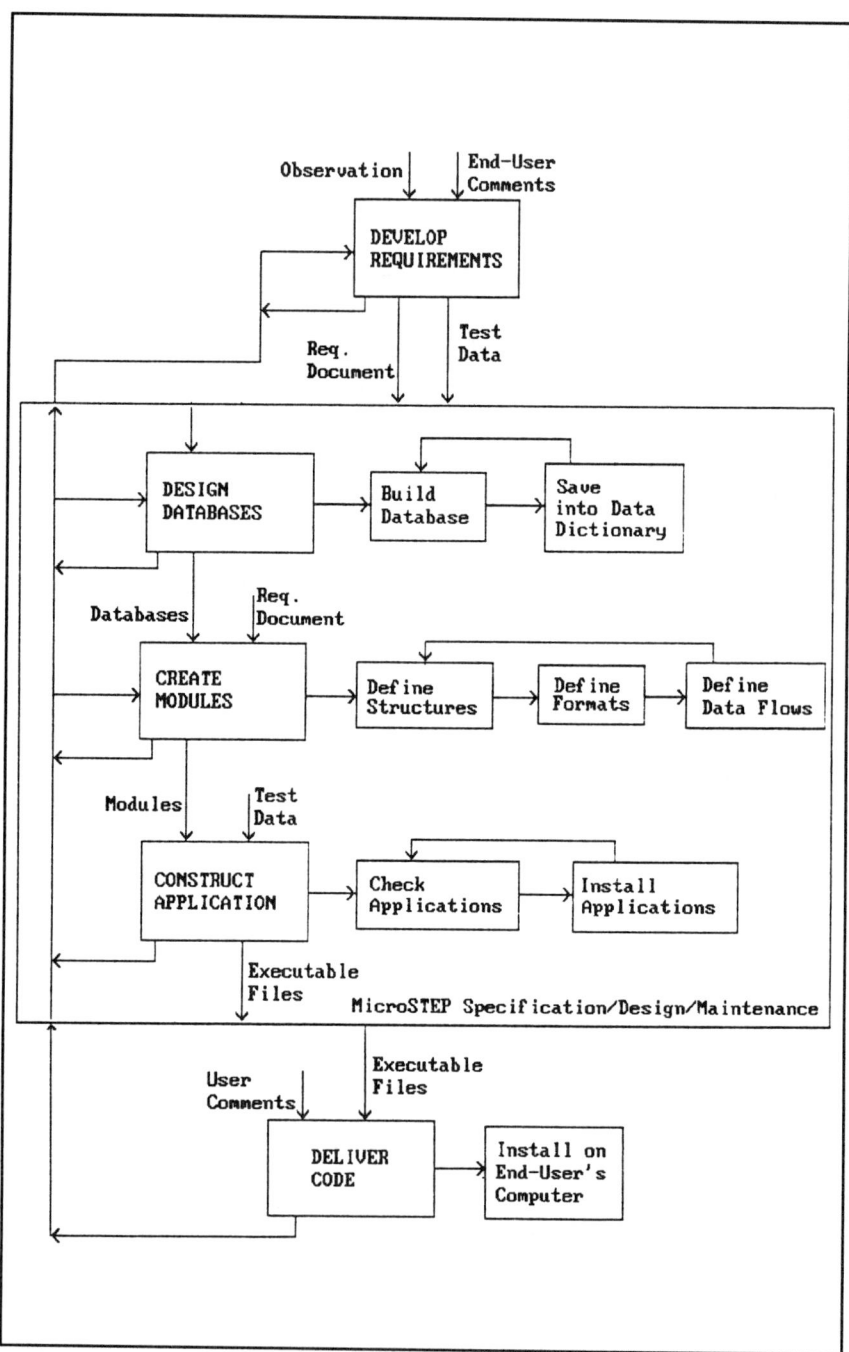

Figure 14: MicroSTEP Rapid Prototyping Methodology (MRPM)

Step Two: Design Databases. The next step was to design the database structures which would be the framework of the application. Again, getting them as close to "right" as possible at the start, allows for small modifications instead of major overhauls later. The correct and complete design of the databases associated with the application, established a foundation for the entire project. The input for this design process was the requirements developed in Step One. A feedback loop allowed the developer to consult the requirements as the design process evolved into a final database design for achieving the desired level of functionality. The newly constructed databases were stored in the Data Dictionary so that they could be reused. These databases were the output of Step Two.

Step Three: Create Modules. Stored databases and requirements are the input needed for this step. Since the initial prototype's goal is to achieve functionality as soon as possible, we allowed MicroSTEP to generate default screen formats in the Screen Format Builder (Figure 5) and Report Builder (Figure 7). MicroSTEP does this using the structure already entered. This saves time and gets the prototype to the end-user much quicker.

All but the smallest applications will need to break the project up into modules similar to a procedure or function in a high level language. As the developer builds the reports and formats necessary to meet the requirements, the feedback loop may require returning to Step Two, or merely a loop internal to the step where modules are built against the requirements. For a good design, each module should perform a separate function in the application. The output for this step was a MicroSTEP application that consisted of linked modules which accomplished the goals set forth in the requirements specification.

Step Four: Construct the Application. The next step calls for building and testing the new application. The test data from Step One and the completed modules from Step Three made up the input for this step. Each activity and module was checked for correctness as it is completed. In Figure 3, one of the menu options is "Check," and a similar feature is offered in the Regular Activity Builder. Performing this step regularly not only insures syntactic correctness, but helps uncover errors as they occur. If checking fails, return to Step Three, correct the problem, and perform the check again. The installation command causes the specification(s) to be checked and code to be generated and compiled before building the executable files. The command also installs the application in an interactive manner. What emerges as output from Step Four is an executable application file.

Step Five: Deliver Code. After the application is thoroughly tested by the developer, deliver it to the end-user. The *Program Export App* command assists in the effort (see Figure 2). This command can be used to copy the necessary files onto a disk, if the application is to be installed on a different computer than it was developed on. The resulting files were the input to this step. The first prototype required the developer to sit down with the end-user to solicit comments and guide the user through the new software. As the user becomes more familiar with the application, they can do more testing themselves. When the end-user finishes evaluating the software, they should provide feedback to the developer. The developer takes the feedback and may return to Step Two, or Step Three. The extent of the required changes drives the decision of how far back into the loop the developer goes. Through constant interaction with the end-user, the application is molded into usable and useful software. This delivered product was the output of Step Five.

Finally, since the application was designed in a modular fashion, maintenance was simplified. After the DDSS was installed at the Dual Drilling Company, the end-user needed a format change. This change required the developer to enter MicroSTEP at Step Three and modify the appropriate module. Next, Steps Four and Five were repeated by building and testing the application, and then installing it on the user's computer. The end-user comments, and the MicroSTEP modules which needed alteration, were the input for this maintenance process. The feedback loop was completed as often as necessary by returning to Step Three. This was done without disrupting other modules (unless a structural database change is required by returning to Step Two).

Lessons Learned

In evaluating the project and its progress through the development process, some of the lessons learned were due to factors outside the development life cycle. One of these lessons was the "learning curve" for MicroSTEP: the time it took to develop DUAL specification was lengthened because MicroSTEP concepts were new to the developer. Significant time was spent resolving typical "beginner" type problems.

Other lessons learned include a confidence that MicroSTEP is a tool which supports the entire life cycle when a Rapid Prototyping model is used. The iterative requirements specification-design-and-coding/testing cycle effectively automates the requirements specification and design phases of the cycle by making incremental changes in the design and requirements as feedback is obtained from the user about newer versions of the application. Although the MicroSTEP development paradigm automates only two portions of the life cycle, coding and testing, other portions are supported as well. A specification can be edited in order to maintain an application, and there are provisions to include documentation while developing an application in MicroSTEP. Thus, the entire life cycle is accommodated by applying the MRPM with the MicroSTEP tool.

There were some problems which, if they had been recognized and dealt with earlier in the process, would not have detracted from the development time. One problem which was encountered has been called "creeping functionality" (Martin, 1990). As newer and better prototypes are delivered to the user, more helpful and useful operations are added to the requirements list until the project has much greater scope than originally planned. While a form of creeping requirements specification is one of the stated goals of the Rapid Prototyping method, if allowed to go unchecked, it can exceed the bounds of the "necessary" and add development time to the project. If this happens, it may negate the advantage gained by the faster development time.

In Retrospect

The question may be asked, "Was it necessary to develop the DUAL application to derive the methodology?". The answer is that for the methodology to be more than a theory, it had to be shown to work. Since no methodology was specified for use with MicroSTEP, it is up to each developer to arrive at their own "best way" to use the tool to its best advantage. By using it to develop a real world application, the MRPM passed from being a technique that was *potentially* useful to one which *has been demonstrated* to be useful. Moreover, the methodology evolved during the development process.

The importance of establishing a "foundation" of solid databases was driven home by the experience of having to rework the database structure of DUAL application. This experience is what caused Step 2 of the MRPM to be separated from Step 3. Initially, the actions required in these steps were combined. The process of actually building MicroSTEP specifications reinforced the importance of end-user feedback, checking every step, and constant communications between the developer and user.

CONCLUSIONS

When coupled with MicroSTEP, Rapid Prototyping quickly produces consistent, quality software and supports excellent communications with end-users. The user involvement in the process substantially reduces dissatisfaction with the final delivered product. This was the initial attempt to define a methodology to use MicroSTEP to its best advantage. As more experience is gained through developing a wider variety of applications using Rapid Prototyping with MicroSTEP, the methodology will be improved upon and refined. It remains to be discovered if this method of software development can be applied to every software project. However, in the applications developed to this point, it enhanced our productivity and has the potential to contribute substantially in the effort to make all software developers much more productive.

ACKNOWLEDGMENTS
Thanks are due to Ismail Bayraktar and the other members of the Software Engineering and Knowledge Systems (SEK) group at SMU for their support and assistance. Also, the MicroSTEP technicians at SYSCORP were unfailing and liberal with their patience and expertise. We would like to thank Ali H. Dogru for his outstanding help in the time consuming task of document preparation and organizational advice. Lastly, we appreciate Raymond T. Yeh's continuing intellectual support in furthering our understanding of the software development process.

REFERENCES

Boar, B. H. (1984). *Application Prototyping*. New York: John Wiley & Sons.

Carey, J. M. (1990). "Prototyping: Alternative Systems Development Methodology". *Information and Software Technology 32* (March), 119-126.

CASE (1991). "Unix Based CASE Products Survey". *CASE Trends 3* (January/February), 30-31.

Crozier, M., Glass, D., Hughes, J. G., Johnston, W. & McChesney, I. (1989). "Critical Analysis of Tools for Computer-Aided Software Engineering". *Information and Software Technology 31* (November), 486-496.

Doke, E. R. (1990). "An Industry Survey of Emerging Prototyping Methodologies". *Information and Management 18* (April), 169-176.

Fisher, Alan S. (1988). *CASE: Using Software Development Tools*. New York: John Wiley & Sons.

Gould, J. D., Boies, S. J. & Lewis C. (1991). "Making Usable, Useful, Productivity-Enhancing Computer Applications". *CACM 34* (January), 74-85.

Halverson, M. A., Bayraktar, I. & Tanik M. M. (1990). *MicroSTEP with Single Concept Teaching Method. Technical Report 90-CSE-28*, Department of Computer Science and Engineering, Southern Methodist University, (August; revised January 1991).

Key, D. J. (1991). Software Development Life Cycle Issues with the Specification Compiler MicroSTEP. Masters thesis, Southern Methodist University.

Key, D. J. & Tanik M. M. (1991). *A Specification Experience: Dual Drilling Supply System Built with MicroSTEP.* Technical Report 91-CSE-9, Department of Computer Science and Engineering, Southern Methodist University, (March).

Lea R.J., & Chung C. G. (1990). "Rapid Prototyping from Structured Analysis: Executable Specification Approach". *Information and Software Technology,* 32 (November) 589-597.

Lewis, T. G. & Oman P. (1990). "The Challenge of Software Development". *IEEE Software* (November), 9-12.

Martin, J. (1989). "RAD Designed to Facilitate Dynamic Change in Firms". *PC Week,* (18 December), 64.

Martin, J. (1989). "RAD Techniques are a Must for Retooling the IS Factory". *PC Week,* (25 December), 52.

Martin, J. (1990). "User/Analyst Teams Make the Best Systems Developers". *PC Week,* (29 January), 74.

Norman, R. J., & Nunamaker, J. F. Jr. (1989). "CASE Productivity Perceptions of Software Engineering Professionals". *CACM 32* (September), 1102-1108.

Oman, P. W. (1990). "CASE Analysis and Design Tools". *IEEE Software* (May), 37. CASE (1990).

"PC Based CASE Tools Survey". *CASE Trends 2* (January/ February), 25-29.

Pressman, R. S. (1987). *Software Engineering: A Practitioner's Approach.* 2d ed. New York: McGraw-Hill.

Stamps, D. (1989). "CASE vs. 4GLs". *Datamation 35* (August15), 29-31.

Stanford, D., Udell, J., Allen, D., Wszola, S., Joch, A., Apiki, S. & Grehan R. (1989). "Making a Case for CASE". *BYTE 14* (December), 154-171.

Statland, N. (1989). "Payoffs Down the Pike: A CASE Study". *Datamation 35* (April 1), 32-34.

SYSCORP, (1991a). *MicroSTEP Building Blocks: Sample MicroSTEP Specifications.* Austin: SYSCORP International, Inc.

SYSCORP, (1991b). *MicroSTEP Version 1.5 Reference Manual.* Austin: SYSCORP International, Inc., 1991.

Tanik, M. M. & Yeh, R. T. (1989). "Rapid Prototyping in Software Development". *Computer 22* (May), 9-10.

Tate, G. (1990). "Prototyping: Helping to Build the Right Software". *Information and Software Technology 32* (May), 237-244.

Tate G., & Verner, J. (1990). "Case Study of Risk Management, Incremental Development, and Evolutionary Prototyping". *Information and Software Technology 32* (April), 207-214.

Watterson, K. (1989). "New Age Applications with MicroSTEP". *Databased Advisor 7* (December), 64-76.

Whitten, J. L., Bentley, L. D. & Barlow, V. M. (1989). *Systems Analysis and Design Methods.* 2d ed. Boston: Irwin.

Yeh, R. T. (1990). "An Alternative Paradigm for Software Evolution". In *Modern Software Engineering: Foundations and Current Perspectives,* Yeh R. T. & Ng, P. edts, 7-22. New York: Van Nostrand Reinhold.

Yeh, R.T. (1990). "MicroSTEP: A Business Definition Language System". In *Modern Software Engineering: Foundations and Current Perspectives,* Yeh, R. T. & Ng, P. edts, 503-536. New York: Van Nostrand Reinhold.

Yeh, R. T. (1990). "Specification Compilers". *System Builder 3* (April/May): 30-32.

CHAPTER TWENTY-ONE

Integrating Computer-Aided Software Engineering (CASE) Technology into the Information Systems Curriculum: A Case Study

David J. Jankowski
California State University, San Marcos

Douglas L. Dean
University of Arizona

The increasing popularity of computer-aided software engineering (CASE) technology among systems analysis and design practitioners creates the need to expose information systems students to this technology. This chapter describes the integration of CASE technology into the information systems curriculum in the Department of Management Information Systems at The University of Arizona. The integration is traced from the point the authors became involved with the systems analysis and design courses in the fall of 1989 through the complete integration of CASE technology into the department's junior, senior-, and graduate-level systems courses in the fall of 1991. Critical success factors for CASE integration as well as successes and difficulties encountered along the way will be described.

In order to keep up with the advances in hardware and software technology, which occur almost daily, it becomes necessary for information systems departments in academia to modify their curricula to incorporate new technology; CASE is one such technology. The two most influential agencies that provide recommendations for information systems curricula, the Data Processing Management Association (DPMA) and the Association for Computing Machinery (ACM), have recently revised their information systems model curricula. Both have included CASE technology as an

Course #	Course name
IS1	Computer and programming concepts
IS2	Data and file structures
IS3	Systems and information concepts in organizations
IS4	Database management systems
IS5	Fundamentals of systems development
IS6	Computer communication networks and distributed processing
IS7A	Decision, executive, and cooperative work support systems
IS7B	Expert systems and artificial intelligence
IS8	Information systems development tools and techniques
IS9	Information management
IS10	Information systems projects

Table 1: Preliminary 1990 ACM Information Systems Model Curriculum

Course #	Course name
CIS-01	Fundamental concepts of information and computer technology
CIS-02	IS concepts
CIS-03	Computer concepts
CIS-04	Application development
CIS-05	Application design and implementation
CIS-06	System development 1 (single-user systems)
CIS-07	System development 2 (multi-user systems)
CIS-08	Systems project
CIS-09	Management of IS

Table 2: Preliminary 1990 DPMA Information Systems Model Curriculum

essential component of an information systems education (DPMA, 1990; Nunamaker, Cougar, & Davis, 1990). The DPMA curriculum states that "CASE is an important thrust; consequently, it is highly desirable to provide some exposure to this technology" (DPMA, 1990, p. 12). Tables 1 and 2 summarize the ACM and DPMA information systems model curriculuma.

A survey of information systems faculty who teach systems analysis and design courses by Jankowski and Norman (1992) found that 79% of the responding faculty use CASE technology to support their assigned term projects. While this finding is encouraging, this leaves 21% using manual methods which, although possibly sufficient for the systems projects encountered in academia, are not sufficient for the increasingly sophisticated systems the student will encounter in the professional world. Further, many of the faculty using CASE, and all faculty who do not use CASE, reported problems with integrating CASE technology into their curriculum. Problems included the CASE tool learning curve, the lack of texts for CASE, the cost of acquiring CASE tools, and insufficient hardware support for CASE tools.

Because of the need to make CASE technology a more prevalent component of the information systems curriculum, information systems texts at all levels are being modified to incorporate CASE technology. In support of the introductory MIS course, many textbooks include a rudimentary discussion of CASE technology as it relates to systems analysis and design (Capron, 1990; Szymanski, Szymanski, Morris, & Pulschen, 1991). In support of advanced courses, systems analysis and design textbooks include entire chapters devoted to CASE technology (Eliason, 1990b; Martin, 1991; Whitten, Bentley, & Barlow, 1989). These books use output from CASE tools to illustrate the case studies that run throughout the texts. Additionally, CASE workbooks have been developed to accompany systems analysis and design texts (Eliason, 1990a; Schmidt, 1990, 1992; Wenig, 1991; Whitten & Bentley, 1987). For the advanced systems development project course, books such as those by Amadio and Amadio (1990) and Mynatt (1990) are intended to be used in conjunction with CASE technology to support a term project.

CASE tool vendors realize that systems analysts of the future will receive their first exposure to CASE technology while in school. As a result, companies such as Index Technology, Visible Systems, Arthur Andersen, and Cadre Technologies have made it easier for academic departments to adopt their tools by developing educational versions of their products, entering into adoption agreements with publishers, or deeply discounting their tools for the academic market.

While the resources listed above are now available, effectively integrating CASE into a curriculum is no easy endeavor. The following questions must be considered: Which CASE tools should be acquired (professional or educational versions)? How will the tools be acquired (grant, departmental direct purchase, site license, or student purchase)? Where will the tools be installed (new or existing laboratories)? And how will the tools be utilized within the context of a particular course? An important question is, "Of which course (or courses) should CASE technology be a part?" Norman (1989) suggests introducing CASE technology in the introductory systems analysis and design course. Kuehn and Fleck (1989) suggest a new three-course sequence devoted to CASE technology.

Each course would involve working with a progressively more sophisticated and costly CASE tool. The first course would concentrate on the analysis and preliminary design phases. The second course would incorporate prototyping and project management, while the third course would include code generation and PC-mainframe communication. Because of the potential difficulties associated with adding new courses to an existing curriculum, Jankowski (1990) suggests following the previously mentioned information systems model curricula as a framework for the integration of CASE technology into the curriculum. These models, which were developed by some of the most knowledgeable educators and industry leaders, are the basis for many schools' information systems programs[1].

Fortunately for information systems departments getting started with CASE technology, or wishing to further integrate CASE into their curricula, there are several papers that describe individual experiences with integrating CASE tools into the information systems curriculum. Norman (1989) describes the integration of CASE technology into the introductory systems analysis and design course, including planning and installation issues. Reports by Heiat (1989) and Mynatt and Leventhal (1990) also include a student assessment of CASE. Gibson and Capon (1989a, 1989b) concentrate on the installation process of a particular CASE tool and identify procedures for minimizing the overhead associated with initializing group projects each semester. Amadio (1989) looks at extending the software life cycle in a systems development project class, to include actual system implementation using a particular CASE tool. While these papers are all helpful within the context of a particular course, they do not address the issue of using CASE across the information systems curriculum.

This chapter details the authors'[2] experiences with integrating CASE technology throughout the analysis and design courses in the information systems curriculum in the Department of Management Information Systems at The University of Arizona (hereafter referred to as Arizona). Specifically, CASE technology is now being utilized in the introductory undergraduate systems analysis and design course, the capstone undergraduate systems development project course, and the graduate systems analysis and design courses. The first section of this chapter outlines the systems courses offered at Arizona and their relation to the other courses in the information systems curriculum, at Arizona and in the model curricula. The second section describes the status of the systems courses with respect to CASE technology at the time the authors became involved with these courses in the fall of 1989. The third section describes the evolution of the integration of CASE technology into the undergraduate and graduate curricula through the fall of 1991. Finally, future plans for CASE technology will be discussed.

SYSTEMS COURSES AT ARIZONA

There are four systems courses available in the undergraduate and graduate curriculum (described below). The undergraduate systems courses, as well as the additional required undergraduate MIS courses, are listed in Table 3, cross referenced with the ACM model curriculum.

Undergraduate Courses

Information Systems Analysis and Design (MIS 341) serves as an introduction to systems analysis and design. MIS 341 introduces the students to the classical systems development life cycle model with emphasis on the early stages of the model. This course emphasizes requirements specification, analysis, and preliminary design. Students typically take this course late in their junior year or early in their senior year. During their junior year, students have taken courses in data structures and data communications. Additionally, students are required to be concurrently enrolled in the introductory database course (briefly described below).

Arizona Course #	Course name	ACM course #
MIS 111	Introduction to computing	IS1
MIS 121	Business programming	IS1
MIS 301	Program and data structures	IS2
MIS 307	Computer organization and data communications	IS6
MIS 331	Data management systems	IS4
MIS 341	Information systems analysis and design	IS5, IS10
MIS 441	Information systems design and implementation	IS8, IS10
MIS 471	Policy formation and management information systems	IS9

Table 3: Undergraduate MIS Curriculum at Arizona and Corresponding ACM Classes

MIS 341 course work consists of short assignments, which serve to introduce the concepts of structured analysis, and to a lesser extent, structured design. This is followed by a term project which incorporates the early phases of the systems life cycle. CASE technology is not introduced until after the students have been exposed to the systems development life cycle and, especially, a structured methodology such as Yourdon's structured analysis. Before the students are introduced to a specific CASE tool, which they will use in support of their term project, they receive two or three lectures covering such issues as CASE components, CASE as a methodology companion, CASE usage in the professional world and so forth. We have found it beneficial to expose students to the CASE tool they will be using before they begin their term projects. Students are required to use the CASE tool to represent a small system which they have previously decomposed and documented manually. This allows the student to temporarily uncouple the learning of the CASE tool from the intellectual overhead of having to think through a new system. Introducing students to the CASE tool in this way allows them to learn the basics of the tool before becoming involved in the rigors of their term projects.

Term projects, typically taken from books or from the university and/or business community, are assigned by the instructor and are manageable enough to be completed by teams of three to four students during the last two months of the semester. Within a particular course section, all groups work on the same term project. If the system being studied is of sufficient scope and complexity, the instructor will break the system into its component subsystems. Each group is then assigned one subsystem, necessitating inter-group coordination.

As mentioned previously, Data Management Systems (MIS 331), is taken concurrently with MIS 341. The data modeling and normalization techniques learned in MIS 331 are applied to the detailed system design begun in MIS 341 and continued in MIS 441 (described below).

After successful completion of MIS 341, students enroll in Information Systems Design and Implementation (MIS 441). This course picks up where MIS 341 leaves off, concentrating on the later phases of the classical systems development life cycle model, i.e., detailed design and implementation. Course work consists of assigned readings and a semester-long term project. Because the students have already been introduced to CASE technology and a specific CASE tool in MIS 341, the term project may be assigned earlier in the semester than is possible in MIS 341. The term project often extends and implements a preliminary design begun by students in MIS 341.

We have found an enrollment limit of thirty-five students limits the demands a well-run project course can make on one instructor. When multiple sections of a particular course are offered during a semester a different instructor teaches each section; the same textbook is used in each section along with similar exercises and projects to assure that all students receive adequate preparation for succeeding course work. An extensive amount of integration of the undergraduate courses assures that all students are exposed to the same core material.

It should be noted that the ACM and DPMA model curricula (see Tables 1 and 2) contain three systems courses at the undergraduate level. Due to the demands of the students' business core course work and the university's general education requirements, Arizona is only able to offer two analysis and design courses at the undergraduate level. Rather than combining IS5 and IS8 (from the ACM curriculum) into a one-semester life cycle course, the department decided to integrate the project aspects of IS10 into both IS5 and IS8. This integration allows the students to receive adequate exposure to the entire life cycle as well as gain invaluable experience working with non-trivial term projects. Dean and Elder (1991) provide a more complete discussion of the content and philosophy of the undergraduate analysis and design courses beyond the integration of CASE technology.

Graduate Courses

At the graduate level, Computer-Aided Information Systems Analysis and Design (MIS 541A and MIS 541B) make up a one-year sequence taken by students pursuing any of the following degrees: Master of Science (M.S.) in MIS, Master of Business Administration (M.B.A.) with an MIS concentration, and Doctor of Philosophy (Ph.D.) in business administration with a major in MIS. The course material is similar to that in MIS 341 and MIS 441 but is taught from a managerial, rather than a technical, perspective. Due to the varied backgrounds of the students, the entire systems development life cycle is taught in this sequence, albeit in an accelerated mode. Course work consists primarily of assigned readings from MIS literature that emphasize current trends in systems development, as well as a term project which concentrates on the front-end of the classical systems development life cycle, i.e., enterprise analysis, requirements specification and, to a lesser extent, systems analysis. Projects are usually taken from the business or university community. MIS 541A is offered during the fall semester and MIS 541B is offered during the spring semester. The same instructor teaches both courses.

BEFORE CASE TECHNOLOGY

The authors involvement with the analysis and design courses began during the fall of 1989. At that time, CASE technology served as the discussion topic in one or two lectures, depending upon the textbook's emphasis and the instructor's familiarity with CASE technology. At the graduate level, the lectures were typically supplemented by several readings from the trade literature discussing experiences with CASE from the perspective of analysts and managers.

At the time, all undergraduate and graduate systems courses were centered around assigned readings, a midterm examination and a final examination rather than a fundamental analysis, design, and implementation experience. There were some small pencil-and-paper exercises and, occasionally, a small project, which did not count for much of the student's semester grade. Many undergraduate and graduate students criticized the systems courses, claiming there was not enough emphasis on detailed design and implementation. Students also expressed an interest in "actually building a system rather than just reading about building one." What little lecture material the students did receive concerning CASE caused them to feel as if they were not receiving "hands-on" exposure to the technological developments they would encounter in the professional world.

CASE tools were not used in any of the systems courses for several reasons: 1) there were no CASE tools available, 2) the hardware facilities were perceived as inadequate to accommodate commercial CASE products, and 3) the faculty responsible for the systems courses felt they did not have adequate time to bring themselves and their students over the CASE tool learning curve. Arizona was not alone in this, however. A study of information systems departments by Jankowski and Norman (1991) found that 50 departments (out of 202 responding departments) did not use CASE technology in their curriculum. Table 4 contains a list of reasons why CASE was not being used by other information systems departments. The absence of CASE at Arizona was ironic considering that one of the roots of CASE technology can be traced back to the Arizona department head's involvement with PSL/PSA (Dennis, George, Jessup, Nunamaker, & Vogel, 1988).

Reasons (respondents could choose more than one)	Number
Commercial CASE is cost prohibitive	17
High learning curve of CASE tools	16
Insufficient hardware resources	14
CASE unavailable in the department	13
Not convinced of CASE benefits	5
Waiting for further development of CASE	5
Prior negative experience with CASE	2
Manual methods are sufficient	2
Other	4

Table 4: Why CASE Isn't Being Used

INTEGRATION OF CASE TECHNOLOGY

The integration of CASE technology into the curriculum was a gradual process. CASE was brought into the department slowly so as not to overwhelm the faculty, students, lab support staff, and hardware facilities. An eight-phase integration model was followed. Table 5 lists the eight phases and their accompanying critical success factors[3] while Table 6 displays the phases chronologically and also indicates the substantial overlap that occurred between phases. Each phase, and the accompanying critical success factor(s), is described in the following sections.

Phase One - Curriculum Change

The authors were asked to teach one of the offerings of MIS 441 during the fall of 1989. Because the teaching assignment was made rather late in the summer, the authors were not able to fully implement the desired curriculum changes, i.e., using CASE tools as a means of project support. However, some changes to the course content were made in order to ease the transition to CASE technology.

The course was redesigned to emphasize the completion, through implementation, of a small information systems project; all exams and paper and pencil exercises were eliminated. Instead, the students were divided into project teams at the beginning of the semester. A single systems project designed by the instructor was assigned to all groups, and the entire semester grade was based upon the following series of project deliverables: functional specifications, design specifications, source code, and project presentation. A new

CASE and IS Curriculum 603

Phase	Critical success factors
1. Curriculum change	Change course emphasis from exams to projects that can be supported by CASE.
2. Identification of constraints and candidate CASE tools	Identify functional, financial, and hardware constraints. Identify candidate CASE tools based upon functional and hardware constraints.
3. CASE tool acquisition	Acquire CASE tools from candidate list subject to financial constraints.
4. Hardware support	Acquired tools run in existing hardware, network, and operating system environment.
5. Pilot usage	Provide adequate tool instruction for students. Provide adequate tool documentation for students. Students demonstrate tool proficiency. Minimize impact on existing facilities.
6. Tool selection	Choose tool(s) based on instructor evaluations and student evaluations.
7. Coordination and integration	Faculty acceptance. Minimize project overhead for faculty. Minimize faculty learning curve.
8. Dedicated laboratory	Facility must be supported. Eliminate computer contention.

Table 5: Phases and Critical Success Factors in CASE Integration

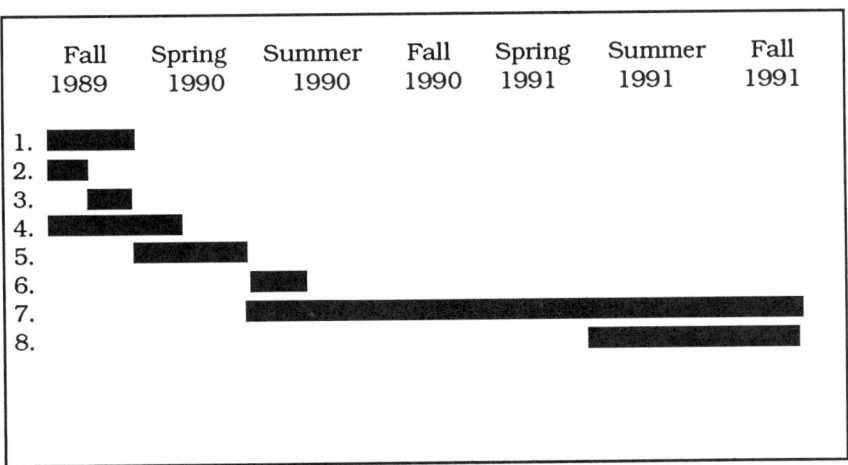

Table 6: Time Table for CASE Integration

textbook (Whitten, Bentley, & Barlow, 1989) was chosen which used a significant amount of CASE output to illustrate analysis and design examples. The text, coupled with a demonstration of the *Excelerator* CASE tool given by the professor, served to expose the students to CASE technology.

Phase Two - Identification of Constraints and Candidate CASE Tools

Before any CASE software was acquired, a needs assessment was performed. Three sets of constraints were identified: functional, financial, and hardware.

In order to maintain continuity between the systems courses, and to minimize the learning curve for students and faculty, we desired to use a single CASE tool. Therefore, it was required that all candidate tools support the analysis and design phases of the life cycle, specifically the Yourdon methodology and its accompanying methods: data flow diagrams, a data dictionary, structure charts and, to a lesser extent, data modeling. The existence of a prototyping facility was deemed desirable but not mandatory; code generation was unnecessary.

While CASE tools were being considered for acquisition, Arizona was in the midst of a state mandated budget tightening. This financial constraint necessitated looking exclusively at vendors that offered academic grants or discounts. Additionally, financial constraints eliminated any possible expenditures for hardware; making it necessary to use existing computing facilities (discussed in detail below).

Once a set of constraints had been determined, a list of candidate CASE tools was found. Gane (1990) includes a product summary of 24 commercially available CASE tools. These summaries were consulted and vendors were identified whose CASE tools fit our functional and hardware constraints.

Phase Three - CASE Tool Acquisition

After a needs assessment was performed and a list of candidate CASE tools was obtained, a search was begun to find affordable commercial products. The goal was to have the tools installed for use during the spring of 1990.

Through the adoption of the Whitten, Bentley, and Barlow text the authors were able to enroll in the *Excelerator* Educational Grant Program sponsored by Index Technology (now Intersolv). This entitled Arizona to one free copy of Excelerator (version 1.9), including documentation and a security device[5].

A second textbook adoption (Flaatten, McCubbrey, O'Riordan, & Burgess, 1989) enabled Arizona to acquire the student version (and site license) of Arthur Andersen's Design/1 CASE tool. The student version was limited in both the functionality of the tool as well as the size and number of projects supported. The site license allowed for unlimited copies to be made without any kind of security restriction. Along with the software, a subset of the professional version of the Design/1 documentation was provided, including a tutorial.

A third CASE tool was acquired from Visible Systems. A beta test version of *Visible Analyst Workbench* (VAW) (version 3.1) was obtained free of charge, including documentation and a security device, in exchange for a brief review of the product. Several other CASE tool vendors were contacted whose products fit both the functional and hardware constraints, but they were unable to provide a grant copy or a sufficient educational discount[6].

Phase Four - Hardware Support

While waiting for the CASE tools to arrive from the vendors, plans were made to acquire space in one of Arizona's microcomputer laboratories. The lab contains 60 microcomputers (IBM PC AT compatible, 60 megabyte hard disk, 640K RAM, EGA monitor, bus mouse) networked with a minicomputer which functions as a print server. There are three laser printers connected to the print server.

Twelve computers were assigned to the systems courses with the understanding that the computers would not be dedicated to the systems courses. Thus, students from other courses could use these computers for their course work. It was especially important to minimize the impact CASE tools would have on the lab. This entailed soliciting input from faculty (from systems and non-systems courses), lab consultants, and lab technicians regarding computer access and contention policies. All parties realized the CASE tools would be used in support of labor intensive activities and allowances would need to be made to give CASE tool users extra computer time.

Excelerator was installed on six computers, Design/1 was installed on five computers, and VAW was installed on one computer. In order to preserve hard disk space, and to protect the students from any hard disk problems, project groups would be required to backup their work onto floppy disks each time they used the tool. Some fine tuning was necessary in order for the CASE tools to function under the microcomputer's memory constraints[7].

Phase Five - Pilot Usage

With the CASE tools installed and the hardware problems resolved, the MIS 441 students in the spring 1990 pilot course were able to begin hands-on CASE tool usage. Project groups of four students were selected by the instructor. Groups were then randomly assigned to a particular CASE tool. The assigned term project required project groups to turn in the following deliverables: functional specifications (data flow diagrams, data dictionary, minispecs), design specifications (structure charts, screens and reports), and documented source code.

After receiving background in CASE technology, the project groups were given a demonstration of their respective CASE tools. At the time of the demonstration, documentation was given to each group. Excelerator groups received Schmidt (1990) and also had access to the complete set of Excelerator documentation provided by Index Technology. Design/1 groups received the student documentation package (a subset of the professional documentation) and also had access to the professional version of the documentation provided by Andersen Consulting. The VAW group received a copy of the professional documentation provided by Visible Systems. Groups were required to demonstrate their proficiency with the CASE tools by presenting their data flow diagrams to their classmates soon after the project was assigned. A similar exercise was performed with prototyped screens and reports. Further, the students were required to give an in-class demonstration of the functionality of their assigned CASE tool.

Phase Six - Tool Selection

The goal of the MIS 441 CASE tool pilot course was twofold: first, to determine the feasibility of using CASE tools to support a semester project given the existing constraints and second, to choose one particular tool, from the three being piloted, for all project groups to use in all systems course work beginning with the following semester (summer 1990). While problems were encountered using CASE, these problems were deemed insignificant in comparison to the invaluable exposure the students were receiving to CASE technology utilized in the professional world.

Throughout the pilot course the students received exposure to all three CASE tools through sample output, in-class demonstrations, and word-of-mouth from their peers. At the end of the semester each group was asked to evaluate its assigned CASE tool. The following four questions were asked:

1. What did you especially like about your CASE tool?
2. What did you especially dislike about your CASE tool?
3. What would have made your time spent with the CASE tool easier?
4. Given what you have seen/heard of the three CASE tools, which would you prefer to work with?

The students all agreed the CASE tools have a high learning curve but, as they practiced drawing diagrams and working with the dictionary, they became proficient with their tool. The students agreed the learning curve might have been less steep if the vendor documentation had been more thorough. There was also concern that the CASE tools were not much of a methodology companion, although this concern may have been due to the students' lack of experience with the methodology. The students also agreed the effort required to gain proficiency with the CASE tools was well worth it. The students overwhelmingly expressed a preference for Excelerator based upon its familiar graphics interface (similar to that used in mouse-driven graphics programs such as MacPaint or PC-Paintbrush) and the ease of entering information into the data dictionary.

Due to the favorable response *Excelerator* received from the students, it was chosen as the sole CASE tool for MIS 441 during the summer of 1990. However, as the integration of *Excelerator* into the other systems courses began, several problems still remained. Lack of lab space posed a difficulty for the pilot class and this problem would be further compounded when additional courses began using CASE tools. Additionally, the new faculty who would be teaching the other systems courses needed to be familiarized with *Excelerator*.

Phase Seven - Coordination and Integration

For the fall of 1990, between MIS 341, MIS 441, and MIS 541A, there were five new faculty members who needed to be adequately exposed to *Excelerator* in order to properly introduce *Excelerator* to their students. While all of the faculty agreed that students need hands-on exposure to CASE technology, the faculty all expressed reluctance to devote the time necessary to learn *Excelerator* well enough to be able to assist their students with learning the tool. Additionally, the faculty were concerned about contention for the *Excelerator* workstations now that there were several classes using it.

In order to provide instructional CASE tool support under these conditions, it was deemed necessary to have one person coordinate all instructional use of *Excelerator*. It was agreed that the analysis and design instructors would learn *Excelerator* on their own time and a CASE tool coordinator would be employed while instructors were becoming familiar with CASE technology. The CASE coordinator would provide class and lab demonstrations of the CASE tools and assist students in the computer lab as well as help the faculty acquire a working knowledge of the CASE tool. Additionally, materials from the authors' previous CASE course experience was provided to the faculty. Beyond providing instructional CASE tool support for students and instructors, the CASE tool coordinator would also be responsible for maintaining the CASE software. As the faculty became comfortable with the CASE tools, the coordinator position would be gradually phased out. Table 7 contains Chikofsky's (1989)

Technique	How applied at Arizona
1. Provide meaningful support to new projects and users.	Coordinator responsible for providing support for students and instructors.
2. Tailor training to the user audience; include meaningful problems and examples.	Provided demonstrations of tools and examples. Students did smaller learning exercises before using tool on course projects. Provided instruction on benefits offered by the CASE tool.
3. Explain standards and conventions; provide "how to" documentation.	Provided instruction on methodology and how CASE tool should be used to support that methodology. Made sure inexpensive documentation was available to students.
4. Make materials from prior projects accessible.	Provided examples for new faculty of previous student CASE projects.
5. Match features of tool to the needs and levels of expertise of new users.	Tools were selected from vendors eager to penetrate educational market. Tools should be easy to learn & support chosen methodology.
6. Avoid the presumption that someone who has been to one class on the tool can train the rest of the users.	The CASE coordinator provided instruction in classes while faculty were becoming familiar with the tool. After establishing proficiency with the tool, faculty provided instruction.
7. Revise conventions and standards to reflect real project experience.	Educated users about how to use the tool as a group. Scoped the difficulty of the projects to be of sufficient complexity for learning, but not so difficult as to be overwhelming.

Table 7: Techniques to Effectively Manage the Learning Curve

techniques for effectively managing the learning curve, and how these techniques were applied to CASE integration by the authors.

The authors volunteered to serve as the CASE tool coordinator during the 1990-1991 academic year. The CASE tool coordinator position proved extremely beneficial to the faculty as it allowed them to learn Excelerator at their own pace while still having a resource the students could turn to for help. Further, the authors' success with CASE served to eliminate the skepticism of the newly involved faculty members who had previously thought CASE to be too difficult to integrate into the systems courses[8].

Although CASE had been successfully integrated into the curriculum, the faculty expressed dissatisfaction with the limited lab resources available for *Excelerator*. The limited lab hours, limited number of workstations and the constraint that Excelerator had to be used in the lab due to the presence of a security block, were all catalysts in the search for both a new facility for CASE tools, as well as a CASE tool the students could use at home.

These problems were partially solved in the summer of 1991 with the introduction of the student version of *Visible Analyst Workbench*. Students in the summer session were able to purchase the student version of VAW and its documentation at a nominal cost and install it on their personal computers at home. The students who were able to work on their home computers were unanimous in their approval of being able to work at their leisure while those students who worked in the lab were able to do so with much less contention than in the preceding two semesters. While the educational version of VAW has some limitations, which are not present in *Excelerator*[9], VAW has no security block restriction and is able to fit into 640K RAM in the presence of a network. The positive response received by VAW led to its being adopted as the instructional CASE tool during the 1991-1992 school year.

Phase Eight - Dedicated Laboratory

During the fall of 1991 a microcomputer laboratory was dedicated to the systems courses. Sixteen IBM PC AT compatible microcomputers and nine dot-matrix printers were installed in the new lab. VAW was installed on each microcomputer in the new lab. All faculty involved with the systems courses were asked to hold their office hours in the new lab in order to supplement the number of funded hours available to keep the lab open. The new lab is currently open approximately seven hours per day, seven days a week.

FUTURE OF CASE AT ARIZONA

While CASE technology has become integrated into teaching and research, the evolution of CASE technology is not yet complete. Future plans call for upgrading hardware facilities to enable CASE tools to run on a network, and the establishment of a library of CASE tools to support various phases of the systems development life cycle. Further plans call for the acquisition of CASE tools to be used with existing MacIntosh computers.

CONCLUSION

Making a commitment to CASE technology has not been easy. Funding and facility constraints have contributed to setbacks during the last two years. Rather than jumping headlong into a commitment to CASE tools, the multi-stage approach to integration described in this chapter has been followed to allow students, faculty, and facilities to adapt to the new technology. By following this integrated approach, we have successfully established CASE technology as an integral component of the entire MIS curriculum at the undergraduate and graduate levels.

A by-product of the classroom exposure to CASE technology has been the extensive use of CASE technology to support research projects. After having been exposed to CASE in the classroom, and after an extensive amount of hands-on experience with a CASE tool, many master's and doctoral students are using CASE tools to assist them with their research projects. Furthermore, work is being done at Arizona to better integrate CASE technology with analysis and design work done in groups (e.g. joint application design (JAD)). With the establishment of an infrastructure to support CASE technology, we are able to expose students to systems analysis and design tools used in support of today's increasingly complicated computer information systems.

ENDNOTES

[1] The implementation described in this chapter generally fits the ACM information systems model curriculum.

[2] Throughout this chapter the word "authors" will be used to refer to one or both of the authors.

[3] Critical success factors (CSF) are the areas in which satisfactory results ensure successful performance. For a detailed discussion of CSF see Rockart (1979).

⁴ It should be noted that the course was a pilot. The other section of MIS 441 was not changed until the following year.

⁵ Academic institutions that qualify for the grant program may make unlimited copies of the software, however, in order for multiple copies to run concurrently, the institution must also purchase an equal number of security blocks. Through the grant program six additional security blocks were ordered allowing for the support of seven concurrent *Excelerator* workstations.

⁶ It should be noted that all companies contacted were willing to provide some form of educational discount and all supported multi-copy discounts for the commercial sector. Most CASE vendors are eager to get involved with the educational market because they realize that academia is the best way to expose future analysts to their product. Intersolv's *Excelerator* is the best-selling commercial CASE product and, perhaps not coincidentally, also has the most generous academic grant program.

⁷ During product installation and subsequent testing, a problem was encountered with loading *Excelerator* and *VAW* into RAM. Between the PC and network operating systems, there was not enough memory for CASE tools. Because of a lack of an extended memory manager, the CPU was unable to take advantage of 364K of extended memory. Since we lacked funds to purchase the necessary memory managers, a work around was designed. A separate boot disk was made for each of the computers reserved for *Excelerator* and *VAW*. When a student desired to use *Excelerator* or *VAW*, they would reboot the computer from the A: drive. Since the AUTOEXEC.BAT file did not contain network loading commands, memory was saved. In this way, students could use the CASE tools although all print jobs had to be spooled to disk files. A student ready to print would reboot from the hard disk, which reconnected the computer to the print server. The student could then print from the DOS prompt using the graphics print utilities supplied with *Excelerator* and *VAW*. Unlike *Excelerator* and *VAW*, *Design/1* was able to fit into memory without disconnecting the computer from the LAN. However, as the students worked on their projects, and the size of the diagrams increased, memory limitations also became a problem for groups using *Design/1*. (With the advanced memory management capabilities of DOS 5.0, this may no longer be a problem.)

A second problem was encountered with the quality of the output generated by *Excelerator* and *VAW*. All graphics output, especially diagram labels, was corrupted by extraneous characters. Because the lab in which the CASE tools were installed was used for many other applications (word processing, database, spreadsheet), the laser printers had to be configured in such a way as to satisfy all applications, including CASE tools. Unfortunately, the IBM PC Graphics font set chosen for the laser printers did not produce the high quality output that had been exhibited when the CASE tools were initially tested. (Testing was initially done on a stand-alone PC directly connected to a near-letter-quality dot matrix printer using the IBM PC Graphics font set.) With the help of the Index Technology *Excelerator* hot-line the problem was determined to be a combination of the printing network and the font set. Since it was not possible to dedicate a laser printer to the CASE tool workstations, dot-matrix printers were connected to each computer.

[8] At this point it must be noted that academia is very different form the professional world. Due to the nature of the teacher-student relationship it is easier for faculty to require students to use a particular CASE tool, programming language, operating system, etc. than to require the same thing of a professional systems analyst. Students may be more receptive to the introduction of new ideas and technologies due to their lack of experience. Contrast this with the professional world, in which an analyst may have been using manual systems development techniques for several years and is quite resistant to a change in techniques. Orlikowski (1989) studied a consulting firm which shifted toward CASE technology. With the introduction of CASE, the firm's technical consultants, who were responsible for supporting the CASE tools, gained increased responsibility and power at the expense of the functional consultants, who were responsible for the development of application systems. This resulted in resentment on the part of the functional consultants.

[9] Only one project per workstation is permitted; there is a limit on the number of diagrams per project and objects per diagram, and there is no data modelling or prototyping utility.

REFERENCES

Amadio, W., & Amadio, C. (1990). *Systems development projects.* New York: McGraw-Hill.

Amadio, W. (1989). Realistic software development in the classroom: A case study using GENIFER. *Interface: The Computer Education Quarterly, 11*(3), 4-15.

Capron, H. L. (1990). *Computers: Tools for an information age.* Redwood City, CA: Benjamin/Cummings.

Chikofsky, E. J. (1989). How to lose productivity with productivity tools. In E. J. Chikofsky (Ed.), *Software development. Computer-aided software engineering (CASE)* (pp. 120-123). Washington, DC: IEEE Computer Society.

Data Processing Management Association. (1990). *The DPMA model curriculum for a four year undergraduate degree.* Park Ridge, IL: Author.

Dean, D. L., & Elder, K. L. (1991). An integrated approach for getting the most out of two systems analysis and design courses: Four critical success factors. In R. W. Stone (Ed.), *Proceedings of the Sixth Annual Conference of the International Academy for Information Management* (pp. 129-141).

Dennis, A. R., George, J. F., Jessup, L. M., Nunamaker, J. F., Jr., & Vogel, D. R. (1988). Information technology to support electronic meetings. *MIS Quarterly, 12*(4), 591-624.

Eliason, A. L. (1990a). *CASE laboratory manual: Using Excelerator.* Glenview, IL: Scott, Foresman.

Eliason, A. L. (1990b). *Systems development: Analysis, design, and implementation.* Glenview, IL: Scott, Foresman.

Flaatten, P. O., McCubbrey, D. J., O'Riordan, P. D., & Burgess, K. (1899). *Foundations of business systems.* Chicago, IL: Dryden Press.

Gane, C. (1990). *Computer-aided software engineering: The methodologies, the products, and the future.* Englewood Cliffs, NJ: Prentice Hall.

Gibson, M., & Capon, C. (1989a). Installing the CASE tool Excelerator in a micro lab for analysis and design courses: Part 1. *Interface: The Computer Education Quarterly, 11*(1), 4-10.

Gibson. M., & Capon, C. (1989b). Installing the CASE tool Excelerator in a micro lab for analysis and design courses: Part 2. *Interface: The Computer Education Quarterly, 11*(2), 4-10.

Heiat, A. (1989). BriefCASE: A CASE tool for MIS curricula. *Interface: The Computer Education Quarterly, 11*(4), 4-9.

Jankowski, D. J. (1990). Mapping CASE technology into the information systems model curriculums. In R. J. Norman & R. V. Ghent (Eds.), *Advance working papers of the Fourth International Workshop on Computer-Aided Software Engineering* (pp. 96-97). Washington, DC: IEEE Computer Society Press.

Jankowski, D. J, & Norman, R. J. (1992). Computer-aided software engineering (CASE) technology in the information systems curriculum: Current practice. *Journal of Computer Information Systems, 32*(3), 6-14.

Kuehn, R., & Fleck, R. (1989). Integrating the CASE methodology into the management information systems curriculum. In John Jenkins (Ed.), *Advance working papers of the Third International Workshop on Computer-Aided Software Engineering* (pp. 16.5-16.8).

Martin, M. P. (1991). *Analysis and design of information systems.* New York: MacMillan.

Mynatt, B. T. (1990). *Software engineering with student project guidance.* Englewood Cliffs, NJ: Prentice Hall.

Mynatt, B. T., & Leventhal, L. M. (1990). An Evaluation of a CASE-based approach to teaching undergraduate software engineering. In D. T. Joyce (Ed.) *The papers of the Twenty-first SIGCSE Technical Symposium on Computer Science Education* (pp. 48-52). New York: Association for Computing Machinery.

Norman, R. J. (1989). CASE software: A tool for the systems analysis course. *The Journal of Computer Information Systems, 30*(2), 8-10.

Nunamaker, J. F., Jr., Couger, J. D., & Davis, G. B. (1990). *Information systems curriculum recommendations for the 90s:* Undergraduate and graduate programs. Draft.

Orlikowski, W. J. (1989). Division among the ranks: The social implications of CASE tools for system developers. In J. I. DeGross, J. C. Henderson & B. R. Konsynski (Eds.), *Proceedings of the Tenth International Conference on Information Systems* (pp. 199-210).

Rockart, J. F. (1979). Chief executives define their own data needs. *Harvard Business Review, 57*(2), 81-93.

Schmidt, A. (1990). *Working with Excelerator.* Englewood Cliffs, NJ: Prentice Hall.

Schmidt, A. (1992). *Working with Excelerator Version 1.9.* Englewood Cliffs, NJ: Prentice Hall.

Szymanski, R., Szymanski, D., Morris, N., & Pulschen, D. (1991). I*ntroduction to computers and information systems.* New York: Macmillan.

Wenig, R. (1991). *Introduction to C.A.S.E. technology using Visible Analyst.* New York: MacMillan.

Whitten, J. L., & Bentley, L. D. (1987). *Using Excelerator for systems analysis and design.* St. Louis: Times Mirror/Mosby.

Whitten, J. L., Bentley, L. D., & Barlow, V. M. (1989). *Systems analysis and design methods.* Homewood, IL: Irwin.

Section V

CASE and the Future

CHAPTER TWENTY-TWO

Critical Factors Influencing the Future of Computer-Aided Software Engineering

Robert L. Crosslin
The American University

Thomas J. Bergin
The American University

Jack W. Stott
University of Maryland Baltimore County

This chapter reports the results of a survey of CASE experts in the United States and Europe. The purpose of the research is to identify and rank the critical factors that the experts believe will influence the future of CASE. This study does not attempt to predict the future course of CASE development, rather, we identify those factors the experts believe will significantly influence the future development of software engineering generally, and computer-aided software engineering specifically. To the extent that these factors and their rankings are accurate, the results of this survey will help CASE users and researchers identify, anticipate, and understand marginal changes in CASE technology over the next five to ten years. The results of the survey may also aid CASE developers in their consideration of new and improved methodologies and tools.

Predicting the future is always a risky business. Predicting the future of a technology which is changing as rapidly as CASE borders on insanity. Those involved in the discipline, such as tool designers, tool users, and academics teaching systems engineering, however, need some idea of what the future might bring, in order to properly plan for it. To provide some guidance on the future of CASE, this paper reports the results of a survey of CASE experts in the United

States and Europe (about fifty experts participated in the survey).

The purpose of the survey was to determine and rank the **critical factors** influencing the future of CASE, focusing on the **process of CASE evolution** rather than attempting to predict specific outcomes. In this way, readers can evaluate the critical factors from their own perspective, and moreover, draw their own conclusions with respect to the future of software development, software engineering, and CASE.

No attempt has been made to predict the future course of CASE tool development. However, the paper does identify those factors that our panel of experts believe will significantly influence the future development of software engineering as a methodology, and computer-aided software engineering. To the extent that these factors and their rankings are accurate, the results of this survey will help CASE users and researchers identify, anticipate, and understand marginal changes in CASE technology over the next five to ten years. The results of the survey may also aid CASE developers in their consideration of new and improved methodologies and tools.

The respondents to our survey are individuals actively engaged in CASE research and use, both in the United States and Europe. Participants include both academic researchers and industry consultants. Their combined expert views provide a unique glimpse of the factors that will influence the course of CASE development in the coming decade. The American experts are about evenly split between authors of the chapters of this book and industry consultants actively engaged in helping organizations to apply CASE tools. The majority of the European experts are academic researchers, however the European response does include a significant number of industry consultants.

In the next section we briefly trace the development of CASE over the last two decades as a backdrop to our discussion of critical factors in the future of CASE. The third section of the paper explains our methodology: the structure of the survey used to identify and rank the critical factors, and how the survey was carried out. The results of the survey are presented and analyzed in the fourth section. A final section draws implications and conclusions about the future of CASE.

REVIEW OF CASE DEVELOPMENT AND FUTURE CASE ISSUES

As an approach to tracking the term "CASE tool," we have followed its use in the popular trade magazine *Datamation*. Our assumption was that this magazine is representative of the industry's interest in various topics, especially at a management level. From examining past issues of *Datamation,* some interesting insights begin to appear about the use and interest in CASE. It might be noted, by the reader, that we wanted a general management-oriented perspective on CASE rather than the specialist perspective of other more technical periodicals, such as *Software Magazine, IEEE Software, Communications of the ACM,* or *CASE Outlook.* The authors also believe that an attempt to comprehensively examine the specific CASE literature exceeded the purpose of this chapter. Indeed, given the constant and rapidly changing nature of the CASE arena, we were afraid that the results would be meaningless.

Gaining Acceptance and Importance

Although many academics were talking about automated tools for system development and several tool developers were marketing "CASE" tool products much earlier, the initial references to CASE in *Datamation* occurred in June, 1986. The first reference that we found was to Ed Yourdon's article, "Whatever Happened to Structured Analysis?" Although the article was mainly concerned with the reasons why industry was not using *structured analysis techniques,* Yourdon observed that: "Just as CAD/CAM technologies have helped revolutionize various engineering industries, CASE (Computer-Aided Software Engineering) technologies will help revolutionize the software industry. At present, there are an estimated 6,000 CASE workstations installed in the U.S."

Later that same year, in the October 15th issue, Daniel Klinger, in an article entitled "Rapid prototyping revisited," listed a number of automated tools which he believed were necessary to properly support successful rapid prototyping:

- database management systems (DBMS)
- data dictionaries coupled to DBMS's
- ad hoc query facilities
- non-procedural data manipulation languages
- screen generators
- batch report generators
- procedural languages
- text editors

It is important for the reader to remember that, by late 1986, there were numerous CASE tools capable of supporting specific parts of the systems development life cycle. Indeed, the specific technical literature identified above had extensive discussion of **integrated case tools (I-CASE)**, and some vendors were marketing I-CASE products. Interestingly enough, there was no mention of CASE, per se, by Klinger in this article.

The first article devoted to CASE appeared in the July 1, 1987 issue. Written by David Stamps, and entitled "CASE: Cranking out productivity," the article speaks about the application backlog and a new tool, *Computer-Aided Software Engineering*, which promised to help reduce the software development backlog. Stamps listed 24 CASE tools offered by 21 different vendors. Many of these tools were limited in scope or were job specific tools, such as CICS screen generators. It is interesting to see that the market for tools was well ahead of the popular interest in the tools, atleast as expressed in a general industry periodical.

In the ensuing 5 years, *Datamation* has published 16 articles about CASE and many more references to CASE in other articles and news bites. The latest review of the "state of the CASE art" appeared in the March 1, 1992 issue. The cover story focused on the question "Can Intersolv Excelerate On OS/2?", and a special report looked at "Open CASE Emerges as AD/Cycle Lags". In addition, a buyer's guide entitled "A World of CASE Tools" identified 400+ CASE products from over 100 different vendors.

A Merging of Software Technologies

This is not to say, however, that the beginnings of CASE were in the mid to late 1980's. As stated above, the software literature, and ultimately a literature specific to CASE, contained in-depth treatments of CASE topics. Software engineering and computer-supported software development do, however, have deeper roots.

In 1971, Daniel Teichroew and Hasan Sayani wrote an article for *Datamation* describing current research on an ongoing project called Information System Design and Optimization System (ISDOS). Teichrow and Sayani's vision was a set of languages and processors of those languages that would ultimately produce a complete working system from a non-procedural system specification. Although the term *computer-aided software engineering* was never used, they do say "...the system building process itself should be automated or at least computer-aided."

During this period, there were several other efforts to automate the system development life cycle. These efforts all seemed to set goals that were too ambitious, given the technology available. As a result, many of these efforts were abandoned or sidetracked, and others failed due to a lack of support, i.e., because industry management could not see any immediate results or benefits.

The late 1970's saw the beginning of several other research efforts into the automation of the software development process. These efforts were more focused, and set more realistic goals than the earlier efforts. Generally speaking, these research projects focused on the following areas:

- data dictionaries
- higher level languages (4th Generation Languages)
- automatic code generation
- business planning tools
- screen generators
- generalized software packages
- re-usable code and code libraries
- graphics-oriented diagramming packages

What we consider a true CASE system today is an integrated set of tools which perform a wide variety of tasks. The key concept is **integration**. Early CASE tool development efforts resulted in stand-alone tools which supported narrow segments of the system development life cycle. In order to use more than one such tool, the metadata contained in the data dictionary of one tool needed to be converted to the format of the tool supporting the next stage in the software development process.

Some Major Discoveries

Two discoveries radically changed the direction of CASE tools in the mid- to late-1980's: using application domains to allow the maximization of reusable modules, and standardizing on a data management platform. The original developers of CASE tools believed that the CASE tool should generate the entire target system from scratch, i.e., from the information contained in the "design repository." As time went on, and a better understanding of "automated systems engineering" developed, CASE tool developers realized that it was much more productive to develop CASE tools for domains of applications, such as real-time systems or business data processing applications. Indeed, some tool developers focused their efforts on application-domains within specific industries. Given a particular domain, much of the design and some of the lower level code could be pre-established.

In addition, most of the original CASE tool developers placed no restrictions on the resulting system. If the system designers were planning to build a system using some kind of hybrid database, then the CASE tool should support that decision. In the late 80's, CASE tool developers began to standardize on the relational database model for the storage and manipulation of metadata. This allowed CASE tool developers to make many more assumptions about the underlying nature of the target system.

In the early batch oriented application systems, often referred to today as *legacy systems*, almost all of the code dealt with the data management and data manipulation required by the user application. Newer, online systems place increasingly heavy requirements on the user interface. In fact, in modern systems, as much as 80% of the system is devoted to the user interface. These changes in the systems development *process* have allowed CASE vendors to offer a wide variety of tools that make it easier for application developers to create applications in less than 10% of the time than it used to take.

Now that the data management, user interface, and data type manipulations are taken care of by re-usable, pluggable modules, the developer's attention can shift to the business rules that glue all of these things together. Business rules supply the underlying logic and flow requirements that create each individual target system. These business rules are captured using "Upper CASE" tools and translated into high level system code.

An Old Problem: Maintaining Old Systems

At present, the CASE marketplace is maturing, and contains a relatively complete set of tools for "forward engineering" systems. One of the major problems for Information Systems managers, however, is the tremendous amount of existing applications code that needs to be maintained, or retro-fitted, using modern techniques and tools. One of the major thrusts, at present, is the desire in many organizations to *reverse engineer*, or *re-engineer* this old code. The primary objective of reverse engineering is to salvage the business rules embedded in these old systems, while re-engineering results in replacing old code with new, modern, reusable modules developed using current I-CASE tools. In most cases, such efforts will result in improved functionality, as well as allowing applications to be downsized, or operate on new platforms.

That brings us up to the present. As our brief of CASE development has shown, the evolution of CASE has occurred rapidly during just the last eight years, with much of the latest development focused on the integration of functionality and methodology to cover the entire system development life cycle, i.e. Integrated Computer-Aided Software Engineering or I-CASE.

Where will CASE development go in the future? The following section describes the methodology which we used to gain insights into the possible answers to that question.

METHODOLOGY

Predicting the future is risky in any field, especially one that seems to be changing at an increasing rate of speed. Therefore, we have not attempted to predict the future course of CASE development, but instead, we surveyed a number of CASE experts in an attempt to identify those **factors** that are likely to have a significant influence on the course of CASE development during the coming decade.

The purpose of the survey was to determine and rank the **critical factors** influencing the future of CASE, focusing on the **process of CASE evolution** rather than attempting to predict specific outcomes. In this way, readers could evaluate the critical factors from their own perspective, and draw their own conclusions with respect to the future of software development, software engineering, and CASE.

Since we believe that the relative ranking of the identified factors is just as important as identifying the factors themselves, we asked the experts to identify and rank the critical factors with respect to three areas: *methodology, tools* and *process*.

> **Methodology** refers to the underlying conceptual and theoretical basis for software or system development. A methodology identifies *what* needs to be done and *when* it should be done, e.g., the numerous *structured design* and *information engineering* methodologies in use throughout the industry. Methodologies usually prescribe specific *techniques* to be used to capture specific information during specific phases of the systems development life cycle. For example, data flow diagramming (DFD) and entity-relationship diagramming (ERD) are diagramming *techniques* common to all *structured* methodologies.

> **Tools** are software packages which support the use of specific techniques. All present CASE packages contain tools which assist users in developing and maintaining data flow and entity relationship diagrams (DFDs and ERDs). Some vendors identify their products as *upper, middle, and lower CASE tools;* such products support the different techniques used during the different phases of the systems development life cycle (SDLC).

Integrated-CASE (I-CASE) tools provide support across the entire SDLC.

Process refers to how organizations implement CASE methodologies and tools. Organizations may adopt formal or informal rules and procedures for one project or for all projects across the entire organization. For example, one organization may use an upper CASE tool to support individuals working on stand-alone workstations during the analysis phase of a single project. Another organization may adopt an I-CASE tool and use it in a network environment to support all analysts and designers throughout the entire systems development life cycle.

In addition to the three areas of *methodology, tools* and *process*, we wanted to solicit our experts' views with respect to the practical dimensions of *decision making* about the use of CASE tools, now and in the future. To this end, we asked the respondents to group their critical factors with respect to the following subject areas which we believe drive decisions about the adoption and use of CASE methodologies, tools and procedures:

Existing CASE Products
Future CASE Products
The Economics of CASE
The Implementation of CASE in Organizations

Existing CASE products have a future, at least in the short-run, and users are making daily decisions with respect to using these CASE products. In addition, present users have gained enough experience in using existing CASE tools to have concerns and desires with respect to future CASE tools and products. CASE economics has many dimensions, but the most obvious are the relative costs and benefits of adopting CASE as a strategy for software development and maintenance. Implementation of CASE in organizations is of critical importance because this is where the success of CASE will ultimately be decided.

Results of the Survey

The first round of the survey asked the experts to identify the factors "that you believe will be *critical* to the future of [a] particular aspect of CASE." In addition, we also asked the experts to provide a one or two sentence description of each factor. The description was used by the authors to assure that we captured the correct meaning

---

Methodology Factors
Software analysis and design through graphical representations.
Clearer links between tools and specific supported methodologies.
Improved project management support.

Tool Factors
Allow configuration to a methodology.
File standards to allow integration of tools.
Better support for software reengineering.
Improve user interface.
Lower learning curves.
Free availability to universities.
Clear interfaces between phases.
Code/frame generation.

Process Factors
Support Groupware concepts of security, file sharing, version control, noting, etc.
Capability to expand scope and functionality of tools.
Connection of tools and phases.
Clarification of role of CASE in maintenance.
Support for planning activities.

Table 1: Existing CASE Factors

for each listed factor. The first round of the survey was mailed to experts in the United States at the end of November, 1991.

We sent requests to identify factors to 31 experts in the United States. We received responses from 19 of these experts (61%). These respondents identified dozens of factors. After comparison of the two-sentence descriptions of each factor, we were able to reduce the list to the 55 unique factors shown in Tables 1, 2, 3 and 4.

As can be seen in Table 1, sixteen factors were identified as important for Existing CASE. The experts identified the importance of methodologies which define the use of graphic representations, and highlighted the need for clearer linkages between CASE tools and the methodologies they are designed to support. Indeed, a concern was voiced about the extent of that support, and the need for improved support of project management activities.

The tools factors identified are directly related to the methodology factors, i.e. the need for flexible CASE tools which can be configured or tailored to specific methodologies. Since the experts perceived a need for using multiple tools, assumedly from different vendors, the development of file standards so that tools can communicate at the meta-data level is deemed critical. Concern was also expressed for improved support for the software re-engineering and code generation processes throught the development of new tools and improvements to existing CASE products. Finally, the experts called for improved user interfaces in order to lower the learning curve.

With repect to the process of applying CASE, the experts see the need for tools which support the efforts of development groups by providing file sharing, version control, noting, and appropriate levels of security. The need for improvements in the relationships between tools and methods is identified as a process factor as well as a methodology factor and a tool factor. Specifically the need for improved support during the planning and maintenance phases of the SDLC were identified as major areas for future improvements.

As can be seen in Table 2, the experts believe that it is important that newer methodologies, such as object oriented analysis and design, be incorporated into, or supported by, future CASE products. There is a lingering concern that present methodologies and tools are not sufficiently integrated and, specifically, that they do not provide sufficient support for techniques such as rapid prototyping and Joint Application Design. Some experts expressed a belief that CASE must support the use of automated software metrics, while others saw CASE as a potential fifth-generation (graphic) language. Finally, some experts called for the continued development of domain-

---

Methodology Factors
Incorporation of new methodologies, including those based on object-oriented methods.
Integration of methodologies and tools.
Incorporation of automated software metrics.
Integration with Joint Application Development (JAD).
Integration with rapid prototyping.
CASE as a graphic fifth-generation language (5GL).
Development of domain-specific methodologies.

Tool Factors
UNIX environments with cross-compilation of applications.
Reuse of analysis and design efforts.
AI assisted tools.
Reduce the increase in hardware requirements.
Capture more model semantics.
Enterprise modeling capabilities.
Domain-specific tools.

Process Factors
Reverse engineering using a variety of methodologies.
Develop automated CASE tools.
More automatic consistency and completeness checking.

Table 2: Future CASE Factors

specific methodologies.

UNIX was identified as a development environment which could support multiple platform environments. This could also enhance the trend toward the reuse of analysis and design efforts. A major improvement in CASE tools is expected to result from the development of artificial intelligence techniques to assist the user as well as the developer. Improvements in the tools themselves should include support for enterprise modeling, the ability to capture more model semantics, and the development of tools for use in specific domains.

With respect to the process of using CASE, the experts called for the development of newer strategies and tools to support reverse engineering activities, including more automatic checking of designs for completeness and consistency.

The Economic factors associated with methodology include the incorporation of cost-benefit analysis in the decision to adopt CASE as a methodology, as well as a factor in the decision to acquire and use CASE tools. Our respondents also identified a need to apply CASE to the development and maintenance of information systems, as opposed to scientific, process control or other applications.

A concern was expressed that economic factors often mitigate aginst the availability of a "universal compliment" of CASE tool features. To assist in the economic evaluation of CASE, our experts called for additional (in-depth) case studies of tool selection processes in real organizations, and the need for tools devoted to specific problem domains as well as improved price-performance relationships.

Finally, the experts identified the need for improved execution efficiency through improved "smart" designs, i.e., to incorporate

---

Methodology Factors
Incorporation of cost-benefit analysis.
Focus on IS development and maintenance.

Tool Factors
Universal complement of features in all CASE products.
Pre-written analysis and design models by problem domain.
Studies of CASE tool selection.
Improve performance/price relationship.

Process Factors
Execution efficiency through smart designs.
Total quality management.
Exploit cheap computing power of PCs.
Activity (dynamic) base accountability.

Table 3: Economics of CASE Factors

> **Methodology Factors**
> Customize to an organization.
> Top management support.
> Open systems architectures.
> Increased use of Joint Application Development techniques.
> **Tool Factors**
> Customize to an organization.
> Integration of CASE within organizations.
> End-user construction & maintenance.
> Improved and expanded training.
> **Process Factors**
> CASE tool standards.
> Improved and expanded training.
> Automatic design generation from transaction flows.
> Active Prototyping.

Table 4: Implementation of CASE in Organizations Factors

artificial intelligence techniques as mentioned in the discussion on future CASE tools. There is also a concern that CASE users and vendors accept and apply the principles of total quality management and dynamic activity base accountability.

With respect to the implementation of CASE in organizations, the experts believed that a number of factors influenced successful adoption of CASE: first, that CASE needs to be customized to the organization, and not adopted wholesale from a vendor or system integrator, and second, that the support of top management is critical to the successful CASE adoption. The experts also called for open systems architectures and the increased use of the Joint Application Development technique.

Our respondents also believe that CASE must be integrated with the culture of the organization, including increased involvement of end-users in the construction and maintanance of applications. For this to be successful, end-user training and support for CASE tool use must be improved and expanded.

Finally, the lack of CASE tool standards are identified as a major factor inhibiting the use of CASE in organizations. The experts also called for increased use of active prototyping as a strategy for promoting the process of CASE adoption.

Ranking the Factors

In the second round of the survey, we asked the 31 American experts to rank the critical factors with respect to each of the three areas: *methodology, tools, and process*. In addition, we sent the same list of factors to the 45 European experts and asked that they rank the factors in the same way. We received 19 responses (60%) from the American experts and 23 responses (49%) from the European experts. The factors, grouped by methodlogy, tools, and process, are provided in Tables 5, 6, and 7. The ranking document is included as an Appendix to this chapter. The results of the ranking process, the

Existing CASE:
Software analysis and design through graphical representations.
Clearer links between tools and specific supported methodologies.
Improved project management support.
Future of CASE:
Incorporation of new methodologies, including those based on object-oriented methods.
Integration of methodologies and tools.
Incorporation of automated software metrics.
Integration with Joint Application Development (JAD).
Integration with rapid prototyping.
CASE as a graphic fifth-generation language (5GL).
Development of domain-specific methodologies.
Economics of CASE:
Incorporation of cost-benefit analysis.
Focus on IS development and maintenance.
Implementation of CASE in Organizations:
Customize to an organization.
Top management support.
Open systems architectures.
Increased Joint Application Development.

Table 5: Methodology Factors

Existing CASE:
Allow configuration to a methodology.
File standards to allow integration of tools.
Better support for software reengineering.
Improve user interfaces and lower learning curves.
Free availability to universities.
Clear interfaces between phases.
Code/frame generation.
Future CASE:
UNIX environments with cross-compilation of applications.
Reuse of analysis and design efforts.
AI assisted tools.
Reduce the increase in hardware requirements.
Capture more model semantics.
Enterprise modeling capabilities.
Domain-specific tools.
Economics of CASE:
Universal complement of features in all CASE products.
Pre-written analysis and design models by problem domain.
Studies of CASE tool selection.
Improve performance/price relationship.
Implementation of CASE in Organizations:
Customize to an organization.
Integration of CASE within organizations.
End-user construction & maintenance.
Improved and expanded training.

Table 6: Tool Factors

> ***Existing CASE:***
> Support Groupware concepts of security, file sharing, version control, noting, etc.
> Capability to expand scope and functionality of tools.
> Connection of tools and phases.
> Clarification of role of CASE in maintenance.
> Support for planning activities.
> ***Future CASE:***
> Reverse engineering using a variety of methodologies.
> Develop automated CASE tools.
> More automatic consistency and completeness checking.
> ***Economics of CASE:***
> Execution efficiency through smart designs.
> Total quality management.
> Exploit cheap computing power of PCs.
> Activity (dynamic) base accountability.
> ***Implementation of CASE in organizations:***
> CASE tool standards.
> Improved and expanded training.
> Automatic design generation from transaction flows.
> Active Prototyping.

Table 7: Process Factors

American and European experts, are shown in Tables 8, 9 and 10.

The Methodology Factors. The European and American experts are in fairly close agreement on methodology factor rankings for the first five factors. *Improved project management support* is the most important methodology factor, according to the American experts. Those experts apparently believe strongly that existing CASE methodologies have neglected this practical aspect of software/systems projects, and that successful projects must be well managed, whether supported by CASE or not. The European experts are in close agreement, since they ranked *improved project management support* third.

The European experts ranked *customization to an organization* as the most important *methodology* factor; the American experts also ranked this factor high (fourth). This finding, we believe, invites two interpretions: first, that IS organizations need to adapt CASE *tools* to the systems development process of the IS organization, i.e. to see CASE as more than a technical tool (or toy); and second, that this finding reflects the broader maturation process which calls for the IS organization to reflect the overall organization culture, i.e. to focus on business process rather than technological advantage. This finding is further reinforced by the fact that domain-specific methodologies is ranked sixth (seventh) by the American (European)

Rank	USA Experts	Rank	European Experts
1	Improved project management support (E)	1	Customize to an organization (O)
2	Integration of methodologies and tools (F)	2	Integration of methodologies and tools (F)
3	Clearer links between tools and specifically supported methodologies (E)	3	Improved project management support (E)
4	Customize to an organization (O)	4	Incorporation of new methodologies, including object-oriented (F)
5	Incorporation of new methodologies, including object-oriented (F)	5	Focus on IS development and maintenance (Ec)
6	Domain-specific methodologies (F)	6	Clearer links between tools and specifically supported methodologies (E)
7	Incorporation of automated software metrics (F)	7	Domain-specific methodologies (F)
8	Focus on IS development and maintenance (Ec)	8	Open systems architectures (O)
9	Top management support (O)	9	Increased Joint Application Development (O)
10	Integration with Joint Application Development (F)	10	Integration with rapid prototyping (F)

Note: (E) Existing CASE
(F) Future CASE
(Ec) Economics of CASE
(O) Implementation of CASE in Organizations

Table 8: Ranking of Methodology Factors

experts. Domain-specific methodologies are obviously easier to customize to an organization. Apparently, CASE experts on both sides of the Atlantic want CASE methodologies and tools that can be made more specific to the way organizations carry out software/systems projects.

Interestingly, both the American and European experts ranked *integration of methodologies and tools* as the second most critical methodology factor. Although, historically, there has been no linkage between the evolution of *methodologies, techniques, and tools*, the results are obvious to experts on both sides of the Atlantic. We have techniques for which there are no tools; we have tools which do not fully support any standardized (non-vendor specific) methodology.

The importance of improving the *integration of methodologies and tools* is reinforced by the fact that *clearer links between tools and specifically supported methodologies* is ranked third (sixth) by the American (European) experts. This finding bodes well for tool providers who tie their products to a particular methodology, particularly those which support a full, standardized methodology, and especially for those methodologies which have received wide acceptance.

Incorporation of new methodologies, including object-oriented methods, and a *focus on IS development and maintenance* round out the top five critical methodology factors. These factors are beginning to receive more attention in the CASE arena, and our experts believe that these factors should be fully incorporated into CASE future methodologies. The incorporation of new areas into methodologies is to be expected as a young area such as CASE grows and matures.

Although we do not place any significance on the fact that the European and American experts did not select all 10 of the same factors, we do believe that the selected factors are important nevertheless. Thus, the experts agree that there is a need for standards and for increased use of prototyping support by appropriate CASE tools.

The Tool Factors. *Customization to an organization* is clearly the most important tool factor in both the American and European markets. We interpret this as another bit of evidence for the growing demand for domain- or organization-specific tools and methods. However, after this most important factor, our experts agree less on tool factors than on methodology and process factors.

Four of the top ten factors for each group were not among the top

Rank	USA Experts	Rank	European Experts
1	Customize to an organization (O)	1	Customize to an organization (O)
2	Re-use of analysis and design efforts (F)	2	Enterprise modeling capabilities (F)
3	Code/frame generation (E)	3	Integration of CASE within organizations (O)
4	Clear interfaces between phases (E)	4	Allow configuration to a methodology (E)
5	File standards to allow integration of tools (E)	5	Re-use of analysis and design efforts (F)
6	Integration of CASE within organizations (O)	6	Capture more model semantics (F)
7	Allow configuration to a methodology (E)	7	Code/frame generation (E)
8	AI-assisted tools (F)	8	Reduce the increase in hardware requirements (F)
9	Better support for software re-engineering (E)	9	Better support for software re-engineering (E)
10	Lower learning curves (E)	10	Improve user interface (E)
Note:	(E) Existing CASE, (F) Future CASE, (Ec) Economics of CASE, (O) Implementation of CASE in Organizations		

Table 9: Ranking of Tool Factors

ten for the other group. This is most evident by the fact the Europeans ranked *enterprise modeling capabilities* second while this factor did not even make the top ten list for the American experts. Similarly, *file standards to allow integration of tools* is the fifth most important factor for USA experts and this factor did not make the top ten list for the Europeans.

Despite these differences, there were still a lot similarities. *Reuse of analysis and design efforts* was ranked second (fifth) by the American and European experts. Both groups obviously see this as an important productivity and time-saving feature that should be part of future CASE tools. This is a logical next step-moving from automating analysis and design efforts to reusing those automated efforts. *Code and frame generation* from existing CASE tools is the third (seventh) most critical factor. Our respondents obviously believe that it is crucial for current tool manufacturers to continue to improve the capabilities of current and future CASE products in the area of automatic generation of executable modules.

The *integration of CASE within organizations* and *allowing configuration to a methodology*, are tool factors which we believe support the findings in the discussion on methodology, i.e. that integrated tools and methods support the organization's processes.

Although both sets of experts see the need for *better support for software re-engineering* as important, the Europeans are more concerned with the *re-use of analysis and design efforts* and the *capturing of more model semantics*. The American experts see the *need for file standards to allow the integration of tools* and the development of *AI-assisted tools as important*. Even though the factors differ, we believe that all these factors point to a need for more intelligent CASE tools. Both sets of experts are looking for more intelligent systems with improved user interfaces which will result in lower learning curves.

A significant finding is that none of the economics factors were among the top ten. This seems to imply that costs and benefits are not important to decisions about CASE tools, or that CASE users are more concerned with performance and productivity of tools rather than their costs.

The Process Factors. The process factor rankings are shown in Table 10. The American and European experts are very close in their respective rankings. The one exception is that the American experts ranked *CASE tool standards* as the most important factor while this factor did not even make the top ten for the Europeans. Is it that users in the American group try to use a wider variety of tools within the same organization than do Europeans? This would make an interesting topic for future research. *Connection of tools and*

Rank	USA Experts	Rank	European Experts
1	CASE tool standards (O)	1	Connection of tools and phases (E)
2	Connection of tools and phases (E)	2	Support groupware concepts of security, file sharing, version control, noting (E)
3	More automated consistency and completeness checking (F)	3	More automated consistency and completeness checking (F)
4	Total Quality management (Ec)	4	Capability to expand scope and functionality of tools (E)
5	Reverse engineering using a variety of methodologies (F)	5	Clarification of role in maintenance (E)
6	Support groupware concepts of security, file sharing, version control, noting (E)	6	Total Quality management (Ec)
7	Support for planning activities (E)	7	Reverse engineering using a variety of methodologies (F)
8	Automatic CASE processing (F)	8	Open systems architectures (O)
9	Active prototyping of CASE-based designs (O)	9	Active prototyping of CASE-based designs (O)
10	Capability to expand scope and functionality of tools (E)	10	Automatic design generation from transactions flows

Note: (E) Existing CASE
(F) Future CASE,
(Ec) Economics of CASE,
(O) Implementation of CASE in Organizations

Table 10: Ranking of Process Factors

phases is the second most important factor for the American group and it is ranked first by the Europeans. This is consistent with the high ranking of *improved project management support* in the methodology factor rankings (Table 8). Apparently tool users on both sides of the Atlantic are having difficulty managing the use of existing CASE as part of their current life-cycle software/systems development process—existing CASE does not seem to match their life-cycle phases. The second most critical factor for the Europeans is *support for groupware concepts*; that factor was ranked sixth by our American experts. This is consistent with the fact that *increased/integrated joint application development* made the top ten methodology factor list (Table 8) for both the American and European groups.

More automatic consistency and completeness checking is high on the list (third) for both groups of experts. Our experts believe that more rigor is needed in CASE processes, similar to their belief that more intelligent tools are needed. Another process factor ranking high (fourth/sixth) is *total quality management (TQM)*. This is not surprising given the recent, and continuing focus on this issue in software/systems development. Users on both sides of the Atlantic have a strong desire to incorporate TQM into CASE processes. This is definitely an area for future study and development in the CASE field.

CONCLUSIONS

Our survey of American and European experts on the critical factors that will influence future CASE provides interesting and important insights into what CASE researchers and practitioners believe may happen as CASE evolves in the 1990's. The findings appear to us to be internally consistent since those factors ranked as highly critical in the methodology area had highly ranked related factors in the tool and/or process areas.

An overall conclusion that places the rest of our conclusions in context is that our experts place more importance on CASE methods and processes than on tools. Our experts believe that the tools should be integrated with standard methodologies and processes within the organization. Our experts believe that integration, standard methodologies, and domain/organization specificity are the critical factors that will form the foundation for successful evolution of CASE in the future.

Customization to the organization is clearly one of the most important factors, according to our experts. They believe that both methodologies and tools should be integrated with the business and system development processes of the organization.

Our experts also believe that it is important to improve the *integration of methodologies and tools,* especially *clearer links between tools and specifically supported methodologies*. This indicates that tool providers who tie their products to a widely accepted standard methodology may be most successful in the CASE product market.

Our experts want more intelligent CASE tools. Improved facilities for code re-use, reverse engineering, AI assistance, and other intelligent features are considered important tool factors by our experts.

There was more agreement than disagreement between our American and European experts, at least in the top five or six factors for each area. We did not collect information that would allow us to draw conclusions about the reasons for any differences between the two groups. That subject should be researched in the future because it may have implications for tool developers and marketers.

Critical Factors 635

RANKING SHEET FOR CRITICAL FACTORS INFLUENCING THE FUTURE OF CASE

Rank	Methodology Factors	Rank	Tool Factors	Rank	Process Factors
	Existing CASE:		**Existing CASE:**		**Existing CASE:**
	Software analysis and design through graphical representations		Allow configuration to a methodology		Support Groupware concepts of security, file sharing, version control, noting etc.
	Clearer links between tools and specifically supported methodologies		File standards to allow integration of tools		Capability to expand scope and functionality of tools
	Improved project management support		Better support for software reengineering		Connection of tools and phases
			Improve user interface		Clarification of role of in maintenance
			Lower learning curves		Support for planning activities
			Free availability to universities		
			Clear interfaces between phases		
			Code/frame generation		
	Future CASE:		**Future CASE:**		**Future CASE:**
	Incorporation of new methodologies, including object-oriented		UNIX environments with cross-compilation of applications		Reverse engineering using a variety of methodologies
	Integration of methodologies and tools		Reuse of analysis and design efforts		Develop automated CASE tools
	Incorporation of auto. software metrics		AI-assisted tools		More auto. consistency & completeness checking
	Integration with JAD		Reduce the increase in hardware requmts		
	Integration with rapid prototyping		Capture more model semantics		
	CASE as a graphic 5GL		Enterprise modeling capabilities		
	Domain-specific methodologies		Domain-specific tools		
	Economics of CASE:		**Economics of CASE:**		**Economics of CASE:**
	Incorporation of cost-benefit analysis		Universal complement of features in all CASE products		Execution efficiency through smart designs
	Focus on IS development and maintenance		Pre-written analysis and design models by problem domain		Total quality management
			Studies of CASE tool selection		Exploit cheap computing power of PCs
			Improve performance/price relationship		Activity (dynamic) base accountability
	Implementation of CASE in organizations:		**Implementation of CASE in organizations:**		**Implementation of CASE in organizations:**
	Customize to an organization		Customize to an organization		CASE tool standards
	Top management support		Integration of CASE within organizations		Improved and expanded training
	Open systems architectures		End-user construction & maintenance		Auto. design generation from trans flows
	Increased Joint Application Development		Improved and expanded training		Active prototyping of CASE-based designs

The results of our survey may or may not accurately predict the future of CASE in the 1990's. However, it is a first attempt to gather expert opinion on the critical factors that may influence that development. We anticipate that future research, as well as the actual evolution of CASE over the coming decade, will add to our body of knowledge.

REFERENCES

Davis, Dwight. Safe Deposit For Enterprise Data. *Datamation*, 38, 5, March 1, 1992, 67-70.

Fosdick, Howard. Ten Steps to AD/Cycle. *Datamation*, 36, 23, December 1, 1990, 59-64.

Francis, Bob. A Window Into CASE. *Datamation*, 38, 5, March 1, 1992, 43-44

Forte, Gene, Mazim H. Madhavji, and Hausi A. Muller (eds) CASE '92 - 5th International Workshop on Computer-Aided Software Engineering. (Proceedings). Los Alamitos, IEEE Press.

Klinger, Daniel. Rapid prototyping revisited. *Datamation*, 32, 20, October 15, 1986, 131-132.

Lindholm, Elizabeth. A World of CASE Tools. *Datamation*, 38, 5, March 1, 1992, 75-81.

Ronald J. Norman and Minder Chen. Working Together to Integrate CASE. *IEEE Software*, 9, 2., March 1992. This special issue contains 9 articles on Integrating CASE. (see also special issue on CASE, March 1988)

> Minder Chen and Ronald J. Norman. A Framework for Integrated CASE
> Alan W. Brown and John A. McDermid. Learning from IPSE's Mistakes
> Ian Thomas and Brian A. Nejmeh. Definitions of Tool Integration for Environments
> Christer Fernstrom, Kjell-Haken Narfelt and Lennart Ohlsson. Software Factory Principles, Architectures, Experiments
> Peiwei Mi and Walt Scacchi. Process Integration in CASE Environments
> Matthias Jarke. Strategies for Integrating CASE Environments
> Jacob L. Cybulski and Karl Reed. A Hypertext-Based Software-Engineering Environment
> Alan R. Hevner, Shirley A. Becker and Lenard B. Pedowitz. Integrated CASE for Cleanroom Development

Norman, Ronald J. and Gene Forte (eds) Automating the Software Development Process: CASE in the 90's. *Communications of the ACM*, 35, 4. April 1992. This special issue contains 8 articles focusing on CASE.

> Gene Forte and Ronald J. Norman. A Self Assessment by the Software Engineering Community
> Terry Shepard, Steve Sibbald and Colin Wortley. A Visual Software Process Language.
> Clifford C. Huff.Elements of a Realistic CASE Tool Adoption Budget
> Neil A. Maiden and Alistair G. Sutcliffe. Exploiting Reusable Specifications Through Analogy
> Graham Tate, June Verner and Ross Jeffery. CASE: A Testbed for Modeling, Measurement and Management
> Ira D. Baxtyer. Design Maintenance Systems.

Iris Vessey, Sirkka I. Jarvenpaa and Noam Tradctinsky. Evaluation of Vendor Products: CASE Tools as Methodology Companions

Pinella, Paul. The Race For Client/Server CASE. *Datamation*, 38, 5, March 1, 1992, 51-54.

Prakash, Jay. How Europe is Using CASE. *Datamation*, 36, 15, August 1, 1990, 79-80.

Ricciuti, Mike. A CASE for Client/Server. *Datamation*, 37, 17, September 1, 1991, 28-30.

Ricciuti, Mike. (1992). Can Intersolv Excelerate On OS/2? *Datamation*, 38, 5, March 1, 1992, 24-27.

Ricciuti, Mike. (1992). Database Vendors Make Their CASE. *Datamation*, 38, 5, March 1, 1992, 59-60.

Schussel, George. The Promise and the Reality of AD/CYCLE.*Datamation*, 36, 18, September 5, 1990, 69-74.

Semich, J. William. (1992) Open CASE Emerges as AD/Cycle Lags. *Datamation*, 38, 5, March 1, 1992, 30-38.

Snell, Ned. Quality Tools for Quality Software. *Datamation*, 38, 1, January 1, 1992, 53-54.

Stamps, D. (1987). CASE: Cranking Out Productivity. *Datamation*, 33, 13, July 1, 1987, 55-58.

Statland, Norman. Payoff Down the Pike: A CASE Study. *Datamation*, 35, 7, April 1, 1989, 32, 33, 52.

Teichrow, Daniel and Hasan Sayani. Automation of System Building. *Datamation*, 17, 17, August 15 1971, 25-30.

The, Lee. Bridging The CASE/OOP Gap. *Datamation*, 38, 5, March 1, 1992, 63-64.

Yourdon, Ed. Whatever happened to Sturctured Analysis. *Datamation*, 32, 11, June 1, 1986, 133-138.

Weber, Herbert. From CASE to Software Factories.*Datamation*, 35, 7, April 1, 1989, 34-36, 52.

Author Biographies

Macedonio Alanis is currently Chief Information Officer (Director de Informatica) for the government of the state of Nuevo Leon, Mexico. He also works as adjunct faculty for the Universidad de Nuevo Leon and for the Instituto Tecnologico y de Estudios Superiores de Monterrey, in Monterrey, Mexico. He has held a position as Assistant Professor of Management Information Systems at the University of Detroit Mercy. His current research interests include information requirements determination, software development tools and methodologies, and the diffusion of information technologies.

Cyrus H. Azani has a B.S degree in engineering and Masters and Doctoral degrees in Engineering Management from The George Washington University. He is currently teaching at the College of Business and Public Management, University of the District of Columbia and is adjunct professor at the Graduate School of Management and Technology, University of Maryland and at the Kogod College of Business Administration, The American University. He has published more than 20 articles in various journals and periodicals and has done variety of consulting for U.S. companies. His current research interests are man-machine interaction, implementation of modern computer-based technologies such as CIM, CAD/CAM, and CASE tools.

Ismail Bayraktar is a software engineer at Agent Systems, Inc. in Dallas, Texas. He has published several papers and technical reports. He obtained his M.S. in Computer Science from Southern Methodist University.

Shirley A. Becker is an assistant professor of computer science and information systems at The American University. Her research interests include system modeling using Petri-nets, cleanroom systems engineering, group dynamics of system development, and systems development in software product firms. Becker received a Ph.D. in information systems from the University of Maryland at College Park. She is a member of the IEEE Computer Society and ACM.

Author Biographies

Thomas J. (Tim) Bergin is associate professor of Information Systems in the Department of Computer Science and Information Systems, The American University. Prior to this, he served as the Director of the Quantitative Teaching and Research Laboratory of the College of Public Affairs (TAU). He began his career as a systems analyst with the Veterans Administration in 1966. Dr. Bergin's research interests include the history of computing, the ethical and social impacts of computer use, and information resources management. He is a co-author of *A Microcomputer-Based Primer on Structural Behavior* (Prentice-Hall, 1986) and over 50 book chapters, articles, papers and reviews.

David Chender Chou is an associate professor in the Department of Computer Information Systems at West Texas State University. His research interests center on applying model-based expert systems, decision support systems, artificial intelligence and software engineering related areas. He has published several articles in journals such as *Interfaces* and *Information Executive*, and numerous papers in Proceedings. He received the research excellence award at West Texas State University in 1989-1990. He received his BA from Feng Chia University in 1978, his MS from National Taiwan University in 1980, and MS and PhD from Georgia State University in 1987.

Robert L. Crosslin received his Ph.D. in Economics from the University of Missouri in 1973. His research interests are CASE economics and evaluation, group decision support systems, and modeling and simulation of information systems. He previously taught at the University of Maryland Baltimore County, Phillips University and Mississippi State University.

Gordon C. Everest is associate professor of MIS and Database Management Systems in the Carlson School of Management at the University of Minnesota. He has published several articles and a textbook entitled, *Database Management: Objectives, System Functions, and Administration* (McGraw-Hill, 1986). He is also a contributing author of the CODASYL Systems Committee technical report entitled, *A Framework for Distributed Database Systems: Distribution Alternatives and Generic Architectures*. His lecturing and research interests include logical database design methods and diagramming conventions, high-level data languages, selection and use of database management systems, object-oriented databases, CASE tools and the repository, data-centered systems development, organization and functions of database administraiton, data privacy and security, and the legal aspects of computing.

Gene Forte is the president of Portland, Oregon-based CASE Consulting Group (CCG), publisher of the CASE OUTLOOK® International Report on computer-Aided Systems Engineering. As a researcher and analyst, Forte specializes in the latest tools and techniques for systems planning, development and management, and is a frequent speaker at industry conferences and workshops worldwide. CCG acts as a primary source of information on the practical use of systems design automation in both commercial and engineering applications. Consulting clients include IBM, Hewlett-Packard, Cadre Technologies, CitiCorp, the Yankee Group, Mentor Graphics, The Institute for Information Industry, R.O.C. and British Columbia Telephone.

Raoul J. Freeman is professor and chair of Computer Information Systems at California State University, Dominguez Hills. Previously, he was Assistant Superintendent of the Los Angeles Unified School District. Prior to that, he held executive positions with Systems Applications, Inc. and General Electric. During his career, he has managed multi-million dollar systems development efforts and large scale data centers. Dr. Freeman received his Ph.D. from MIT. His extensive publication and speaking record includes 35 refereed articles, 2 books and numerous technical reports. He acts as a consultant to major clients in the private and public sectors, on a world-wide basis, specializing in the use of CASE, the implementation of large scale systems, and managerial audits of data processing organizations. Dr. Freeman is the National Chairman of the EXCELERATOR Academic Users Group. Recently, he headed a blue ribbon Task Force to advise Los Angeles County regarding the future of its 250 million dollar per annum data processing activities.

BJ Gleason is an instructor of Computer Science and Information Systems at The American University in Washington, DC. His research interests include programming languages, object-oriented design techniques, and education technologies. Gleason holds a Master's degree in Computer Science form the New Jersey Institute of Technology and is currently completing his Ph.D. in education administration at the American University.

Oscar Gutierrez is in the Faculty of the Management Science and Information Systems Department in the College of Management at the University of Massachusetts at Boston. He received his Ph.D. in Information Systems from the London School of Economics and Political Science. He holds an M.Sc. in Analysis, Design and Management of Information Systems from the LSE and a B.Sc. in Computer Systems for Administration from the Monterrey Institute of Technology. Dr. Gutierrez has published in *Information and Management* and *The Journal of Systems Management*. He has contributed to several edited volumes on information analysis and CASE technology, and to numerous national and international proceedings on the topic of experimental techniques for systems development. He has lectured in Europe, the United States, and Latin America. He has worked as systems analyst and is currently consulting for the Department of Health and Hospitals of the city of Boston. Dr. Gutierrez is former president of the Boston chapter of the Institute of Management Sciences.

Mary J. Granger is an assistant professor in the Information Systems Technology Program in the Management Science Department of the School of Business and Public Management of the George Washington University. Dr. Granger received her PHD in Information Systems from the University of Cincinnati. Her research interests include CASE, metrics, system development, user interface design, curriculum development and international information systems. She is a member of IEEE and ACM.

Reginald L. Hobbs is a computer scientist on the Software Engineering Team (SWT) at the Army Research Laboratory, Software Technology Branch. The ARL Software Technology Branch was formerly known as AIRMICS. He gained experience in information systems at the Air Force Space Command headquarters, Cheyenne Mountain Complex, Colorado and as a Systems Administrator/Systems Programmer at the Army Research Institute, Alexandria, Virginia. Mr. Hobbs has a B.S. in Electronics from Chapman College. He has research interests in the areas of software development methods, re-engineering, Computer-Aided Software Engineering (CASE) tools, and software metrics.

Christopher G. Jones, CPA, is currently assistant professor of Computer Science and Information Systems at Utah Valley Community College, Orem, Utah, where he teaches Object-Oriented Systems Analysis and Design. Before relocating to Utah, he was the Director of the Computer Information Systems Academic Program at Woodbury University, Los Angeles, California. He has also taught for the University of Phoenix, Los Angeles Pierce College, and California State University, Northridge. Besides teaching, Mr. Jones has significant industry experience in Information

Author Biographies 641

Systems. He has been a Senior Systems Consultant for Arthur Andersen & Company; Director of Management Information at Good Will Publishers, North Carolina; Co-founder of InfoPro, Inc., a Los Angeles-based systems consulting firm; and, the CFO for Sybervision Seminar Systems, responsible for all accounting and information systems design. Most recently, he has been a Senior Analyst at Erudite Software Corporation, responsible for a review of the administrative systems for the State of Utah court system. Mr. Jones holds an MBA from Brigham Young University and a B.S. in Accounting from California State University, Northridge. He is currently a Ph.D. candidate in Business Information Systems at Utah State University. He is the coauthor of two college texts and has published several articles. He is a member of the American Institute of Certified Public Accountants, the Utah Association of Certified Public Accountants (UACPA), and the Association for Computing Machinery. He currently serves as Vice-Chair of the Consulting Services Committee of the UACPA.

Vijay Kanabar is an assistant professor in the Department of Business Comuting and Administrative Studies at the University of Winnipeg, and specializes in database systems, fourth generaiton techniques and software engineering. He has published papers in the *Information Resources Management Journal, ACM-SIGCSE, ICCI*, as well as co-authored a book on Structured Query Language.

Reza Khorramshahgol received a B.Sc. in Mathematics from Tehran University and an M.Sc. in Engineering Management and a D.Sc. in systems analysis from the George Washington University. While there, he taught graduate and undergraduate courses in the School of Engineering and Applied Science for four years. From 1984 to 1987 he was an Assistant Professor of Computer Information Systems in the School of Business, North Carolina Central University. From 1987 to 1989 he was a Member of the Technical Staff at AT&T Bell Laboratories, in the Operations Planning and Architecture Department. Since 1989 he has been with the Department of Computer Science and Information Systems at the American University, Washington D.C. He is a senior member of the IEEE and serves on the editorial board of the *IEEE Transactions on Engineering Management.*

Anita J. LaSalle is chair and associate professor of the Computer Science and Information Systems Department at the American University. She holds a BS in Mechanical Engineering from the Newark College of Engineering, an MS in mechanical Engineering from the New Jersey Institute of Technology and a Ph.D. in Computer Science from Stevens Institute of Technology. She has worked in industry, government and academia. Before joining the American University in 1988, Dr. LaSalle was a program manager at the National Science Foundation. Her research interests are concentrated in software engineering and expert systems development. She has over 50 publications, conference presentations, media interviews and invited talks to her credit.

John Parkinson is the Chief Scientist at the Ernst & Young Methods Development Center in Dallas, Texas. He has been involved with a variety of CASE tools and IS methodologies as a salesman, a developer, a consultant, and a user in over 100 organizations in the UK, Europe, and the United States. Parkinson was one of the principal architects for the Ernst & Young Navigator System Seriessm (an IE methodology).

Parviz Partow-Navid is professor of Computer Information Systems at California State University, Los Angeles. He received his MBA and Ph.D. from the University of Texas at Austin. His research and teaching interests are in the fields of information systems, decision support systems, and expert systems.

Roger Alan Pick earned a B.S. in Mathematics from the University of Oklahoma, an M.S. in Mathematics from Purdue University, and a Ph.D. in Management Science from Purdue. He is presently an associate professor of Management Information Systems at Louisiana Tech University. His research interests are in decision support systems, computer economics, and software engineering. He has authored seven journal articles, two book chapters, and eight conference proceedings papers.

Hasan H. Sayani, PhD, is president of Advanced Systems Technology Corp. (ASTEC), based in Crofton, Maryland. He desgined the graduate curriculum in information systems management at the University of Maryland, and designed and directed the development of a semantic-based repository and a reverse engineering tool to interpret COBOL and FORTRAN code into a formal specification language, as well as several software utilities. He consults with Fortune 100 and governmental agencies on software engineering, operations research, and system development life cycle management. Sayani has co-authored with Cyril Svoboda over 32 courses, 3 seminars, and 24 workshops and has taught these to over 6000 students. He is author and/or co-author of over thirty papers presented at conferences or published in journals or edited books on software engineering.

Robert Schooley, currently an adjunct professor of Management Information Systems at the University of Tulsa, founded (in 1984) and currently directs the Anova Consulting Group. Dr. Schooley's firm specializes in the area of *development effectiveness* (MIS-related, business process innovation).

Ludwig Slusky is professor of Computer Information Systems at California State University, Los Angeles. His specialization is in CASE technology, systems development methodologies, and database design. He published *Practical Applications for Database Design* (1988, 1992) and articles on CASE technology. Ludwig Slusky is also a CASE consultant.

Jack Stott received his Ph.D. in management from the University of Arizona in 1984. His research interests are CASE evaluation, decision support systems, and modeling and simulation of information systems. He previously taught at the University of Hawaii.

Mary Sumner is chairperson of the Department of Management Information systems at Southern Illinois University at Edwardsville. She is also Director of Academic computing for the university. Her teaching and research interests include the impact of computer-mediated communications networks on organizational communications, the management of end-user computing, and software engineering strategies in information systems design. Dr. Sumner has authored three textbooks, including a management information systems text. In addition, she has delivered over 50 speeches and written over 35 articles in professional journals and conference proceedings. Some of her recent research deals with critical success factors in making the transition to computer-assisted software engineering.

Robert A. Stegwee studied at DePauw University and at the University of Amsterdam, from which he holds a Masters degree in Computer Science, with a specialization in Management Information Systems. Currently he is an assistant professor of MIS with the Faculty of Management and Organization at the University of Groningen, the Netherlands. In 1992 he obtained a doctoral degree in Management and Organization from the same University. His doctoral research has focused on the development of a decision support system for information architecture specification. Related research topics are information systems strategy and information systems planning. In conjunction with his work at the University of Groningen Robert has (had) affiliations with Moret Ernst & Young management consultants in Utrecht, the Institute of Knowledge Systems in Groningen, and Information Management Consultancy in Glimmen, (all in the Netherlands). These affiliations have enabled him to carry out applied research, consultancy, and professional training.

Cyril P. Svoboda, PhD, is vice president of Advanced Systems Technology Corp. (ASTEC). He has directed the development of a software bridge between a leading CASE tool and any target repository, and has developed a methodology for information modeling to solve large-scale information problems. He consults with both commercial organizations and governmental agencies on enterprise analysis, strategic planning, requirements analysis, and preliminary design of information systems. He was a co-author of the software engineering curriculum for National Technological University and has conducted needs assessments and designed curricula for three federal agencies. He has authored and/or co-authored over fifteen papers presented at conferences or published in journals and edited books of readings on software engineering.

Murat M. Tanik is an associate professor of Computer Science and Engineering at Southern Methodist University, and is director of the department's software engineering and knowledge-based systems research group. His interest in software development environment research started with the NASA-DOMONIC software development environment project in the early 1970's. Since then, he has worked on related projects for Collins (Rockwell), International Software Systems Inc., Northern Telecom, and Texas Instruments. His publications include several books, numerous papers and technical reports funded by goverment and private agencies. His most recent book *Fundamentals of Computing for Software Engineers* published by Van Nostrand Reinhold addresses the need for more interdisciplinary cooperation for integrated systems development.

Ria M.C. van Waes received her Masters degree in Social Economics from the Agricultural University in Wageningen, the Netherlands, in 1987. Subsequently she joined the Free University in Amsterdam to embark on doctoral research on the role of architectures in information management. Parts of this research have been sponsored by Philips Electronics in Eindhoven, which was also the host organization for several case studies she carried out. Meanwhile, Ria was also active as an information management consultant, and has given several courses on the construction of architectures for information management purposes. After receiving her Ph.D. from the Free University in 1991, she joined Coopers and Lybrand Management Consultants in Utrecht, the Netherlands, where she advises on issues relating to information technology and project management.

J. Philip Vidrine is a senior manager in Ernst & Young's Cleveland, Ohio practice. He has assisted a number of organizations with the selection, implementation, and application of a variety of CASE tools. Vadrine, who has extensive experience across the systems development life cycle, was one of the authors on the Ernst & Young Navigator Systems Series[sm] project.

James R. Warren received the B.S. degree in computer science and the Ph.D. degree in information systems from the University of Maryland. He is currently an assistant professor with the Department of Computer Science and Information Systems at The

American University in Washington, DC. His research interests are in methods of supporting the development of information systems, particularly the application of computer simulation models to the system design process. Dr. Warren is a member of the Society for Computer Simulation.

J. Christopher Westland is currently an assistant professor of Information Systems at the University of Southern California. Previously he worked in industry for eight years, first as a certified public accountant for Touche Ross in Chicago and later as database administrator and computer security analyst for Rockwell International He has been awarded an Andersen Foundation Fellowship, a FLAS Fellowship by the U.S. Department of Education, several Paton Fellowships, a Dykstra Fellowship for Teaching Excellence, and a FRIF Grant to study politics and conflict resolution in information systems resource sharing. His current research focuses on the economics of information systems management and information technologies, on new technologies for software engineering, and on organizational and strategic applications of information technology.

Roy Youngman is a senior manager at the Ernst & Young Methods Development Center in Dallas, Texas. He managed the design and construction of the Ernst & Young Development Effectivenesssm service offering. Youngman has designed and taught classes on Data Modeling and Organization Change Management and he is also the author of the Ernst & Young Navigator System Series[sm] Knowledge Coordination Monograph.

Index

A

abstraction 321
acquisition mechanism 379
active encyclopedia 364
Activity Builder 576
AD/Cycle 46
analytical models 320
Apple's DrawShapes 333
Application Development Workbench 289
application factors 299
application software generators 296, 572
architectures 249
archiving 18
Arthur Andersen's Design/1 CASE tool 605
artificial intelligence 368
assessment plan 217
Association for Computing Machinery 594
association matrices 259

B

barriers to integration 5
box structure methodology 109
bridge tools 65
Buhr diagrams 519, 324
business analysts 177
business information model 277
business information systems 400
business models 264, 265
business paradigm in systems development 181
Business Systems Planning (BSP) 250

C

C++ 319
Cadre Teamwork/Ada CASE 520
case adaptation plan 216
CASE Data Interchange Format 50, 65
CASE environment administrator 7

646 Index

CASE evolution 617
CASE integration standard 50
CASE methodology 177
CASE technology 177
CASE/simulation 428
CDD/Administrator 47
central repository 75
Characteristics of EU-CASE 202
Class Window 349
Class-Responsibility-Collaboration 324
classification abstraction 321
Cleanroom System Development Process (CSDP) 108
Cleanroom Systems Engineering 107
COBOL Structuring Facility 119
COBOL to Ada 510
Common APSE Interface Specification 50
Common User Interface 18
computer-based information systems 474
configuration management 365
control integration 15
cost benefit process 164
cost models 296
creeping functionality 591
critical factors 617
critical success factors 252, 261, 594

D

data analysis 207
data dictionary 555
data flow diagram 261, 339, 383, 572
data integration services 30
Data Processing Management Association 594
data sharing 18
decision support system 284
decomposition diagrams 259

design phase 474
development environments 473
development strategy 182, 187
disintegrated CASE 365
dynamic encyclopedia 364
dynamic modeling 431

E

Economics of CASE: 628
encapsulation 322
End-User CASE 177, 199, 298
enterprise modeling 31, 177
enterprise ownership of information 160
entity relationship diagrams (ERDS) 259, 261, 339
EU-CASE 203
Excelerator 604, 259, 435
Excelerator's PC-Prism 259
experimental systems development 187
Expert System CASE Tool Integrator 96
expert system support 432
expert systems 94, 106, 307, 361, 379, 384

F

file interchange formats 356
flexible manufacturing cell 9
Flow Control 578
Format Builder 576
forward engineering 94, 98, 362, 512, 516
Fourth Generation Languages 297
fourth-generation tools 293
function point methodology 542
functional analysis 206
functional decomposition 278, 528
future of CASE 617, 628

G

globalization 182
GOSSIP 284
Graphic User Interface 345
graphical definition language 280
graphical specifications 552

H

hierarchical inheritance 322
hierarchical object-oriented design 324
HyperCard 333

I

I-CASE/ES platform 360
IDE's Software Through Pictures 511
impact analysis 8
Implementation of CASE in organizations 628
inference engine 379, 386
information architecture 7, 161, 252, 265
Information Engineering Facility 260
Information Engineering Workbench 260, 285
information management 13
Information models 265, 266, 320, 366
Information Resource Directory Services 51
information system development life cycle 61
information systems model curricula 594
information systems planning 249
integrated CASE (I-CASE) Environment 4, 74, 94
Integrated Project Support Environment 17, 68
interface-compatible CASE components 365
ISAC Activity and Information schemata 261
ISMOD 259, 261
integrated systems planning (ISP) 249, 250, 252, 264

K

knowledge acquisition 371
knowledge base 379, 285, 286
knowledge engineering 379, 384
knowledge representation 385
knowledge validation 385
knowledge-based support 432
Kurtz-Woodfield-Embley notation 324

L

"layered" model 94
LEGASY Project 310
life cycle phases 63
lower CASE toolsets 363

M

Maestro, 49, 260
Message Flow Decomposition 324
meta-activity model 277
meta-meta-model 280
meta-modeling 27, 65, 271
methodology factors 624
methodology-dependent CASE 361
MicroSTEP 552, 569
MicroSTEP Rapid Prototyping methodology 580
model hierarchy 283
model integrator 74

modeling processes 13, 257, 261, 427
multi-dimensional models 13

N

n-ary relationship 76
Nastec's DesignAid 77
natural language processors 373
needs assessment 380
NEST 431

O

object management system 27, 49
object-oriented analysis 323, 357
object-oriented database management systems 36
Object-oriented modeling 320
object-oriented paradigm 321
Object-oriented design 324
OOATool 319, 338, 343
OOWorkbench 337
open architecture 65, 68
Oracle's SQL*Design Workstation 280
organizational architecture 253

P

passive encyclopedia 364
performance modeling 427
physical and logical models 383
Pilot 338
Portable Common Tool Environment 50
presentation integration 15
presentation systems 379
Problem Statement Language/Problem Statement Analyst (PSL/PSA) 77
procedural model 320
process factors 624
process model 571
product paradigm 179
Project Factors Expert System 307
project management 198, 293
property matrices 259
prototype 386, 429
prototype simulation environment 427
prototyping 179, 572

Q

QASE RT 431

R

rapid application development 569, 580
rapid prototyping 553, 569, 580
Report Builder 578
repository 14, 361
Repository Manager 46
requirements specification 323
requirements traceability 365
restructuring 98, 512
reusability 579
reverse engineering 94, 512
role analysis 205

S

semantic data model 321, 76
Shlaer/Mellor Information Structure Diagrams 324
simulation environment 430
Smalltalk 333, 349
software (re)engineering 94
Software BackPlane 45
software crisis 320
software development methodologies 474, 571

Software Industrialized Generator & Maintenance Aids (SIGMA) 51
software metrics 294, 542
software quality 475
spiral model 553
stage model approach 213
structured analysis and design 320
structured specification 528
Synchronized Refinement 513
system analysis 383
system design 384
system development life cycle 362, 380
System Development Workbench 259
system dynamics 439
system modelling 383
system quality 473
systems architecture 252, 266, 284

T

Teamwork 511
Teamwork/SA 531
Teamwork/SD CASE 531
Teamwork/SIM 431
technical architecture 266
technology adoption model 215
TESS 430
tool factors 624
TopSTEP 573
total quality management 215
traceability 22

U

Uniform Object Notation 324
upper CASE toolsets 363

V

version management 365
Visible Analyst Workbench 605
Visible Systems 605

W

Ward-Mellor methodology 324
waterfall model 107
Windows Print Manager 352
workbenches 259

GUIDELINES FOR BOOK PROPOSALS

Idea Group Publishing (IGP) is continually looking for new authors to join us in our pursuit of providing innovative, up-to-date, quality publications to the information technology management community. If you have a topic or idea that you feel would be a good subject for a book, we would like to talk to you. With IGP it's easy to pursue your publication dream. Just furnish us with a 4-6 page proposal addressing the following areas:

- **Mission:** What is the purpose of the book?
- **Audience:** Whom do you intend this book to address? Included in this section should be a description of the specific group as well as your estimate of the total core audience.
- **Competition:** What other books are on the market that address this same topic, and how will yours differ? What unique characteristics will your proposed book contain to place it above the competition?
- **Timetable for Production:** Give an estimate of when you would have the initial manuscript finished and when the final manuscript would be delivered.
- **Outline:** This section should contain the overall framework or summary of your proposed book as well as a comprehensive list of the table of contents.
- **Sample chapters:** A copy of several chapters of the proposed book (if available) is requested to allow the editorial staff to assess your proposed publication in a more constructive, efficient manner.

Submit your book proposal to:
IDEA GROUP PUBLISHING
Olde Liberty Square • 4811 Jonestown Road, Suite 230
Harrisburg, PA 17109 U.S.A.
Tel: (717) 541-9150 • Fax (717) 541-9159.